A CASEBOOK ON
SCOTTISH CRIMINAL LAW

A CASEBOOK ON SCOTTISH CRIMINAL LAW

BY

CHRISTOPHER H. W. GANE,

LL.B.,

Lecturer in Scots Law, University of Edinburgh

and

CHARLES N. STODDART,

LL.B., LL.M. (McGill), Ph.D.,

Solicitor and Notary Public, Lecturer in Scots Law,
University of Edinburgh

EDINBURGH

W. GREEN & SON LTD.

ST. GILES STREET

1980

First published   .   .   1980

© 1980.   C. H. W. Gane
C. N. Stoddart

ISBN 0 414 00664 X

PREFACE

It is often said that Scots law is a system based on principle, rather than precedent. But with regard to Scots criminal law, this shibboleth becomes harder to justify as the years pass; indeed it is doubtful whether it ever applied even at the time of Hume, who is generally regarded as the father of our criminal law.

The primary sources for Hume's *Commentaries* were the Books of Adjournal for the previous century, in which there were recorded the actual decisions of the Court of Justiciary from its inception in 1672. In the late eighteenth century two selections of criminal cases, by Maclaurin and Arnot respectively, were published in an attempt to illustrate the then practice of the court; the strong influence of the case law on crimes has persisted ever since. In the twentieth century the publication of textbooks on criminal law was intermittent and unsatisfactory until the first edition of Gordon's *Criminal Law* appeared in 1967, to be followed by a second edition 11 years later. However no modern collection of Scottish criminal cases has been compiled, and so we decided to attempt the task.

The present work is intended primarily for students of criminal law in Scottish universities, although we hope it will appeal to a wider readership. The experience of teaching the subject which each of us has gained over the past few years has convinced us of the need for such a volume, as an aid to study and as a supplement to other teaching materials. As will be seen from the table of contents, we cover both the general theory and the law relating to those crimes commonly encountered in practice. For many of these topics Scottish authority abounds, but where none is available we have not hesitated to include materials drawn from other jurisdictions.

Two matters are however outwith the scope of the work. First, we have dealt only in passing with criminal procedure, because the system seems likely to be altered in a number of material respects by the Criminal Justice (Scotland) Bill which is presently before Parliament. Although the basic division into solemn and summary cases will continue, the mechanics of trials and appeals under both will be affected by the new provisions to such a marked extent that a sizeable body of case law will be rendered obsolete, doubtless to be succeeded by new and, as yet, unforeseen problems. Secondly, we have deliberately excluded road traffic law from our collection. Many of the points which have arisen recently before the Scots courts on this subject have related to procedure and sentence, not least of all in connection with the breathalyser provisions of the Road Traffic Act 1972. These too are to be made the subject of legislation in the near future, and so it seemed singularly inapt to include cases thereon in this work.

v

We have however managed to assemble a certain amount of unreported material including a Full Bench decision in 1949 on the question of automatism which graces the pages of neither the *Justiciary Cases* nor the *Scots Law Times*. Where appropriate, we have also included excerpts from the Institutional writers and references to other cases and statutes.

We are pleased to acknowledge here the assistance given to us by Mr W. Howard and the staff of the Justiciary Office in making much material available to us and for their patience in dealing with our repeated requests. We are also obliged to the publishers for their assistance at every turn in the preparation of the work. Each of us has been responsible for different sections of this volume but we have each read and commented on the work of the other; we hereby accept "art and part" liability for the contents.

The cases included are those decided up to 31 May 1980.

Edinburgh   C. H. W. GANE
June 1980   C. N. STODDART

TABLE OF CONTENTS

vii

TABLE OF CASES

Page numbers of cases set out in the text are in **bold** type.

TABLE OF STATUTES

ABBREVIATIONS

CHAPTER 1

SOURCES AND GENERAL PRINCIPLES

a. General features of Scots criminal law

The Royal Commission on Capital Punishment

Memorandum submitted by the Lord Justice-General (Cooper) (Minutes of Evidence, p.428):

"The Scottish law of crime is not statutory but almost exclusively common law, which has been and is still being evolved by judicial decisions applied with anxious care to the precise facts of actual cases. It is contrary to the tradition and genius of our criminal law to deal with its basic conceptions *in vacuo.* No two cases are exactly alike, and very slight distinctions in the circumstances may tilt the balance as between murder and culpable homicide, and even as between innocence and guilt. By the application of our native methods to our native principles, it has proved possible (within the limits of human fallibility) to keep the law sufficiently flexible and elastic to enable a just discrimination to be applied to the ascertained facts of each case, and sufficiently rigid to prevent proved guilt from escaping the just consequences on any mere technicality . . .

10. As regards the main distinctive features of Scottish criminal practice, I would refer to two published statements by Lord Normand, my immediate predecessor in office—'The Public Prosecutor in Scotland', *Law Quarterly Review,* July, 1938, and 'Scottish Judicature and Legal Procedure' (*Holdsworth Club of the University of Birmingham,* 1941).

In supplement of these fuller statements and of the memorandum submitted by the Crown Office with which I am in general agreement, and with a view to clarifying matters raised before the Commission, I would add the following brief comments:—

(*a*) Private prosecution is unknown in Scotland, the Lord Advocate being in complete control in the public interest, subject only to a measure of oversight by the High Court of Justiciary.

(*b*) The authority of the Lord Advocate as public prosecutor (exercised in important matters personally and in normal business through the Solicitor General, Crown Counsel, the Crown Office staff and the local Procurators Fiscal), has been employed for generations in obedience to jealously guarded traditions of fairness and independence; and a challenge of the propriety of the Lord

1

Advocate's discretion as public prosecutor is in modern times unknown.

(c)   The complete control of prosecutions confided to the Lord Advocate has several important results—(a) the whole of the preliminary investigation into suspected crime is conducted subject to absolute confidentiality, and there is no publication of the evidence prior to a murder trial—coroner's inquests and the preliminary proceedings in lower Courts being unknown in Scotland; (b) the Lord Advocate is 'master of the instance' in the sense that he can in his discretion indict for culpable homicide instead of for murder, if his investigations justify such a course; or, having indicted for murder, he can in course of the trial reduce the charge to any degree that seems appropriate or depart from the charge entirely; or he can in theory refrain from moving for sentence, in which case the accused would have to be discharged.

This last-mentioned power, like the ancient power 'to restrict the pains of law' (by substituting an arbitrary penalty for a statutory penalty of death), never nowadays arises in trials for murder, the modern course being to reduce the charge, should occasion arise, before the jury retire.

11. At the stage of the actual trial in Scotland the following specialities fall to be noted: (a) neither Judge nor Jury know anything of the evidence to be adduced against the accused until the witnesses are in the box; (b) the Crown is not allowed to preface the evidence by any opening speech; (c) at the conclusion of the evidence Crown counsel addresses the jury first, leaving the last word to counsel for the defence; (d) the jury have the choice of three verdicts, the verdict of not proven being less illogical than is commonly supposed, and calculated in many a narrow case to cause an acquittal where there would otherwise have been a conviction; (e) a majority verdict is accepted."

NOTE
The last successful challenge to the Lord Advocate's discretion as public prosecutor was in 1909 (*J. & P. Coats Ltd.* v. *Brown*, 1909 S.C. (J.) 29). Such challenges have become more frequent in recent years. See, *e.g. McBain* v. *Crichton*, 1961 J.C. 25, *Trapp* v. *M.*, *Trapp* v. *Y.*, 1971 S.L.T. (notes) 30, *Meehan* v. *Inglis and Ors.*, 1974 S.L.T. (Notes) 61.

b. The status and powers of the High Court

1.   Mackintosh v. Lord Advocate
(1876) 3 R. (H.L.) 34

The appellant wished to raise a private prosecution against a doctor who, he alleged, had conspired to have the appellant committed to an asylum as insane, in the knowledge that he was in fact sane. He applied to the Lord Advocate for his concurrence to the Bill for Criminal Letters which he was presenting to the High Court. The Lord Advocate refused his concurrence. The appellant then applied to the High Court for an order obliging the Lord Advocate to give his consent. The High Court refused (on two occasions) to make such an order. The appellant took an appeal to the House of Lords. The Lord Advocate presented a petition to the House praying that the appeal be refused as incompetent.

LORD CHANCELLOR (LORD CAIRNS): "My Lords, the broad question which has been argued at your Lordships' bar is this,—whether an appeal lies to this House from an order or sentence of the Court of Justiciary, the Criminal Court in Scotland . . .
The answer to that question appears to me to lie in a very narrow compass. Your Lordships have asked for all the information which could be given as to what the precedents were before the Act of Union with Scotland for any appeal from the Court of Justiciary; and, going back as far as any precedent can usefully be searched for, and considering everything that can be adduced, I think your Lordships will agree with me in saying that there has been no precedent whatever adduced of any appeal maintained before the Union from the Court of Justiciary to the Parliament of Scotland. It may be quite true that during the whole of that time it was not the habit to have appeals from other Courts to the Parliament of Scotland. But certainly, even during the time when appeals, or what were called protestations for remeid of law, which in substance were quite the same as appeals, were brought to the Parliament of Scotland from the other Scotch tribunals,—in those times there is no instance of any appeal from the Court of Justiciary.
I apprehend, looking to the state of Scotland at that time, and to the occupations of the Court of Justiciary, if it had occurred to any person that an appeal would lie, the chance of an appeal certainly would have been taken.
The Act of Union provides by the 19th article, with regard to the Court of Justiciary and the other Courts, upon what footing they shall stand. It provides, first, that the Court of Session or College of Justice do after the Union remain 'in all time coming within Scotland as it is now constituted by the law of that kingdom, and with the same authority and privileges as before the Union.' Now, my Lords, if it was the case that before the Union the Court of Session stood as a tribunal subject to protests for remeid of law, which led to the review of its decisions by the Parliament of Scotland, and that that was its position the proceedings which took place between the Scotch Estates and King William III abundantly shew, and if at the

same time the Court of Justiciary stood as the criminal tribunal, from which there was no appeal to Parliament or elsewhere,—then I apprehend that the 19th article of the Act of Union, continuing both these Courts with the same powers and authority which they had before, would naturally be taken to be a statute continuing the Court of Session with its decisions subject to review, and continuing the Court of Justiciary with its decisions as final and conclusive.

How, then, does it stand, my Lords, as a matter of precedent since the Union? Your Lordships have now the experience of upwards of one hundred and seventy years since the Union. Is there any instance produced of any appeal from an order of the Court of Justiciary during that time? No instance has been found, notwithstanding the diligence used by the learned counsel for the appellant. On the contrary, your Lordships have a most exhaustive and conclusive argument, delivered in this House by Lord Mansfield in Bywater's case, upon this very point. Lord Mansfield went through every case that was supposed to bear upon the question up to the time at which he spoke, and he shewed that there was no case of an appeal from an order of the Court of Justiciary, and that one or two cases, the case of Mr Dempster and the earlier case of Elgin, which were supposed to bear an appearance to an appeal of that kind, really were no authorities whatever for holding that an appeal would lie. With regard to one of those cases, the case of Dempster, it appears to me to afford the strongest possible argument that an appeal would not lie, for that was a case in which, if this House could have exercised an appellate jurisdiction, it was obviously extremely well inclined to do so. But it found that it could not do so, and it therefore resorted to a very singular proceeding, which Lord Mansfield describes, and which was quite inconsistent with any assertion of an appellate right by this House.

From the time of Bywater's case down to the present day there is no instance of any appeal to this House from the Court of Justiciary, and it would be somewhat strange to imagine that during the period up to the Union, and during the period of nearly two centuries which have elapsed since the Union, down to the present time, there should during all that time have been slumbering a right to maintain an appeal from the Court of Justiciary, either to the Scottish Parliament in the first period, or to this House since the Union, and that that right should never have been resorted to by any of the hundreds and thousands of those persons to whose interest it would have been to resort to it.

To that, my Lords, I will only add one other observation. Your Lordships have, in the printed cases before you, the statutory enactments which have been made with regard to the Court of Justiciary in modern times—statutory enactments which have been provided sometimes by way of definition, sometimes by way of enlargement, for the jurisdiction to be exercised by the Court of Justiciary. In all of those statutes the orders and sentences of the Court of Justiciary were made final and conclusive. It appears to have been assumed, whenever the Court of Justiciary was legislated for, that it was a final Court, from which no appeal lay. It would be very strange indeed if an appeal were to lie from the decisions and sentences of the Court of Justiciary outside those statutes, and not from the decisions of that Court under those statutes.

My Lords, these considerations appear to me entirely sufficient for disposing of this case. I think that the attempt to maintain the right of appeal from an order of the Court of Justiciary is a pure experiment, altogether unwarranted by precedent, and which must fail the moment the history which I have attempted to narrate to your Lordships is looked into. I think that the petition of the Lord Advocate, to have the appeal dismissed as incompetent, ought to succeed, and that an order to that effect should now be made, and I move your Lordships accordingly."

Appeal dismissed.

NOTES

The authorities referred to by Lord Cairns are: *Bywater* v. *The Crown* (1781) 2 Paton 563, *Geddie & Mackintosh* v. *Dempster* (1767) (referred to in *Bywater*) and *Magistrates of Elgin* v. *H.M. Advocate and Ors.* (1713) Robertson's App. 69.

The supremacy of the High Court, and the absence of a final appeal court common to Scotland and England can present difficulties in respect of United Kingdom statutory offences, since there is the risk of divergent interpretations of such statutes. From the Scottish point of view it is clear that there is no obligation to follow the English construction (see, *e.g.*, *Keane* v. *Gallacher,* 1980 S.L.T. 144). Not surprisingly, displays of Scottish judicial independence have provoked a peevish response amongst some English commentators (see Blom-Cooper and Drewry, *Final Appeal,* pp. 376-377).

2. Bernard Greenhuff
(1838) 2 Swin. 236

The panel was charged, along with three others, with the crime of keeping a common gaming house for the playing of games of chance for money, for the profit of the keepers, and where games of chance were commonly and publicly played for money. The accused objected to the relevancy of the indictment.

LORD JUSTICE-CLERK (BOYLE): "I have come to be decidedly of opinion, that this is a relevant charge by the common law of Scotland. It does not appear to me to be a matter of any signification in the present question, that we have found that the statutes formerly libelled on do not extend to Scotland. For, in innumerable instances in this Court, charges have been found irrelevant under statutes, and yet relevant at common law. In determining whether or not what is here charged is a crime, we are bound to consider what the nature of a common gambling-house, of the description set forth in this Indictment, is,—what are its effects, —and what its consequences to the public at large. Now, it appears to me, that an establishment of the nature here described, the doors of which are open at all times to the young and to the thoughtless, is necessarily productive of the greatest evil, and must tend to the corruption, not only of individual, but of public morals. And when I call to mind the disgraceful scenes which take place in some of the streets of London, and at the Palais Royal in Paris, I have no hesitation in saying, that the attempt to carry on an establishment of this description within the city, is so great an invasion of the rights of public morality, and threatens such serious evils to the public at large, and to the particular community among whom it is sought to be introduced, as to be clearly cognisable by this Court . . .

I have looked into the authorities on this subject, and I have found enough to satisfy my mind, that there are solid principles in our law to justify a charge of this nature. It is of no consequence that the charge is now made for the first time. For there are numerous instances, in which crimes which had never before been the subject of prosecution, have been found cognisable by the common law of this country. On this point I refer particularly to the authority of Baron Hume. (Vol. i. p. 12.) It appears that the learned author had not been sufficiently aware of the power of the common law in England; for after stating, that 'It seems to be held in England that no Court has power to take cognisance of any new offence, although highly pernicious, and approaching very nearly to others which have been prohibited, until some statute has declared it to be a crime, and assigned a punishment,' he continues—'With us the maxim is directly the reverse; that our Supreme Criminal Court have an inherent power, as such, competently to punish (with the exception of life and limb) every act which is obviously of a criminal nature, though it be such which in time past has never been the subject of prosecution.''

LORD MEADOWBANK: "I cannot say that I have arrived at the opinion which I have formed in this case without difficulty; but it now concurs with that which has been delivered by the Lord Justice-Clerk. I agree with his Lordship as to the inherent power of this Court to repress whatever are, by the law of God, and the laws of morality, *mala in se*. That the Court has always possessed such a power, has been more than once distinctly enunciated by our predecessors on this Bench; and the matter is not now open for consideration or discussion . . ."

LORD COCKBURN (dissenting): "No public prosecutor, though it be his special duty to protect the public morals, has ever charged this as an offence. The record of this Court is an entire blank on the subject. Nor is there any mention of such an offence in any legal work. Not one of our institutional writers, though gathering together every crime, in order that the whole penal code might be known to the people in all its details, ever allude to it as a common law offence. There is not a trace of it anywhere.

In this situation, whatever may be my wishes, I can find no legal ground for *our beginning* now to add it to our criminal catalogue.

It has been said, that it is in the power of this Court to declare, that is, to *introduce*, new crimes; and that if it be in our power, it is our duty to do so on fitting occasions. I dissent utterly from this doctrine; and, if a proper occasion for discussing it shall ever arise, I shall endeavour to explain why I do so. I may only say at present, that I am far from holding that the Court can never deal with any thing as a crime, unless there be a fixed *nomen juris* for the specific act, or unless there be a *direct precedent*. An old crime may certainly be committed in a new way; and a case, though never occuring before in its facts, may fall within the *spirit* of a previous decision, or within an established *general principle*. And such is the comprehensiveness of our common law, that it is no easy matter for any newly invented guilt to escape it. But this is not the meaning of the doctrine, as usually announced, when it is said that this Court can declare new crimes. There is no such declaration, nor the exercise of any extraordinary power needed, in the Court's merely determining that an act that has never presented itself before, *comes within the range of a known term, case, or principle*. The meaning of the doctrine is this,—that though vice may invent a *totally original offence*,—never heard of before,—and for which law has not only no name, but which is not included within any known penal description or principle, *but which is in its whole nature entirely new,—* still, *if it imply wickedness and be hurtful*, the Court of Justiciary, *treating it as an entirely unheard of thing*, may, in virtue of what is termed its "*inherent powers*," introduce it as a new crime.

It is from this that I dissent. I conceive the power ascribed to us to be inconsistent with the proper constitutional limits of any British court. I am aware of the opinion of Mr. Baron Hume, and of the weight due to it; but, *upon such a subject*, I care little for the theory, or the doctrine, of any modern institutional writer; or even for occasional *obiter dicta* from the Bench. I must see the power recognised by Parliament, or practised by the Court *so long and so directly*, that the sanction of Parliament, and the acquiescence of the public are implied . . . If every thing dangerous, or we shall say, dangerous to *public morals*, be a point of dittay in the Court of Justiciary, how does it happen, since we have always had a public prosecutor, whose duty it has been to see the criminal law enforced, that anything dangerous to public morals remains unpunished. There are innumerable notorious overt acts, with which society is quite familiar, that are deeply injurious to individuals, and to the public, to which, nevertheless, it would be considered utterly extravagant to attempt to apply the penalties of the common law. Many examples are given in the Information for the pannels, and others might, on a moment's recollection, be stated. They are so numerous that the selection of instances seems only to weaken the force of the general fact. The prosecutor's principle could not be applied fairly to all cases, without making the administration of law capricious and ludicrous. For it will always be kept in view, that *dangerousness* is to be judged of *by the Court*. It must be what *the Judges may think* hurtful, that is to be dealt with judicially as criminal. Now, how many things are there which society tolerates and enjoys, that are condemned and avoided by wise and good men, on the ground of their immorality? Would it be difficult to obtain, at this moment, a Court composed of able, upright, and learned lawyers, in the sight of every one of whom, the race-course, the hunting-field, and above all, the theatre, is each an abomination, purely from what they think its audacious and profligate corruption of public morals? I see no ground for supposing that the law ever meant to subject the people to so arbitrary a rule, as that their conduct, even in doing what had been done by others with impunity for ages, was to be deemed criminal or not, solely according to the varying and speculative views of Courts."

Plea to relevancy repelled.

NOTES

Cf. Shaw v. *D.P.P.* [1962] A.C. 220. In so far as the declaratory power conflicts with the general principle of legality (*nullum crimen sine lege*) the alleged power of the High Court to declare new crimes is clearly objectionable (*cf.* Gordon, paras. 1-16 to 1-19). The exact limits of the power in modern practice are unclear (Gordon, paras. 1-20 *et seq.*), but it appears that it (or something very like it) was used in the following case.

3. Strathern v. Seaforth
1926 J.C. 100

The respondent was charged with clandestinely taking possession of a motor car, the property of another, knowing that he had not received permission from the owner, and that he would not have obtained such permission to do so. An objection to the relevancy of the complaint, on the grounds that it did not disclose a crime known to the law of Scotland, was sustained by the sheriff-substitute who, at the request of the prosecutor, stated a case to the High Court. The question of law for the High Court was whether the sheriff was right in sustaining the objection to the relevancy of the complaint.

LORD JUSTICE-CLERK (ALNESS): "Counsel for the Crown say that that complaint discloses a crime which the Court was bound to investigate, and that that crime consists in taking and using something clandestinely, without the permission of the owner having been given. It appears to me that the proposition for which the Crown contends is supported by the authorities which were cited. But, speaking for myself, I should not have required any authority to convince me that the circumstances set out in this complaint are sufficient, if proved and unexplained, to constitute an offence against the law of Scotland.

The matter may be tested by considering what the contention for the respondent involves. It plainly involves that a motor car, or for that matter any other article, may be taken from its owner, and may be retained for an indefinite time by the person who abstracts it and who may make profit out of the adventure, but that, if he intends ultimately to return it, no offence against the law of Scotland has been committed. I venture to think that, if that were so, in these days when one is familiar with the circumstances in which motor cars are openly parked in the public street, the result would be not only lamentable but absurd. I am satisfied that our common law is not so powerless as to be unable to afford a remedy in circumstances such as these.

All that we are deciding, and I understand your Lordships agree, is that this is a relevant complaint. All defences will be open to the accused. We merely decide that the learned Sheriff-substitute has gone too fast in dismissing the complaint as irrelevant at this stage. It appears to me that investigation is necessary; and, in that view, I suggest to your Lordships that we should answer the question put to us in the negative."

LORD HUNTER: "I agree in thinking that the learned Sheriff-substitute ought not to have thrown out this complaint without inquiry. It is, under section 5 of the Act of 1887 and also section 5 of the Summary Jurisdiction Act of 1908, not necessary in any indictment or complaint to specify by any *nomen juris* the crime which is charged; but it is sufficient if the indictment sets forth facts relevant to constitute an indictment of a crime.

As your Lordship has pointed out, it is not merely said that the respondent took the car without getting the owner's permission, but also that he did so clandestinely and knowing quite well that the owner would not have given permission. If the contention of the respondent is right, then no offence is committed under the criminal law of Scotland if anyone goes to a garage and takes a car and petrol clandestinely. It would be very unfortunate if that were the state of the law, when we know how so many cars are parked in cities like Glasgow and Edinburgh. I am satisfied, however, that the common law of Scotland does not consider that an act of that sort is not crime. It may turn out that the offence is more or less venial or more or less criminal, but it is not for us to speculate."

The court answered the question in the negative.

NOTES
"Joy-riding" of the above type is now dealt with under s.175 of the Road Traffic Act 1972, but the principle enunciated in *Strathern* v. *Seaforth*, not being limited to road traffic cases, remains unaffected. *Cf. Murray* v. *Robertson*, 1927 J.C. 1.

The court's willingness to deal with a new and growing form of wrong-doing may be contrasted with efforts to deal with the problem of "glue-sniffing"—see *Skeen* v. *Malik, post,* ch. 10. See also *Sweenie* (1858) 3 Irv. 109, *post,* ch. 16, *Kerr* v. *Hill,* 1936 J.C. 71, *post,* ch. 18, and *H.M. Advocate* v. *Martin and Ors.,* 1956 J.C. 1, *ibid.,* for further examples of judicial creativity.

c.   *The presumption of innocence and the burden of proof*

1.   Slater v. H.M. Advocate
1928 J.C. 94

The appellant was charged with the murder of an old woman by striking her on the head with a hammer. The alleged motive for the killing was theft, the old lady having in her home a large quantity of jewellery. Evidence was led that the appellant lived by gambling and dealing in jewels. There was also evidence that he was supported by the earnings of a prostitute. These circumstances were remarked upon by the Lord Advocate in his speech to the jury as indicating a character depraved enough to commit the crime in question. In his charge to the jury, the presiding judge (Lord Guthrie) made the following remarks (*inter alia*):

"That is the kind of man, and you will see at once that his character is double-edged. The Lord Advocate takes it in his own favour, and he may quite fairly do so because, in the first place, a man of that kind has not the presumption of innocence in his favour which is not only a form in the case of every man but is a reality in the case of the ordinary man. Not only is every man presumed to be innocent, but the ordinary man has a strong presumption in his favour. Such a man may be capable of having committed this offence, and that man also may be capable from his previous character of exhibiting a callous behaviour after the offence. That was founded upon by Mr McClure. A man of such a character does not exhibit the symptoms that a respectable man who has been goaded into some serious crime of violence does after the crime is over, and so you will consider that matter from both points of view, telling in favour of the prisoner and telling against him. [After dealing with the pursuer's financial circumstances his Lordship continued]—Gentlemen, all these circumstances are relevant to the case, but I think if you make up your minds to convict the prisoner you will be wise to be in this position; to be able to say to yourselves, 'we have disregarded his character, we have disregarded his financial circumstances, we have convicted him without regard to these.' Having reached that conclusion, it might very well strengthen the conclusion to reflect on the two elements that I have mentioned, but I do not think they should be factors in enabling you to reach a conclusion, although they might support it after the conclusion had been reached."

The jury returned a verdict of guilty of murder. The appellant appealed on the ground, *inter alia*, of misdirection by the trial judge:

LORD JUSTICE-GENERAL (CLYDE): "It would be absurd to hold that a miscarriage of justice occurs whenever, in the report of a speech by counsel to the jury, anything is found which can be read as involving either a misstatement of some fact, or as presenting a wrong view of the relevancy of some piece of evidence; and there are many other passages in the prosecutor's speech which put the case against the appellant independently of any reference to any of the points in the evidence which were other than strictly relevant. But the specialty in this trial was that some of the aspects of the life which the appellant lived were relevant, while others were irrelevant, to the question of his guilt. Thus, the circumstance that the appellant never had a dentistry practice in Glasgow, but dealt in some way in articles of jewellery, was relevant to the motive which, according to the prosecution, drew the appellant to Miss Gilchrist's house in search of the valuables she kept there. But that other aspect of his life, with its peculiarly heinous implications, in which he was shown to be partly dependent on the proceeds of prostitution, was as remote from any bearing on the question of his guilt as it was suggestive of prejudice against his case. Both the former

aspects of the appellant's mode of life, and the latter aspect, un-
avoidably came—together and immixed—to the knowledge of the
jury; and this made the possibility of misunderstanding on the jury's
part the more likely if the odious (and irrelevant) aspect was
referred to in the prosecutor's address to the jury for any other
purpose than to distinguish it from the others as one which was
irrelevant, and which must be put entirely out of their consideration. So far from this, it was unfortunately made the point of the
opening passage of the presentation of the case for the prosecution.

We have already indicated our view that the decision of the
case—particularly with regard to the vital point of satisfactory proof
of identity—presented an unusually difficult and narrow issue,
upon which the balance of judgment might easily be influenced in
one direction or the other. It follows that the danger of allowing the
minds of the jury to be distracted by considerations which were at
once so irrelevant and so prejudicial as those connected with the
relations of the appellant to his female associates was real and great;
and in these circumstances we are of opinion that the clearest and
most unambiguous instruction by the presiding judge was impera-
tively demanded, to prevent the possibility of any misunderstanding
on the part of the jury with regard to so important a matter. As
appears from the shorthand report of the judge's charge, however,
the matter in question was the only one on which the directions
given to the jury were open to serious criticism. They did nothing to
remove the erroneous impression which the opening passages of the
speech for the prosecution might so easily have produced in the
minds of a jury. On the contrary, they were calculated to confirm
them. No distinction was made between those aspects of the
appellant's life which were relevant to the charge of murdering Miss
Gilchrist, and those which were not. It was pointed out—quite
justly—that the considerations arising out of the appellant's mode
of life, as exhibited at the trial, were double-edged, and were
founded on (for different purposes) by the prosecution and the
defence alike. But the jury were told that what is familiarly known
as the presumption of innocence in criminal cases applied to the
appellant (in the light of his ambiguous character) with less effect
than it would have applied to a man whose character was not open
to suspicion. This amounted, in our opinion, to a clear misdirection
in law. The presumption of innocence applies to every person
charged with a criminal offence in precisely the same way, and it can
be overcome only by evidence relevant to prove the crime with the
commission of which he is charged. The presumption of innocence
is fundamental to the whole system of criminal prosecution, and it
was a radical error to suggest that the appellant did not have the

benefit of it to the same effect as any other accused person. It is true that an accused person of evil repute has not the advantage, enjoyed by an accused person of proved good character, of being able to urge on the jury in his defence the improbability that a person of good character would commit the crime charged. The passage in the charge at present under discussion is suggestive that this was what was in the judge's mind. But, however that may be, he put the appellant's bad character as a consideration upon which the prosecution was entitled to found as qualifying the ordinary presumption of innocence . . . That a man should support himself on the proceeds of prostitution is regarded by all men as blackguardism, but by many people as a sign of almost inhuman depravity. It cannot be affirmed that any members of the jury were misled by feelings of this kind in weighing the question of the appellant's guilt, but neither can it be affirmed that none of them was. What is certain is that the judge's charge entirely failed to give the jury the essential warning against allowing themselves to be misled by any feelings of the kind referred to. It is manifestly possible that, but for the prejudicial effect of denying to the appellant the full benefit of the presumption of innocence, and of allowing the point of his dependence on the immoral earnings of his partner to go to the jury as a point not irrelevant to his guilt of Miss Gilchrist's murder, the proportion of nine to five, for 'guilty' and 'not proven' respectively, might have been reversed."

Appeal allowed: conviction quashed.

NOTES

Slater's case is one of the most notorious in Scottish criminal law. After his conviction (in 1909) Slater received a conditional pardon and his death sentence was commuted to life imprisonment. Disquiet over his trial and ultimate disposal contributed to the setting up of a criminal appeal court (under the Criminal Appeal (Scotland) Act 1926) to hear appeals from conviction on indictment. Slater's was one of the first cases to be dealt with by the new court.

In certain circumstances Parliament has seen fit to elide the presumption of innocence and has placed upon accused persons the burden of proving their innocence. See, *e.g.*, the Electricity (Scotland) Act 1979, s. 41, and the Debtors (Scotland) Act 1880, s. 13.

2. **Lambie** v. **H.M. Advocate**
1973 S.L.T. 219

An accused person was charged on indictment with theft. He pled not guilty and lodged a special defence of incrimination naming certain other persons as the perpetrators of the crime. By a majority the jury found him guilty as libelled. He presented an application for leave to appeal based on two alleged misdirections to the jury by the presiding judge, the first of which related to certain evidence given by a Crown witness. The second ground was that in his charge the judge indicated to the jury that there was an onus upon the panel to establish the special defence of incrimination which he had tendered.

THE COURT (The Lord Justice-General, the Lord Justice-Clerk, Lord Cameron, Lord Milligan and Lord Kissen): "What we have already said is sufficient for the disposal of the appeal but since the case was specially remitted to this court for consideration of the second of the alleged misdirections, and since the full argument which we heard upon it disclosed need for guidance from us on a matter of general importance, we propose to examine the second alleged misdirection in a little detail now.

The relevant passage in the sheriff's charge is in the following terms—'Reverting now, ladies and gentlemen, to the accused Lambie, and the charge upon which he faces you, he has given evidence himself. Now, if you believe what he says and if what he says is consistent with innocence, then, of course, you will acquit him. He has put forward a special defence of impeachment—this means that he is saying it was not he who committed the crime, but that it was some others. In order that he may succeed in this he must produce evidence and corroborated evidence. Now, it seems to me that he certainly has not done the second thing, and it is doubtful if he has done the first thing. There is no corroborated evidence which would entitle you to come to a decision on the special defence of impeachment put in by the first accused. Therefore you will not consider that special defence. Now, in saying that I am not in any way saying that you have not to consider the allegations—because that is really what his evidence amounted to—with regard to other people being involved. All I am saying is that there is insufficient evidence to entitle you to find the accused not guilty on the basis that he has made out a special defence of impeachment. The other evidence, and the inference which Mr McSherry invited you to draw from the evidence relating to some other people having been involved, is still before you, and if that evidence produced in your minds a reasonable doubt then, of course, you will acquit the accused because, as I say, it is for the Crown to prove beyond reasonable doubt that the accused person is guilty.'

As will be seen from the quoted passage the direction plainly asserts (i) that there is an onus on the accused to prove his special defence; (ii) that the onus can only be discharged by corroborated evidence; and (iii) that there is no corroboration of the accused's evidence incriminating any of the persons named in the special defence. For the applicant it was conceded that the third of these propositions was accurate. It was conceded further, for the purposes of the argument, that in presenting the first two of these propositions to the jury the sheriff was merely following a widespread practice among trial judges which appears to have developed since the cases of *H.M. Advocate* v. *Lennie,* 1946 J.C. 79, 1946 S.L.T. 212 and *H.M. Advocate* v. *Owens,* 1946 J.C. 119, 1946 S.L.T. 227. Against the background of these concessions the submission was that a proper charge required the sheriff to proceed to tell the jury that although they could not hold the special defence to have been affirmatively proved, they must still consider the appellant's uncorroborated evidence on incrimination and if they believed him or if, while not wholly believing him, found that his evidence created a reasonable doubt as to his guilt of the crime charged, they must acquit him. In this case, however, the sheriff followed up his first three directions by saying: 'Therefore you will not consider that special defence.' Now, it was not disputed by the Crown that, had the charge stopped there, there would have been a plain and grave misdirection by the sheriff, and the question at the end of the day came to be whether the sufficiency of the charge was saved by reading the quoted sentence in the context of the whole passage dealing with the special defence and, in particular, in conjunction with the sentences which immediately follow it. Upon this question we have come to be of opinion, albeit with some hesitation, that, standing the practice to which we have referred, the charge on the special defence read as a whole would sufficiently inform an intelligent lay jury, in spite of the quoted sentence which might otherwise have misled them, that they *were* to consider the applicant's evidence of incrimination and to acquit if it produced in their minds a reasonable doubt of his guilt. In these circumstances we would not have been disposed to sustain the appeal on the second ground.

The matter cannot, however, be allowed to rest there since in course of the argument the soundness of the practice to which we have referred, and the soundness of the observations in *Lennie* (supra) and *Owens* (supra) on which it was based, were seriously questioned. Suffice it to say that the criticisms made were such that it is desirable to look afresh at the whole matter of the proper charge which should be given where there has been lodged by an accused person a special defence of alibi, self-defence or incrimination.

It must be accepted that it has been the practice of many judges since the cases of *Lennie* and *Owens* to direct juries, where any of these special defences is in issue, (i) that there is an onus upon the accused to prove it by evidence sufficient in law on a balance of the probabilities, but (ii) that even if the special defence is not established, the jury must, nevertheless, consider even the evidence of a single witness speaking to alibi, self-defence or incrimination, and if they believe that witness, or find that his evidence creates in their minds a reasonable doubt of the guilt of the accused, they must acquit him, since the burden of proof of guilt is on the Crown throughout. The critical question is whether it is at all appropriate to introduce into a criminal trial, where such a special defence has been lodged, any suggestion that there is at any time any onus on an accused person.

In searching for the answer to this question we begin by noticing what was said in *Lennie* and *Owens*. In *Lennie*, which was a case involving alibi, the Lord Justice-General (Normand) in delivering the opinion of the court said this—'As regards the question of onus, there is no doubt that the onus is throughout on the Crown to prove its case. But it is also true that the onus of proving the alibi was on the appellant. That that has been from the earliest times our law is made clear by the passages in Hume on *Crimes* upon the proving of alibi in olden days. I refer particularly to Vol. II, pp. 298 et seq. and pp. 410 et seq., and these passages also show that it was not uncommon in olden times to take the proof of alibi separately and before remitting the libel to assize. To lay on the Crown the onus of disproving the alibi of which the defence has given notice would be a complete inversion of the rules for the conduct of proofs or trials of which one of the most fundamental and most rational is semper praesumitur pro negante. But, if the jury deals first with the defence of alibi and decides not to sustain it, so that they must then address themselves to the Crown evidence, they must not treat the onus as transferred or affected by the failure of the defence of alibi. The question whether the jury are entitled to reconsider the evidence for the alibi in connection with the evidence for the Crown and in rebuttal of it does not admit of a simple answer yea or nay.'

In *Owens* where self-defence was in issue the same Lord Justice-General in giving the opinion of the court said this—'When we speak of the onus being on the panel to set up self-defence we merely mean that the accused must take the sting out of his own admission that he delivered the fatal blow. If he does this by proving that he was attacked and put in danger of his life (or had reasonable apprehension of danger to his life), he has set up his defence so that he must be acquitted. But, although he may choose to undertake complete legal proof as the best line of defence in the circumstances of his case, he is not bound to lead such evidence as would amount to a discharge of proof. He can rely on his own sworn statement that he was acting in self-defence and rely on his own credibility to outweigh any colourable case the Crown has laid before the jury; and the jury, if satisfied on a review of the whole evidence in the case of his credibility, is entitled to accept the panel's single sworn explanation and to reject evidence which would probably, without the explanation, have been sufficient for a conviction. . . . It may therefore be necessary for the presiding judge, not only to ask the jury to consider whether the special defence has been made out but to ask them also to consider whether it has not had the effect of so shaking reliance on the Crown evidence as to warrant an acquittal from the charge.'

In our opinion there can be no doubt that in *Lennie* and less explicitly in *Owens* the court did subscribe to the proposition that the onus of proving not only alibi but self-defence affirmatively rests on the accused although the judgments at the same time emphasise that the onus of proof of guilt remains on the Crown throughout and that even if proof of the special defence fails for want of corroboration the jury must still consider, in the context of the evidence as a whole, the evidence of even a single witness speaking to alibi or self-defence; and if the evidence of that witness creates in their minds a reasonable doubt of guilt, must acquit. We must accordingly consider whether there was, in law, any warrant for these references to an onus upon the defence, since it is from these references that the charging practice to which we have referred has been derived. What, then, was the state of the law with regard to special defences before 1946? In posing this question we ignore the special defence of insanity at the time since it is quite clear that there is in such a case an onus upon the defence to establish it, since proof of insanity is required before the presumption of sanity can be displaced.

Special defences in our law derive from the requirements of the law in earlier centuries for written defences in answer to a criminal libel when accused persons were limited in their defence to evidence in support of these defences, the relevancy of which had to be affirmed by a court before the matter was remitted to an assize. The 'special defence' of today is the vestigial survivor in modern criminal practice of the written defences of our earlier criminal procedures.

An examination of the earlier authorities discloses no trace of a rule that couples putting forward of a 'special defence' with the necessary acceptance by an accused of an onus of proof of that defence by sufficient, i.e., corroborated evidence, far less of any statement that, should he fail to discharge that onus, the defence as such must fail. It is not to be found in Hume in the passages dealing with 'special defences' (see Hume, Vol. II, pp. 283 and 301) nor in Burnett's *Criminal Law* (published 1811) p. 596, Alison, Vol. II, pp. 369 and 624 nor Macdonald's *Criminal Law* in any edition, nor is it to be found in Anderson's *Criminal Law of Scotland*, p. 274. It is to be observed also that in summary proceedings no notice of such special defences as self-defence or incrimination is required of an accused. In the most recent editions of Renton and Brown, *Criminal Procedure,* the matter is put thus—'The burden of proof that the accused committed the crime libelled against him rests upon the prosecutor throughout the trial. The standard required is proof beyond reasonable doubt. This onus is not transferred or affected by any common law defence pleas other than insanity or diminished responsibility.' The only current statutory requirement relative to the presentation of a special defence in solemn procedure is contained in s. 36 of the Criminal Procedure Act 1887.

By the time Hume was writing, the function of a special defence was limited to giving fair notice to the prosecutor of the line which an accused's defence might take and the requirement of the law was that due notice should be given to the prosecution of such an intention. As put by Hume (Vol. II, p. 301) it was (and is) because 'to let him maintain silence in that respect, till the proof in support of the libel has been closed, would be downright injustice to the prosecutor, who might thus lose the fair means of meeting the defences and strengthening his own case with evidence, in the relative and proper parts.'

It is of course true, as is pointed out in the judgment of the court in *Lennie,* that in earlier times, for reasons which are set out in the passages from Hume cited in that judgment, when in his written defences an accused pleaded alibi, a preliminary proof on the separate issue of alibi was frequently held and if the plea succeeded the libel fell and was not proceeded with. This practice, however, had, at least by the time Hume was writing, fallen into desuetude.

In the case of *H.M. Advocate* v. *Hillan,* 1937 J.C. 53, 1937 S.L.T. 396 one of the grounds of appeal was that the presiding sheriff in a charge of assault had misdirected the jury in respect that he directed the jury on a plea of self-defence to this effect—'that defence (self-defence) is entirely shouldered and must be discharged by the panel. . . . He must have corroborative evidence before you can accept it as established that he did this in self-defence.' The appeal on this point succeeded and Lord Justice-Clerk Aitchison said this at p. 398: 'I think that this direction was unsound. Many cases occur in which from their very circumstances a plea of self-defence must depend upon the evidence of the panel himself. . . . It is no doubt true that a plea of self-defence cannot be affirmatively established upon the evidence of the panel himself, but great injustice might arise if the jury were left with a direction that the plea must fail from want of corroboration. Wherever a plea of self-defence is put forward and supported by evidence, the jury should be explicitly directed that the special defence must be weighed by them in light of the whole proved facts in the case.'

This opinion was before the court in the subsequent cases of *Lennie* and *Owens* and no doubt was cast upon the accuracy of Lord Justice-Clerk Aitchison's statement of the law or of the decision at which the court arrived.

In light of this review of the law and practice before 1946 we have come to be of opinion that the references in *Lennie* and *Owens* to there being an onus upon the defence were unsound. It follows that the passage in Walkers' *Law of Evidence,* § 83 (b) to the effect that 'when a special defence is stated by the accused, the onus of proving it is upon him' can now be regarded as an accurate statement of the law only in the case of the plea of insanity at the time. Apart from the unsoundness of its source the practice of referring at all to an onus being upon the defence inevitably complicated the directions of the presiding judge to such an extent as to be calculated to confuse most juries.

The only purpose of the special defence is to give fair notice to the Crown and once such notice has been given the only issue for a jury is to decide, upon the whole evidence before them, whether the Crown has established the accused's guilt beyond reasonable doubt. When a special defence is pleaded, whether it be of alibi, self-defence or of incrimination, the jury should be so charged in the appropriate language, and all that requires to be said of the special defence, where any evidence in support of it has been given, either in course of the Crown case or by the accused himself or by any witness led for the defence, is that if that evidence, whether from one or more witnesses, is believed, or creates in the minds of the jury reasonable doubt as to the guilt of the accused in the matters libelled, the Crown case must fail and that they must acquit.

Thus, for example, evidence given of acting in self-defence, as this is defined by law, is in no different position from any other evidence consistent with the innocence of the accused and ought to be considered by the jury in precisely the same way."

Appeal allowed: conviction quashed.

NOTE
   Cf. Woolmington v. *D.P.P.* [1935] A.C. 462.

CHAPTER 2

CRIMINAL CONDUCT

a. Criminal acts

Hogg v. Macpherson
1928 J.C. 15

The appellant was the driver of a horse-drawn furniture van for a firm in Edinburgh. While he was leading his horse and van along a street a violent gust of wind blew the van over. The van struck a lamp post, and flattened it to the ground, breaking the lantern. Nothing that the appellant could have done could have averted the damage. A demand was made for payment for the damage, which the appellant refused to pay. He was convicted of failing to pay the sum demanded, contrary to the Edinburgh Municipal and Police Act 1879, s. 93(3). On appeal:

LORD JUSTICE-GENERAL (CLYDE): "This case arises out of a prosecution raised upon one of the sections of the General Police Act, 1862, which is brought by way of incorporation into the scheme of the municipal legislation of this city. The purpose of the enactment is to enable the municipality to recoup itself for accidental or negligent damage done to its street lamps. It is obvious that, in any enactment designed for that object, it is essential that there should be some means or other of selecting a debtor in the obligation to recoup the damage; and, accordingly, what the section in question does is to define the debtor as the person who breaks the lamp, whether the act by which he breaks it be a negligent or an accidental one. The section reads: 'If any person shall, through negligence or accident, break any lamp set up in any street, public or private . . . and shall not, upon demand, make satisfaction for such damage, it shall be lawful for any of the Magistrates, upon complaint thereof being established in the police court, under the summary procedure authorised by this Act, to award such sum of money as the damage proved shall amount to.' In short, the person who breaks a lamp pays for the damage he has done, whether the act by which he breaks it is a negligent act or a purely accidental act. In the present case the appellant was driving a horse-drawn furniture-van along the street on one of those very windy days which occurred not long ago in this city, and one of the more furious of the blasts overturned the lorry. It happened to be near a lamp at the time, and the lamp suffered. The ground of the complaint is that the breaking of the lamp in that way was the act of the driver of the lorry—not (it is admitted) negligent, but (as is alleged) accidental. All I can say is that it seems to me as plain as can be from the circumstances of the case that the breaking of the lamp was not the appellant's act at all, either negligent or accidental, and that, accordingly, upon the facts found proved, there was no justification for the award made."

Appeal allowed.

NOTES

Attempts to define an "act" are not usually successful (see, *e.g.*, the criticisms contained in Gross, *A Theory of Criminal Justice,* ch. 2). The above case does, however, illustrate the minimum requirement of criminal responsibility, *i.e.* some conduct attributable to the accused. See also the cases on automatism (*post*, ch. 8).

b. Criminal omissions

1. R. v. Gibbins and Proctor
(1918) 13 Cr. App. R. 134

Gibbins, and his mistress, Proctor, were convicted of the murder of Gibbins' seven-year-old daughter Nelly, by starving her to death. The relevant facts are outlined in the judgment of Darling J. on appeal.

DARLING J.: "It has been said that there ought not to have been a finding of guilty of murder against Gibbins. The Court agrees that the evidence was less against Gibbins than Proctor, Gibbins gave her money, and as far as we can see it was sufficient to provide for the wants of themselves and all the children. But he lived in the house and the child was his own, a little girl of seven, and he grossly neglected the child. He must have known what her condition was if he saw her, for she was little more than a skeleton. He is in this dilemma; if he did not see her the jury might well infer that he did not care if she died; if he did he must have known what was going on. The question is whether there was evidence that he so conducted himself as to shew that he desired that grievous bodily injury should be done to the child. He cannot pretend that he shewed any solicitude for her. He knew that Proctor hated her, knew that she was ill and that no doctor had been called in, and the jury may have come to the conclusion that he was so infatuated with Proctor, and so afraid of offending her, that he preferred that the child should starve to death rather than that he should be exposed to any injury or unpleasantness from Proctor. It is unnecessary to say more than that there was evidence that Gibbins did desire that grievous bodily harm should be done to the child; he did not interfere in what was being done, and he comes within the definition which I have read, and is therefore guilty of murder.

The case of Proctor is plainer. She had charge of the child. She was under no obligation to do so or to live with Gibbins, but she did so, and receiving money, as it is admitted she did, for the purpose of supplying food, her duty was to see that the child was properly fed and looked after, and to see that she had medical attention if necessary. We agree with what Lord Coleridge C.J. said in *Instan* [1893] 1 Q.B. 450 [see *post*]. 'There is no case directly in point, but it would be a slur upon, and a discredit to the administration of, justice in this country if there were any doubt as to the legal principle, or as to the present case being within it. The prisoner was under a moral obligation to the deceased from which arose a legal duty towards her; that legal duty the prisoner has wilfully and deliberately left unperformed, with the consequence that there has been an acceleration of the death of the deceased owing to the non-performance of that legal duty.' Here Proctor took upon herself the moral obligation of looking after the children; she was *de facto* , though not *de jure*, the wife of Gibbins and had excluded the child's own mother. She neglected the child undoubtedly, and the evidence shews that as a result the child died. So a verdict of manslaughter at least was inevitable."

Appeals dismissed.

NOTE

While the criminal law does not normally penalise omissions, in certain circumstances the law imposes a duty to act. Failure to observe that duty may have criminal consequences. The duty arising from the parent-child relationship is one of the clearest examples. The duty element in other relationships (*e.g.* spouses) is less clear.

2.   R. v. Russell
[1933] V.L.R. 59

The appellant was charged with the murder of his wife and two young children by drowning them in a swimming pool. Evidence was given by the appellant to the effect that his wife had jumped into the pool herself, taking the children with her, and that he had made four unsuccessful attempts to save them, and that he had only given up when he realised that the children were dead. The jury were directed that the appellant would be guilty of murder if he drowned his wife and children, and (in response to a question from the jury) that he would be guilty of manslaughter if he merely stood by and did nothing while his wife drowned herself and the children. If, however, he had encouraged his wife's suicide and murder of the children he would be guilty of murder as an aider and abettor. The jury returned a verdict of manslaughter on all three counts. On appeal:

MANN J. (the trial judge): "The question of the jury was: 'Assuming that the woman took the children into the water without the assistance of putting them in the water by the man, but that he stood by, conniving to the act, what is the position from the standpoint of the law?' This question, heard with knowledge of the course of the trial, including the addresses of counsel and my own charge to the jury, was clearly directed, as I thought and still think, to the second and third counts only, which charged the accused with murder of his two children.

Upon the further consideration given to the matter upon this appeal, I am of opinion that the proper answer for me to have given to the question was that in the case supposed the accused would be guilty of murder.

But apart altogether from the question of murder or manslaughter, it is important that a decision as to the criminal liability of the accused in given circumstances should be referred to the right legal principles. I rested my answer to the jury in effect upon the principles of such cases as *R. v. Instan* [*post*], *R. v. Gibbins and Proctor* [*ante*] and *R. v. Bubb* (1850) 4 Cox C.C. 455. These cases may be regarded as defining the legal sanctions which the law attaches to the moral duty of a parent to protect his children of tender years from physical harm. If applicable to the present case, those authorities would point to the accused's being guilty of what I may call an independent crime of murder. The outstanding difference between the facts of such cases as I have cited and the facts of the present case is the interposition in the latter of a criminal act of a third person which is the immediate cause of death; and the difficulty in such a case is in saying, in the absence of express authority, that the inaction of the accused has caused the death of the children, within the meaning of the criminal law.

I think the more correct view in the present case is that the prisoner on the facts supposed, while perhaps guilty of an independent crime, was certainly guilty as participator in the murder committed by his wife. The moral duty of the accused to save his children, the control which by law he has over his wife, and his moral duty to exercise that control, do not in this view cease to be elements in his crime. On the contrary, it is these elements which as a matter of law give to the acquiescence of the father in the acts of the mother committed in his presence the quality of participation. The control which the law recognizes as exercisable by a husband over his wife is well illustrated in the doctrine that the mere presence of the husband at the commission by his wife of a felony, other than murder, is generally enough to exempt the wife altogether from criminal liability. The physical presence and the 'connivance' of a parent in the position of the accused has in law, in my opinion, a criminal significance not attaching to the presence and connivance of the mere 'passer-by' referred to in some of the cases.

It follows that the case put by me to the jury by way of contrast, though based upon a sound theoretical distinction, was not applicable to the special facts. The facts necessary to constitute aiding and abetting were too narrowly conceived, since no legal distinction can be made between tacit and oral concurrence, and a correct direction would be that not only was the accused morally bound to take active steps to save his children from destruction, but by his deliberate abstention from so doing, and by giving the encouragement and authority of his presence and approval to his wife's act, he became an aider and abettor and liable as a principal offender in the second degree.

I agree therefore with the view expressed by the Acting Chief Justice that upon the case put by the jury the accused was properly convicted, and that it is not necessary to determine finally whether the verdict can also be justified upon those different principles to which I referred in what I said to the jury. I also agree with him in thinking that the two views as to the foundation of liability did not in this case involve any different findings of fact, and that upon any view of the law no injustice can arise from the direction given at the trial."

McARTHUR J.: "The question whether the verdict of manslaughter can stand depends, in my opinion, upon whether the learned Judge's charge to the jury on that subject was correct in law, and whether, having regard to His Honour's charge, the jury were justified in finding that the death of the prisoner's wife and children or any of them was caused by the prisoner's gross culpable neglect.

Leaving over for the moment the question of the prisoner's responsibility for the death of his wife, I am of opinion that the learned Judge's charge with regard to the prisoner's responsibility for the death of the children was correct, and that the conviction on the second and third counts should stand. The learned Judge bases the responsibility primarily upon the duty of the father, by reason of his parenthood, of caring for the safety of his children, who were in his charge and power. So far that is quite correct; and his direction that neglect of that duty would constitute manslaughter and not murder is also, in my opinion, correct.

The authorities which establish the principle of criminal responsibility for the death of one person caused by the neglect of another are mostly cases where young and helpless children or helpless adults were placed under the care and control of the prisoner, and death was caused by the prisoner starving or otherwise neglecting to attend properly to the wants of such child or helpless adult—as, for instance, by omitting to provide necessary medical attention. And these authorities make it clear that if the omission to properly feed or otherwise attend such child or helpless adult was deliberate— done with the intention of causing death—then it would be murder. But if it were not deliberate and intentional, but was due merely to gross and culpable neglect on the part of the prisoner, then it would be manslaughter. And so in the present case a similar distinction was drawn by the learned Judge—the distinction being, as already pointed out, between encouraging and persuading, on the one hand, and merely standing by and doing nothing, on the other.

In describing the duty of the prisoner it would perhaps have been more accurate to have said that he came under a duty to take *all reasonable* steps to prevent the commission of the crime. A man is not bound to take steps which in the circumstances no reasonable man would take in an attempt to save the life of his child. But it is clear that the learned Judge's charge would convey nothing more than that to the jury, because he almost immediately pointed out that it was only where he had 'power to interfere' and 'could have saved them,' and 'refrained from interfering,' that he was criminally responsible; and moreover, on the facts and in the circumstances of the case, and having regard to the view which the jury were taking— as indicated by the question they asked—it was obvious that the steps which the prisoner might have taken in order to have prevented his wife from drowning the children were such as any reasonable man would have taken, and could have taken, without risk or serious trouble to himself.

The learned Judge did not expressly tell the jury that in order to convict the prisoner of manslaughter they must be satisfied that the neglect was gross and culpable, but I think this omission is of no substantial importance in the present case, because on the facts and in the circumstances of the case, and having regard to the view the jury were taking, as indicated by the question they asked, it is obvious that the neglect of the prisoner to make any effort whatever to save the lives of his children was gross and culpable neglect. . . .

I think the conviction on the first count, manslaughter of the wife, cannot stand. Having regard to the questions asked by the jury and to the whole conduct of the case, we must assume, I think, that the jury were of opinion that the wife committed suicide. For the reasons already given I am of opinion that the jury have either found that the prisoner was not a participator in that crime committed by the wife, or they have, at least, not found that he was. And I am not prepared to say that the rules applicable to persons having the care and control of young and helpless children or of helpless adults can be applied to persons having the care of, or having under their protection adults who are not helpless, but are quite capable mentally and physically of looking after themselves. I am therefore of opinion that the prisoner cannot be convicted of the manslaughter of his wife merely because he stood by and did nothing while she committed suicide.

For these reasons I am of opinion that the conviction on the first count should be quashed, and that the convictions on the second and third counts should stand."

Appeal dismissed.

NOTES

Russell raises a number of difficult issues: (a) How does one distinguish between failing to prevent X from committing an act and encouraging him to do it? (b) The problem of causation—How does one establish the causal link between the accused's omission and the death of the children, given the intervention of the wife's act? (c) The ambit of any duty owed by the husband to the wife.

3.   **R. v. Instan**
[1893] 1 Q.B. 450

The accused was convicted of the manslaughter of her seventy-three year-old aunt. The facts are fully outlined in the case stated by Day J. for the Court for Crown Cases Reserved.

DAY J.: "At the time of the committal of the alleged offence, and for some time previous thereto, she had been living with and had been maintained by the deceased. Deceased was a woman of some seventy-three years of age, and until a few weeks before her death was healthy and able to take care of herself. She was possessed of a small life income, and had in the house in which she lived some little furniture, and a few other articles of trifling value. The two women lived together in a house taken by the deceased; no one lived with them or in any way attended to them.

The deceased shortly before her death suffered from gangrene in the leg, which rendered her during the last ten days of her life quite unable to attend to herself or to move about or to do anything to procure assistance. No one but the prisoner had previous to the death any knowledge of the condition in which her aunt thus was.

The prisoner continued to live in the house at the cost of the deceased, and took in the food supplied by the tradespeople; but does not appear to have given any to the deceased, and she certainly did not give or procure any medical or nursing attendance to or for her, or give notice to any neighbour of her condition or wants, although she had abundant opportunity and occasion to do so.

The body of the deceased was on August 2, while the prisoner was still living in the house, found much decomposed, partially dressed in her day clothes, and lying partly on the ground and partly prone upon the bed. The death probably occurred from four to seven days before August 3, the date of the post-mortem examination of the body. The cause of death was exhaustion caused by the gangrene, but substantially accelerated by neglect, want of food, of nursing, and of medical attendance during several days previous to the death. All these wants could and would have been supplied if any notice of the condition of the deceased had been given by the prisoner to any of the neighbours, of whom there were several living in adjoining houses, or to the relations of the deceased, who lived within a few miles. It was proved that the prisoner, while the deceased must have been just about dying, had conversations with neighbours about the deceased, but did not avail herself of the opportunities thus afforded of disclosing the condition in which she then was."

LORD COLERIDGE C.J.: "We are all of the opinion that this conviction must be affirmed. It would not be correct to say that every moral obligation involves a legal duty; but every legal duty is founded on a moral obligation. A legal common law duty is nothing else than the enforcing by law of that which is a moral obligation without legal enforcement. There can be no question in this case that it was the clear duty of the prisoner to impart to the deceased so much as was necessary to sustain life of the food which she from time to time took in, and which was paid for by the deceased's own money for the purpose of the maintenance of herself and the prisoner; it was only through the instrumentality of the prisoner that the deceased could get the food. There was, therefore, a common law duty imposed upon the prisoner which she did not discharge.

Nor can there be any question that the failure of the prisoner to discharge her legal duty at least accelerated the death of the deceased, if it did not actually cause it. There is no case directly in point; but it would be a slur upon and a discredit to the administration of justice in this country if there were any doubt as to the legal principle, or as to the present case being within it. The prisoner was under a moral obligation to the deceased from which arose a legal duty towards her; that legal duty the prisoner has wilfully and deliberately left unperformed, with the consequence that there has been an acceleration of the death of the deceased owing to the non-performance of that legal duty. It is unnecessary to say more than that upon the evidence this conviction was most properly arrived at."

Conviction affirmed.

NOTES

Gordon (para. 3.36) objects to Lord Coleridge's confusion of law and morality, and suggests that a better ratio for *Instan* is that "where people related as were the accused and the deceased live in the circumstances in which they lived, the law imposes an obligation—perhaps because it implies an undertaking—on the healthy person to look after the invalid." Is the relationship necessary for the existence of a duty? *Cf.* the cases of *Stone and Dobinson* [1977] Q.B. 354, *Bonnyman* (1942) 28 Cr.App.R. 131, and the statement of principle in the case of *Charlotte Smith* (1865)10 Cox C.C. 82 (*per* Erle C.J.): "The law is undisputed that, if a person having the care and custody of another who is helpless, neglects to supply him with the necessaries of life and thereby causes or accelerates his death, it is a criminal offence. But the law is also clear, that if a person having the exercise of free will, chooses to stay in a service where bad food and lodging are provided, and death is thereby caused, the master is not criminally liable."

c. *States of affairs*

1. **R. v. Larsonneur**
(1933) 24 Cr. App. R. 74

The appellant, a Frenchwoman, was granted leave to enter the United Kingdom on certain conditions. These conditions were subsequently varied, requiring her to leave the U.K. immediately. She went to the Irish Free State, from whence she was deported and brought under arrest to Holyhead by the Irish Police, where she was handed over to English police officers. She was convicted of an offence contrary to the Aliens Order 1920, Arts. 1(3) (*g*) and 18 (1) (*b*) as amended, the terms of which are set out in the opinion of Hewart L.C.J. On appeal:

HEWART L.C.J.: "The fact is, as the evidence shows, that the appellant is an alien. She has a French passport, which bears this statement under the date March 14, 1933, 'Leave to land granted at Folkestone this day on condition that the holder does not enter any employment, paid or unpaid, while in the United Kingdom,' but on March 22 that condition was varied and one finds these words: 'The condition attached to the grant of leave to land is hereby varied so as to require departure from the United Kingdom not later than March 22, 1933.' Then follows the signature of an Under-Secretary of State. In fact, the appellant went to the Irish Free State and afterwards, in circumstances which are perfectly immaterial, so far as this appeal is concerned, came back to Holyhead. She was at Holyhead on April 21, 1933, a date after the day limited by the condition on her passport.

In these circumstances, it seems to be quite clear that Art. 1 (4) of the Aliens Order 1920 (as amended by the Orders of March 12, 1923, and August 11, 1931), applies. The Article is in the following terms: 'An immigration officer, in accordance with general or special directions of the Secretary of State, may, by general order or notice or otherwise, attach such conditions as he may think fit to the grant of leave to land, and the Secretary of State may at any time vary such conditions in such manner as he thinks fit, and the alien shall comply with the conditions so attached or varied. An alien who fails to comply with any conditions so attached or varied, and an alien who is found in the United Kingdom at any time after the expiration of the period limited by any such condition, shall for the purposes of this Order be deemed to be an alien to whom leave to land has been refused.'

The appellant was, therefore, on April 21, 1933, in the position in which she would have been if she had been prohibited from landing by the Secretary of State and, that being so, there is no reason to interfere with the finding of the jury. She was found here and was, therefore, deemed to be in the class of persons whose landing had been prohibited by the Secretary of State, by reason of the fact that she had violated the condition on her passport. The appeal, therefore, is dismissed and the recommendation for deportation remains."

Appeal dismissed.

NOTES

The decision in *Larsonneur* has been almost universally condemned for its refusal to consider how or why Miss Larsonneur came to be in the United Kingdom (see, *e.g.* Gordon, para. 8.28, Smith and Hogan, p.44). For a reappraisal and attempted rehabilitation of the decision, see Lanham, "Larsonneur Revisited" [1976] Crim.L.R. 276.

2.   O'Sullivan v. Fisher
[1954] S.A.S.R. 33

The respondent was charged with being unlawfully drunk in a public place contrary to s. 74(1) of the Police Act 1936-51. The respondent was in a room on private premises at about 10.30 p.m. when the police arrived. He had been drinking. After some conversation with the police the respondent and the officers left the building and went out into the street where he was very soon arrested. The complaint against him was dismissed by the magistrate. The prosecutor appealed.

REED J.: "Section 74(1) of the Police Act 1936-1951 (as amended in 1946) provides that 'any person who is drunk in any road, street, thoroughfare or public place shall be guilty of an offence'. It was contended for the appellant that (to use the commonly accepted expression) *mens rea* is no part of the offence. By that, as I understand the argument, is meant that it is not necessary for the prosecution to prove either that the defendant intended to get drunk, or intended to be in the public p‧ce, and further, that it is not obligatory for the prosecution to establish that the defendant knew where he was. I have no hesitation in holding that the prohibition contained in s. 74(1) is absolute and is not conditional on the defendant having a guilty mind. If, therefore, a defendant to a charge under s. 74(1) is proved to have been drunk in a road, street, thoroughfare or public place he will, in the usual case, be convicted. The question still remains, however, whether any defence, not founded on a denial of either of the two elements just mentioned, is nevertheless open on a charge under this section.

The Special Magistrate found that the respondent was in Morphett Street for the reason that 'the police told him to go there from a private house where they found him'. After saying that no justification for that order had been proved, but whether or not there was any justification, and whether or not there was any purported arrest of the respondent on the premises (as alleged by him), the Special Magistrate said that the respondent 'may well have felt under compulsion to comply'. The respondent's evidence was that one of the constables told him in the upstairs room that he was under arrest. That was denied by the two police officers who gave evidence for the prosecution, and although the respondent said there were three constables present, it does not appear to be at all probable that that part of his evidence was accurate. The decision of the Special Magistrate does not rest upon a finding on that disputed issue, as the question is excluded in so many words. What did influence him appears to be that he could not believe that 'by the amendment to s. 74 (in 1946) on which the prosecutor relies, namely, the substitution of the words "who is" for the word "found," Parliament intended to give the police authority to order a drunken person into a public place and then arrest him and have him convicted for being there.' I may say that I share that view, as it is not to be supposed that by the alteration of s. 74 effected in 1946

Parliament intended to confer upon members of the police force powers that they did not previously possess in relation to persons on private property. To say that, however, does not decide this case. Mr Chamberlain put the common occurrence of the closing of a hotel bar at 6 p.m., when those who are in it are required to leave. If a man who has been drinking in the bar is drunk, he may go through the door into a street, and his exit may be expedited by a policeman in the bar who has told him to go. In such a case, as it seems to me, it would clearly be no defence to a charge under s. 74 of the Police Act for the defendant to answer that he had been ordered out of the bar by a police officer, or that he believed he had been so ordered out and for that reason only he had gone into the street. So also, if a licensee acts under the provisions of s. 143 of the Licensing Act and turns out of his licensed premises a person who is drunk by obtaining the assistance of a member of the police force, or if that person is expelled by a member of the police force on the demand of the licensee (*cf.* sub-s. (3)), that person has been lawfully evicted, and surely cannot succeed, on a charge under s. 74 of the Police Act, by answering that he was, or believed he was, in the street by the order of a police officer.

Then again a drunken person may be in a public place after leaving a private residence, having been ejected therefrom by the occupier, who has used such force only as was reasonable to get rid of an unwelcome visitor. Whatever the powers of a police constable may be, I see no reason why an occupier who desires to eject a drunken person from his property should not request a police officer to assist him in removing such a person, and give him authority to use reasonable force in doing so. In such a case I cannot see that the person so ejected would have a defence to a charge under s. 74, on the ground that he was in the public place as the result of the action of the occupier or of the police officer.

In all the cases I have taken as examples, the drunken person is in the public place by reason of some act that is lawful. Whatever may be the limits of compulsion as an answer to a charge of an offence against the law (to which I will refer later) I am unable to agree that, as a general proposition, a drunken person who comes into a public place because of a lawful action on the part of some other person is entitled to succeed on a charge of being drunk in a public place on the ground that he was lawfully compelled to be there. It may be that if a man who is drunk is arrested in a house for some offence and is taken in custody into the street, where he is detained until a police vehicle arrives, he would have an answer to a charge under this section, if the zeal of some police officer led him to lay such a charge. Such a defence, if valid, would I think rest upon a general ground not of the same nature as that which has been discussed.

The question whether compulsion is a defence to this charge has been debated. Mr Chamberlain contended, for the appellant, that the charge was established upon proof that the defendant was drunk, and was in a public place, and it was irrelevant how he came to be there.

For the present purpose, however, it appears to be sufficient to say that actual physical compulsion is recognised as an answer to a charge of murder in certain circumstances, as where A by force takes the hand of B, in which is a weapon, and therewith kills C—this is murder in A, but B is not guilty: *cf.* 1 Hale P.C. 434; *Russell on Crimes* (10th ed., 1950) Vol. 1, p. 60: *Archbold on Criminal Pleading* (32nd ed., 1949), p. 20. In *Halsbury's Laws of England* (2nd ed.), Vol. 9, p. 23, the rule is stated as being: 'A person compelled by physical force to do an act which, if voluntarily done, would be a crime, is free from criminal responsibility, but the person compelling him is criminally liable'. In the case of murder above supposed, A is guilty. If, on the other hand, B, who is drunk, is sitting on the verandah of his house, which abuts on the street, and A by force, and without any lawful authority, takes him into the street, it does not appear to be just to hold that B is guilty of an offence against s. 74 of the Police Act. Furthermore, A would not be guilty of that offence, although he might be charged with assault, or some other offence. Being called upon to express an opinion, I state my view as being that if the respondent in the present case proved that he was compelled by physical force, used by a person or persons having no lawful right or authority to remove him from the premises, to go out into the street, he has established an answer to the charge.

With all respect to any who may hold the contrary view, it seems to me that the answer of duress or compulsion to a charge of an offence rests upon the right of an accused person to show that the act is one which in law cannot be imputed to him; and that the answer may be made in certain cases even though the person exercising the compulsion is not guilty of the offence with which the accused is charged (*cf. Cambridge Law Journal*, Vol. 6, at p. 91).

For these reasons the appeal will be allowed, and the order of dismissal will be set aside. I think the proper course to take is to remit the matter for rehearing. There are passages in the evidence that suggest that the two police officers acted at the request and upon the authority of the occupier of the premises, and it is possible that the respondent left voluntarily without the use of any force."

Appeal allowed.

NOTES

Cf. clause 67 of the Criminal Justice (Scotland) Bill 1979 which provides: "(1) Where a vehicle, being a public service vehicle which is being used as a contract carriage, is engaged on a journey the principal purpose of which is to convey passengers to or from a designated sporting event, then . . . (c) any person who is drunk on the vehicle shall be guilty of an offence".

Would an offence be committed by X if (a) he was carried on to the bus by friends while unconscious through drink, or (b) he was required to get on to the bus by a police officer who was trying to clear the crowd after a designated sporting event?

d. Voluntariness

In so far as the *actus reus* of an offence consists in conduct, the general principle is that that conduct must be voluntary before it will attract criminal sanctions. Many of the cases which raise this issue also involve questions of automatism and mental abnormality, and the issue in Scotland has become confused with insanity in some cases. These cases are, therefore, discussed in the chapter on criminal capacity (*post*). The two following cases are included here to illustrate (a) that not all cases of involuntariness involve mental abnormality, and (b) that the issue can arise in relation to omissions as well as acts.

1. Middleton v. Tough
(1908) 5 Adam 485 (Full Bench)

LORD JUSTICE-GENERAL (DUNEDIN): "My Lords, the question brought before your Lordships is whether there ought to have been a conviction on the following facts as stated by the learned Sheriff-Substitute who states the case.

In the county of Ross and Cromarty, at the Geanies salmon fishery, there is in operation, by force of law, the bye-law contained in schedule D of the Salmon Fisheries (Scotland) Act of 1868. The section of that statute which imposes the penalty is the 24th, and it puts upon the proprietor or occupier of every fishery the obligation of doing all acts for the due observance of the weekly close time required by any bye-law in force within the district. The bye-law imposed by Schedule D provides that, with regard to the due observance of the weekly close time, which is a close time imposed from six o'clock on Saturday afternoon till six o'clock on Monday morning, 'the netting of the leader of each and every bag-net shall be entirely removed and taken out of the water.' Your Lordships will therefore observe that a positive duty is put upon the owner or the occupier of every fishing. The occupier, who is the respondent in this case, is a Mrs Tough, and she admittedly upon the occasion specified did not take out the leaders of her bag-nets during the whole of the specified period, but left them there from six o'clock on Saturday evening till a very early period on Monday morning. *Prima facie*, therefore, it is quite clear that she has contravened the statute, and consequently is liable to conviction. What, then, is her excuse? She says, and the learned Sheriff-Substitute holds that it is proved, that at six o'clock on Saturday evening the state of the weather was such that it was a physical impossibility to remove the leaders. Then he goes on to say that the leaders could have been removed without danger on Sunday—as a matter of fact, one of them was removed by the Fishery Board people on that day—and he further finds that there was no evidence that the respondent's men were ever asked by her to remove the leaders on the Sunday, or that they refused to do so, or that it was impossible for the respondent to hire men willing to remove leaders on the Sunday.

Upon the state of the facts I think there must be a conviction here, because the *onus* upon the prosecutor is satisfied as soon as he shows that there was a contravention of the bye-law. That he does by showing that the leaders were not removed. No doubt there may be an answer to that which has always been held as an answer satisfactory to avoid conviction, namely, that there was impossibility. Physical impossibility there undoubtedly was at six o'clock on Saturday evening, by reason of the weather, but it was not according to the stated facts impossible on the Sunday morning. Therefore, there must have been some other class of impossibility which the respondent was bound to table, and she had not proved either that she took the slightest trouble to try and get her men to remove the leaders, or, failing them, that she could not get others. Practically speaking, that is enough for the decision of the case.

But Mr Hunter has appealed to us not to decide the case upon that matter alone, because I understand that this case has been brought up in order to review the decision in *Middleton* v. *Paterson* (1904) 4 Adam 321. I have no hesitation in saying that I agree with the opinion of Lord Moncreiff in *Middleton* v. *Paterson*, and that I do not think that case was rightly decided. There are various grounds for my opinion. The argument for inability is admittedly entirely based upon the Scottish statutes against Sunday labour. These are certain old statutes of the Scottish Parliament. I am bound to say that for myself I am greatly in doubt whether these statutes are still in operation, or whether they have not fallen into desuetude. But I do not think it is necessary to decide that question, as I shall presently explain. *Prima facie*, I do not think that these statutes have anything to do with it, because the question is not as to whether a conviction could be secured under these statutes for doing a certain thing, but whether this person was prevented from doing what she should otherwise have done by *vis major*. I use that expression because it comprehends laws of every kind, physical or otherwise. It may be that you could find persons who would be content to work on the Sunday and take their risk of a conviction under the statutes, and looking at the general state of affairs as matters go nowadays, I do not think the risk would be a very great one. But it was argued that this was so clearly against the statutes that really it becomes tantamount to an impossibility, because if you engage anybody to do that thing you would be engaging him to do a thing which was in itself unlawful. My Lords, I cannot follow that, because, assuming, as I do for the moment, that the statutes are still in observance and not in desuetude, I cannot say that the act here would ever be struck at by the statutes. What may be called the leading case for the statutes is that of *Phillips* v. *Innes* (1837) 2 Sh. & MacL. 465, where it was held that, looking to the prohibitions of the statutes, a barber's apprentice in Dundee, who had been engaged to do his master's work, holidays excepted, was justified in refusing to shave customers as an ordinary business on Sunday before ten o'clock in the morning. The one point was that shaving customers before ten o'clock on Sundays was ordinary work, and that if he had been obliged to do it, he would have had to shave Sunday after Sunday just as on other days. In point of fact, he might have had to shave more than on ordinary days, because there are men of peculiar habits who prefer shaving on Sundays rather than on other days. But the learned Lords who decided that case seem to have been very careful to distinguish between ordinary and regular labour, and labour of a casual sort, which might be called for in an emergency, because the Lord Ordinary and one of the noble and learned Lords, Lord Wynford, put as an exception the particular case of a man being called upon to shave some one suffering from acute illness, and the shaving of whose head became more or less a work of necessity. I am of opinion that this particular operation of taking up the leaders on a Sunday, when it has been rendered impossible on Saturday by the state of the weather, is just such a work of necessity, and there again I agree with the opinion of Lord Moncreiff in *Middleton* v. *Paterson*.

Mr Hunter read a passage in Lord Brougham's opinion in *Phillips'* case, in which the noble and learned Lord used some expressions which seem to mean that the necessity must be that of the person called upon to work and not that of the person whom he serves. That view, I think, is absolutely untenable. It is perfectly evident that you cannot so limit it, for it is possible, not only to have works of necessity where the necessity is for the weal of the public in general, but also to identify the interests of the master and servant. If it were not so, the feeding of cattle, for example, would not be lawful, because there is no necessity, so far as the servant is concerned, it being the master's loss, and not his, if the cattle die.

But the matter does not end there, because I think there is another ground which takes this case out of the decision in the case of *Phillips*, and it is this. These old statutes may not be in desuetude, but they certainly are not, to say the least of it, rigorously enforced. Then, in 1868 Parliament passed another Act which shows upon the face of it that something must be done by somebody on Sunday, because Parliament must be held to have had the common sense to know that occasionally there would be states of the weather which would make it impossible to remove the leaders on Saturday. Still, Parliament has held that the leaders must be taken out of the water during the weekly close time. That is equivalent to a positive enactment not necessarily repealing the old statutes, but holding that such a work is a work of necessity. Upon that ground I come to the opinion clearly that there was here no justifiable excuse for not complying with the Act of Parliament. Of course, whether a person could get a servant or not to do the work is another matter. The duty is put upon the occupier or owners, and if they cannot do it themselves they must get some one who will. You might find certain persons who would not work for you on Mondays, but you may contract with those who will. Or, take one religion and you will find a person who refuses to work on a Saturday. But that is your affair. All that is necessary to say here is that such an excuse is not *vis major*. Whether you can get a servant to do the work or not is simply a matter of contract."

Appeal allowed.

2. **Kilbride** v. **Lake**
[1962] N.Z.L.R. 590 (Supreme Court of New Zealand)

The appellant was convicted on a charge of operating a motor vehicle on which there was no current warrant of fitness carried, contrary to reg. 52(1) of the Traffic Regulations 1956. He appealed against conviction. The circumstances of the alleged offence are fully set out in the opinion of Woodhouse J.

WOODHOUSE J.: "On Thursday, 15 June 1961, the appellant drove his wife's car into Queen Street in the city of Auckland where he left it parked. He returned to it a short time later to find stuck to the inside of the windscreen a traffic offence notice drawing his attention to the fact that a current warrant of fitness was not displayed in terms of Reg. 52 of the Traffic Regulations 1956 (S.R. 1956/217). It was agreed before me that the warrant had been in its correct position when he left the vehicle, but that it could not be found upon his return. It was further agreed that during the period of his absence from the car the warrant had become detached from the windscreen in some way and been lost, or it had been removed by some person unknown. The fact that it was a current warrant was proved conclusively by records showing that on 13 April it had been issued by the Auckland Municipal Motor Vehicle Testing Station under No. 4513, and in respect of voucher No. 115456. Thus it had been issued for only two months, and four months would elapse before it required to be renewed. Despite a written explanation to this general effect which he had forwarded on the same day, a prosecution followed and he was convicted before Justices on an information alleging that he 'did operate a motor vehicle . . . and did fail to display in the prescribed manner a current warrant of fitness'. The proceedings were defended, but no note of the evidence was taken and no reasons for the decision were given. In these circumstances the appeal was argued on agreed facts as I have summarised them.

So far as it is applicable the Regulation reads: '(1) . . . No person shall operate a motor vehicle . . . unless there is carried on the vehicle a current warrant of fitness as described in subclause (2) of this Regulation.' Subclause (2) provides that in the case of a vehicle fitted with a windscreen the warrant shall be affixed to the inside of the windscreen. The word 'operate' is defined in Reg. 3 as meaning 'to use or drive or ride, or cause or permit to be driven or ridden, or to permit to be on any road whether the person operating is present in person or not.'

The appeal was argued on the basis that the appellant operated the vehicle by permitting it to be on the road, and the facts do not support any wider application of the word 'operate'. Accordingly the regulation under review may be written, for the present purpose, as follows: 'No person shall permit a motor vehicle to be on a road whether the person operating it is present or not unless there is carried on the vehicle a current warrant of fitness'.

The case for the appellant was that if he could show an absence of *mens rea*, then he could not be convicted, and he had succeeded in doing this as the warrant had disappeared without his knowledge during his absence from the car. On the other hand it was claimed for the respondent that this statutory offence was one which excluded *mens rea* as an ingredient to be proved. On this basis it was submitted that the offence was one of strict liability, and therefore the knowledge or the intention of the appellant was irrelevant. The issue thus raised on these simple facts directly poses the important question as to whether something done perfectly lawfully by the appellant could become an offence on his part by reason of an intervening cause beyond his influence or control, and which produced an effect entirely outside his means of knowledge.

It has long been established, of course, that if there is an absolute prohibition, and the prohibited act is done by the defendant, then the absence of *mens rea* affords no defence. This principle derives its justification from the general public interest, and any consequential injustice which might seem to follow in individual cases has necessarily been accepted. In the present case the respondent has conceded that the appellant had no opportunity of dealing with the situation which arose. But, it is said, however unfair a conviction might be to him personally, this offence has been made one of absolute liability as it is essential to put strong pressure on drivers of motor vehicles to do their whole duty. He permitted the car to be on the road, it was found there without a warrant and accordingly he is guilty of the offence. With all respect to the arguments of both counsel, however, I am of the opinion that the emphasis which has been put on the matter of *mens rea* has obscured the real issue in this case.

It is fundamental that quite apart from any need there might be to prove *mens rea*, 'a person cannot be convicted for any crime unless he has committed an overt act prohibited by law, or has made default in doing some act which there was a legal obligation upon him to do. The act or omission must be voluntary': *10 Halsbury's Laws of England*, 3rd ed., 272. He must be shown to be responsible for the physical ingredient of the crime or offence. This elementary principle obviously involves the proof of something which goes behind any subsequent and additional inquiry that might become necessary as to whether *mens rea* must be proved as well. Until that initial proof exists arguments concerning *mens rea* are premature. If the first decision to be made is that the offence excludes *mens rea*, then that finding is likely to disguise the fact that there is an absence of proof showing that the accused has done all that is charged against him, should this in fact be the case. The missing link in the chain of causation, if it is noticed at all, appears to be provided by notions of absolute liability. But it is impossible, of course, to prove the one ingredient by eliminating the need to prove another. It appears to me that this confusion has arisen in this case. The primary question arising on this appeal, in my opinion, is whether or not the physical element in the offence was produced by the appellant. This physical element may be described by the convenient term *actus reus*, in contrast to the mental element or *mens rea* which is also an ingredient of a crime or offence, unless expressly excluded by its statutory definition.

In considering whether the *actus reus* can be attributed to a defendant, it is important to recognise that this is something which occurs following acts or omissions. It is not the line of conduct which produces the prohibited event, but it is the event itself. It is an occurrence brought about by some activity or inactivity, or by both. The crime therefore (excluding for the moment the possible ingredient of *mens rea*) is constituted by the event, and not by the discrete acts or omissions which preceded it: *Russell on Crime*, 11th ed., pp. 25, *et seq.* Accordingly it is not sufficient to show by some single act or omission that the accused produced the event. It is this fact which produces difficulties of causation when attempting to attribute responsibility for the *actus reus* to a given person. It is easy to do this when the *actus reus* can result from a single act, as, for example, a death by shooting. When it depends, however, upon supervening acts, and particularly when omissions are added to them, then the difficulties tend to multiply. Of course, when *mens rea* is an ingredient to be proved against an accused person, all these difficulties disappear as soon as they arise, because he usually cannot be proved to have intended acts done by others. He is thereupon acquitted on that ground. As *mens rea* is so frequently an ingredient of crimes and offences, this is a problem which rarely arises, and for that reason is not always recognised.

In the present case the definition of the offence takes the form of a prohibition followed by an exception. The prohibited event, however, in the sense of the term *actus reus* is not merely to permit a vehicle to be on the road. It is the doing of that act accompanied by an omission to observe the obligation to carry the current warrant of fitness. The *actus reus* occurs only when the second of these factual ingredients co-exists with the first. There must be the presence of the car combined with the absence of the warrant. Did this appellant produce that prohibited event, or did he merely set the stage?

There can be no doubt that the appellant permitted the vehicle to be on the road, and his conduct in this respect was a continuing act which did not end when he left the vehicle. Nevertheless, at this latter point of time the warrant was on the car, and there was no unlawful situation. Only when some extraneous cause subsequently removed the warrant did the event occur which the regulation is directed to prevent. If he is to be regarded as responsible for that *actus reus*, therefore, the decision must be made on the basis that he omitted immediately to replace the warrant.

It is, of course, difficult to demonstrate that an omission to act was not, in a causal sense, an omission which produced some event. All omissions result from inactivity, and in this matter of the warrant the appellant was necessarily inactive. But, in my opinion, it is a cardinal principle that, altogether apart from the mental element of intention or knowledge of the circumstances, a person cannot be made criminally responsible for an act or omission unless it was done or omitted in circumstances where there was some other course open to him. If this condition is absent, any act or omission must be involuntary, or unconscious, or unrelated to the forbidden event in any causal sense regarded by the law as involving responsibility. See for example *Salmond on Jurisprudence*, 11th ed. 401, *Causation in the Law* by Hart and Honore 292, *et seq.*, and the passage in *10 Halsbury's Laws of England*, 3rd ed., 272 cited above. In my opinion a correct emphasis is now given by this last paragraph to the need for the act or omission making up the *actus reus* to be voluntary, whereas in the corresponding paragraph of the second edition this distinction was blurred in discussion of *mens rea*. Naturally the condition that there must be freedom to take one course or another involves free and conscious exercise of will in the case of an act, or the opportunity to choose to behave differently in the case of omissions. But this mental stimulus required to promote acts or available to promote omissions if the matter is adverted to, and consequently able to produce some forbidden condition, is entirely distinct from the mental element contained in the concept of *mens rea*. The latter is the intention or the knowledge behind or accompanying the exercise of will, while the former is simply the spark without which the *actus reus* cannot be produced at all. In the present case there was no opportunity at all to take a different course, and any inactivity on the part of the appellant after the warrant was removed was involuntary and unrelated to the offence. In these circumstances I do not think it can be said that the *actus reus* was in any sense the result of his conduct, whether intended or accidental. There was an act of the appellant which led up to the prohibited event (the *actus reus*), and that was to permit the car to be on the road. The second factual ingredient was not satisfied until the warrant disappeared during his absence. The resulting omission to carry the warrant was not within his conduct, knowledge, or control: on these facts the chain of causation was broken.

For the foregoing reasons I am of the opinion that the physical ingredient of this charge was not proved against the appellant. Accordingly, I express no opinion on the submission that *mens rea* is excluded as an ingredient of the offence. On the view I have taken of the case the point does not arise."

Appeal allowed.

Chapter 3

CAUSATION

As far as criminal responsibility is concerned, the question of causation has been most frequently discussed in the context of causing death in homicide. The problem is not, however, confined to this area, and questions of causality may present themselves, for example, in the law of fraud (*Mather* v. *H.M. Advocate* (1914) 7 Adam 525, *post*, ch. 14) and offences of causing damage to property.

a. *"Taking the victim as you find him"*

1. **H.M. Advocate** v. **Robertson and Donoghue**
High Court, August 1945, *unreported*

The accused were charged with, *inter alia*, assault, robbery and murder. The case against the first accused was that he had assaulted an elderly shopkeeper in his shop, struggled with him and inflicted certain slight injuries on him. As a result of this attack the old man died of heart failure. The first accused was also charged with assaulting the deceased's wife, and stealing a sum of money from the shop. The case against a second accused was that he was art and part in these offences. The medical evidence disclosed that the deceased had a very weak heart. In his charge to the jury the presiding judge made the following remarks on the question of causation:

LORD JUSTICE-CLERK (COOPER): "The first point you have to address your mind to is not, I think, the question whether murder or culpable homicide was committed, but whether the old man died as a direct result of the violence used against him—for this reason, ladies and gentlemen: whether the criminal taking of life is charged as murder or culpable homicide, in either event it is indispensable that the victim should have died as a result of the injury inflicted—obviously so. The death must result from real violence used against the victim. To take obvious examples, if in any case death was due to, say, natural causes, or to some subsequent accident or maltreatment or neglect, which broke the chain of causation between the so-called crime and the death, then the death cannot be laid to the door of the assailant. Such a death would be, to borrow [counsel's] phrase, an act of God or a mischance. On the other hand, you have to keep very steadily in view that somewhat different considerations apply in a case like this if it be the case that the

41

assailant was engaged at the time in committing a crime of violence. What I mean is this: we know that Mr. Demarco (the deceased) was an old man of 82; we know as a result of the post-mortem examination what probably nobody knew, not even Mr. Demarco, before that examination was made . . . that his heart was in a very serious condition, and that he was, to use Dr. Wright's words, a frail, old man. Now it cannot be sufficiently emphasised, ladies and gentlemen, that if an intruder or aggressor, acting from some criminal intent and in pursuance of some criminal purpose, makes a violent attack upon any man or woman he must take his victim as he finds him. It is every whit as criminal to kill a feeble and infirm old man, or a new born infant as it is to kill an adult in the prime of life. However precarious the victim's hold on life may be, no person dare extinguish the spark by violent means but at his peril. It would never do for it to go forth from this Court that house-breakers or robbers, or others of that character, should be entitled to lay violent hands on very old or very sick or very young people, and, if their victim died as a result, to turn round and say that they would never have died if they had not been very weak or very old or very young. That is not the law, and I think you will agree with me that it is not common sense. And so this point, ladies and gentlemen, very much turns on the view you as a jury take both of the background and general circumstances under which the assault was committed and of the evidence we have heard with regard to Mr. Demarco and his condition. . . .

On that medical evidence it is for you to consider . . . whether, so to put it, the violence which I assume you hold proved to have been inflicted by Robertson on Mr. Demarco was or was not the direct cause of his death, or whether, to put it from the opposite standpoint, Mr. Demarco's death was a pure mischance and an act of God. . . . The question is for you on the medical and other evidence, but . . . if you are satisfied that the applied violence, the violence applied by Robertson, was the effective cause of Mr. Demarco's death, then you would pass to the next stage, which is to consider whether . . . Robertson is answerable for the crime of murder or only for the lesser crime of culpable homicide. It was said by one of the witnesses . . . that Demarco might have died any moment in his sleep. I suppose the same is true of any of us, although in a lesser degree I hope, but the point I wish to make is that it is none the less homicide to accelerate or precipitate the death of an ailing person than it is to cut down a healthy man who might have lived for fifty years."

Verdict: Robertson guilty of culpable homicide; case against Donoghue found not proven.

NOTES

Similar statements of the law are to be found in *H.M. Advocate* v. *Rutherford*, 1947 J.C. 1 (*post*, ch. 11), *Bird* v. *H.M. Advocate*, 1952 J.C. 23 (*post*, ch.11). The rule that an assailant cannot rely on the weakness or illness of his victim as an exculpatory circumstance applies even where the weakness is self-induced, or due to some fault on the part of the victim. In *James Williamson* (1866) 5 Irv. 326 (*post*) it was argued by the accused that the victim's health had been impaired by excessive drinking, so that a blow which might not otherwise have been very serious proved fatal to her. The Lord Justice-Clerk (Inglis) rejected the argument, stating, "because a person is weaker than his neighbours, either from natural constitution or bad habit, can never make the slightest difference in the question of guilt or innocence in a case of this kind."

2. R. v. Blaue
[1975] 3 All E.R. 446

The appellant was charged, *inter alia*, with the murder of a young woman, by stabbing her. At his trial the evidence disclosed that the victim was a Jehovah's Witness, who, on being taken to hospital, refused the blood transfusion which she was advised was essential if she was to survive. She did not receive a transfusion, and died four hours later. It was accepted that she would have survived if she had accepted the transfusion when it was suggested. The appellant was found to be suffering from diminished responsibility, and was convicted of manslaughter. On appeal against conviction:

LAWTON L. J.: "The physical cause of death in this case was the bleeding into the pleural cavity arising from the penetration of the lung. This had not been brought about by any decision made by the deceased girl but by the stab wound.

Counsel for the appellant tried to overcome this line of reasoning by submitting that the jury should have been directed that if they thought the girl's decision not to have a blood transfusion was an unreasonable one, then the chain of causation would have been broken. At once the question arises—reasonable by whose standards? Those of Jehovah's Witnesses? Humanists? Roman Catholics? Protestants of Anglo-Saxon descent? The man on the Clapham omnibus? But he might well be an admirer of Eleazar who suffered death rather than eat the flesh of swine or of Sir Thomas Moore who, unlike nearly all his contemporaries, was unwilling to accept Henry VIII as Head of the Church of England. Those brought up in the Hebraic and Christian traditions would probably be reluctant to accept that these martyrs caused their own deaths.

As was pointed out to counsel for the appellant in the course of argument, two cases, each raising the same issue of reasonableness because of religious beliefs, could produce different verdicts depending on where the cases were tried. A jury drawn from Preston, sometimes said to be the most Catholic town in England, might have different views about martyrdom to one drawn from the inner suburbs of London. Counsel for the appellant accepted that this might be so; it was, he said, inherent in trial by jury. It is not inherent in the common law as expounded by Sir Matthew Hale and Maule J. It has long been the policy of the law that those who use violence on other people must take their victims as they find them. This in our judgment means the whole man, not just the physical man. It does not lie in the mouth of the assailant to say that his victim's religious beliefs which inhibited him from accepting certain kinds of treatment were unreasonable. The question for decision is what caused her death. The answer is the stab wound. The fact that the victim refused to stop this end coming about did not break the causal connection between the act and death.

If a victim's personal representatives claim compensation for his death the concept of foreseeability can operate in favour of the wrongdoer in the assessment of such compensation; the wrongdoer is entitled to expect his victim to mitigate his damage by accepting treatment of a normal kind: see *Steele* v. *R. George & Co. Ltd.* [1942] A.C. 497. As counsel for the Crown pointed out, the criminal law is concerned with the maintenance of law and order and the protection of the public generally. A policy of the common law applicable to the settlement of tortious liability between subjects may not be, and in our judgment is not, appropriate for the criminal law.

The issue of the cause of death in a trial for either murder or manslaughter is one of fact for the jury to decide. But if, as in this case, there is no conflict of evidence and all the jury has to do is to apply the law to the admitted facts, the judge is entitled to tell the jury what the result of that application will be. In this case the judge would have been entitled to have told the jury that the appellant's stab wound was an operative cause of death. The appeal fails."

Appeal dismissed.

NOTES

Is it only religious conviction that is to be accorded this respect? Suppose that the victim was a racial bigot and refused to accept treatment because the only available medical staff were coloured? Would this be materially different from *Blaue?*

Is causation properly a question of fact for the jury or one of law for the court? Compare *Blaue* with the remarks of the Lord Justice-Clerk in *Robertson and Donaghue (ante)*, and see also Williams, pp. 331-332.

b. Malregimen

1. James Williamson
(1866) 5 Irv. 326

The panel was charged with the murder, or alternatively culpable homicide, of a woman by stabbing her. On his behalf it was argued, *inter alia*, that the wound only proved fatal because of the bad medical treatment she received. In his charge to the jury the presiding judge made the following remarks:

LORD JUSTICE-CLERK (INGLIS): "Then, in the second place, it is said that this woman, after she received the wound was not well treated, and that if she had been better treated she would have recovered. Now, it is necessary to explain to you how the law stands about this. If a person receives a wound from the hand of another which is not fatal in itself—it may be a simple and easily cured wound—and then afterwards by unskilful and injudicious treatment this wound assumes a more serious aspect, and finally terminates in death, it is possible to say, and to say with perfect truth, that the wound inflicted by the hand of the prisoner is not the cause of death, because it would not by itself have produced death but for the bad treatment which followed on it. But it will never do, on the other hand, if a wound calculated to prove mortal in itself is afterwards followed by death, to say that every criticism that can be made on the treatment of the patient after the wound is received is to furnish a ground for aquitting the person who inflicted the wound of either murder or culpable homicide."

Verdict: guilty of culpable homicide.

2. Heinrich Heidmeisser
(1879) 17 S.L.R. 266

The panel was charged with the murder of a man by stabbing him. The view of the medical witnesses was that the wounds were not necessarily fatal, but that they were dangerous. It was argued on behalf of the panel that the cause of death was not the wounds but improper medical treatment. It was established that his nurses had been replaced by an old man, described as "quite inefficient," and that his condition might have been seriously affected by exposure to a chill, the hospital being a draughty building. One of the medical witnesses was of the view that the deceased was "out of danger" when the improper treatment began.

LORD JUSTICE-CLERK (MONCREIFF): "The first point to consider is, what was the cause of this man's death. The defence as to this seemed to be that the deceased with proper treatment in the hospital would have recovered, but that his death had resulted from improper treatment after the danger from the wound had been removed. This defence is what is technically known as *mal regimen* —that is to say, where an injury has become mortal or fatal by reason of improper treatment. With regard to such a defence there are distinctions to be observed, which I think have been properly and clearly laid down in the cases referred to—*A. Dingwall*, September 1867, 5 Irv. 466; *J. Williamson*, November 1866, 5 Irv. 326—and which will commend themselves to your common sense. If a man inflicts an injury on another which is not in itself mortal, or which if left to its own operation could not be said to be likely to lead to death, and if that injury becomes fatal by reason of improper treatment, then it does not necessarily follow that the man who inflicted the wound was the cause of death. I do not lay it down more strongly than that, because every case depends on its own circumstances. On the other hand, if a man inflicts an injury which if left to itself will result in death, or of which death is the probable result— which is calculated to lead to death, though it may be capable of cure by the best attention of the best medical skill—then though the man might have recovered if he had had these, it will not relieve the person who inflicted the wound from the guilt of homicide that that best medical skill or care had not been got. That is the general rule, and it will, I think, commend itself to your own common sense, as well as being a sound legal proposition. If a man fights a duel and wounds his antagonist, and by reason of the mode of carrying him off the field haemorrhage set in, though the wound might not in itself have caused death, and haemorrhage is the direct cause, the man who inflicts the wound is responsible.

To apply this doctrine to the present case, you will see that it is a hard one for the prisoner. This man had not recovered from the injury in any popular or reasonable sense, but he was fairly within the grasp of proper medical care. He had been brought through the danger, and nothing more was required but ordinary skill and care,—but he had not recovered, and if a chill was sufficient to carry him off, as in point of fact it seems to have done, the man who put his fellow-man in a position where a chill would carry him off is responsible."

Verdict: guilty of culpable homicide.

NOTES

Does Lord Moncreiff's charge imply that there may be cases of slight injury followed by improper treatment where the original wound might remain the cause of death?

Do the above cases adequately deal with the situation where death results from the combined effects of a dangerous (but not necessarily fatal) wound and treatment which is not merely negligent but totally wrong?

In *R*. v. *Jordan* (1956) 40 Cr. App. R. 152 the appellant stabbed a man who subsequently received treatment described by medical witnesses as "palpably wrong," resulting in death from pneumonia. In quashing his conviction for murder, the Court of Criminal Appeal stated: "We are disposed to accept it as the law that death resulting from any normal treatment employed to deal with a felonious injury may be regarded as caused by the felonious injury. . . . It is sufficient to point out here that this was not normal treatment. Not only one feature, but two separate and independent features of treatment were, in the opinion of the doctors, palpably wrong and these produced the symptoms discovered at the post-mortem examination which were the direct and immediate cause of death, namely, the pneumonia resulting from the condition of oedema which was found."

In *R*. v. *Smith* [1959] 2 All E.R. 193 the appellant was convicted of the murder of a man by stabbing him. One of the wounds penetrated the lung. On the way to a medical station the injured man was dropped twice, and in the medical station he received treatment which was described as "thoroughly bad" and which "might well have affected his chances of recovery." In dismissing the appeal, the Courts-Martial Appeal Court stated: "It seems to the court that, if at the time of death the original wound is still an operating cause and a substantial cause, then the death can properly be said to be the result of the wound, albeit that some other cause of death is also operating. Only if it can be said that the original wounding is merely the setting in which another cause operates can it be said that the death does not result from the wound. Putting it in another way, only if the second cause is so overwhelming as to make the original wound merely part of the history can it be said that the death does not flow from the wound. . . . The court is satisfied that *R*. v. *Jordan* was a very particular case depending on its exact facts."

3.   James Wilson
(1838) 2 Swin. 16

The panel was charged, along with another man, with culpable homicide or, alternatively, assault to the danger of life. The charge of culpable homicide alleged that they struck the deceased with their fists and feet and cut him with a bayonet, "or at least [the deceased] in consequence of the injuries so suffered . . . contracted or was infected with erysipelas of the head . . . and of which disease he died . . ." and was thus killed by the accused. It appeared that there was a mild case of erysipelas in the hospital to which the deceased was taken for treatment. The medical witnesses took the view that the deceased did not contract the disease through infection from the other patient, although it was possible that he might have done so. In his charge to the jury the presiding judge made the following remarks:

LORD COCKBURN: "It is argued by the public prosecutor, that but for the wounds inflicted by the pannel, the sufferer never would have died, and they are, therefore, not only the remote, but, properly speaking, the real and only cause of his death. For the pannel, on the other hand, it is argued, that the wounds cannot be blamed for the effects of a disease, which is not the natural consequence of them, and but for which they would have proved comparatively harmless. Now, this latter doctrine is not to be taken without some limitation. Suppose a man to die of apoplexy, but that apoplexy to have been produced by a blow. It will not, surely, do for the prisoner, in that case, to say, I gave you a blow, but I did not give you apoplexy. He must stand the peril of the consequences of his act. Death seldom follows directly from a blow, or even a wound. Some supervening disease is generally the immediate cause . . . You must apply this principle to the present case. If the wound caused the disease, the pannel must be found guilty of culpable homicide. If it had no effect in producing it—the verdict cannot go that length. Now, the medical witnesses tell us that the disease was not contracted by infection, and their report describes the wounds as the primary cause of death. Before you can acquit the pannel of the more serious charge standing against him, you must be satisfied that the disease was an entirely new disease—not produced by the wounds, but by infection, or some other external cause."

Verdict: guilty of assault as libelled.

NOTES

Cf. Heidmeisser (ante). Gordon's view is that the remarks of Lord Moncreiff there are wrong, and that the law is probably contained in *Wilson* (Gordon, para. 4-46). In *Bush* v. *Commonwealth*, 78 Ky. 268 (1880) the accused shot and wounded his victim. The latter was infected with scarlet fever by a member of the medical staff treating him, and died. It was held that death had been caused by the disease, and not by the accused's wound, which was not in itself mortal.

c.   *The victim's contribution*

1. **Jos. and Mary Norris**
(1886) 1 White 292

Two accused were charged with the culpable homicide of a man by striking him with their fists and stones, and knocking him to the ground and kicking him about the back and head. It appeared that none of the wounds inflicted by the accused were serious, and that he received prompt medical treatment. However, the victim died eight days later, of lockjaw (tetanus). Evidence was led on behalf of the accused that the victim had not followed medical advice by consuming alcohol, and also that he had removed his own bandages. On two occasion he walked home late at night, having consumed a quantity of beer. In his charge to the jury the presiding judge gave the following direction:

LORD CRAIGHILL: "If you are of opinion that the prisoners inflicted the wounds on the deceased, the medical testimony is clear that wounds of so apparently trivial a character have been known to cause tetanus, and had produced tetanus in this case. There is also no doubt at all that the deceased died of tetanus.

If therefore you believe that tetanus was the natural result of the injuries the deceased received on that occasion, and would have ensued whether the deceased had behaved in the manner spoken to by the witnesses Keith and Taylor or not, then it is my duty to tell you that the legal result is that the prisoners are liable for the consequences of their assault on the assumption that it was unjustifiable. On the other hand, if you believe that the tetanus was not a natural result, but was brought on by the deceased's own indiscretion, then the prisoners would be entitled to a verdict in their favour."

Verdict: not proven.

NOTE

In this case the victim appears to have deliberately ignored medical advice. What would be the result if he had not received any such advice but had acted as he did?

2. People v. Lewis
124 Cal. 551; 57 Pac. 470 (1899) (Supreme Court of California)

The accused shot his brother-in-law in the stomach, inflicting a wound which, according to medical evidence, would have resulted in death within one hour. The victim was put to bed, and a few minutes later cut his own throat, inflicting a wound which, according to medical evidence, must necessarily have resulted in death within five minutes. The deceased died a few minutes later. The accused was convicted of manslaughter, and appealed.

TEMPLE J.: "Now, it is contended that this is a case where one languishing from a mortal wound is killed by an intervening cause, and therefore deceased was not killed by Lewis. To constitute manslaughter, the defendant must have killed some one, and if, though mortally wounded by the defendant, Farrell actually died from an independent intervening cause, Lewis, at the most, could only be guilty of a felonious attempt. He was as effectually prevented from killing as he would have been if some obstacle had turned aside the bullet from its course, and left Farrell unwounded. And they contend that the intervening act was the cause of death, if it shortened the life of Farrell for any period whatever. The attorney general does not controvert the general proposition here contended for, but argues that the wound inflicted by the defendant was the direct cause of the throat-cutting, and therefore defendant is criminally responsible for the death. He illustrates his position by supposing a case of one dangerously wounded, and whose wounds had been bandaged by a surgeon. He says, suppose, through the fever and pain consequent upon the wound, the patient becomes frenzied, and tears away the bandage, and thus accelerates his own death, would not the defendant be responsible for a homicide? Undoubtedly he would be, for in the case supposed the deceased died from the wound, aggravated, it is true, by the restlessness of the deceased, but still the wound inflicted by the defendant produced death. Whether such is the case here is the question. The attorney general seems to admit a fact which I do not concede,— that the gunshot wound was not, when Farrell died, then itself directly contributing to the death. I think the jury were warranted in finding that it was. But, if the deceased did die from the effect of the knife wound alone, no doubt the defendant would be responsible, if it was made to appear, and the jury could have found from the evidence, that the knife wound was caused by the wound inflicted by the defendant, in the natural course of events. If the relation was causal, and the wounded condition of the deceased was not merely the occasion upon which another cause intervened, not produced by the first wound, or related to it in other than in a casual way, then defendant is guilty of a homicide. But, if the wounded condition only afforded an opportunity for another unconnected person to kill, defendant would not be guilty of a homicide, even though he had inflicted a mortal wound. In such case, I think, it would be true that the defendant was thus prevented from killing.

The case, considered under this view, is further complicated from the fact that it is impossible to determine whether deceased was induced to cut his throat through pain produced by the wound. May it not have been from remorse, or from a desire to shield his brother-in-law? In either case the causal relation between the knife wound and the gunshot wound would seem to be the same. In either case, if defendant had not shot the deceased, the knife wound would not have been inflicted. Suppose one assaults and wounds another, intending to take life, but the wound, though painful, is not even dangerous, and the wounded man knows that it is not mortal, and yet takes his own life to escape pain, would it not be suicide only? Yet the wound inflicted by the assailant would have the same relation to death which the original wound in this case has to the knife wound. The wound induced the suicide, but the wound was not, in the natural course of things, the cause of the suicide. Though no case altogether like this has been found, yet, as was to have been expected, the general subject has often been considered. In 1 Hale, P. C. 428, the law is stated. So far as material here, his views may be thus summarized: (1) If one give another a dangerous wound, which might, by very skillful treatment, be cured, and is not, it is a case of homicide. (2) If one inflicts a dangerous wound, and the man dies from treatment, 'if it can clearly appear that the medicine, and not the wound, was the cause of the death, it seems it is not homicide; but then it must appear clearly and certainly to be so.' (3) If one receives a wound, not in itself mortal, and fever or gangrene sets in because of improper treatment or unruly conduct of the patient, and death ensues, it is homicide, 'for that wound, though it was not the immediate cause of his death, yet it was the mediate cause thereof, and the fever or gangrene was the immediate cause of his death, yet the wound was the cause of the gangrene or fever, and so, consequently, is causa causati.' (4) One who hastens the death of a person languishing with a mortal disease is guilty of a homicide, for the death is not merely by a visitation of Providence, but the hurt hastens it, and the wrongdoer cannot thus apportion the responsibility, etc. It would make no difference, I presume, if the person killed was languishing from a mortal wound, rather than from an ordinary disease. . . . The facts of this case do not bring it strictly within any of the propositions found in 1 Hale, P. C. 428. The second and third propositions both predicate a wound not necessarily mortal. What the law would have been in the second case, had the wound been mortal, and the applications had hastened the death, is not stated. It seems to me, however, the case of a person already languishing from a mortal wound is precisely that of one suffering from a mortal disease. Certainly, the willful and unlawful killing of such a person would be a felony, and it cannot be true that the first offender and the last can each be guilty of murdering the same man, if they had no connection with each other, and both wounds were not actively operating to produce death when it occurred.

But why is it that one who inflicts a wound not mortal is guilty of a homicide, if through misconduct of the patient or unskillful treatment gangrene or fever sets in, producing a fatal termination, when, if it can be clearly made to appear that the medicine, and not the wound, was the cause of the death, he is not guilty of a homicide? In each case, if the wound had not been, the treatment would not have been, and the man would not then have died. In each case the wound occasioned the treatment which caused or contributed to the death. The reason, I think, is found in the words advisedly used in the last sentence. In the one case the treatment caused the death, and in the other it merely contributed to it. In one case the treatment aggravated the wound, but the wound thus aggravated produced death. In the other the wound, though the occasion of the treatment, did not contribute to the death, which occurred without any present contribution to the natural effect of the medicine from the wound. Take, for instance, the giving of a dose of morphine, by mistake, sufficient to end life at once. In such case it is as obvious that the treatment produced death as it would have been had the physician cut off his patient's head. But see People v. Cook. 39 Mich. 236. In this case it appears that defendant had inflicted a dangerous wound, but it was contended by the defense that death was caused by an overdose of morphine. Defendant asked an instruction as follows: 'If the jury believe that the injury inflicted by the prisoner would have been fatal, but if death was actually produced by morphine poisoning, they must acquit.' The instruction was refused, but the jury were told that if the wound was not in itself mortal, and death was caused solely by the morphine, they must acquit. The action of the trial court was sustained on the ground that a mortal wound had been given, which necessitated medical treatment; that the physicians were competent, and acted in good faith; and that it was not made clearly to appear that the morphine solely produced death, and that the wound did not at all contribute to the death at that time. Under the authorities, this was equivalent to a finding that the wound did not contribute to the death. This case differs from that in this: that here the intervening cause, which it is alleged hastened death, was not medical treatment, designed to be helpful, and which the deceased was compelled to procure because of the wound, but was an act intended to produce death, and did not result from the first wound in the natural course of events. But we have reached the conclusion by a course of argument unnecessarily prolix, except from a desire to fully consider the earnest and able argument of the defendant, that the test is—or, at least, one test— whether, when the death occurred, the wound inflicted by the defendant did contribute to the event. If it did, although other independent causes also contributed, the causal relation between the unlawful acts of the defendant and the death has been made out. Here, when the throat was cut, Farrell was not merely languishing from a mortal wound; he was actually dying; and after the throat was cut he continued to languish from both wounds. Drop by drop the life current went out from both wounds, and at the very instant of death the gunshot wound was contributing to the event. If the throat-cutting had been by a third person, unconnected with the defendant, he might be guilty; for, although a man cannot be killed twice, two persons, acting independently, may contribute to his death, and each be guilty of a homicide. A person dying is still in life, and may be killed; but, if he is dying from a wound given by another, both may properly be said to have contributed to his death."

Appeal dismissed: conviction affirmed.

NOTES

Suppose that the first wound had not been fatal. How should the court have dealt with the causation problem then?

Cf. the case of *Blaue (ante).*

3. **Commonwealth v. Atencio and Marshall**
189 N.E. 2d. 223 (1963) (Supreme Judicial Court of Massachusetts)

The defendants were convicted, *inter alia,* of the manslaughter of a third man with whom they had been playing "Russian roulette". The circumstances of the death are outlined in the judgment of Wilkins C.J., on appeal.

WILKINS C.J: "Facts which the jury could have found are these. On Sunday, October 22, 1961, the deceased, his brother Ronald, and the defendants spent the day drinking wine in the deceased's room in a rooming house in Boston. At some time in the afternoon, with reference to nothing specific so far as the record discloses, Marshall said, 'I will settle this,' went out, and in a few minutes returned clicking a gun, from which he removed one bullet. Early in the evening Ronald left, and the conversation turned to 'Russian roulette.'

The evidence as to what happened consisted of testimony of police officers, who took statements of the defendants, and testimony of one defendant, Atencio. The evidence did not supply all the facts. For example, the source and ownership of the revolver were not made clear. The jury could have found that it was produced by the deceased and that he suggested the 'game,' or they might have found neither to be the fact. There was evidence that Marshall earlier had seen the revolver in the possession of the deceased, and that the latter handed it to Marshall, who put it in the bathroom under the sink. Later when the deceased accused him of stealing it, he brought it back from the bathroom, and gave it to the deceased. Any uncertainty is not of prime importance. The 'game' was played. The deceased and Atencio were seated on a bed, and Marshall was seated on a couch. First, Marshall examined the gun, saw that it contained one cartridge, and, after spinning it on his arm, pointed it at his head, and pulled the trigger. Nothing happened. He handed the gun to Atencio, who repeated the process, again without result. Atencio passed the gun to the deceased, who spun it, put to his head, and pulled the trigger. The cartridge exploded, and he fell over dead . . .

The defendants argue as if it should have been ruled, as matter of law, that there were three 'games' of solitaire and not one 'game' of 'Russian roulette.' That the defendants participated could be found to be a cause and not a mere condition of Stewart Britch's death. It is not correct to say that his act could not be found to have been caused by anything which Marshall and Atencio did, nor that he would have died when the gun went off in his hand no matter whether they had done the same. The testimony does not require a ruling that when the deceased took the gun from Atencio it was an independent or intervening act not standing in any relation to the defendants' acts which would render what he did imputable to them. It is an oversimplification to contend that each participated in something that only one could do at a time. There could be found to be a mutual encouragement in a joint enterprise. In the abstract, there may have been no duty on the defendants to prevent the deceased from playing. But there was a duty on their part not to cooperate or join with him in the 'game.' Nor, if the facts presented such a case, would we have to agree that if the deceased, and not the defendants, had played first that they could not have been found guilty of manslaughter. The defendants were much more than merely present at a crime. It would not be necessary that the defendants force the deceased to play or suggest that he play.

We are referred in both briefs to cases of manslaughter arising out of automobiles racing upon the public highway. When the victim is a third person, there is no difficulty in holding the drivers, including the one whose car did not strike the victim (Brown v. Thayer, 212 Mass. 392; 99 N.E. 237), or in whose car a victim was not a passenger. Nelson v. Nason, 343 Mass. 220, 221; 177 N.E.2d 887.

In two cases the driver of a non-colliding car has been prosecuted for the death of his competitor, and in both cases an appellate court has ruled that he was not guilty of manslaughter. In Commonwealth v. Root, 403 Pa. 571; 170 A.2d 310; 82 A.L.R.2d 452, the competitor drove on the wrong side of the road head-on into an oncoming truck and was killed. The court held (p. 580; 170 A.2d p. 314) that 'the tort liability concept of proximate cause has no proper place in prosecutions for criminal homicide and more direct causal connection is required for conviction. . . . In the instant case, the defendant's reckless conduct was not a sufficiently direct cause of the competing driver's death to make him criminally liable therefor.' In Thacker v. State, 103 Ga. App. 36; 117 S.E.2d 913, the defendant was indicted for the involuntary manslaughter of his competitor in a drag race who was killed when he lost control of his car and left the highway. The court said (p. 39, 117; S.E.2d p. 915) that the indictment 'fails to allege any act or acts on the part of the defendant which caused or contributed to the loss of control of the vehicle driven by the deceased, other than the fact that they were engaged in a race at the time.'

Whatever may be thought of those two decisions, there is a very real distinction between drag racing and 'Russian roulette.' In the former much is left to the skill, or lack of it, of the competitor. In 'Russian roulette' it is a matter of luck as to the location of the one bullet, and except for a misfire (of which there was evidence in the case at bar) the outcome is a certainty if the chamber under the hammer happens to be the one containing the bullet."

Appeal dismissed: conviction affirmed.

d. Intervention by a third party

1. People v. Fowler
174 Pac. 892 (1918) (Supreme Court of California)

The defendant was convicted of murder in the first degree, by striking his victim on the head with a club and leaving him lying in the roadway where he was subsequently struck on the head by a passing car. The defendant's case was that he struck the blow in self-defence. On appeal:

SHAW J.: "The court gave an instruction as follows: 'In this case it is not denied that the defendant struck the blow by which the deceased received the wound in the head, but it is claimed in his behalf that he was justified in so doing, and that the act was committed in defense of his own life, or to prevent infliction upon him, by the deceased, of great bodily injury.'

The claim that the statement that 'the defendant struck the blow by which the deceased received the wound in the head' is an instruction on a question of fact upon which the evidence was in conflict is not sustained by the record. The defendant himself testified that he struck Duree a blow on the head with a heavy club; that it felled him to the ground; that he then left him there unconscious, supposing that he was dead. Duree was found shortly afterwards lying as he fell, with the pistol near his hand, as the defendant had arranged it to make it appear that Duree had a pistol at the time he was struck. There was no controversy or dispute at the trial over these facts. The court was authorized to state the testimony, if it was uncontradicted, and declare the law, on any subject involved in the case. Const. art. 6 § 19. The statement was appropriate as an introduction to the instructions on the law of self-defense which immediately followed it. The argument on the point really is that it was an instruction concerning the immediate cause of the death, or one which might have been so understood by the jury. The persons who discovered the body were passing along the public road in an automobile. The body, when found, lay with the head on the grass at the roadside and the feet extending out into the macadamized portion of the roadway. The driver of the automobile, Albert Due, who lived in that neighbourhood, testified that the automobile wheel ran over the shoes or feet of the body, as he passed along, and at the time he at first thought it was only a wet spot in the road. It was in the nighttime, cloudy and dark. As he proceeded, it occurred to him that it might have been a man lying there, so he turned back and found him, as above stated. There was no other direct evidence on the subject. The evidence which suggested the automobile wheel theory was that of the physician who performed the autopsy on the body. He testified that there were two severe wounds on the head, caused by the impact of some blunt instrument, and that one of them was, in his opinion, broader than would be caused with the club wielded by the defendant, and that it might have been made by the wheel of an automobile. From this it is argued that the larger wound was probably caused by the wheel of the automobile of Due, or some other person, passing over Duree's head as he lay in the public road, that this wound, and not the blow of the defendant, was the immediate cause of the death, and that the court should not have said to the jury that 'the defendant had struck *the* blow by which the deceased received the wound in the head.'

This, of course, would have no bearing on the question of the propriety of the statement as an introduction to the subject of the law of self-defense. The question whether or not the blow was given in self-defense must be determined by a consideration of the circumstances as they existed at the time the blow was struck, without regard to any subsequent injury as the cause of death. To the suggestion that the statement in the instruction may have been understood by the jury to indicate that the court believed that the blow of the defendant was the cause of the death and not the injury, if any, from the wheel of the automobile, the answer is that in that aspect the instruction is not injurious to the defendant. There is no evidence, and no claim, that the automobile was purposely driven over the body. If it was the cause of the death, it was not a felonious cause. If it were, the defendant might not have been responsible for the homicide. It was the natural and probable result of the defendant's conduct in leaving Duree lying helpless and unconscious in a public road, exposed to that danger. This conduct of the defendant would then be criminal or not, according to the character of the blow he gave Duree. If it was done in self-defense, it would be justifiable. If it was felonious, it would be murder or manslaughter, according to the intent and the kind of malice with which it was inflicted. This, as we have said, would depend upon the circumstances attending and preceding the blow, and not on the subsequent passing of the automobile over the body. The case in that event would be similar to many that are given in the books, where the defendant was held responsible for the natural and probable result of his unlawful acts. . . .

There are numerous cases to the effect that where one with felonious intent inflicts a wound upon another, not necessarily fatal, but by reason of the poor treatment given in good faith in the attempt to heal it death results, the person who inflicted the wound is responsible for the death, in a criminal prosecution. . . .

For these reasons we conclude that the instruction was not erroneous, and that the claim that the death might possibly have been caused by the wheel of an automobile was not sufficient to exonerate the defendant from the charge."

Appeal dismissed: conviction affirmed.

NOTE

Shaw J. suggests that the defendant might not be responsible if the victim were deliberately run over by a third party. What would be the case if he were struck by a vehicle being driven negligently or recklessly?

2. Finlayson v. H.M.Advocate
1978 S.L.T. (Notes) 60

The appellant was convicted of culpable homicide by injecting into another man (with his consent) a mixture of morphine and diazepam. There was evidence that after the deceased had been injected with the drugs he had been taken to a hospital where he was placed on a life-support machine. A decision had subsequently been taken to switch the machine off and the patient died. The appellant argued that the trial judge should have directed the jury to find him not guilty, since the chain of causation between his unlawful act and death was broken by the actions of the doctors.

LORD JUSTICE-GENERAL (EMSLIE): "Before we come to the
alleged misdirection it is proper to give a brief summary of the
essential background against which the argument was presented.
The result of injecting the drug into the person of Wilson was that it
caused such serious brain damage that brain death occurred and
that the heart would have inevitably failed for lack of oxygen unless
means were available and taken to prolong heart function and to
delay physical death by artificial mechanisms. In the event, when
Wilson was taken to hospital he was placed on a life support
machine in, we imagine, the intensive care unit of the hospital
concerned. After a relatively short period on the life support
machine and after serious consultation among responsible and
highly qualified consultants, and after discussions with the parents
of Wilson himself, a decision was taken to discontinue the artificial
life support on the grounds that the brain damage was seen to be
complete and irreversible and that all that a life support machine
could do in the circumstances was to prolong the physical life of a
person who was by then in a totally vegetative state. The decision
having been taken the artificial life support was discontinued.
Nature took control and the patient in due course died. For the
applicant the submission of counsel was this. Even if the reckless
injection of the drug would have led to the death of the deceased
had matters been left to nature, matters were not left to nature. In
short once the deceased had been placed on the life support
machine it was the fact that his physical life could have been maintained indefinitely. In these circumstances what caused the death of
the deceased was not the act of the applicant, but the deliberate
discontinuance of the life support treatment which had been
applied. This then, it was said, was an extraneous and extrinsic act
which broke any chain of causation between the act of the applicant
which caused the brain injury and the patient's death. That being so
the trial judge should have directed the jury to bring in a verdict of
not guilty of culpable homicide. This it was said, and by this we
mean the act of discontinuing the life support treatment, was a
deliberate act which could not be foreseen. In presenting this submission counsel for the appellant relied upon the case of *R*. v. *Smith*
[1959] 2 Q.B. 35 and he cited it in particular for the quotation by
Parker L.J. with approval of a test enunciated by Lord Wright in the
well-known case of *The Oropesa*. The test is in these terms. 'To
break the chain of causation it must be shown that there is something which I will call ultroneous, something unwarrantable, a new
cause which disturbs the sequence of events, something which can
be described as either unreasonable or extraneous or extrinsic.'
    In our judgment the argument for the applicant is unsound. On
the face of it, it appears that the effects of the applicant's act were a

substantial and operating and continuing cause of the death which occurred. It must be remembered that the decision which was taken to place the patient on a life support machine was taken, no doubt, with a view to keeping the patient physically alive until it could be ascertained with certainty whether there were any prospects of recovery of brain function. The argument further conceded that the decision to discontinue life support was in all the circumstances a perfectly reasonable one. It follows accordingly that the act of disconnecting the machine can hardly be described as an extraneous or extrinsic act within the meaning of these words as they were used by Lord Wright in their context. Far less can it be said that the act of disconnecting the machine was either unforeseeable or unforeseen and it certainly cannot be said that the act of disconnecting the machine was an unwarrantable act. If we read the definition or test of Lord Wright properly the key to the test is to be found in the word unwarrantable. Once the initial reckless act causing injury had been committed the natural consequence which the perpetrator must accept is that the victim's future depended on a number of circumstances, including whether any particular treatment was available and if it was available whether it was medically reasonable and justifiable to attempt it and to continue it. Having said all that, we are perfectly satisfied that upon the evidence led in this case it was not in any event a matter for the judge to determine ab ante whether, as matter of fact, it could be said that the chain of causation had been broken. That was a matter inexplicably bound up with the other facts in the case which were for determination by the jury and what the judge did was to leave the very question of the chain of causation to the jury with, as we see it, proper directions. We have little doubt that the jury reached the correct conclusion, but, in any event, no misdirection has been demonstrated and we have not the slightest hesitation in saying that it would have been a gross misdirection if the judge had, in the circumstances we have narrated, directed the jury that they must on his instruction return a verdict of not guilty of culpable homicide."

Appeal dismissed.

NOTES

For earlier stages in this case see *H.M. Advocate* v. *Finlayson,* 1978 S.L.T. (Notes) 18, *post,* ch. 11.

Cf. the case of *Lafferty* v. *H.M. Advocate,* High Court, June 1973, unreported (but see *Glasgow Herald,* June 2, 1973). The appellant was convicted of the culpable homicide of his infant daughter by striking her head against her cot. The child had been placed on a life-support machine in hospital, but a decision was subsequently taken to withdraw the life-support system. The High Court held that death was caused by the injuries inflicted by the appellant, and not by the withdrawal of the life-support system.

For a full discussion of the problems involved in such cases, see: Skegg, "The Termination of Life-Support Measures and the Law of Murder" (1978) 41 M.L.R. 423, Watson *et al.,* "Brain Stem Death" (1978) 23 J.L.S. 433, and Kennedy, "Switching Off Life-Support Machines: The Legal Implications" [1977] Crim.L.R. 443.

CHAPTER 4

ART AND PART

a.   The logic of art and part guilt

1.   Young v. H.M.Advocate
1932 J.C. 63

The appellant was charged along with a number of other persons with, *inter alia,* making a fraudulent allotment of shares in a limited company. The appellant's co-accused were all associated with the company either as directors or, in one case, as secretary, but he had no such connection with the company. He was convicted on this charge, while the other accused were all acquitted. On appeal against conviction:

LORD JUSTICE-GENERAL (CLYDE): *"Charge* (2).—This is a charge of fraud upon the new company, and of fraudulent misappropriation of its funds to an extent exceeding in all £500,000. The fraud upon the new company is said to have consisted in the directors going to allotment at all in the circumstances known to them, and particularly in allotting shares to certain of the applicants; and the fraudulent misappropriation is said to have consisted in the making of certain payments by the said directors out of the new company's funds, for their own purposes, and without value or consideration. The appellant Todd was the new company's secretary, and he is charged along with the directors. The appellant Young was not a director of, or otherwise officially connected with, the new company; but he is charged with being 'art and part,' both in the fraud and in the fraudulent misappropriation, and—as regards the latter—the charge was laid against the directors and secretary, and all of them, 'acting in concert' with the appellant Young. The verdict was one of not guilty in favour of all the accused except the appellant Young, who was found guilty of the charge 'but not guilty of acting in concert with the others.'

The result thus arrived at is a remarkable one; and counsel for the appellant Young not only subjected it to attack, but (not unnaturally) used it to reinforce the argument (already dealt with in connexion with charge (1)) that there was an unjust discrimination in the verdict against the appellant Young. Dealing, however, with charge (2), the result was to convict the appellant Young of being art and part in acts (namely, the allotment of the company's shares, and the sanction of payments out of its funds) to which—whether inspired by fraudulent intent or not—he (not being a director) could not possibly be a party, and, moreover, of being art and part in a

fraud which the principal persons charged with it are found by the
jury not to have committed. That the charge of concert between the
directors and secretary and the appellant Young was disposed of by
the verdict in his favour may have been due to the general direction
given by the trial Court to the jury that there was no evidence of any
common fraudulent design among the accused; but, inasmuch as
(particularly as regards the fraudulent misappropriation of the company's funds) the only possible link between the exclusive domain
of the directors and the actings of the appellant Young was the
alleged concert, it is difficult to understand how a verdict could be
arrived at against him on this charge at all. The Crown sought to
justify the conviction on the ground that a person accused as art and
part might be convicted notwithstanding the failure of the prosecutor to bring home the commission of the crime to the principals
charged, provided the fact that the crime was committed (even by
persons unknown) is proved. It was suggested that the jury may
have been convinced that fraud and fraudulent misappropriation
had been committed, although not by the directors and secretary
who were indicted. This is an afterthought. If the crime was committed at all, it must have been by some person or persons who were
in the position of directors; and it is incredible that individual
directors, who were either not charged in the indictment, or whose
names were withdrawn from it by the Crown, could be sanely
regarded as the guilty parties. Whatever be the explanation of what
happened in connexion with this charge, it is clear that the conviction of the appellant Young under it is neither reasonable nor
intelligible, and it must be quashed accordingly."

Appeal allowed, *quoad* conviction on charge (2).

2.   McAuley v. H.M.Advocate
1946 J.C. 8

The appellant was charged with being concerned, along with two
other named persons, in a scheme whereby a number of greyhounds
were doped and bets were placed on other dogs running in the same
race "fraudulently to the prejudice of the . . . company owning said
greyhounds and sponsoring said race and of persons betting or
receiving bets on said greyhounds." The alleged accomplices had
already been tried summarily for the same scheme, and one of them
had been acquitted. The appellant was convicted and appealed.

LORD JUSTICE-CLERK (COOPER): "Nine reasons of appeal are
stated against the conviction and sentence in this case, but we have
only heard argument on the first. That reason arises from the

following circumstances:—The appellant was charged on indictment that, while acting in concert with two men, James Preston and
Archibald Ralston, he did certain acts in pursuance of a fraudulent
scheme involving the doping of greyhounds. On that charge he was
convicted. Some time previous to his trial the same two men with
whom the appellant is alleged to have fraudulently conspired,
namely James Preston and Archibald Ralston, were charged on
summary complaint with forming, in concert with the appellant, the
identical fraudulent scheme, and carrying it out in exactly the same
method detailed in the indictment against the appellant. In that
prosecution James Preston was acquitted. The objection now for-
mulated in the first reason of appeal is that it was contrary to the
fundamental principles of fairness that the appellant should have
been tried on indictment on the charge of acting in concert in this
fraudulent scheme with Preston and Ralston who had already been
separately tried on substantially the same charge; and in particular
that the later indictment was vitiated by the fact that it charged the
appellant with being a fraudulent co-conspirator with a man who
had been acquitted of being a fraudulent co-conspirator with the
appellant in relation to the same subject-matter.

On the wider question of practice to which the argument was
directed, Mr Cameron founded upon the case of *His Majesty's
Advocate* v. *Clark*, 1935 J.C. 51, in which this Court, while
expressing reluctance to interfere with the discretion of the Crown,
would not allow two separate indictments in two separate trials to
proceed against several persons alleged to be involved in the same
crime or criminal schemes. In that case Lord Murray said this (at p.
59): 'Counsel for the Crown stated in answer to an invitation by the
Court, that they were not aware of any authority to the effect that
the Crown, when all parties concerned in an alleged crime are in fact
within its power and can be brought to trial under one and the same
indictment, is entitled under our criminal law and procedure to
bring the case to trial under several and separate indictments. So far
as I am aware, the rule in our practice is directly to the contrary, and
this rule, in my opinion, is a just and salutary one.'

It will be observed that in *Clark's* case, and in the observations of
Lord Murray which I have just quoted, the emphasis was laid upon
the bringing of two or more several and separate *indictments*, and
the distinction was sought to be drawn between such a case and the
present case, in which what I might call the full dress rehearsal took
place in a summary Court against certain of the accused, and the
subsequent proceedings took place before a jury under the solemn
procedure. I have two observations to make on the case of *Clark*.
The first is this, that it seems to me that the mischief which the Court
sought to remedy in that case did not arise from the accident that

two indictments were there in question, but from the objection on the ground of fairness which it was thought attached to taking what was in essence one criminal investigation in two or more separate stages. The second observation is that, so far as my own personal knowledge goes, the practice between 1935 and 1941 was the same as Lord Murray found it to have been prior to 1935. But, without for a moment desiring to give the authority of this Court to the new practice which was followed in this case, and which the Solicitor-General sought to defend, it seems to me that there is a specialty here which renders it strictly unnecessary for us to pronounce upon the wider question. That specialty arises from the fact that in the summary proceedings against Preston and Ralston, Preston was acquitted; and once that happened it seems to me to be quite unjustifiable for this Court to applaud or countenance the subsequent service of an indictment upon McAuley for having engaged in a fraudulent scheme with a person who after, I must presume, a fair and proper trial was found not guilty of having fraudulently conspired with McAuley in that very scheme.

On that ground, and without finally committing myself on the wider propositions addressed to us, it seems to me that the proceedings in this case must be regarded as vitiated and the conviction should be quashed."

Conviction quashed.

NOTES

It was clearly improper for the Crown in the above case to seek to obtain a conviction of the appellant for a crime allegedly committed with a man who had already been found not guilty, but would it have been possible for the Crown to seek a conviction on the basis that the appellant was acting with the already convicted accomplice? *Cf.* the following case.

3.   Greig v. Muir
1955 S.L.T. 99

The appellant was convicted of fraudulently obtaining board and lodging to the value of £35 10s. Prior to his conviction, however, the Crown had already brought a charge of fraud against another party, in respect of the same set of facts, and had accepted a plea of guilty thereto. On appeal by stated case to the High Court:

LORD JUSTICE-CLERK (THOMSON): "The appellant was convicted of a charge of obtaining board and lodging to the value of £35 10s., without paying and intending not to pay therefor and so defrauding an hotel-keeper. The complaint is in the statutory form and in the ordinary case it would be enough for the prosecutor to establish that the appellant obtained the board and lodging to the value stated, that he did not pay and that he intended not to pay for it. The stated case, however, discloses that a woman, Patricia Williams, was separately charged in respect of the same *species facti* and having pleaded guilty was sentenced. Two people cannot be guilty of the same offence unless they were art and part in its commission. The recognised practice when all parties concerned in an alleged crime are in fact within the power of the Crown is to bring them to trial under one and the same indictment or complaint. This was a matter of concession by the Crown in *H.M. Advocate* v. *Clark,* 1935 J.C. 51, 1935 S.L.T. 143, see per Lord Murray, at page 59. In the same case Lord Justice-Clerk Aitchison said in terms (at page 56): 'There can, I think, be little doubt that the better practice, where persons are accused of acting with a common fraudulent purpose, is to try them together unless there are very strong and cogent reasons to the contrary.' In *McAuley* v. *H.M. Advocate,* 1946 J.C. 8, 1946 S.L.T. 50, Lord Justice-Clerk Cooper said: '. . . so far as my own personal knowledge goes, the practice between 1935 and 1941 was the same as Lord Murray found it to have been prior to 1935.' I am in a position to bring the practice down to 1947. It also falls to be noted that where any of the parties who are art and part are not available for trial, the practice is to name them in the indictment. The principle is that the Crown puts before the court and at the same time certiorates the accused who in its view were the whole participators in the offence charged. If one of the actors who has disappeared is later recaptured and put on trial, his indictment would likewise name the others involved.

The reason which the Lord Advocate gave for the procedure followed in the present case was that as Patricia Williams had a criminal record and was implicated in other charges, she was put on indictment and that as the appellant was a first offender it was undesirable in his own interests to include him in that indictment.

I can appreciate the force of that, but I am not satisfied that it follows that the proper course was to charge the appellant on a complaint which *ex facie* represented him as the only person implicated in the fraud. As the Crown were bringing proceedings against both in respect of the same set of circumstances the only possible theory on which they could proceed was that the two were acting with a common fraudulent purpose. I think that it would have been better in the circumstances if the case against the appellant had been presented to the court on the footing that they were art and part. While the Crown's anxiety to avoid the appellant's being charged on indictment is to be commended, I think that in the peculiar circumstances the possibility cannot be excluded that if the two had been tried at the same time, or if the appellant had been charged on a complaint that narrated that he was acting along with the woman, the appellant might have been acquitted. The facts found show that the woman was the prime mover in the business. Moreover the Sheriff makes no finding that the appellant knew that the woman did not intend to pay and if she was the prime mover some such finding was necessary to make him art and part in her fraud. Accordingly, I think that it would be safer in the circumstances to quash the conviction."

Conviction quashed.

NOTES

How far does the principle enunciated by Lord Justice-Clerk Thomson extend? Consider the following example: A is convicted of murder (on the basis that he committed the murder with B, although the latter is not tried). X is later charged with the murder (on the basis that he committed it with Y who is likewise not tried). Is A's conviction any bar to the proceedings against X? Does this situation fall under the principle that "two people cannot be guilty of the same offence unless they were art and part in its commission"? *Cf. H.M.Advocate* v. *Waddell and Anor.*, High Court, November 1976 (reported on another point at 1976 S.L.T. (Notes) 61).

b. Establishing the common purpose

1. **H.M.Advocate v. Lappen and Ors.**
1956 S.L.T. 109

Lappen and five others were charged, *inter alia,* with assault and robbery. In the course of his charge to the jury the presiding judge gave the following directions on the question of art and part guilt:

LORD PATRICK: "The Crown's case is that all the accused except Thomson together with this man George Grey of whom we have heard so much, were parties to a common plan to rob the van and to assault the guard. If that was proved, that they were parties to such a common plan, each of those five with whom I am now dealing would be responsible for the acts of all the others in carrying out the robbery and the assault; the acts of each of them in that case would in law be the acts of every one of them, and it would not matter at all that all of them did not actually take part in the attack and seizure of the property, or were not proved to have taken part in the attack and the seizure of the property. To illustrate this doctrine of the law, though I do not for a moment suggest that the illustration is what happened in this case—that has to be proved—if a number of men form a common plan whereby some are to commit the actual seizure of the property, and some according to the plan are to keep watch, and some according to the plan are to help to carry away the loot, and some according to the plan are to help to dispose of the loot, then, although the actual robbery may only have been committed by one or two of them, every one is guilty of the robbery, because they joined together in a common plan to commit the robbery. But such responsibility for the acts of others under the criminal law only arises if it had been proved affirmatively beyond reasonable doubt that there was such a common plan and that the accused were parties to that common plan. If it has not been proved that there was such a common plan, or if it has not been proved that the accused were parties to this previously conceived common plan, then in law each is only responsible for what he himself did, and bears no responsibility whatever for what any of the other accused or any other person actually did.

It becomes, ladies and gentlemen, a somewhat difficult business when a jury is considering such a case as this, where a common plan to commit a crime is alleged, it becomes a somewhat difficult business to keep what each has done quite clearly and separately before the jury's eyes, so that there is always a danger, unless one is careful, that they might before they have arrived at the conclusion that there was a common plan to which the accused were parties, they might before they have arrived at that conclusion tend to ascribe to some of the accused acts which had been done by others, and that would be wrong. The way to approach the problems you have to decide is this: you should first of all consider each of the accused quite separately and one after the other. Make up your minds what each of these accused is himself proved to have done, then take all these facts which you find each of the accused severally and separately is proved to have done, and against the general background of circumstances which are proved in the case, and which have no particular reference to one or the other, say whether you are convinced beyond reasonable doubt that there was a common plan to commit this robbery, and whether it is proved that the accused, or some of them, and, if so, which of them were parties to that common plan.

You may not have very much difficulty in holding it proved that this robbery was carried out in pursuance of a common plan conceived between certain persons. In some cases that is an initial difficulty, but it may be that you will not have any difficulty in this case, because if you accept the evidence, undoubtedly more than one person took part in the actual attack and the seizure. If you accept the evidence, the attackers were using overalls to disguise their ordinary clothing, which they discarded, or some of them discarded, at 7 Dumbreck Road when they left the van. The timing of the affair was as near perfect as could be. We are told the driver and one guard had gone inside the bank. Then the paper was slapped by one of the men into his hand, a signal for the attack—if you think it was a signal. Then came the sudden rush, two into the back of the van to overpower the only guard who was left, two into the front to whip the van away in a moment of time, the cosh, the rope, the adhesive plaster were there; the cosh, to overpower, if necessary, the guard, and the rope and the plaster to tie and gag him. There was the discovery or knowledge of the existence of an unoccupied house very close to the scene of the crime, and the use of it to take the van quickly there, where under partial cover at the back of the house the loot could be transferred to some other less questionable form of conveyance than the van. Do you think that all these things prove that there was here a previously conceived common plan to commit this robbery, or do you think all these things could possibly have been done with such perfect timing and co-ordination although there had not been such a common plan between some persons? The critical question remains, of course, between whom?

Suppose you do not, as I have said to you before, hold that a common plan has been proved, then no question can possibly arise of holding any man responsible except for what he himself is proved to have done, but if you do hold that there was here a common plan between some, more than one, and possibly a good number more than one, persons to commit this robbery then the next question which you will have to determine is which, if any, of the accused is proved to have been a party to that common plan. Any one of the accused, again I am speaking of the first five—any one of them whom you hold to have been a party to a common plan to commit this robbery would then be responsible for the commission of the robbery, and would be guilty of the fifth charge, no matter what part he played in the actual execution of the robbery, and no matter though it had not been proved that he played a part in the actual execution of the robbery. The critical things are, has it been proved that there was such a common plan, and secondly, is it proved that the accused, and if so, which of them, were parties to that common plan?"

Verdict: three accused convicted.

2. **H.M.Advocate v. Kerr and Ors.**
(1871) 2 Couper 334

Three accused were charged with assault with intent to ravish. One of them, Donald, was charged with being "present, in company with" the principal offender, "aiding and abetting him whilst he was attempting to ravish" the victim, "by looking on and failing to interfere in her behalf, or to call for assistance." The accused had taken no direct part in the attack, but had stood at the other side of a hedge, watching the attack. He did not speak either to the girl or to his companions during the attack.

The accused Donald objected to the relevancy of the charge against him.

LORD ARDMILLAN: "I noticed the peculiarity in respect of which this objection has been taken when I first read this indictment, and think it has been properly brought under consideration of the Court. I will not attempt to decide the general question which has been adverted to, whether a man is a *particeps criminis* who sees a crime committed and passes by or looks on without doing anything. The answer to that question can not be given in general terms, for it may depend upon a variety of circumstances. Here I think it proper that the charge should go to the Jury in order that all the circumstances may be disclosed in evidence. It may be, that Donald actually encouraged the other prisoners by his language, or by his presence,—being in such a position as to indicate readiness to give assistance, not to the girl but to her assailants, if necessary, and thus intimidating the girl. This is quite possible, and is not excluded by the terms of the indictment. It may yet be proved. If nothing of that kind appears in the course of the evidence for the prosecution, that will be for the benefit of the accused, who can raise, with reference to the ascertained facts, the objection which he has now stated on the relevancy."

The indictment having been held relevant, the case went to the jury. In his charge to the jury, Lord Ardmillan gave the following directions with regard to the accused Donald:

LORD ARDMILLAN: "If Donald had been in the field standing close beside the other panels, and during the commission of their offence on the girl, the English authorities quoted would not have deterred me from regarding the present case against Donald as a case to go to the Jury, leaving it to them to decide on the question of participation; for if there was participation the case is a serious one. But it seems to be proved that he was not in the field, but only looking through the hedge; and although this was an improper thing to do, it would, I think, not be safe for you to convict the prisoner Donald on this charge."

Verdict: the jury found the charge against Donald not proven.

NOTES

Mere presence at, or failure to prevent the commission of, an offence will not, in the absence of any special duty, result in responsibility for that offence (but see the discussion of criminal omissions, *ante*, ch. 2).

Cf. the cases of *Coney*(1882) 8 Q.B.D. 534 and *Clarkson and Ors.* [1971] 1 W.L.R. 1402. In the latter case (almost identical to *Kerr* in its essential facts) it was held that while mere presence at the commission of such an offence might in fact amount to encouragement to the attackers, it was essential that the Crown proved an intention to encourage them, or to discourage the victim.

3.   H.M.Advocate v. Johnstone and Stewart
1926 J.C. 89

The two accused were charged with procuring an abortion while acting in concert. The accused were in fact unknown to each other. The first accused took no part in the actual operation, which was performed by the second accused, but had merely passed on her name (which she had received from a third party) to persons interested in obtaining an abortion. She received no reward for such referral. In his charge to the jury the presiding judge gave the following directions on the issue of art and part guilt:

LORD MONCRIEFF: "If you are satisfied that Mrs Johnstone and Mrs Stewart were entire strangers, and are further satisfied that no money passed, then I think it would be straining the law to hold that the mere communication of a name by a party who was not in actual communication with the party named was actual participation in the illegal act. . . . Accordingly, on the question raised, you have to consider, Is there any evidence, of association between these two women? If you find there is not such evidence, you must next consider, Is there proper legal proof which can be relied on that money had passed for the giving of the name? And if you find in the negative on that question also—that there was nothing except, upon solicitation, communication of the name to the parties—then I have to direct you that it will be your duty in that case to find a verdict in favour of the prisoner Johnstone."

Verdict: Johnstone, not guilty, Stewart, guilty.

NOTES

Clearly the required *nexus* for art and part guilt was not present in the above case, but how much more was required? Suppose, for example, that the first accused had regularly made such referrals?

4. R. v. Bainbridge
[1959] 1 Q.B. 129

The appellant bought some oxygen cutting equipment on behalf of some thieves who used it to break into and rob a bank. He was convicted of being an accessory before the fact. He admitted that he suspected the equipment was to be used for something unlawful, perhaps the breaking up of stolen metal, but it was his contention that he did not contemplate its use for the purposes of breaking into the bank. On appeal:

LORD PARKER C.J.: "The complaint here is that Judge Aarvold, who tried the case, gave the jury a wrong direction in regard to what it was necessary for them to be satisfied of in order to hold the appellant guilty of being an accessory before the fact. The passages in question are these. He said: 'To prove that the prosecution have to prove these matters: first of all they have to prove the felony itself was committed. Of that there is no doubt. That is not contested. Secondly, they have to prove the defendant, this man Bainbridge, knew that a felony of that kind was intended and was going to be committed, and with that knowledge he did something to help the felons commit the crime. The knowledge that is required to be proved in the mind of this man Bainbridge is not the knowledge of the precise crime. In other words, it need not be proved he knew the Midland Bank, Stoke Newington branch, was going to be broken and entered and money stolen from that particular bank, but he must know the type of crime that was in fact committed. In this case it is a breaking and entering of premises and the stealing of property from those premises. It must be proved he knew that sort of crime was intended and was going to be committed. It is not enough to show that he either suspected or knew that some crime was going to be committed, some crime which might have been a breaking and entering or might have been disposing of stolen property or anything of that kind. That is not enough. It must be proved he knew the type of crime which was in fact committed was intended.'

There are other passages to the same effect, in particular when the jury returned for further directions before they came to their verdict. Later the judge said this: 'If, in fact, before it has happened he, knowing what is going to happen, with full knowledge that a felony of that kind is going to take place, deliberately and wilfully helps it on its way, he is an accessory.' Then a little further on: 'If he was not present he would not be guilty as a principal, but then you would have to decide whether he helped in purchasing this equipment for Shakeshaft knowing full well the type of offence for which it was going to be used, and with that knowledge, buying it and helping in that way.'

Mr. Simpson, who has argued this case very well, contends that that direction is wrong. As he puts it, in order that a man should be convicted of being accessory before the fact, it must be shown that at the time he bought the equipment in a case such as this he knew that a particular crime was going to be committed, and by a particular crime Mr. Simpson means that the premises in this case which were going to be broken into were known to the appellant and contemplated by him, and not only the premises in question but the date when the breaking was going to occur; in other words, that he must know that on a particular date the Stoke Newington branch of the Midland Bank is intended to be broken into.

The court fully appreciates that it is not enough that it should be shown that a man knows that some illegal venture is intended. To take this case, it would not be enough if he knew—he says he only suspected—that the equipment was going to be used to dispose of stolen property. That would not be enough. Equally, this court is quite satisfied that it is unnecessary that knowledge of the particular crime which was in fact committed should be shown to his knowledge to have been intended, and by 'particular crime' I am using the words in the same way in which Mr. Simpson used them, namely, on a particular date and particular premises.

It is not altogether easy to lay down a precise form of words which will cover every case that can be contemplated but, having considered the cases and the law this court is quite clear that the direction of Judge Aarvold in this case cannot be criticised. Indeed, it might well have been made with the passage in Foster's Crown Cases (3rd ed. (1809) at p. 369) in mind, because there the author says: 'If the principal totally and substantially varieth, if being solicited to commit a felony of one kind he wilfully and knowingly committeth a felony of another, he will stand single in that offence, and the person soliciting will not be involved in his guilt. For on his part it was no more than a fruitless ineffectual temptation, 'the converse, of course, being that if the principal does not totally and substantially vary the advice or the help and does not wilfully and knowingly commit a different form of felony altogether, the man who has advised or helped, aided or abetted, will be guilty as an accessory before the fact.'

Judge Aarvold in this case, in the passage to which I have referred, makes it clear that there must be not merely suspicion but knowledge that a crime of the type in question was intended, and that the equipment was bought with that in view. In his reference to the felony of the type intended it was, as he stated, the felony of breaking and entering premises and the stealing of property from those premises. The court can see nothing wrong in that direction.''

Appeal dismissed.

NOTES

The problem with this approach is, of course, to determine whether the offence contemplated is of the same type as that committed. Suppose, for example, that X borrows Y's credit card. Y thinks X is going to use it to commit fraud. X in fact uses it to open a "Yale" lock to steal from a house. Is Y art and part in X's offence?

b. Responsibility for the consequences

1. H.M.Advocate v. Welsh and McLachlan
(1897) 5 S.L.T. 137

The two accused were charged, *inter alia,* with the murder of an old woman by striking her on the head with an iron bar or other weapon, having broken into her house and stolen certain articles therein. In the course of his charge to the jury, the presiding judge, Lord Young stated that there could be no doubt on the evidence that the house, 81 Abbotsford Place, was broken into. Neither did there appear to be any question that the men, whoever they were, who broke into the house, struck Jane Cumming, so that she died within a fortnight. The question was—whether or not it was proved that both or either of the prisoners were the persons who broke into the house, and whether both or either of them struck the old woman? If the jury held it proved that the prisoners were the men who broke into the house, and that one of them struck the blow which proved fatal, then the further question arose as to whether both the prisoners could be held legally responsible for the violent act of one of them. If one of the prisoners in this case struck the woman, that would not necessarily lead to the conviction of both on the charge of murder. If two men, both with pistols, stop a man on the highway and demand his money or his life, and one shoots the man, then both would be responsible. If two housebreakers went with pistols or knives, or anything which satisfied the jury that they were prepared, by violence, to overcome any resistance which was offered, regardless of human life, then, though only one inflicted the fatal injury, both would be responsible. That did not appear to his lordship to be applicable in the present case, in which a helpless, feeble old woman who could not offer any resistance was struck by one of the men, and there was no evidence by which of them. In such a case the other could not be held responsible. If the jury were convinced that both prisoners went into the house with the intent to inflict such violence as was inflicted upon the woman, then both the prisoners would be responsible if only one had done what both were prepared to do. There was no evidence to indicate a case of that kind here, and the jury would take it that, in law, they could not convict either prisoner of the murder without being satisfied that he was the man who had inflicted the blow. It was sad enough if they should come to the conclusion that one or other did the deed, but they could not tell which. Still, if that were so, it would be their duty not to convict either. The evidence was as weak and slender as his lordship had seen on so serious a charge.

Verdict: not proven on the charge of murder.

2. Webster and Anor. v. Wishart
1955 S.L.T. 243

The appellants stole seven cwts. of coal from a distillery and made their escape in a lorry belonging to the second appellant. The lorry was involved in a collision with a car and a motor cycle. Both the appellants were charged with reckless driving, contrary to s.11(1) of the Road Traffic Act 1931. There was no evidence as to who was driving at the time of the offence. The sheriff convicted them both, and they appealed by stated case to the High Court.

LORD JUSTICE-CLERK (THOMSON): "Counsel for appellants' next point was that . . . there was not enough evidence to convict of [the second charge] because one did not really know anything about the situation, who was driving, or who was the passenger, or how these offences came to be committed. The Solicitor-General put before us the broad proposition that where people are engaged in a criminal enterprise and make their escape from the scene of the crime by car all the occupants of the car become liable for such breaches of the Road Traffic Act as the driver commits, and that that doctrine applied even in a case of this kind where it is not known who the actual driver was. The Solicitor-General's proposition is that all the parties who were acting in concert took the risk of the driver's conduct. It seems to me that that is too wide a proposition. I have no doubt at all that there may be cases where a passenger in a car which is being used for criminal purposes may become liable for what the driver does, but before convicting such a passenger one would require to know something about the facts. One would have to apply this doctrine with some knowledge of the particular facts. It does not seem to me that it is a doctrine which one can apply indiscriminately and I am not prepared to apply it here where we do not know which was driving or the circumstances surrounding the commission of the offence."

Appeal allowed.

NOTES

Presumably the concert involved in the theft did not extend to the escape from the scene of the crime. But would this be so if, for example, the theft had been an armed robbery necessitating a speedy escape?

3. Docherty v. H.M.Advocate
1945 S.L.T. 247

The appellant was convicted of murder. The circumstances of the offence and the grounds of appeal are fully set out in the opinion of Lord Moncrieff:

LORD MONCRIEFF: "In this case the appellant was charged on an indictment, the charge against him being that he, while acting in concert with a person whose name and address were to the prosecutor unknown, on a day in December last and in a one-roomed house occupied by him at an address in Greenock, did assault a man named Davies, offering him various acts of violence, and in particular attacking him with a hatchet, did rob him of a cigarette case and other property, and did murder him. He was tried before the High Court in Glasgow, and on 1st March of this year was convicted of murder by the verdict of a jury and was sentenced to death. It is against that conviction that this appeal is taken.

In the note of application for leave to appeal, three reasons of appeal are set forth. The third of these reasons is that the verdict was contrary to the evidence. Senior counsel, however, eventually found himself unable to withhold an admission that, subject to affirming concert which the jury were entitled to affirm, there was material in the evidence upon which the jury could competently return that verdict; but he insisted—and this was the proposition upon which he particularly relied—that unless concert was so affirmed, there was no evidence which could support the verdict.

The special feature of this case is the need for affirming concert in the circumstances in which the act is said to have occurred. That need arose as follows. When the blow with the hatchet which caused death was struck, assuming that it in fact was struck in the house and in the presence of the appellant, there were present in that single room not only Davies, who lost his life, and the appellant, but also and along with them the unknown associate referred to in the indictment. For all that appears in the evidence the fatal blow may as well have been struck by the associate as struck by the appellant. To establish guilt on the part of the appellant it was thus conceded that it was essential to prove concert; and this in order that, if he was not guilty in respect of his own act, he might yet remain guilty under the doctrine of law which ascribes to associates in crime in certain cases responsiblity for the criminal acts of their associate. As might thus be expected, the reasons of appeal which are still maintained are two reasons which are both associated with the concert which is alleged as a principal element in the indictment; and both of these reasons are founded upon objections to the charge to the jury by the presiding judge.

The first reason of appeal, which is that the presiding judge failed to give adequate directions, was, I think, expanded so as to become a complaint of what amounted to misdirection. That this was the purport of the objection is made clear by the case which was relied on in support of this objection, namely, the case of *Tobin* (1934 J.C. 60). In that case a charge to a jury was given by a learned sheriff in a case in which concert was alleged; and it was held that his failure as presiding judge to direct the jury to consider the evidence against each of the accused separately, and to explain that it was competent to convict certain of the accused without convicting the others, had amounted to a misdirection. It was argued that a similar misdirection was to be found in the charge of the presiding judge to the jury in this case. I have great difficulty in understanding what is supposed to be the foundation of that objection. The learned judge at the outset of his charge proceeds to deal with legal questions, and in particular with the legal consequences of an individual act by one of two parties who are acting in concert; and he points out that proof of a previous plan or arrangement to commit the act is not required, and that concert may be demonstrated by the fact that people have joined together in doing what is done. Then he says in terms, 'Although a number of persons are charged as acting in concert, it does not follow that all may be found guilty. Some may be guilty and some may not be guilty, and, just because of that, where concert is charged the first thing a jury has to determine is whether each—and they must consider each separately—whether each is in the concert or in the plot or took part in the crime which was committed.' I cannot think of words which could more clearly direct a jury to have in view the plea in defence which the learned judge had failed to bring to the notice of the jury in the case of *Tobin (supra);* and accordingly, so far as this reason of appeal is dependent upon a contention that the error made in the case of *Tobin* was again made in this case, it is one which very clearly, in my opinion, should not be sustained.

But then there is maintained under this reason a further objection to the charge; because it was urged by learned counsel that a particular illustration which the learned judge immediately proceeds to give is one which does not correctly formulate the law, and which therefore gives a misdirection on a point of law which may properly have been thought of critical importance by the jury. The illustration is in the following terms: 'If without premeditation two or three men set on to someone in the street with the intention, just perhaps entered into at the time of causing him injury, and one stabs him fatally, then all are equally guilty although there was not really an intention, until the man came along, to attack him at all.' Now, if one were considering the academic question of whether that illustration correctly formulates a doctrine of law, I think it might be recognised that perhaps the proposition is too widely and too unguardedly framed. I think the proposition should have been stated less universally. It is true that if people acting in concert have reason to expect that a lethal weapon will be used—and their expectation may be demonstrated by various circumstances, as, for example, if they themselves are carrying arms or if they know that arms and lethal weapons are being carried by their associates—they may then under the law with regard to concert each one of them become guilty of murder if the weapon is used with fatal results by one of them. In view of their assumed expectation that it might be used, and of their having joined together in an act of violence apt to be completed by its use, they will be assumed in law to have authorised the use of the fatal weapon, and so to have incurred personal responsibility for using it. If, on the other hand, they had no reason so to expect that any one among them would resort to any such act of violence, the mere fact that they were associated in minor violence will not be conclusive against them; and the lethal act, as being unexpected, will not be ascribed to a joint purpose so as to make others than the principal actor responsible for the act.

This distinction has the support of many authorities. In his Commentaries on the Law of Crimes, at page 270 of the first volume, Baron Hume, after dealing with the question of joint liability for the act of one member of a group of persons using violence, says: 'In all that has been said this limitation is plainly implied, that to affect all concerned, the homicide must be done in pursuance of the common enterprise. For if the killer strike on some accidental and peculiar quarrel of his own, nowise connected with or subservient to the original design; or, though it be in some sort connected with that design, if a resolution of the whole party to accomplish their object by such extreme means cannot reasonably be inferred in the whole circumstances of the case; certainly all the reasons fail for which, by the construction of law, the act of one of them may be carried over into the persons of his associates.' In like manner Lord Anderson, in his work on the Criminal Law of Scotland, at page 48, lays down the law as follows: 'But persons acting together are not always guilty of the acts of one of them. If a sudden brawl arise, *rixa per plures,* sticks and fists being used, and one draws a knife and stabs another, the friends of the man who used the knife are not guilty of murder if the injured man dies.' In this passage Lord Anderson thus gives a concise illustration of the doctrine that secondary responsibility for a criminal act arises only in cases of reasonable expectation. The case of *Welsh* (1897, 5 S.L.T. 137) affords an excellent illustration of the limitation of the application of the doctrine to cases in which the special act of violence might reasonably be anticipated. In that case two men broke into a house, the old lady of the house was wakened, and one of the men, seizing a crowbar, assaulted her so violently that she died from her injuries. It was suggested that the act of the man who used the crowbar should be regarded, under the doctrine of concert in violence, as being the act also of the man who did not use the crowbar; but Lord Young negatived that view, and told the jury that so unexpected an act as such a violent attack upon one who was so incapable of resistance, need not be within the reasonable expectation of anyone other than the man who himself did the act. Upon consideration of these authorities, if one were dealing with the exact formulation of a proposition in law, it might thus be open to comment whether the illustration put before the jury by the presiding judge was not too broadly and too generally stated; and had this been a case in which the act of violence which caused death had been perpetrated with a weapon which had been concealed by the man who used it and had been suddenly and unexpectedly produced, then I think that the illustration might well have been regarded as misleading. But in this case the weapon which was used was a hatchet which was the property of the appellant and which must have been present visibly in the room; and it seems to me that in these circumstances either of the assailants must have ascribed against him a common expectation that in the stress of the event the other might snatch up anything which was handy and which was adapted to achieve the joint purpose. I am thus enabled to take the view that, while the illustration might have been a misleading one in certain circumstances, it in this case rather acted as a useful guide to the jury, and did not operate as a misdirection. In any event, I regard the giving of the illustration as one which in the circumstances could in no sense have caused a miscarriage of justice; and so, if there should be thought to be any ground for this attack upon the charge, it is one which I think may be disregarded under the provisions of section 2 (1) of the Act of 1926 (16 & 17 Geo. V. cap. 15)."

Appeal allowed, conviction quashed.

NOTES

The appellant's conviction was quashed on the ground that the trial judge had failed to direct the jury adequately on the proper course to adopt if they did not find that concert had been proved. There was no direct evidence to show who struck the blow and it was therefore essential to the Crown's case against the appellant to establish at least that the appellant was art and part responsible for the death. It was the court's view that the jury should have been directed that if they failed to find concert they were obliged, on the evidence, to return a verdict of acquittal. This result does not follow, of course, where proof of concert is not essential: *Shaw* v. *H.M.Advocate*, 1953 J.C. 51.

c.   Limits to art and part guilt

1.   R. v. Tyrrell
[1894] 1 Q.B. 710

The defendant was convicted of aiding and abetting a man to have unlawful carnal knowledge of her, contrary to s. 5 of the Criminal Law Amendment Act 1885. The case was reserved for the Court for Crown Cases Reserved, the question for the opinion of the court being, "Whether it is an offence for a girl between the ages of thirteen and sixteen to aid and abet a male person in the commission of the misdemeanor of having unlawful carnal connection with her, or to solicit and incite a male person to commit that misdemeanor."

LORD COLERIDGE C.J.: "The Criminal Law Amendment Act, 1885, was passed for the purpose of protecting women and girls against themselves. At the time it was passed there was a discussion as to what point should be fixed as the age of consent. That discussion ended in a compromise, and the age of consent was fixed at sixteen. With the object of protecting women and girls against themselves the Act of Parliament has made illicit connection with a girl under that age unlawful; if a man wishes to have such illicit connection he must wait until the girl is sixteen, otherwise he breaks the law; but it is impossible to say that the Act, which is absolutely silent about aiding or abetting, or soliciting or inciting, can have intended that the girls for whose protection it was passed should be punishable under it for the offences committed upon themselves. I am of opinion that this conviction ought to be quashed."

MATHEW J.: "I am of the same opinion. I do not see how it would be possible to obtain convictions under the statute if the contention for the Crown were adopted, because nearly every section which deals with offences in respect of women and girls would create an offence in the woman or girl. Such a result cannot have been intended by the legislature. There is no trace in the statute of any intention to treat the woman or girl as criminal."

Conviction quashed.

NOTES

Cf. Gordon's view (para. 5-05) that: "So far as sexual offences are concerned the law probably is that where an offence is created in order to protect a particular class of persons a member of that class cannot be convicted of being art and part in its commission against herself." It is difficult to see why this should be so if the "victim" genuinely encourages the offence. The practical problem alluded to by Mathew J. may be overcome by the discretion not to prosecute where the "victim" is required as a witness.

2. R. v. Cogan and Leak
[1975] 3 W.L.R. 316

At the instigation of Leak, Cogan had intercourse with Leak's wife, without her consent. Cogan was charged with rape, and Leak with aiding and abetting that offence. They were both convicted, but Cogan's conviction was subsequently quashed, in accordance with the decision in *R.* v. *Morgan (post)*, on the ground of misdirection. Leak appealed against his conviction on the ground, *inter alia*, that since Cogan's conviction had been quashed he could not stand convicted of aiding and abetting that offence.

LAWTON L.J.: "Leak's appeal against conviction was based on the proposition that he could not be found guilty of aiding and abetting Cogan to rape his wife if Cogan was acquitted of that offence as he was deemed in law to have been when his conviction was quashed: see section 2 (3) of the Criminal Appeal Act 1968. Leak's counsel, Mr. Herrod, conceded, however, that this proposition had some limitations. The law on this topic lacks clarity as a perusal of some of the textbooks shows: see *Smith and Hogan, Criminal Law.* 3rd. ed. (1973). pp. 106-109; *Glanville Williams, Criminal Law,* 2nd ed. (1961), pp. 386-390, 406-408; *Russell on Crime,* 12th ed. (1964), vol. 1, p. 128. We do not consider it appropriate to review the law generally because, as was said by this court in *Reg.* v. *Quick* [1973] Q.B. 910, 923, when considering this kind of problem: 'The facts of each case . . . have to be considered and in particular what is alleged to have been done by way of aiding and abetting.'

The only case which Mr. Herrod submitted had a direct bearing upon the problem of Leak's guilt was *Walters* v. *Lunt* [1951] 2 All E.R. 645. In that case the respondents had been charged, under section 33 (1) of the Larceny Act 1916, with receiving from a child aged seven years, certain articles knowing them to have been stolen. In 1951, a child under eight years was deemed in law to be incapable of committing a crime: it followed that at the time of receipt by the respondents the articles had not been stolen and that the charge had not been proved. That case is very different from this because here one fact is clear—the wife had been raped. Cogan had had sexual intercourse with her without her consent. The fact that Cogan was innocent of rape because he believed that she was consenting does not affect the position that she was raped.

Her ravishment had come about because Leak had wanted it to happen and had taken action to see that it did by persuading Cogan to use his body as the instrument for the necessary physical act. In the language of the law the act of sexual intercourse without the wife's consent was the actus reus: it had been procured by Leak who had the appropriate mens rea, namely, his intention that Cogan should have sexual intercourse with her without her consent. In our judgment it is irrelevant that the man whom Leak had procured to do the physical act himself did not intend to have sexual intercourse with the wife without her consent. Leak was using him as a means to procure a criminal purpose.

Before 1861 a case such as this, pleaded as it was in the indictment, might have presented a court with problems arising from the old distinctions between principals and accessories in felony. Most of the old law was swept away by section 8 of the Accessories and Abettors Act 1861 and what remained by section 1 of the Criminal Law Act 1967. The modern law allowed Leak to be tried and punished as a principal offender. In our judgment he could have been indicted as a principal offender. It would have been no defence for him to submit that if Cogan was an 'innocent' agent, he was necessarily in the old terminology of the law a principal in the first degree, which was a legal impossibility as a man cannot rape his own wife during cohabitation. The law no longer concerns itself with niceties of degrees in participation in crime; but even if it did Leak would still be guilty. The reason a man cannot by his own physical act rape his wife during cohabitation is because the law presumes consent from the marriage ceremony: see *Hale, Pleas of the Crown* (1778), vol. 1, p. 629. There is no such presumption when a man procures a drunken friend to do the physical act for him. Hale C.J. put this case in one sentence, at p. 629: 'tho in marriage she hath given up her body to her husband, she is not to be by him prostituted to another': see loc. cit. Had Leak been indicted as a principal offender, the case against him would have been clear beyond argument. Should he be allowed to go free because he was charged with 'being aider and abettor to the same offence'? If we are right in our opinion that the wife had been raped (and no one outside a court of law would say that she had not been), then the particulars of offence accurately stated what Leak had done, namely, he had procured

Cogan to commit the offence. This would suffice to uphold the conviction. We would prefer, however, to uphold it on a wider basis. In our judgment convictions should not be upset because of mere technicalities of pleading in an indictment. Leak knew what the case against him was and the facts in support of that case were proved. But for the fact that the jury thought that Cogan in his intoxicated condition might have mistaken the wife's sobs and distress for expressions of her consent, no question of any kind would have arisen about the form of pleading. By his written statement Leak virtually admitted what he had done. As Judge Chapman said in *Reg.* v. *Humphreys* [1965] All E.R. 689, 692: 'It would be anomalous if a person who admitted to a substantial part in the perpetration of a misdemeanor as aider and abettor could not be convicted on his own admission merely because the person alleged to have been aided and abetted was not or could not be convicted.' In the circumstances of this case it would be more than anomalous: it would be an affront to justice and to the common sense of ordinary folk. It was for these reasons that we dismissed the appeal against conviction."

Appeal dismissed.

NOTES

How far did the court depart from the principle *actus non facit reum nisi mens sit rea* in this case? After all, it was accepted that the accused who committed the *actus* did not have the *mens rea*. How then can there have been an *actus reus* without an unprecedented interference with the requirement of coincidence of *actus reus* and *mens rea* (as to which, see *post*, ch. 6).

The case illustrates a modification of the doctrine of art and part, in that in some cases an accused may be convicted of being art and part in an offence which he could not himself legally commit. In this respect, see *Vaughan* v. *H.M.Advocate*, 1979 S.L.T. 49 *(post*, ch. 16).

Whether this is true with regard to statutory offences, where criminal liability is restricted to a particular class of persons is a matter of doubt. In *Robertsons* v. *Caird* (1885) 5 Couper 4 it was held that a person who was not a "debtor in a process of sequestration or cessio" within the meaning of s. 13 of the Debtors (Scotland) Act 1880, could not be guilty art and part of an offence contrary to that section, where the offence was limited to persons of that class. In *Vaughan* v. *H.M. Advocate,* however, it was held that an accused, who was not within the limited class of persons envisaged by the Incest Act 1567 could nonetheless be guilty art and part of an offence committed by a person who was within that class. (See below, ch. 16.)

CHAPTER 5

INCHOATE OFFENCES

a.   Incitement

H.M. Advocate v. Tannahill and Neilson
1943 J.C. 150

A partner in a firm of contractors who were carrying out work for a government department was charged, *inter alia*, with attempting to induce certain sub-contractors who had done work for him to charge the government for this work, and thereby attempting to defraud the department. In his charge to the jury the presiding judge gave the following directions on attempt and incitement:

LORD WARK: "The Advocate-Depute maintained, upon certain authorities from text-books which he quoted, that it is criminal by the law of Scotland to instigate a person to do a criminal act, but you will observe that the alleged instigation here is charged not merely as instigation but also as attempt to defraud. If you turn to the end of charge 1 (*f*) you will see the charge is, 'Did thus instigate and attempt to induce said William Napier Samuels and Robert Nimmo M'Lean to render to said firm false and fabricated accounts in relation to said amounts for inclusion by said firm in said claim form . . . and you did attempt to defraud said Department thereof.' So that this is set forth as an attempt to defraud. I have to direct you that there is no evidence on this part of the charge which would entitle you to bring in a verdict of an attempt to defraud, because in order to get so far as that I think you would require to have some overt act, the consequences of which cannot be recalled by the accused, which goes towards the commission of the crime, before you can convict even of attempt. The question came up in a famous case in 1911 known as the Pearl Necklace Case, and the direction which was there given by the learned Lord Justice-General, Lord Dunedin, was that, before you get into the region of attempt, matters must have proceeded from a mere act of preparation to an act of perpetration, and I am going to direct you that matters in this case did not get so far. But I think there is authority—and the learned Advocate-Depute has referred me to it—that instigation to a crime may in itself be criminal even although the crime is never committed and never attempted to be committed."

Verdict: not guilty.

NOTES

The "Pearl Necklace Case" referred to by his Lordship is the case of *H.M. Advocate* v. *Camerons*, 1911 S.C. (J.) 110 (*post*). *Tannahill and Neilson* is discussed in *Morton* v. *Henderson*, 1956 J.C. 55 (*post*).

b. Conspiracy

The law relating to conspiracy in Scotland is still in a relatively early state of development, when compared with, for example, English law. For that reason alone it is difficult to state with any certainty what is the law. This difficulty is exacerbated by the fact that few if any of the modern conspiracy cases have been reported. The cases included here are illustrative of the current Scottish practice.

1. H.M. Advocate v. Wilson, Latta and Rooney
High Court, February 1968, *unreported*

Wilson, Latta and Rooney were charged with conspiracy to have false evidence given at a trial and thus to defeat the ends of justice, "and in pursuance of said conspiracy," (a) subornation of perjury, (b) attempted subornation, and (c) attempted subornation, in relation to a number of witnesses. In his charge to the jury the presiding judge gave the following directions on conspiracy:

LORD JUSTICE-CLERK (GRANT): "I turn now to the indictment which you have before you. It is a long indictment and on the face of it a rather complicated indictment, as any conspiracy indictment is bound to be . . .

The indictment libels one single charge, and that is a charge of conspiracy . . . It is one single charge, but it is in two parts. The conspiracy is narrated in that part of the indictment which finishes up 'and thus to defeat the ends of justice.' It then goes on to narrate certain things that were done in pursuance of said conspiracy, and these matters are subdivided in the three heads (a), (b) and (c).

Your first duty, I think, will be to decide whether the Crown have established a conspiracy either between all three of the accused or between any two of them (you will appreciate that it takes more than one to make a conspiracy). A criminal conspiracy arises when two or more persons agree to render one another assistance in doing an act, whether as an end or as a means to an end, which would be criminal if done by a single individual. Perhaps I might just read you another definition which is, I think, to the same effect; it comes from a speech of the late Viscount Simon, when he was Lord Chancellor, in a Scottish case in the House of Lords; it was a civil case, although what he is dealing with here is criminal conspiracy. 'Conspiracy, when regarded as a crime, is the agreement of two or more persons to effect any unlawful purpose whether as their ultimate aim or only as a means of it; and the crime is complete if there is such agreement even if nothing is done in pursuance of it.' So you can have a criminal conspiracy even although it is never in any way carried into effect. In the present case, of course, the Crown say that the conspiracy was in fact carried into effect in the manner stated in the sub-heads (a), (b) and (c). That I think is important—I think you will see it is important when I read a sentence which is later in Viscount Simon's speech: 'The crime consists in the agreement, though in most cases overt acts done in pursuance of the combination are available to prove the fact of agreement.' In effect, let's face it, you won't often get eye-witnesses of the agreement being made or eavesdroppers who actually heard it being made. Accordingly, in many cases it is a question of judging from the acts of the alleged conspirators whether in fact there was a conspiracy between them in pursuance of which they are acting. It is by their acts, as frequently happens in other spheres of life, that we know them.

I should perhaps add this, that it is not necessary that all the conspirators should have reached the agreement at the same time. For example, if two men agree to carry out a criminal purpose and they decide that they need a larger team, they may approach C and D and say, 'We, A and B, have agreed to do this. Would you also agree to come into the plot, conspiracy or what have you, along with us?' If C and D agree to carry out this criminal purpose, then of course all four are in it. But, as Mr Stewart pointed out, it is not enough merely that C and D should be sitting by and doing nothing. He read you a passage which is perhaps more apt to heads (a), (b) and (c) than it is to conspiracy, although you will keep it in mind with regard to both: 'Presence on the scene of the crime, coupled with a failure to prevent the crime, does not of itself constitute art and part guilt.' But the next sentence, as Mr Stewart quite frankly admitted, is of some importance: 'But the circumstances of A's presence may be such as to enable the Court to infer that he was "in it" '—'in it' is in inverted commas—'with the principal offenders.' I think probably in Rooney's case that is the sort of question which you will have to answer, because there is, I think, no evidence that he actively persuaded any witness to make any particular state-ment—I think that is right. He was a constant attender, but if he was a henchman, he was a silent henchman most of the time.

As I have already indicated, the evidence in regard to the facts alleged in heads (a), (b) and (c) are of course very relevant to your consideration of whether there was a conspiracy or not. And if you found that a conspiracy is established, then you would of course go on to consider heads (a), (b) and (c), which in a sense you have considered already. You see, it might be, for example, that you could find conspiracy between all three, but you might find, for example, that in pursuance of the conspiracy only heads (a) and (b) were in fact carried out and that (c) was not—I just give that as an example. But once you find a conspiracy a slightly different situation arises. Normally a man is responsible only for what he himself does, but if he is involved in a conspiracy he may be responsible not merely for what he himself does but for what his fellow-conspirators do. For example, if you found Rooney was in the conspiracy, and found further that Latta and Wilson took an active part under head (a), you could find Rooney equally guilty even though his part was a passive one, merely because he was in the conspiracy to carry out what is set forth in head (a).

Now in order to try and make this a little clearer for you I am not going to put it in my own words but I am going to read what was said in a conspiracy trial of some note in 1953 by my predecessor, the Lord Justice-Clerk, Lord Thomson. . . . I quote: 'Once two or more people are brought together as conspirators, or indeed as art and part in any kind of crime, they are each and all liable for all the acts done in furtherance of the conspiracy.' That is to say, once you are in a conspiracy or a plot or whatever you like to call it, you have to shoulder responsibility not only for what you yourself do in furtherance of the conspiracy, but for what your fellow-conspirators or plotters do; and the only way you could escape responsibility would be if it appeared that your fellow-plotters had gone beyond the bounds of the conspiracy. But it is essential, members of the Jury, that each man's case be considered separately. There must be evidence, satisfying you, that makes him a member of the plot. If he is not proved to be a member of the plot then, of course, you cannot saddle on him what other plotters did, and he remains liable only for what he himself did. . . .

Now, I have already indicated that what are called overt acts may be evidence of whether there was a conspiracy or not. It is a matter for you, but you may think that the question of whether or not A and B, or A and B and C, have agreed to carry out a common criminal purpose is a matter to which their actings, their criminal actings, are highly relevant. So, as I have already indicated, in deciding whether or not any of the accused was a party to the conspiracy libelled you are entitled and should take into account any evidence as to his participation in the various matters alleged in heads (a), (b) and (c) of the indictment.

The next matter is . . . there is always a possibility that you would find no conspiracy proved against any of the accused. Now, if that be so, that is not a complete end of the matter. You would have to consider in regard to each man individually and separately whether he committed the acts set out in heads (a), (b) and (c). The reason is this . . . that if conspiracy is not established, nevertheless there are in heads (a), (b) and (c) of the indictment a separable part of the indictment which constitutes indictable crimes. In effect, if conspiracy goes out of the window, you will still have to consider in each case whether there was subornation under (a), attempted subornation under (b) and attempted subornation under (c); and as I say you will do that taking each accused separately and on the basis of individual responsibility in each case. If it came to that you would, of course, return a separate verdict under each head in respect of each accused. And I think I have already told you that I think one of the three was not in the conspiracy but the other two were, then the case of the third would have to be considered in the same way. . . .

Now I come to the verdicts which it is open to you to return. You will return a separate verdict in respect of each accused. If conspiracy is established against any particular accused and in addition the matters set out in heads (a), (b) and (c), you will find him guilty as libelled on the indictment as amended. . . .

Secondly, if in the case of any accused you find conspiracy established and also one or two but not all of these sub-heads (a), (b) and (c), then your verdict would be guilty as libelled under deletion of the particular sub-head which you had not found established.

Thirdly, if in the case of any accused you find that conspiracy is not established but that he is guilty of subornation or attempted subornation in regard to the matters narrated in heads (a), (b) and (c), you would find him guilty of subornation or attempted subornation accordingly, deleting of course any sub-head which was not established. Supposing conspiracy went out of the window against one particular accused and you found he was guilty of subornation under head (a) but that heads (b) and (c) were not established, your verdict would be guilty of subornation under head (a) full stop—and that means not guilty of the rest.

Now, if none of these three conditions applies, that is if in the case of any accused neither conspiracy nor subornation or any attempted subornation is established, you have alternative verdicts of not guilty or not proven." Verdict: the jury found the accused Wilson guilty as libelled, the accused Latta guilty under deletion of head (b), and the accused Rooney guilty under deletion of head (c).

NOTES

The competency of convicting of the separate "heads" depended on s. 60 of the Criminal Procedure (Scotland) Act 1887 which permitted a conviction to be returned on any part of an indictment which disclosed an indictable crime (see now the 1975 Act, ss. 61(2) and 312(*n*)).

The case is authority for the competency of convicting of the "heads" included in a conspiracy charge, provided these heads are themselves crimes, even if the conspiracy is not proved (Gordon, para. 6-58). But a number of questions remain: (1) What happens if, as in fact happened in this case, the conspiracy and any of the "heads" are proved? (2) What is the effect of a finding by the jury that X is not part of the conspiracy, but did carry out one of the "heads" where that "head" does not disclose a criminal offence? (3) Whether it is competent to return a cumulative verdict—guilty both of conspiracy and any substantive crime disclosed in the "heads"? See, generally on these questions, Gordon, paras. 6-57 to 6-61, and the following case.

2.   H.M. Advocate v. Milnes and Ors.
High Court, Glasgow, January 1971, *unreported*

Ronald Milne, David Brannan, and three others were charged on an indictment which libelled a conspiracy to pervert the course of justice by offering inducements to potential witnesses at a forthcoming trial, by intimidating and coercing them and finally by murder and "in pursuance of said conspiracy" a number of acts, some criminal, some not, numbered (A) to (G). The case went to the jury, against Milne under deletion of heads (F) and (G), and against Brannan under deletion of all the heads except (F). In the course of his charge to the jury the presiding judge gave the following directions on conspiracy:

LORD AVONSIDE: "[The] crime libelled in the indictment is conspiracy to pervert the course of justice. It has not been disputed, and no one would dispute it, that it is a crime to pervert the course of justice, to interfere with the proper administration of justice, to impede it or distort or prevent the pursuit of justice.

In this case the method which the Crown say was used to carry out the crime was, put simply, to induce, intimidate, coerce, and when these failed, resort to murder of certain witnesses who were going to give evidence in the High Court on circuit at Glasgow. If that were proved there should be no clearer case of the crime of perverting or attempting to pervert the course of justice. . . .

If—now, this is sheer assumption—if you find Ronald Milne guilty of conspiracy to pervert the course of justice, then you must look at the indictment as I have restricted it in relation to him, and you will see as a conspirator he is said to have done or to be responsible as a conspirator for doing, the various acts which are grouped under the five separate heads (A) to (E), the acts which the Crown say were carried out in pursuance of the conspiracy. You must look at the evidence relating to Ronald Milne in respect of each of these acts and in relation to each you must ask yourself whether the Crown has proved that he, as a conspirator, is guilty of any of these acts, part of the acts contained in any individual head. So far as Brannan is concerned, your concentration is focussed on head (E) alone. Here you will have in mind the law which I explained fully and when I again do in a condensed form. A conspirator is guilty of acts done by himself or by his fellows in pursuance of a conspiracy, but not guilty of acts done by his fellows which were outwith what might be reasonably anticipated to be done in pursuance of that conspiracy.

Just assuming—and again this is pure assumption—assuming that you found Ronald Milne guilty of conspiracy. You may then, depending on your view of the evidence before you, find him guilty of the actings set out under heads (A) to (E), or some of them. I am merely using entirely random examples, but you might, for example, find him guilty under head (B) or head (D) and the rest not guilty or not proven; or, if this were your view, that the charges under heads (A) to (E) in the case of Ronald Milne, which I am merely taking as an example, are not proved, and in respect of that your verdict in relation to him would be not guilty or not proven. If you found charge (E) not proved against Brannan then your verdict in relation to that head is not guilty or not proven.

I must go on now to assume that a charge of conspiracy has not been proved—has not been proved against Milne or Brannan. If that be so you, of course, find them not guilty of conspiracy. That, however, is not the end of the case, because each of the heads (A) to (E) libels an act or combination of acts each of which by themselves constitute indictable crimes, irrespective of the issue of conspiracy. This is very plain under head (E), for example, which you may think is the important one, because really how the indictment would read is: Neil Milne and Ronald Milne (sic), not guilty of conspiracy, but charged with: 'On 27 September 1970, in Everard Drive aforesaid, assault said William Murray and discharge a loaded shotgun at him to his severe injury and attempt to murder him.' That, quite clearly, standing on its own feet is a criminal charge, irrespective of whether that was done in relation to a conspiracy or not. When you are considering, if you come to consider, head (E) in isolation you will remember that the same rules regarding people acting together apply in relation to it as apply in relation to a conspiracy. If you are of the view that under head (E) Milne and Brannan acted together with a common purpose then they are both guilty although only one fired the shot, unless you are of the view that the shooting was something outwith the reasonable contemplation of the man who did not fire the shot. . . .

If you find the conspiracy has not been proved your verdict will be not guilty or not proven as regards the conspiracy, but then you will want to consider the various heads against Ronald Milne and head (E) against Brannan; and if you find the heads, or some of them, against Ronald Milne not proved then you will find him not guilty on those which are not proved, but guilty on those which are, if any. If you find Brannan not guilty on charge (E) then there, of course, is the end of the case so far as he is concerned, he is not guilty or not proven of the whole charge. If you find Ronald Milne guilty of conspiracy and of all or some or one of heads (A) to (E), then you will find him guilty of conspiracy as libelled and guilty of the heads in which your verdict is that.

So far as head (E) is concerned, the same of course applies to Brannan, and once more I will remind you that you can, if you find guilt, restrict head (E) to an assault to serious injury, if that be your view.

If, in the end of the day, you come to this conclusion, that they are not guilty of conspiracy and guilty of only (E), then you will so find."

> Verdict: the jury found the accused Milne guilty of conspiring to pervert the course of justice, on head (A) by a majority, on (B), (C) and (D) not proven, and unanimously guilty of (E); the accused Brannan was found guilty of conspiring to pervert the course of justice, and guilty of head (E).

NOTES

Gordon (para. 6-60) describes the above case as a "mishmash." It is difficult to disagree. It appears that in fact the jury achieved a result held not to be competent in *Wilson, Latta and Rooney, viz.,* a cumulative verdict of guilty of the conspiracy and a substantive offence in one of the heads. A number of important questions remain unanswered with regard to the law of conspiracy in general. Thus the problem of the "one-man" conspiracy is not clearly settled. In *Wilson, Latta and Rooney (ante)* Lord Grant remarked that "it takes more than one to make a conspiracy," but would it be possible to overcome this by charging X along with "persons unknown"? And what would happen if A and B were convicted of conspiracy, and B's conviction later quashed? See, on these points, the English cases of *Anthony* [1965] 2 Q.B. 189, *Shannon* [1974] 2 All E.R. 1009, and *O'Brien* (1974) 59 Cr. App. R. 222. For further doubts on the Scottish law, see Gordon, paras. 6-57 to 6-61.

c.   Attempts

1.   H.M. Advocate v. Camerons
1911 S.C. (J.) 110

Two persons, husband and wife, formed a scheme to defraud insurance underwriters by insuring a necklace, staging a fake robbery, and claiming the insurance money by pretending to the underwriters that the necklace had been stolen. They were charged with attempting to defraud the underwriters of the sum of £6500. At the trial, however, the Crown failed to prove that a claim had actually been made. In charging the jury the Lord Justice-General gave the following directions on attempt:

LORD JUSTICE-GENERAL (DUNEDIN): "You must take it that it is a blunder; but it is a bad blunder, because you are bound to take it from me that it is not proved that any claim was made against the underwriters by Mrs Cameron. It is not only that no formal claim has been made but no claim has been made. As I tell you, I foresaw this some time ago,—as it happened really, I think, on the first day of the trial,—and it gave me very great anxiety, because it certainly was a question whether it did not ruin the case altogether. I not only considered the matter very carefully myself, but I did what I have a perfect right to do, I consulted with several of my brethren on the matter, and therefore what I am now to lay down to you is very carefully considered law, and at any rate, as you know, you are bound to take the law from me. I am bound to say that although I have nothing to complain of—I have already said what I thought of counsel's speeches—I cannot say that the law here was correctly stated by either of the learned counsel who addressed you. Mr Morison said that there was no crime at all unless a claim had been put forward, and Mr Clyde said that four things had to be proved before you could have a conviction, and the fourth was the making of the claim. Now, I cannot lay down either of those propositions as correct law. The thing that is charged here is an attempt, it is not success. The underwriters have not been defrauded, because they have not paid a penny. Fraud and an attempt to commit a fraud are both crimes according to the law of Scotland. Now, I am going to read to you first the words of a writer who wrote more than a hundred years ago, and who is still one of the greatest authorities on the criminal law in Scotland, viz., Baron Hume. What he said is this: 'I have now said enough concerning the nature of that inordinate and vicious will which is essential to the guilt of every crime. But the vicious will is not sufficient, unless it is coupled to a wrongful act. And here the question arises, How far must the culprit have proceeded in the prosecution of his wicked purpose to make him answerable in the tribunals of this world? This may on many occasions be a difficult inquiry.' Then he goes on thus, after giving some illustrations of where a person trying to do one thing did something less, I mean trying to murder and only wounding: 'Even when no harm ensues on the attempt, still the law rightly takes cognisance of it . . . if there has been an inchoate act of *execution* of the meditated deed.' After going through many cases, and in particular the case of *Maciver and Macallum* for boring holes in a ship's bottom and drawing the plugs to sink the vessel and cheat the insurers, he goes on: 'Between these extremes there lie a great variety of ambiguous cases with respect to which it is very difficult to say where preparation ends and perpetration begins.' Now, that is really the root of the whole matter; it is to discover where preparation ends and where perpetration begins. In other words, it is a question of degree, and when it is a question of degree it is a jury question, a question for you.

Applying these observations to the matter in hand, mere conception of a fraudulent scheme is not enough; that fraudulent scheme, in order to be criminal, must be carried into some effect by overt act; but if it has begun to be carried into effect by overt act it need not come to final fruition. The mere conceiving of the scheme—if you think a scheme was conceived—is not enough; but if that scheme is so far carried out as that a false insurance is taken, and that a false robbery is gone through, very little more will do. At the same time you must remember that the actual claim has not been made. I give an illustration to show you how particular this is. Supposing that after getting that letter from Price & Gibbs saying that they wanted a formal claim, Dundas & Wilson had gone down to the parties and said, 'We want a formal claim,' and they said, 'No, we have changed our minds, and we give it up; we are not to claim at all'—do you think there would have been much chance of convicting them? Well, of course, they are not in that happy position, but, through the omission of the Crown to prove any claim, they are in the same position, as you must just take it, as if they had been arrested after they had made the communications to which I am now going to refer. Now, the communications which are libelled other than those which you must read out as not proved—you must read out the Dundas & Wilson letters—are, first of all, an intimation to Mr Munt by telegram on the night of the occurrence, 'Regret to report pearl necklace snatched off wife's neck in street 6.15 p.m. to-night local police informed immediately. Will you set your own detectives to work?' And then that is followed by a confirming letter: 'In confirmation of my wire of to-night I greatly regret to report that my wife's pearls were snatched from her to-day in the circumstances explained in the enclosed statements.' Then the two statements are enclosed in that letter. They do not say anything about asking for money, but they give an account of the robbery in the street. I do not read them again, because they have been read before. Then there is a letter of 14th February, which is after Mr Leach had been down. 'My dear Mr Munt,—We are disappointed at the result of your man's visit. He only stayed one day and seemed even sceptical because the thing seemed so wonderful. My solicitors here, Dundas & Wilson, who keep the police up to the mark and take charge of my papers, would very much like a copy of the policy just for form. May I have one please?' And he gets the copy of the policy. The last letter is the one in which he says that Mr Munt is quite right in his story, and then he says, 'We will now be able to show our hand more or less, and, if necessary, declare war.' Well, now, you are entitled to take all those communications into consideration, and you are entitled to consider what is the true meaning of them. You do not as a rule write to an insurance broker to say that there has been a theft except with a view to following it up by making a claim. Mr Munt is not the actual representative of the underwriters, as counsel were quite right in saying, but still there you are, and that is how the matter rests. Assuming that you find that there is a conspiracy at all, you have to consider whether what was done had got beyond the stage of preparation into the stage of perpetration."

Verdict: both accused were found guilty.

NOTES

Gordon (paras. 6-26 to 6-27) critises the "perpetration theory" as being "meaningless" and "vague" and leading to unsatisfactory results. It might also be added that if an attempt to commit a crime is itself a crime it is unsatisfactory that a major element in the definition of the crime (the stage at which attempt is reached) should be a matter of fact for the jury, as is suggested by Lord Dunedin. But, *cf.* Lord Reid's approach in *Haughton* v. *Smith* [1975] A.C. 476 (*post*).

2. H.M. Advocate v. Mackenzies
1913 S.C. (J.) 107

A husband and wife were charged on an indictment which, *inter alia*, charged the husband with making copies of certain secret recipes which he had taken from his employers, in breach of his contractual obligations to his employers, "with intent to dispose of said copies for valuable consideration to trade rivals." An objection was taken to the relevancy of this charge.

LORD JUSTICE-CLERK (MACDONALD): "I am quite unable to hold that this is a relevant charge of crime, either completed crime or attempted crime. It is a charge covering a preparation for crime only—assuming that the completed act or actual attempt would infer crime—but it is not a charge of anything done that can be called an overt act. The law does not strike at preparation to commit a crime unless by special statutory enactment such preparation is placed in the category of crime. The analogy which comes nearest to the present case is that of forgery. No successful prosecution can take place so as to secure punishment for the preparation of a forgery. The overt act of uttering is essential to a conviction. The forger is not amenable to the law because he has made a forgery or has a forgery in his possession, whatever may be his intent to make use of it to effect a felonious end. Thus in the indictments, although forgery and uttering were charged, there could be no conviction of the forgery unless the uttering was proved. It must have gone beyond his power to abstain from using by his having used it, by actually presenting it, or posting it, or so putting it out of his own possession that there is no longer any *locus poenitentiae*. Till this is done, however much the making or the possession of the fabricated document may indicate moral delinquency, his act does not bring him within the grasp of the law. He has not proceeded to put his nefarious intention into operation. He is like a man who has prepared false keys in order to enter the premises of another for a felonious purpose, but has never used them. This well-established and most just rule of law, which does not allow of punishment for unfulfilled intents and preparations which have not culminated in an irrevocable act of commission or attempt, is only, as I have said, set aside in certain cases by statutory enactments for special reasons. Thus the manufacture of spurious banknotes is constituted a criminal offence without there being any proof of uttering. The statute strikes at the manufacture of false banknotes as being a thing highly dangerous to the general community, and calling for special State intervention. That a statute should be necessary to check such wholesale manufacture illustrates the rule that the preparation of a fraudulent document, or a document intended to be fraudulently used, is not in itself a punishable crime, and that it requires an overt act of use to constitute an indictable offence. In this indictment the statement that he made the copies with an intent to dispose of them to trade rivals, is not an averment of any act done, but only of a state of mind, which might be gone back upon, and nothing done to carry out the intent. I have therefore no hesitation in holding the second charge against the male prisoner to be irrelevant."

Objection to the relevancy of the
second charge sustained.

NOTE

In what sense had the Camerons proceeded further in their scheme than Mackenzie (given that the Camerons had not made a claim)?

3. Samuel Tumbleson
(1863) 4 Irv. 426

The accused was charged with attempting to murder his wife by giving a quantity of poisoned oatmeal to an innocent third party to give to his wife. Objections were taken to the relevancy of the indictment, on the ground, *inter alia*, that there was no averment that the poisoned food had reached, or been taken by the intended victim, or, at least, that it had been placed, by some overt act, beyond the control of the accused.

LORD NEAVES: "With regard to the second objection, it is true that the mere resolution to commit a crime is not indictable. It requires, of course, to be expressed in some overt act, more or less proximate, before the law can take cognizance of it; but when, as in the present case, machinery is put in motion, which, by its own nature, is calculated to terminate in murder,—when this agency is let out of the party's hands to work its natural results,—that is a stage of the operation by which he shows that he has completely developed in his own mind a murderous purpose, and has done all that in him lay to accomplish it."

LORD DEAS: "As regards the major proposition, which in substance charges an attempt to administer poison with the intent of committing murder, or with the intent of committing great bodily injury, I have no doubt at all, any more than your Lordship, that the attempt to administer poison with either of these views is a crime according to the law of Scotland. It has always, I think, been so held, and it is common sense that it should be so. So much for the major proposition. But the more important question relates to the minor proposition, namely, whether, assuming that such an attempt as I have mentioned is a crime in law, the facts set forth in the minor amount to that offence? Now, the facts stated just come to this,— that the panel mixed in a quantity of oatmeal this strychnia or other deadly poison, and that he gave it to the woman (Mrs Tumbleson) named in the indictment, directing and instructing her to give it (that is to say, the meal containing the poison) to his wife, 'in order that it might be partaken of by her as an article of food.' Now I can have no doubt that if the wife had partaken of the oatmeal and died, the panel would have been guilty of murder. I recollect a case from

Dundee conducted by myself as Advocate-Depute, in which the circumstances were very analogous. There the man (Leith I think was his name) was indicted in the High Court for the murder of his wife by means of poison. The mode of administration libelled was the mixing the poison with a quantity of oatmeal, and leaving the oatmeal in a place where he expected his wife would find it and use it, which she did, and consequently died. The panel was convicted and executed. Here, as there, the panel, if what be said is true, had done his part. He had mixed the poison with the meal, and given it to a third party, to be handed to his wife, intending and expecting that she would partake of it as food. If the woman to whom the panel gave the meal had done what he intended her to do, and his wife had used the meal, his alleged purpose would have been accomplished; and it was not owing to him, so far as we can see, that these results did not follow. Now, it would be a sad state of the law, if, after a man has done all which it lies with him to do to poison his wife or anybody else, and put the result beyond his own power, but through some providential cause over which he had no control, the result intended does not follow, it should be held that the law cannot take cognizance of what has been done with a view to punishment, but must allow him to repeat the attempt with impunity as often as he pleases, until he ultimately succeeds. I cannot hold this to be the law of this country."

Objection to relevancy repelled.

NOTES

Camerons and *Mackenzies* are not inconsistent with this case. *Tumbleson* had clearly reached beyond preparation. The case may, however, support the "last act" theory of attempt, *i.e.*, that the accused commits an attempt once he has done all that is required of *him* to commit the full offence. What would happen, however, if the accused, having committed this "last act" repented, and took steps to prevent his plans being fulfilled?

4.   H.M. Advocate v. Baxter
(1908) 5 Adam 609

In order to procure an abortion for a pregnant woman, the accused obtained a quantity of drugs, which he sent to a third party with instructions on how they were to be administered in order to bring about an abortion. He was charged with attempting to procure an abortion. An objection was taken to the relevancy of the indictment.

LORD JUSTICE-CLERK (MACDONALD): "This is a very peculiar case, but I have no difficulty in holding that the indictment is irrelevant. It appears on the face of it to be a charge of an attempt to commit a crime. The attempt consisted solely in supplying a person with a drug which, if used in a certain way, would be likely to cause a pregnant woman to abort. It is not said the drug ever reached the person to whom it was sent; indeed, we are told at the bar that it never did reach him, and I should have gathered that from the indictment without being told it. The indictment is based on this, that one person sent to another person something which, if used in the way directed, would be likely to cause abortion. No one can doubt that is a reprehensible act, and if Parliament were to make such a thing illegal by statute, probably no one would be found to express disapproval of the enactment. But the sole question we are now dealing with is whether at common law this constitutes an attempt to commit a crime. There are many crimes for which preparation is necessary; but mere preparation is not enough to constitute attempt. Suppose a man is employed by housebreakers to make instruments for the purpose of housebreaking. It is not a crime at common law to make a jemmy or a brace or any other housebreaking tool, or to sell it to a man who is going to commit housebreaking. But it is said by the Advocate-Depute that if the man knows that the tools are to be used for the purposes of breaking into a house, and hands them to the housebreaker for that purpose, then he renders himself liable to a charge of attempt. That can be tested in this way. If it were so, the attempt to commit house-breaking could only be at the place the housebreaker told told the man that the tools were to be used, and nowhere else. Now, no burglar could be charged with housebreaking because the police found him going along the street to the house he intended to break into, and were able to prove that it was his intention to break into the house. Supposing he had gone to the house and peeped through the keyhole, and then, because he had seen a watchman, went away again. Could it be said he had made an attempt at housebreaking? I do not think it could. And if the burglar went to another house and broke into it with the tools, the man who made the tools could certainly not be charged with attempt to break into that house, because they were not made for that purpose. There must be some direct act applied at the place where it could be said the manu-facturer of the tools intended them to be used, before he could be charged with attempt as art and part.

The moment the instrument has been used on the house for which it was intended, then that moment you have something on which a jury can say whether the two men were engaged in attempting to break into it. Up to the time when something is done there is no attempt, because there is nothing except the burglar with his tools being in the particular locality. Unless it is said that an attempt is made at the time of serving out the drug or other article for use to commit the crime to some man who may thereafter commit it, I do not see how what is not a crime can become one by anything which subsequently happens, except where conspiracy can be charged and proved to do the particular deed. And I am unable to see how it can be said that there was an attempt to commit crime. There was plenty of room for going back on what was done. The sender of the drugs might immediately afterwards have sent a letter to the man to whom they were sent forbidding him to use them for the purpose for which he sent them, and saying that, if he did not get an undertaking at once that they would not be so used, he would himself inform the police of the matter. It is quite plain that, if he had done that, it could not be said that an attempt to commit the crime had been made. If that is so, it is equally plain that it cannot be said an attempt was made if nothing took place. The fact that he did not or did express repentance could not make what was done a crime or not a crime.

Cases have been referred to where a person, being himself a principal in the act, did something which if followed out was such as could be dealt with as a completed crime. It is sufficient to say that these cases seem to me to have no bearing on the present question. A man who has done something by way of overt act with the purpose of committing a crime, but does not complete it, is punishable for attempt to commit the crime. Examples were cited of putting poison in a teapot or sending explosives addressed to a person in such a way that they would go off when the packet was opened. But these were acts done by a person who is in course of committing the full crime, and the person attempting had by overt act directly taken steps, not merely to prepare for the perpetration of a crime, but to put his machinations into practical action. It could not be said that he made an attempt to commit the crime of murder by buying the poison or the explosives unless he followed that up by making use of what he had bought, so as to be in the act of perpetrating the crime, which, failing to effect it, reduced the case to an attempt only.

The Advocate-Depute was in a difficulty about the different cases of an accessory and a principal. But this is not a case of an accessory, but entirely one of a principal, and being so, I cannot say that it can be said on the facts stated in the indictment that he made an attempt to commit the crime of abortion when he supplied a person with materials for that purpose and nothing further took place. It might be well if such an act was made criminal by the Legislature although no actual attempt was made. But it certainly does not constitute an attempt at common law.''

Objection to relevancy sustained.

If, as his Lordship suggests, it is possible for an attempt to be thwarted or nullified by the repentance of the wrongdoer, then the "last act" theory as explained above must be subject to some qualification in respect of possible repentance.

5. Morton v. Henderson
1956 J.C. 55

The appellant and another man suggested to the owner of a greyhound that she should "doctor" it before a race by giving it a concoction which would impair its racing ability. The request was not acceded to, and the dog was not tampered with. The appellants were charged with, and convicted of, attempting to defraud bookmakers accepting bets on the race in which the dog was running, and also members of the public placing bets in respect of the race. On appeal by stated case to the High Court:

LORD JUSTICE-GENERAL (CLYDE): "The appellants' contention before us was that the facts fell short of what constitutes attempted fraud by the law of Scotland. There is no doubt that the mere formulation of a fraudulent scheme is not a crime by the law of Scotland. No one can be prosecuted for what merely goes on in his own head. As Hume on *Crimes*, 1. 1. 26, says: 'The vicious will is not sufficient, unless it is coupled to a wrongful act. And here the question arises, how far must the culprit have proceeded in the prosecution of his wicked purpose, to make him answerable in the tribunals of this world? This may on many occasions be a difficult inquiry. . . . Between these extremes there lie a great variety of ambiguous cases, with respect to which it is very difficult to say where preparation ends, and perpetration begins.' This same test is adopted by the Lord Justice-General in *H.M. Advocate* v. *Camerons*, 1911 J.C. 110, 6 Adam 456. At page 485, after quoting this passage from Hume, he proceeds: 'Applying these observations to the matter in hand, mere conception of a fraudulent scheme is not enough; that fraudulent scheme, in order to be criminal, must be carried into some effect by overt act: but if it has begun to be carried into effect by overt act it need not come to final fruition'. In *H.M. Advocate* v. *Tannahill and Neilson*, 1943 J.C. 150, the same view was expressed by Lord Wark, the presiding judge at the trial. The indictment, in that case, *inter alia* charged the accused with attempting to defraud a Government Department in various ways. One of these was by improper entries in claims for work done which they submitted to the Department, and another method was by instigating and attempting to induce subcontractors to render false and fabricated accounts. Lord Wark directed the jury in regard to the instigation of subcontractors that there was 'no overt act, the consequences of which cannot be recalled by the accused', and the basis therefore was not laid upon which a verdict of attempt to defraud under this head of the indictment could be pronounced. But he left it to the jury to decide whether on the evidence instigation to commit a crime under this latter part of the indictment had been proved, apart from any question of attempt to defraud.

In the present case, in my opinion, the formulation of a fraudulent scheme is adequately established. But my difficulty is whether any overt act, as required by the decisions, is proved. I have come to the conclusion that it is not. It is true that the appellants visited the place where the dog was kept with an apparently preconceived scheme and sought to persuade Mrs Duffin to commit a crime. But they did no more with her than the accused did with the subcontractors in *Tannahill's* case, and in my opinion, the facts do not warrant the conclusion that the scheme had passed out of the stage of preparation into perpetration. If so, attempt to defraud is not proved."

Appeal allowed.

NOTES

What is the significance of Lord Wark's direction in *Tannahill and Neilson*? Is it, for example, to the effect that the stage of perpetration is reached only once the accused has committed an "overt act, the consequences of which [cannot] be recalled by the accused"? Lord Clyde expressly refers with approval both to Lord Wark's definition and that of Lord Dunedin in *Camerons*.

The cases may, however, be authority for the proposition that an attempt is only committed once the accused has not only reached the "last stage," but in addition, is no longer in a position to repent effectually.

d.   Impossibility

The problem of impossibility is most frequently discussed in the context of attempted crimes. It should be apparent, however, that the issue may arise in respect of the other forms of inchoate offence.

1.   Lamont v. Strathern
1933 J.C. 33

The appellant was charged along with two others, with stealing £2 from a man in the street. The sheriff found them guilty of an attempt to steal. One of the accused had put his hand towards the pocket of the intended victim, but had been prevented from getting anything by the victim himself. It was not, however, proved that there was anything in the pocket at the time which could have been stolen. On appeal by stated case:

LORD SANDS: "In this case I am satisfied that the learned Sheriff-substitute was warranted upon the evidence in finding that the three accused men, while acting in concert, dogged the man Dunbar with the intention of stealing from him, and that one of the three, Wilkie, made an attempt upon Dunbar's pocket with the view of stealing any money he might find therein. The sole question is whether, in these circumstances, the Sheriff-substitute was warranted in convicting the accused of an attempt to steal money, in the absence of satisfactory evidence that the pocket contained money.

I confess that I understood the law to be as stated by a recent commentator:—'It is no answer to a charge of attempt that there was nothing to steal as, for example, where the accused had rifled the pockets of some person who had nothing in his pockets.' I recall a case where I was prosecutor of a man who was charged with theft and attempt to steal, and who was convicted of both. He had been noticed to put his hands into the pockets of two persons. From the one he got a purse, the other missed nothing. I have no recollection of this second witness being asked whether he had anything upon his person which a thief might have stolen if he had found it, and it certainly seems odd if this ought to have been a determining factor. I am not, I confess, impressed by the metaphysical argument that, whereas one cannot take what is not there, therefore one cannot attempt to take what is not there. I apprehend that, if men were charged with illegally attempting to take salmon with a net from a certain pool, contrary to any Act which declared any such attempt to be illegal, it would be a futile defence that, as they caught nothing, the pool proving to be empty, they did not attempt to take salmon. Nor, I think, would it be reasonable to deny to Mother Hubbard the credit of an attempt to fetch a bone for her dog.

In the Criminal Procedure (Scotland) Act, 1887, forms of charge are provided which are directed to be followed as nearly as may be. These forms, as I understand, were not invented, but were culled from indictments in the Justiciary Office. The form for attempted theft is:—'You did place your hand in one of the pockets of Thomas Kerr, commercial traveller, 115 Main Street, Perth, and did thus attempt to steal.' In all the other forms for offences against property the property is specified and the charges are relevant charges, which they would not be without such specification. But this form as it stands would be irrelevant if proof as to a specific article in the pocket be necessary, for the accused is just as much entitled to

notice of this as of anything else of which proof is necessary in order
to substantiate the charge.

Very frequently the would-be thief has no knowledge of what, if
anything is in the pocket. But it will hardly be suggested, in any
view, that, if there is anything of value in the pocket, he might not
be accused of an attempt to steal it. It may, however, have been
something he did not want and would on no account appropriate.
Some pilferers will not appropriate any identifiable trinket or even
bank notes. It is difficult to think that, in the case of a pocket pilferer
in a church porch, the presence in the pocket of a pew notice of a
collection for the following Sunday, or even of a hymn book, might
be material as rendering the charge relevant. I am not, I confess,
troubled by the dilemma—what does the dishonest person attempt
to steal if there is nothing there? He attempts to steal whatever he
may happen to find there. The analogy of housebreaking and
opening lockfast places is imperfect, for these are offences themselves. Walking round the counter of a shop may be an intrusion,
but it is not an offence. I figure, however, the case of a dishonest
person who, in the absence of the shopman, steps round the counter
and rummages in the open drawer in which the shopman usually
places his drawings. It happens that he finds nothing. Was there not
an attempt to steal?

There is no authority upon the particular point in Scotland. This
is not perhaps remarkable, as in former times there could not be
conviction of the attempt when the full crime of theft was charged,
and attempt to steal, not being a *nomen juris*, was not relevant as the
major premiss, although a relevant premiss might have been framed
by detailing the particular facts alleged—Compare *Etch* v. *Burnet*
(1849) J. Shaw 201, and *Ure* (1858) 3 Irv. 10. The question has,
however, come up more than once in England. In *R.* v. *Collins*
(1864) 9 Cox C.C. 497 it was held that a charge of attempted theft
failed when there was nothing in the pocket to steal. But this case
was expressly overruled in *R.* v. *Brown* (1889) L.R. 24 Q.B.D. 357.
Some doubt seems to have been subsequently felt in a lower Court
owing to the entirely different character of the offence in *Brown's*
case (an attempt to commit an offence which it was alleged was
physically impossible to carry out). Accordingly the matter came up
again in *R.* v. *Ring* (1892) 17 Cox C.C. 491. This case is exactly in
point, and in one way was weaker than the present one. Two men
who had been observed to be fumbling in ladies' pockets were
convicted of attempt to steal. The ladies were not traced and it was
impossible to affirm that anything was contained in the pockets.
The conviction was sustained, and *R.* v. *Collins* was again declared
to be overruled, the Lord Chief Justice pointing out that two courts
of five judges had now unanimously disapproved of that judgment.

We do not always attach high importance to judgments of the Courts of England in matters of criminal law, but in these two cases the English Courts do not appear to have proceeded upon any principles or precedents foreign to our system.

Our attention was called to a ruling of Lord Anderson in a recent case, that a charge of attempt to bring about abortion was not relevant when it was not set forth that the woman was pregnant. In that case the charge was 'you did insert pieces of slippery elm bark or other substance into the private parts of A.M. . . . in the belief that she was then pregnant, and for the purpose of causing her to abort, and did attempt to cause her to abort.' As it seems to me, this is a somewhat confusing form of charge, but I think that, if the words 'and did attempt to cause her to abort' were deleted the charge might be a relevant one. In other words, I think that it would be a relevant charge that an accused, in the belief that a woman was pregnant, penetrated her person with intent to cause her to abort. But the charge of 'attempt to cause her to abort' introduces a different consideration, and it seems to have been upon this that Lord Anderson proceeded. A charge of attempt at criminal abortion is a charge of an attempt to make a pregnant woman abort. A charge of attempt to steal is a charge of attempting to steal anything of value that might be found. The completed acts may be on the same footing. One cannot cause abortion if the womb be empty, or steal a valuable if the pocket be empty. But the attempts may be on a different footing. As regards abortion, I understand that the view taken was that attempt to commit abortion must be an attempt to cause a pregnant woman to abort. A pregnant woman is a condition of the offence. On the other hand, in the case of attempted theft from a pocket, that is an attempt to steal whatever may be found there. A pocket which *may* contain something of value is the only condition.

On the whole matter I am of opinion that the conviction and sentence cannot be disturbed."

Appeal refused; conviction affirmed.

NOTE

The "recent case" referred to by his Lordship was the case of *H.M. Advocate* v. *Anderson*, 1928 J.C. 1, which is discussed and approved in the following case.

2. H.M. Advocate v. Semple
1937 J.C. 41

The accused was charged on an indictment which contained a number of charges relating to the supply of drugs to a woman for the purpose of causing her to abort. Objections were taken to the relevancy of all but one of the charges. These were repelled, except in relation to charges 6 and 7.

LORD JUSTICE-CLERK (AITCHISON): "That leaves charges 6 and 7, which, in addition to the first point generally ruled, raise a point by themselves. I take charge 6 as typical. It sets out that the panel did on the date libelled supply to the woman named a number of powders and pessaries, the nature of which was to the prosecutor unknown, in the belief that she was then pregnant, with intent to cause her to abort, and then the libel sets out instigation and use as before, and then representations made to the panel by the woman that what had been supplied to her had been without effect, and a further supply, and so on, and then the charge concludes, ' and this you did with intent to cause her to abort.' Now, I think it is quite plain that an attempt to procure abortion is not libelled in this charge. I think it was rightly not libelled, because it is an essential element of the crime of attempting to procure abortion that there be something to abort; in other words, the woman must be pregnant. We were referred to the case of *Anderson*. In that case, upon a libel which did not set out that the woman was pregnant, but merely, as here, that the panel did certain things in the belief that she was pregnant, Lord Anderson held the libel to be irrelevant, but there the charge was laid as a charge of attempting to procure abortion. I have not the slightest doubt that Lord Anderson was right in holding, on the terms of the libel with which he had to deal, that it did not set out the crime of attempt to procure abortion. Now, in this case the Crown has not libelled pregnancy, only a belief in the mind of the panel that the woman was pregnant, and it is said that what was done was done in that belief and with the intent to cause an abortion. In my judgment, that does not disclose a crime as the law of Scotland at present stands. It may be reprehensible conduct; it may be injurious to private and public morality; it may be conduct which ought to be criminal conduct; but that will not make it a crime by the law of Scotland. We were referred to no case in which a charge of this kind has been sustained as a relevant charge. The matter is not free from difficulty, but I think we ought not to declare new offences in this branch of the law. If that is to be done, it should, in my view, be done by the Legislature. But I wish to reserve my opinion as to whether there might not have been a crime if what was done had caused death or injury to the woman. In such a case different considerations might apply, especially if the death or injury arose from want of skill or any degree of negligence. I take such a case to be reserved.

Upon the whole matter, I move your Lordships that we sustain the plea of the panel with regard to the relevancy of charges 6 and 7 in the libel; that quoad ultra we repel the objections to the relevancy; and that, with the exception of charges 6 and 7, we remit the libel to the knowledge of an assize."

Objections to the relevancy
of charges 6 and 7 sustained.

NOTES

Can the two sets of circumstances discussed in the above cases be distinguished in the way suggested by Lord Justice-Clerk Aitchison? Why is a pregnant woman a "condition" of the offence of attempted abortion while the existence of property which could be stolen not a condition of attempted theft? The cases would seem to be irreconcilable. For further consideration of these, and other, authorities, see, *Maxwell and Ors.* v. *H. M. Advocate, (unreported), post.*

3. Haughton v. Smith
[1975] A.C. 476

A lorry carrying stolen goods was intercepted by the police. It was allowed to continue its journey, with two police officers on board, and a following escort of police. The respondent was one of a number of persons who met the lorry, with a view to the future disposal of the stolen goods. He was charged with, and convicted of, attempting to handle stolen goods. It was conceded by the Crown that at the time of the alleged offence the goods had ceased to be "stolen," by virtue of s. 24(3) of the Theft Act 1968, having been taken into lawful custody by the police. His conviction was set aside by the Court of Appeal. The Crown appealed to the House of Lords.

LORD HAILSHAM OF ST. MARYLEBONE L.C.: "An attempt to commit a criminal offence is itself a criminal offence at common law, and by section 6(4) of the Criminal Law Act 1967, it remains an offence as an attempt notwithstanding that the accused person is shown to have been guilty of the completed offence. But what is an attempt? The earliest attempt at definition in comparatively modern times is in *Reg.* v. *Eagleton* (1855) Dears.C.C. 515, 538, *per* Parke B. when he said: 'The mere intention to commit a misdemeanour is not criminal. Some act is required, and we do not think that all acts towards committing a misdemeanour are indictable. Acts remotely leading towards the commission of the offence are not to be considered as attempts to commit it, but acts immediately connected with it are; and if, in this case, after the credit with the relieving officer for the fraudulent overchange, any *further step* [emphasis his] on the part of the defendant had been necessary to obtain payment, . . . we should have thought that the obtaining credit . . . would not have been sufficiently proximate to the obtaining the money. But, on the statement in this case, no other act on the part of the defendant would have been required. It was the last act, *depending on himself*, [emphasis his] towards the payment of the money, and therefore it ought to be considered as an attempt.'

A more modern definition is to be found in the judgment of Lord Parker C.J. in *Davey* v. *Lee* [1968] 1 Q.B. 366, 370 where he said: 'What amounts to an attempt has been described variously in the authorities, and for my part I prefer to adopt the definition given in *Stephen's Digest of Criminal Law,* 5th ed. (1894), art. 50, where it says that: "An attempt to commit a crime is an act done with intent to commit that crime, and forming part of a series of acts which would constitute its actual commission if it were not interrupted." As a general statement that seems to me to be right, although it does not help to define the point of time at which the series of acts begins. That as Stephen said, depends upon the facts of each case. A helpful definition is given in paragraph 4104 in the [then] current (36th) edition (1966) of *Archbold, Criminal Pleading, Evidence & Practice* where it is stated in this form: "It is submitted that the actus reus necessary to constitute an attempt is complete if the prisoner does an act which is a step towards the commission of a specific crime, which is immediately and not merely remotely connected with the commission of it, and the doing of which cannot reasonably be regarded as having any other purpose than the commission of the specific crime." ' . . . From the two definitions cited above, I derive the following propositions relevant to the present appeal.

(1) There is a distinction between the intention to commit a crime and an attempt to commit it. Thus, in this case, the respondent intended to commit a crime under section 22 of the Theft Act. But this dishonest intention does not amount to an attempt. This distinction has not always been observed in the discussion of cases on the law affecting attempts.

(2) In addition to the intention, or mens rea, there must be an overt act of such a kind that it is intended to form and does form part of a series of acts which would constitute the actual commission of the offence if it were not interrupted. In the present case the series of acts would never have constituted and in fact did not constitute an actual commission of the offence, because at the time of the handling the goods were no longer stolen goods.

(3) The act relied on as constituting the attempt must not be an act merely preparatory to commit the completed offence, but must

bear a relationship to the completion of the offence referred to in *Reg.* v. *Eagleton,* Dears.C.C. 515, 538 as being 'proximate' to the completion of the offence and in *Davey* v. *Lee* [1968] 1 Q.B. 366, 370 as being 'immediately and not merely remotely connected' with the completed offence. I do not think that the present case turns on the test of proximity at all, although, as will be seen, many of the arguments canvassed involve a discussion of it. Obviously whenever the test of proximity becomes crucial in a particular case, difficult questions of fact and degree will arise which will call for considerable skill on the part of the trial judge in directing the jury. I do not think these problems arise here.

In his discussion in the present case of the legal implications of inchoate, but uncompleted, sequences of actions in cases which might or might not amount to criminal attempts, Lord Widgery C.J. attempted to analyse them into two categories (see [1973] 2 W.L.R. 942, 944) namely:

(1) 'The first class is the type of case where the accused has embarked on a course of conduct which, if completed, will result in an offence but for some reason breaks off that course of conduct and never completes the action required to amount to the offence.' In this first class of case, Lord Widgery C.J. classified the 'pickpocket who puts his hand in a man's pocket only to find it empty; the burglar who is disturbed by the police when he is in the process of trying to break open the window; the safebreaker who finds when he gets to the safe, it is too difficult for him and he cannot open it.' 'In general,' and Lord Widgery C.J. emphasised that he dealt only in generalities in this context, he thought 'a charge of attempt can properly be laid in that type of case.' But it was otherwise, he thought, in the second class of case which he described as follows, at p. 945:

(2) 'Where the accused has meticulously and in detail followed every step of his intended course believing throughout that he was committing a criminal offence and when in the end it is found that he has not committed a criminal offence because in law that which he planned and carried out does not amount to a criminal offence at all.' Lord Widgery C.J. placed the present case in this second class and, after discussing a number of divergent authorities, came to the conclusion that in such a case a criminal attempt had not been committed.

With respect, I do not altogether agree that this dual classification is adequate, and if it were, I am not quite sure why all the examples given should be classified as they were. I note that in the New Zealand case of *Reg.* v. *Donnelly* [1970] N.Z.L.R. 980, which, except in so far as it relates to the construction of the relevant New Zealand statutes, is very much on all fours with this, Turner J., adopts a six-fold classification. He says, at p. 990: 'He who sets out to commit a crime may in the event fall short of the complete commission of that crime for any one of a number of reasons. *First,* he may, of course, simply change his mind before committing any act sufficiently overt to amount to an attempt. *Secondly,* he may change his mind, but too late to deny that he had got so far as an attempt. *Third,* he may be prevented by some outside agency from doing some act necessary to complete commission of the crime—as when a police officer interrupts him while he is endeavouring to force the window open, but before he has broken into the premises. *Fourth,* he may suffer no such outside interference, but may fail to complete the commission of the crime through ineptitude, inefficiency or insufficient means. The jemmy which he has brought with him may not be strong enough to force the window open. *Fifth,* he may find that what he is proposing to do is after all impossible—not because of insufficiency of means, but because it is for some reason physically not possible, whatever means be adopted. He who walks into a room intending to steal, say a specific diamond ring, and finds that the ring is no longer there, but has been removed by the owner to the bank, is thus prevented from committing the crime which he intended, and which, but for the supervening physical impossibility imposed by events he would have committed. *Sixth,* he may without interruption efficiently do every act which he set out to do, but may be saved from criminal liability by the fact that what he has done, contrary to his own belief at the time, does not after all amount in law to a crime.' On the whole, though I hope it will never be subjected to too much analysis, as it is merely a convenient exposition and illustration of classes of case which can arise, I find this classification more satisfactory than Lord Widgery's dual classification. Applying the three principles derived from my primary definitions, I would seek to obtain the following results. (1) In the first case no criminal attempt is committed. At the relevant time there was no mens rea since there had been a change of intention, and the only overt acts relied on would be preparatory and not immediately connected with the completed offence. (2) In the second case there is both mens rea and an act connected immediately with the offence. An example would be an attempted rape where the intended victim was criminally assaulted, but the attacker desisted at the stage immediately before he had achieved penetration. It follows that there is a criminal attempt. (3) The third case is more difficult because, as a matter of fact and degree, it will depend to some extent on the stage at which the interruption takes place, and the precise offence the attempt to commit which is the subject of the charge. In general, however, a criminal attempt is committed, assuming that the proximity test is passed. (4) In the fourth case there is ample authority for the proposition that, assuming the proximity test is passed, a criminal attempt is committed. But here casuistry is possible. Examples were given in argument of shots at an intended victim which fail because he is just out of range, or because, as in the case of the well known popular novel, *The Day of the Jackal,* the intended victim moves at the critical moment, or when a dose of poison insufficient to kill is administered with intent to murder. In all these cases the attempt is clearly criminal. (5) The fifth case is more complicated. It is clear that an attempt to obtain money by a false pretence which is not in fact believed, is criminal notwithstanding that the consequences intended were not achieved: see *Reg.* v. *Hensler* (1870) 11 Cox C.C. 570. The same would be true of an attempted murder when the victim did not actually die for whatever reason. But I do not regard these as true, or at least not as typical, examples of the fifth class. They belong rather to the fourth, since the criminal had done all that he intended to do, and all that was necessary to complete the crime was an act or event wholly outside his control. . . .

In addition to the reported cases, we postulated in argument a number of real and imaginary instances of this class. In *The Empty Room*, Sherlock Holmes' enemy, Colonel Maron, was induced to fire at a wax image of the detective silhouetted in the window, though Holmes prudently rejected Inspector Lestrade's advice to prefer a charge of attempted murder and so the matter was never tested; in *Rex.* v. *White* [1910] 2 K.B. 124, a man who put a small quantity of cyanide in a wine glass, too small to kill, was held guilty of attempted murder. This was an example of the fourth of Turner J.'s cases and therefore criminal. But quaere, what would have been the position if the glass administered had contained pure water, even though the accused believed falsely that it contained cyanide? We discussed the situation when a would be murderer attempts to assassinate a corpse, or a bolster in a bed, believing it to be the living body of his enemy, or when he fires into an empty room believing that it contained an intended victim; and we had our attention drawn to an American case where the accused fired at a peephole in a roof believed to be in use by a watching policeman who was in fact a few yards away. In most of these cases, a statutory offence of some kind (e.g. discharging a firearm with intent to endanger life) would be committed in English law, but in general I would think that a charge of an attempt to commit the common law offence of murder would not lie since, if the contemplated sequence of actions had been completed (as in some of the supposed instances they were) no substantive offence could have been committed of the type corresponding to the charge of attempt supposed to be laid. . . .

(6) Turner J.'s sixth class of case was where a man efficiently does 'without interruption every act which he set out to do, but may be saved from criminal liability by the fact that what he has done, contrary to his own belief at the time, does not after all amount to a crime.' This is really equivalent to Lord Widgery's second class. I have already explained that I consider that the present appeal fails on the proper construction of section 22 of the Theft Act 1968. But I think that this is a special example of a wider principle, and I agree with Turner J.'s conclusion about it. . . .

In my view, it is a general principle that Turner J.'s sixth class of attempts are not criminal, not because the acts are not proximate or because the intention is absent, but because the second of the three propositions I derive from the two judical definitions I cited above is not satisfied. The acts are not part of a series 'which would constitute the actual commission of the offence if it were not interrupted.' In this event the often discussed question whether the legal impossibility derives from a mistake of fact or law on the part of the accused is hardly relevant. . . .

I agree with the decision in *Rex* v. *Percy Dalton* (*London*) *Ltd.* (1949) 33 Cr.App.R. 102, and particularly with the quotation from Birkett J., cited by Lord Widgery C.J. in the present case, where he said, at p. 110: 'Steps on the way to the commission of what would be a crime, if the acts were completed, may amount to attempts to commit that crime, to which, unless interrupted, they would have led; but steps on the way to the doing of something, which is thereafter done, and which is no crime, cannot be regarded as attempts to commit a crime.' I would add to the last sentence a rider to the effect that equally steps on the way to do something which is thereafter *not* completed, but which if done would not constitute a crime cannot be indicted as attempts to commit that crime. It is, of course, true that, at least in theory, some villains will escape by this route. But in most cases they can properly be charged with something else—statutory offences like breaking and entering with intent etc., or loitering with intent etc., using an instrument with intent etc., discharging or possessing a firearm with intent etc., or as here, common law offences like conspiring to commit the same offence as that the attempt to commit which is charged, or even committing a substantive offence of a different kind, as here, stealing or attempting to steal."

LORD REID: "What, then, is meant by an attempt to commit a crime? Normally when a person commits a deliberate crime he begins by making any necessary preparations and then he sets out to take the various steps which culminate in the final act which accomplishes the crime. But he may stop or be interrupted at some stage. Then the question will be whether he has gone so far that he can be said to have attempted to commit the crime. It is well settled that mere preparation is not criminal. A few statutes have made acts preparatory criminal but otherwise the accused must have gone beyond that stage. It has often been said that to constitute an attempt the act must be proximate to and not remote from the crime itself. But that is hardly illuminating. It can be said that the accused must have begun to perpetrate the crime. But no words, unless so general as to be virtually useless, can be devised which will fit the immense variety of possible cases. Any attempted definition would, I am sure, do more harm than good. It must be left to common sense to determine in each case whether the accused has gone beyond mere preparation.

But this theory attaches a very different meaning to the word 'attempt.' The accused has done, as he did here, everything which he intended to do. There is no question of drawing a line so that remote acts of preparation are not attempts but acts proximate to the crime are attempts. The crime is impossible in the circumstances, so no acts could be proximate to it. The theory confuses attempt with intent. If the facts had been as he believed they were the man would have committed a crime. He intended to commit it. But he took no step towards the commission of a crime because there was no crime to commit.

I would not, however, decide the matter entirely on logical argument. The life blood of the law is not logic but common sense. So I would see where this theory takes us. A man lies dead. His enemy comes along and thinks he is asleep, so he stabs the corpse. The theory inevitably requires us to hold that the enemy has attempted to murder the dead man. The law may sometimes be an ass but it cannot be so asinine at that. And take another case. A man marries a woman believing that her husband is still alive; but in fact he died last week. The theory requires us to hold him guilty of attempted bigamy. Then suppose that the husband disappeared some time ago. The man who marries the wife may have a variety of beliefs. He may think it is highly probable that the husband is still alive or he may think it is quite likely or he may think the chance that the husband is still alive is small. In fact the husband is dead. I do not know how the theory would deal with those three possible cases.

The theory is really an attempt to punish people for their guilty intention. The man who stabs the corpse may be as deserving of punishment as a man who attempts to murder a living person. The accused in the present case may be as deserving of punishment as he would have been if the goods had still been stolen goods. But such a radical change in the principles of our law should not be introduced in this way even if it were desirable.

In my judgment this theory must be rejected. I think that the law was properly stated in *Rex* v. *Percy Dalton* (*London*) *Ltd.*, 33 Cr.App.R. 102, 110: 'Steps on the way to the commission of what would be a crime, if the acts were completed, may amount to attempts to commit that crime, to which, unless interrupted, they would have led; but steps on the way to the doing of something, which is thereafter done, and which is no crime, cannot be regarded as attempts to commit a crime.'

I do not say that that is an exhaustive definition. It requires some explanation or expansion in at least one class of case. A man may set out to commit a crime with inadequate tools. He finds that he cannot break in because the door is too strong for him. Or he uses poison which is not strong enough. He is certainly guilty of attempt: with better equipment or greater skill he could have committed the full crime. Or the person whom he attempted to murder has moved a short distance away and he shoots at the place where the person was a short time earlier. There may well be borderline cases of that kind. We are not applying a rule but a principle and it must be applied sensibly. I would not seek to lay down the law in detail beyond what is necessary for the present case."

Appeal dismissed.

NOTES

The argument that the general statements made by their Lordships were strictly speaking *obiter* (an argument based on the view that the case turned on a proper construction of ss. 22 and 24 of the 1968 Act) was rejected by Lord Widgery C.J. in *Partington* v. *Williams* (1975) 62 Cr. App. R. 220. The appellant had been convicted of attempting to steal from an empty wallet. On appeal, the Divisional Court held it now to be "settled law" in England that on such facts the accused could not be convicted of attempted theft because the commission of the substantive offence was in the circumstances impossible.

The current approach of the courts to this problem has not been uncritically accepted. Smith and Hogan, for example, described the recent authorities as "a deplorable and unnecessary change in the law" (p. 258), and *Partington* v. *Williams* has been recently criticised by the House of Lords in *D.P.P.* v. *Nock (post)* as erring in its interpretation of *Haughton* v. *Smith*.

4.   **D.P.P. v. Nock and Anor.**
[1978] 3 W.L.R. 57

The appellants were convicted of conspiracy to produce a Class A controlled drug, namely cocaine, in contravention of s. 4 of the Misuse of Drugs Act 1971. They had entered into an arrangement to produce cocaine from a quantity of powder which they believe to be a mixture of cocaine and lignocaine. On analysis the powder was found to contain no cocaine whatsoever, and none could have been produced from it. Their conviction was upheld by the Court of Appeal. On appeal to the House of Lords:

LORD SCARMAN: "My Lords, the headnote to the report of *Reg.* v. *Smith (Roger)* [*ante, sub nom. Haughton* v. *Smith*] [1975] A.C. 476 accurately records that the second of the holdings of your Lordships' House in that case was that steps on the way to the doing of something, which was thereafter done (or would have been done, if not interrupted by some supervening event) and which is no crime, cannot be regarded as attempts to commit a crime. In dismissing the two appeals which are now under consideration by your Lordships, the Court of Appeal declined to apply this principle to cases of conspiracy, but certified the point as one of general public importance. The Court of Appeal has certified the point in terms specific to the facts of this case. It is, however, a general question, which, with respect, I think is better put as follows: when two or more persons agree upon a course of conduct with the object of committing a criminal offence, but, unknown to them, it is not possible to achieve their object by the course of conduct agreed upon, do they commit the crime of conspiracy? The question falls to be considered at common law, the relevant events having occurred before the coming into force of the Criminal Law Act 1977, section 1 (1) of which contains a statutory definition of conspiracy superseding the common law. Nevertheless the point is of some importance for the reason given by the Court of Appeal—that the common law may have to be investigated for the purpose of construing the section.
The classic description of the crime of conspiracy at common law is that it consists of an agreement to do an unlawful act or a lawful act by unlawful means: *Mulcahy* v. *The Queen*, L.R. 3 H.L. 306, 317. The agreement itself constitutes the offence. The mens rea of the offence is the intention to do the unlawful act: the actus reus is the fact of agreement. The Court of Appeal—correctly, in my judgment—stressed that it is the factor of agreement which distinguishes conspiracy from attempt. But were they also correct in concluding that because of the factor of agreement the principle accepted by your Lordships' House in *Reg.* v. *Smith* [1975] A.C. 476 as applying to attempts is not to be applied to conspiracy. I have reached the conclusion that the Court of Appeal fell into error on this point, and that *Reg.* v. *Smith* is applicable to cases of conspiracy. . . .

The appellants made a number of attempts—all of them, of course, unsuccessful—to extract cocaine from their powder. It was not until after they had been arrested and the powder seized by the police and sent for analysis that they learnt to their surprise that there was no way in which cocaine could be produced from it.

The trial judge in his direction to the jury, and the Court of Appeal in their judgment dismissing the two appeals, treated this impossibility as an irrelevance. In their view the agreement was what mattered: and there was plain evidence of an agreement to produce cocaine, even though unknown to the two conspirators it could not be done. Neither the trial judge nor the Court of Appeal thought it necessary to carry their analysis of the agreement further. The trial judge described it simply as an agreement to produce cocaine. The Court of Appeal thought it enough that the prosecution had proved 'an agreement to do an act which was forbidden by section 4 of the Misuse of Drugs Act 1971.' Both descriptions are accurate, as far as they go. But neither contains any reference to the limited nature of the agreement proved: it was an agreement upon a specific course of conduct with the object of producing cocaine, and limited to that course of conduct. Since it could not result in the production of cocaine, the two appellants by pursuing it could not commit the statutory offence of producing a controlled drug. The appellants, who did get a chemist to take on the impossible job of extracting cocaine from the powder, may perhaps be treated as having completed their agreed course of conduct: if so, they completed it without committing the statutory offence. Perhaps, however, it would be more accurate to treat them as having desisted before they had completed all that they had agreed to do: but it makes no difference because, had they completed all that they had agreed to do, no cocaine would have been produced.

If, therefore, their agreement, limited as it was to a specific course of conduct which could not result in the commission of the statutory offence, constituted (as the Court of Appeal held) a criminal conspiracy, the strange consequence ensues, that by agreeing upon a course of conduct which was not criminal (or unlawful) the appellants were guilty of conspiring to commit a crime.

Upon these facts the appellants submit that the evidence reveals no 'conspiracy at large,' by which they mean an agreement in general terms to produce cocaine if and when they could find a suitable raw material, but only the limited agreement, to which I have referred. Counsel for the appellants concedes that, if two or more persons decide to go into business as cocaine producers, or, to take another example, as assassins for hire (e.g. 'Murder Incorporated'), the mere fact that in the course of performing their agreement they attempt to produce cocaine from a raw material which could not possibly yield it or (in the second example), stab a corpse, believing it to be the body of a living man, would not avail them as a defence: for the performance of their general agreement would not be rendered impossible by such transient frustrations. But performance of the limited agreement proved in this case could not in any circumstances have involved the commission of the offence created by the statute.

The answer sought to be made by the Crown (and accepted by the Court of Appeal) is that the offence of conspiracy is committed when an agreement to commit, or to try to commit, a crime is reached, whether or not anything is, or can be, done to perform it. It is wrong, upon their view, to treat conspiracy as a 'preliminary' or 'inchoate' crime: for its criminality depends in no way upon its being a step towards the commission of the substantive offence (or, at common law, the unlawful act). Upon this view of the law the scope of agreement is irrelevant: all that is needed to constitute the crime is the intention to commit the substantive offence and the agreement to try to do so.

If the Court of Appeal is right, *Reg.* v. *Smith* [1975] A.C. 476 can have no application in cases of conspiracy. But neither history nor principle supports this view of the law. In *Board of Trade* v. *Owen* [1957] A.C. 602, 623-625 Lord Tucker, quoting with approval some observations from R. S. Wright J.'s little classic, *The Law of Criminal Conspiracies and Agreements* (1873) and some passages from Sir William Holdsworth's (somewhat larger) work, *The History of English Law*, accepted that the historical basis of the crime of conspiring to commit a crime (the case with which we are now concerned) was that it developed as an 'auxiliary' (R. S. Wright's word) to the law which creates the crime agreed to be committed. Lord Tucker accepted Holdsworth's comment (at p. 625) that 'It was inevitable therefore, as Stephen has said, that conspiracy should come to be regarded as a form of attempt to commit a wrong.' Lord Tucker concluded his survey with these words, at p. 626: 'Accepting the above as the historical basis of the crime of conspiracy, it seems to me that the whole object of making such agreements punishable is to prevent the commission of the substantive offence before it has even reached the stage of an attempt. . . .'

Lord Tucker, in whose opinion the other noble and learned Lords sitting with him concurred, by stressing the 'auxiliary' nature of the crime of conspiracy and by explaining its justification as being to prevent the commission of substantive offences, has placed the crime firmly in the same class and category as attempts to commit a crime. Both are criminal because they are steps towards the commission of a substantive offence. The distinction between the two is that, whereas a 'proximate' act is that which constitutes the crime of attempt, agreement is the necessary ingredient in conspiracy. The importance of the distinction is that agreement may, and usually will, occur well before the first step which can be said to be an attempt. The law of conspiracy thus makes possible an earlier intervention by the law to prevent the commission of the substantive offence. But the distinction has no relevance in determining whether the impossibility of committing the substantive offence should be a defence. Indeed upon the view of the law authoritatively explained and accepted in *Owen's* case [1957] A.C. 602, logic and justice would seem to require that the question as to the effect of the impossibility of the substantive offence should be answered in the same way, whether the crime charged be conspiracy or attempt.

It is necessary, therefore, to analyse the decision in *Reg.* v. *Smith* [1975] A.C. 476 in order to determine whether it can reasonably be applied to cases of conspiracy. The Court of Appeal thought that there were difficulties. But I do not agree.

It was—somewhat half-heartedly—suggested by the Crown that the House might reconsider the decision, which we were told is causing difficulties in some respects. It is, however, a very recent decision; and a unanimous one reached after full argument which brought to the attention of this House the relevant case law and exposed the difficulties. More importantly, the decision is, in my respectful opinion, correct in principle. I would not question the decision, though its proper limits may have to be considered. The House decided the case upon two grounds, either of which would have sufficed, standing alone, to support the decision, but both of which commended themselves to the House. They may be described as the statutory (and narrower) ground and the common law principle.

The statutory ground was provided by sections 22 and 24 (3) of the Theft Act 1968. The offence being considered by the House was one of attempting to handle stolen goods. At the time of the attempted handling, the goods had been (this was conceded) restored to lawful custody. The House ruled that, in the case of a statutory offence: 'The only possible attempt would be to do what Parliament has forbidden. But Parliament has not forbidden that which the accused did, i.e., handling goods which have ceased to be stolen goods. . . . Here the mens rea was proved but there was no actus reus so the case is not within the scope of the section,' *per* Lord Reid at p. 498C. With all respect to the Court of Appeal, there is no difficulty in applying this line of reasoning to a case in which the allegation is not an attempt but a conspiracy to commit a statutory offence. First, there is no logical difficulty in applying a rule that an agreement is a conspiracy to commit a statutory offence only if it is an agreement to do that which Parliament has forbidden. It is no more than the application of the principle that an actus reus as well as mens rea must be established. And in the present case there was no actus reus, because there was no agreement upon a course of conduct forbidden by the statute. Secondly, the application of such a rule is consistent with principle. Unless the law requires the actus reus as well as mens rea to be proved, men, whether they be accused of conspiracy or attempt, will be punished for their guilty intentions alone. I conclude the consideration of this ground of decision with a further quotation from Lord Reid's speech, at p. 500: 'But such a radical change in the principles of our law should not be introduced in this way even if it were desirable.'

The second ground of decision—the common law principle—can be summarised in words which commended themselves to all the noble and learned Lords concerned with the case. In *Rex* v. *Percy Dalton (London) Ltd.* Birkett J., giving the judgment of the Court of Criminal Appeal said (1949) 33 Cr.App.R. 102, 110: 'Steps on the way to the commission of what would be a crime, if the acts were completed, may amount to attempts to commit that crime, to which, unless interrupted, they would have led; but steps on the way to the doing of something, which is thereafter done, and which is no crime, cannot be regarded as attempts to commit a crime.' In his speech Lord Hailsham of St. Marylebone L.C. added the rider (a logical one) to the effect 'that equally steps on the way to do something which is thereafter *not* completed, but which if done would not constitute a crime cannot be indicted as attempts to commit that crime,' [1975] A.C. 476, 497C. As in the case of the statutory ground, there is no logical difficulty in the way of applying this principle to the law relating to conspiracy provided it is recognised that conspiracy is a 'preliminary' or 'auxiliary' crime. And again, as with the statutory ground, common sense and justice combine to require of the law that no man should be punished criminally for the intention with which he enters an agreement unless it can also be shown that what he has agreed to do is unlawful.

The Crown's argument, as developed before your Lordships, rests, in my judgment, upon a misconception of the nature of the agreement proved. This is a case not of an agreement to commit a crime capable of being committed in the way agreed upon, but frustrated by a supervening event making its completion impossible, which was the Crown's submission, but of an agreement upon a course of conduct which could not in any circumstances result in the statutory offence alleged, i.e. the offence of producing the controlled drug, cocaine.

I conclude therefore that the two parallel lines of reasoning upon which this House decided *Reg.* v. *Smith* [1975] A.C. 476 apply equally to criminal conspiracy as they do to attempted crime. We were referred to a recent case in the Court of Appeal, *Reg.* v. *Green* (*Harry*) [1976] Q.B. 985, in which the contrary view was expressed, but not developed at any length. The court in that case, as also the Court of Appeal in this case, attached importance to some observations of Lord Hailsham of St. Marylebone L.C. in *Reg.* v. *Smith* [1975] A.C. 476, where the indictment undoubtedly included, as the second count, a charge of conspiracy with persons unknown to handle stolen goods. The Lord Chancellor (p. 489F) remarked that he was unable to understand why the prosecution did not proceed with this charge. He reverted to the point at p. 497D, and there is an echo of it in Viscount Dilhorne's speech at p. 503E. In *Green's* case [1976] Q.B. 985, 993 Ormrod L.J. treated these remarks as an indication that *Reg.* v. *Smith* [1975] A.C. 476 is not applicable in cases of conspiracy. The Court of Appeal in the instant case took the same view. But I do not think that either the Lord Chancellor or Viscount Dilhorne was saying anything of the sort. The conspiracy charged in the second count must have ante-dated the police seizure of the van and the return of the goods to lawful custody. Smith must have agreed to help in the disposal of the goods at a time when they were stolen goods and the agreement could be performed. It was an agreement to commit an offence which, but for the police interruption, would have been committed. There is nothing in *Reg.* v. *Smith* which would prevent such an agreement in such circumstances from being treated as a criminal conspiracy."

Appeal allowed.

NOTES

Should such importance have been placed on the limited nature of the appellants' agreement? What should happen in the following example:

A and B agree to rob every branch of the Royal Bank of Scotland in Paisley. Unknown to them, the first one they plan to rob has been closed for months. X and Y agree to rob that same branch (and only that branch). They too are unaware that the branch has been closed. Would the approach of the House of Lords in *Nock* lead to the conviction of A and B for conspiracy, but not X and Y?

5.   Maxwell and Ors. v. H.M. Advocate
High Court, 21 March 1980, *unreported*

Three accused persons were convicted of a conspiracy to bribe or otherwise improperly influence members of the City of Glasgow District Licensing Board improperly to approve the transfer of a gaming licence. At the date of the offence, it was not within the legal competence of the board to approve the transfer since the matter of issue of the licence was itself under appeal to the sheriff. The ultimate object of the conspiracy was thus factually impossible to achieve. All three appealed against conviction on the ground, *inter alia,* of misdirection by the trial judge. Their principal argument was that the jury should have been directed to acquit, since an agreement (however dishonest in intent) to achieve a result which was impossible to effect could not amount to a criminal conspiracy.

OPINION OF THE COURT: "The major charge in the indictment in the first alternative was essentially one of conspiracy to bribe members of the licensing board to do something, namely, improperly to approve the transfer of a gaming licence to certain premises in favour of the company named in that charge. The essence of the matter was therefore the transfer of the licence and that was the object of the conspiracy . In this charge, the presiding judge presented the issue to the jury on the basis that it was admittedly impossible to achieve the stated object of the conspiracy which it was said was to obtain, in January 1978, the desired transfer. The reason for this, as to which there was no dispute, was that at this time the issue of the transfer of the particular licence was out of the hands of the licensing board whose decision made as the result of an application in May 1977 was under appeal to the sheriff.

The procedure for transfer was governed by the provisions of Sched. 2 to the Gaming Act 1968, and there was no doubt that the objective of the scheme was impossible of achievement in January 1978. In these circumstances, while the presiding judge was correct in directing the jury that it was factually impossible for anyone to bribe members of the licensing board and as a result to get the desired transfer at the end of January, he was wrong in leaving the matter to the jury and leaving it open to them to convict the applicants on the charge as laid against them in the first alternative in the indictment. The admitted fact that the objective of the scheme libelled could not be achieved in January 1978 should have led the presiding judge to direct the jury that upon the first alternative of the charge of conspiracy they must acquit the applicants. Where an alleged criminal purpose is physically impossible of achievement then a charge of conspiracy to achieve such a purpose is necessarily irrelevant and should it appear on evidence in support of an indictment ex facie relevant that such was the fact, then the only proper direction must be one to aquit. Such a direction was required in this case and was not given. Indeed the presiding judge directed the jury precisely in the contrary sense. This was a fatal misdirection, and the jury's verdict given on such a misdirection could not stand. On this ground alone the applicants' conviction should be quashed. The argument was thus simple and pointed. A result which could not be achieved could not be criminal. Therefore an agreement however dishonest in intent to achieve a result which was impossible to effect could not amount to a criminal conspiracy.

In support of this submission the learned Dean relied on decisions in certain well-known Scottish authorities and on two recent English decisions of the House of Lords which were thought to be persuasive.

The Scottish cases on which the Dean relied were *H.M. Advocate* v. *Anderson* [1928 J.C. 1, 1927 S.L.T. 651]; *H.M. Advocate* v. *Semple* [1937 J.C. 41, 1937 S.L.T. 48] and *Lamont* v. *Strathern* [1933 J.C. 33, 1933 S.L.T. 118]. In the case of *Anderson* an indictment charged the accused with the performance of an operation on a woman believing her to be pregnant for the purpose of causing her to abort, and so attempt to cause abortion was held to be irrelevant for lack of the averment that the woman was in fact pregnant at the time. In the later case of *Semple* a charge of supplying powders to a woman, in the belief that she was pregnant and with intent to cause her to abort, was held to be irrelevant for the same reason, namely the absence of any averment that the woman was pregnant. *Anderson* was expressly approved in *Semple*. The intervening case of *Lamont* was one of attempting to steal from the pocket. It was there held that it was not necessary for relevance or conviction that it should be libelled that there was anything in the pocket to be stolen.

The English cases of *R.* v. *Smith* [[1975] A.C. 476] and *D.P.P.* v. *Nock* [[1978] A.C. 979] were concerned with very different matters. The decision in the first turned on an interpretation of s. 24(3) of the Theft Act 1968 which, of course, has no application to Scotland, and the second was concerned with an alleged conspiracy to produce the controlled drug cocaine (a statutory offence) by extracting it from a particular powder which, unknown to the accused, contained no cocaine at all.

In order to deal with the Dean's argument and the authorities on which that argument relied, it is necessary to consider what constitutes the crime of conspiracy according to the law of Scotland. That crime is constituted by the agreement of two or more persons to further or achieve a criminal purpose. A criminal purpose is one which if attempted or achieved by action on the part of an individual would itself constitute a crime by the law of Scotland. It is the criminality of the purpose and not the result which may or may not follow from the execution of the purpose which makes the crime a criminal conspiracy.

In the present case the stated object of the conspiracy was to corrupt persons holding public office entrusted by statute with the honest discharge of comparatively important administrative functions. The method of corruption libelled was bribery. There can be no doubt, of course, that to bribe or attempt to bribe such persons to act improperly or dishonestly in the discharge of their official duties is itself a crime of extreme gravity. Whether corruption attempted or achieved has the further consequence of actual perversion or dereliction of duty, or of the exercise of improper or dishonestly motivated influence, raises a separate and independent question, and the results or objective of the corruption are themselves very different matters. The vital element in the crime is corruption actual or attempted. Corruption is the purpose and corruption the object: it is therefore difficult to see how it does not necessarily follow that once this is done or attempted to be done the crime is complete. The criminal intent is there—the actus is the offer or acceptance of the bribe or inducement and the mens rea in respect of the criminal intent is sufficient to make the actus reus. Should the bribe fail for any reason to lead to the desired result or should the bribe offered be refused the consequence can scarcely absolve the act of its criminal quality. The corruption or attempt to corrupt has taken place and, therefore, the crime is complete if it is a crime to corrupt or to attempt to corrupt. Nothing can undo what has in fact been done, and if what in fact has been done is itself criminal that would seem to be the end of the matter. What has been done and cannot be undone is to strike a blow at the integrity of public administration.

The argument that because of the accident of events or physical causes beyond or outwith the control or even the knowledge of the corrupting agent, the ultimate objective of the plan to corrupt or attempt to corrupt cannot be achieved, is itself enough to deprive what otherwise is a completed criminal act of its criminal quality appears on the face of it somewhat startling. If sound, this could place criminal responsibility at the whim of extraneous events wholly divorced from the criminally directed actions of the participants themselves. The fallacy in this argument lies in the confusion between the criminal purpose of the conspiracy, i.e. corruption by bribery and the intended result or consequence of that corruption. Once a bribe has been offered, accepted, or received or even rejected, the crime of corruption or attempted corruption has been committed. Suppose the situation in which the recipient of a bribe has been arrested on information received by the Police before he was able to take any action to earn his bribe: in such a case, upon what basis of reason could it be said that he and those responsible for bribing him were thereby absolved from the initial criminality of their actions? To argue thus would appear to confuse the criminal act of corruption with the results which it was hoped would follow a successful act of bribery.

It was urged however by the learned Dean that his proposition was to be deduced from the authorities he cited. When these are examined, however, they do not provide the support which he claims. The basis of the decision in the case of *Anderson* is to be found in Lord Anderson's opinion. He said (1927 S.L.T. at pp. 651-652): "The ground of my judgment is that, in a charge of procuring or attempting to procure abortion, which is a charge of an attempt to commit a well-known crime, the prosecutor must libel, and to secure a conviction must prove, that the patient was pregnant. This proposition seems to be made good by consideration of what is involved in the crime, and by having regard to the presumptive reasons whereby the acts resulting in abortion are regarded as criminal. Abortion, in the sense of the criminal law, is held to be criminal because its successful accomplishment results in the destruction of potential human life. That is the main consideration". As we have said the case of *Anderson* was approved in *Semple* in which the Lord Justice-Clerk (Aitchison) said (1937 S.L.T. at p. 51): "I have not the slightest doubt that Lord Anderson was right in holding on the terms of the libel with which he had to deal that it did not set out the crime of attempting to procure abortion".

Lords Fleming and Moncrieff agreed with the Lord Justice-Clerk and no doubt was cast on Lord Anderson's reasoning or the main consideration on which he based his judgment. These authorities have now stood unchallenged on reasoning or decision for almost half a century. The last Scottish case founded on by the Dean is that of *Lamont*, which decided that an attempt to steal from a pocket is still an attempt to steal and therefore a criminal act even if it be shown that there is nothing in the particular pocket to be stolen, i.e. that the intended result of the act can be frustrated by an event or events which lay beyond the control of the actor or were even unknown to him. The case of *Anderson* was cited but distinguished, but nothing was said by Lord Sands to cast doubt on the soundness of the decision or the reasoning on which it was based. If *Lamont* is sound in its reasoning, then it matters not that for reasons beyond their control the result which the applicants represented as being possible of achievement by bribery could not be so achieved because 'the pocket was empty', which is the same thing as saying that the pocket had been emptied before the thief or intended thief got at it.

So far as the cases of *Smith* and *Nock* decide the particular issues which arose in them, it does not appear to us that the decisions are of material assistance in the solution of the problem raised in the present appeal. In the case of *Smith* the decision turned upon the fact that owing to the somewhat curious terms of s. 24(3) of the Theft Act 1968 the goods which formed the subject-matter of a charge of handling stolen goods in contravention of s. 22(1) of that Act, could not be treated as stolen. The facts disclosed that the goods in question had been in the custody of the police when the alleged offence took place. Section 24(3) provided that no goods should be regarded as having continued to be stolen goods after they have been restored to the person from whom they were stolen or to other lawful possession or custody.

The basis of the decision, therefore, was that the accused were handling goods—albeit with dishonest intent—which at the time were not, in law, stolen goods. There is no parallel here with what the applicants were found to have done. They were 'handling' or seeking to 'handle' or manipulate dishonestly members of the licensing board—not persons who turned out to be something other than members of that board—so the attempted parallel is fatally halted. The case of *Nock* is equally far off the mark. The substance which was libelled as that which the accused were seeking to produce could not be produced by the means which were of the essence of the plan. Therefore to enter into an agreement to produce that substance in the mistaken belief that it could be produced in a particular way constituted no crime. Here there was no mistake as to the character of the persons to be corrupted. We do not think it necessary or helpful to the decision of this case to enter upon consideration of the full and valuable discussions in the opinions of their Lordships beyond the actual decisions at which they arrived.

In our opinion the argument presented upon the relevant authorities on behalf of this applicant, Maxwell, is not supported by them nor is it supported upon what we regard as a correct application to this indictment of the learned judge's charge and the common law of conspiracy in our law.

But in addition to this there is a further obstacle in the way of the applicant's success. The indictment does not specify at what sitting or date was the transfer of the licence referred to to come before the licensing board. The presiding judge, while indicating very rightly that, as the evidence disclosed this, the question of transfer on an application already made and refused by the board, and in fact under appeal to the sheriff, could not be dealt with by the board in January 1978, also rightly pointed out that this did not disable the jury from considering the first alternative of the charge of conspiracy libelled in the indictment. As things stood a renewed application could be made in May and there is nothing in the language of the indictment which, in relation to the first alternative of the conspiracy charge purported to limit the proposed action to any specific date or sitting. Therefore, the fact that no application for transfer could competently be presented to or determined by the board in January was not in any sense fatal to the relevancy or competency of the charge libelled in the first alternative in the indictment."

NOTES

It is respectfully submitted that, in the circumstances of this case, the court's analysis was the correct one. It might well have been different if, for example, the accused had offered a bribe to an individual who was not a member of the licensing board. The apparent conflict in the Scottish approach to impossibility remains, therefore, unresolved.

CHAPTER 6

THE MENTAL ELEMENT IN CRIME

a. "Dole"—Hume's views

Hume, i, 21-22

"In determining the extent of that part of the Law of Scotland, which has relation to CRIMES, I shall take that term in its ordinary acceptation; and shall consider every act as a crime, for which our practice has appointed the offender to make some satisfaction to the public, beside repairing, where that is possible, the injury sustained by the individual. It is obvious, that in exacting any such atonement, the law always supposes that the delinquent has infringed, in some respect, those duties which he owes to the community: He has set a dangerous example of violence, dishonesty, falsehood, indecency, irreligion; or he has trespassed with respect to some of those other articles of wholesome discipline, or wise economy, which affect the public welfare, and are matters of general concernment.

It does not seem necessary for me to say more, in this place, concerning the nature of crimes, as distinguished from civil wrongs; and I therefore proceed to submit a few remarks on the character of that *Dole,* as it is called,—that corrupt and evil intention, which is essential (so the light of nature teaches, and so all authorities have said) to the guilt of any crime. Now, in delivering this precept, those authorities are not to be understood in this sense, as if it were always necessary for the prosecutor to bring evidence of an intention to do the very thing that has been done, and to do it out of enmity to the individual who has been injured. In this more favourable sense to the prisoner, the maxim cannot be received into the law; for it would screen many great offenders from the due punishment of their transgressions. And I think it is only true in this looser and more general, but a practical and a reasonable sense, in which an English author of the first judgment in those matters has explained it; that the act must be attended with such circumstances, as indicate a corrupt and malignant disposition, a heart contemptuous of order, and regardless of social duty."

NOTES

The English author referred to by Hume is Foster, *Crown Law,* pp. 256 *et seq.*

Despite the fact that these views were first expressed in 1797, they are still influential in the courts. See, for recent examples: *Cawthorne* v. *H.M. Advocate,* 1968 J.C. 32, (*post,* ch. 11), *Gray* v. *Hawthorn,* 1961 J.C. 13 (*post,* ch. 10). Hume's views on mental abnormality have likewise been recently approved by the High Court—see *Brennan* v. *H.M. Advocate,* 1977 S.L.T. 151 (*post,* ch.8).

b.   *The modern judicial approach*

The Scottish courts tend to avoid extensive theoretical examinations of such concepts as intention and recklessness (but see *Allan* v. *Patterson,* 1980 S.L.T. 77, *post*), and indeed there is an increasing reliance on such notions as "evil intent" or "wickedness" (see *e.g., Smart* v. *H.M.Advocate,* 1975 S.L.T. 65, *post,* ch. 10). Most judicial discussions of *mens rea* tend also to be closely linked to the particular offence in question, and it is therefore necessary to examine particular areas of the law in order to obtain a general impression of current judicial thinking. The cases noted here are not, therefore, the sum total of the courts' efforts, but simply illustrate the approach of the courts to certain general issues.

1.   **Allan v. Patterson**
1980 S.L.T. 77

The respondent was charged with reckless driving, contrary to s.2 of the Road Traffic Act 1972, as amended by s.50 of the Criminal Law Act 1977. The sheriff acquitted the respondent, and the Crown appealed by way of stated case to the High Court. The circumstances of the offence, and the grounds for the sheriff's acquittal are outlined in the opinion of the court.

OPINION OF THE COURT: "In this appeal by the Crown this court is required for the first time to consider s.2 of the Road Traffic Act 1972 as that section has been amended by the Criminal Law Act 1977, s.50. Before the amendment the section read as follows: 'If a person drives a motor vehicle on a road recklessly, or at a speed or in a manner which is dangerous to the public, having regard to all the circumstances of the case, including the nature, condition and use of the road, and the amount of traffic which is actually at the time, or which might reasonably be expected to be, on the road, he shall be guilty of an offence.' It now reads: 'A person who drives a motor vehicle on a road recklessly shall be guilty of an offence.'

At the hearing before us the appellant and the respondent joined issue on the proper interpretation of this section and in particular as to the test to be applied by a judge or a jury in determining whether the offence created by s.2 in its amended form has been established by the prosecutor.

These questions come before us in this way, The respondent went to trial in the sheriff court at Jedburgh upon a summary complaint in which he was charged in these terms—'that on 11 September 1978 on the Kelso to Ednam Road and Edenside Road, Kelso, District of Roxburgh, you did drive a motor vehicle, namely a motor cycle, recklessly and at a place where a child on his way to or from school was seeking to cross the road, and having been required to stop said motor cycle by a school crossing patrol in uniform, and exhibiting a prescribed sign, did fail to stop said motor cycle: Contrary to the Road Traffic Act 1972, s.2.'

After trial the sheriff acquitted the respondent. According to the Crown the sheriff in so doing misdirected himself as to the meaning and implications for the prosecutor of s.2 as amended. The particular submission was that although the sheriff appears to have found in fact that the respondent drove his motor cycle with a high degree of negligence in all the circumstances of the case he acquitted the respondent only because on his construction of s.2 in its new form he concluded that no person can be convicted of driving 'recklessly' unless it is shown: (a) that he knew that there were material risks in driving in a particular manner and (b) that he deliberately decided to drive in that manner regardless of the possible consequences. In short, it was contended, the sheriff applied what has been called a subjective test. Upon the assumption that the sheriff so directed himself we shall now come to the competing submissions.

For the Crown the submission can be stated shortly. There is no doubt that the question whether a person has committed the offence created by s.3 of the Act, i.e. of driving a motor vehicle on a road without due care and attention or without reasonable consideration for other persons using the road, must be answered by the application of an objective test. A judge or a jury, accordingly, must simply ask themselves whether the particular act of driving established in evidence demonstrated a want on the part of the driver of that degree of care and attention or consideration for other persons to be expected of a competent and careful driver. In considering a charge brought under ss.1 and 2 of the Act in their unamended form (and such a charge normally included the word 'recklessly' as well as the succeeding words 'or at a speed or in a manner etc.') the simple task of a judge or a jury was to consider the act of driving proved and ask themselves, quite objectively, whether it was driving which, by reason of speed or otherwise, was in their judgment dangerous to the public having regard to all the circumstances of the case including those specially mentioned in the sections. In its amended form there is nothing in the language of s.2 (and similar considerations apply to s.1 as amended) to indicate an intention on the part of Parliament that the test to be applied is no longer to be objective. The word 'reckless' in its ordinary meaning is well understood. The adverb 'recklessly' is an adverb of manner qualifying the verb 'drives.' In its context it plainly means a piece of driving which, judged objectively, is eloquent of a high degree of negligence much more than a mere want of due care and attention and supports the inference that material risks were deliberately courted or that these risks which ought to have been obvious to any observant and careful driver were not noticed by reason of gross inattention. Driving 'recklessly' accordingly, is driving which demonstrates a gross degree of carelessness in the face of dangers.

For the respondent counsel resolutely defended the proposition that no man can be said to drive 'recklessly' unless it is shown that he actually knew of certain material risks in driving in a particular way and nevertheless elected to drive in that way with complete indifference to the possible consequences.

We have no difficulty in reaching the conclusion that the Crown submission must receive effect. There is nothing in the language of s.2 as amended to suggest an intention on the part of Parliament to penalise thereunder only a course of driving embarked upon wilfully or deliberately in the face of known risks of a material kind. Inquiry into the state of knowledge of a particular driver accused of the offence created by the section as amended and into his intention at the time is not required at all. The statute directs attention to the quality of the driving in fact but not to the state of mind or the intention of the driver. If it were otherwise, the section, and indeed s.1, would virtually become inoperable in all but the rarest of instances. Neither is the skill or capacity of the particular driver in issue: the offence can be committed whether or not the event is followed or demonstrated by a casualty. All that is in issue and all that Parliament requires the court or the jury to consider and determine is the degree to which the driver in question falls below the standard to be expected of a careful and competent driver in all the circumstances of the particular case and whether the degree is such as properly to attach in the judgment of court or jury the epithet or label of 'reckless.'

Section 2, as its language plainly, we think, suggests, requires a judgment to be made quite objectively of a particular course of driving in proved circumstances, and what the court or a jury has to decide, using its commonsense, is whether that course of driving in these circumstances had the grave quality of recklessness. Judges and juries will readily understand, and juries might well be reminded, that before they can apply the adverb 'recklessly' to the driving in question they must find that it fell far below the standard of driving expected of the competent and careful driver and that it occurred either in the face of obvious and material dangers which were or should have been observed, appreciated and guarded against, or in circumstances which showed a complete disregard for any potential dangers which might result from the way in which the vehicle was being driven. It will be understood that in reaching a decision upon the critical issue a judge or jury will be entitled to have regard to any explanation offered by the accused driver designed to show that his driving in the particular circumstances did not possess the quality of recklessness at the material time.

We ought, we think, to mention that in the course of his submission the learned advocate-depute drew our attention to a passage in Wilkinson's *Road Traffic Offences* (9th ed.) p. 287, where the author suggests that in respect of the offence now defined by s.2, as amended, a court will require to consider a driver's state of mind. With that suggested construction we profoundly disagree. The author also declares that the following definition proposed by the Law Commission (of England) is perhaps as satisfactory as any other: 'A person is reckless if (a) knowing that there is a risk that an event may result from his conduct or that a circumstance may exist, he takes that risk, and (b) it is unnecessary for him to take it having regard to the degree and nature of the risk which he knows to be present.' The author goes on to say 'The test in (a) is subjective and the test of necessity of (b) is objective.' It will be appreciated from what we have said that the section is concerned with the quality of a proved course of driving and that there is nothing in its language to indicate that that quality is to be assessed otherwise than objectively. We cannot accordingly approve of the definition as an aid in deciding whether a s.2 offence has been committed. Apart from this it appears to us that the editor falls into the error of failing to appreciate that the proposed definition is apparently intended, as it says, to define a reckless person. What this statute is defining or seeking to define is a manner of driving—a very different matter. The Law Commission's definition is, in any event, one which, if it did not confuse a judge would bemuse most juries. Finally, we have only to add that although we were very properly referred to the English cases of *R. v. Clancy* [1979] R.T.R. 312 and *R. v. Davis (William)* [1979] R.T.R. 316, it is evident that in neither was the Court of Appeal called upon to decide whether the relevant test in respect of a s.2 offence is in whole, or even in part, subjective, and, indeed, there is much in the opinion delivered in the latter case by Geoffrey Lane L.J. (as he then was) to indicate that, as we think, the approach must be totally objective."

> Case remitted to the sheriff in order that he might inform the court whether, in the light of their opinion, he would have convicted; the High Court subsequently ordered him to convict.

NOTES

The court's opinion suggests that recklessness may be either subjective (in the sense of deliberate risk-taking) or objective (in the sense, probably, of gross negligence). The court's distinction between a "reckless person" and a reckless manner of driving is highly suspect. What is reckless about a manner of driving except the driver?

There is no Scottish judicial discussion of intention—the Scottish courts tend to take the view that it does not require definition. Furthermore, reliance on the concept of "wicked recklessness," especially in the law of murder, tends to minimise the importance of intention as a concept. *Cf.* the English approach: *Hyam* v. *D.P.P.* [1975] A.C. 55; *R.* v. *Mohan* [1976] Q.B. 1.; *R.* v. *Murphy (Williams)* [1980] 2 All E.R. 325.

2.   H.M.Advocate v. Byfield and Ors.
High Court, January 1976, *unreported*

The accused was charged, *inter alia*, with the murder of a man called Ewart. A number of pleas were raised in defence, notably self-defence and provocation. The case is noted here for what was said by Lord Thomson on the subject of the mental element in murder during his charge to the jury.

LORD THOMSON: "Now, I come to the serious charge and that is No. 4. It is right that I should repeat to you because I think you have already heard it from the learned advocate-depute and perhaps Mr. Gow as well what is the classic definition of murder. I will read it to you. Murder is constituted by any wilful act causing the destruction of life, whether intended to kill or displaying such wicked reckless-ness as to imply a disposition depraved enough to be regardless of the consequences. Now, all that means is this: in the first place, it is a wilful act, not an accidental act. If it is an accident the thing can't be murder. It is a wilful act, and, in this case, it means a deliberate stabbing with a knife. That is the application of that in this case. The second thing is, causing the destruction of life. Well, we know it did cause the destruction of life because he died within a minute or so. Whether intended to kill—this is to cover the case where there is a deliberate intention to kill, what sometimes you read of as deliberate cold-blooded murder where there might be pre-meditated . . . or at least, it is done with the deliberate intention of killing. The learned advocate-depute did not suggest that that was so in this case. You then get 'or displaying such wicked recklessness as to imply a disposition depraved enough to be regardless of the consequences.' The test of that is, what that means is really this: You can get murder even if the wielder of the weapon does not deliberately intend to kill, if he acts in such a way as to show that he wasn't really caring what the consequences were going to be, and that is the category into which the advocate-depute would put this stabbing here. It won't do for somebody who stabbed somebody else simply to say 'Well, I didn't mean to kill him, I just didn't think about it at all, I just stuck a knife in him.' If the circumstances are such as to suggest that that evidences a degree of wicked recklessness showing that he just didn't care whether the victim lived or died then, in law, the act would be murder."

Verdict: guilty of murder.

NOTE

The tendency to treat the mental element in crime, or at least recklessness, as an objective question, to be determined by reference to such matters as the nature of the weapon used, etc., is particularly marked in directions such as the above.

3.   Latta v. Herron
High Court, October 1967, *unreported*

The appellant was convicted of the reset of two guns, and appealed by stated case to the High Court. The circumstances of the appeal are set out in the opinion of the court.

OPINION OF THE COURT: "This is a stated case in which the appellant was charged and found guilty of reset of a revolver and a shotgun, the same having been dishonestly appropriated by theft. The sheriff substitute, after the evidence had been led, found the charge of reset proved and the question argued before us is whether on the facts admitted or proved the sheriff substitute was entitled to find the appellant guilty of reset of the firearms.

The only issue argued before us was whether the sheriff substitute was entitled to hold on these facts that the appellant knew that the goods had been stolen. According to Alison on *Criminal Law*, Vol. I, p. 330, it is stated that 'it is sufficient if circumstances are proved which to persons of ordinary understanding and situated as the panel was must have led to the conclusion that they were theftuously acquired.' In the present case I find it unnecessary to examine the facts in any detail as in the case the learned sheriff substitute states 'I was inclined to believe that when the appellant purchased the firearms he was not conscious of the fact that they had been stolen, but, it seems to me that if this were so he had wilfully blinded himself to the obvious and that the inescapable inference from the circumstances in which the transaction was carried out, the price paid, and the fact that the appellant knew the character of the persons with whom he was dealing was that, after a reasonable time for reflection and certainly before the firearms were seized by the police on 24 November, he must have come to realise that they were dishonestly obtained.'

It appears to me that this view of the evidence, which the facts narrated in the case seem to me ample to warrant, does more than satisfy the criterion set out in the passage from Alison to which I referred. The matter is essentially one of fact for the sheriff substitute and the facts led him to an inescapable inference which those facts certainly warranted, and with which this court cannot possibly interfere. In my view, accordingly, the question falls to be answered in the affirmative.''

Appeal dismissed.

NOTE

    Cf. Knox v. *Boyd,* 1941 J.C. 82, and *Mackay Bros.* v. *Gibb,* 1969 S.L.T. 216 and Gordon's comments, paras. 7-72 to 7-74.

4.   **Clark v. H.M. Advocate**
1968 J.C. 53

The appellants neglected to provide food and medical aid for their child, as a result of which the child was caused suffering and injury to health, and eventually died. They were convicted under s.12 of the Children and Young Persons (Scotland) Act 1937 of "wilfully neglecting the child in a manner likely to cause her unnecessary suffering and injury to health.''

LORD JUSTICE-CLERK (GRANT): "The applicants were convicted by a jury in the sheriff court in Edinburgh on a charge under section 12(1) of the Children and Young Persons (Scotland) Act, 1937, to the effect that they did "wilfully neglect" their infant child 'in a manner likely to cause her unnecessary suffering and injury to health.' The neglect libelled was failure to provide adequate food and medical aid, and in the outcome the child died. In the course of the defence case the defending solicitor sought to adduce as a witness Dr Parry, a psychiatrist, who had seen the applicants for the first time on the previous Saturday and had no personal knowledge of the facts of the case. After argument the sheriff-substitute, on the ground that Dr Parry's proposed evidence was not relevant to the question of guilt or innocence, refused to allow him to be called as a witness at that stage, but without prejudice to the right of the defence to call him to give evidence in mitigation in the event of the accused being found guilty.

Even assuming that the proposed evidence was irrelevant to the question of guilt or innocence, it would, I think, have been preferable to allow Dr Parry to give evidence, so far as relevant to mitigation before the jury retired, in order that, if they thought fit and as they were entitled to do, they might add a recommendation to leniency when returning their verdict. Indeed, it would appear from the transcript that the basic objection of the procurator-fiscal was not to the witness being adduced at that stage, but to the relevance of the proposed line of evidence to the question of guilt or innocence. However, it appears that in passing sentence the Sheriff-substitute took into account Dr Parry's report, no complaint is made in regard to sentence, and this procedural matter is not in issue in the present applications.

From the transcript, the grounds upon which the defending solicitor sought to uphold the relevance of the proposed evidence to the merits of the case are not wholly clear. Insanity was not pleaded, there was no question of diminished responsibility in the legal sense, and it appears that the object of the evidence was to establish some lesser state of mental irresponsibility which would negative wilfulness and justify an acquittal. The Sheriff-substitute in rejecting the defence submission followed the *dicta* of the Lord Justice-General (Clyde) in *H.M.Advocate* v. *Cunningham*, 1963 J.C. 80 at p. 84, to the effect that 'any mental or pathological condition short of insanity—any question of diminished responsibility owing to any cause, which does not involve insanity—is relevant only to the question of mitigating circumstances and sentence . . . diminished responsibility is a plea applicable to murder. It is not open in the case of a lesser crime . . .'

Before us, Mr Gow did not challenge the *dicta* above quoted, but contended that, so far as the present case is concerned, '*Cunningham* is a red herring.' His argument centred on the word 'wilful' and was to the effect that, just as the Crown have to establish *wilful* neglect here, equally the defence were entitled to lead psychiatric evidence of a mental state on the part of the applicants, short of insanity, which would justify the jury in holding that the acts and omissions constituting the neglect complained of, if established, had not been shown to be wilful. He equiparated such evidence with evidence tending to establish accident, but conceded that, if his argument be right, it was an argument which would be open, not merely in the case of statutory offences which are not absolute but involve wilfulness, but also in the wide field of common law crimes and offences in which *mens rea* is of the essence. In that event, the new hazards and difficulties involved in accepting the argument would be immense.

It is not disputed that the applicants neglected their child, that they failed to provide adequate food and medical aid for her and, as I understand it, that unnecessary suffering and injury to her health were caused as a result and that she died. Nor is it suggested that the medical evidence sought to be led was designed to counter any of these facts. What is said is that evidence would have been to the effect that the applicants were so feckless and incompetent that they did not appreciate what the result of their failure would be and that accordingly their neglect was not wilful. On that basis, it was said the jury would have been entitled to acquit. Although the passage was not cited to us, I think that the argument for the applicants can be found, put in a nutshell, in Gordon's Criminal Law at p.208. The passage in a paragraph dealing with 'Wilful Neglect' reads thus:

'Neglect may be negligent or intentional: the man who neglects his children by deliberately keeping them short of food and clothing has neglected them wilfully; the man who keeps them short of food and clothing because he is too feckless to look after them properly has neglected them negligently.'

That, in my opinion, is not the test to apply in a case of an offence under section 12(1) of the 1937 Act. The argument for the applicants seems to me to proceed on a confusion between the two ingredients of such an offence: (a) that there should be neglect (or ill-treatment, abandonment, assault, etc.) which is *wilful*—though it is difficult to conceive of conduct which is not wilful constituting assault; and (b) that this should be in a manner likely to cause the child unnecessary suffering or injury to health. As the Sheriff-substitute pointed out, 'neglect is the want of reasonable care, that is the omission of such steps as a reasonable parent would take, such as are usually taken in the ordinary experience of mankind. That is what neglect is, but before you can bring a criminal charge, you have got to prove that it was wilful in the sense of being deliberate or intentional, *but . . .without necessarily having any intent to harm the child.*' In other words, while proof of wilfulness is essential to establish head (a), the test under head (b) is an objective one. That test is whether the neglect *was* 'in a manner *likely* to cause . . .' and not whether it was 'in a manner *intended* to cause . . .' It is not suggested here that the applicants did not appreciate the nature of their acts or omissions or that these were not deliberate and intentional. The argument is, and the evidence proposed to be led was, to the effect that the *consequences* were not intended or foreseen. Mr Gow in support of his argument founded mainly on the case of *Reg.* v. *Senior,* [1899] 1 Q.B. 283, which was an appeal which was concerned with the effect and meaning of certain statutory provisions which were, for all relevant purposes, in the same terms as section 12(1) of the 1937 Act. That decision, however, seems to me to be against the applicants' contentions here. Mr Senior, who was an affectionate parent, had taken all reasonable steps for the care of his dangerously ill child except the vital step of calling in medical aid. This he had deliberately omitted to do, not because he wished or intended any harm to the child (who in fact died), but because of religious convictions which he held as a member of a sect known as the 'Peculiar People'. Nevertheless his conviction was upheld. In the words of Lord Russell of Killowen C.J. (at pp. 290-291), ' "Wilfully" means that the act is done deliberately and intentionally, not by accident or inadvertence, but so that the mind of the person who does the act goes with it.' The test of 'wilful neglect' was thus satisfied (head (*a*) referred to above) and it was no defence that, acting on strongly held religious principles, he had no intention of causing unnecessary suffering or harm. The absence of such intention where, as is said to be the case here, the actings or omissions are due, not to religious principles, (however mistaken), but to fecklessness and incompetence is, in my opinion, equally no defence. This present case is, in my opinion, an attempt, wholly lacking in any merit, to prise ajar a door which was firmly shut in *Cunningham*. I agreed and still agree with what was said in *Cunningham* and I would refuse both applications for leave to appeal."

Application for leave to appeal dismissed.

NOTES

While one might agree with the court's view that the offence contains a subjective element and an objective element, one might disagree with their treatment of the applicants' argument, since the evidence of their inadequacy might well have gone to affect the question of "wilfulness."

As to the case of *Cunningham* v. *H.M.Advocate*, see *post*, ch. 8.

c. Error

(i) **Error of fact.** Error of fact may operate to negative *mens rea*, as, for example, where X mistakenly takes Y's umbrella, thinking it is his own. His mistake negatives any intention to steal. (Where, of course, recklessness is a sufficient *mens rea* for the offence, then an error arrived at recklessly would not exclude *mens rea*.) Error of fact may also have the effect of inducing on the part of the accused a belief as to circumstances justifying his conduct—*e.g.*, a mistaken belief that one is being attacked could support a plea of self-defence. The principal difficulties in relation to errors of fact are (a) whether such errors to be relevant must be reasonable, and (b) whether there is any onus on the accused to establish his error.

1.   Dewar v. H.M.Advocate
1945 J.C. 5

The appellant, the manager of a crematorium, was convicted of the theft of two coffins and a large number of coffin lids which, along with the bodies contained therein, had been consigned to him for cremation. The lids had been disposed of "in various utilitarian ways." In his defence he stated that he believed that the coffins and their lids, once delivered to him, were completely within his jurisdiction for disposal, and also that he believed he was merely following a practice commonly adopted at other crematoria throughout Britain. On appeal:

LORD JUSTICE-GENERAL (NORMAND): "The next objection was that there was no appropriation by the appellant of the coffins or of the lids. This is, in my opinion, an unstatable proposition—unstatable both in law and in fact. It is contrary to the appellant's own evidence that the coffins were completely under his jurisdiction for disposal, and that he was merely following a usual practice in removing the lids, storing them, and using them as firewood or employing them in some other 'economic way,' as he called it, rather than destroying them. His evidence is a plain assertion of his unlimited right of property in a thing which he knew was sent to him under contract for the purpose of destruction, and of destruction only along with the bodies, and this applies both to the coffins and to the lids. Accordingly, in my opinion, there was misappropriation of property which he knew was sent to him merely for destruction by a prescribed method. That being so, there is no doubt that there was evidence upon which the jury were entitled to find the appellant guilty of theft, and I have very great doubt whether there was any relevance in the further contention that it was necessary to establish a guilty intent by other facts and circumstances. In my opinion, the presiding judge would have been perfectly entitled to instruct the jury that the evidence about the alleged practice in other crematoria and the evidence of the appellant's belief in the alleged practice was irrelevant and that they were bound to disregard it. That was not, however, the course taken by the learned judge, and he left to the jury the question whether the felonious intent was established by other evidence, or, more correctly, whether the appellant had by other evidence established that his intent had been innocent. There was evidence led on behalf of the appellant to show that he only did what others do elsewhere, or at least that he believed that he only followed the common practice in other crematoria, and further, that he had not practised any concealment. The presiding judge took a lenient view when he instructed the jury to consider whether the appellant might have entertained an honest and reasonable belief, based on colourable grounds, that he was entitled to treat the coffins, as 'scrap.' The presiding judge pointed out that the jury must not exculpate the appellant merely because he entertained an erroneous belief founded on some singular notions of his own, but that they must discover some evidence that he had rational and colourable grounds for believing that he was entitled to remove, retain and dispose of the coffin lids. The direction could not have been more favourable to the appellant than it was. The onus is rightly placed on him. What had to be proved by him was stated and reiterated with the most careful moderation, and I think that there is no possible objection to the direction on the ground of unfairness."

Appeal dismissed.

NOTES

It is not entirely clear what sort of error Dewar made. It appears to have been a combination of error of fact (as to the practice at other crematoria) which induced an error of law (as to his right to dispose of the lids in any way he chose).

The case is, however, authority for two propositions: (a) that an error to be relevant must be "reasonable" and (b) that the onus of establishing the erroneous belief rests with the accused, rather than there being any onus on the Crown to disprove such a belief.

As to the meaning of "reasonable" in this context, it seems that really only fantastic errors with no objective foundation whatsoever will be held to be unreasonable—see Alison, i. 272, and Hume, i. 74 who were founded on by the presiding judge at the trial, and the cases of *Crawford* v. *H.M. Advocate*, 1950 J.C. 67 (*post*, ch. 11) and *Owens* v. *H.M. Advocate*, 1946 J.C. 119 (*post*, ch. 11).

2. **R. v. Morgan and Ors.**
    [1976] A.C. 182

Morgan invited three junior colleagues to come to his house and have intercourse with his wife. He warned them that she would struggle, but advised them that she did this because she was "kinky" and did this to heighten her sexual pleasure. They all had intercourse with her, during which time she did not consent and was for most of the time forcibly restrained. The three associates were charged with rape, and Morgan with aiding and abetting rape. All were convicted, and this conviction was upheld by the Court of Appeal. They appealed to the House of Lords.

LORD HAILSHAM OF ST. MARYLEBONE: "The certified question arises because counsel for the appellants raised the question whether, even if the victim consented, the appellants may not have honestly believed that she did. As I have pointed out, the question was wholly unreal, because if there was reasonable doubt about belief, the same material must have given rise to reasonable doubt about consent, and vice versa. But, presumably because, at that stage, the jury's view of the matter had not been sought, the matter was left to them, as the appellants complain, in a form which implied that they could only acquit if the mistaken belief in consent was reasonable, and it was not enough that it should be honest. This ruling was originally made at the close of the case for the prosecution, but, as it was subsequently embodied in the summing up, it is sufficient to refer to this.

I will quote the principal passage in extenso from the record. The learned judge said:

'First of all, let me deal with the crime of rape. What are its ingredients? What have the prosecution to prove to your satisfaction before you can find a defendant guilty of rape? The crime of rape consists in having unlawful sexual intercourse with a woman without her consent and by force. By force. Those words mean exactly what they say. It does not mean there has to be a fight or blows have to be inflicted. It means that there has to be some violence used against the woman to overbear her will or that there has to be a threat of violence as a result of which her will is overborne. You will bear in mind that force or the threat of force carries greater weight when there are four men involved than when there is one man involved. In other words, measure the force in deciding whether force is used. One of the elements to which you will have regard is the number of men involved in the incident.

Further, the prosecution have to prove that each defendant intended to have sexual intercourse with this woman without her consent, not merely that he intended to have intercourse with her but that he intended to have intercourse without her consent. Therefore if the defendant believed or may have believed that Mrs. Morgan consented to him having sexual intercourse with her, then there would be no such intent in his mind and he would be not guilty of the offence of rape, but such a belief must be honestly held by the defendant in the first place. He must really believe that. And, secondly, his belief must be a reasonable belief; such a belief as a reasonable man would entertain if he applied his mind and thought about the matter. It is not enough for a defendant to rely upon a belief, even though he honestly held it, if it was completely fanciful; contrary to every indication which could be given which would carry some weight with a reasonable man. And, of course, the belief must be not a belief that the woman would consent at some time in the future, but a belief that at the time when intercourse was taking place or when it began that she was then consenting to it.'

No complaint was made of the first paragraph where the learned judge is describing what, to use the common and convenient solecism, is meant by the actus reus in rape. Nor is there any complaint by the appellants of the judge's first proposition describing the mental element.

It is upon the second proposition about the mental element that the appellants concentrate their criticism. An honest belief in consent, they contend, is enough. It matters not whether it be also reasonable. No doubt a defendant will wish to raise argument or lead evidence to show that his belief was reasonable, since this will support its honesty. No doubt the prosecution will seek to cross examine or raise arguments or adduce evidence to undermine the contention that the belief is reasonable, because, in the nature of the case, the fact that a belief cannot reasonably be held is a strong ground for saying that it was not in fact held honestly at all. Nonetheless, the appellants contend, the crux of the matter, the factum probandum, or rather the fact to be refuted by the prosecution, is honesty and not honesty plus reasonableness. In making reasonableness as well as honesty an ingredient in this 'defence' the judge, say the appellants, was guilty of a misdirection.

My first comment upon this direction is that the propositions described 'in the first place' and 'secondly' in the above direction as to the mental ingredient in rape are wholly irreconcileable. In practice this was accepted by both counsel for the appellants and for the respondent, counsel for the appellants embracing that described as 'in the first place' and counsel for the respondent embracing the 'secondly,' and each rejecting the other as not being a correct statement of the law. In this, in my view, they had no alternative.

If it be true, as the learned judge says 'in the first place,' that the prosecution have to prove that 'each defendant intended to have sexual intercourse without her consent, not merely that he intended to have intercourse with her but that he intended to have intercourse without her consent,' the defendant must be entitled to an acquittal if the prosecution fail to prove just that. The necessary mental ingredient will be lacking and the only possible verdict is 'not guilty.' If, on the other hand, as is asserted in the passage beginning 'secondly', it is necessary for any belief in the woman's consent to be 'a reasonable belief' before the defendant is entitled to an acquittal, it must either be because the mental ingredient in rape is not 'to have intercourse and to have it without her consent' but simply 'to have intercourse' subject to a special defence of 'honest and reasonable belief,' or alternatively to have intercourse without a reasonable belief in her consent. Counsel for the Crown argued for each of these alternatives, but in my view each is open to insuperable objections of principle. No doubt it would be possible, by statute, to devise a law by which intercourse, voluntarily entered into, was an absolute offence, subject to a 'defence' of belief whether honest or honest and reasonable, of which the 'evidential' burden is primarily on the defence and the 'probative' burden on the prosecution. But in my opinion such is not the crime of rape as it has hitherto been understood. The prohibited act in rape is to have intercourse without the victim's consent. The minimum mens rea or guilty mind in most common law offences, including rape, is the intention to do the prohibited act, and that is correctly stated in the proposition stated 'in the first place' of the judge's direction. In murder the situation is different, because the murder is only complete when the victim dies, and an intention to do really serious bodily harm has been held to be enough if such be the case.

The only qualification I would make to the direction of the learned judge's 'in the first place' is the refinement for which, as I shall show, there is both Australian and English authority, that if the intention of the accused is to have intercourse nolens volens, that is recklessly and not caring whether the victim be a consenting party or not, that is equivalent on ordinary principles to an intent to do the prohibited act without the consent of the victim.

The alternative version of the learned judge's direction would read that the accused must do the prohibited act with the intention of doing it without an honest and reasonable belief in the victim's consent. This in effect is the version which took up most of the time in argument, and although I find the Court of Appeal's judgment difficult to understand, I think it the version which ultimately commended itself to that court. At all events I think it the more plausible way in which to state the learned judge's 'secondly.' In principle, however, I find it unacceptable. I believe that 'mens rea' means 'guilty or criminal mind,' and if it be the case, as seems to be accepted here, that mental element in rape is not knowledge but intent, to insist that a belief must be reasonable to excuse is to insist that either the accused is to be found guilty of intending to do that which in truth he did not intend to do, or that his state of mind, though innocent of evil intent, can convict him if it be honest but not rational. Even if full value is to be given to the 'probative' burden as defined in *Woolmington* v. *Director of Public Prosecutions* [1935] A.C. 462, this is to insist on an objective element in the definition of intent, and this is a course which I am extremely reluctant to adopt, especially after the unhappy experience of the House after the decision in *Director of Public Prosecutions* v. *Smith* [1961] A.C. 290, a case which is full of warnings for us all, and which I fully discussed in *Reg.* v. *Hyam* [1975] A.C. 55. . . .

Once one has accepted, what seems to me abundantly clear, that the prohibited act in rape is non-consensual sexual intercourse, and that the guilty state of mind is an intention to commit it, it seems to me to follow as a matter of inexorable logic that there is no room either for a 'defence' of honest belief or mistake, or of a defence of honest and reasonable belief and mistake. Either the prosecution proves that the accused had the requisite intent, or it does not. In the former case it succeeds, and in the latter it fails. Since honest belief clearly negatives intent, the reasonableness or otherwise of that belief can only be evidence for or against the view that the belief and therefore the intent was actually held, and it matters not whether, to quote Bridge J. in the passage cited above, 'the definition of a crime includes no specific element beyond the prohibited act.' If the mental element be primarily an intention and not a state of belief it comes within his second proposition and not his third. Any other view, as for insertion of the word 'reasonable' can only have the effect of saying that a man intends something which he does not.

By contrast, the appellants invited us to overrule the bigamy cases from *Reg.* v. *Tolson*, 23 Q.B.D. 168 onwards and perhaps also *Reg.* v. *Prince*, L.R. 2 C.C.R. 154 (the abduction case) as wrongly decided at least in so far as they purport to insist that a mistaken belief must be reasonable. The arguments for this view are assembled, and enthusiastically argued, by Professor Glanville Williams in his treatise on *Criminal Law,* 2nd ed. (1961) between pages 176 and 205, and by Smith and Hogan (see *Smith and Hogan* at pp. 148, 149 of their text book).

Although it is undoubtedly open to this House to reconsider *Reg.* v. *Tolson* and the bigamy cases, and perhaps *Reg.* v. *Prince* which may stand or fall with them, I must respectfully decline to do so in the present case. Nor is it necessary that I should. I am not prepared to assume that the statutory offences of bigamy or abduction are necessarily on all fours with rape, and before I was prepared to undermine a whole line of cases which have been accepted as law for so long, I would need argument in the context of a case expressly relating to the relevant offences. I am content to rest my view of the instant case on the crime of rape by saying that it is my opinion that the prohibited act is and always has been intercourse without consent of the victim and the mental element is and always has been the intention to commit that act, or the equivalent intention of having intercourse willy-nilly not caring whether the victim consents or no. A failure to prove this involves an acquittal because the intent, an essential ingredient, is lacking. It matters not why it is lacking if only it is not there, and in particular it matters not that the intention is lacking only because of a belief not based on reasonable grounds. I should add that I myself am inclined to view *Reg.* v. *Tolson* as a narrow decision based on the construction of a statute, which prima facie seemed to make an absolute statutory offence, with a proviso, related to the seven year period of absence, which created a statutory defence. The judges in *Reg.* v. *Tolson* decided that this was not reasonable, and, on general jurisprudential principles, imported into the statutory offence words which created a special "defence" of honest and reasonable belief of which the "evidential," but not the probative burden lay on the defence. I do not think it is necessary to decide this conclusively in the present case. But if this is the true view there is a complete distinction between *Tolson* and the other cases based in statute and the present."

Appeals dismissed.

NOTES

Their Lordships held, by a majority of three to two, that there had been a misdirection, and that the appellants' belief need not have been reasonable if honestly held. They did, however, uphold the convictions and dismiss the appeal by applying the proviso to s. 2(1) of the Criminal Appeal Act 1968.

As far as the English law of rape is concerned, the actual decision in *Morgan* was given statutory approval in the Sexual Offences (Amendment) Act 1976, s.1, both as to the basic requirement of an "honest" mistake, and also to the issue of reasonableness as a test of honesty.

(ii) Errors of law. The maxim *ignoratia juris neminem excusat* is rigorously applied in the criminal law (see, for example, the case of *R.* v. *Bailey* (1800) Russ & Ry 1, in which ignorance of the criminal law was held to be no defence even where it was impossible for the accused to have known that what he did was against the law), but it is probably the case that a distinction ought to be drawn between ignorance of the criminal law and ignorance of the civil law.

1. **Clark v. Syme**
1957 S.L.T. 32

The respondent was charged with maliciously shooting and killing a sheep belonging to a neighbour. The latter had received complaints by the respondent about damage to his crops from trespassing sheep, and the respondent had delivered an ultimatum warning the neighbour that he would shoot sheep which wandered on to his land in the future. The sheriff-substitute found the respondent not guilty, on the view that any inference of malice in the respondent's actions was displaced by the respondent's genuine misconceptions as to his legal rights in such cases. The prosecutor appealed by stated case to the High Court.

LORD JUSTICE-GENERAL (CLYDE): "The Sheriff-Substitute's ground for holding the respondent 'not guilty' is stated by him in the following terms:—'The presumption of malice which is essential and is normally inferred in such cases was adequately displaced by the respondent's explanation (which I accepted) that in the circumstances he genuinely misconceived his legal rights in the matter, and further that his desire to vindicate his own property for the future in the face of such persistent provocation was excusable.'

I am quite unable to accept either of these grounds as justifying the Sheriff-Substitute in finding the respondent not guilty. A misconception of legal rights, however gross, will never justify the substitution of the law of the jungle for rules of civilised behaviour, or even of common sense. The Sheriff-Substitute, indeed, appears to have misunderstood the nature of the facts which require to be proved to establish the crime charged in this case. No question of a presumption of malice is involved in this crime at all. Malicious mischief either involves a deliberate and wicked intent to injure, or it may equally be established by proof of a wilful disregard of, or indifference to, the rights of others (see the opinion of the Lord Justice-Clerk in the case of *Ward* v. *Robertson*, 1938 J.C. 32, at page 36). I accept this statement of the law as sound. If, as in the case of *Ward* v. *Robertson*, it was not clear whether the appellant knew that by doing what he did he was doing, or likely to do, damage, the Crown might fail as they failed in that case. For the necessary wilfulness might not then be present. But in this case no such doubt could possibly arise. The respondent in this case acted deliberately. He knew what he was doing and he displayed in his actings a complete disregard of the rights of others. The mere fact that his criminal act was performed under a misconception of what legal remedies he might otherwise have had does not make it any the less criminal. So far, therefore, as concerns the first of the two grounds for his conclusion set out by the Sheriff-Substitute it appears to me quite unfounded in law.

As regards his second reason for finding the respondent 'not guilty', namely, the respondent's desire to vindicate his own property for the future in the face of persistent provocation being excusable, I have found in the case no facts which would warrant any such conclusion. A desire to vindicate his own rights of property is all very well in its proper place, but when that involves the deliberate destruction of the property and rights of others it ceases, in my view, to be excusable.

We were referred to two other authorities on the question of malicious mischief. The first of these was *Black* v. *Laing,* 4 Couper, page 276. But in that case, which was concerned with the destruction of a fence across an access to the appellants' garden, the Court held that the conviction should be quashed upon the ground that the appellants were on the whole justified in removing the fence, since the only access to their garden was through the gap where that fence had been erected. This case affords no analogy nor assistance in the circumstances before us to-day. The other case referred to was a case of *Speid* v. *Whyte* in 4 Irvine, page 584. It was concerned with a relatively trivial injury to part of the harness attached to a vehicle, and here again the Court held that the circumstances did not warrant the conviction. But the ground upon which that conclusion was reached was that there was not in that case, in view of the trivial nature of the injury done, that degree of recklessness and wilful destruction of property which is essential to the constitution of the crime of malicious mischief. The killing of the sheep in the present case affords just that link which was missing in *Speid* v. *Whyte*.

In the whole circumstances, accordingly, in my view, the question put to us in this case should be answered in the negative, and I so move your Lordships."

Appeal allowed.

NOTES

What would have been the decision if the respondent had mistakenly believed that the sheep became his once they wandered onto his land? *Cf.* the case of *Dewar, ante,* and the following case.

2. R. v. Smith (David)
[1974] 1 Q.B. 354

The appellant was convicted of causing criminal damage, contrary to s.1 of the Criminal Damage Act 1971. The circumstances of the offence are fully set out in the judgment of James L.J. in the Court of Appeal.

JAMES L.J.: "The question of law in this appeal arises in this way. In 1970 the appellant became the tenant of a ground-floor flat at 209, Freemason's Road, E.16. The letting included a conservatory. In the conservatory the appellant and his brother, who lived with him, installed some electric wiring for use with stereo equipment. Also, with the landlord's permission, they put up roofing material and asbestos wall panels and laid floor boards. There is no dispute that the roofing, wall panels and floor boards became part of the house and, in law, the property of the landlord. Then in 1972 the appellant gave notice to quit and asked the landlord to allow the appellant's brother to remain as tenant of the flat. On September 18, 1972, the landlord informed the appellant that his brother could not remain. On the next day the appellant damaged the roofing, wall panels and floorboards he had installed in order—according to the appellant and his brother—to gain access to and remove the wiring. The extent of the damage was £130. When interviewed by the police, the appellant said: 'Look, how can I be done for smashing my own property. I put the flooring and that in, so if I want to pull it down it's a matter for me.'

The offence for which he was indicted is in these terms: 'Damaging property contrary to section 1 (1) of the Criminal Damage Act 1971. *Particulars of Offence:* David Raymond Smith and Steven John Smith on September 19, 1972, in Greater London, without lawful excuse, damaged a conservatory at 209, Freemason's Road, E.16, the property of Peter Frank Frand, intending to damage such property or being reckless as to whether such property would be damaged.' The Steven John Smith jointly charged is the appellant's brother. He was acquitted.

The appellant's defence was that he honestly believed that the damage he did was to his own property, that he believed that he was entitled to damage his own property and therefore he had a lawful excuse for his actions causing the damage. In the course of his summing up the deputy judge directed the jury in these terms:

'Now, in order to make the offence complete, the person who is charged with it must destroy or damage that property belonging to another, "without lawful excuse," and that is something that one has got to look at a little more, members of the jury, because you have heard here that, so far as each defendant was concerned, it never occurred to them, and, you may think, quite naturally never occurred to either of them, that these various additions to the house were anything but their own property. . . . But members of the jury, the Act is quite specific, and so far as the defendant David Smith is concerned lawful excuse is the only defence which has been raised. It is said that he had a lawful excuse by reason of his belief, his honest and genuinely held belief that he was destroying property which he had a right to destroy if he wanted to. But, members of the jury, I must direct you as a matter of law, and you must, therefore, accept it from me, that belief by the defendant David Smith that he had the right to do what he did is not lawful excuse within the meaning of the Act. Members of the jury, it is an excuse, it may even be a reasonable excuse, but it is not, members of the jury, a lawful excuse, because, in law, he had no right to do what he did. Members of the jury, as a matter of law, the evidence, in fact, discloses, so far as David Smith is concerned, no lawful excuse at all, because, as I say, the only defence which he has raised is the defence that he thought he had the right to do what he did. I have directed you that that is not a lawful excuse, and, members of the jury, it follows from that that so far as David Smith is concerned, I am bound to direct you as a matter of law that you must find him guilty of this offence with which he is charged.'

It is contended for the appellant that that is a misdirection in law, and that, as a result of the misdirection, the entire defence of the appellant was wrongly withdrawn from the jury.

Section 1 of the Criminal Damage Act 1971 reads: '(1) A person who without lawful excuse destroys or damages any property belonging to another intending to destroy or damage any such property or being reckless as to whether any such property would be destroyed or damaged, shall be guilty of an offence.'

The offence created includes the elements of intention or recklessness and the absence of lawful excuse. There is in section 5 of the Act a partial 'definition' of lawful excuse. Section 5 applies to offences under section 1 (1) and, not relevant for present purposes, to offences under sections 2 and 3 with certain exceptions. Section 5 (2), so far as it is relevant, reads: '(2) A person charged with an offence to which this section applies shall, whether or not he would be treated for the purposes of this Act as having a lawful excuse apart from this subsection, be treated for those purposes as having a lawful excuse—(a) if at the time of the act or acts alleged to constitute the offence he believed that the person or persons whom he believed to be entitled to consent to the destruction of or damage to the property in question had so consented, or would have so consented to it if he or they had known of the destruction or damage and its circumstances; . . .' Section 5 (3) reads: 'For the purposes of this section it is immaterial whether a belief is justified or not if it is honestly held.' Section 5 (5) reads: 'This section shall not be construed as casting doubt on any defence recognised by law as a defence to criminal charges.'

It is argued for the appellant that an honest, albeit erroneous, belief that the act causing damage or destruction was done to his own property provides a defence to a charge brought under section 1 (1). The argument is put in three ways. First, that the offence charged includes the act causing the damage or destruction and the element of mens rea. The element of mens rea relates to all the circumstances of the criminal act. The criminal act in the offence is causing damage to or destruction of 'property belonging to another' and the element of mens rea, therefore, must relate to 'property belonging to another.' Honest belief, whether justifiable or not, that the property is the defendant's own negatives the element of mens rea. Secondly, it is argued that by the terms of section 5, in particular the words of subsection (2), 'whether or not he would be treated for the purposes of this Act as having a lawful excuse apart from this subsection,' and the words in subsection (5), the appellant had a lawful excuse in that he honestly believed he was entitled to do as he did to property he believed to be his own. This it seems is the way the argument was put at the trial. Thirdly, it is argued, with understandable diffidence, that if a defendant honestly believes he is damaging his own property he has a lawful excuse for so doing because impliedly he believes that he is the person entitled to give consent to the damage being done and that he has consented: thus the case falls within section 5 (2) (*a*) of the Act.

We can dispose of the third way in which it is put immediately and briefly. Mr. Gerber for the Crown argues that to apply section 5 (2) (*a*) to a case in which a defendant believes that he is causing damage to his own property involves a tortuous and unjustifiable construction of the wording. We agree. In our judgment, to hold that those words of section 5 (2) (*a*) are apt to cover a case of a person damaging the property of another in the belief that it is his own would be to strain the language of the section to an unwarranted degree. Moreover, in our judgment, it is quite unnecessary to have recourse to such a construction.

Mr. Gerber invited our attention to *Cambridgeshire and Isle of Ely County Council* v. *Rust* [1972] 2 Q.B. 426, a case under section 127 of the Highways Act 1959, concerning the pitching of a stall on a highway without lawful excuse. The case is cited as authority for the proposition that in order to establish a lawful excuse as a defence it must be shown that the defendant honestly but mistakenly believed on reasonable grounds that the facts were of a certain order, and that if those facts were of that order his conduct would have been lawful. Applying that proposition to the facts of the present case, Mr. Gerber argues that the appellant cannot be said to have had a lawful excuse because in law the damaged property was part of the house and owned by the landlord. We have no doubt as to the correctness of the decision in the case cited. The proposition is argued here in relation to the appellant's contention that he had a lawful excuse and does not touch the argument based on absence of mens rea.

It is conceded by Mr. Gerber that there is force in the argument that the element of mens rea extends to 'property belonging to another.' But, it is argued, the section creates a new statutory offence and that it is open to the construction that the mental element in the offence relates only to causing damage to or destroying property. That if in fact the property damaged or destroyed is shown to be another's property the offence is committed although the defendant did not intend or foresee damage to another person's property.

We are informed that so far as research has revealed this is the first occasion on which this court has had to consider the question which arises in this appeal.

It is not without interest to observe that, under the law in force before the passing of the Criminal Damage Act 1971, it was clear that no offence was committed by a person who destroyed or damaged property belonging to another in the honest but mistaken belief that the property was his own or that he had a legal right to do the damage. In *Reg.* v. *Twose* (1879) 14 Cox C.C. 327 the prisoner was indicted for setting fire to furze on a common. Persons living near the common had occasionally burned the furze in order to improve the growth of grass but without the right to do so. The prisoner denied setting fire to the furze and it was submitted that even if it were proved that she did she could not be found guilty if she bona fide believed she had a right to do so whether the right were a good one or not. Lopes J. ruled that if she set fire to the furze thinking she had a right to do so that would not be a criminal offence.

Upon the facts of the present appeal the charge, if brought before the Act of 1971 came into force, would have been laid under section 13 of the Malicious Damage Act 1861, alleging damage by a tenant to a building. It was a defence to a charge under that section that the tenant acted under a claim of right to do the damage.

If the direction given by the deputy judge in the present case is correct, then the offence created by section 1 (1) of the Act of 1971 involves a considerable extension of the law in a surprising direction. Whether or not this is so depends upon the construction of the section. Construing the language of section 1 (1) we have no doubt that the actus reus is 'destroying or damaging any property belonging to another.' It is not possible to exclude the words 'belonging to another' which describes the 'property.' Applying the ordinary principles of mens rea, the intention and recklessness and the absence of lawful excuse required to constitute the offence have reference to property belonging to another. It follows that in our judgment no offence is committed under this section if a person destroys or causes damage to property belonging to another if he does so in the honest though mistaken belief that the property is his own, and provided that the belief is honestly held it is irrelevant to consider whether or not it is a justifiable belief.

In our judgment, the direction given to the jury was a fundamental misdirection in law. The consequence was that the jury were precluded from considering facts capable of being a defence to the charge and were directed to convict."

Appeal allowed, conviction quashed.

NOTES

The distinction between *R.* v. *Smith (David)* and *Clark* v. *Syme* could be said to lie in the different nature of the erroneous beliefs involved. Smith's belief is akin to a "claim of right" as in theft where the accused claims he cannot be guilty of theft because he believed the goods to be his own (due to an error of law). Syme's belief is rather just a general misapprehension as to his legal remedies. There are better policy grounds for convicting Syme than Smith since, as Lord Sorn pointed out in *Clark* v. *Syme,* "It would never do if the Courts were to countenance farmers taking the law into their own hands and destroying other people's animals in this sort of way. If the respondent found the situation intolerable the proper thing for him to do was to invoke the assistance of the civil law in the ordinary way."

d.   Motive

Palazzo v. Copeland
1976 J.C. 52

The appellant fired a shotgun in the air in the early hours of the morning to disperse a crowd of youths who were creating a disturbance in the street outside. He was convicted of breach of the peace, and appealed by stated case to the High Court.

OPINION OF THE COURT: "The appellant was convicted after trial on summary complaint upon a charge of breach of the peace. The particulars of the charge were that at a late hour at night, indeed in the early hours of the morning on 29th November, he discharged a shotgun into the air to the alarm of the lieges. The Sheriff, as we have indicated, convicted and the question in the case is whether on the facts stated he was entitled so to do. Mr Booker-Milburn has argued that it is perfectly plain from the case that the gun was fired in the air to try to stop a breach of the peace which was being committed by a number of unsavoury and drunken youths in the vicinity. The findings show that the appellant had been caused trouble before by youths who had damaged his property and that in course of the breach of the peace some of the drunken youths were shouting abusive expressions in the direction of his premises. The proposition was that an act which is committed to stop a breach of the peace ought not to be regarded itself as a breach of the peace. While the proposition is attractive, however, we regret to say that we cannot give effect to it in law. Undoubtedly a gun was fired in the air in an urban situation in the early hours of the morning. Undoubtedly certain lieges, however undesirable they might have been, were put in a state of fear and alarm. But more importantly, the act of firing a gun in the air in an urban situation at that time in the morning was calculated to be likely to put lieges in general in a state of fear and alarm. In these circumstances the fact that the appellant's motive was the sound one of trying to stop a breach of the peace is irrelevant. The fact that the only persons put in a state of fear and alarm were those committing the breach of the peace is equally irrelevant. A man may not take the law into his own hands. Furthermore a man may not commit an offence in an attempt to stop another. In the event, as the case shows, what the appellant did, did not end the fracas outside his premises, and it might be thought to have aggravated an already unsatisfactory situation. In the whole matter, while we have considerable sympathy for the appellant, we have no alternative but to answer the question in the case in the affirmative."

Appeal dismissed.

NOTE

   Cf. Chandler v. D.P.P. [1964] A.C. 763.

e.   Coincidence of actus reus and mens rea

The principle of *actus non facit reum nisi mens sit rea* is generally understood to require a coincidence of the two elements in point of time. As the following cases illustrate, however, this requirement may not always be easily satisfied.

1.   Thabo Meli and Ors. v. The Queen
[1954] 1 W.L.R. 228

The appellants, acting on a preconceived plan, attacked a man and, believing him to be dead, rolled his body over a cliff to make the death look like an accident. It was established that the initial juries were not sufficient to cause death, and that death was due in fact to exposure. The appellants were convicted of murder, and appealed, arguing that the acts which caused death were not accompanied with malice aforethought since they believed the victim to be already dead. On appeal to the Privy Council from the High Court of Basutoland.

LORD REID: "The point of law which was raised in this case can be simply stated. It is said that two acts were necessary and were separable: first, the attack in the hut; and, secondly, the placing of the body outside afterwards. It is said that, while the first act was accompanied by mens rea, it was not the cause of death; but that the second act, while it was the cause of death, was not accompanied by mens rea; and on that ground it is said that the accused are not guilty of any crime except perhaps culpable homicide.

It appears to their Lordships impossible to divide up what was really one transaction in this way. There is no doubt that the accused set out to do all these acts in order to achieve their plan and as parts of their plan; and it is much too refined a ground of judgment to say that, because they were under a misapprehension at one stage and thought that their guilty purpose had been achieved before in fact it was achieved, therefore they are to escape the penalties of the law. Their Lordships do not think that this is a matter which is susceptible of elaboration. There appears to be no case either in South Africa or England, or for that matter elsewhere, which resembles the present. Their Lordships can find no difference relevant to the present case between the law of South Africa and the law of England, and they are of opinion that by both laws there could be no separation such as that for which the accused contend, so as to reduce the crime from murder to a lesser crime, merely because the accused were under some misapprehension for a time during the completion of their criminal plot.

Their Lordships must, therefore, humbly advise Her Majesty that this appeal should be dismissed."

Appeal dismissed.

NOTE

Cf. *H.M.Advocate* v. *McPhee*, 1935 J.C. 46.

2.   **R. v. Church**
[1966] 1 Q.B. 59

Church attempted unsuccessfully to have sexual intercourse with a woman. When she reproached him, and slapped him he struck her, knocking her unconscious. After making unsuccessful attempts to revive her he panicked, and threw her body in a river, where she died of drowning. At his trial he stated that he thought she was dead when he put her in the river. The trial judge directed the jury that if that was what he genuinely thought when he disposed of the body he could not be convicted of murder, since "he obviously was not actuated by any intention to cause death or grievous bodily harm; you cannot cause death or serious bodily harm to a corpse." The jury convicted him of manslaughter. On appeal against conviction and sentence:

EDMUND DAVIES J. "In the light of *Meli* v. *The Queen* [1954] 1 W.L.R. 228 it is conceded on behalf of the appellant that, on the murder charge, the trial judge was perfectly entitled to direct the jury, as he did: 'Unless you find that something happened in the course of this evening between the infliction of the injuries and the decision to throw the body into the water, you may undoubtedly treat the whole course of conduct of the accused as one.'

But for some reason not clear to this court, appellant's counsel denies that such an approach is possible when one is considering a charge of manslaughter. We fail to see why. We adopt as sound Dr. Glanville Williams' view in his book, Criminal Law (1961), 2nd ed., p. 174 that, 'If a killing by the first act would have been manslaughter, a later destruction of the supposed corpse should also be manslaughter.' Had Mrs. Nott died of her initial injuries a manslaughter verdict might quite conceivably have been returned on the basis that the accused inflicted them under the influence of provocation or that the jury were not convinced that they were inflicted with murderous intent. All that was lacking in the direction given in this case was that, when the judge turned to consider manslaughter, he did not again tell the jury that they were entitled (if they thought fit) to regard the conduct of the appellant in relation to Mrs. Nott as constituting throughout a series of acts which culminated in her death, and that, if that was how they regarded the accused's behaviour, it mattered not whether he believed her to be alive or dead when he threw her in the river. Having regard to the summing-up as a whole, the difference between what was said to the jury and that which, in the opinion of this court, should have been said is so minimal that we consider that no substantial miscarriage of justice resulted."

Appeal dismissed; sentence of fifteen years' imprisonment upheld.

NOTES

See also *Fagan* v. *Metropolitan Police Commissioner* [1969] 1 Q.B. 439 (*post*, ch. 10), *Shoukatallie* v. *R.* [1962] A.C. 81, *R.* v. *Chiswibo* [1961] (2)

S.A. 714, *S.* v. *Masilela* 1968 (2) S.A. 558, and *Brennan* v. *H.M.Advocate*, 1977 S.L.T. 151.

These cases all deal with the problem of coincidence in point of time. For the further problem of coincidence in point of the actor, see *R.* v. *Cogan and Leak* [1976] Q.B. 217 *(ante,* ch. 4). *(Actus reus* committed by A, accompanied by *mens rea* on part of B.)

CHAPTER 7

MENS REA IN STATUTORY OFFENCES

a.   The presumption in favour of mens rea

It has been stressed in many cases both in Scotland and England that strict responsibility for a statutory criminal offence is the exception rather than the rule, and that penal statutes should normally be construed as requiring *mens rea* as to the elements which give rise to guilt. As was said by Lord Justice-Clerk Cooper in *Duguid* v. *Fraser,* 1942 J.C. 1 at p. 5: "Our reports already contain many examples of cases in which it has been held that a *malum prohibitum* has been created by statutory enactment in such terms and under such circumstances as to impose an absolute obligation of such a kind as to entail this wider liability. In all such cases it has, I think, been the practice to insist that the Crown should show that the language, scope and intendment of the statute require that an exception should be admitted to the normal and salutary rule of our law that *mens rea* is an indispensable ingredient of a criminal or quasi-criminal act; and I venture to think that it would be a misfortune if the stringency of this requirement were relaxed." The House of Lords has also confirmed this view.

Sweet v. Parsley
[1970] A.C. 132

Cannabis was found on property let out by the appellant who did not know her tenants were using the premises for the purposes of smoking cannabis. She was convicted of being concerned in the management of premises used for smoking cannabis, under s. 5 of the Dangerous Drugs Act 1965, and appealed to the House of Lords.

LORD REID: "Where it is contended that an absolute offence has been created, the words of Alderson B. in *Attorney-General* v. *Lockwood* (1842) 9 M. & W. 378, 398 have often been quoted: 'The rule of law, I take it upon the construction of all statutes, and therefore applicable to the construction of this, is, whether they be penal or remedial, to construe them according to the plain, literal, and grammatical meaning of the words in which they are expressed, unless that construction leads to a plain and clear contradiction of the apparent purpose of the Act, or to some palpable and evident absurdity.'

That is perfectly right as a general rule and where there is no legal presumption. But what about the multitude of criminal enactments

154

where the words of the Act simply make it an offence to do certain things but where everyone agrees that there cannot be a conviction without proof of mens rea in some form? This passage, if applied to the present problem, would mean that there is no need to prove mens rea unless it would be 'a plain and clear contradiction of the apparent purpose of the Act' to convict without proof of mens rea. But that would be putting the presumption the wrong way round: for it is firmly established by a host of authorities that mens rea is an essential ingredient of every offence unless some reason can be found for holding that that is not necessary.

It is also firmly established that the fact that other sections of the Act expressly require mens rea, for example because they contain the word 'knowingly', is not in itself sufficient to justify a decision that a section which is silent as to mens rea creates an absolute offence. In the absence of a clear indication in the Act that an offence is intended to be an absolute offence, it is necessary to go outside the Act and examine all relevant circumstances in order to establish that this must have been the intention of Parliament. I say 'must have been' because it is a universal principle that if a penal provision is reasonably capable of two interpretations, that interpretation which is most favourable to the accused must be adopted.

What, then, are the circumstances which it is proper to taken into account? In the well known case of *Sherras* v. *De Rutzen* [1895] 1 Q.B. 918, Wright J. only mentioned the subject matter with which the Act deals. But he was there dealing with something which was one of a class of acts which 'are not criminal in any real sense, but are acts which in the public interest are prohibited under a penalty' (p.922). It does not in the least follow that when one is dealing with a truly criminal act it is sufficient merely to have regard to the subject matter of the enactment. One must put oneself in the position of a legislator. It has long been the practice to recognise absolute offences in this class of quasi-criminal acts, and one can safely assume that, when Parliament is passing new legislation dealing with this class of offences, its silence as to mens rea means that the old practice is to apply. But when one comes to acts of a truly criminal character, it appears to me that there are at least two other factors which any reasonable legislator would have in mind. In the first place a stigma still attaches to any person convicted of a truly criminal offence, and the more serious or more disgraceful the offence the greater the stigma. So he would have to consider whether, in a case of this gravity, the public interest really requires that an innocent person should be prevented from proving his innocence in order that fewer guilty men may escape. And equally important is the fact that fortunately the Press in this country are vigilant to expose injustice and every manifestly unjust conviction

made known to the public tends to injure the body politic by
undermining public confidence in the justice of the law and of its
administration. But I regret to observe that, in some recent cases
where serious offences have been held to be absolute offences, the
court has taken into account no more than the wording of the Act
and the character and seriousness of the mischief which constitutes
the offence.

The choice would be much more difficult if there were no other
way open than either mens rea in the full sense or an absolute
offence; for there are many kinds of case where putting on the
prosecutor the full burden of proving mens rea creates great difficulties and may lead to many unjust acquittals. But there are at least
two other possibilities. Parliament has not infrequently transferred
the onus as regards mens rea to the accused, so that, once the
necessary facts are proved, he must convince the jury that on
balance of probabilities he is innocent of any criminal intention. I
find it a little surprising that more use has not been made of this
method: but one of the bad effects of the decision of this House in
Woolmington v. *Director of Public Prosecutions* [1935] A.C. 462
may have been to discourage its use. The other method would be in
effect to substitute in appropriate classes of cases gross negligence
for mens rea in the full sense as the mental element necessary to
constitute the crime. It would often be much easier to infer that
Parliament must have meant that gross negligence should be the
necessary mental element than to infer that Parliament intended to
create an absolute offence. A variant of this would be to accept the
view of Cave J. in *Reg.* v. *Tolson* (1889) 23 Q.B.D. 168, 181. This
appears to have been done in Australia where authority appears to
support what Dixon J. said in *Proudman* v. *Dayman* (1941) 67
C.L.R. 536, 540: 'As a general rule an honest and reasonable belief
in a state of facts which, if they existed, would make the defendant's
act innocent affords an excuse for doing what would otherwise be an
offence.' It may be that none of these methods is wholly satisfactory
but at least the public scandal of convicting on a serious charge
persons who are in no way blameworthy would be avoided.

If this section means what the Divisional Court have held that it
means, then hundreds of thousands of people who sublet part of
their premises or take in lodgers or are concerned in the management of residential premises or institutions are daily incurring a risk
of being convicted of a serious offence in circumstances where they
are in no way to blame. For the greatest vigilance cannot prevent
tenants, lodgers or inmates or guests whom they bring in from
smoking cannabis cigarettes in their own rooms. It was suggested in
argument that this appellant brought this conviction on herself
because it is found as a fact that when the police searched the

premises there were people there of the 'beatnik fraternity.' But surely it would be going a very long way to say that persons managing premises of any kind ought to safeguard themselves by refusing accommodation to all who are of slovenly or exotic appearance, or who bring in guests of that kind. And unfortunately drug taking is by no means confined to those of unusual appearance.

Speaking from a rather long experience of membership of both Houses, I assert with confidence that no Parliament within my recollection would have agreed to make an offence of this kind an absolute offence if the matter had been fully explained to it. So, if the court ought only to hold an offence to be an absolute offence where it appears that that must have been the intention of Parliament, offences of this kind are very far removed from those which it is proper to hold to be absolute offences."

LORD PEARCE: "The notion that some guilty mind is a constituent part of crime and punishment goes back far beyond our common law. And at common law mens rea is a necessary element in a crime. Since the Industrial Revolution the increasing complexity of life called into being new duties and crimes which took no account of intent. Those who undertake various industrial and other activities, especially where these affect the life and health of the citizen, may find themselves liable to statutory punishment regardless of knowledge or intent, both in respect of their own acts or neglect and those of their servants. But one must remember that normally mens rea is still an ingredient of any offence. Before the court will dispense with the necessity for mens rea it has to be satisfied that Parliament so intended. The mere absence of the word 'knowingly' is not enough. But the nature of the crime, the punishment, the absence of social obloquy, the particular mischief and the field of activity in which it occurs, and the wording of the particular section and its context, may show that Parliament intended that the act should be prevented by punishment regardless of intent or knowledge.

Viewing the matter on these principles, it is not possible to accept the prosecution's contention. Even granted that this were in the public health class of case, such as, for instance, are offences created to ensure that food shall be clean, it would be quite unreasonable. It is one thing to make a man absolutely responsible for all his own acts and even vicariously liable for his servants if he engages in a certain type of activity. But it is quite another matter to make him liable for persons over whom he has no control. The innocent hotel-keeper, the lady who keeps lodgings or takes paying guests, the manager of a cinema, the warden of a hostel, the matron of a hospital, the house-master and matron of a boarding school, all these, it is conceded, are, on the prosecution's argument, liable to conviction the moment that irresponsible occupants smoke cannabis cigarettes. And for what purpose is this harsh imposition laid on their backs? No vigilance by night or day can make them safe. The most that vigilance can attain is advance knowledge of their own guilt. If a smell of cannabis comes from a sitting-room, they know that they have committed the offence. Should they then go at once to the police and confess their guilt in the hope that they will not be prosecuted? They may think it easier to conceal the matter in the hope that it may never be found out. For if, though morally innocent, they are prosecuted they may lose their livelihood, since thereafter, even though not punished, they are objects of suspicion. I see no real, useful object achieved by such hardship to the innocent. And so wide a possibility of injustice to the innocent could not be justified by any benefit achieved in the determent and punishment of the guilty. If therefore, the words creating the offence are as wide in their application as the prosecution contend, Parliament cannot have intended an offence to which absence of knowledge of mens rea is no defence.''

LORD DIPLOCK: "The expression 'absolute offence' used in the first question is an imprecise phrase currently used to describe an act for which the doer is subject to criminal sanctions even though when he did it he had no mens rea, but mens rea itself also lacks precision and calls for closer analysis than is involved in its mere translation into English by Wright J. in *Sherras* v. *De Rutzen* [1895] 1 Q.B. 918, 921 as 'evil intention or a knowledge of the wrongfulness of the act'—a definition which suggests a single mental element common to all criminal offences and appears to omit thoughtlessness which, at any rate if it amounted to a reckless disregard of the nature or consequences of an act, was a sufficient mental element in some offences at common law.

A more helpful exposition of the nature of mens rea in both common law and statutory offences is to be found in the judgment of Stephen J. in *Reg.* v. *Tolson* (1889) 23 Q.B.D. 168, 187. He said: 'The full definition of every crime contains expressly or by implication a proposition as to a state of mind. Therefore, if the mental element of any conduct alleged to be a crime is proved to have been absent in any given case, the crime so defined is not committed; or, again, if a crime is fully defined, nothing amounts to that crime which does not satisfy that definition.'

Where the crime consists of doing an act which is prohibited by statute the proposition as to the state of mind of the doer which is contained in the full definition of the crime must be ascertained from the words and subject-matter of the statute. The proposition, as Stephen J. pointed out, may be stated explicitly by the use of such qualifying adverbs as 'maliciously,' 'fraudulently,' 'negligently' or 'knowingly'—expressions which in relation to different kinds of conduct may call for judicial exegesis. And even without such adverbs the words descriptive of the prohibited act may themselves connote the presence of a particular mental element. Thus, where the prohibited conduct consists in permitting a particular thing to be done the word 'permit' connotes at least knowledge or reasonable grounds for suspicion on the part of the permitter that the thing will be done and an unwillingness to use means available to him to prevent it and, to take a recent example, to have in one's 'possession' a prohibited substance connotes some degree of awareness of that which was within the possessor's physical control: *Reg.* v. *Warner* [1969] 2 A.C. 256.

But only too frequently the actual words used by Parliament to define the prohibited conduct are in themselves descriptive only of a physical act and bear no connotation as to any particular state of mind on the part of the person who does the act. Nevertheless, the mere fact that Parliament has made the conduct a criminal offence gives rise to some implication about the mental element of the conduct proscribed. It has, for instance, never been doubted since *McNaghten's* case (1843) 10 Cl. & F. 200, that one implication as to the mental element in any statutory offence is that the doer of the prohibited act should be sane within the McNaghten rules; yet this part of the full defintion of the offence is invariably left unexpressed by Parliament. Stephen J. in *Reg.* v. *Tolson* (1889) 23 Q.B.D. 168 suggested other circumstances never expressly dealt with in the statute where a mental element to be implied from the mere fact that the doing of an act was made a criminal offence would be absent, such as where it was done in a state of somnambulism or under duress, to which one might add inevitable accident. But the importance of the actual decision of the nine judges who constituted the majority in *Reg.* v. *Tolson,* which concerned a charge of bigamy under section 57 of the Offences Against the Person Act, 1861, was that it laid down as a general principle of construction of any enactment, which creates a criminal offence, that, even where the words used to describe the prohibited conduct would not in any other context connote the necessity for any particular mental element, they are nevertheless to be read as subject to the implication that a necessary element in the offence is the absence of a belief, held honestly and upon reasonable grounds, in the existence of facts which, if true, would make the act innocent. As was said by the Privy Council in *Bank of New South Wales* v. *Piper* [1897] A.C. 383, 389, 390, the absence of mens rea really consists in such a belief by the accused.

This implication stems from the principle that it is contrary to a rational and civilised criminal code, such as Parliament must be presumed to have intended, to penalise one who has performed his duty as a citizen to ascertain what acts are prohibited by law (ignorantia juris non excusat) and has taken all proper care to inform himself of any facts which would make his conduct lawful.

Where penal provisions are of general application to the conduct of ordinary citizens in the course of their everyday life the presumption is that the standard of care required of them in informing themselves of facts which would make their conduct unlawful, is that of the familiar common law duty of care. But where the subject-matter of a statute is the regulation of a particular activity involving potential danger to public health, safety or morals in which citizens have a choice as to whether they participate or not, the court may feel driven to infer an intention of Parliament to impose by penal sanctions a higher duty of care on those who choose to participate and to place upon them an obligation to take whatever measures may be necessary to prevent the prohibited act, without regard to those considerations of cost or business practicability which play a part in the determination of what would be required of them in order to fulfil the ordinary common law duty of care. But such an inference is not lightly to be drawn, nor is there any room for it unless there is something that the person on whom the obligation is imposed can do directly or indirectly, by supervision or inspection, by improvement of his business methods or by exhorting those whom he may be expected to influence or control, which will promote the observance of the obligation (see *Lim Chin Aik* v. *The Queen* [1963] A.C. 160, 174).

The numerous decisions in the English courts since *Reg.* v. *Tolson* (1889) 23 Q.B.D. 168 in which this later inference has been drawn rightly or, as I think, often wrongly are not easy to reconcile with others where the court has failed to draw the inference, nor are they always limited to penal provisions designed to regulate the conduct of persons who choose to participate in a particular activity as distinct from those of general application to the conduct of ordinary citizens in the course of their everyday life. It may well be that had the significance of *Reg.* v. *Tolson* been appreciated here, as it was in the High Court of Australia, our courts, too, would have been less ready to infer an intention of Parliament to create offences for which honest and reasonable mistake was no excuse. . . .

It has been objected that the requirement laid down in *Reg.* v. *Tolson* (1889) 23 Q.B.D. 168 and the *Bank of New South Wales* v. *Piper* [1897] A.C. 383 that the mistaken belief should be based on reasonable grounds introduces an objective mental element into mens rea. This may be so, but there is nothing novel in this. The test of the mental element of provocation which distinguishes man-slaughter from murder has always been at common law and now is by statute the objective one of the way in which a reasonable man would react to provocation. There is nothing unreasonable in requiring a citizen to take reasonable care to ascertain the facts relevant to his avoiding doing a prohibited act."

Appeal allowed; conviction quashed.

NOTE

Section 5 of the Dangerous Drugs Act 1965, under which Ms Sweet was charged, is no longer in force. See now Misuse of Drugs Act 1971, s.8.

b.   Words importing mens rea

As will be observed, the mere fact that a statute fails to prescribe that an offence can only be committed "wilfully", or "maliciously" or under a similar condition, does not mean that it does not require *mens rea*. The major problem here has arisen in relation to know-ledge of possession of an article or its character.

1.   **Black and Another v. H.M. Advocate**
1974 S.L.T. 247

The accused were charged with contraventions of s.3(*b*), or alterna-tively s.4(1), of the Explosive Substances Act 1883. They appealed against their convictions for contravention of s.3(*b*) on the ground *inter alia* that the presiding judge failed to distinguish in his charge to the jury between "knowledge that explosives were in the house and proof that the accused had in their possession and control an explosive substance."

OPINION OF THE COURT: "Upon either branch of the indictment it was essential for a conviction that the possession or control libelled against the accused should be knowing possession or control of the explosive substances libelled in the indictment. In addition, upon the first alternative not only was it necessary that the Crown should establish that knowledge, but also that possession or control should be with a specific intent in mind. In that very important respect the first charge differed materially from the second. In the alternative charge of contravention of s. 4 (1), in addition to proving knowing possession or control the Crown required only to establish circumstances which gave rise to a par-ticular reasonable suspicion which, in the absence of satisfactory explanation to the contrary, warranted conviction.

Thus, the two charges are materially different in respect of what must be proved in order to establish them.

In the alternative charge of breach of s. 4 (1) the positive proof of particular intention is not necessary to conviction. In the charge of breach of s. 3 (*b*), on the contrary, it is of the essence of the charge to prove the particular and geographically limited intention. Not only so, but in the present case this distinction was, in our opinion, of particular importance and required to be brought clearly to the notice of the jury. As we have already noted, the learned advocate-depute, in his submissions upon the issues of misdirection, disclaimed any intention to treat the case as one of concert between the accused or of actor and actor, art and part. He maintained that he presented and was presenting the case against each accused separately and as being each a principal responsible for his own actions alone and in so doing drew our attention to the fact that the presiding judge more than once in the course of his charge emphasised to the jury that they must treat each charge in the indictment and each accused separately. This being the manner in which the case was presented then, it necessarily follows that there can be no question of evidence incriminatory of one accused being available to the Crown as evidence against the other, and it also follows from this that the jury required definite direction that in considering the case against one accused they must ignore any evidence which might be incriminatory of the other.

Upon the alleged breach of s. 3 (*b*) it was, therefore, all the more necessary that there should be sufficient evidence to establish the relevant intent independently against Black and against Megeary, even if this evidence should proceed from common sources, either in whole or in part, proof of the intent being a vital constituent of proof of guilt of contravention of the section.

For the same reasons, and especially in light of the Crown's presentation of the case, it was necessary that, as against each accused, there should be proof of individual possession or control of the explosives libelled upon either alternative charge, and clear direction that proof of possession or control by the one accused was by itself of no relevance or avail in proof of possession or control by the other.

But however the matter be viewed, and whether or not the case is to be treated as one of concert or, as the Crown insisted, solely of individual guilt and responsibility, upon either view it is vital that 'possession or control' of the explosive substance should be established and, in our opinion, it is necessary that a jury should receive adequate guidance and direction as to what may, in the particular case, be held by them to be sufficient to constitute such possession and control. Counsel for both applicants maintained that no such direction was given and further that such direction as was given by the judge was erroneous, in that it equiparated knowledge of the presence of explosives in the house with possession or control of these explosives by both accused. The passages to which counsel drew attention do not indicate that anything more than knowledge of the presence of explosives is required to establish possession or control. Indeed the last sentence of the judge's charge, dealing specifically with the charge of breach of s. 4 (1), is in these terms: '. . . in relation to the alternative charge, you cannot convict of the alternative charge unless you hold it proved that there was knowledge on the part of one or other of the accused, if you are disposed to convict either of these under head B.' This statement puts the matter negatively—it is not difficult to imply from the negative that the positive would suffice in terms of knowledge (of the presence of explosives) to establish that which would suffice for convictions at least on the alternative charge. We observe also that this sentence was added after the judge inquired of counsel for Black whether he wished him 'to add anything *further* [our italics] about knowledge as opposed to possession and control?' Now the only passage in the charge which bears upon this materially or at all is one at which the learned judge referred to a statement alleged to have been made by Megeary after caution but outwith the presence or hearing of Black, to this or a similar effect, 'I suppose you found the stuff in the cupboard', i.e., in the room occupied as a bedroom by Black. What the judge said was: 'It is for you, ladies and gentlemen, to decide . . . what is the proper construction to be put on the evidence whether it indicates knowledge on the part of Megeary that his lodger was keeping these explosives in the house.' In these circumstances we think it is the legitimate, if not the only inference to be drawn from this passage in the charge, and we can find no other which deals with the question of possession or control, that proof of knowledge of the presence of explosives could be sufficient at least to establish such possession and control as to satisfy the requirements of proof of breach of s. 4 (1). The English cases cited by counsel for the applicants support the proposition that mere knowledge of the presence of explosives on occupied premises or in a vehicle is not by itself sufficient to bring home a charge of possession or control of those explosives. As it was put in the case of *Searle* [1971] Crim. L.R. 592, 'mere knowledge of the possession of a forbidden article in the hands of a confederate is not enough for joint possession to be established'. We would agree with that proposition, and with the deduction from it that knowledge alone is not proof of either possession or control in the case of the individual charged alone. In our opinion, where an individual is charged with possession or control of explosives which are found in premises occupied by him

and another or others, the mere fact that it is proved that at the time
when he is interrogated or charged in respect of the presence of the
explosives he has knowledge of their presence on the premises is
not, by itself, sufficient to establish possession or control of those
explosives. Proof of knowledge is certainly essential to conviction
either of breach of s. 3 (*b*) or s. 4 (1) of the Act, but more must be
proved to saddle an accused with responsibility as for possession or
control, be it joint or individual. What more is necessary must
depend upon the circumstances of the particular case, but whatever
the nature or amount of the evidence required to be adduced, it
must be more than, and in addition to, mere knowledge. In our
opinion, therefore, it is necessary that a judge, when charging a jury
in a case of alleged breaches of these sections of the Explosives Act,
should give to the jury a direction which makes it clear that there
must be corroborated evidence which demonstrates either that the
accused has himself acquired or been in possession of and retained
the possession of explosives or, if they are found in premises, that
fixes the accused not only with knowledge of the presence of the
substance in premises which he occupies or over which he exercises
or is able to exercise control, but with acceptance of the substance
into his premises or at least permission for or connivance at its
remaining there in the knowledge of its character. What in a particular case will suffice to satisfy the requirements of 'possession or
control' must be a matter of circumstance, but, in our opinion, it is
essential that there should be proved facts and circumstances from
which a jury can infer that the accused is in a position to exercise
practical control over the presence or dispose of the substance in
question, and that this is not established by mere proof of knowledge of the presence of the substance and of its character. Even if a
man is knowingly in possession of a box or parcel containing explosives that knowledge by itself is insufficient to establish the quality of
knowledge necessary to constitute the knowledge which is of the
essence of the offence, that knowledge must include knowledge of
the fact that the substance or substances are explosives. This is a
matter on which, in our opinion, a jury should receive clear and
unequivocal direction. In the present case it is plain that they did not
receive directions as to the quality of the knowledge necessary to
fulfil the requirement of the statute nor that proof of such knowledge, though a relevant and essential ingredient of proof of the
offences upon either of the alternatives libelled, was not by itself
sufficent to warrant conviction. On the contrary, a fair reading of
what the presiding judge said would or at least might well lead to an
impression on minds which were unenlightened as to the law, that
proof of knowledge of the presence of sealed box and bags in the
bedroom cupboard in Megeary's house was sufficient to warrant

conviction of both accused on either branch of the indictment. This, in our opinion, was a serious misdirection and goes to the root of the verdict against both applicants, and unless the provision of s. 2 (1) of the Criminal Appeal (Scotland) Act 1926 can be applied, is of such a character that the verdict cannot stand.

But before determining whether this is a case in which the proviso should be applied to save the verdict, we think it is necessary to consider the other grounds of alleged misdirection founded upon by the applicants. There is a very clear and important distinction between the alternative charges in the indictment. Without proof of the specific intent libelled there can be no conviction of either accused for breach of s. 3 (b) of the statute. That intent is specific in substance and in geographical limitations. As the Crown maintained that this was not a case in which the charges against the applicants were charges of acting in concert or of common criminal purpose but were charges to fix individual responsibility, and the learned judge properly emphasised to the jury that the evidence against each accused had to be considered separately on both charges, it was essential therefore, in our opinion, that the attention of the jury should be directed not only to the differing requirements in proof of the two charges—and apart from reading the charges as set out in the indictment the learned judge made no comment on the substantial differences between the two—but also to the need for proof in the individual case of each applicant of the intent, proof of which was essential for conviction for breach of s. 3 (b). This, in our view, was all the more necessary in this case and particularly in the case of Black if, as was matter of admission by the Crown, the evidence of the intent on which the Crown relied consisted of certain documents and objects found by the police in a suitcase which was not in the room occupied by Black and, so far as identification went, related only to Megeary. As the jury convicted Black under the charge of breach of s. 3 (b) and if, as was admitted by the Crown, the only evidence bearing on the specified intent was as we have indicated, then clearly the jury treated that evidence as available as proof of guilt of both applicants on the first charge of the indictment. In our opinion, the failure to make clear to the jury that it was essential in proof of a breach of s. 3 (b) against either accused that there should be sufficient evidence in law to establish individual intent was itself a serious misdirection."

Convictions quashed.

2. R. v. Warner
[1969] 2 A.C. 256

The appellant was charged with having drugs in his possession without being duly authorised contrary to s. 1(1) of the Drugs

(Prevention of Misuse) Act 1964. There was evidence that a police officer had stopped the appellant who was driving a van in the back of which were found three cases, one of which contained scent bottles and another a plastic bag containing 20,000 amphetamine sulphate tablets. The appellant had been to a café where he was accustomed to collect scent from B, was told by the proprietor that a parcel from B was under the counter, and had found two parcels there, namely the one containing scent and the other which was found to contain the drugs. He said that he had assumed that both contained scent. On the question of possession the chairman directed the jury that if he had control of the box which turned out to be full of amphetamine sulphate, the offence was committed and it was only mitigation that he did not know the contents.

The accused was convicted and appealed, ultimately, to the House of Lords.

LORD REID (dissenting): "I understand that this is the first case in which this House has had to consider whether a statutory offence is an absolute offence in the sense that the belief, intention, or state of mind of the accused is immaterial and irrelevant. It appears from the authorities that the law on this matter is in some confusion, there being at least two schools of thought. So I think it necessary to begin by making some observations of a general character.

There is no doubt that for centuries mens rea has been an essential element in every common law crime or offence. Equally there is no doubt that Parliament, being sovereign, can create absolute offences if so minded. But we were referred to no instance where Parliament in giving statutory form to an old common law crime has or has been held to have excluded the necessity to prove mens rea. There are a number of statutes going back for over a century where Parliament in creating a new offence has transferred the onus of proof so that, once the facts necessary to constitute the crime have been proved, the accused will be held to be guilty unless he can prove that he had no mens rea. But we were not referred to any except quite recent cases in which it was held that it was no defence to a charge of a serious and truly criminal statutory offence to prove absence of mens rea.

On the other hand there is a long line of cases in which it has been held with regard to less serious offences that absence of mens rea was no defence. Typical examples are offences under public health, licensing and industrial legislation. If a person sets up as say a butcher, a publican, or a manufacturer and exposes unsound meat for sale, or sells drink to a drunk man, or certain parts of his factory are unsafe, it is no defence that he could not by the exercise of reasonable care have known or discovered that the meat was unsound, or that the man was drunk or that his premises were unsafe. He must take the risk and when it is found that the statutory prohibition or requirement has been infringed he must pay the penalty. This may well seem unjust but it is a comparatively minor injustice, and there is good reason for it as affording some protection to his customers or servants or to the public at large. Although this man might be able to show that he did his best, a more skilful or diligent man in his position might have done better, and when we are dealing with minor penalties which do not involve the disgrace of criminality it may be in the public interest to have a hard and fast rule. Strictly speaking there ought perhaps to be a defence that the defect was truly latent so that no one could have discovered it. But the law has not developed in that way, and one can see the difficulty if such a defence were allowed in a summary prosecution. These are only quasi-criminal offences and it does not really offend the ordinary man's sense of justice that moral guilt is not of the essence of the offence."

LORD PEARCE: "Lord Parker C.J. ([1967] 2 Q.B. 243, 248) was right (and this is conceded by both sides) in taking the view that a person did not have possession of something which had been 'slipped into his' bag without his knowledge. One may, therefore, exclude from the 'possession' intended by the Act the physical control of articles which have been 'planted' on him without his knowledge. But how much further is one to go? If one goes to the extreme length of requiring the prosecution to prove that 'possession' implies a full knowledge of the name and nature of the drug concerned, the efficacy of the Act is seriously impaired, since many drug pedlars may in truth be unaware of this. I think that the term 'possession' is satisfied by a knowledge only of the existence of the thing itself and not its qualities, and that ignorance or mistake as to its qualities is not an excuse. This would comply with the general understanding of the word 'possess'. Though I reasonably believe the tablets which I possess to be aspirin, yet if they turn out to be heroin I am in possession of heroin tablets. This would be so I think even if I believed them to be sweets. It would be otherwise if I believed them to be something of a wholly different nature. At this point a question of degree arises as to when a difference in qualities amounts to a difference in kind. That is a matter for a jury who probably decide it sensibly in favour of the genuinely innocent but against the guilty.

The situation with regard to containers presents further problems. If a man is in possession of the contents of a package, prima facie his possession of the package leads to the strong inference that he is in possession of its contents. But can this be rebutted by evidence that he was mistaken as to its contents? As in the case of goods that have been 'planted' in his pocket without his knowledge, so I do not think that he is in possession of contents which are quite different in kind from what he believed. Thus the prima facie assumption is discharged if he proves (or raises a real doubt in the matter) either (a) that he was a servant or bailee who had no right to open it *and* no reason to suspect that its contents were illicit or were drugs or (b) that although he was the owner he had no knowledge of (including a genuine mistake as to) its actual contents or of their illicit nature and that he received them innocently and also that he had had no reasonable opportunity since receiving the package of acquainting himself with its actual contents. For a man takes over a package or suitcase at risk as to its contents being unlawful if he does not immediately examine it (if he is entitled to do so). As soon as may be he should examine it and if he finds the contents suspicious reject possession by either throwing them away or by taking immediate sensible steps for their disposal. . . .

The direction to which the accused was entitled would, in my opinion, be approximately as follows. The Act forbids possession of these drugs. Whether he possessed them with an innocent or guilty mind or for a laudable or improper purpose is immaterial since he is not allowed to possess them. If he possessed them he is guilty. If a man has physical control or possession of a thing that is sufficient possession under the Act provided that he knows that he has the thing. But you do not (within the meaning of the Act) possess things of whose existence you are unaware. The prosecution have here proved that he possessed the parcel, but have they proved that he possessed its contents also? There is a very strong inference of fact in any normal case that a man who possesses a parcel also possesses its contents, an inference on which a jury would in a normal case be justified in finding possession. A man who accepts possession of a parcel normally accepts possession of the contents.

But that inference can be disproved or shaken by evidence that, although a man was in possession of a parcel, he was completely mistaken as to its contents and would not have accepted possession had he known what kind of thing the contents were. A mistake as to the qualities of the contents, however, does not negative possession. Many people possess things of whose exact qualities they are unaware. If the accused knew that the contents were drugs or were tablets, he was in possession of them, though he was mistaken as to their qualities. Again if, though unaware of the contents, he did not open them at the first opportunity to ascertain (as he was entitled to do in this case) what they were, the proper inference is that he was accepting possession of them. (It would be otherwise if he had no right to open the parcel.) Again, if he suspected that there was anything wrong about the contents when he received the parcel, the proper inference is that he was accepting possession of the contents by not immediately verifying them. (This would, in my opinion, apply also to a bailee.)"

Conviction affirmed,
although magistrates' direction defective.

NOTES

The problems thrown up in *Warner* have now been cured by legislation, at least in the field of drugs. See Misuse of Drugs Act 1971, s.28. For a comment on the difficulties which arise in connection with offences involving possession, see Gordon, para. 8-25.

c. *Vicarious* mens rea

Apart from the doctrine of art and part (*ante*, ch.4) the general rule is that an accused is only answerable for his own acts. In some circumstances, however, statute may impose liability on a superior (usually an employer) for the acts of persons under his direction and control.

Noble v. Heatly
1967 J.C. 5

OPINION OF THE COURT: "This appeal was put out before a Court of five judges in order to consider the soundness of the decision in the case of *Greig* v. *Macleod,* 1908 S.C. (J.) 14, particularly in the light of the recent decision in the House of Lords of *Vane* v. *Yiannopoullos*[1965] A.C. 486.

The material facts in the present case which bear upon this issue are simple. The appellant is the holder of a public house certificate. In the complaint he is charged with knowingly permitting drunkenness in this public house, contrary to the terms of his certificate and section 131 of the Licensing (Scotland) Act, 1959. One of the terms of his certificate was (see the 1959 Act, Second Schedule, article 10 of the form of certificate for a public house): 'The certificate-holder shall not knowingly permit any . . . drunkenness . . . in the premises'. He was found guilty of this charge.

The magistrate has held that two persons were found drunk on the premises when the police were admitted about an hour and half after closing time. Drunkenness was consequently clearly established. But the certificate-holder was not present that evening. He had delegated the running of the public house to a supervisor experienced in the management of public houses. This supervisor some weeks before the incident in question in this case had appointed a Mr Welch to manage the public house and its staff, the supervisor merely visiting the premises occasionally. Full instructions had been issued by the supervisor to Mr Welch regarding the steps necessary to comply with the licensing law, *inter alia*, in regard to drunkenness.

Mr Welch was in sole charge of the premises when the police visited them.

It is clear in these circumstances that the appellant had himself no personal knowledge of the drunkenness that evening in this public house, and the question in the case is whether the magistrate was entitled to convict him of knowingly permitting the drunkenness which occurred there. The decision of the magistrate is sought to be justified by the decision of the Court in *Greig* v. *Macleod*, 1908 S.C. (J.) 14. In that case the High Court upheld the conviction of the holder of a public house certificate charged with knowingly allowing an assistant in the premises to sell exciseable liquor to a girl under fourteen years of age, in breach of section 59 of the Licensing (Scotland) Act, 1903. The sale took place outwith the certificate-holder's presence and actual personal knowledge. He had given no sufficient instructions as to the supply of liquor to persons under fourteen. Lord McLaren, who gave the leading opinion, with which the rest of the Court agreed, stated his reason for upholding the conviction in the following words:—'In the case of *Emary* v. *Nolloth*, [1903] 2 K.B. 264 we have the authority of Lord Alverstone for this construction of the provisions of the section, that if a person in the position of the appellant delegates the conduct of his business to another, he is responsible for the acts of the person to whom he has given the institorial power, as if he had made the sale himself. Now I think it is not an illegitimate extension of the rule thus laid down if I say that every licensee who delegates the conduct of a part of his business, is at least responsible to the extent that he must give instructions to his assistant as to compliance with Acts of Parliament which regulate the spirit trade.'

Although the result at which the Court arrived in that case appears to be sound in the light of the facts found proved, Lord McLaren's grounds for reaching the decision are in our opinion unsound. In the first place Lord Alverstone's observations were not necessary for the decision of the case of *Emary,* which was not a case of delegation by the licence-holder. They were therefore strictly *obiter.* In the second place these *dicta* were pronounced in an English case, and related to rules of English Law which have never been part of the law of Scotland, and which, so far as appears from the decided cases reported in Scotland, have never been applied in Scotland except in *Greig's* case. In the third place Lord McLaren in this latter case sought to extend the English rule in a way which would conflict with other passages in Lord Alverstone's opinion and for which there is no warrant in what Lord Alverstone had said.

In the result, therefore, 'knowingly' must in our opinion mean what it says, and, unless there is express statutory warrant for holding it to mean something else, an offence is not committed where 'knowingly' is of its essence, unless there is personal knowledge on the part of the accused person. Considerable support for this conclusion is to be found in the speeches in the recent House of Lords decision in *Vane* v. *Yiannopoullos* regarding the meaning of 'knowingly' in a similar provision in an English Licensing Act."

Conviction quashed.

d.   Defences to charges involving vicarious responsibility

These are usually provided by express statutory provision and are often encountered in the field of consumer protection.

1.   **Tesco Supermarkets Ltd. v. Nattrass**
[1972] A.C. 153

Section 24 of the Trade Descriptions Act 1968 provides:

"(1) In any proceedings for an offence under this Act it shall, subject to subsection (2) of this section, be a defence for the person charged to prove—

   (a) that the commission of the offence was due to a mistake or to reliance on information supplied to him or to the act or default of another person, an accident or some other cause beyond his control; and

   (b) that he took all reasonable precautions and exercised all due diligence to avoid the commission of such an offence by himself or any person under his control.

(2) If in any case the defence provided by the last foregoing subsection involves the allegation that the commission of the offence was due to the act or default of another person or to reliance on information supplied by another person, the person charged shall not, without leave of the court, be entitled to rely on that defence unless, within a period ending seven clear days before the hearing, he has served on the prosecutor a notice in writing giving such information identifying or assisting in the identification of that other person as was then in his possession.

S.C.L.—13

(3) In any proceedings for an offence under this Act of supplying or offering to supply goods to which a false trade description is applied it shall be a defence for the person charged to prove that he did not know, and could not with reasonable diligence have ascertained, that the goods did not conform to the description or that the description had been applied to the goods."

A supermarket company was charged under the Trade Descriptions Act 1968 and pleaded in defence that s. 24 (1) of the Act applied in that the offence was due to the act or default of their store manager and that they had taken all reasonable precautions and used due diligence to avoid breaking the law. The store manager did not hold a high executive position within the company which had however instituted a proper system for avoidance of offences under the Act. The store manager had been properly trained to operate the system and was supervised on a regular basis.

In the magistrates' court it was held that the defendants had complied with s. 24 (1) (b) of the Act in that the system was properly organised but that the manager had failed to carry out his part in the running thereof. The magistrates however convicted on the view that the store manager could not be "another person" within the wording of s. 24(1) (a).

On appeal to the House of Lords:

LORD REID: "Over a century ago the courts invented the idea of an absolute offence. The accepted doctrines of the common law put them in a difficulty. There was a presumption that when Parliament makes the commission of certain acts an offence it intends that mens rea shall be a constituent of the offence whether or not there is any reference to the knowledge or state of mind of the accused. And it was and is held to be an invariable rule that where mens rea is a constituent of any offence the burden of proving mens rea is on the prosecution. Some day this House may have to re-examine that rule, but that is another matter. For the protection of purchasers or consumers Parliament in many cases made it an offence for a trader to do certain things. Normally those things were done on his behalf by his servants and cases arose where the doing of the forbidden thing was solely the fault of a servant, the master having done all he could to prevent it and being entirely ignorant of its having been done. The just course would have been to hold that, once the facts constituting the offence had been proved, mens rea would be presumed unless the accused proved that he was blameless. The courts could not, or thought they could not, take that course. But they could and did hold in many such cases on a construction of the statutory provision that Parliament must be deemed to have intended to depart from the general rule and to make the offence absolute in the sense that mens rea was not to be a constituent of the offence.

This has led to great difficulties. If the offence is not held to be absolute the requirement that the prosecutor must prove mens rea makes it impossible to enforce the enactment in very many cases. If the offence is held to be absolute that leads to the conviction of persons who are entirely blameless: an injustice which brings the law into disrepute. So Parliament has found it necessary to devise a method of avoiding this difficulty. But instead of passing a general enactment that it shall always be a defence for the accused to prove that he was no party to the offence and had done all he could to prevent it, Parliament has chosen to deal with the problem piece-meal, and has in an increasing number of cases enacted in various forms with regard to particular offences that it shall be a defence to prove various exculpatory circumstances.

In my judgment the main object of these provisions must have been to distinguish between those who are in some degree blame-worthy and those who are not, and to enable the latter to escape from conviction if they can show that they were in no way to blame. I find it almost impossible to suppose that Parliament or any reason-able body of men would as a matter of policy think it right to make employers criminally liable for the acts of some of their servants but not for those of others and I find it incredible that a draftsman, aware of that intention, would fail to insert any words to express it. But in several cases the courts, for reasons which it is not easy to discover, have given a restricted meaning to such provisions. It has been held that such provisions afford a defence if the master proves that the servant at fault was the person who himself did the pro-hibited act, but that they afford no defence if the servant at fault was one who failed in his duty of supervision to see that his subordinates did not commit the prohibited act. Why Parliament should be thought to have intended this distinction or how as a matter of construction these provisions can reasonably be held to have that meaning is not apparent.

In some of these cases the employer charged with the offence was a limited company. But in others the employer was an individual and still it was held that he, though personally entirely blameless, could not rely on these provisions if the fault which led to the commission of the offence was the fault of a servant in failing to carry out his duty to instruct or supervise his subordinates.

Where a limited company is the employer difficult questions do arise in a wide variety of circumstances in deciding which of its officers or servants is to be identified with the company so that his guilt is the guilt of the company.

I must start by considering the nature of the personality which by a fiction the law attributes to a corporation. A living person has a mind which can have knowledge or intention or be negligent and he has hands to carry out his intentions. A corporation has none of these: it must act through living persons, though not always one or the same person. Then the person who acts is not speaking or acting for the company. He is acting as the company and his mind which directs his acts is the mind of the company. There is no question of the company being vicariously liable. He is not acting as a servant, representative, agent or delegate. He is an embodiment of the company or, one could say, he hears and speaks through the persona of the company, within his appropriate sphere, and his mind is the mind of the company. If it is a guilty mind then that guilt is the guilt of the company. It must be a question of law whether, once the facts have been ascertained, a person in doing particular things is to be regarded as the company or merely as the company's servant or agent. In that case any liability of the company can only be a statutory or vicarious liability.

In *Lennard's Carrying Co. Ltd.* v. *Asiatic Petroleum Co. Ltd.* [1915] A.C. 705 the question was whether damage had occurred without the 'actual fault or privity' of the owner of a ship. The owners were a company. The fault was that of the registered managing owner who managed the ship on behalf of the owners and it was held that the company could not dissociate itself from him so as to say that there was no actual fault or privity on the part of the company. Viscount Haldane L.C. said, at pp. 713, 714: 'For if Mr. Lennard was the directing mind of the company, then his action must, unless a corporation is not to be liable at all, have been an action which was the action of the company itself within the meaning of section 502. . . . It must be upon the true construction of that section in such a case as the present one that the fault or privity is the fault or privity of somebody who is not merely a servant or agent for whom the company is liable upon the footing respondeat superior, but somebody for whom the company is liable because his action is the very action of the company itself. . . .'

In some cases the phrase alter ego has been used. I think it is misleading. When dealing with a company the word alter is I think misleading. The person who speaks and acts as the company is not alter. He is identified with the company. And when dealing with an individual no other individual can be his alter ego. The other individual can be a servant, agent, delegate or representative but I know of neither principle nor authority which warrants the confusion (in the literal or original sense) of two separate individuals. . . .

In *John Henshall (Quarries) Ltd.* v. *Harvey* [1965] 2 Q.B. 233 a company was held not criminally responsible for the negligence of a servant in charge of a weighbridge. In *Magna Plant* v. *Mitchell* (unreported) April 27, 1966, the fault was that of a depot engineer and again the company was held not criminally responsible. I think these decisions were right. In the *Magna Plant* case Lord Parker C.J. said: '. . . knowledge of a servant cannot be imputed to the company unless he is a servant for whose actions the company are criminally responsible, and as the cases show, that only arises in the case of a company where one is considering the acts of responsible officers forming the brain, or in the case of an individual, a person to whom delegation in the true sense of the delegation of management has been passed'.

I agree with what he said with regard to a company. But delegation by an individual is another matter."

LORD DIPLOCK: "What amounts to the taking of all reasonable precautions and the exercise of all due diligence by a principal in order to satisfy the requirements of paragraph (*b*) of section 24(1) of the Act depends upon all the circumstances of the business carried on by the principal. It is a question of fact for the magistrates in summary proceedings or for the jury in proceedings on indictment. However large the business, the principal cannot avoid a personal responsibility for laying down the system for avoiding the commission of offences by his servants. It is he alone who is party to their contracts of employment through which this can be done. But in a large business, such as that conducted by the appellants in the instant appeal, it may be quite impracticable for the principal personally to undertake the detailed supervision of the work of inferior servants. It may be reasonable for him to allocate these supervisory duties to some superior servant or hierarchy of supervisory grades of superior servants, under their respective contracts of employment with him. If the principal has taken all reasonable precautions in the selection and training of servants to perform supervisory duties and has laid down an effective system of supervision and used due diligence to see that it is observed, he is entitled to rely upon a default by a superior servant in his supervisory duties as a defence under section 24(1), as well as, or instead of, upon an act of default of an inferior servant who has no supervisory duties under his contract of employment. . . .

To establish a defence under section 24 a principal who is a corporation must show that it 'took all reasonable precautions and exercised all due diligence'. A corporation is an abstraction. It is incapable itself of doing any physical act or being in any state of mind. Yet in law it is a person capable of exercising legal rights and of being subject to legal liabilities which may involve ascribing to it not only physical acts which are in reality done by a natural person on its behalf but also the mental state in which that person did them. In civil law, apart from certain statutory duties, this presents no conceptual difficulties. Under the law of agency the physical acts and state of mind of the agent are in law ascribed to the principal, and if the agent is a natural person it matters not whether the principal is also a natural person or a mere legal abstraction. Qui facit per alium facit per se: qui cogitat per alium cogitat per se.

But there are some civil liabilities imposed by statute which, exceptionally, exclude the concept of vicarious liability of a principal for the physical acts and state of mind of his agent; and the concept has no general application in the field of criminal law. To constitute a criminal offence, a physical act done by any person must generally be done by him in some reprehensible state of mind. Save in cases of strict liability where a criminal statute, exceptionally, makes the doing of an act a crime irrespective of the state of mind in which it is done, criminal law regards a person as responsible for his own crimes only. It does not recognise the liability of a principal for the criminal acts of his agent: because it does not ascribe to him his agent's state of mind. Qui peccat per alium peccat per se is not a maxim of criminal law.

Due diligence is in law the converse of negligence and negligence connotes a reprehensible state of mind—a lack of care for the consequences of his physical acts on the part of the person doing them. To establish a defence under section 24(1) (b) of the Act, a principal need only show that he personally acted without negligence. Accordingly, where the principal who relies on this defence is a corporation a question to be answered is: What natural person or persons are to be treated as being the corporation itself, and not merely its agents, for the purpose of taking precautions and exercising diligence?

My Lords, a corporation incorporated under the Companies Act 1948 owes its corporate personality and its powers to its constitution, the memorandum and articles of association. The obvious and the only place to look to discover by what natural persons its powers are exercisable, is in its constitution. The articles of association, if they follow Table A, provide that the business of the company shall be managed by the directors and that they may 'exercise all such powers of the company' as are not required by the Act to be exercised in general meeting. Table A also vests in the directors the right to entrust and confer upon a managing director any of the powers of the company which are exercisable by them. So it may also be necessary to ascertain whether the directors have taken any action under this provision or any other similar provision providing for the co-ordinate exercise of the powers of the company by executive directors or by committees of directors and other persons, such as are frequently included in the articles of association of companies in which the regulations contained in Table A are modified or excluded in whole or in part.

In my view, therefore, the question: what natural persons are to be treated in law as being the company for the purpose of acts done in the course of its business, including the taking of precautions and the exercise of due diligence to avoid the commission of a criminal offence, is to be found by identifying those natural persons who by the memorandum and articles of association or as a result of action taken by the directors, or by the company in general meeting pursuant to the articles, are entrusted with the exercise of the powers of the company. . . .

Any legal duty, whether arising at common law or imposed by statute, may generally be performed by the person upon whom it is imposed through the agency of some other person. But if it is not performed, the person upon whom the duty is imposed is liable for its non-performance. It is irrelevant that he instructed a servant or agent to perform it on his behalf, if that servant or agent failed to do so. All that is relevant is that the duty was not performed. When the duty is imposed upon a person by statute and non-performance is made a criminal offence without any requirement of mens rea this is what is meant by an offence of 'strict liability'.

The fallacy lies in the next step of the argument. Where Parliament in creating an offence of 'strict liability' has also provided that it shall be a defence if the person upon whom the duty is imposed proves that *he* exercised all due diligence to avoid a breach of the duty, the clear intention of Parliament is to mitigate the injustice, which may be involved in an offence of strict liability, of subjecting to punishment a careful and conscientious person who is in no way morally to blame. To exercise due diligence to prevent something being done is to take all reasonable steps to prevent it. It may be a reasonable step for an employer to instruct a superior servant to supervise the activities of inferior servants whose physical acts may in the absence of supervision result in that being done which it is sought to prevent. This is not to delegate the employer's duty to exercise all due diligence; it is to perform it. To treat the duty of an employer to exercise due diligence as unperformed unless due diligence was also exercised by all his servants to whom he had reasonably given all proper instructions and upon whom he could reasonably rely to carry them out, would be to render the defence of due diligence nugatory and so thwart the clear intention of Parliament in providing it. For, pace *R. C. Hammett Ltd.* v. *London County Council,* 97 J.P. 105, there is no logical distinction to be drawn between diligence in supervising and diligence in acting, if the defaults of servants are to be treated in law as the defaults of their employer."

Conviction quashed.

NOTES

Here the company were ultimately successful in establishing that the contravention was due to the act or default of another person and that they had used due diligence to prevent contraventions. On the question of corporate responsibility, see Gordon, paras. 8-84 to 8-93.

2.   Readers' Digest Association Ltd. v. Pirie
1973 J.C. 42

The accused were charged with contravening the Unsolicited Goods and Services Act 1971 by continuing to send to, and claim payment for, copies of a magazine from someone who had cancelled his subscription, "not having reasonable cause to believe there was a right to payment." On appeal against conviction:

LORD JUSTICE-CLERK (WHEATLEY): " I accordingly approach the question on the basis that there was a demand for payment for goods which were unsolicited. That leaves for consideration whether the appellants had or had not reasonable cause to believe that there was a right to payment and whether they knew that the goods were unsolicited. The time at which the test of knowledge that the goods were unsolicited is gauged must be the time at which the demand for payment was made. It is at that point of time, too, that the issue of whether the accused did or did not have reasonable cause to believe that there was a right to payment has to be determined. The facts are that the letter from the subscriber cancelling the order, and the letter from his solicitors reinforcing the cancellation were in the possession of the company up to the time when the prosecution proceedings were commenced. There is a finding that it was the policy of the appellants not to send out unsolicited copies of the publication or to demand payment from customers for goods not ordered by them or on their behalf, or otherwise deliberately to ignore instructions from their customers. Their system was to feed into a computer all relevant information relating to orders for the publication, including orders of cancellation, and, if the system worked properly in due course the computer in appropriate cases would produce the demand for payment by the individual customer. . . .

There was obviously an initial mistake by someone in the appellants' organisation, as a result of which incomplete information was fed into the computer, and the inaccurate and offending result was produced in consequence of which the demand for payment was sent out. Miss Calkin was at fault in not checking to see whether the customer's instructions were still among the records, and if so whether these were properly implemented in the information produced by the computer. Mr. Holland's secretary was also at fault in not passing to him Miss Calkin's memorandum.

Against that background the competing submissions were made. Counsel for the appellants submitted that the employees who had made the mistakes were so relatively junior in the company's establishment that they could not be said to be acting as the company even if they were acting *for* the company. In that situation two consequences followed. Firstly, it could not be said that the *company* knew that the goods were unsolicited. Secondly, it could not be said that the company had no reasonable cause to believe that there was no right to payment. The Advocate-depute on the other hand argued that since all the relevant information was with the company, i.e., within its organisation, at all material times, it must be held that the company knew that the goods were unsolicited, and that there was in the circumstances no reasonable excuse for the appellants not knowing that there was no right to payment.

What then is the position in relation to a company, which can only operate through its board of directors and employees at different levels?

As I read section 2(1) the prosecution has to prove (1) that a demand for payment was made by the company, (2) that the goods in respect of which the demand was made were unsolicited, and (3) that the company knew that the goods were unsolicited. If the prosecution fails to prove any of these, the prosecution must fail. But even if the prosecution proves all of them, the question of reasonable cause has to be considered. The Advocate-depute accepted that the onus was on the prosecution to establish that there was no reasonable cause. The question of where the onus lies might have been a point worthy of debate, in view of the decision in *Kennedy* v. *Clark*, 1970 J.C. 55, 1970 S.L.T. 260, but since it was not argued, I need not deal with it. In any event it may be that the point is academic here.

It has been found in fact that it was the policy and practice of the company not to send out unsolicited copies of the publication, not to demand from customers payment for goods not ordered by them or on their behalf, and not to ignore deliberately instructions from customers (which would include instructions to cancel a particular order). The company had set up a system of operations, whereby, if it was properly carried out, no improper demand for payment would be made. Here the improper demand for payment was made in respect of unsolicited goods not as a result of anything that was wrong with the company's policy, practice or system of operation, but because of a mistake or mistakes by relatively junior employees as a result of which the company's system of operation broke down, and its policy and practice were defeated. In these circumstances I do not consider that it can be said that the *company* did not have reasonable cause to believe that there was a right to payment. On the contrary I think that it has been shown that the *company* acted in good faith, but were let down by the mistakes of their junior staff. That seems to me to constitute reasonable cause within the meaning of the sub-section.

The facts to which I have adverted clearly show that there was no *mens rea* on the part of the company, or anyone who could be said to be the 'mind' of the company in relation to the dispatch of the demand for payment. The observations of Lord Reid on the position of a company *vis-à-vis* its employees, and the limited circumstances in which the 'mind' of an employee can be said to be the 'mind' of the company *(Tesco Supermarkets Limited* v. *Nattrass* [1972] A.C. 153, at pp. 170) are relevant to this point. I am therefore of the opinion that the Sheriff was wrong in holding that the appellants had no reasonable cause to believe that there was a right to payment. He based this finding on the proposition that the knowledge which was available to junior employees if they had carried out their duties properly can be imputed to the company. In this I think he erred. In the circumstances I find it unnecessary to consider the other aspects of the complaint, and in particular whether the company knew that the goods were unsolicited. I accordingly answer the third and fourth questions of law in the negative, finding it unnecessary to answer the other questions, and move your Lordships to quash the conviction."

Appeal allowed; conviction quashed.

e.   *Causing and permitting*

The main problem (until recently) in this area of law is in cases where the accused did not know of the contravention which he is charged with causing or permitting.

Smith of Maddiston Ltd. v. MacNab
1975 S.L.T. 86

OPINION OF THE COURT (nine judges): "The appellants are a limited company who carry on business as haulage contractors. They were convicted in the sheriff court at Greenock on a complaint that they caused or permitted to be used by their employee, John Lamont, a motor vehicle with an insecure load. On the same complaint, John Lamont pled guilty to using the vehicle whilst in this condition. The complaint bore that both offences were contrary to Regulation 90 (2) of the Motor Vehicles (Construction and Use) Regulations 1973. . . .

At the time of the offence the appellants had hired the vehicle with the driver Lamont for the purpose of transporting an 8-ton tiller from Greenock to Ardrossan. The appellants through their responsible officials knew that in order to secure the load safely and prevent it falling off, a chain and dwang should be used. They did not specifically instruct Lamont to secure the load by this means. He was an experienced driver and had done similar work before. Chains and dwangs were available in the appellants' central store depot. Lamont knew that he could, at any time, draw the equipment he required to secure a load from that depot. The appellants took it for granted that he would know to use a chain and dwang. Lamont did not do so but secured the load by a rope. In the course of the journey the load broke loose and fell off, struck a passing car and injured its occupants. Lamont admitted to the operations manager of the appellants that he had not used a chain and a dwang. He also said he was not satisfied with the way the load had been secured.

The sheriff convicted the appellants on the ground that the decision in *Hunter* v. *Clark*, 1956 J.C. 59, 1956 S.L.T. 188, compelled him to conclude that the obligation imposed by Regulation 90 (2) of the 1973 Regulations as applied by s. 40 (5) of the Act of 1972 is absolute both upon the person who uses the vehicle and the person who causes or permits its use. In the sheriff court the Crown case was presented on the basis that the appellants were guilty if they caused the vehicle to be used although they were unaware that it was being used in breach of the regulation. In view of that, the Solicitor-General stated that he would not argue before this court that the conviction should, in any event, stand because the appellants had not given sufficient directions to Lamont as to how the load should be secured.

The case of *Hunter* v. *Clark* (supra) related to a breach of the Motor Vehicles (Construction and Use) Regulations 1955, made under the Road Traffic Act 1930. Regulation 104 created the offence by stating that if any person used or caused or permitted to be used on any road a motor vehicle in contravention of the regulations he should be liable to penalties. The regulations alleged to be contravened were Regulation 76 relating to the braking system and Regulation 61 relating to the painting of certain markings on vehicles. It was proved that the vehicle was used in contravention of these regulations. There was no proof that the owner knew of the defective brakes. He had given instructions to a painter to paint all his vehicles with the markings required by Regulation 61.

In dealing with the alleged contravention of Regulation 76 the Lord Justice-General stated that, in his view, the matter was analogous to the situation in the seven judge case of *Mitchell* v. *Morrison*, 1938 J.C. 64, 1938 S.L.T. 201. It was this observation which led to the present case being heard before a Bench of nine judges. In *Mitchell* v. *Morrison* (supra) the court were concerned with the provisions of the Road and Rail Traffic Act 1933 and the relevant regulations which required the holder of a licence for the carriage of goods to keep or cause to be kept certain records regarding drivers and others. It was held that these provisions imposed an absolute obligation. This obligation, however, is a direct personal one imposed by Parliament upon the holder of a licence and differs from the obligation considered in *Hunter* v. *Clark* where, as in the present case, the offence consisted in causing or permitting another to use a vehicle in contravention of regulations. *Mitchell* v. *Morrison* does not, therefore, require to be reviewed by this court. The Solicitor-General and counsel for the appellants both accepted this. The distinction between *Mitchell* v. *Morrison* and *Hunter* v. *Clark* was noted in the English case of *Ross Hillman Ltd.* v. *Bond* [1974] Q.B. 435. The analogy sought to be drawn by the Lord Justice-General in *Hunter* v. *Clark* is therefore unsound.

In addition, the Lord Justice-General drew a distinction between causing and permitting as used in Regulation 104. His view was that in the case of causation responsibility remained with the person who caused the use even if he had no knowledge of the use in contravention; whereas permission to use in contravention necessarily involved knowledge of that contravention. We agree with the second part of this proposition but not the first. In our opinion a person cannot permit the use of a vehicle in contravention of a regulation unless he knows or should know of the contravention. In *Hunter* v. *Clark* the Crown conceded that this was correct and, in the present case, the sheriff, following the Lord Justice-General in *Hunter* v. *Clark*, accepted the accuracy of the proposition. Before this court the Solicitor-General did not renew the concession, but in our view the proposition is accurate and is supported by authority. We agree with the opinion of the majority of the court in *James & Son Ltd.* v. *Smee* [1955] 1 Q.B. 78. That case was concerned with Regulation 101 of the Motor Vehicles (Construction and Use) Regulations 1951 which made it an offence for any person to use or cause or permit to be used on a road a motor vehicle in contravention of the regulations. The majority held that a charge of permitting the use in contravention imported a state of mind and required knowledge on the part of the person who permitted not only the use of the vehicle but its use in contravention. Knowledge in this connection includes the state of mind of a man who shuts his eyes to the obvious and allows another to do something in circumstances where a contravention is likely, not caring whether a contravention takes place or not. It may be inferred where the permittor has given no thought to his statutory obligations at all (*Houston* v. *Buchanan*, 1940 S.C. (H.L.) 17, 1940 S.L.T. 232, per Lord Wright, at p. 236).

Accepting that permission requires knowledge in the sense above described it is our opinion that the same consideration must apply to the interpretation of the word 'causes' in s. 40 (5) of the Road Traffic Act 1972. To 'cause' involves some express or positive mandate from the person 'causing' to the other person, or some authority from the former to the latter arising in the circumstances of the case (*Houston* v. *Buchanan* (supra), per Lord Wright, at p. 236; *Shave* v. *Rosner* [1954] 2 Q.B. 113). In *Lovelace* v. *D.P.P.* [1954] 1 W.L.R. 1468, Lord Goddard, C.J. applied this definition to a situation where the licensee and manager of a theatre was convicted of causing to be presented part of a play without the approval of the Lord Chamberlain. The departure from the approved script took place at the instance of one of the actors without the knowledge of the appellant. Indeed, it was contrary to his express instructions to adhere strictly to the script. In allowing the appeal Lord Goddard stated at p. 1471 that if a man is charged with causing or permitting something, it follows that that must result by reason of some act of his which is equivalent to causing, such as a command or direction to do the act. We respectfully agree with this proposition. It follows from it, in our opinion, that a person cannot be said to have caused another to do something in contravention of a regulation without knowledge, actual or constructive, that it will be done in such contravention. This view also appealed to the court in *Ross Hillman Ltd.* v. *Bond* (supra).

For these reasons we do not agree with the distinction drawn by the Lord Justice-General in *Hunter* v. *Clark* between causing and permitting so far as the question of knowledge is concerned. Also, we do not agree with the conclusion of Lord Russell in the same case to the effect that if absence of knowledge were to be an offence the regulations would have said so. In our opinion the correct approach is to construe the regulation in the first instance. If that construction points to absolute liability on the part of the person who merely causes or permits the vehicle to be used on the road, the question of a statutory defence based on absence of knowledge may then be important. We prefer the approach and reasoning of Lord Sorn in his dissenting judgment. His conclusion was that the words 'causes to be used . . . in contravention' contained in Regulation 104 of the 1955 Regulations denote a person who causes not only use but use in contravention.

The Solicitor-General pointed out that in the present case the statutory provision under consideration, viz. s. 40 (5) of the Road Traffic Act 1972, is worded differently from Regulation 104 of the 1955 Regulations considered in *Hunter* v. *Clark*. Section 40 (5) makes it an offence to use on a road a motor vehicle which does not comply with the regulations, or to cause or permit a vehicle to be so used. Regulation 104 provides that if any person uses or causes or permits to be used on any road a motor vehicle in contravention of the defined regulations he shall be liable to penalties. This distinction was not considered by the court in *Ross Hillman Ltd.* v. *Bond*. The Crown argument was that the decision in *Hunter* v. *Clark*, whether correct or incorrect, was not directly relevant to the differently worded s. 40 (5) now being considered. It was said that as a matter of plain construction a breach of that section necessarily followed on proof of two facts—(a) that the vehicle was caused or permitted to be used on a road, and (b) that it did not comply with the regulations. This argument proceeded on the basis that knowledge of the second fact need not be established either in causing or in permitting. *Hunter* v. *Clark* and other Scottish decisions in which such knowledge was recognised as necessary to permitting were decided on a concession to that effect which was not made in the present case. It was also urged that the English decisions on the matter should not be followed. We do not consider that the difference in wording involves a different construction of the words 'causes or permits' in s. 40 (5) to that given to the same words in Regulation 104. Also, for the reasons already given, we are satisfied that a necessary ingredient of permission in this context is knowledge, actual or imputed, not only of the use of the vehicle on a road but of the use of that vehicle which does not comply with the relevant regulation. The Solicitor-General accepted that, if this were so, it is equally a necessary ingredient of causation in the same context and we so conclude.

We allow the appeal and answer the question in the stated case in the negative."

Conviction quashed.

CHAPTER 8

CRIMINAL CAPACITY

a. Non-age

Criminal Procedure (Scotland) Act 1975, ss. 170 and 369

"It shall be conclusively presumed that no child under the age of eight years can be guilty of any offence."

NOTES

Sections 170 and 369 ought not to be construed as meaning that once the age of criminal responsibility is reached the age of a child ceases to be relevant to criminal responsibility. Where, for example, *mens rea* is a necessary element of an offence, the youthfulness of a child even over the age of eight ought to be relevant in determining whether the child formed the requisite criminal intent.

A child who is alleged to have committed an offence may be dealt with by means of a children's hearing under Part III of the Social Work (Scotland) Act 1968 (which is not a criminal proceeding) or by prosecution. The latter course may only be adopted on the instructions of the Lord Advocate or at his instance, and no court other than the High Court or the sheriff court has jurisdiction in such cases (Social Work (Scotland) Act 1968, s. 31 (1)). Criminal prosecutions involving children are governed by the Criminal Procedure (Scotland) Act 1975.

For the above purposes, a "child" is defined, principally, as a person under the age of sixteen years (Social Work (Scotland) Act 1968, s. 30 (1) (*a*)). Presumably a person who is over the age of sixteen, but whose mental age is below sixteen does not fall within the definition. *(Cf. State* v. *Schabert*, 24 N.W. 2d. 846 (1947): on a murder charge, a defendant whose chronological age was 28 years, but whose mental age was only 8 years, sought to avail herself of a rebuttable statutory presumption that children over seven and under twelve years of age were incapable of committing crime. The court held that "age" referred to chronological age.) A case such as this may come within the doctrine of diminished responsibility (see *post*).

b. Insanity

Insanity may arise either as a defence to a criminal charge, or as a plea in bar of trial. In the first case the issue is whether or not the panel's mental condition *at the time of the offence* was such as to justify a verdict of acquittal on the ground of insanity. In the second the issue is whether the panel is presently fit to stand trial, irrespective of his mental condition at the time of the offence.

(i)   The defence

1.   H.M. Advocate v. Kidd
1960 J.C. 61

The panel was charged with the murder of his wife and his daughter by administering chloroform to them and asphyxiating them. A special defence of insanity was raised by the panel. At the trial, Lord Strachan gave the following directions to the jury on the special defence:

LORD STRACHAN: "You are concerned not only with the question of whether the accused committed the acts charged against him; you are also concerned with his mental condition at the time of the alleged offences. It is not suggested that the accused is insane now, and you must proceed upon the footing that he is now sane. If he were insane now he could not have given instructions for his defence, and the case would not have proceeded before you in the form which it has taken. If this special defence that he was insane at the time is established that would mean that even if he did commit the acts charged, he was not responsible for his actions in law, and he could not be convicted of the crimes. . . .

On the question whether the accused committed the acts with which he is charged, the burden of proof lies wholly on the Crown. On the special defence of insanity there is a burden upon the accused, but different considerations apply there, and I shall deal with these later. In the proof of the Crown case, the burden of proof lies wholly on the Crown. It is a fundamental principle of our law that an accused person is presumed to be innocent until he is proved to be guilty. It is for the Crown to prove guilt, and not for the accused to prove his innocence. . . .

The question is—Was he responsible in law for his actions? His special defence is that he was insane. If he was insane he was not responsible, and he could not then be convicted, but he would not of course be set at liberty. If he committed the acts charged and was insane, he would be detained in a way with which you are not concerned. On this matter of the special defence of insanity, the burden of proof lies on the accused. He is presumed to be sane unless he proves that he was insane. It is for the accused to establish his special defence of insanity, but you must particularly note that the standard of proof which is required from the accused is a lower standard than that which you are to require from the Crown. You do not need proof beyond reasonable doubt on this question of insanity. The special defence will be sufficiently established if you think that, on a balance of probabilities, the accused was insane at the time. You are entitled here to base your decision upon the probabilities which in your view arise upon the evidence. In other words, if there is a doubt in your mind between sanity and insanity, you must decide in favour of that which you think is the more probable. The question is, in the light of the whole evidence—Is it probable that the accused was insane? . . .

Well now, has the accused shown that it is probable that he was insane at the time of the acts charged? In answering that question it is obviously necessary that you should know what is meant by insanity in that connexion. What nature and degree of mental illness is sufficient in law to excuse a person from responsibility for his actions? That is a question of law upon which I have to direct you. You have to say whether the accused did in fact suffer from such insanity. . . .

The question really is this, whether at the time of the offences charged the accused was of unsound mind. I do not think you should resolve this matter by inquiring into all the technical terms and ideas that the medical witnesses have put before you. Treat it broadly, and treat the question as being whether the accused was of sound or unsound mind. The question is primarily one of fact to be decided by you, but I have to give you these directions. First, in order to excuse a person from responsibility for his acts on the ground of insanity, there must have been an alienation of the reason in relation to the act committed. There must have been some mental defect, to use a broad neutral word, a mental defect, by which his reason was overpowered and he was thereby rendered incapable of exerting his reason to control his conduct and reactions. If his reason was alienated in relation to the act committed, he was not responsible for that act, even although otherwise he may have been apparently quite rational. What is required is some alienation of the reason in relation to the act committed. Secondly, beyond that, the question in this case whether the accused's mind was sound or unsound is to be decided by you in the light of the evidence, in the exercise of your common sense and knowledge of mankind, and it is to be judged on the ordinary rules on which men act in daily life. Thirdly, the question is to be decided in the light of the whole circumstances disclosed in the evidence. You must have regard to the evidence which has been given by the medical witnesses, but the medical evidence by itself is not conclusive. The question is to be decided by you and not by the mental specialists. In coming to your decision you are entitled, and indeed bound, to regard the whole evidence. You are entitled in particular to consider the nature of the acts committed and the conduct of the accused at and about the relevant times, and his previous history. Those are the directions which I give you on this matter.

At one time, following English law, it was held in Scotland that if an accused did not know the nature and quality of the act committed, or if he did know it but did not know he was doing wrong, it was held that he was insane. That was the test, but that test has not been followed in Scotland in the most recent cases. Knowledge of the nature and quality of the act, and knowledge that he is doing wrong, may no doubt be an element, indeed are an element in deciding whether a man is sane or insane, but they do not, in my view, afford a complete or perfect test of insanity. A man may know very well what he is doing, and may know that it is wrong, and he may none the less be insane. It may be that some lunatics do an act just because they know it is wrong. I direct you therefore that you should dispose of this question in accordance with the directions which I have given, which briefly are, that there must be an alienation of reason in regard to the act committed, otherwise the question is one for you to decide whether the accused was at the time of sound or unsound mind."

NOTES

Lord Strachan's rejection of a test of insanity based on the M'Naghten Rules of English law *(M'Naghten's Case* (1843) 10 Cl. & F. 200) was confirmed by the approach of the Second Division in the civil case of *Breen* v. *Breen,* 1961 S.C. 158 and by the High Court in *Brennan* v. *H.M. Advocate,* 1977 S.L.T. 151 *(post).*

Is it possible to reconcile the statement that "it is for the Crown to prove guilt, and not for the accused to prove his innocence" with the statement that "on this matter of the special defence of insanity, the burden of proof lies on the accused"?

Is the test of legal insanity one of "sound or unsound mind" or is it "alienation of reason in relation to the act committed"? *Cf.* the following case.

2.   **Brennan v. H.M. Advocate**
1977 S.L.T. 151

The appellant was charged with the murder of his father by stabbing him. On the day on which the killing took place the appellant had consumed between twenty and twenty-five pints of beer, a glass of sherry and, about half-an-hour before the killing, a microdot of LSD. A special defence of insanity was lodged on his behalf, and it was also contended that the effect of his self-induced intoxication might be to reduce the quality of the crime from murder to culpable homicide. At the trial, Lord Wylie withdrew the special defence from the jury, and directed them that the evidence of the accused's state of intoxication did not entitle them to return a verdict of culpable homicide. The accused appealed against conviction.

THE COURT (FULL BENCH): "What was said was that the appellant, at the time he stabbed his father, was so much under the influence of the drink and the drug he had taken as to be insane. This case accordingly is one in which the state of the appellant's mind was, according to the evidence, attributable merely to the transitory effects of alcohol and LSD deliberately consumed by the appellant with knowledge, from his previous experience of both, that they were bound to intoxicate him. It will be seen therefore that the first submission for the appellant raises the single and important question whether a temporary impairment of mental faculties, resulting merely from self-induced intoxication, may in our law amount to insanity for the purposes of a special defence such as the appellant tabled in this case. . . .

In the development of the first submission the particular proposition was that if a person suffers total alienation of reason as the result of self-induced intoxication he will be regarded by our law as insane and thus free from any criminal responsibility. On the assumption that this proposition was sound it was then argued that there was evidence on which a jury would have been entitled to hold on a balance of probability that the special defence had been made out.

We ask ourselves first of all the fundamental question: 'What is insanity, according to the law of Scotland, for the purpose of a special defence of insanity at the time?' The question has nothing to do with any popular view of the meaning of the word insanity, nor indeed is it a question to be resolved upon medical opinion for the time being. It is, on the contrary, a question which has been resolved by the law itself as a matter of legal policy in order to set, in the public interest, acceptable limits upon the circumstances in which any person may be able to relieve himself of criminal responsibility.

In discovering what is insanity within the meaning of our criminal law we cannot do better than begin by noticing that Hume treated the nature of the plea, in vol. I, p. 37, of the third edition of his work on *Crimes*, thus: 'Which condition, if it is not an assumed or imperfect, but a genuine and thorough insanity, and is proved by the testimony of intelligent witnesses, makes the act like that of an infant, and equally bestows the privilege of an entire exemption from any manner of pain. . . . I say, where the insanity is absolute, and is duly proved: For if reason and humanity enforce the plea in these circumstances, it is no less necessary to observe such a caution and reserve in applying the law, as shall hinder it from being understood, that there is any privilege in a case of mere weakness of intellect, or a strange and moody humour, or a crazy and capricious or irritable temper. In none of these situations does or can the law excuse the offender: . . . To serve the purpose of a defence in law, the disorder must therefore amount to an absolute alienation of reason . . . such a disease as deprives the patient of the knowledge of the true aspect and position of things about him,—hinders him from distinguishing friend or foe,—and gives him up to the impulse of his own distempered fancy.' It is clear from the discussion which follows that Hume is speaking of absolute alienation of reason in relation to the act charged. It is abundantly clear, too, whatever may be comprehended within the word 'disease' as Hume used it that it does not include deliberate and self-induced intoxication, for in the passage immediately following his treatment of insanity, Hume (p. 45) contrasts insanity with 'that sort of temporary madness, which is produced by excess in intoxicating liquors', and says of the latter: 'certain it is, that the law of Scotland views this wilful distemper with a quite different eye from the other, which is the visitation of Providence; and if it does not consider the man's intemperance as an aggravation, at least sees very good reasons why it should not be allowed as an excuse, to save him from the ordinary pains of his transgression. Not to mention that one cannot well lay claim to favour, on the ground of that which shows a disregard of order and decency. . . .'

We have no doubt that the law as stated by Hume is and has always been the law of Scotland, and neither our own researches, nor those of the learned Solicitor-General and senior counsel for the appellant, have revealed that the accuracy of Hume's statement has ever been called in question. On the contrary it has constantly been accepted and applied, and with the increasing misuse of drugs in these times, it would be wholly irresponsible to alter or modify it in any way. . . .

In short, insanity in our law requires proof of total alienation of reason in relation to the act charged as the result of mental illness, mental disease, or defect or unsoundness of mind and does not comprehend the malfunctioning of the mind of transitory effect, as the result of deliberate and self-induced intoxication."

Appeal refused.

NOTES

To the extent that voluntary intoxication cannot found a plea of insanity at the time of the offence, the charge to the jury in *H.M. Advocate* v. *Aitken*, 1975 S.L.T. (Notes) 86 was disapproved by the court in *Brennan*. See also, *McGowan* v. *H.M. Advocate*, 1976 S.L.T. (Notes) 8.

See below under "intoxication" for the court's views on the appellant's alternative plea.

Is the "absolute" or "total" alienation of reason referred to by the court in *Brennan* a different, or more stringent, requirement than the alienation of reason referred to by Lord Strachan in *Kidd*?

In *Brennan,* Lord Emslie seems to lay more stress on alienation of reason, and less on unsoundness of mind. Is this not a move towards the M'Naghten approach, despite the court's explicit rejection of the Rules? *Cf.* the remarks of the Butler Committee on Mentally Abnormal Offenders (Cmnd. 6244, 1975), para. 18.6: "the main defect of the M'Naghten test is that it was based on the now obsolete belief in the pre-eminent role of reason in controlling social behaviour."

Brennan should also be considered in relation to automatism or "temporary dissociation." See *H.M. Advocate* v. *Ritchie (post), H.M. Advocate* v. *Cunningham (post),* and R. B. Ferguson "Intoxication and Criminal Liability" (1977) 22 J.L.S. 380.

3.   H.M. Advocate v. Harrison
High Court, Dundee, October 1967, *unreported*

The panel was charged with the murder of his father's housekeeper by striking her on the head with an axe. At the trial, he sought to rely on a plea of diminished responsibility, while the Crown led evidence which tended to establish that he was insane at the time of the offence. Expert witnesses described him as having a psychopathic personality and at the time of the killing he was suffering from a depressive illness. He was said to be impulsive and explosive, and there was a possibility that he might commit the same sort of act again.

LORD AVONSIDE: "Ladies and Gentlemen, you have heard the advocate-depute address you on behalf of the Crown and Mr. Bell on behalf of the Panel, and it is now for me to sum up. And I should say at once that this I think is a unique case in this sense, that as I understand it the Crown in effect are pressing for a verdict of acquittal, which would have certain consequences, whereas the Defence are pressing for a verdict of guilty, albeit a verdict of culpable homicide and not of murder. . . .

What [the Crown] assert, and this is essentially a question for your final determination, is that when this act of killing was committed Harrison was insane. Now plainly enough this question only arises if you come to the conclusion that Harrison not only killed [the deceased] but that the act of killing would have been murder if he had been a normal person. If Harrison was insane at the time when the act took place, he was not and is not criminally responsible, because a man who is insane cannot be held to form an intention, open or otherwise, of committing a crime. The question of whether or not Harrison was insane at that time is one which you must determine on the evidence, and your determination of this rests on the balance of probability. And this is not a matter which is

determined beyond reasonable doubt, it is on the balance of probability looking at all the evidence you have heard where does it
swing on this particular issue? Was it insanity or not?"

Verdict: Guilty of culpable homicide.

NOTES

See also (1968) 32 J.C.L. 119. The accused was ordered to be detained in
the state mental hospital without limit of time under ss. 55 and 60 of the
Mental Health (Scotland) Act 1960 (see now ss. 174(3) and 174(4) of the
Criminal Procedure (Scotland) Act 1975).

In both solemn and summary proceedings the prosecutor has a duty to
bring before the court such evidence as may be available of the mental
condition of the accused, where it appears to the prosecutor that that person
may be suffering from mental disorder (1975 Act, ss. 175(2) and 376(5)).

If the Crown were to be successful in obtaining a verdict of not
guilty by reason of insanity in a case such as *Harrison,* by what means could
the accused obtain a review of this finding? He cannot, after all, appeal
against his acquittal. *Cf.* the English Criminal Appeal Act 1968, s. 12 of which
gives a right of appeal in such cases. See also the Second Report of the
Thomson Committee on Criminal Procedure in Scotland (Cmnd. 6218/
1975), paras. 52-18 to 52-23. (It should be noted that although an accused
cannot appeal against an acquittal on the ground of insanity he may appeal
against a hospital order made pursuant to such a finding: 1975 Act, s. 280,
and see *Smith* v. *H.M. Advocate,* 1980 S.L.T. (Notes) 56.)

The above case suggests that the standard of proof of insanity remains
that of a balance of probabilities where the Crown raises the issue. Ought
this to be so?

(ii)　The plea in bar of trial

1.　**H.M. Advocate v. Brown**
1907 S.C. (J.) 67

The panel was charged with the murder of a woman who had eaten a
piece of shortbread containing poison which the panel had sent to
the deceased's employer for his consumption. At the first diet
before the sheriff, the procurator fiscal produced a certificate
signed by two doctors certifying that the accused was not fit to plead
to the indictment because of unsound mind. The sheriff reserved
the matter for the High Court at the second diet and did not call
upon the accused to plead. At the second diet, counsel for the
Crown informed the court that the panel's mental condition had not
changed. Counsel for the panel objected to the intervention, stating
that his client had instructed him, and wished to be tried.
(Full Bench)

LORD JUSTICE-GENERAL (DUNEDIN): "It seems to me quite clear from the decided cases that from a very early period the court considered it always competent, if they thought it expedient, to make an inquiry into the state of a prisoner's sanity with the view of seeing whether the prisoner should be allowed to plead, which, of course, is the first step to be taken in order to his being put on trial. The source of the information which in the various cases prompted the Court to take that course seems to have varied, but I agree with the Solicitor-General when he said that neither at common law nor under the Lunacy Act of 1857 is there any limitation to these sources of information. The counsel for the prisoner sought to distinguish the decided cases, with the exception of the case of *Robertson*, 3 White 6, from the present case, upon the ground that in all the other cases the source of information was either what may be called an outside source or was a source of information which the Court derived from its own eyes and ears. *Robertson's* case, Mr Hunter maintained, was badly decided. I am satisfied that the power of the Court in this matter is well settled. I am also satisfied that the conduct of the Crown in this case was not only justified but was in every respect eminently proper, because it seems to me that if the Crown had in their possession certificates from doctors to the effect of the certificate produced, it would not have been right to have left the Court in ignorance of the contents of these certificates. But it does not seem to me that that ends the matter. It is not a rule binding on the Court to order an investigation where a prisoner's sanity is put in question. It is a question of expediency, and I think that the Court having got information from any source—from the Lord Advocate or anyone else— must always decide in each particular case, and upon the circumstances of that particular case, as to the expediency of going on with a preliminary investigation. . . . The prisoner is defended by an eminent member of the Bar in whom your Lordships have confidence, and he has been able to say that he has received instructions from the prisoner personally, and although he very properly declined to take up the position of a medical expert, he stated to your Lordships upon his professional responsibility that the instructions which he received from the prisoner were just such instructions, as far as he could judge, as a sane man would give. He informed your Lordships that there was no reason, as far as he could see, why the prisoner should not be allowed to plead, that the prisoner had given sane instructions for his defence, and on behalf of the prisoner he intimated his wish that the trial should proceed. In these circumstances I think it would be inexpedient that your Lordships should, against the wish of the prisoner, proceed to have a preliminary investigation. If the absence of such an investigation could make any difference in the long run my opinion would be very much altered, because if it is the case that the prisoner is truly in the condition in which these doctors' certificates say he was, then undoubtedly he ought not to be subjected to trial, and still less ought he to be punished for the offence if he committed it. But it is quite clear that the absence of a preliminary investigation will not make any difference in the long run because of the provisions of the Act of 1857. Taking sections 87 and 88 of that Act together, it is perfectly clear that if this trial proceeds the jury will be able to follow one or other of several courses. They will be able to say at the conclusion of the evidence, if they reach that result, that the prisoner is insane at the present moment, and if they say so that will end the matter; or they will be able, without saying that he is insane at the present moment, to find that he did not commit the crime, and that also will end the matter; or they will be able to say that he did commit the crime, and that he was insane at the date when he committed it, and that also will end the matter. These three courses exhaust the possibilities of the case. . . . I hold that each case must depend on its own circumstances, and that in the present case it would not be expedient to have a preliminary inquiry."

The panel pleaded not guilty, and the trial proceeded before the Lord Justice-General and a jury. In charging the jury his Lordship gave the following directions as to how the question of insanity should be disposed of.

LORD JUSTICE-GENERAL: "If you come to the conclusion that the ravages of the disease are such that it cannot be said that this man is in the same condition that a sane man would be, and that he is not able to tell fully about his actions, then you are bound to state that he is insane, and not proceed to the other portion of the case. . .

The first question you must answer is, Is the prisoner now insane? If you answer that question in the affirmative, you must not, whatever you think, proceed to any of the other questions."

> Verdict: The jury were unanimously
> of the opinion that the accused was
> presently insane.

NOTES

Is it any advantage to the accused to dispense with a preliminary inquiry into his fitness to plead if, after the evidence has been led, the jury must decide this issue before considering the rest of the evidence? What should the jury do if they consider that the accused is unfit to plead but that on the evidence he has a good defence? *Cf.* the Criminal Procedure (Insanity) Act 1964, s.4(2), which allows in England the issue of fitness to be postponed

until any time up to the opening of the case for the defence, and see also
Roberts (1953) 37 Cr. App. R. 86. The Thomson Committee (Second
Report) made proposals for a new Scottish procedure to overcome this
problem (see paras. 52.14 *et seq.*).

2.   H.M. Advocate v. Wilson
1942 J.C. 75

The panel was charged with robbery and murder. There was
evidence that not only was he almost completely deaf and dumb,
but also that he suffered from a state of feeble-mindedness, and
considerable difficulty was encountered in communicating with
him. No plea of unfitness was raised by the panel whose counsel
contended that he was fit to be tried. The issue was, however, put to
the High Court as a preliminary question, by way of certification by
the trial judge. The court elected to let the issue go to the jury at the
trial. In charging the jury Lord Wark gave the following directions
on the issue of fitness:

LORD WARK: "Now what exactly is meant by saying that a man is
unfit to plead? The ordinary and common case, of course, is the case
of a man who suffers from insanity, that is to say, from mental
alienation of some kind which prevents him from giving the instructions which a sane man would give for his defence, or from following
the evidence as a sane man would follow it, and instructing his
counsel as the case goes along upon any point that arises. Now, no
medical man says, and no medical man has ever said, that this
accused is insane in that sense. His reason is not alienated, but he
may be insane for the purposes of the section of the Lunacy Act to
which counsel referred, although his reason is not alienated, if his
condition be such that he is unable either from mental defect or
physical defect, or a combination of these, to tell his counsel what
his defence is and instruct him so that he can appear and defend
him; or if, again, his condition of mind and body is such that he does
not understand the proceedings which are going on when he is
brought into court upon his trial, and cannot intelligibly follow what
it is all about."

3.   Russell v. H.M. Advocate
1946 J.C. 37

The appellant was charged with a series of frauds extending over a
period of more than three years. At the first diet she lodged a plea in
bar of trial that she was suffering from hysterical amnesia and was
on that account unable to plead to the libel or give instructions for
her defence. At her trial the presiding judge held a preliminary

inquiry into the issue of her fitness to plead. Having heard evidence from medical witnesses to the effect that she had no recollection of events from the period during which the frauds were allegedly committed, but that she was mentally normal at the time of the trial, his Lordship repelled the plea. The panel was convicted, and appealed on the ground that the presiding judge misdirected himself in refusing to sustain the plea in bar of trial.

LORD JUSTICE-CLERK (COOPER): "The onus is always on the accused to justify a plea in bar of trial, and to do so not to the satisfaction of expert witnesses but to the satisfaction of the Court; and it appears to me that the evidence summarised above was insufficient to support the plea, and, indeed, that it was in the main incompetent and inadmissible. I cannot see how the basis in fact for such a plea, directed as it proved to be to showing that a sane accused person was now handicapped in her defence by a partial loss of memory, could ever be established without adducing the accused as a witness for examination and cross-examination, or without adducing the husband and nurse on whose statements, reported as hearsay, the doctors proceeded. Nor do I think that such an inquiry could properly be concluded without investigation into the facts and circumstances of the course of criminal conduct alleged to have been forgotten. The presiding Judge would doubtless have been deeply affected by these considerations but for the remarkable attitude of the Crown. So far from attacking the value or contesting the sufficiency of the evidence adduced in support of the plea, the Advocate-Depute, apparently on instructions, contented himself with perfunctory cross-examination directed to minor points, and tendered (though he did not prove) a report by another medical witness (Dr Garrey) which he stated was to a like effect as the evidence already led. In effect (and later almost in so many words), the Crown thus admitted that the facts on which the plea rested were sufficiently established. Not only so, but the Advocate-Depute further intimated that he could not seriously contest that the plea, so stated and supported, was a 'good' plea in bar of trial, and the argument was ultimately directed to the question what order should be pronounced on the plea being sustained.

The presiding Judge was thus placed in a position of serious difficulty. The Lord Advocate is master of the instance, and he can, if he so determines on his own responsibility, depart from any criminal charge. But in relation to an important question of criminal law and practice now admitted to be unprecedented in the history of this Court, I do not consider that the Crown can properly invite a judicial decision on the basis of admissions of crucial facts which are not proved, and of concessions of equally crucial legal principles; for to do so is in effect to ask that on certain unvouched hypotheses the Court should submissively interpone authority to an administrative decision taken in the Crown Office. Before us the Solicitor-General accepted this position, for he completely repudiated the attitude of the Advocate-Depute and executed a double *volte-face* by contending (*a*) that the plea was not a good plea in bar of trial, and (*b*) that in any event it was unsupported by evidence.

What the presiding Judge actually did was to accept the conceded basis of the plea in fact but to reject the concession in law, holding that the plea, though in his view vouched in fact, was not a good plea in bar of trial. He indicated, however, that it would be open to the accused to tell the jury that she had now no recollection of the events forming the subject of the charges and to lead corroborative evidence. On the accused being called upon to plead, counsel adhered to the plea of not guilty but tendered in addition a special defence to the effect that at the time of the crimes libelled the accused was suffering from hysterical amnesia and was not responsible for her actions, and that she was still so suffering and was unable to instruct her defence. As the presiding Judge had formally repelled the plea in bar of trial, the second branch of this special defence should not have been put to the jury.

Though no point is taken as to the subsequent proceedings, we have thought it right to obtain a transcript of the Judge's charge in order to see what eventually happened. From this it appears that the medical evidence on hysterical amnesia was led over again to the jury with the addition of the evidence of Dr Garrey and of the accused herself; that there was no evidence at all to justify the first branch of the special defence; but that the attention of the jury was pointedly directed to the evidence as to alleged loss of memory— *not* as bearing upon the question whether the appellant was a fit object for trial, but as increasing the onus on the Crown to prove the charges, and the obligation on the jury to see to it that the appellant suffered no prejudice from her handicap, assuming they held the handicap to be real and not feigned. . . .

It is, I think, plain from the unbroken practice followed from the earliest dates to which our records extend that, in dealing with pleas in bar of trial founded on some abnormal condition in the accused, the Court has balanced against each other two major considerations, viz., (1) fairness to the panel, who should not be tried if and so long as he is not a fit object for trial, and (2) the public interest which requires that persons brought before a criminal Court by a public prosecutor should not be permitted to purchase complete immunity from investigation into the charge by the simple expedient of proving the existence at the diet of trial of some mental or physical incapacity or handicap. When fairness to the accused requires that the trial should not then and there proceed, the public interest equally requires that the accused should not there and then be virtually acquitted untried. That is the only principle which can be derived from the consistent practice of our law, and it is a salutary and necessary principle. It is possible that the advance of certain branches of medical science may lead to the presentation of new reasons in fact as the basis of pleas in bar of trial of this type, but whatever its basis in fact no such plea in bar can by our law result in the panel's unconditional discharge.

It remains to deal with the extreme argument in theory presented for the appellant. That argument, founded on Lord Dunedin's charge to the jury in *Brown*, 1907 S.C. (J.) 67 [*ante*], was that no person can be tried who cannot not only intelligently but 'without obliteration of memory as to what has happened in his life, give a true history of the circumstances of his life at the time the supposed crime was committed' or who 'cannot tell his counsel, with the certainty of not being deceived, what he was really doing at the time'. These *dicta* are to be found in a case in which the Crown had produced a medical certificate by two doctors to the effect that the accused was in the full sense insane, and in which the jury ultimately held the accused to be 'now insane,' with the result that he was ordered to be detained during His Majesty's pleasure. I do not consider that they were intended to be understood, or capable of being understood, literally as applying to the case of a sane prisoner—in this case one whom all the medical witnesses adduced have pronounced to be completely sane and normal—for so to read them would come near to paralysing the administration of criminal justice. On any such reading the plea in bar would require to be sustained in most cases in which the accused has been under the influence of drink, or had sustained a head injury, at the time of the crime, or even if he was naturally a person of unreliable memory. I am confident that Lord Dunedin would have been the first to repudiate the idea that the law of Scotland is concerned only to investigate and punish crimes of the perpetration of which the criminal has a perfect recollection on which his counsel can 'with certainty' rely. It has further to be kept in view that the appellant's theory will not fit the fact that mental deficiency cannot be pleaded as a plea in bar—*Breen*, 1921 J.C. 30—though many classes of mental defectives, such as idiots and imbeciles, could never satisfy Lord Dunedin's *dictum*. Further, weakmindedness, sufficient to reduce murder to culpable homicide or to justify other inferences of reduced responsibility, has never been a plea in bar, while intoxication, unless so extreme as to render the accused incapable of forming the requisite criminal intent, will not even suffice to reduce murder to culpable homicide, whatever its effects on the reliability of the accused's memory of the crime—*Kennedy,* 1944 J.C. 171.

The conclusions which I feel bound to draw are that loss of memory may be an important element in leading to the conclusion that a panel is insane within the meaning of section 87 of the Lunacy (Scotland) Act, 1857. But if it falls short of that, loss of memory in a person otherwise normal and sane plays its full part, if it is sufficiently proved, in increasing the onus on the Crown and in raising doubts to which it may be the duty of a jury to give effect in a verdict of acquittal after investigation of the whole case. But as our law stands, it can have no further or other effect. I would only add that in such a case the onus of proof of loss of memory is necessarily a very heavy one when, as in this case, it rests ultimately on the assertion of a person with a powerful motive to feign or exaggerate a condition incapable of objective test.

Returning in the light of these observations to the question of the disposal of this appeal, I repeat that the only issue properly before us, is whether the presiding Judge ought to have sustained the plea as a plea in bar of trial and to have discharged the appellant as if she had been tried and acquitted. To this question I consider that there can only be a negative answer. The appellant could only succeed by satisfying us (*a*) that the facts on which she relies are proved; (*b*) that these facts, if established, reveal·in the circumstances of this case such a degree of unfairness to the appellant that she was not a fit object for trial; and (*c*) that she should have been set at liberty unconditionally and free from liability to trial at any future time. In my view, she has failed on all three heads. I desire to add that, in view of the unusual and in some respects unsatisfactory course which the proceedings took, we have anxiously examined the case from a much wider standpoint than was required by the single ground of appeal presented to us, and that, in common with your Lordships, I am satisfied that no miscarriage of justice occurred. The appeal should therefore be refused.

This is the opinion of the Court."

Appeal refused.

NOTES

Russell was followed by the Court of Criminal Appeal in the case of *R.* v. *Podola* [1960] 1 Q.B. 325. The question of amnesia in relation to a defence of insanity at the time was fully discussed in *H.M.Advocate* v. *Kidd,* 1960 J.C. 61, noted *ante.* In that case Lord Strachan directed the jury that amnesia, if established on the evidence, was an important element to be considered in deciding whether the accused was sane or insane at the time of the offence, and could have the effect of lessening the burden on the accused in establishing his special defence of insanity.

A successful plea of insanity in bar of trial is not the equivalent of an acquittal. The accused may, *e.g.*, be detained under a hospital order and, indeed, may later be put on trial should he recover his sanity. (See, e.g., *H.M. Advocate* v. *Bickerstaff*, 1926 J.C. 65).

c. *Diminished responsibility*

This plea of mental abnormality verging on, though not amounting to, insanity, has an interesting history. "Invented" in its modern form by Lord Deas in *Alex Dingwall* (1867) 5 Irv. 466, it developed steadily until the early post-war period, at which stage there was a marked retrenchment. The plea was adopted into English law by the Homicide Act 1957 (s.2), where it has continued to develop in marked contrast to its status in Scots law.

1.   Carraher v. H.M. Advocate
1946 J.C. 108

The appellant was charged with the murder of a man by stabbing him. Evidence was led at the trial to the effect that the appellant suffered from a psychopathic personality, and that on the day in question he had taken a considerable amount of drink. He was convicted of murder and appealed. The circumstances of the appeal are outlined by the Lord Justice-General who gave the opinion of the High Court (Full Bench).

LORD JUSTICE-GENERAL (NORMAND): "I come next to the question of diminished responsibility. The ground of appeal here is that the presiding Judge erred in his directions to the jury on the issue of diminished responsibility. The facts are that there was evidence that the appellant had that evening taken a considerable amount of drink, and that there was also evidence of opinion by medical men that he was suffering from a psychopathic personality which they said was associated with diminished responsibility. The presiding Judge's direction on diminished responsibility is as follows:— 'The accused, as I say,is perfectly sane, but our law does recognise, and it is a comparatively recent introduction into our law, that, if a man suffers from infirmity or aberration of mind or impairment of intellect to such an extent as not to be fully accountable for his actions, the result is to reduce the quality of the evidence in a case like this, which, if you think so, would be otherwise murder, to reduce it to culpable homicide.'

That is an adequate formulation of the law as it has been recognised in previous decisions. The learned Judge then goes on to describe by reference to previous decisions the essential elements in diminished responsibility. He quotes from an opinion of the Lord Justice-Clerk in *Braithwaite's* case. (*H.M. Advocate* v. *Braithwaite,* 1945 J.C. 55). The Lord Justice-Clerk there cites with approval the following passage from the charge of Lord Justice-Clerk Alness in *Savage's* case (*H.M. Advocate* v. *Savage,* 1923 J.C. 49): 'It is very difficult to put it in a phrase, but it has been put this way: that there must be aberration or weakness of mind; that there must be some form of mental unsoundness; that there must be a state of mind which is bordering on, although not amounting to, insanity; that there must be a mind so affected that responsibility is diminished from full responsibility to partial responsibility—in other words, the prisoner in question must be only partially accountable for his actions. And I think one can see running through the cases that there is implied that there must be some form of mental disease.' The presiding Judge in a later passage directed the jury to treat as tests of the responsibility possessed by the appellant these elements which he had taken from previous decisions. Another element was a condition of partial insanity, and yet another the existence of a condition of great mental peculiarity of mind.

He dealt with the medical evidence in this case, and he says that the evidence of one of the witnesses was to the effect that he was inclined to place the accused in the category of a psychopathic personality; that a psychopathic personality is a clinical condition in which are included persons who from childhood or early youth show all the gross abnormality in their social behaviour and emotional reaction, and who do not as a rule show enough insanity to be certifiable as insane; that, broadly speaking, it is a condition in which there is an inability on the part of the person affected to adapt himself to the ordinary social conditions, that it is usually less than certifiable insanity, and that it is associated with emotional instability. The charge also reminds the jury of this passage in the evidence of the same witness:— 'If you asked me does the accused know the difference between right and wrong intellectually, does he know if he commits a wrong act he is liable to punishment, I say yes, and then he is responsible, but if responsibility means that he has a proper appreciation of his social responsibility, that he is capable of resisting temptation, capable of exercising control over his actions, then, in my opinion, he is not as responsible as a normal person.'

The presiding Judge, after a direction dealing with the question of drink, comes back again to the question of diminished responsibility, and he says:— 'On the remaining elements which the doctors described as amounting to diminished responsibility they referred to various peculiarities which they said they found in the accused, or at least suspected, that he did not seem to appreciate the consequences of the charge hanging over him, that he had difficulty in resisting temptation, that he could not withstand frustration, and the description, you may remember, was such that it led me to ask whether there were not a great many people in this country who do not act just as good citizens, and whether he would include these in the category of psychopathic personality, and he said "Yes".' The learned Judge felt, as he says, difficulty about remitting this evidence for consideration to the jury as a ground for reducing the charge from one of murder to one of culpable homicide. I also have great doubt whether it was evidence of anything approaching to mental disease, aberration or great peculiarity of mind, and whether the Judge might not have been warranted in withdrawing the issue from the jury. The Court has a duty to see that trial by judge and jury according to law is not subordinated to medical theories; and in this instance much of the evidence given by the medical witnesses is, to my mind, descriptive rather of a typical criminal than of a person of the quality of one whom the law has hitherto regarded as being possessed of diminished responsibility."

Appeal refused.

NOTES

If the decision in *Carraher* did not put an end to the development of the doctrine of diminished responsibility it imposed severe restraints upon it, particularly in relation to the psychopathic personality. See, however, *H.M. Advocate* v. *Gordon* (1967) 31 J.C.L. 270, which suggests that in some cases the Crown is prepared to ignore *Carraher* in this respect. *Cf.* the development of the doctrine in English law after the Homicide Act 1957. See, for example, *R.* v. *Byrne* [1960] 2 Q.B. 396: Smith & Hogan, p. 181.

2.   **H.M. Advocate v. Braithwaite**
1945 J.C. 55

The panel was charged with the murder of his wife by stabbing her after a quarrel. Evidence was led to support a plea of diminished responsibility.

LORD JUSTICE-CLERK (COOPER) [His Lordship quoted the passage from *H.M. Advocate* v. *Savage* mentioned above and similar tests, and then continued:] "To carry the matter just a stage further in view of the evidence, . . . I am going to take the responsibility of telling you, in so many words, that it will *not* suffice in law for the purpose of this defence of diminished responsibility merely to show that an accused person has a very short temper, or is unusually excitable and lacking in self-control. The world would be a very convenient place for criminals and a very dangerous place for other people if that were the law. It must be much more than that. . .

If the Crown have established that the accused did this thing, it is not for the Crown to go further and show that he was fully responsible for what he did; it is for the accused to make good his defence of partial responsibility, and that means that he must show you that the balance of probability on the evidence is in favour of the view that his accountability and responsibility were below normal."

Verdict: Guilty of murder.

3. H.M. Advocate v. Macleod
1956 S.L.T. 24

The panel was charged with the murder of his wife. It was contended on his behalf, *inter alia,* that at the time of the killing he was under the influence of drink and suffering from diminished responsibility. In the course of his charge to the jury the presiding judge gave the following directions:

LORD HILL WATSON: "My direction is in these terms, if a man is not shown by the evidence to be within the category of one with a diminished responsibility when sober he cannot place himself within the category of diminished responsibility by taking drink. That is a direction in law, and I give you that. My view is this on the law, because it was definitely done in that case about psychopathic personality (*Carraher* v. *H.M. Advocate,* (*ante*)) that you had to leave drink out of account, that if you found upon the evidence that this man suffered from a diminished responsibility without any question of drink at all then that would be a good defence, but if on the evidence you came to the conclusion that this diminished responsibility resulting in what he calls these blackouts only arises when the man takes drink then it is not diminished responsibility as known to the law of Scotland, and it would be your duty not to give effect to that plea. . . . You see, there is a recognised category of diminished responsibility that is a ground in the law of Scotland for reducing a charge of murder to one of culpable homicide, but if an accused person can only seek to take advantage of that doctrine by proving that he took drink, even if only a little drink, and so lost the restraint which he otherwise would have had, then that in the law of Scotland does not amount to a good defence of diminished responsibility."

NOTES

Certain of the statements in *Carraher* v. *H.M. Advocate* on the issue of intoxication must be read with caution in the light of *Brennan* v. *H.M.*

Advocate (see below). As regards the relationship between intoxication and diminished responsibility, however, *Brennan* confirms *Macleod*. Cf. *R.* v. *Fenton* (1975) 61 Cr.App.R. 261.

For evidential and procedural problems involved in setting up diminished responsibility, see *Gemmill* v. *H.M. Advocate*, 1979 S.L.T. 217.

d. *Intoxication*

Brennan v. H.M. Advocate
1977 S.L.T. 151

(For the facts of this case, see above under "Insanity.")

THE COURT: "The second and alternative submission for the appellant was that in any event the trial judge should have left to the jury the possibility of returning a verdict of guilt of culpable homicide because, it was said, there was evidence on which the jury would have been entitled to conclude that the appellant was intoxicated to such a degree that he was deprived of all capacity to form the 'specific intent' which is of the essence of the crime of murder.

The argument for the appellant in support of this submission was necessarily founded upon the cases of *H.M. Advocate* v. *Campbell* (1921 J.C. 1) and *Kennedy* v. *H.M. Advocate* (1944 J.C. 171) in which it was said that, according to the law of Scotland, if a man accused of murder was shown to have been incapable, by reason of self-induced intoxication, of forming the intention to kill or do serious injury to the deceased, he will be guilty only of culpable homicide. According to these cases the laws of Scotland and England are the same on this matter, and attention was drawn to the case of *D.P.P.* v. *Beard* [1920] A.C. 479, the judgment in which has recently been explored and explained in the case of *D.P.P.* v. *Majewski* [1977] A.C. 443 to which reference has already been made. Before us the correctness of the statements of the law to be found in *Campbell* and *Kennedy* was challenged by the Crown and fully debated, but before we come to examine these cases it is, we think, important to remind ourselves of the law as it clearly appeared to be when Campbell went to trial on 27 September 1920, and to notice certain differences between the laws of Scotland and England.

As we have already shown, impairment of the mental faculties of an accused person caused merely by self-induced intoxication however gross the impairment may be, is not insanity in our law. Further, proof of the mere effects of such intoxication, whatever their degree, cannot in our law support a defence of diminished responsibility—a defence available only where the charge is murder and which, if it is established, can result only in the return of a verdict of guilt of the lesser crime of culpable homicide. In both branches, insanity and diminished responsibility, the attitude of the law of Scotland has accordingly been entirely consistent, and has remained true to the sound general rule enunciated by Hume and Alison that self-induced intoxication is no defence to any criminal charge, at least for an offence in itself perilous or hurtful. In these circumstances it would be surprising if our law were to admit proof of self-induced intoxication as a defence to a charge of murder in circumstances in which it could not be held that the criminal responsibility of the accused was in law diminished.

The law of England as we understand it was until the late 19th century at one with the law of Scotland in refusing to countenance self-induced intoxication as any kind of defence to a criminal charge, and embarked upon the same search for a modification and mitigation of the law in those cases where the only penalty for the crime of murder was capital. In Scotland the search led to the recognition of the concept of diminished responsibility as early as 1867 in the case of *H.M. Advocate* v. *Dingwall,*—a concept which was only introduced into the law of England by statute in the latter half of this century. In England, it appears, the law took a different route and the formula adopted was that of permitting, where the charge was murder, a verdict of guilty of manslaughter to be returned where it was shown that the effects of self-induced intoxication had deprived the accused of all capacity to form the 'specific intent' which had to be proved to establish the crime of murder *(D.P.P.* v. *Beard).* This relaxation was, it seems, applied to all crimes involving proof of 'specific intent' as distinct from 'basic intent' but to no others, and the rule in *Beard* which was conceived in the days of capital punishment has rightly been recognised as illogical. We have only to add that in crimes of 'basic intent' we understand the law of England to be at one with the law of Scotland in refusing to admit self-induced intoxication as any kind of defence.

The next matters to be noticed before we proceed to an examination of the cases of *Campbell* and *Kennedy* are these. Our law has never recognised a distinction between 'specific' and 'basic' intent in crime. Further, the definition of the crime of murder in Scotland is not the same as the definition of that crime in the law of England. In England the crime involves 'malice aforethought', a technical expression which requires proof of either the specific intention to kill or to do serious injury. In the law of Scotland, however, the crime of murder is constituted by any wilful act causing the destruction of life whether intended to kill or displaying such wicked recklessness as to imply a disposition depraved enough to be regardless of the consequences. Our definition of murder includes the taking of human life by a person who has an intent to kill or to do serious injury or whose act is shown to have been wickedly reckless as to the consequences.

The case of *Cawthorne* v. *H.M. Advocate*, 1968 S.L.T.330, where the charge was of attempted murder by a man who fired rifle shots at random into a room where he knew that there were several persons, is a good example of actings so wickedly reckless that if they resulted in the taking of life the crime would be murder. The charge of the trial judge in that case was affirmed by the court on appeal and the following passage appears in the opinion of the Lord Justice-General (Clyde) at p.331: 'The crimes of murder and attempted murder are common law crimes in Scotland and I do not find it helpful to seek to draw analogies from alien systems of law where the rules may for various reasons be different. The issue must be determined by the rules applicable to Scots law. In our law murder is constituted by any wilful act causing the destruction of life (Macdonald, *Criminal Law* (5th ed.), p 89). The mens rea which is essential to the establishment of such a common law crime may be established by satisfactory evidence of a deliberate intention to kill or by satisfactory evidence of such wicked recklessness as to imply a disposition depraved enough to be regardless of consequences. (See Macdonald in the same passage.) The reason for this alternative being allowed in our law is that in many cases it may not be possible to prove what was in the accused's mind at the time, but the degree of recklessness in his actings, as proved by what he did, may be sufficient to establish proof of the wilful act on his part which caused the loss of life.'

Finally we must dispel any suspicion that what was said in *Campbell* and *Kennedy* was merely an echo of a passage in the charge of the Lord Justice-Clerk in *McDonald*, in which he directed the jury that 'if the means adopted were not of themselves likely to lead to bad results and if there were no malice aforethought then the fact that the man was in a drunken state may be considered in determining the question between murder and culpable homicide'. The initial hypothesis presented to the jury is of crucial importance: (1) absence of malicious or criminal intent to kill; and (2) use of modes of assault not of themselves likely to lead to bad results. The case of *McDonald* therefore lays down and professes to lay down no general principle of law, and the direction is one related precisely to a particular combination of facts. It might indeed have been argued that without any evidence of drunkenness that combination of facts would have made a verdict of culpable homicide a proper one.

We come now to the case of *Campbell*. In that case the Lord Justice-Clerk was dealing with a charge of murder by violent blows of the fist. There was no evidence to support a contention that the accused was in any way suffering from mental disease or disorder causing total or partial alienation of reason related to the crime charged. The only alleged mitigating circumstance was the accused's intoxication at the time of the event. It was pleaded for the accused that his drunkenness was of such a degree as to warrant the jury in returning a verdict of culpable homicide. The report bears that 'Counsel for the Crown contended that the drunkenness of the accused did not reduce the crime from that of murder to culpable homicide. Reference was made to *H.M. Advocate* v. *McDonald* and *Director of Public Prosecutions* v. *Beard.*' It also appears that counsel for the accused founded on the passage in the charge in *McDonald* which we have already examined. There is in the report no trace of any argument that *Beard* did not represent the law of Scotland and in directing the jury without having had the advantage of a full debate or further examination of the relevant Scots authorities on the place of self-induced intoxication in our law, the Lord Justice-Clerk said this: 'If a man strikes and wounds another and a fist may be just as dangerous, if it is sufficiently used, as a weapon—if he strikes him in such a way and kills him there and then on the spot, with the intent to kill, that is murder. But it is also the law that if a man proceeds to strike another fellow-being, it may be without the intent to kill, but with the intent to cause serious injury, then, although he did not mean to kill, or had no intention of killing, if he struck with the intent to bring about serious injury, and the result is that his victim died, then that too is murder. The question which you have to consider is whether from the blows which this man undoubtedly inflicted upon this woman, his wife, who was six months gone in pregnancy at the time—whether he had the intention to cause her serious injury. If you think he was so drunk that he could not form any intention about it, you may reduce it to culpable homicide; the question for you is, was he so drunk as to be incapable of forming any intention on the subject, or was there any other intention on the part of this man but to cause serious injury to the woman.'

Later he referred to the case of *Beard* and said this: 'Quite recently there was a very important case . . . decided in England, by the House of Lords, where this question came up as to what was the effect of drunkenness when a man had killed a fellow human being, and the case was considered of such importance that it was dealt with by eight judges in the House of Lords. Two of them were Scotsmen, one being a Scottish lawyer, Lord Dunedin, and the other Lord Haldane, and one judgment was delivered expressing

the views of the whole Court. On this matter there is no difference
between the law of England and the law of Scotland. It would be
most unfortunate indeed if, as to the effect of drunkenness, where
injuries are due to the violence of a drunk person, there was such a
difference; but there is no difference at all. The result of that case
may be summed up thus—that insanity, of course, is a complete
answer, to this effect, that the man or person who has committed a
crime cannot be found guilty if he was insane at the time even
though the insanity is caused by drink, and he will be dealt with as an
insane person; but so far as drunkenness was concerned, their
lordships said this, that evidence of drunkenness which renders the
accused incapable of forming the specific intent required to
constitute the crime—that is in this case the intention to kill or to do
serious injuries—should be taken into consideration with the other
facts proved in order to determine whether or not he had that
intention.'

From our examination of the charge as a whole and in particular
the passages we have quoted it is plain that the Lord Justice-Clerk
omitted to notice that *Beard* was a special case not involving a need
to prove specific intent as that is understood by the law of England
for by that law, differing from the law of Scotland, it was only
necessary to show that the act of causing death was done in furtherance of rape. He omitted to notice also that the definition of murder
in Scotland is not the same as that of the law of England and that the
concept of 'specific intent' is only intelligible if the crime may only
be constituted by proof of actual intention to kill or do serious
injury. Further he gave no reasons why what was said in *Beard*
coincided with the law of Scotland, unless perhaps it was because
two of the eight judges were Scotsmen! Finally he did not appreciate
that there was no trace in the law of Scotland before 1920 of
self-induced intoxication being a recognised defence to a charge of
murder, and that evidence of the effects of such intoxication, by
itself, was not even admitted by our law to be a foundation for a plea
of diminished responsibility. The charge accordingly contained for
the first time a proposition of law contrary to the whole tract of
previous authority on the subject, and inconsistent with the broad
general principle upon which self-induced intoxication had always
been treated in the law of Scotland. If according to our law the mens
rea in murder may be deduced from the wicked recklessness of the
actings of the accused, it is extremely difficult to understand how
actings may lose the quality of such recklessness because the actor
was in an intoxicated state brought about by his own deliberate and
conscious purpose. . . .

The case of *Campbell* was however approved in the later case of
Kennedy, but here again it was apparently agreed by both prosecu-

tion and defence for the purposes of the argument that the law with regard to the effects of drunkenness upon criminal responsibility was accurately set out in *Campbell. Kennedy* involved a charge of murder by stabbing, and the defence was that the verdict should be one of culpable homicide in respect of the accused's drunkenness which, it was maintained, had deprived him of the capacity to form the specific intent to kill or inflict serious injury. The presiding judge refused to allow that plea to be considered by the jury on the ground that, in his opinion, there was no relevant evidence to support it. The appeal was concerned only with the question whether the judge was entitled to take the course he did. It is clear therefore that the appeal was conducted before the Full Bench of five judges of eminence and long experience upon agreement and concession as to the applicability of the law as it was stated in *Campbell's* case and as to the applicability in Scotland of the ratio of *Beard.* This is expressly recorded in the Lord Justice-General's opinion. In particular there was no reference at all to, or examination of, the differences and distinctions between the elements which constitute the crime of murder in the criminal law of Scotland, and those which, according to *Beard,* constitute that crime in England. More important still, there was no discussion or examination of the applicability to the law of Scotland of the distinction drawn in *Beard's* case between crimes of 'specific intent' of which murder is apparently one, and all other crimes described as crimes of 'basic intent'. We have already pointed out how inappropriate that distinction is in any proper consideration of the crime of murder in the law of Scotland. In the result, notwithstanding the great weight which is normally to be accorded to any statement of the law by Lord Justice-General Normand and his distinguished colleagues, we are unable to find in *Kennedy's* case any more sound foundation for the law stated in *Campbell.* We have no doubt that the law was therein incorrectly stated, and that what was said in *Beard's* case as to the effect of self-induced intoxication in relation to a charge of murder, does not and never did represent the law of Scotland. There is nothing unethical or unfair or contrary to the general principle of our law that self-induced intoxication is not by itself a defence to any criminal charge, including in particular the charge of murder. Self-induced intoxication is itself a continuing element and therefore an integral part of any crime of violence, including murder, the other part being the evidence of the actings of the accused who uses force against his victim. Together they add up or may add up to that criminal recklessness which it is the purpose of the criminal law to restrain in the interests of all the citizens of this country.

For the reasons we have given, the learned trial judge gave directions to the jury which were entirely in accordance with our law and which were in the circumstances properly given. We shall accordingly refuse the appeal.''

Appeal refused.

NOTES

Is it possible to argue that the decision in *Brennan* only extends to those offences which can be committed recklessly? Would intoxication be a defence to a charge of, say, assault, which requires intention? (see below, ch. 10).

Would the adoption of such a view involve one in saying that *Brennan* holds gross intoxication as being equivalent to recklessness. Is that what the case says? Suppose X kills Y while grossly intoxicated, but in circumstances which would otherwise point to a verdict of culpable homicide. What verdict ought to be returned?

e.   Automatism

1.   Simon Fraser
(1878) 4 Couper 70

The panel was charged with the murder of his eighteen-month-old son by fracturing his skull. A special plea was entered that at the time the crime was committed the panel was asleep. The panel stated that he had had a nightmare during which he believed he was being attacked by an animal. He had a history of somnabulism, accompanied on occasions by violent behaviour. Medical witnesses, however, disagreed on the question of his sanity. In addressing the jury:

THE LORD JUSTICE-CLERK: "I suppose, gentlemen, you have not the slightest doubt that the prisoner at the time was totally unconscious of the act that he was doing. There is not the slightest doubt that he was labouring under one of those delusions which occurred in a state of somnambulism—he was under the impression that some animal had got into the bed. I see no reason to doubt, and I do not suppose you, gentlemen, have any doubt, that the account as given is correct. It is a matter of some consequence to the prisoner whether he is found responsible or not, because you are aware that his future must to a great extent depend upon the verdict you shall return. The question whether a state of somnambulism such as this is to be considered a state of insanity or not is a matter with which I think you should not trouble yourselves. It is a question on which medical authority is not agreed. But what I would suggest is, that you should return a verdict such as this—that the Jury find the panel killed his child, but that he was in a state in which he was unconscious of the act which he was committing by reason of the condition of somnambulism, and that he was not responsible."

> The jury returned a verdict in accordance with the above direction.

NOTES

Fraser was dismissed from the bar, having given an undertaking to sleep alone in future. What action was open to the court if he refused to give such an undertaking, or failed to abide by it, is not clear. A similar approach has, however, been sanctioned by a Full Bench of the High Court (see *H.M. Advocate* v. *Hayes,* November 1949, *unreported, post*).

2. H.M. Advocate v. Ritchie
1926 J.C. 45

The panel was charged with the culpable homicide of a pedestrian by reckless driving. A special defence was tendered to the effect that "by the incidence of temporary mental dissociation due to toxic exhaustive factors he was unaware of the presence of the deceased on the highway and of his injuries and death, and was incapable of appreciating his immediately previous and subsequent actions." In the course of his charge to the jury, the presiding judge gave the following directions:

LORD MURRAY: [After a summary of the facts] "Now, however, you have to consider the more difficult aspect of the case—the special defence, which is a somewhat novel one, based upon the alleged abnormal and irresponsible condition of the accused at the time of the accident. Such irresponsibility may create criminal immunity and form the ground of a good defence; but there is a strong presumption in favour of normality and responsibility. The presumption may be overcome, but the onus of proof lies, as indeed was conceded by counsel for the defence, upon the person who pleads that he is abnormal and irresponsible.

Turning now to the question of a man's responsibility or irresponsibility for his actions, irresponsibility need not be confined to what to us is the most familiar example, viz., the case of a person who is, in popular language, 'out of his mind'. It may be useful for me to remind you of the general basis on which the defence of irresponsibility rests. Putting it in language which is both legal and intelligible, it amounts to this, that, owing to some disordered condition of the mind which affects its working, the afflicted person does not know the nature of his act, or, if he does know what he is doing he does not know that what he is doing is wrong. The most familiar case is where reason has been upset and the person is, in common parlance, out of his mind, a condition which may be permanent or passing. This condition may be induced by various causes. It may be congenital; it may be induced by illness, fever, palsy, accident, injury, or shock; all these may induce a condition in which, in popular language, a man is 'not fully responsible for his action'. This condition may be brought about by a man's own action, *e.g.* over-indulgence in drink; but in the present case I am glad to say we are relieved from considering that question, as both sides are in agreement that the question of drink does not enter into the case. It being then the law that there may be irresponsibility—temporary or permanent— where the reason is so affected as to make the person who has committed the act unaware of the nature of his act, I must remind you shortly of conditions which fall short of inferring irresponsibility. As was pointed out by counsel for the Crown, there are certain things which will not excuse. If a person, being normal, runs over someone because he did not see him, the fact that he did not see the person he ran over affords no excuse, for the law holds that he ought to have seen him. If a person is abnormal, in the sense merely that he is below the ordinary or average standard, that affords no excuse. The degree of care which the law imposes is always proportionate to the risk of the operation. In the event of an accident it would be no defence for a man to say, 'I happened to be tired and rather exhausted and therefore less attentive'. It would be no defence for a woman to say, 'I had overestimated the strength of my nerves; a situation arose in which my nerves were unequal to the strain, and that was the cause of the accident'. The law says to such persons that they were bound to take account of such possibilities. But where the defence is that a person, who would ordinarily be quite justified in driving a car, becomes—owing to a cause which he was not bound to foresee, and which was outwith his control— either gradually or suddenly not the master of his own action, a question as to his responsibility or irresponsibility for the con- sequences of his action arises, and may form the ground of a good special defence. The question, accordingly, which you have to determine is whether, at the time of the accident, the accused was or was not master of his own action. So put the question becomes a pure question of fact.

Now it is not disputed that there may be such a thing as a condition of irresponsibility induced by what has been referred to as mental dissociation. The admission, however, of the possibility of such a condition does not relieve the case of difficulty. As regards the period immediately following the accident, it is common ground between the factors examined on behalf of the Crown and the accused respectively that the actions of the accused during this period are typical of a state of mental dissociation. The period to which you must turn your attention is the crucial period which elapsed from the time the accused left the young lady at her door until the moment of the accident. What happened thereafter, it is common ground, may be regarded as typical of mental dissociation. You must draw your conclusions as best you can from the facts, as the question you have to decide does not admit of definite proof. Upon the facts proved you must decide whether after leaving the young lady and until the accident, the accused, being then in a normal condition, was just driving carelessly and inattentively, and whether it was not the shock of the accident which induced a state of dissociation; or whether, on the contrary, the state of dissociation, which admittedly existed after the accident, was not a continuation of a state which had existed prior to the accident, and which had supervened and was in operation from some time after the accused left the young lady at her house. On leaving her house did something supervene in the mind and condition of the accused for which he was not responsible and which he could not foresee, and did this something exist at the time of the accident; or is the true view that it was not until after the accident that the abnormality supervened? That appears to me to be the problem with which you are confronted. Admittedly, the facts in the case are open to more than one interpretation. For instance, take the question of excessive speed. It is within your knowledge that persons, who as a rule are careful, are sometimes careless, and it is a perfectly rational view of the facts in this case that we have here an instance of a careful man betrayed from mere fatigue into a situation in which he was not paying proper attention. On the other hand, as the defence contends, the apparent carelessness may not have been carelessness at all, but the result of some abnormal influence at work in the accused from some time after he left the young lady and became the sole occupant of the car. It is between these two views you have got to choose, and I shall now touch on the facts which I think you should keep in mind as bearing on the situation. [His Lordship reviewed the facts, drawing the jury's attention, *inter alia,* to the marked inconsistency between the reckless and apparently callous conduct of the accused at the time of, and immediately after, the accident and the character and record of the accused up to that date.]

Upon the question of the form of verdict which you are to return, it would be competent for you, under my direction, to return a special verdict; but I prefer the course suggested by counsel for the defence, that you should return a general verdict. If there were no question of abnormality in the case, I have little doubt your verdict would be one of guilty, but the question of abnormality is present and must be dealt with. If you think that, at the time of the accident, the accused was master of his own actions, it is your duty to return a verdict of guilty. If, on the other hand, you think that the condition of mental dissociation, which admittedly was present after the accident, was also actively present prior to the accident, then your view would preclude the existence of culpability on his part. If you affirm irresponsibility there can be no culpability, and the proper verdict for you to return is one of 'not guilty'. I do not think that there is any difficulty on the law of the case, but only on its application to the facts. The question you have to solve is really one of fact, and it is for you to arrive at a just inference from the facts laid before you."

Verdict: Not guilty.

NOTE

The directions in *Ritchie* are in accordance with the principle that where an offence consists of conduct, that conduct must be voluntary, and the accused's plea—"non-insane automatism"—leads logically to the result achieved in this case, *i.e.*, simple acquittal.

3.   H.M. Advocate v. Hayes
High Court, November 1949, *unreported*

The accused was charged on an indictment which libelled culpable homicide, or alternatively reckless driving, contrary to s. 11 of the Road Traffic Act 1930. The facts alleged were that he was the driver of a bus which, due to his neglectful driving, collided with two stationary vehicles and overturned, killing some of the passengers, and injuring several others. A special defence was tabled to the effect that the accused pleaded not guilty "and further pleads . . . that at the time the crime charged is said to have been committed by the incidence of temporary dissociation due to masked epilepsy or other pathological condition, he was unaware of the presence of the stationary motor lorries with which the motor bus driven by him collided."

The presiding judge (Lord Carmont) directed the jury that in returning their verdict they should answer the following questions:

(1)   Has the Crown proved against the accused the charge of culpable homicide, or the alternative charge of reckless driving, and if so, which?

If the answer to question 1 is that either charge has been proved, the jury must go on to answer the following question:

(2)   Do you find the special defence proved or do you not so find?

The jury found the charge of culpable homicide proved against the accused, and also found the special defence proved. After some debate as to the effect of the jury's findings the verdict was allowed to stand. In respect of the difficulty occasioned by the findings of the jury, as to their correct interpretation and the consequent disposal of the case, Lord Carmont, in accordance with a memorandum previously issued by the Lord Justice-General, certified the case to the High Court (Full Bench).

OPINION OF THE COURT: "If we had been left in any doubt as to the true effect of the verdict returned by this jury under the special circumstances which have been described by Lord Carmont, it would have been necessary to re-affirm the salutary rule that, once a verdict has been recorded and assented to, it is no longer open to challenge or discussion except through the medium of an appeal under the Act of 1926. That, however, is a matter which has ceased to be significant in this case, because it is sufficiently plain from the record and from the shorthand note that the view of the jury was that, if the pannel had been a normal man, they would have found him guilty of culpable homicide, but that they were satisfied on the medical evidence that the special defence was established and therefore that he was not a normal man. It is on the footing that that was the jury's conclusion that we approach the question as to the advice we should give to Lord Carmont as to his duty in this case.

We are faced, as always happens in these cases, with a twofold responsibility, our duty to the pannel on the one side, and our duty to do what in us lies for the protection of the public interest on the other side; and the proposal I am about to announce is the one that seems appropriate in this case but is by no means to be regarded as a necessary precedent in any other case. Our advice is that, if the pannel will give an undertaking of the type indicated by his learned counsel, namely, that he will now surrender his public service licence and his driving licence and undertake that he will engage no more in driving cars or public service vehicles of any kind, he should be discharged from the bar; and we also consider that an intimation of the decision should be sent to the Licensing Authority and to the Road Traffic Commissioners. With that conclusion and advice we shall adjourn to enable Lord Carmont to carry through the concluding stages of the trial."

NOTES

The method of disposal is in essence the same as that employed in *Simon Fraser (ante)*. Subject to the problem of enforcing such undertakings, it seems that the solution adopted by the court is not unattractive.

While the court was at pains to point out that it did not wish its decision to be adopted as a necessary precedent, it is submitted that it should have received more serious consideration by the court in *H.M. Advocate* v. *Cunningham*, 1963 J.C. 80 *(post)*, where a similar plea was in effect rejected. This is particularly so in view of the fact that it is a decision of seven judges, and the court in *Cunningham* were at pains to point out that the case of *Ritchie (ante)*, which they refused to follow, was a decision of a single judge.

4.   H.M. Advocate v. Cunningham
1963 J.C. 80

LORD JUSTICE-GENERAL (CLYDE): "The panel in this case is indicted on three charges. In the first place, he is charged with taking and driving away a motor van without the owner's consent or other lawful authority, contrary to section 217 of the Road Traffic Act, 1960; secondly, he is charged with reckless driving and causing his vehicle to mount the footpath and collide with several persons (one of whom was so severely injured that he died immediately thereafter), contrary to section 1 of the Act; and the third charge is that he was unfit to drive through drink or drugs, contrary to section 6(1) of the Act.

The panel pleaded 'not guilty' and has tabled what is described as a 'special defence', that, throughout the period during which the crimes libelled are said to have been committed, he was not responsible for his actings on account of the incidence of temporary dissociation due to an epileptic fugue or other pathological condition.

When the case came before the High Court in Glasgow, the presiding Judge reported it to this Court, as the Crown had challenged the competency and meaning of such a 'special defence'. By the law of Scotland a 'special defence', if established to the satisfaction of a jury, leads to a verdict of 'not guilty'. The onus of proving such a defence is, of course, upon the defence, but, if that onus is discharged, the verdict is one of 'not guilty'. The categories of special defences are well known and have long been recognised in our law. As I see it, the so-called 'special defence' in the present case constitutes an attempt to extend the categories of special defences in order to include a new one, namely, something short of insanity, which would lead to an acquittal. For this I can see no warrant in principle. On the contrary, as has been pointed out more than once in previous cases, such a novel type of special defence would be a startling innovation which could lead to serious consequences so far as the safety of the public is concerned. After all, that safety is one of the considerations to which we have to have regard when we are asked to sanction a complete acquittal, if a defence of this nature is sustained by the jury on the facts.

In my opinion, this present defence is not a competent special defence at all. To constitute a valid special defence the proof of the factors in it should lead to a verdict of 'not guilty'. Proof of all the factors in the present special defence would not, in my opinion, justify a verdict of not guilty. On the contrary, these factors only bear upon mitigation of sentence and not upon guilt. It follows, therefore, in my view, that the case of *H.M. Advocate* v. *Ritchie* [*ante*] where an opposite view was taken by Lord Murray sitting alone, was wrongly decided. To affirm, or even extend, that decision would lead to laxity and confusion in our criminal law which could do nothing but harm.

It follows that if this present so-called special defence is to be made into a true special defence, as understood in the law of Scotland, it would require to include an averment of insanity at the time the offence was committed. If that were pleaded and if that defence were sustained by a jury, the verdict would be acquittal and a finding in terms of the Mental Health (Scotland) Act, 1960, requiring the panel's detention in a state hospital. Any mental or pathological condition short of insanity—any question of diminished responsibility owing to any cause, which does not involve insanity—is relevant only to the question of mitigating circumstances and sentence. An argument was presented to us in regard to diminished responsibility. But diminished responsibility is a plea applicable to murder. It is not open in the case of a lesser crime such as culpable homicide or of a contravention of section 1 of the Road Traffic Act, 1960. In my view, accordingly, the so-called special defence is not a competent special defence at all. At the very highest, it only raises matters which are appropriate for consideration in relation to sentence."

NOTES

Cunningham has been subjected to much criticism (see, generally, Gordon, paras. 3-18 to 3-27.) Is the objection to treating automatism of the *Cunningham* variety as legal insanity? (In *H.M. Advocate* v. *Mitchell,* 1951 J.C. 53 an accused, charged with murder, pleaded insanity. He alleged that at the time of the offence he was in a state of unconsciousness due to a condition described as "psychic epilepsy." The Lord Justice-Clerk directed the jury that if they accepted this plea he could not be held responsible and they should acquit him on the ground of insanity.) Or is the objection to the failure to distinguish between insane and non-insane automatism? (This distinction was drawn to the attention of the court by the advocate-depute who distinguished *Ritchie* on the ground that his dissociation was due to external factors.) Would it in fact be possible for someone in Ritchie's situation to plead insanity today, in view of the decision in *Brennan (ante)?*

5.   Farrell v. Stirling
1975 S.L.T. (Sh.Ct.) 71

The driver of a car was involved in a collision with another vehicle. He failed to stop, and having driven on for about another four miles he collided with two more vehicles. He was charged, *inter alia*, with driving without due care and attention contrary to s.3 of the Road Traffic Act 1972. Evidence was led in his defence to the effect that he was a diabetic and at the time of the incidents he was suffering from hypoglycaemia.

THE SHERIFF (A.L. STEWART): "So far as the charges under s. 3 were concerned, the solicitor for the Crown submitted and the solicitor for the accused conceded that mens rea or criminal intention was not a necessary ingredient for a contravention of s. 3. In my view this is correct. Section 3 imposes absolute liability on any person who 'drives' in the manner described in the section. Both parties agreed further that the standard to be applied was an objective one and there was really no dispute that the driving of the accused's car fell within the manner described in the section.

The only question which, in my opinion, arises in the present case is whether the accused was at the time of the three collisions 'driving' his car. Prima facie he clearly was. He was sitting in the driving seat and his hands and feet were controlling the movements of the vehicle. If, however, the evidence showed that the movements of the vehicle were the result of no action of conscious will on the part of the accused, he could, in my opinion, not be said to be driving within the meaning of s. 3 and would therefore be entitled to acquittal. The state where a person is in apparent control of the vehicle but in fact has no voluntary control over his actions or the movements of the vehicle has been described as 'automatism' but that is a word without any clearly defined meaning (see, e.g., the case of *Watmore* v. *Jenkins* [1962] 2 Q.B. 572) and I prefer not to use it.

I was referred to several authorities and I have taken the opportunity to look at certain other authorities to which I was not referred. The Crown founded on the case of *H.M. Advocate* v. *Cunningham,* 1963 S.L.T. 345 as authority for the proposition that the accused's state of mind, where insanity was not alleged, was not relevant. *Cunningham* [*ante*], is, of course, a decision which is binding on me although I must say that it reaches a conclusion with which I have little sympathy. However, I am not persuaded that it is a decision which has relevance to the present case. In the first place, it was concerned with the competency of a special defence, and a special defence properly so called is a concept unknown in summary procedure. Secondly, the decision of the court in *Cunningham* was, in my opinion, appropriate to a case where the Crown required to prove mens rea, but not a case such as the present where criminal intention is irrelevant. In this connection I refer to Professor Gordon's *Criminal Law*, at pp. 252-3, where the learned author indicates his opinion that insanity at the time of the alleged crime may be irrelevant in an offence of strict responsibility. I agree with him that, as a matter of practice, insanity would almost certainly be accepted as a defence to such a charge, but it would not be logical to do so. I appreciate that at p. 69 of the same work Professor Gordon indicates that in his view *Cunningham* is relevant to a case such as the present, but I must, with respect, disagree with him for the reasons which I have set forth above.

The case, most similar to the present, to which I was referred was *Watmore* v. *Jenkins* (cit. supra). In that case the court placed considerable weight on a finding-in-fact by the justices to the effect that the defendant continued to perform the functions of driving after a fashion after the commencement of the state of hypo- glycaemia, and on the fact that there was no specific finding that during the relevant period the defendant's actings were involuntary or unconscious. The decision reached by the court appears to have depended very much on the particular facts stated and the case cannot, in my opinion, be put forward as an authority for the proposition that a state of hypoglycaemia is not a possible defence to a charge such as the present one. Rather, I take it to suggest that a person is entitled to be acquitted if he is in such a state and the evidence shows that the movements of his hands, body and legs in 'driving' were involuntary and wholly uncontrolled by any conscious effort of will on his part.

I have looked at the case of *Hill* v. *Baxter* [1958] 1 Q.B. 277 which again depended on its own particular facts but which confirms the proposition that a person can be in the driving seat without 'driving' within the meaning of s. 3. I was referred to Wilkinson's *Road Traffic Offences* (7th edition), at pp. 21 and 219. The position adopted by the English courts in such cases as *Hill* (supra) and *Watmore* is there summarised.

The only other Scottish case to which I was referred was *Stevenson* v. *Beatson*, 1965 S.L.T. (Sh.Ct.) 11. In that case Sheriff Peterson deals with the question of onus of proof of a state of automatism and concludes that the onus is on the accused to prove it on a balance of probabilities. In my opinion this is not correct. The approach which recommends itself to me and which I have adopted in this case is that laid down by the High Court in the recent case of *Lambie* v. *H.M. Advocate*, 1973 S.L.T. 219 in relation to a special defence, viz., that if the evidence led is believed or creates a reasonable doubt in the mind of the court the Crown case must fail and the accused must be entitled to a verdict of acquittal. As I have already indicated, what is involved here is not a special defence but the principle in my view must be the same. I bear in mind, of course, that the general rule enunciated in *Lambie* (supra) does not apply to a special defence of insanity at the time of the alleged crime, but, as I have already indicated, such a special defence would logically be irrelevant in a case, such as this, of strict liability."

Verdict: Not guilty.

NOTES

Is the sheriff's attempt to exclude *Cunningham* from strict liability offences convincing? If, because of automatism, the accused's conduct lacks the basic requirement of voluntariness does it matter whether the offence is one of strict liability or requires proof of *mens rea*? The basic question seems to be this: Is insane automatism insanity (which affects *mens rea*) or automatism (which affects voluntariness as well as *mens rea*)? Which approach did the sheriff adopt?

6. Bratty v. Attorney-General for Nothern Ireland
[1963] A.C. 386

The appellant was charged with murder. At his trial he pleaded that he was not guilty because at the time of the offence he was in a state of automatism due to an attack of psychomotor epilepsy, or alternatively that he was insane within the M'Naghten Rules. The presiding judge refused to leave the plea of automatism to the jury, but left the plea of insanity to them. The jury convicted the appellant of murder. On appeal:

LORD DENNING: "My Lords, in the case of *Woolmington* v. *Director of Public Prosecutions* [1935] A.C. 462 at p. 482 Viscount Sankey L.C. said that: 'when dealing with a murder case the Crown must prove (a) death as the result of a voluntary act of the accused and (b) malice of the accused'. The requirement that it should be a voluntary act is essential, not only in a murder case, but also in every criminal case. No act is punishable if it is done involuntarily: and an involuntary act in this context—some people nowadays prefer to speak of it as 'automatism'—means an act which is done by the muscles without any control by the mind, such as a spasm, a reflex action or a convulsion; or an act done by a person who is not conscious of what he is doing, such as an act done whilst suffering from concussion or whilst sleep-walking. The point was well put by Stephen J. in 1889: 'Can anyone doubt that a man who, though he might be perfectly sane, committed what would otherwise be a crime in a state of somnambulism, would be entitled to be acquitted? And why is this? Simply because he would not know what he was doing', see *R.* v. *Tolson* (1889) 23 Q.B.D. 168 at p. 187. The term 'involuntary act' is, however, capable of wider connotations and to prevent confusion it is to be observed that in the criminal law an act is not to be regarded as an involuntary act simply because the doer does not remember it. When a man is charged with dangerous driving, it is no defence for him to say 'I don't know what happened. I cannot remember a thing,' see *Hill* v. *Baxter* [1958] 1 Q.B. 277. Loss of memory afterwards is never a defence in itself, so long as he was conscious at the time; see *Russell* v. *H.M. Advocate* (1946 J.C. 37); *R.* v. *Podola* [1960] 1 Q.B. 325. Nor is an act to be regarded as an involuntary act simply because the doer could not control his impulse to do it. When a man is charged with murder and it appears that he knew what he was doing, but he could not resist it, then his assertion 'I couldn't help myself' is no defence in itself, see *Attorney-General for South Australia* v. *Brown* [1960] A.C. 432: though it may go towards a defence of diminished responsibility, in places where that defence is available, see *Reg.* v. *Byrne* ([1960] 2 Q.B. 396): but it does not render his act involuntary so as to entitle him to an unqualified acquittal. Nor is an act to be regarded as an involuntary act simply because it is unintentional or its consequences are unforeseen. When a man is charged with dangerous driving, it is no defence for him to say, however truly, 'I did not mean to drive dangerously'. There is said to be an absolute prohibition against that offence, whether he had a guilty mind or not, see *Hill* v. *Baxter* [1958] 1 Q.B. 277 per Lord Goddard C.J. But even though it is absolutely prohibited, nevertheless he has a defence if he can show that it was an involuntary act in the sense that he was unconscious at the time, and did not know what he was doing, see *H.M. Advocate* v. *Ritchie*, 1926 J.C. 45, *Reg.* v. *Minor* (1955) 15 W.W.R. (N.S.) 433) and *Cooper* v. *McKenna, Ex parte Cooper* [1960] Qd. R. 406.

Another thing to be observed is that it is not every involuntary act which leads to a complete acquittal. Take first an involuntary act which proceeds from a state of drunkenness. If the drunken man is so drunk that he does not know what he is doing, he has a defence to any charge, such as murder or wounding with intent, in which a specific intent is essential, but he is still liable to be convicted of manslaughter or unlawful wounding for which no specific intent is necessary, see *Beard's* case.

Again, if the involuntary act proceeds from a disease of the mind, it gives rise to a defence of insanity, but not to a defence of automatism. Suppose a crime is committed by a man in a state of automatism or clouded consciousness due to a recurrent disease of the mind. Such an act is no doubt involuntary, but it does not give rise to an unqualified acquittal, for that would mean that he would be let at large to do it again. The only proper verdict is one which ensures that the person who suffers from the disease is kept secure in hospital so as not to be a danger to himself or others. That is, a verdict of guilty but insane.

Once you exclude all the cases I have mentioned, it is apparent that the category of involuntary acts is very limited. So limited, indeed, that until recently there was hardly any reference in the English books to this so-called defence of automatism. There was a passing reference to it in 1951 in *Rex* v. *Harrison-Owen* ([1951]2 All E.R. 726) where a burglar, who broke into houses, said that he did not know what he was doing. . . . The next is the singular case of *Reg.* v. *Charlson* ([1955] 1 W.L.R. 317). Stanley Charlson, a devoted husband and father, hit his ten-year-old son on the head with a hammer and threw him into the river and injured him. There was not the slightest cause for the attack. He was charged with causing grievous bodily harm with intent, and with unlawful wounding. The evidence pointed to the possibility that Charlson was suffering from a cerebral tumour in which case he would be liable to a motiveless outburst of impulsive violence over which he would have no control at all. Now comes the important point—no plea of insanity was raised, but only the defence of automatism. Barry J. directed the jury in these words: 'If he did not know what he was doing, if his actions were purely automatic and his mind had no control over the movement of his limbs, if he was in the same position as a person in an epileptic fit then no responsibility rests upon him at all, and the proper verdict is "Not Guilty".' On that direction the jury found him not guilty. In striking contrast to *Charlson's* case is *Reg.* v. *Kemp* ([1957] 1 Q.B. 399). A devoted husband of excellent character made an entirely motiveless and irrational attack upon his wife. He struck her violently with a hammer. He was charged with causing grievous bodily harm. It was found that he suffered from hardening of the arteries which might lead to a congestion of blood in the brain. As a result of such congestion, he suffered a temporary lack of consciousness, so that he was not conscious that he picked up the hammer or that he was striking his wife with it. It was therefore an involuntary act. Note again the important point—no plea of insanity was raised but only the defence of automatism. Nevertheless, Devlin J. put insanity to the jury. He held that hardening of the arteries was a 'disease of the mind' within the M'Naughten Rules and he directed the jury they ought so to find. They accordingly found Kemp guilty but insane...

It is to be noticed that in *Charlson's* case and *Kemp's* case the defence raised only automatism, not insanity. In the present case the defence raised both automatism and insanity. And herein lies the difficulty because of the burden of proof. If the accused says he did not know what he was doing, then, so far as the defence of automatism is concerned, the Crown must prove that the act was a voluntary act, see *Woolmington's* case. But so far as the defence of insanity is concerned, the defence must prove that the act was an involuntary act due to disease of the mind, see *M'Naughten's* case [*ante*]. This apparent incongruity was noticed by Sir Owen Dixon, the Chief Justice of Australia, in an address which is to be found in 31 Australian Law Journal, p. 255, and it needs to be resolved. The defence here say: Even though we have not proved that the act was involuntary, yet the Crown have not proved that it was a voluntary act: and that point at least should have been put to the jury.

My Lords, I think that the difficulty is to be resolved by remembering that, whilst the *ultimate* burden rests on the Crown of proving every element essential in the crime, nevertheless in order to prove that the act was a voluntary act, the Crown is entitled to rely on the *presumption* that every man has sufficient mental capacity to be responsible for his crimes: and that if the defence wish to displace that presumption they must give some evidence from which the contrary may reasonably be inferred. Thus a drunken man is presumed to have the capacity to form the specific intent necessary to constitute the crime, unless evidence is given from which it can reasonably be inferred that he was incapable of forming it, see the valuable judgment of the Court of Justiciary in *Kennedy* v. *H.M. Advocate* (1944 J.C. 171) which was delivered by Lord Normand. So also it seems to me that a man's act is presumed to be a voluntary act unless there is evidence from which it can reasonably be inferred that it was involuntary. To use the words of Devlin J. the defence of automatism 'ought not to be be considered at all until the defence has produced at least prima facie evidence,' see *Hill* v. *Baxter;* and the words of North J. in New Zealand 'unless a proper foundation is laid,' see *Reg.* v. *Cottle* ([1958] N.Z.L.R. 999). The necessity of laying the proper foundation is on the defence: and if it is not so laid, the defence of automatism need not be left to the jury. . . .

What, then, is a proper foundation? The presumption of mental capacity of which I have spoken is a provisional presumption only. It does not put the legal burden on the defence in the same way as the presumption of sanity does. It leaves the legal burden on the prosecution, but nevertheless, until it is displaced, it enables the prosecution to discharge the ultimate burden of proving that the act was voluntary. Not because the presumption is evidence itself, but because it takes the place of evidence. In order to displace the presumption of mental capacity, the defence must give sufficient evidence from which it may reasonably be inferred that the act was involuntary."

Appeal dismissed.

7.   Regina v. Quick and Paddison
[1973] Q.B. 910

The appellants were nurses at a mental hospital. They were charged with assault occasioning actual bodily harm to one of the patients. They both pleaded not guilty and Quick, a diabetic, relied on a defence of automatism. The evidence suggested that at the time of the assault he was in a state of hypoglycaemia, possibly due in part to his failure to follow medical advice. The trial judge ruled that this defence was one of insanity, rather than automatism. Quick changed his plea to guilty, and Paddison was convicted of aiding and abetting him. On appeal:

LAWTON L.J. [His Lordship considered the circumstances of the case, and the English and Commonwealth authorities, and continued]: "In this quagmire of law seldom entered nowadays save by those in desperate need of some kind of a defence, *Bratty* v. *Attorney-General for Northern Ireland*[1963] A.C. 386, 403, 412, 414 provides the only firm ground. Is there any discernible path? We think there is. Judges should follow in a common sense way their sense of fairness. This seems to have been the approach of the New Zealand Court of Appeal in *Reg.* v. *Cottle* [1958] N.Z.L.R. 999, 1011 and of Sholl J. in *Reg.* v. *Carter* [1959] V.R. 105, 110. In our judgment no help can be obtained by speculating (because that is what we would have to do) as to what the judges who answered the House of Lords' questions in 1843 meant by disease of the mind, still less what Sir Matthew Hale meant in the second half of the 17th century. A quick backward look at the state of medicine in 1843 will suffice to show how unreal it would be to apply the concepts of that age to the present time. Dr. Simpson had not yet started his experiments with chloroform, the future Lord Lister was only 16 and laudanum was used and prescribed like aspirins are to-day. Our task has been to decide what the law means now by the words 'disease of the mind'. In our judgment the fundamental concept is of a malfunctioning of the mind caused by disease. A malfunctioning of the mind of transitory effect caused by the application to the body of

some external factor such as violence, drugs, including anaes-
thetics, alcohol and hypnotic influences cannot fairly be said to be
due to disease. Such malfunctioning, unlike that caused by a defect
of reason from disease of the mind, will not always relieve an
accused from criminal responsibility. A self-induced incapacity will
not excuse, see *Reg.* v. *Lipman* [1970] 1 Q.B. 152, nor will one
which could have been reasonably foreseen as a result of either
doing, or omitting to do something, as, for example, taking alcohol
against medical advice after using certain prescribed drugs, or
failing to have regular meals while taking insulin. From time to time
difficult border line cases are likely to arise. When they do, the test
suggested by the New Zealand Court of Appeal in *Reg.* v. *Cottle*
[1958] N.Z.L.R. 999, 1011 is likely to give the correct result, viz.,
can this mental condition be fairly regarded as amounting to or
producing a defect of reason from disease of the mind?

In this case Quick's alleged mental condition, if it ever existed,
was not caused by his diabetes but by his use of the insulin
prescribed by his doctor. Such malfunctioning of his mind as there
was, was caused by an external factor and not by a bodily disorder in
the nature of a disease which disturbed the working of his mind. It
follows in our judgment that Quick was entitled to have his defence
of automatism left to the jury and that Bridge J.'s ruling as to the
effect of the medical evidence called by him was wrong. Had the
defence of automatism been left to the jury, a number of questions
of fact would have had to be answered. If he was in a confused
mental condition, was it due to a hypoglycaemic episode or to too
much alcohol? If the former, to what extent had he brought about
his condition by not following his doctor's instructions about taking
regular meals? Did he know that he was getting into a hypoglycaemic episode? If yes, why did he not use the antidote of eating
a lump of sugar as he had been advised to do? On the evidence
which was before the jury Quick might have had difficulty in
answering these questions in a manner which would have relieved
him of responsibility for his acts. We cannot say, however, with the
requisite degree of confidence that the jury would have convicted
him. It follows that this conviction must be quashed on the ground
that the verdict was unsatisfactory."

Appeal allowed; conviction quashed.

NOTES

Paddison's conviction was also quashed, the court holding that in the
circumstances of the case he could not be held to have aided and abetted an
offence.

Cf. the views of the High Court in *Brennan* v. *H.M. Advocate (ante)* on
insanity, and on the relevance of early authorities on mental abnormality to
modern conditions.

CHAPTER 9

EXCUSES

a.   Necessity

1.   Hume, i, 54-55 (1797)

"Last of all, let me take notice of another sort of constraint, that which arises from the pressure of extreme want: I mean where the person has done some thing which serves to the support of nature for the time. As might be expected, lawyers have differed about the justice of punishing in such a case: some affirming that the notion of dole is excluded in these circumstances of personal distress, or at least that they afford a good plea for a mitigation of the ordinary pains; while others deny that such considerations are at all available in law. With us, reference is made in support of the merciful opinion, to that chapter of the *Regiam Majestatem,* entitled *de Lege Burthynsack,* under which, according to one construction, a man is not to be punished for the theft of a calf, or a ram, or as much meat as he can carry on his back. But the passage does not distinguish whether the thief be or be not necessitous; and taking the whole sections of the chapter in connection, the meaning rather seems to be, that for a theft to this amount the offender shall not be answerable with his life: . . . Whatever may be the true meaning of the passage, it cannot now be of great weight in the solution of this question; which does not seem to be attended with much difficulty, if it is taken up on those obvious and substantial grounds, which present themselves on the least reflection. Certainly there is a wide difference between a single act of theft, committed to relieve the cravings of nature, and the rapacious invasion of the property of others, by one who makes a trade of such injustice. Yet, it is evident how dangerous, or rather how impracticable it is to incorporate such an exception into the common law and practice of the land; and subject it, like other defences, to a discussion with the judge and jury. If there were no other obstacles, by what possible rule can we settle the due measure of distress, which shall serve to excuse? Or how shall the true be known from the pretended necessity; or that which is blameless and unavoidable, from that which is the just consequence of a vicious or a criminal course of conduct? Yet to distinguish in this matter, according to the source and occasion of the indigence, and thus to investigate the whole history of the offender's life, would be indispensable to justice, if the law were in any case to listen to such an excuse.

But there are truly far higher considerations against admitting such a rule—a rule which would subvert all security of property, by confounding the common notions of honesty among our people, and throwing into every man's own hand the estimation of his own wants and distresses, and of the impossibility of relieving them in any more lawful course. It is grounded, therefore, in sound reason, and substantial justice, and is, as I understand, the settled law of Scotland, that the judge shall apply the ordinary pains of law in this, as in every other case, where a person knowingly, and for his own advantage, has taken the property of his neighbour; leaving it to the necessitous offender to supplicate his relief from his Majesty, who is the source of mercy, and will not refuse to listen, in any case where it is fit for him to interpose. Thus the rigid and salutary precept of the law is maintained entire; and humanity is at the same time consulted; without the risk of any of those manifold evils and disorders, which would follow on a more enlarged scheme of indulgence."

NOTES

Compare Hume's views with the following remarks, made nearly 200 years later.

2.   London Borough of Southwark v. Williams and Anor.
[1971] Ch. 734

The defendants were unable to obtain housing and "squatted" in empty houses owned by the borough council. The council obtained an order for possession against the defendants who were trespassers. The defendants appealed, relying, *inter alia*, on a defence of necessity.

LORD DENNING M.R.: "The doctrine [necessity] so enunciated must, however, be carefully circumscribed. Else necessity would open the door to many an excuse. It was for this reason that it was not admitted in *R. v. Dudley and Stephens* [noted *post*], where the three shipwrecked sailors, in extreme despair, killed the cabin-boy and ate him to save their own lives. They were held guilty of murder. The killing was not justified by necessity. Similarly, when a man who is starving enters a house and takes food in order to keep himself alive. Our English law does not admit the defence of necessity. It holds him guilty of larceny. Lord Hale said that 'if a person, being under necessity for want of victuals or clothes, shall upon that account clandestinely, and *animus furandi,* steal another man's food, it is a felony.' (*Pleas of the Crown,* i. 54) The reason is because, if hunger were once allowed to be an excuse for stealing, it would open a way through which all kinds of disorder and lawlessness would pass. So here. If homelessness were once admitted as a defence to trespass, no one's house could be safe. Necessity would open a door which no man could shut. It would not only be those in extreme need who would enter. There would be others who would imagine that they were in need, or would invent a need, so as to gain entry. Each man would say his need was greater than the next man's. The plea would be an excuse for all sorts of wrongdoing. So the courts must, for the sake of law and order, take a firm stand. They must refuse to admit the plea of necessity to the hungry and the homeless; and trust that their distress will be relieved by the charitable and the good."

Appeal dismissed.

3. **R. v. Dudley and Stephens**
(1884) 14 Q.B.D. 273

The defendants, along with a third man called Brooks and a seven-teen year old boy called Parker were cast adrift in an open boat after their yacht went down in a storm 1,600 miles from the Cape of Good Hope. On the twentieth day after the shipwreck, when they had been for eight days without food and for six without water, the defendants killed the boy. The latter did not consent to their act, but did not offer any resistance, being already too ill to do so. The defendants and Brooks fed on the flesh and blood of the boy until they were picked up four days later. At the trial the jury returned a special verdict which stated, *inter alia*:

"If the men had not fed upon the body of the boy, they would probably not have survived to be so picked up and rescued, but would within the four days have died of famine; the boy, being in a much weaker condition was likely to have died before them; at the time of the act in question there was no sail in sight nor any reasonable prospect of relief; under the circumstances there appeared to the prisoners every probability that, unless they then fed, or very soon fed, upon the boy or one of themselves, they would die of starvation; there was no appreciable chance of saving life except by killing someone for the others to eat; assuming any necessity to kill anybody, there was no greater necessity for killing the boy than any of the three men."

LORD COLERIDGE C.J.: "From these facts, stated with the cold precision of a special verdict, it appears that the prisoners were subjected to terrible temptation, to suffering which might break down the bodily power of the strongest man, and try the conscience of the best . . . But nevertheless this is clear, that the prisoners put to death a weak and unoffending boy upon the chance of preserving their own lives by feeding upon his flesh and blood after he was killed, and with the certainty of depriving *him* of any possible chance of survival. The verdict finds in terms that 'if the men had not fed upon the body of the boy they would *probably* not have survived,' and that 'the boy being in a much weaker condition was *likely* to have died before them.' They might possibly have been picked up next day by a passing ship; they might possibly not have been picked up at all; in either case it is obvious that the killing of the boy would have been an unnecessary and profitless act. It is found by the verdict that the boy was incapable of resistance, and, in fact, made none; and it is not even suggested that his death was due to any violence on his part attempted against, or even so much as feared by, those who killed him . . . (His Lordship dealt with certain objections taken on behalf of the defendants which are not relevant to the present question, and the state of the authorities on the question, and then continued) . . . Now except for the purpose of testing how far the conservation of a man's own life is in all cases and under all circumstances, an absolute, unqualified, and paramount duty, we exclude from our consideration all the incidents of war. We are dealing with a case of private homicide, not one imposed upon men in the service of their Sovereign and in the defence of their country. Now it is admitted that the deliberate killing of this unoffending and unresisting boy was ʻclearly murder, unless the killing can be justified by some well-recognised excuse admitted by the law. It is further admitted that there was in this case no such excuse, unless the killing was justified by what has been called 'necessity.' But the temptation to the act which existed here was not what the law has ever called necessity. Nor is this to be regretted. Though law and morality are not the same, and many things may be immoral which are not necessarily illegal, yet the absolute divorce of law from morality would be of fatal consequence; and such divorce would follow if the temptation to murder in this case were to be held by law an absolute defence of it. It is not so. To preserve one's life is generally speaking a duty, but it may be the plainest and highest duty to sacrifice it. War is full of instances in which it is a man's duty not to live, but to die. The duty, in case of shipwreck, of a captain and his crew, of the crew to the passengers, of soldiers to women and children, as in the noble case of the *Birkenhead*; these duties impose on men the moral necessity, not of preservation, but of the sacrifice of their lives for others, from which in no country, least of all, it is to be hoped, in England, will men ever shrink, as indeed, they have not shrunk. It is not correct, therefore, to say that there is any absolute or unqualified necessity to preserve one's life . . . It is not needful to point out the awful danger of admitting the principle which has been contended for. Who is to be the judge of this sort of necessity? By what measure is the comparative value of lives to be measured? Is it to be strength, or intellect, or what? It is plain that the principle leaves to him who is to profit by it to determine the necessity which will justify him in deliberately taking another's life to save his own. In this case the weakest, the youngest, the most unresisting, was chosen. Was it more necessary to kill him than one of the grown men? The answer must be 'No'—

'So spake the Fiend, and with necessity,
The tyrant's plea, excused his devilish deeds.'

It is not suggested that in this particular case the deeds were 'devilish', but it is quite plain that such a principle once admitted might be made the legal cloak for unbridled passion and atrocious crime. There is no safe path for judges to tread but to ascertain the law to the best of their ability and to declare it according to their judgments; and if in any case the law appears to be too severe on individuals, to leave it to the Sovereign to exercise that prerogative of mercy which the Constitution has intrusted to the hands fittest to dispense it.

It must not be supposed that in refusing to admit temptation to be an excuse for crime it is forgotten how terrible the temptation was; how awful the suffering; how hard in such trials to keep the judgment straight and the conduct pure. We are often compelled to set up standards we cannot reach ourselves, and to lay down rules which we could not ourselves satisfy. But a man has no right to declare temptation to be an excuse, though he might himself have yielded to it, nor allow compassion for the criminal to change or weaken in any manner the legal definition of the crime. It is therefore our duty to declare that the prisoners' act in this case was wilful murder, that the facts as stated in the verdict are no legal justification of the homicide; and to say that in our unanimous opinion the prisoners are upon this special verdict guilty of murder.''

Verdict: Guilty.

NOTES

The defendants were sentenced to death. This sentence was afterwards commuted to six months' imprisonment. Was this the most just result?

Did his Lordship hold that as a matter of law necessity was not a defence to murder, or only that in the facts of this case the defendants had no defence? Suppose that the boy had fought off his assailants and killed one of them. Presumably he could plead self-defence. Would this consideration have any relevance in determining the effect of the plea of necessity?

4.　U.S. v. Holmes
26 Fed. Cas. 360 (1842)

The defendant was a member of the crew of an American ship, the *William Brown*. While bound for Philadelphia from Liverpool with a crew of seventeen, sixty-five passengers and a heavy cargo, the ship struck an iceberg and sank. Nine of the crew (including Homles and the mate) and thirty-two passengers crowded into the ship's longboat. About twenty-four hours after the wreck, Holmes, along with other members of the crew, acting on the orders of the mate, began to throw out some of the male passengers in order to lighten the boat which was in serious danger of being swamped by the rising sea. In all, fourteen male passengers (and possibly two female passengers) were thrown out. None of the crew members suffered this fate. All those who were in the boat were picked up by another ship the following morning. Holmes was charged with the man-slaughter of one of the men he put overboard. In his charge to the jury the presiding judge gave the following directions:

BALDWIN, CIRCUIT JUSTICE: "It is a different thing, when we are asked, not to extenuate, but to justify, the act. In the former case, as I have said, our decisions may in some degree be swayed by feelings of humanity; while, in the latter, it is the law of necessity alone which can disarm the vindicatory justice of the country. Where, indeed, a case does arise, embraced by this 'law of necessity,' the penal laws pass over such a case in silence; for law is made to meet the ordinary exigencies of life. But the case does not become ' a case of necessity,' unless all ordinary means of self-preservation have been exhausted. The peril must be instant, over-whelming, leaving no alternative but to lose our own life, or take the life of another person. An illustration of this principle occurs in the ordinary case of self-defence against lawless violence, aiming at the destruction of life, or designing to inflict grievous injury to the person; and within this range may fall the taking of life under other circumstances where the act is indispensably requisite to self-existence. For example, suppose that two persons who owe no duty to one another that is not mutual, should, by accident not attributable to either, be placed in a situation where both cannot survive. Neither is bound to save the other's life by sacrificing his own, nor would either commit a crime in saving his own life in a struggle for the only means of safety . . .

But in applying this law, we must look, not only to the jeopardy in which the parties are, but also to the relations in which they stand. The slayer must be under no obligation to make his own safety secondary to the safety of others. A familiar application of this principle presents itself in the obligations which rest upon the owners of stages, steamboats, and other vehicles of transportation. In consideration of the payment of the fare, the owners of the vehicle are bound to transport the passengers to the place of con-templated destination. Having, in all emergencies, the conduct of

the journey, and the control of the passengers, the owners rest
under every obligation for care, skill, and general capacity; and if,
from defect of any of these requisites, grievous injury is done to the
passenger, the persons employed are liable. The passenger owes no
duty but submission. He is under no obligation to protect and keep
the conductor in safety, nor is the passenger bound to labour,
except in cases of emergency, where his services are required by
unanticipated and uncommon danger . . .

The passenger stands in a position different from that of the
officers and seamen. It is the sailor who must encounter the hard-
ships and perils of the voyage. Nor can this relation be changed
when the ship is lost by tempest or other danger of the sea, and all on
board have betaken themselves, for safety to the small boats; for
imminence of danger cannot absolve from duty. The sailor is
bound, as before, to undergo whatever hazard is necessary to
preserve the boat and the passengers. Should the emergency
become so extreme as to call for the sacrifice of life, there can be no
reason why the law does not still remain the same. The passenger,
not being bound either to labour or to incur the risk of life, cannot
be bound to sacrifice his existence to preserve the sailor's. The
captain, indeed, and a sufficient number of seamen to navigate the
boat, must be preserved; for, except these abide in the ship, all will
perish. But if there be more seamen than necessary to manage the
boat, the supernumerary sailors have no right, for their safety, to
sacrifice the passengers. The sailors and passengers, in fact, cannot
be regarded as in equal positions. The sailor (to use the language of
a distinguished writer) owes more benevolence to another than
himself. He is bound to set a greater value on the life of others than
on his own. And while we admit that sailor and sailor may lawfully
struggle with each other for the plank which can save but one, we
think that, if a passenger is on the plank, even 'the law of necessity'
justifies not the sailor who takes it from him. This rule may be
deemed a harsh one towards the sailor, who may have thus far done
his duty, but when the danger is so extreme, that the only hope is in
sacrificing either a sailor or a passenger, any alternative is hard; and
would it not be the hardest of any to sacrifice a passenger in order to
save a supernumerary sailor?

But in addition, if the sources of the danger have been obvious,
and destruction ascertained to be certainly about to arrive, though
at a future time, there should be consultation, and some mode of
selection fixed, by which those in equal relations may have equal
chance for their life. By what mode, then, should selection be
made? The question is not without difficulty; nor do we know of any
rule prescribed, either by statute or by common law, or even by
speculative writers on the law of nature. In fact, no rule of general

application can be prescribed for contingencies which are wholly unforeseen. There is, however, one condition of extremity for which all writers have prescribed the same rule. When the ship is in no danger of sinking, but all sustenance is exhausted, and a sacrifice of one person is necessary to appease the hunger of others, the selection is by lot. This mode is resorted to as the fairest mode, and, in some sort, as an appeal to God, for the selection of the victim . . .

When the selection has been made by lots, the victim yields of course to his fate, or, if he resists, force may be employed to coerce submission. Whether or not 'a case of necessity' has arisen, or whether the law under which death has been inflicted have been so exercised as to hold the executioner harmless, cannot depend on his own opinion; for no man may pass upon his own conduct when it concerns the rights, and especially, when it affects the lives, of others."

Verdict: Guilty (with recommendation to mercy).

NOTES

The defendant was sentenced to six months' solitary confinement at hard labour, and a twenty dollar fine. The sentence was later remitted.

The process of selection suggested in *Holmes* was rejected by Lord Coleridge in *Dudley and Stephens* in the following terms: "The American case . . . in which it was decided, correctly indeed, that sailors had no right to throw passengers overboard to save themselves, but on the somewhat strange ground that the proper mode of determining who was to be sacrificed was to vote upon the subject by ballot, can hardly . . . be an authority to a court in this country." His Lordship appears to have misunderstood the case.

Does Justice Baldwin's method completely validate the proceedings? How should a person who refuses to draw a lot be dealt with? Suppose that it became necessary to eject some passengers and the wife of a victim attacked those who were trying to eject her husband. Would that attack be a criminal assault?

For further discussions of the plea of necessity see *Buckoke* v. *Greater London Council* [1971] Ch. 655; *Wood* v. *Richards* [1977] Crim. L.R. 295; Gordon, ch. 13; G. Williams "The Defence of Necessity" 1953 Current Legal Problems 216; P.R. Glazebrook, "The Necessity Plea in English Criminal Law" [1972] C.L.J. 87; and Law Commission Report on Defences of General Application (Law Com. No. 83) (which recommends that there should be no general defence of necessity in English law, and that to the extent that it exists at common law it should be abolished, para. 4.33).

b. Coercion

1. Hume, i, 52

Of the plea of compulsion:

"But generally, and with relation to the ordinary condition of a well-regulated society, where every man is under the shield of the law, and has the means of resorting to the protection, this is at least somewhat a difficult plea, and can hardly be serviceable in the case of a trial for any atrocious crime, unless it have the support of these qualifications: an immediate danger of death or great bodily harm; an inability to resist the violence; a backward and an inferior part in the perpetration; and a disclosure of the fact, as well as restitution of the profit, on the first safe and convenient occasion. For if the pannel take a very active part in the enterprise, or conceal the fact, and detain his share of the profit, when restored to a state of freedom, either of these replies will serve in a great measure to elide his defence."

2. H.M. Advocate v. Docherty and Others
Glasgow High Court, June 1976, *unreported*

Two youths, aged fifteen and sixteen, and an older man were charged with a number of offences which included two charges of assault and armed robbery and a charge of attempted robbery. The two younger accused raised a defence of coercion, alleging that they participated unwillingly in the offence through fear of the third accused. Both of the youths admitted that they had not been threatened, nor had any violence been used against them, but they both stated that they were "scared" of the third accused. There was a suggestion of veiled threats involving the mothers of the youths, but no specific threats had ever been made. In charging the jury the presiding judge made the following remarks:

LORD KEITH: "Now, another chapter of law which has been raised by this trial is the law about coercion because the two younger accused—Docherty and Kerr—have made it their defence in so far as they did the acts charged in the indictment charged against them, they did these acts under coercion on the part of the accused Neil. Now, ladies and gentlemen, coercion can be a defence to a criminal charge, there is no doubt about that but in order that it may be a defence the position must be that the accused who is pleading this defence acted in a situation created by a threat to him which he had reason to believe, and did believe, would be carried out. Ladies and gentlemen, people act for different reasons and for various motives but they are, in the eyes of the law, to be treated—if they are sane—as acting under the influence of their own will. It can happen that the will of an individual is overborne by the will of another in certain circumstances so he is not acting of his own free will. Well, if his will has been overborne by a threat of the kind that I have mentioned then that may be a defence to a crime which he would otherwise be guilty of, but, ladies and gentlemen, it must be the situation that his will has been overborne by a threat to him, that he had reason to believe—and believed—it would be carried out. This is not a plea which has been very often accepted but it is acceptable in appropriate circumstances. Usually the cases where it is accepted are pretty extreme and pretty obvious, where somebody has been dragged away at the point of a gun and forced to drive a car— something of that sort—which is carrying people to a murder, but the circumstances can vary. The essence of the matter is that the will of the accused should be overborne by threats which he believed would be carried out . . .

Of course, Docherty and Kerr admitted in the witness box that they went into this shop with a gun and received a sum of money as a result of the theft and they incriminated Neil by their evidence. They said it was he who put them up to it and took them there and encouraged them—indeed, almost obliged them—to go in and do it. That was their evidence. Neil on the other hand denies everything. . . . As regards Docherty and Kerr, you have to consider very carefully their evidence, of course, and it will be convenient for you to consider this first in relation to this charge—although it arises in connection with the other charges too—but keep in mind the definition of coercion which I gave you and consider carefully the evidence which they gave you on this matter. Consider, first of all, how far you accept it either in whole or in part. That is entirely up to you, and having decided what you accept of it, then make up your mind what it amounts to. Remember, if you are absolutely satisfied, if you are satisfied on their evidence, even though not corroborated, that they acted as a result of their will being overborne by threats they believed would be carried out to them, or, indeed, to their mothers, that would be sufficient—you would be entitled to acquit. Even if you don't altogether believe it, you would still be entitled to acquit if a reasonable doubt was raised in your minds as to whether they were acting as free agents . . .

Now, there was some talk on the part of the learned advocate-depute that you might, in relation to the accused Docherty and Kerr, bring in some such verdict as guilty subject to coercion, or something like that. Well, ladies and gentlemen, that is not so: either you acquit them by reason of coercion or you find them guilty. It is, of course, always open to you to make any recommendations but there is no question of giving any particular verdict on that matter: it is either guilty, not proven or not guilty."

> Verdict: The jury returned a verdict of guilty, adding a rider that "In the opinion of the jury Docherty and Kerr were badly influenced by older persons and were easily led."

NOTES

Lord Keith's directions concentrate very much on the *effect* of the alleged coercion, nothing being said about the nature of the threats required to constitute coercion. Was his Lordship right in leaving the defence to the jury in the absence of evidence of clear threats of "death or great bodily harm"? *Cf. H.M. Advocate* v. *Peters and Ors.* (1969) 33 J.C.L. 209.

3. **R. v. Hudson and Taylor**
[1971] 2 Q.B. 202

LORD PARKER C.J.: "The judgement of the court which I am about to read was prepared by Widgery L.J.

These appellants were convicted of perjury at the Manchester Crown Court on May 18, 1970, and each was granted a conditional discharge. They now appeal against their convictions by leave of the single judge.

On April 6, 1969, a fight took place in a Salford public house between one Wright and one Mulligan with the result that Wright was charged with wounding Mulligan. Each of the present appellants gave statements to the police and they were the principal prosecution witnesses at Wright's trial. Elaine Taylor is 19, and Linda Hudson is 17.

Wright's trial took place on August 4, 1969, but when called to give evidence the appellants failed to identify Wright as Mulligan's assailant. Taylor said that she knew no one called Jimmy Wright, and Hudson said that the only Wright she knew was not the man in the dock. Wright was accordingly acquitted and, in due course, the appellants were charged with perjury. At their trial they admitted that the evidence which they had given was false but set up the defence of duress. The basis of the defence was that, shortly after the fight between Wright and Mulligan, Hudson had been approached by a group of men including one Farrell who had a reputation for violence and was warned that if she 'told on Wright in court' they would get her and cut her up. Hudson passed this warning to Taylor who said that she had also been warned by other girls to be careful or she would be hurt. The appellants said in evidence that in consequence of these threats, they were frightened and decided to tell lies in court in order to avoid the consequences which might follow if they testified against Wright. This resolve was strengthened when they arrived at court for Wright's trial and saw that Farrell was in the gallery.

The recorder directed the jury as a matter of law that the defence of duress was not open to the appellants in these circumstances. He said: 'In my direction to you which you have to obey I tell you that duress can only arise when there is a threat made of death or serious personal injury and that threat must be a present immediate threat.' Later he continued: 'Assuming everything in favour of these two girls . . . assuming that Farrell did make this threat to Hudson . . . assuming that the information was passed on by Hudson to Taylor and assuming that the girls believed it; assuming in favour of Elaine Taylor and Linda Hudson that Elaine Taylor was approached on various occasions by young women who said to her 'Be careful and watch it' . . . assuming all that to be 100 per cent. in their favour I direct you as a matter of law that that does not amount to duress. These girls may very well have thought that if they did not tell lies something very unpleasant might happen to them in the future, but that is not a present immediate threat capable of being then and there carried out because when they told lies they were in a court of law with the recorder of Salford there for protection and with the police there in court and, members of the jury, I direct you that that does not amount to duress.'

It is now submitted that this was a misdirection in law and that the case should have been left to the jury to determine, as a fact, whether the appellants had acted under duress.

We have been referred to a large number of authorities and to the views of writers of text books. Despite the concern expressed in *Stephen's History of the Criminal Law of England*, vol. 2 (1883) p. 107 that it would be 'a much greater misfortune for society at large if criminals could confer [immunity] upon their agents by threatening them with death or violence if they refuse to execute their commands' it is clearly established that duress provides a defence in all offences including perjury (except possibly treason or murder as a principal) if the will of the accused has been overborne by threats of death or serious personal injury so that the commission of the alleged offence was no longer the voluntary act of the accused.

This appeal raises two main questions; first, as to the nature of the necessary threat and, in particular, whether it must be 'present and immediate'; secondly, as to the extent to which a right to plead duress may be lost if the accused has failed to take steps to remove the threat as, for example, by seeking police protection.

It is essential to the defence of duress that the threat shall be effective at the moment when the crime is committed. The threat must be a 'present' threat in the sense that it is effective to neutralise the will of the accused at that time . . . Similarly a threat of future violence may be so remote as to be insufficient to overpower the will at that moment when the offence was committed, or the accused may have elected to commit the offence in order to rid himself of a threat hanging over him and not because he was driven to act by immediate and unavoidable pressure. In none of these cases is the defence of duress available because a person cannot justify the commission of a crime merely to secure his own peace of mind.

When, however, there is no opportunity for delaying tactics, and the person threatened must make up his mind whether he is to commit the criminal act or not, the existence at the moment of threats sufficient to destroy his will ought to provide him with a defence even though the threatened injury may not follow instantly, but after an interval. This principle is illustrated by *Subramaniam v. Public Prosecutor* [1956] 1 W.L.R. 965, when the appellant was charged in Malaya with unlawful possession of ammunition and was held by the Privy Council to have a defence of duress, fit to go to the jury, on his plea that he had been compelled by terrorists to accept the ammunition and feared for his safety if the terrorists returned.

In the present case the threats of Farrell were likely to be no less compelling because their execution could not be effected in the court room, if they could be carried out in the streets of Salford the same night. In so far, therefore, as the recorder ruled as a matter of law that the threats were not sufficiently present and immediate to support the defence of duress we think that he was in error. He should have left the jury to decide whether the threats had overborne the will of the appellants at the time when they gave the false evidence.

Mr. Franks, however, contends that the recorder's ruling can be supported on another ground, namely, that the appellants should have taken steps to neutralise the threats by seeking police protection either when they came to court to give evidence, or beforehand. He submits on grounds of public policy that an accused should not be able to plead duress if he had the opportunity to ask for protection from the police before committing the offence and failed to do so. The argument does not distinguish cases in which the police would be able to provide effective protection, from those when they would not, and it would, in effect, restrict the defence of duress to cases where the person threatened had been kept in custody by the maker of the threats, or where the time interval between the making of the threats and the commission of the offence had made recourse to the police impossible. We recognise the need to keep the defence of duress within reasonable bounds but cannot accept so severe a restriction upon it. The duty, of the person threatened, to take steps to remove the threat does seem to have arisen in an English case but, in a full review of the defence of duress in the Supreme Court of Victoria (*Reg.* v. *Harley and Murray* [1967] V.R. 526), a condition of raising the defence was said to be that the accused 'had no means, with safety to himself, of preventing the execution of the threat.'

In the opinion of this court it is always open to the Crown to prove that the accused failed to avail himself of some opportunity which was reasonably open to him to render the threat ineffective, and that upon this being established the threat in question can no longer be relied upon by the defence. In deciding whether such an opportunity was reasonably open to the accused the jury should have regard to his age and circumstances, and to any risks to him which may be involved in the course of action relied upon.

In our judgment the defence of duress should have been left to the jury in the present case, as should any issue raised by the Crown and arising out of the appellants' failure to seek police protection."

Appeals allowed;
convictions quashed

NOTES

The Law Commission (Law Com. No. 83) took the view (para. 2.29) that the decision in *Hudson and Taylor* undesirably widened the ambit of the defence: "In our view there would be considerable danger in admitting as exoneration a threat of harm to be inflicted in the future in circumstances which allow time for steps to be taken to avoid the harm." They therefore recommended (para. 2.46) that the defendant must believe (*inter alia*) that "the threat will be carried out immediately, or, if not immediately, before he can have any real opportunity of seeking official protection." *Cf.* the following case.

4. R.v. Carker (No. 2)
[1967] 2 C.C.C. 190

Section 17 of the Canadian Criminal Code provides (*inter alia*) that a person who commits an offence "under compulsion by threats of immediate death or grievous bodily harm from a person who is present when the offence is committed is excused for committing the offence if he believes that the threats will be carried out."

The respondent was convicted of unlawfully and wilfully damaging public property and thereby committing mischief. On appeal his conviction was quashed. The Crown appealed to the Supreme Court of Canada. The circumstances of the case are set out in the judgment of Ritchie J.

RITCHIE J.: "At the outset of the proceedings at trial in the present case and in the absence of the jury, Mr. Greenfield, who acted on behalf of the accused, informed the court that he intended to call evidence of compulsion and duress and he elected to outline the nature of this evidence which was that the offence had been committed during a disturbance, apparently organized by way of protest, to damage property at the Prison Farm in the course of which a substantial body of prisoners, shouting in unison from their separate cells, threatened the respondent, who was not joining in the disturbance, that if he did not break the plumbing fixtures in his cell he would be kicked in the head, his arm would be broken and he would get a knife in the back at the first opportunity.

The question which the learned trial Judge was required to determine on Mr. Greenfield's application was whether the proposed evidence which had been outlined to him indicated a defence or excuse available at law; he decided that it did not and the majority of the Court of Appeal having taken a different view, the Attorney-General now appeals to this Court.

There can be little doubt that the evidence outlined by Mr. Greenfield, which was subsequently confirmed by the evidence given by the ringleaders of the disturbance in mitigation of sentence, disclosed that the respondent committed the offence under the compulsion of threats of death and grievous bodily harm, but although these threats were 'immediate' in the sense that they were continuous until the time that the offence was committed, they were not threats of 'immediate death' or 'immediate grievous bodily harm' and none of the persons who delivered them was present in the cell with the respondent when the offence was committed. I am accordingly of opinion that the learned trial Judge was right in deciding that the proposed evidence did not afford an excuse within the meaning of s. 17 of the *Criminal Code*.

In the course of his most thoughtful judgment in the Court of Appeal . . . Norris J. had occasion to say: 'The question as to whether or not the person threatening was present goes to the question of the grounds for the fear which the appellant might have. In my opinion a person could be present in making a threat although separated by the bars of the cell. These are all matters which should have gone to the jury, as was the question of whether or not the threat of death or grievous bodily harm was an immediate one—a question of degree. They might well consider that the threat was immediate as being continuous, as it was in this case, that it would be all the more frightening because of the uncertainty as to when it actually might happen, and therefore force him to act as he did.'

With the greatest respect it appears to me that the question of whether immediate threats of future death or grievous bodily harm constitute an excuse for committing a crime within the meaning of s. 17 and the question of whether a person can be 'present' within the meaning of that section when he is locked in a separate cell from the place where the offence is committed are both questions which depend upon the construction to be placed on the section and they are therefore questions of the law and not questions of fact for the jury . . .

In support of the suggestion that the threat in the present case was 'immediate and continuous' Norris J. relied on the case of *Subramaniam* v. *Public Prosecutor* [1956] 1 W.L.R. 965, in which the Privy Council decided that the trial Judge was wrong in excluding evidence of threats to which the appellant was subjected by Chinese terrorists in Malaya. In that case it was found that the threats were a continuous menace up to the moment when the appellant was captured because the terrorists might have come back at any time and carried them into effect. Section 94 of the *Penal Code* of the Federated Malay States, which the appellant sought to invoke in that case provided [see p. 968]: 'Except murder and offences included in Chapter VI punishable with death, nothing is an offence which is done by a person who is compelled to do it by threats, which, at the time of doing it, reasonably cause the apprehension that instant death to that person will otherwise be the consequence; . . .'

The distinctions between the *Subramaniam* case and the present one lie in the fact that Subramaniam might well have had reasonable cause for apprehension that instant death would result from his disobeying the terrorists who might have come back at any moment, whereas it is virtually inconceivable that 'immediate death' or 'grievous bodily harm' could have come to Carker from those who were uttering the threats against him as they were locked up in separate cells, and it is also to be noted that the provisions of s. 17 of the *Criminal Code* are by no means the same as those of s. 94 of the *Penal Code* of the Federated Malay States; amongst other distinctions the latter section contains no provision that the person who utters the threats must be present when the offence is committed in order to afford an excuse for committing it.

Both Norris, J., and Branca, J., in delivering their separate reasons for judgment in the Court of Appeal, expressed the view that the evidence which was tendered should have been admitted on the issue of whether the respondent acted wilfully in damaging the prison plumbing or whether he was so affected by the threats uttered against him as to be incapable of adopting any other course than the one which he did . . .

In this regard it is important to bear in mind the fact that 'wilful' as it is used in Part IX of the *Criminal Code* is defined in s.371 (1) which reads, in part, as follows: 'Every one who causes the occurrence of an event by doing an act or by omitting to do an act that it is his duty to do, knowing that the act or omission will probably cause the occurrence of the event and being reckless whether the event occurs or not, shall be deemed, for the purposes of this Part, wilfully to have caused the occurrence of the event.'

The evidence outlined to the learned trial Judge discloses that the criminal act was committed to preserve the respondent from future harm coming to him, but there is no suggestion in the evidence tendered for the defence that the accused did not know that what he was doing would 'probably cause' damage. Accepting the outline made by defence counsel as being an accurate account of the evidence which was available, there was in my view nothing in it to support the defence that the act was not done 'wilfully' within the meaning of s. 371 (1) and 372 (1) of the *Criminal Code* and there was accordingly no ground to justify the learned trial Judge in permitting the proposed evidence to be called in support of such a defence.

In view of all the above, I would allow this appeal, set aside the judgment of the Court of Appeal and restore the conviction."

Appeal allowed; conviction restored.

NOTES

Would the respondent's defence be upheld (*a*) under Scots law, (*b*) under the ruling in *R.* v. *Hudson and Taylor, ante,* (*c*) under the Law Commission's proposal?

For the underlying basis of the plea of duress, compare what is said in *Carker* (*ante*) with the views of Lord Wilberforce in *Lynch* v. *D.P.P. for Northern Ireland* [1975] A.C. 653 (*post*).

5.   Lynch v. D.P.P. for Northern Ireland
[1975] A.C. 653

The appellant was charged with murder. The case against him was that he had aided and abetted those who actually killed the victim. At his trial he relied on the plea of duress. The trial judge decided not to leave this defence to the jury, on the view that, as a matter of law, duress was not available on a charge of murder. The appellant was convicted. The facts of the case are fully set out in the opinion of Lord Morris of Borth-y-Gest.

On appeal to the House of Lords:

LORD MORRIS OF BORTH-Y-GEST: "[The appellant] said that while at his house he had received a message that one Sean Meehan required his presence. It was in the forefront of his case that Sean Meehan was and was known to be both a member of the I.R.A. and a ruthless gunman. The appellant had not previously known Meehan personally but had known of him. He said that what Meehan asked to be done had to be done. 'You have no other option. I firmly believe that I would have been shot for defying him.' So he went with the messenger to an address in Belfast and there saw Meehan and two other men. Meehan, he said, had a rifle in his hand. After it was learned that the appellant could drive a car he was told to go with another man named Mailey (who had a small automatic gun) and seize a car. They went away. Mailey held up a car and ordered its driver to get out. The appellant was told to drive the car to the address where Meehan had remained. The appellant did so. He parked the car and was told that he would not be doing any more driving. So he returned to his own house. Some half-hour later the messenger returned and told the appellant that Meehan wanted him. He went to the same house as before. Meehan, Bates, Mailey and another man were there. Meehan, who had a rifle told the appellant that he was to drive the car which he then did after Mailey (who had a gun in his pocket) had got in beside him and after Bates and Meehan had got into the back. Meehan, Bates and Mailey had combat jackets and balaclava helmets. The appellant was told to go to a particular road. He asked Meehan what he was going to do and was told: 'Bates knows a policeman'. Following directions given to him he drove past a garage (at which point Bates said: 'That's him') and then stopped near to the garage. Meehan told him to stay there. The other three pulled up their woollen helmets and left the car and ran across the road. Then there were a number of shots fired in quick succession. The three men came running back to the car and got into it. The appellant was told to drive on—which he did. They returned to their starting point . . .

In a series of decisions and over a period of time courts have recognised that there can be circumstances in which duress is a defence. In examining them and more particularly in approaching the issue raised in this appeal the question naturally presents itself—why and on what basis can duress be raised? If someone acts under duress—does he intend what he does? Does he lack what in our criminal law is called mens rea? If what he does amounts to a criminal offence ought he to be convicted but be allowed in mercy and in mitigation to be absolved or relieved from some or all of the possible consequences?

The answer that I would give to these questions is that it is proper that any rational system of law should take fully into account the standards of honest and reasonable men. By those standards it is fair that actions and reactions may be tested. If then someone is really threatened with death or serious injury unless he does what he is told to do is the law to pay no heed to the miserable, agonising plight of such a person? For the law to understand not only how the timid but also the stalwart may in a moment of crisis behave is not to make the law weak but to make it just. In the calm of the court-room measures of fortitude or of heroic behaviour are surely not to be demanded when they could not in moments for decision reasonably have been expected even of the resolute and the well disposed.

In posing the case where someone is 'really' threatened I use the word 'really' in order to emphasise that duress must never be allowed to be the easy answer of those who can devise no other explanation of their conduct nor of those who readily could have avoided the dominance of threats nor of those who allow themselves to be at the disposal and under the sway of some gangster-tyrant. Where duress becomes an issue courts and juries will surely consider the facts with care and discernment.

In my view the law has recognised that there can be situations in which duress can be put forward as a defence. Someone who acts under duress may have a moment of time, even one of the utmost brevity, within which he decides whether he will or will not submit to a threat. There may consciously or subconsciously be a hurried process of balancing the consequences of disobedience against the gravity or the wickedness of the action that is required. The result will be that what is done will be done most unwillingly but yet intentionally. Terminology may not, however, much matter. The authorities show that in some circumstances duress may excuse and may therefore be set up as a special defence.

A tenable view might be that duress should never be regarded as furnishing an excuse from guilt but only where established as providing reasons why after conviction a court could mitigate its consequences or absolve from punishment. Some writers including Stephen (see *History of the Criminal Law in England* (1883), vol. 2, pp. 107-108) have so thought. It is, however, much too late in the day, having regard to the lines of authority, to adopt any such view. But apart from this—would such an approach be just? I think not. It is said that if duress could not be set up as a defence there would be difficulties in the way of bringing evidence of the relevant facts and circumstances before the court. I am not greatly impressed by this. A judge could ensure that after a conviction full opportunity would be given to adduce all material evidence. If, however, what a person has done was only done because he acted under the compulsion of a threat of death or of serious bodily injury it would not in my view be just that the stigma of a conviction should be cast on him. As

Blackstone put it (*Commentaries on the Laws of England* (1862), vol. 4, p. 23): '. . . it is highly just and equitable that a man should be excused for those acts which are done through unavoidable force and compulsion.'

The law must, I think, take a common sense view. If someone is forced at gun-point either to be inactive or to do something positive—must the law not remember that the instinct and perhaps the duty of self-preservation is powerful and natural? I think it must. A man who is attacked is allowed within reason to take necessary steps to defend himself. The law would be censorious and inhumane which did not recognise the appalling plight of a person who perhaps suddenly finds his life in jeopardy unless he submits and obeys.

The issue in the present case is therefore whether there is any reason why the defence of duress, which in respect of a variety of offences has been recognised as a possible defence, may not also be a possible defence on a charge of being a principal in the second degree to murder. I would confine my decision to that issue. It may be that the law must deny such a defence to an actual killer, and that the law will not be irrational if it does so.

Though it is not possible for the law always to be worked out on coldly logical lines there may be manifest factual differences and contrasts between the situation of an aider and abettor to a killing and that of the actual killer. Let two situations be supposed. In each let it be supposed that there is a real and effective threat of death. In one a person is required under such duress to drive a car to a place or to carry a gun to a place with knowledge that at such place it is planned that X is to be killed by those who are imposing their will. In the other situation let it be supposed that a person under such duress is told that he himself must there and then kill X. In either situation there is a terrible agonising choice of evils. In the former to save his life the person drives the car or carries the gun. He may cling to the hope that perhaps X will not be found at the place or that there will be a change of intention before the purpose is carried out or that in some unforeseen way the dire event of a killing will be averted. The final and fatal moment of decision has not arrived. He saves his own life at a time when the loss of another life is not a certainty. In the second (if indeed it is a situation likely to arise) the person is told that to save his life he himself must personally there and then take an innocent life. It is for him to pull the trigger or otherwise personally to do the act of killing. There, I think, before allowing duress as a defence it may be that the law will have to call a halt. May there still be force in what long ago was said by Hale? 'Again, if a man be desperately assaulted, and in peril of death, and cannot otherwise escape, unless to satisfy his assailant's fury he will kill an innocent person then present, the fear and actual force will not acquit him of the crime and punishment of murder, if he commit the fact; for he ought rather to die himself, than kill an innocent' (see *Hale's Pleas of the Crown*, vol. 1, p. 51). Those words have over long periods of time influenced both thought and writing but I think that their application may have been unduly extended when it is assumed that they were intended to cover all cases of accessories and aiders and abettors.

Writers on criminal law have generally recorded that whatever may be the extent to which the law has recognised duress as a defence it has not been recognised as a defence to a charge of murder (see *Russell on Crime*, 12th ed. (1964), p. 90; *Kenny's Outlines of Criminal Law*, 19th ed. (1966), p. 70; *Glanville Williams, Criminal Law*, 2nd ed. (1961), p. 759, and *Smith and Hogan, Criminal Law*, 3rd ed. (1973), pp. 164-168).

It may be a matter for consideration whether the offences of being accesssory before the fact to murder and of aiding and abetting murder might not be constituted as separate offences involving a liability to the imposition of life imprisonment but not as a mandatory sentence.

I fully appreciate that, particularly at the present time, situations may arise where the facts will be much less direct and straight-forward than those which, as examples, I have described. I see no advantage in giving illustrations of them. They will be situations presenting greater difficulties of fact than those presented in the present case. But where there have been threats of the nature that really have compelled a person to act in a particular way and he has only acted because of them I think that the approach of the law should be to recognise that the person may be excused in the cases that I have supposed.

It is most undesirable that, in the administration of our criminal law, cases should arise in which, if there is a prosecution leading to a conviction, a just conclusion will only be attained by an exercise thereafter of the prerogative of granting a pardon. I would regret it, therefore, if upon an application of legal principles such cases could arise. Such principles and such approach as will prevent them from arising would seem to me to be more soundly based. . . .

I see no reason to question the law as laid down in *R.* v. *Dudley and Stephens* [noted *ante*], the authority of which will in my view be in no way disturbed if duress is held to be a possible defence in the case of someone charged with having aided and abetted the commission of murder. . . .

We are only concerned in this case to say whether duress could be a possible defence open to Lynch who was charged with being an aider and abettor. Relying on the help given in the authorities we must decide this as a matter of principle. I consider that duress in such a case can be open as a possible defence. Both general reasoning and the requirements of justice lead me to this conclusion."

LORD WILBERFORCE: "It is clear that a possible case of duress, on the facts, could have been made. I say 'a possible case' because there were a number of matters which the jury would have had to consider if this defence had been left to them. Among these would have been whether Meehan though uttering no express threats of death or serious injury, impliedly did so in such a way as to put the appellant in fear of death or serious injury; whether, if so, the threats continued to operate throughout the enterprise; whether the appellant had voluntarily exposed himself to a situation in which threats might be used against him if he did not participate in a criminal enterprise (the appellant denied that he had done so); whether the appellant had taken every opportunity open to him to escape from the situation of duress.

In order to test the validity of the judge's decision to exclude this defence, we must assume on this appeal that these matters would have been decided in favour of the appellant.

What, then, does exclusion of the defence involve? It means that a person, assumedly not himself a member of a terrorist group, summoned from his home, with explicit or implied threats of death or serious injury at gunpoint, to drive armed men on what he finds to be a criminal enterprise, having no opportunity to escape, but with the certainty of being shot if he resists or tries to get away, is liable to be convicted of murder. The same would be true of a bystander in a street, or an owner of a car, similarly conscripted, once it is shown that he, or she, knew the nature of the enterprise. One may multiply examples of the possible involvement of persons, whom the normal man would regard as without guilt, under threats of death or violence, in violent enterprises—examples unfortunately far from fanciful at this time. Does the law require all these to be changed with murder and call for their conviction? It would be our duty to accept such a law if it existed, but we are also entitled to see if it does.

Does then the law forbid admission of a defence of duress on a charge of murder whether as a principal in the first degree or as a principal in the second degree or as an accessory?. Consistently with the method normal in the development of the common law, an answer to this question must be sought in authority, and in the principles upon which established authority is based. I look first at the principle. The principle upon which duress is admitted as a defence is not easy to state. Professor Glanville Williams indeed doubts whether duress fits in to any accepted theory: it may, in his view, stand by itself altogether outside the definition of will and act. (*Criminal Law*, 2nd ed. 1961, p.751). The reason for this is historical. Duress emerged very early in our law as a fact of which account has to be taken, particularly in times of civil strife where charges of treason were the normal consequence of defeat, long before the criminal law had worked out a consistent or any theory of 'mens rea' or intention. At the present time, whatever the ultimate analysis in jurisprudence may be, the best opinion, as reflected in decisions of judges and in writers, seems to be that duress per minas is something which is superimposed upon the other ingredients which by themselves would make up an offence, i.e., upon act and intention. 'Coactus volui' sums up the combination: the victim completes the act and knows that he is doing so; but the addition of the element of duress prevents the law from treating what he has done as a crime. One may note—and the comparison is satis-factory—that an analogous result is achieved in a civil law context: duress does not destroy the will, for example, to enter into a contract, but prevents the law from accepting what has happened as a contract valid in law. . . .

What reason then can there be for excepting murder? One may say—as some authorities do (cf. *Attorney-General* v. *Whelan* [1934] I.R. 518, 526 *per* Murnaghan J., *Reg.* v. *Hurley and Murray* [1967] V.R. 526, 543 *per* Smith J.) that murder is the most heinous of crimes: so it may be, and in some circumstances, a defence of duress in relation to it should be correspondingly hard to establish. Indeed, to justify the deliberate killing by one's own hand of another human being may be something that no pressure or threat even to one's own life which can be imagined can justify—no such case ever seems to have reached the courts. But if one accepts the test of heinousness, this does not, in my opinion, involve that all cases of what is murder in law must be treated in the same way. Heinousness is a word of degree, and that there are lesser degrees of heinousness, even of involvement in homicide, seems beyond doubt. An accessory before the fact, or an aider or abettor, may (not neces-sarily must) bear a less degree of guilt than the actual killer: and even if the rule of exclusion is absolute, or nearly so in relation to the latter, it need not be so in lesser cases. Nobody would dispute that the greater the degree of heinousness of the crime, the greater and less resistible must be the degree of pressure, if pressure is to excuse. Questions of this kind where it is necessary to weigh the pressures acting upon a man against the gravity of the act he commits are common enough in the criminal law, for example with regard to provocation and self-defence: their difficulty is not a reason for a total rejection of the defence. To say that the defence may be admitted in relation to some degrees of murder, but that its admission in cases of direct killing by a first degree principal is likely to be attended by such great difficulty as almost to justify a ruling that the defence is not available, is not illogical. It simply involves the recognition that by sufficiently adding to the degrees, one may approach an absolute position.

So I find no convincing reason, on principle, why, if a defence of duress in the criminal law exists at all, it should be absolutely excluded in murder charges whatever the nature of the charge; hard to establish, yes, in case of direct killing so hard that perhaps it will never be proved: but in other cases to be judged, strictly indeed, on the totality of facts. Exclusion, if not arbitrary, must be based either on authority or policy. I shall deal with each.

As to authority, this has been fully examined by others of your Lordships and I shall not duplicate the process. The stream is reasonably clear if not deep. I do not think it open to controversy (i) that a defence of duress is known to English law and has been so known since the 14th century. (In one form or another it seems to be admitted in all common law and civil law jurisdictions.); (ii) that the defence is admitted in English law as absolving from guilt, not as diminishing responsibility or as merely mitigating the punishment. Some authors do indeed suggest the latter, at least in relation to homicide (cf. *East's Pleas of the Crown* (1803), p. 225) and there may be a case (not an unanswerable case) for saying, generally, that this ought to be the law. It clearly, however, is not the law and, particularly where sentence is mandatory, whether of death or life imprisonment, Parliamentary action would be necessary if proof of duress were to operate upon the sentence. It would also be necessary if duress were to be admitted as diminishing responsibility; (iii) that there is no direct English judicial authority against its application to charges of murder . . .

The broad question remains how this House, clearly not bound by any precedent, should now state the law with regard to this defence in relation to the facts of the present case. I have no doubt that it is open to us, on normal judicial principles, to hold the defence admissible. We are here in the domain of the common law: our task is to fit what we can see as principle and authority to the facts before us, and it is no obstacle that these facts are new. The judges have always assumed responsibility for deciding questions of principle relating to criminal liability and guilt, and particularly for setting the standards by which the law expects normal men to act. In all such matters as capacity, sanity, drunkenness, coercion, necessity, provocation, self-defence, the common law, through the judges, accepts and sets the standards of right-thinking men of normal firmness and humanity at a level which people can accept and respect. The House is not inventing a new defence: on the contrary, it would not discharge its judicial duty if it failed to define the law's attitude to this particular defence in particular circumstances. I would decide that the defence is in law admissible in a case of aiding and abetting murder, and so in the present case. I would leave cases of direct killing by a principal in the first degree to be dealt with as they arise."

LORD SIMON OF GLAISDALE (dissenting): "Any sane and humane system of criminal justice must be able to allow for all such situations as the following, and not merely for some of them. A person, honestly and reasonably believing that a loaded pistol is at his back which will in all probability be used if he disobeys, is ordered to do an act prima facie criminal. Similarly, a person whose child has been kidnapped, and whom as a consequence of threats he honestly and reasonably believes to be in danger of death or mutilation if he does not perform an act prima facie criminal. Or his neighbour's child in such a situation. Or any child. Or any human being. Or his home, a national heritage, threatened to be blown up. Or a stolen masterpiece of art destroyed. Or his son financially ruined. Or his savings for the old age of himself and his wife put in peril. In other words, a sane and humane system of criminal justice needs some general flexibility, and not merely some quirks of deference to certain odd and arbitrarily defined human weaknesses. In fact our own system of criminal justice has such flexibility, provided that it is realised that it does not consist only in the positive prohibitions and injunctions of the criminal law, but extends also to its penal sanctions. May it not be that the infinite variety of circumstances in which the lawful wish of the actor is overborne could be accommodated with far greater flexibility, with much less anomaly, and with avoidance of the social evils which would attend acceptance of the appellant's argument (that duress is a general criminal defence), by taking those circumstances into account in the sentence of the court? Is not the whole rationale of duress as a criminal defence that it recognises that an act prohibited by the criminal law may be morally innocent? Is not an absolute discharge just such an acknowledgment of moral innocence? Nor should one even stop short at the sentence of the court. Does not our system of criminal justice extend more widely still—to the discretion of prosecutors, to the exercise of the prerogative of mercy, to the operations of the Parole Board?

I spoke of the social evils which might be attendant on the recognition of a general defence of duress. Would it not enable a gang leader of notorious violence to confer on his organisation by terrorism immunity from the criminal law? Every member of his gang might well be able to say with truth, 'It was as much as my life was worth to disobey.' Was this not in essence the plea of the appellant? We do not, in general, allow a superior officer to confer such immunity on his subordinates by any defence of obedience to orders: why should we allow it to terrorists? Nor would it seem to be sufficient to stipulate that no one can plead duress as a defence who had put himself into a position in which duress could be exercised on himself. Might not his very initial involvement with, and his adherence to, the gang be due to terrorism? Would it be fair to exclude a defence of duress on the ground that its subject should have sought police protection, were the police unable to guarantee immunity, or were co-operation with the police reasonably believed itself to be a warrant for physical retribution? (If *Reg.* v. *Hudson* [1971] 2 Q.B. 202 is to be taken as a growing point for this part of the law, it suggests that the impossibility of recourse to the police is not a necessary precondition for the defence of duress). In my respectful submission your Lordships should hesitate long lest you may be inscribing a charter for terrorists, gang-leaders and kidnappers.

As Stephen pointed out, coercion lies at the very basis of the criminal law itself. The criminal law is itself a system of threats of pains and penalties if its commands are disregarded. Is it to abdicate because some subject institutes a countervailing system of threats? The answer might well be a reluctant Yes, if the only alternative were to require something more than ordinary human nature can reasonably be expected to bear. But is that the only alternative? Are prosecutors bound to indict? Have English courts no power and duty to reflect moral guilt in the sentence? (I shall deal later with murder, where the penalty is a fixed one.) . . .

There is, however, an apparent exception to such flexibility. This is constituted where a crime has a fixed penalty—specifically, murder with its fixed penalty of life imprisonment. It is true that prosecutors have a discretion whether to indict; but such discretion is hardly real in the circumstances which fall for your Lordships' instant consideration. It is true that the Home Secretary can advise exercise of the royal prerogative of mercy, and that the Parole Board can mitigate the rigour of the penal code; but these are executive not forensic processes, and can only operate after the awful verdict with its dire sentence has been pronounced. Is a sane and humane law incapable of encompassing this situation? I do not believe so.

An infraction of the criminal code under duress does not involve that the conduct is either involuntary or unintentional. The actor is therefore responsible for his act. But his responsibility is diminished by the duress. Provocation operates similarly to diminish the responsibility, transmuting the great crime of murder to the lesser crime of manslaughter with no fixed penalty."

LORD KILBRANDON(dissenting): "The next aspect of the matter leads me to the little I have to say on policy. The difference between the defence of duress, which comes from coercion by the act of man, and that of necessity, which comes from coercion by the forces of nature, is narrow and unreal. Counsel for the appellant was, in my opinion, right to concede that if his argument succeeded, the case of *Reg.* v. *Dudley and Stephens,* 14 Q.B.D. 273 must be held to have been wrongly decided. It seems clear that, if the argument for the appellant is sound, the judge in that case ought to have directed the jury that in law the defence of necessity was available, and to have taken a plain verdict of 'guilty' or 'not guilty.' If that be so it will then become essential, at some time or other, to decide how far the doctrine of necessity is to extend. Unless, for example, want is to be allowed to excuse theft, a strange situation would arise. Suppose that in the instant case the accused had acted under the threat of violence to his family. Then, although if he had taken a loaf from a supermarket to feed his starving children he would have been a thief, he is guiltless if, for his family's safety, he kills the father of Constable Carroll's children. Again, it is impossible not to be deeply impressed by the circumstances, dramatically figured by your Lordships, which are especially liable to occur at this moment in Northern Ireland; the coercion of otherwise law-abiding citizens could, under present law, turn them into unwilling murderers. On the other hand, if the present law be altered, coercion will be a good defence to one who, at the behest of a mafia or I.R.A. boss, places a bomb in an aircraft and 250 people are killed. It is more likely, too, that the accused will have assisted by preparing and delivering the bomb knowing its intended use; in that case the question would be, is coercion a good defence to murder as a principal in the second degree or as accessory? This situation was long ago foreseen. The closing passage of the judgment in *Reg.* v. *Dudley and Stephens* points out that, if the defence were a good one, the strongest man on board the boat might have eaten his way through all the crew, killing them one by one, and after his rescue have been held guiltless. How many may a man kill in order to save his own life? I pose such a question for the purpose of suggesting that it cannot be answered in this place. It raises issues, some legal, others social, even more ethical, upon which the public will clamour to be heard. It would probably be necessary, too, to lay down that coercion would not avail one who, e.g., took orders from the head of the gang of which he was a voluntary member. Such a provision figures in the codes; I do not see how it could become part of English law save by legislation. In short, the policy questions are so deeply embedded in the legal doctrines we are being asked to review that we may be in danger of reforming the law upon an inadequate appreciation of public needs and public opinion. What would purport to be a judgment declaratory of the common law would in reality be a declaration of public policy."

Appeal allowed; new trial ordered.

NOTES

Lynch was in fact convicted when re-tried.

Compare the views of Lord Simon on the proper effect of a plea of duress with those of Lord Keith in *Docherty and Ors.* (*ante*).

To what extent is Lord Kilbrandon question—begging when he uses the expression "unwilling murderers"?

6. **Abbot v. The Queen**
[1976] 3 All E.R. 140

The appellant was a member of a commune in Trinidad, which was presided over by a man called Malik. On the orders of the latter, the appellant, along with other members of the commune and a hired killer, took a leading part in the murder of a young woman. The appellant held her while she was stabbed by a third party, and helped to bury her alive. At his trial on a charge of murder, the appellant raised a defence of duress, the substance of which was that he had participated in the killing because of threats made by Malik against the appellant and his mother. The trial judge refused to leave this defence to the jury and the appellant was convicted. He appealed to the Privy Council.

LORD SALMON: "Whilst their Lordships feel bound to accept the decision of the House of Lords in *Lynch* v. *Director of Public Prosecutions for Northern Ireland* [noted *ante*] they find themselves constrained to say that had they considered (which they do not) that that decision was an authority which required the extension of the doctrine to cover cases like the present, they would not have accepted it.

Their Lordships will now consider the question whether *Lynch* v. *Director of Public Prosecutions for Northern Ireland* can properly be regarded as any authority for the proposition advanced on behalf of the appellant that duress affords him a complete defence although he was a principal in the first degree, having clearly taken an active, prominent and indispensable part in the actual killing of Gale Benson.

The majority of the noble and learned Lords who decided *Lynch* v. *Director of Public Prosecutions for Northern Ireland* certainly said nothing to support the contention now being made on behalf of the appellant. At best, from the appellant's point of view, they left the point open. Indeed, there are passages in some of their speeches which suggest that duress can be of no avail to a charge of murder as principal in the first degree. Lord Morris of Borth-y-Gest said: 'It may be that the law must deny such a defence [i.e. duress] to an actual killer, and that the law will not be irrational if it does so.' He went on to explain the difference between the situation in which a man under a real threat of death or serious violence (a) carries a gun or drives a car to a place with the knowledge that at such place those exercising the duress plan to kill and (b) the man who under the same threat is the actual killer. Of the former he said: 'The final and fatal moment of decision has not arrived. He saves his own life at time when the loss of another life is not a certainty.' Of the latter he said: '. . . the person is told that to save his life he himself must personally . . . pull the trigger or otherwise . . . do the act of killing. There, I think, before allowing duress as a defence it may be that the law will have to call a halt.' Of the dissenting judgement of Bray C.J. in *R. v. Brown and Morley* [1968] S.A.S.R. 467 he said: 'In a closely reasoned judgment, the persuasive power of which appeals to me, [Bray C.J.] held that it was wrong to say that no type of duress can ever afford a defence to any type of complicity in murder though he drew a line of limitation when he said: "I repeat also that as at present advised I do not think duress could constitute a defence to one who actually kills or attempts to kill the victim." '

Lord Wilberforce said: 'Indeed, to justify the deliberate killing by one's own hand of another human being may be something that no pressure or threat even to one's own life . . . can justify—no such case ever seems to have reached the courts. But if one accepts the test of heinousness, this does not, in my opinion, involve that all cases of what is murder in law must be treated in the same way. Heinousness is a word of degree, and that there are lesser degrees of heinousness, even of involvement in homicide, seems beyond doubt. An accessory before the fact, or an aider or abettor, may (not necessarily must) bear a less degree of guilt than the actual killer: and even if the rule of exclusion is absolute, or nearly so in relation to the latter, it need not be so in lesser cases . . . The conclusion which I deduce is that although, in a case of actual killing by a first degree principal the balance of judicial authority at the present time is against the admission of the defence of duress, in the case of lesser degrees of participation, the balance is, if anything, the other way.'

It seems to their Lordships that if one adds these passages from the speeches of Lord Morris of Borth-y-Gest and Lord Wilberforce to those of Lord Simon of Glaisdale and Lord Kilbrandon, who disssented in *Lynch* v. *Director of Public Prosecutions for Northern Ireland,* the majority of the House was of the opinion that duress is not a defence to a charge of murder against anyone proved to have done the actual killing. However this may be, their Lordships are clearly of the opinion that in such a case, duress, as the law now stands, affords no defence. For reasons which will presently be explained their Lordships, whilst loyally accepting the decision in *Lynch's* case, are certainly not prepared to extend it. . . .

Counsel for the appellant has argued that the law now pre-supposes a degree of heroism of which the ordinary man is incapable and which therefore should not be expected of him and that modern conditions and concepts of humanity have rendered obsolete the rule that the actual killer cannot rely on duress as a defence. Their Lordships do not agree. In the trials of those responsible for wartime atrocities such as mass killings of men, women or children, inhuman experiments on human beings, often resulting in death, and like crimes, it was invariably argued for the defence that these atrocities should be excused on the ground that they resulted from superior orders and duress: if the accused had refused to do these dreadful things, they would have been shot and therefore they should be acquitted and allowed to go free. This argument has always been universally rejected. Their Lordships would be sorry indeed to see it accepted by the common law of England.

It seems incredible to their Lordships that in any civilised society, acts such as the appellant's, whatever threats may have been made to him, could be regarded as excusable or within the law. We are not living in a dream world in which the mounting wave of violence and terrorism can be contained by strict logic and intellectual niceties alone. Common sense surely reveals the added dangers to which in this modern world the public would be exposed, if the change in the law proposed on behalf of the appellant were effected. It might well, as Lord Simon of Glaisdale said in *Lynch* v. *Director of Public Prosecutions for Norther Ireland* prove to be a charter for terrorists, gang leaders and kidnappers. A terrorist of notorious violence might, e.g., threaten death to A and his family unless A obeys his instructions to put a bomb with a time fuse set by A in a certain passenger aircraft and/or a thronged market, railway station or the like. A, under duress, does obey his instructions and as a result, hundreds of men, women and children are killed or mangled. Should the contentions made on behalf of the appellant be correct, A would have a complete defence and, if charged would be bound to be acquitted and set at liberty. Having now gained some real experience and expertise, he might again be approached by the terrorist who would make the same threats and exercise the same duress under which A would then give a repeat performance, killing even more men, women and children. Is there any limit to the number of people you may kill to save your own life and that of your family?

We have been reminded that it is an important part of the judge's role to adapt and develop the principles of the common law to meet the changing needs of time. We have been invited to exercise this role by changing the law so that on a charge of murder in the first degree, duress shall entitle the killer to be acquitted and go scot-free. . . . Their Lordships, however, are firmly of the opinion that the invitation extended to them on behalf of the appellant goes far beyond adapting and developing the principles of the common law. What has been suggested is the destruction of a fundamental doctrine of our law which might well have far-reaching and disastrous consequences for public safety, to say nothing of its important social, ethical and maybe political implications. Such a decision would be far beyond their Lordships' powers even if they approved —as they certainly do not—of this revolutionary change in the law proposed on behalf of the appellant. Judges have no power to create new criminal offences nor, in their Lordships' opinion, for the reasons already stated, have they the power to invent a new defence to murder which is entirely contrary to fundamental legal doctrine, accepted for hundreds of years without question . . .

Their Lordships, however, consider that the law relating to duress is in an unsatisfactory state. . . .

Any murderer who kills under duress would be less, in many cases far less, blameworthy than another who has killed of his own free will. Should not the law recognise this factor? A verdict of guilty of murder carries with it a mandatory sentence, in this country life imprisonment, in other parts of the Commonwealth death. There is much to be said for the view that on a charge of murder, duress, like provocation, should not entitle the accused to a clean acquittal but should reduce murder to manslaughter and thus give the court power to pass whatever sentence might be appropriate in all the circumstances of the case."

LORDS WILBERFORCE AND EDMUND-DAVIES (dissenting): "*Lynch* v. *Director of Public Prosecutions for Northern Ireland* having been decided as it was, the most striking feature of the present appeal is the lack of any indication, in the judgement of the majority, *why* a flat declaration that in no circumstances whatsoever may the actual killer be absolved by a plea of duress makes for sounder law and better ethics. In truth, the contrary is the case. For example, D attempts to kill P but, though injuring him, fails. When charged with attempted murder he may plead duress (*R.* v. *Fegan,*

September 20, 1974, unreported and several times referred to in *Lynch's* case). Later P dies and D is charged with his murder; if the majority of their Lordships are right, he now has no such plea available. Again, no one can doubt that our law would today allow duress to be pleaded in answer to a charge, under s.18 of the Offences against the Person Act 1861, of wounding with intent. Yet here again, should the victim die after the conclusion of the first trial, the accused when faced with a murder charge would be bereft of any such defence. It is not the mere lack of logic that troubles one. It is when one stops to consider why duress is ever permitted as a defence even to charges of great gravity that the lack of any moral reason justifying its *automatic* exclusion in such cases as the present becomes so baffling—and so important.

The majority have deemed it right to resurrect in the present appeal objections to the admissibility of a plea of duress which, if accepted, would leave *Lynch* v. *Director of Public Prosecutions for Northern Ireland* with only vestigial authority, even though the decision resulted from their demolition. One example of this is the alleged ease with which bogus pleas of duress can be advanced, and the so-called 'charter for terrorists, gang-leaders and kidnappers' originally raised by Lord Simon of Glaisdale in *Lynch's* case, just as though the pleas of duress had merely to be raised for an acquittal automatically to follow. But the realistic view is that, the more dreadful the circumstances of the killing, the heavier the evidential burden of an accused advancing such a plea, and the stronger and more irresistible the duress needed before it could be regarded as affording any defence (cf. *Lynch's* case, per Lord Wilberforce). That the learned trial judge in the present case was perfectly capable of dealing searchingly with any pleas of duress is clearly established by his admirable summing-up on those issues which he in fact left to the jury as well as by the remarks he made on the evidence of duress which he did not leave to the jury. And those who are forever apprehensive of the gullibility of juries need to be reminded yet again of the wise words of Dixon J. in *Thomas* v. *R.* (1937) 59 C.L.R. 279 at 309: 'a lack of confidence in the ability of a tribunal correctly to estimate evidence of states of mind and the like can never be sufficient ground for excluding from inquiry the most fundamental element in a rational and humane criminal code.' "

Appeal dismissed.

NOTES

Cf. H.M. Advocate v. *Peters and Ors.* (1969) 33 J.C.L. 209: question reserved whether, on a charge of murder, coercion could be a defence. The evidence of coercion was, in any event, insufficient, and the defence was withdrawn from the jury.

Is there necessarily a "lack of logic" in the approach of the majority in *Abbot?* If one treats duress as a matter of excuse rather than something which affects *mens rea,* or which justifies the accused's actions, is it illogical to say that attempted murder, or wounding with intent may be excused, but that murder may not?

Scots law makes no distinction between principals and accessories, but is there room for the *Lynch—Abbot* distinction in Scots law in view of Hume's statement about a "backward and inferior part in the perpetration"?

c.   *Superior orders*

1.   **H.M. Advocate v. Hawton and Parker**
(1861) 4 Irv. 58

The accused were, respectively, a boatswain in the Royal Navy, and a marine. They were sent out at night with a party of seamen to intercept persons who were illegally trawl fishing in Lochfyne. On the orders of the boatswain the marine fired on the trawlers to make them stop fishing and come to the shore. Blank shot was used at first, then live rounds were fired, with the intention of going wide of the trawlers. One shot, however, hit and killed one of the fishermen. The accused were charged with murder or alternatively culpable homicide. The Crown passed from the charge of murder, but sought a conviction on the latter charge.

THE LORD JUSTICE-GENERAL (MCNEILL): "There was no doubt that, on this occasion, the prisoners went out in the performance of their duty, and that they were armed in the usual manner; and also, that the fishermen were at the time engaged in an unlawful occupation; and it was also beyond question that a person in one of these boats had been killed by a shot fired by Parker. The question was, were either of the prisoners responsible?

The prisoners were enlisted in the naval service of the country, and were bound to follow the rules of that service. It was not necessary to discuss how far the employment of persons in the naval service in such a duty as suppressing trawling, imported into that employment the rules of the naval service. But subordinate officers or privates were not persons who were entitled to consider whether the rules to which they had been accustomed were imported into this duty, unless that were explained to them by their superior officers. One of the prisoners in this case had a certain command, the other was in the position of a subordinate; and it was the duty of the subordinate to obey his superior officer, unless the order given by his superior was so flagrantly and violently wrong that no citizen could be expected to obey it. But that principle extended also to the other prisoner, the officer then in command, because he was there also as a subordinate to fulfil the duty entrusted to him according to the rules of the service. And, therefore, if, when the prisoners fired the shots with the view of making the fishermen yield to legal authority, they were acting in accordance with the usage of the naval service, they were not guilty of any violation of the law.

But then in doing that it was incumbent on them to take due care of the lives of the fishermen; their object in firing was not to produce death or injury, but merely to give notice to these persons that they were required to submit to the law; and they were bound to take care that the shots fired for that purpose were not so carelessly fired as to produce injury or death. . . . [If the jury] were of opinion that the prisoners had acted in accordance with the rules of the naval service, and had not acted carelessly or recklessly, the prisoners were entitled to an acquittal. If, on the other hand, they were of opinion that they had deviated from the rules of the service, or that, in acting according to the rules of the service, they had failed to use due caution, they were then bound to give a verdict against the prisoners."

Verdict: Not guilty.

2. H.M. Advocate v. Sheppard
1941 J.C. 67

The accused, a private in the Pioneer Corps, was part of an escort under the charge of a lance-corporal, whose duty it was to return a deserter from the Corps to their regiment. The accused was left alone with the deserter for a few minutes, during which time the deserter tried to escape and the accused shot and killed him. It appeared from the evidence that no clear orders had been given as regards shooting at escaping prisoners, but it was established that the lance-corporal had told the accused to stand no nonsense and to shoot if necessary. The accused explained that he had not intended to kill, but merely to frighten, the prisoner who had already made two abortive attempts to escape (both of which had been thwarted by the accused). The accused was charged with assault and murder (the latter being reduced by the Crown to culpable homicide during the trial).

In his charge to the jury the presiding judge made the following remarks.

LORD ROBERTSON: "Now, first of all, about culpable homicide. Here, the killing of Fitzgerald is not in dispute, but the question for you on the charge of culpable homicide that is made against the accused is: Was the accused culpable, and was he culpable in the degree required to make the crime . . . of culpable homicide? Now that degree of culpability is higher than mere negligence such as would suffice to substantiate, for instance, a civil claim of damages by let me say, the widow of a person who had been killed by negligence on the part of the person accused. The degree is higher than that. To make the crime of culpable homicide, the degree of culpability must be what is described by Lord Justice-Clerk Alness in the case to which the learned Dean of Faculty referred me *(H.M. Advocate* v. *Cranston,* 1931 J.C. 28) as 'gross and palpable careless-ness'; or, to take an expression from another judge, Lord Justice-Clerk Aitchison . . . the position is this, that 'a person is not criminally liable for a mere act of negligence. He may be civilly liable, but he would not be criminally liable. Before you can convict of the second charge'—that is, culpable homicide—'you must be able to say that the accused acted with such gross and wicked recklessness that his conduct ought properly to be regarded as criminal conduct'.

Now that is the position which you have to consider generally before you come to the facts of the case on the charge made against the accused of culpable homicide; and I would just like to add a little as to what Lord Justice-Clerk Aitchison said in the case to which I have referred, *H.M. Advocate* v. *Macpherson* (Edinburgh High Court, September 1940, *unreported).* It was the case of a soldier not on duty, but on leave. He had come up from the south, somewhere in England, to Edinburgh, and in the course of the black-out, and while an air-raid alert was in progress, he took it upon himself, having a rifle and ammunition, to shoot at a motor-car which was proceeding along the road, as he thought at an excessive rate of speed, and, as he thought, with its lights not sufficiently dimmed. It so happened that the motor-car was a police car, and contained the Assistant Chief Constable of Edinburgh, and the Assistant Chief Constable was shot and killed, and the accused man was accused of culpable homicide. In that case what Lord Aitchison said to the jury, amongst other things, was this: 'If the shot was deliberately directed at the car, as it was, in which these people were travelling, that was criminal recklessness in the sense of the indictment unless there are proved facts in the case that will justify you in saying that the act of the accused can be excused upon some reasonable ground, but I must emphasise the words "upon some reasonable ground." It won't do for a soldier on leave to discharge a loaded rifle in the public street and take human life and then seek to evade the responsibility for his act by saying that he thought he was doing his duty. You must ask yourselves whether there were any reasonable grounds, such as might influence a man in his sober senses, for the accused acting as he did.' . . . His Lordship went on: 'Now I am bound to tell you that there are no facts proved in this case that would justify a plea of justifiable homicide.' You will remember, however, the soldier there was on leave with no duty to perform at the moment. He added: 'We are not in the region of justifiable homicide at all. The question is not—Was the accused justified in taking Thomson's life?'—Thomson was the Assistant Chief Constable—'That is not the question. The question is—Is it proved that he acted with criminal recklessness? And that just comes down to the other question—Had he, looking at it broadly, some kind of just excuse for what he did?' And then I ask you to note that his Lordship added this: 'Even in a case where the soldier was on leave and had no specific duty to perform, if you are able to say that the accused acted under a mistaken sense of duty and that he had some reasonable cause for what he did, you would be entitled to acquit him.' . . . Now the accused was on duty, unlike the accused in the case of *Macpherson* when the Assistant Chief Constable of Edinburgh was shot. The accused was on duty, and his immediate duty was to keep in custody, and to deliver up, the man whom he was escorting. In such a case it is obviously not impossible by any means for a jury to take the view that, if the circumstances were such as to require the accused, for the due execution of his duty, to shoot in order to keep this man in custody, then the homicide was justifiable, and so to acquit the accused entirely of the crime charged against him. The question is—and it is a question for you, the jury—whether on the facts the conclusion that there was no crime in the matter, but only the execution, painful as it might be, of a duty imposed upon the accused—whether that conclusion is a proper one. In considering it, it will be right for you to keep in view the situation in which the accused was placed. He was a soldier on duty in charge of a deserter and under obligation to deliver up the body of the deserter to headquarters. It would be altogether wrong to judge his actings, so placed, too meticulously—to weigh them in fine scales. If that were to be done, it seems to me that the actings of soldiers on duty might well be paralysed by fear of consequences, with great prejudice to national interests. . . .

[His Lordship referred to Hume's treatment of superior orders (Hume, *Commentaries,* i, p. 205) and continued:] and on the facts now the question for you will be whether, making the allowance to which the accused as a soldier on duty is properly entitled, you must nevertheless convict him of the crime of culpable homicide: or whether you can acquit him entirely of crime. Now that comes down to this, I think. Was this shooting, in a proper sense, in the line of the accused's duty as reasonably understood by him, or was it an act which, while falling short of murder, is yet proved to have been of such gross and wicked recklessness that the conduct of the accused must properly be regarded as criminal conduct? These are the two alternatives. In the former case, that is, if the shooting was in the line of the accused's duty, then the homicide was justified and the proper verdict would be one of not guilty—applying to the whole of the indictment. In the latter case, that is if there is to your satisfaction proof of gross and wicked recklessness, then the proper verdict, as it seems to me, would be one of guilty as libelled on the whole indictment, as now restricted to an indictment of assault and culpable homicide."

Verdict: Not guilty.

NOTES

What would have been the position if the Crown had proved that there was a general order not to shoot at escaping prisoners? Would the more immediate order of the lance-corporal have provided a defence? See Gordon, para. 13-36.

Lord Robertson suggests that acting in the line of duty and criminal recklessness are "alternatives." How does this compare with the views of the Lord Justice-General in *Hawton and Parker?*

In *U.S.* v. *Calley*, 22 U.S.M.C.A. 534 (1973) the following directions by the trial judge were upheld by the military appeal court: "A determination that an order is illegal does not, of itself, assign criminal responsibility to the person following the order for acts done in compliance with it. Soldiers are taught to follow orders, and special attention is given to obedience of orders on the battlefield. Military effectiveness depends upon obedience to orders. On the other hand, the obedience of a soldier is not the obedience of an automaton. A soldier is a reasoning agent, obliged to respond, not as a machine, but as a person. The law takes these factors into account in assessing criminal responsibility for acts done in compliance with illegal orders.

The acts of a subordinate done in compliance with an unlawful order given him by his superior are excused and impose no criminal liability upon him unless the superior's order is one which a man of ordinary sense and understanding would, under the circumstances, know to be unlawful, or if the order in question is actually known to the accused to be unlawful."

d. Entrapment

The defence of entrapment arises where the accused pleads that the offence in question was committed at the instigation of a police officer (or other individual acting for the law enforcement agencies) and that without such instigation he would not otherwise have committed the offence.

As a defence this plea has been widely recognised in the United States. Attempts have been made to establish it in England and other Commonwealth jurisdictions, with little success. The defence has not been expressly raised in any Scottish case. Official instigation of crime may, however, be taken into account in sentencing, or with regard to admissibility of evidence (see below).

1. **Sorrells v. U.S.**
287 U.S. 435, 77 L. ed. 413 (1932)

The defendant was charged with possessing and selling liquor contrary to the National Prohibition Act. At his trial he raised a defence of entrapment, which the court refused to allow to go to the jury, holding that "as a matter of law" there was no entrapment. This decision was upheld by the Circuit Court of Appeals. The defendant appealed to the Supreme Court. The facts are fully set out in the opinion of the Chief Justice.

HUGHES C.J.: "The substance of the testimony at the trial as to entrapment was as follows: For the Government, one Martin, a prohibition agent, testified that having resided for a time in Haywood County, North Carolina, where he posed as a tourist, he visited defendant's home near Canton, on Sunday, July 13, 1930, accompanied by three residents of the county who knew the defendant well. He was introduced as a resident of Charlotte who was stopping for a time at Clyde. The witness ascertained that defendant was a veteran of the World War and a former member of the 30th Division A.E.F. Witness informed defendant that he was also an ex-service man and a former member of the same Division, which was true. Witness asked defendant if he could get the witness some liquor and defendant stated that he did not have any. Later, there was a second request without result. One of those present, one Jones, was also an ex-service man and a former member of the 30th Division, and the conversation turned to the war experiences of the three. After this, witness asked defendant for a third time to get him some liquor, whereupon defendant left his home and after a few minutes came back with a half gallon of liquor for which the witness paid defendant five dollars. Martin also testified that he was 'the first and only person among those present at the time who said anything about securing some liquor,' and that his purpose was to prosecute the defendant for procuring and selling it. The Government rested its case on Martin's testimony. . . .

It is clear that the evidence was sufficient to warrant a finding that the act for which the defendant was prosecuted was instigated by the prohibition agent, that it was the creature of his purpose, that defendant had no previous disposition to commit it but was an industrious, law-abiding citizen, and that the agent lured the defendant, otherwise innocent, to its commission by repeated and persistent solicitation in which he succeeded by taking advantage of the sentiment aroused by reminiscences of their experiences as companions in arms in the World War. Such a gross abuse of authority given for the purpose of detecting and punishing crime, and not for the making of criminals, deserves the severest condemnation, but the question whether it precludes prosecution or affords a ground of defense, and, if so, upon what theory, has given rise to conflicting opinions.

It is well settled that the fact that officers or employees of the Government merely afford opportunities or facilities for the commission of the offense does not defeat the prosecution. Artifice and stratagem may be employed to catch those engaged in criminal enterprises. The appropriate object of this permitted activity, frequently essential to the enforcement of the law, is to reveal the criminal design; to expose the illicit traffic, the prohibited publication, the fraudulent use of the mails, the illegal conspiracy, or other offenses, and thus to disclose the would-be violators of the law. A different question is presented when the criminal design originates with the officials of the Government, and they implant in the mind of an innocent person the disposition to commit the alleged offense and induce its commission in order that they may prosecute.

The Circuit Court of Appeals reached the conclusion that the defense of entrapment can be maintained only where, as a result of inducement, the accused is placed in the attitude of having committed a crime which he did not intend to commit, or where, by reason of the consent implied in the inducement, no crime has in fact been committed. . . .

The Federal courts have generally approved the statement of Circuit Judge Sanborn in the leading case of Butts v. United States (C. C. A. 8th) 18 A.L.R. 143, 273 Fed. 38, supra, as follows: 'The first duties of the officers of the law are to prevent, not to punish crime. It is not their duty to incite to and create crime for the sole purpose of prosecuting and punishing it. Here the evidence strongly tends to prove, if it does not conclusively do so, that their first and chief endeavor was to cause, to create, crime in order to punish it, and it is unconscionable, contrary to public policy, and to the established law of the land to punish a man for the commission of an offense of the like of which he had never been guilty, either in thought or in deed, and evidently never would have been guilty of if the officers of the law had not inspired, incited, persuaded, and lured him to attempt to commit it.' The judgment in that case was reversed because of the 'fatal error' of the trial court in refusing to instruct the jury to that effect. . . .

The validity of the principle as thus stated and applied is challenged both upon theoretical and practical grounds. The argument, from the standpoint of principle, is that the court is called upon to try the accused for a particular offense which is defined by statute and that, if the evidence shows that this offense has knowingly been committed, it matters not that its commission was induced by officers of the Government in the manner and circumstances assumed. It is said that where one intentionally does an act in circumstances known to him, and the particular conduct is forbidden by the law in those circumstances, he intentionally breaks the law in the only sense in which the law considers intent. Ellis v. United States, 206 U.S. 246, 257, 51 L. ed. 1047. Moreover, that as the statute is designed to redress a public wrong, and not a private injury, there is no ground for holding the Government estopped by the conduct of its officers from prosecuting the offender. To the suggestion of public policy the objectors answer that the legislature, acting within its constitutional authority, is the arbiter of public policy and that, where conduct is expressly forbidden and penalized by valid statute, the courts are not at liberty to disregard the law and to bar a prosecution for its violation because they are of the opinion that the crime has been instigated by government officials.

It is manifest that these arguments rest entirely upon the letter of the statute. They take no account of the fact that its application in the circumstances under consideration is foreign to its purpose; that such an application is so shocking to the sense of justice that it has been urged that it is the duty of the court to stop the prosecution in the interest of the Government itself, to protect it from the illegal conduct of its officers and to preserve the purity of its courts. Casey v. United States, 276 U.S. 413, 72 L. ed. 632. But can an application of the statute having such an effect—creating a situation so contrary to the purpose of the law and so inconsistent with its proper enforcement as to invoke such a challenge—fairly be deemed to be within its intendment?

Literal interpretation of statutes at the expense of the reason of the law and producing absurd consequences or flagrant injustice has frequently been condemned. . . . In United States v. Kirby, 7 Wall. 482, 19 L. ed. 278, the case arose under the Act of Congress of March 3, 1825, providing for the conviction of any person who 'shall knowingly and willfully obstruct or retard the passage of the mail, or of any driver or carrier . . . carrying the same.' Considering the purpose of the statute, the Court held that it had no application to the obstruction or retarding of the passage of the mail or of its carrier by reason of the arrest of the carrier upon a warrant issued by a state court. The Court said: 'All laws should receive a sensible construction. General terms should be so limited in their application as not to lead to injustice, oppression, or an absurd consequence. It will always, therefore, be presumed that the legislature intended exceptions to its language which would avoid results of this character. The reason of the law in such cases should prevail over its letter.' ...

We think that this established principle of construction is applicable here. We are unable to conclude that it was the intention of the Congress in enacting this statute that its processes of detection and enforcement should be abused by the instigation by government officials of an act on the part of persons otherwise innocent in order to lure them to its commission and to punish them. We are not forced by the letter to do violence to the spirit and purpose of the statute. This, we think, has been the underlying and controlling thought in the suggestions in judicial opinions that the Government in such a case is estopped to prosecute or that the courts should bar the prosecution. If the requirements of the highest public policy in the maintenance of the integrity of administration would preclude the enforcement of the statute in such circumstances as are present here, the same considerations justify the conclusion that the case lies outside the purview of the Act and that its general words should not be construed to demand a proceeding at once inconsistent with that policy and abhorrent to the sense of justice. This view does not derogate from the authority of the court to deal appropriately with abuses of its process and it obviates the objection to the exercise by the court of a dispensing power in forbidding the prosecution of one who is charged with conduct assumed to fall within the statute ...

Objections to the defense of entrapment are also urged upon practical grounds. But considerations of mere convenience must yield to the essential demands of justice. The argument is pressed that if the defense is available it will lead to the introduction of issues of a collateral character relating to the activities of the officials of the Government and to the conduct and purposes of the defendant previous to the alleged offense. For the defense of entrapment is not simply that the particular act was committed at the instance of government officials. That is often the case where the proper action of these officials leads to the revelation of criminal enterprises, Grimm v. United States, 156 U.S. 604, 39 L. ed. 550. The predisposition and criminal design of the defendant are relevant. But the issues raised and the evidence adduced must be pertinent to the controlling question whether the defendant is a person otherwise innocent whom the Government is seeking to punish for an alleged offense which is the product of the creative activity of its own officials. If that is the fact, common justice requires that the accused be permitted to prove it. The Government in such a case is in no position to object to evidence of the activities of its representatives in relation to the accused, and if the defendant seeks acquittal by reason of entrapment he cannot complain of an appropriate and searching inquiry into his own conduct and predisposition as bearing upon that issue. If in consequence he suffers a disadvantage, he has brought it upon himself by reason of the nature of the defense.

What has been said indicates the answer to the contention of the Government that the defense of entrapment must be pleaded in bar to further proceedings under the indictment and cannot be raised under the plea of not guilty. This contention presupposes that the defense is available to the accused and relates only to the manner in which it shall be presented. The Government considers the defense as analogous to a plea of pardon or of autrefois convict or autrefois acquit. It is assumed that the accused is not denying his guilt but is setting up special facts in bar upon which he relies regardless of his guilt or innocence of the crime charged. This, as we have seen, is a misconception. The defense is available, not in the view that the accused though guilty may go free, but that the Government cannot be permitted to contend that he is guilty of a crime where the government officials are the investigators of his conduct. The Federal courts in sustaining the defense in such circumstances have proceeded in the view that the defendant is not guilty. The practice of requiring a plea in bar has not obtained. Fundamentally, the question is whether the defense, if the facts bear out, takes the case out of the purview of the statute because it cannot be supposed that the Congress intended that the letter of its enactment should be used to support such a gross perversion of its purpose.

We are of the opinion that upon the evidence produced in the instant case the defense of entrapment was available and that the trial court was in error in holding that as a matter of law there was no entrapment and in refusing to submit the issue to the jury."

ROBERTS J.: "Society is at war with the criminal classes, and courts have uniformly held that in waging this warfare the forces of prevention and detection may use traps, decoys, and deception to obtain evidence of the commission of crime. Resort to such means does not render an indictment thereafter found a nullity nor call for the exclusion of evidence so procured. But the defense here asserted involves more than obtaining evidence by artifice or deception. Entrapment is the conception and planning of an offense by an officer, and his procurement of its commission by one who would not have perpetrated it except for the trickery, persuasion, or fraud of the officer. Federal and state courts have held that substantial proof of entrapment as thus defined calls for the submission of the issue to the jury and warrants an acquittal. The reasons assigned in support of this procedure have not been uniform. Thus it has been held that the acts of its officers estop the government to prove the offense. The result has also been justified by the mere statement of the rule that where entrapment is proved the defendant is not guilty of the crime charged. Often the defense has been permitted upon grounds of public policy, which the courts formulate by saying they will not permit their process to be used in aid of a scheme for the actual creation of a crime by those whose duty is to deter its commission.

This court has adverted to the doctrine, but has not heretofore had occasion to determine its validity, the basis on which it should rest, or the procedure to be followed when it is involved. The present case affords the opportunity to settle these matters as respects the administration of the federal criminal law.

There is common agreement that where a law officer envisages a crime, plans it, and activates its commission by one not theretofore intending its perpetration, for the sole purpose of obtaining a victim through indictment, conviction and sentence, the consummation of so revolting a plan ought not to be permitted by any self-respecting tribunal. Equally true is this whether the offense is one at common law or merely a creature of statute. Public policy forbids such sacrifice of decency. The enforcement of this policy calls upon the court, in every instance where alleged entrapment of a defendant is brought to its notice, to ascertain the facts, to appraise their effect upon the administration of justice, and to make such order with respect to the further prosecution of the cause as the circumstances require.

This view calls for no distinction between crimes mala in se and statutory offenses of lesser gravity; requires no statutory construction, and attributes no merit to a guilty defendant; but frankly recognizes the true foundation of the doctrine in the public policy which protects the purity of government and its processes. . . . Neither courts of equity nor those administering legal remedies tolerate the use of their process to consummate a wrong. The doctrine of entrapment in criminal law is the analogue of the same rule applied in civil proceedings. And this is the real basis of the decisions approving the defense of entrapment, though in statement the rule is cloaked under a declaration that the government is estopped or the defendant has not been proved guilty.

A new method of rationalizing the defense is now asserted. This is to construe the act creating the offense by reading in a condition or proviso that if the offender shall have been entrapped into crime the law shall not apply to him. So, it is said, the true intent of the legislature will be effectuated. This seems a strained and unwarranted construction of the statute; and amounts, in fact, to judicial amendment. It is not merely broad construction, but addition of an element not contained in the legislation. . . . It cannot truly be said that entrapment excuses him or contradicts the obvious fact of his commission of the offense. We cannot escape this conclusion by saying that where need arises the statute will be read as containing an implicit condition that it shall not apply in the case of entrapment. The effect of such construction is to add to the words of the statute a proviso which gives to the defendant a double defense under his plea of not guilty, namely, (a) that what he did does not fall within the definition of the statute, and (b) entrapment. This amounts to saying that one who with full intent commits the act defined by law as an offense is nevertheless by virtue of the unspoken and implied mandate of the statute to be adjudged not guilty by reason of someone else's improper conduct. It is merely to adopt a form of words to justify action which ought to be based on the inherent right of the court not to be made the instrument of wrong. . . . Proof of entrapment, at any stage of the case, requires the court to stop the prosecution, direct that the indictment be quashed, and the defendant set at liberty. If in doubt as to the facts it may submit the issue of entrapment to a jury for advice. But whatever may be the finding upon such submission the power and the duty to act remain with the court and not with the jury. . . .

Recognition of the defense of entrapment as belonging to the defendant and as raising an issue for decision by the jury called to try him upon plea of the general issue, results in the trial of a false issue wholly outside the true rule which should be applied by the courts. It has been generally held, where the defendant has proved an entrapment, it is permissible for the government to show in rebuttal that the officer guilty of incitement of the crime had reasonable cause to believe the defendant was a person disposed to commit the offense. This procedure is approved by the opinion of the court. The proof received in rebuttal usually amounts to no more than that the defendant had a bad reputation, or that he had been previously convicted. Is the statute upon which the indictment is based to be further construed as removing the defense of entrapment from such a defendant?

Whatever may be the demerits of the defendant or his previous infractions of law these will not justify the instigation and creation of a new crime, as a means to reach him and punish him for his past misdemeanors. He has committed the crime in question, but, by supposition, only because of instigation and inducement by a government officer. To say that much conduct by an official of government is condoned and rendered innocuous by the fact that the defendant had a bad reputation or had previously transgressed is wholly to disregard the reason for refusing the processes of the court to consummate an abhorrent transaction. It is to discard the basis of the doctrine and in effect to weight the equities as between the government and the defendant when there are in truth no equities belonging to the latter, and when the rule of action cannot rest on any estimate of the good which may come of the conviction of the offender by foul means. The accepted procedure, in effect, pivots conviction in such cases, not on the commission of the crime charged, but on the prior reputation or some former act or acts of the defendant not mentioned in the indictment.

The applicable principle is that courts must be closed to the trial of a crime instigated by the government's own agents. No other issue, no comparison of equities as between the guilty official and the guilty defendant, has any place in the enforcement of this overruling principle of public policy."

Judgment reversed.

NOTES

The dispute between the majority view, and that of Roberts J. (with whom Brandeis and Stone JJ. concurred) was taken up again in *Sherman* v. *U.S.*, 356 U.S. 369, 2 L.Ed. 848 (1958) and *Masciale* v. *U.S.*, 356 U.S. 386, 2 L.Ed. 859 (1958). The dispute has been summarised in the following terms *(Grohman* v. *State,* (1970) 41 A.L.R. 3d. 406 (0) (Maryland), per Finan J.): "The majority opinion of the three Supreme Court cases adopted the 'origin of interest tests', which allows the defense of entrapment only if the criminal act was 'the product of the creative activity' of law enforcement officials. In applying this test the court must make two inquiries: (1) whether there was an inducement on the part of the government officials and if so (2) whether the defendant showed any predisposition to commit the offence. The other criterion adopted by the concurring opinions in the *Sorells* and *Sherman* cases and the dissent in *Masciale* based the defense of entrapment upon an objective test whereby the Court considers only the nature of the police activity involved without reference to the predisposition of the particular defendant."

2. **R. v. Mealey and Sheridan**
(1974) 60 Cr.App.R. 59

The appellants, along with a third man, were convicted, *inter alia*, of conspiracy to rob, and sentenced to ten years' imprisonment. They at first sought leave to appeal against sentence only, but subsequently appealed against conviction on the ground that one of their co-conspirators (a man called Lennon who had since been found dead) was a police informer who had acted as an *agent provocateur* in instigating the commission of the offence.

LORD WIDGERY C.J.: "The first thing which must be made clear in fairness to everybody is that there is no evidence, beyond such fragmentary parts of the statements of Mealey and Sheridan as I have indicated, that Lennon was an agent provocateur in the true sense. I say 'in the true sense' because there is a neat definition contained in the report of the Royal Commission on Police Powers (Cmd. 3297) in 1928 where an agent provocateur is taken to mean 'a person who entices another to commit an express breach of the law which he would not otherwise have committed and then proceeds or informs against him in respect of such offence.' I say, in fairness to Lennon and indeed to the police, that it is not established to our satisfaction that Lennon came into that category, but that he was a police informer passing information to the police and co-operating with them is beyond doubt.

So far as the propriety of using methods of this kind is concerned, we think it right to say that in these days of terrorism the police must be entitled to use the effective weapon of infiltration. In other words, it must be accepted today, indeed if the opposite was ever considered, that this is a perfectly lawful police weapon in appropriate cases, and common sense indicates that if a police officer or anybody else infiltrates a suspect society, he has to show a certain amount of enthusiasm for what the society is doing if he is to maintain his cover for more than five minutes. Accordingly one must expect, if this approach is made by the police, that the intruder who penetrates the suspect organisation does show a certain amount of interest and enthusiasm for the proposals of the organisation even though they are unlawful. But, of course, the intruder, the person who finds himself placed in the organisation, must endeavour to tread the somewhat difficult line between showing the necessary enthusiasm to keep his cover and actually becoming an agent provocateur, meaning thereby someone who actually causes offences to be committed which otherwise would not be committed at all.

It is not possible in this case, as I say, in our judgment to decide positively whether Lennon overstepped the mark or not. We really have no reason to suppose that he did, but are prepared for the purposes of this case to assume that he did without it being established before us.

But what then? Mr. O'Connor has strenuously argued that if Lennon was an agent provocateur, or is supposed to be such for present purposes, that that fact would give rise to a defence available to Sheridan, and a defence, of course, which was not before the trial for obvious reasons.

The fundamental question in this case is whether that proposition, however stated, is true; in other words, whether it is true as a matter of law that a defendant can plead not guilty and entitle himself to an acquittal by showing that he acted in concert with or as a result of the conduct of an agent provocateur.

The submission made by Mr. O'Connor is in these terms, and I read them out because it is only fair to him that his submission should be considered against that background. He said: "If the defendant would not have committed a criminal offence but for the activities of a police officer or an agent provocateur, and where those activities are found to be objectively unacceptable to the court, this constitutes a defence.' I say, with all respect to Mr. O'Connor's argument, that for my part, speaking for myself for the moment, I would find it quite impossible to accept as a principle for the practice of criminal law in this country any test so difficult in its construction and so vague in its scope, I really do not know even now what is meant by 'objectively unacceptable,' or who is going to decide the question.

In fact, if one looks at the authorities, it is in our judgment quite clearly established that the so-called defence of entrapment, which finds some place in the law of the United States of America, finds no place in our law here. It is abundantly clear on the authorities, which are uncontradicted on this point, that if a crime is brought about by the activities of someone who can be described as an agent provocateur, although that may be an important matter in regard to sentence, it does not affect the question of guilty or not guilty."

Application refused; conviction
and sentence upheld.

NOTES

The authorities relied upon by his Lordship were *Browning* v. *J.W.H. Watson (Rochester) Ltd.* [1953] 1 W.L.R. 1172, *McEvilly and Lee* (1973) 60 Cr. App. R. 150, *Wright and Cox*, July 1974 (*unreported*) and Smith and Hogan (3rd. ed.) p. 150.

3.   R. v. Sang
[1979] 2 All E.R. 1222

The appellant was charged (*inter alia*) with conspiracy to utter forged American banknotes. He applied to the trial judge for a trial within a trial, seeking a ruling that evidence in relation to the charges against him should be excluded on the ground that the offences were induced by an *agent provocateur*. The judge ruled that he had no discretion to exclude the evidence, and this ruling was upheld by the Court of Appeal. On appeal to the House of Lords:

LORD DIPLOCK: "The decisions in *R.* v. *McEvilly, R.* v. *Lee* (1973) 60 Cr. App. R. 150 and *R.* v. *Mealey, R.* v. *Sheridan* (noted *ante*) that there is no defence of 'entrapment' known to English law are clearly right. Many crimes are committed by one person at the instigation of others. From earliest times at common law those who counsel and procure the commission of the offence by the person by whom the actus reus itself is done have been guilty themselves of an offence, and since the abolition by the Criminal Law Act 1967 of the distinction between felonies and misdemeanours can be tried, indicted and punished as principal offenders. The fact that the counsellor and procurer is a policeman or a police informer, although it may be of relevance in mitigation of penalty for the offence, cannot affect the guilt of the principal offender; both the physical element (actus reus) and the mental element (mens rea) of the offence with which he is charged are present in his case.

My Lords, this being the substantive law on the matter, the suggestion that it can be evaded by the procedural device of preventing the prosecution from adducing evidence of the commission of the offence, does not bear examination. Let me take first the summary offence prosecuted before magistrates where there is no practical distinction between a trial and a trial within a trial. There are three examples of these in the books, *Brannan* v. *Peek* [1948] 1 K.B. 68; *Browning* v. *J.W.H. Watson (Rochester) Ltd.* [1953] 1 W.L.R. 1172; *Sneddon* v. *Stevenson* [1967] 2 All E.R. 1277. Here the magistrates in order to decide whether the crime had in fact been instigated by an agent provocateur acting on police instructions would first have to hear evidence which ex hypothesi would involve proving that the crime had been committed by the accused. If they decided that it had been so instigated, then, despite the fact that they had already heard evidence which satisfied them that it had been committed, they would have a discretion to prevent the prosecution from relying on that evidence as proof of its commission. How does this differ from recognising entrapment as a defence, but a defence available only at the discretion of the magistrates?

Where the accused is charged on indictment and there is a practical distinction between the trial and a trial within a trial, the position, as it seems to me, would be even more anomalous if the judge were to have a discretion to prevent the prosecution from adducing evidence before the jury to prove the commission of the offence by the accused. If he exercised the discretion in favour of the accused he would then have to direct the jury to acquit. How does this differ from recognising entrapment as a defence, but a defence for which the necessary factual foundation is to be found not by the jury but by the judge and even where the factual foundation is so found the defence is available only at the judge's discretion.

My Lords, this submission goes far beyond a claim to a judicial discretion to exclude evidence that has been obtained unfairly or by trickery; nor in any of the English cases on agents provocateurs that have come before appellate courts has it been suggested that it exists. What it really involves is a claim to a judicial discretion to acquit an accused of any offences in connection with which the conduct of the police incurs the disapproval of the judge. The conduct of the police where it has involved the use of an agent provocateur may well be a matter to be taken into consideration in mitigation of sentence; but under the English system of criminal justice it does not give rise to any discretion on the part of the judge himself to acquit the accused or to direct the jury to do so, notwithstanding that he is guilty of the offence. Nevertheless the existence of such a discretion to exclude the evidence of an agent provocateur does appear to have been acknowledged by the Courts-Martial Appeal Court of Northern Ireland in *R.* v. *Murphy* [1965] N.I. 138. That was before the rejection of 'entrapment' as a defence by the Court of Appeal in England; and Lord McDermott C.J. in delivering the judgment of the court relied on the dicta as to the existence of a wide discretion which appeared in cases that did not involve an agent provocateur. In the result he held that the court-martial had been right in exercising its discretion in such a way as to admit the evidence.

I understand your Lordships to be agreed that whatever be the ambit of the judicial discretion to exclude admissible evidence it does not extend to excluding evidence of a crime because the crime was instigated by an agent provocateur. In so far as *R.* v. *Murphy* suggests the contrary it should no longer be regarded as good law".

LORD SALMON: "I would now refer to what is, I believe, and hope, the unusual case in which a dishonest policeman, anxious to improve his detection record, tries very hard with the help of an agent provocateur to induce a young man with no criminal tendencies to commit a serious crime, and ultimately the young man reluctantly succumbs to the inducement. In such a case, the judge has no discretion to exclude the evidence which proves that the young man has committed the offence. He may, however, according to the circumstances of the case, impose a mild punishment on him or even give him an absolute or conditional discharge and refuse to make any order for costs against him. The policeman and the informer who had acted together in inciting him to commit the crime should however both be prosecuted and suitably punished. This would be a far safer and more effective way of preventing such inducements to commit crimes from being made, than a rule that no evidence should be allowed to prove that the crime in fact had been committed."

LORD FRASER OF TULLYBELTON: "The important question is whether the discretion (a) is limited to excluding evidence which is likely to have prejudicial value out of proportion to its evidential value or (b) extends to excluding other evidence which might operate unfairly against the accused and, if so, how far it extends. On the best consideration that I can give to the authorities, I have reached the opinion that the discretion is not limited to excluding evidence which is likely to have prejudicial effects out of proportion to its evidential value. I take first the judgment of Lord Goddard C.J. in *Kuruma Son of Kaniu* v. *R* [1955] A.C. 197 from which I have already quoted. It is true that immediately after saying the judge has discretion to disallow evidence if the strict rules 'would operate unfairly against the accused', Lord Goddard C.J. referred to *Noor Mohamed* v. *R.* [1949] A.C. 182 and *Harris* v. *Director of Public Prosecutions* [1952] A.C. 694, and might therefore seem to have had in mind only cases that would fall within alternative (a) above. But he went on as follows (at p. 204):
'If, for instance, some admission or some piece of evidence, e.g., a document, had been obtained from a defendant by a trick, no doubt the judge might properly rule it out. It was this distinction that lay at the root of the ruling of Lord Guthrie in *H.M. Advocate* v. *Turnbull,* 1951 J.C. 96. The other cases from Scotland to which their Lordships' attention was drawn, *Rattray* v. *Rattray* (1897) 25 R. 315, *Lawrie* v. *Muir,* 1950 J.C. 19, and *Fairley* v. *Fishmongers of London,* 1951 J.C. 14, all support the view that if the evidence is relevant it is admissible and the court is not concerned with how it is obtained. No doubt their Lordships in the Court of Justiciary appear at least to some extent to consider the question from the point of view whether the alleged illegality in the obtaining the evidence could properly be excused. . . .'
I find this passage difficult to follow. *Lawrie* v. *Muir* was a case in which the court held that evidence obtained by an illegal search of the accused's business premises was not *admissible*, because the illegality could not be excused. With the greatest respect, the case does not seem to me to support the proposition, for which it was cited by Lord Goddard C.J., that if the evidence is relevant it is admissible. On the contrary, I think it is an application of the principle well established in Scots criminal law, that 'An irregularity in the obtaining of evidence does not *necessarily* make that evidence inadmissible': see Lord Justice-General Cooper quoting from Lord Justice-Clerk Aitchison in *H.M. Advocate* v. *M'Guigan,* 1936 J.C.

16 at p. 18. A few lines lower down Lord Cooper said: 'Irregularities require to be excused, and infringements of the formalities of the law in relation to these matters are not lightly to be condoned.' Nor can I agree that what lay at the root of Lord Guthrie's decision in *H.M. Advocate* v. *Turnbull* to exclude documentary evidence was that the evidence had been obtained from the accused by a trick. The case is in my opinion another example of evidence obtained from premises occupied by an accused person, by an irregularity which could not be excused. Lord Guthrie's final reason was that it was unfair to the accused to admit the evidence. He said (at pp. 103-104): 'If such important evidence upon a number of charges is tainted by the method by which it was deliberately secured, I am of opinion that a fair trial upon these charges is rendered impossible.'

The decision in *H.M. Advocate* v. *Turnbull* may be contrasted with the decision in *Jeffrey* v. *Black* [1978] Q.B. 490, where it was held that the justices would not have been entitled to exclude evidence 'simply because the evidence in question had been obtained by police officers who had entered [the accused's residence] without the appropriate authority'. It is not particularly surprising that the two decisions may not be easily reconcilable because the law on this matter is not the same in Scotland as it is in England, as has been judicially recognised on both sides of the border: see *King* v. *R.* [1969] 1 A.C. 304 per Lord Hodson at 315, and *Chalmers* v. *H.M. Advocate*, 1954 J.C. 66 per Lord Justice-General Cooper at 77-78. In *Chalmers* v. *H.M. Advocate* Lord Cooper referred to 'the English courts being in use to admit certain evidence which would fall to be rejected in Scotland'. But the principle of fairness to the accused applied by Lord Guthrie in *H.M. Advocate* v. *Turnbull* seems to be the same as that stated by Lord Widgery C.J. in *Jeffrey* v. *Black*, where he said: '. . . the magistrates sitting in this case, like any other criminal tribunal in England and sitting under the English law, have a general discretion to decline to allow any evidence to be called by the prosecution if they think that it would be unfair or oppressive to allow that to be done.' That was the principle that seems to have been recognised by Lord Goddard C.J. in his reference to *H.M. Advocate* v. *Turnbull* and treated by him as applicable in England. . . .

I recognise that there does not appear to be any decision by an appellate court in England clearly based on an exercise of the discretion except when the excluded evidence either (1) is more prejudicial than probative or (2) relates to an admission or confession. . . . But notwithstanding the absence of direct decision on the point, the dicta are so numerous and so authoritative that I do not think it would be right to disregard them, or to treat them as applicable only to cases where the prejudicial effect of the evidence would outweigh its probative value. If they had been intended to have such a limited application, the references to Scottish cases would be inexplicable. In any event, I would be against cutting down their application to that extent.

On the other hand, I doubt whether they were ever intended to apply to evidence obtained from sources other than the accused himself or from premises occupied by him. Indeed it is not easy to see how evidence obtained from other sources, even if the means for obtaining it were improper, could lead to the accused being denied a fair trial. I accordingly agree with my noble and learned friends that the various statements with regard to the discretion to which I have referred should be treated as applying only to evidence and documents obtained from an accused person or from premises occupied by him. That is enough to preserve the important principle that the judge has an overriding discretion to exclude evidence the admission of which would prevent the accused from having a fair trial."

Appeal dismissed.

NOTES

With the exception of Lord Fraser, their Lordships were unanimous in the view that while a court has the power to exclude evidence when its prejudicial effect outweighs its probative value, this discretion could not operate to exclude evidence of the type in question here, since the ground of exclusion was the effect of the evidence, not how it was obtained.

Lord Fraser's view appears to be that, on the principle of fairness, the discretion to exclude evidence extends to the methods by which it is obtained, but that this is limited to evidence obtained from the accused or from premises occupied by him.

4. **Marsh v. Johnston**
1959 S.L.T. (Notes) 28

Two plain clothes police officers entered the complainer's hotel, where they saw two customers apparently being served with drinks outside the permitted hours. They ordered a drink and were themselves served. They then called uniformed officers and the complainer was charged with an offence contrary to s. 4 of the Licensing Act 1921. On conviction, he presented a bill of suspension to the High Court, complaining, *inter alia,* "that since the two plain clothes police officers had themselves committed an offence in ordering a drink outside permitted hours, their evidence was vitiated."

LORD JUSTICE-GENERAL (CLYDE): "It may be that in ordering a drink outside permitted hours and in tasting it the police were guilty of a technical offence under the Act, but this was a sheer technicality and was not done to procure the commission of an offence but to detect and confirm that offences were being committed. In the circumstances it does not appear to me that there was anything in the conduct of the police which was in the least improper, still less does it make their evidence incompetent. As Lord Young said in the *Southern Bowling Club* v. *Ross* (1902) 4 F. 405 at page 415, 9 S.L.T. 155, in a case of shebeening 'The only way that occurs to me of detecting offences is for the police to employ detectives, and where a club is suspected of shebeening the only mode of discovering the truth of the matter is for detectives to go to the club and ask to be supplied with spirits.' It appears to me that that observation is very much in point in a case where a licence-holder is suspected of selling drinks outside the hours permitted by his licence. The present case itself shows how difficult it would be to prove offences of this nature unless police evidence of this kind were used, for the two customers whom the police saw being supplied with liquor after closing time both denied that they had purchased any liquor after that time. If evidence of this kind was to be regarded by the Court as necessarily being incompetent, there would be a wholesale flouting of the provisions of Acts of Parliament. It would have been a very different matter if any unfairness to the complainer had been established. If, for instance, the police had pressed him to commit the offence or had tricked him into committing an offence which he would not otherwise have committed the position would have been quite different. But there is no question of anything of that kind here. The police officers were instructed not to buy any drink outside hours until they had seen two other customers supplied with drink outside the permitted time. When they intervened the Act of Parliament had already been breached by the complainer, and they were engaged in detecting the commission of an offence against the Act. There can, in my view, be no justification in treating such evidence as being in any way unfair. In cases of this type in Scotland the test for the competency of such police evidence is 'was it fair to the accused', and in determining that matter the Court has got to try to reconcile two important interests which are liable to come into conflict, (1) the interests of the citizen to be protected from illegal or irregular invasion of his liberties by the authorities, and (2) the interest of the State to secure that evidence bearing upon the commission of a crime and necessary to enable justice to be done shall not be withheld from a Court of Law on any mere formal or technical ground. (See Lord Justice-General Cooper in *Lawrie* v. *Muir*, 1950 J.C. 26; *Fairley* v. *Fishmongers of London*, 1951 J.C. 14

at page 24). Reference was made in the course of the argument to a *dictum* of Lord Chief Justice Goddard in the English case of *Brannan* v. *Peek* [1948] 1 K.B. 68 at page 72. In that case, however, the policeman concerned had deliberately misled the accused as to who he was, in order to induce the accused to accept a bet or bets laid by the policeman, and it was in respect of the bets so laid that the police brought the charge in question. The conduct of the policeman in that case was grossly unfair and amounted to a trick upon the accused, in order to induce him to commit an offence . . . But the situation in the present case is quite different and whatever may be the practice in England, where criminal law is administered under a different system from ours, it is settled in practice here that fairness to the accused is the true criterion for the admissibility of police evidence. I see nothing unfair in what took place in the present case."

Appeal refused.

NOTES

In *Brannan* v. *Peek* [1948] 1 K.B. 68 the appellant was convicted of an offence against the Street Betting Act 1906, s.1(4). On two occasions he had taken bets from a police officer in a public house. On both occasions the officer was in plain clothes, and on at least one occasion the appellant was clearly reluctant to accept the bet. Lord Goddard C.J. had this to say about the activities of the police:

"The court observes with concern and strong disapproval the fact that the police authority at Derby thought it right in this case to send a police officer into a public house for the purposes of committing an offence in that house. It cannot be too strongly emphasised that, unless an Act of Parliament provides that for the purposes of detecting offences police officers or others may be sent into premises to commit offences therein . . . it is wholly wrong to allow a practice of that sort to take place. . . . If, as the police authority assumed, a bookmaker commits an offence by taking a bet in a public house, it is just as much an offence for a police constable to make a bet with him in the public house and it is quite wrong that the police officer should be instructed to commit this offence.

I hope the day is far distant when it will become a common practice in this country for police officers who are sent into premises for the purposes of detecting crime to be told to commit an offence themselves for the purpose of getting evidence against another person." (In the All E.R. version of this report the following words appear: "if they do commit offences they ought also to be convicted and punished for the order of their superior would afford no defence.")

5.   Cook v. Skinner
1977 S.L.T. (Notes) 11

The holder of a restricted certificate for a hotel was charged on summary complaint with contravention of s. 1 (3) (*b*) of the Licensing (Scotland) Act 1962 and of s. 131 of the Licensing (Scotland) Act 1959 in that exciseable liquor was sold to a police constable who was neither a resident in the hotel nor a friend of a resident for consumption on or off the premises without having a table meal and also that two cans of lager were sold to the same constable. Two police constables, both dressed in sweater and jeans, had entered the hotel in question at about 9.15 p.m. One wore the badge of a ski school to which he belonged. When they entered the hotel, a disco dance was in progress in the dining room, which contained about 60 or 70 people. Drinks were being served at tables but no food was being served. The police constables took part in the dancing. At about 9.45 p.m. they were offered a table and were asked if they would like a drink. Two drinks were bought and paid for. No inquiry was made as to whether the constables were resident in the hotel. At 10.00 p.m. one of the constables asked for and was supplied with two cans of beer to carry out with him. The hotel had a winter trade in bus parties of skiers and could accommodate 40 or 50 people. It appeared that no hotel register was kept and there was no procedure for ascertaining whether people wishing to buy alcohol were residents in the hotel. At the trial objection was taken to the competency and admissibility of the evidence given by the two police officers. This evidence, which was crucial for conviction, was allowed and the licensee appealed.

THE COURT: "For the appellant the submission was that the evidence of the two police officers was in all the circumstances of the case incompetent. It is not in doubt that in cases of this type in Scotland the test for the competency of such police evidence is 'was it fair to the accused' and that in determining that matter the court has got to try to reconcile two important interests which are liable to come into conflict: (i) the interests of the citizen to be protected from illegal or irregular invasion of his liberty by the authorities; and (ii) the interest of the State to secure that evidence bearing upon the commission of a crime and necessary to enable justice to be done shall not be withheld from a court of law on any mere formal or technical ground. This we take from the case of *Marsh* v. *Johnston*, 1959 S.L.T. (Notes) 28.

For the appellant the submission was that the facts found by the justices demonstrated that the evidence of the police constables was not fair to the appellant in respect that they were parties to a trick to induce the appellant to commit the offence libelled. The trick it was said, consisted of their entering the hotel in casual clothes, mingling with the dancers and thus tacitly inviting the licensee to treat them like the other people in the hotel at the time.

In our opinion there is no substance in this submission. The question of whether the evidence of the police was fairly or unfairly obtained is a question of fact and opinion. It is quite impossible to categorise conduct in the obtaining of evidence which will be regarded as fair and conduct in the obtaining of evidence which will be regarded as unfair. It is clear, however, from the decided cases to which we were referred, that where the court has held that evidence has been obtained unfairly there has been established on the part of the police officers concerned conduct which clearly amounted to a trick upon the accused on the part of the police officers, and in particular a trick which involved positive deception and pressure, encouragement or inducement to commit an offence which, but for that pressure, encouragement or inducement, would never have been committed at all.

In our opinion nothing done by the two police officers in this case can reasonably be regarded as amounting to a trick of the kind to which we have referred. There was no pressure, encouragement or inducement on their part to incite the appellant to commit an offence which she would otherwise not have committed at all. The part played by the police officers in the whole transaction was purely passive, and indeed the appellant took the initiative in the matter of the supply of liquor to the police constables at 9.45 p.m. When the conduct of the police officers is examined in light of the whole findings including in particular the finding as to the approach of the appellant in the matter of observing strictly the conditions of her licence, no inference of unfairness can reasonably be drawn and the appellant had no reasonable grounds for alleging that anything done by the police officers induced her to commit an offence which she would otherwise not have committed at all."

Appeal refused.

NOTES

It would seem that in principle the Scottish courts could censure unfair police methods through the exclusion of evidence thus obtained, on the general ground of "fairness to the accused."

For a full discussion of the issues involved in entrapment see the Law Commission's Report on Defences of General Application (Law Com. No. 83), paras. 5.1 *et seq*. See also, Smith, "Official Instigation and Entrapment" [1975] Crim. L.R. 12, Heydon, "The Problems of Entrapment" [1973] C.L.J. 268, and Barlow, "Entrapment and the Common Law" (1978) 41 M.L.R. 266.

For official policy on the use of police spies, see Home Office Statement, and comment [1969] N.L.J. pp. 513 and 497; H.C. Deb., Vol, col. 142, H.C. Deb., Vol. 784, col. 289 and H.C. Deb., Vol. 785, col. 30 (written answers).

CHAPTER 10

ASSAULT and REAL INJURY

Assault may be very simply defined as an attack upon the person of another (Gordon, para. 29-01, Macdonald, 115). For these purposes, an "attack" ranges from the violent infliction of personal injury to very trivial "attacks," and indeed need not involve any personal injury at all—as where a blow is aimed but does not connect, or a gun pointed without being fired.

a. The actus reus *of assault*

1. **David Keay**
(1837) 1 Swin. 543

The panel was charged with assaulting a boy who was riding a pony in that he did "wickedly, culpably, and reckless of the consequences, whip the said pony, and did give it with his driving-whip repeated lashes on its back or other parts, whereby the animal becoming alarmed, run away with the [rider], and threw him off its back, or fell with or above him, . . . and from [the rider] having fallen off, or fallen with or under the said pony, or from the said pony, in rising from the ground after it fell, having planted one or more of its feet on the body of the [rider], his right leg was severely wounded, to the serious injury of his person, and the great effusion of his blood."

An objection was taken to the relevancy, on the ground, *inter alia,* that "In the case of assault, the party strikes at the individual assaulted. Direct personal injury is intended, whereas here the immediate object was to quicken the pace of the pony, and the ultimate result was imputable to accident."

LORD MONCREIFF: "It is assumed by the counsel for the panel that no injury was intended to the boy. But I cannot see what purpose the panel could have, except either to do him a direct injury, or to put him in alarm. I cannot go quite so far as to say, that every case must be one of assault, which, if death had followed, would be culpable homicide. If a person throws a stone out of a window into the street, and thereby kills a passer by, he would be guilty of culpable homicide. Yet this act, done without intention to hurt anyone, could not be charged as assault. Although I have some difficulty, I think the charge of assault is relevant in this case."

LORD COCKBURN: "I have no doubt at all upon the subject. It may appear on proof that the panel had no actual intention of

282

injuring the boy. But there may be a constructive intention. If he had seized the boy in his arms and carried him away, that would most clearly have constituted an assault, and the fact of his having made the pony the instrument of carrying him off makes no difference. The maxim *qui facit per alium facit per se* makes the act of the pony the act of the panel."

Objection to relevancy repelled.

NOTES

Despite Lord Cockburn's imaginative extension of the doctrine of vicarious responsibility, the case is a good illustration of how even indirect injury may constitute an "attack" for the purposes of assault. It is also worth noting that a person may be subjected to an attack of which he is unaware, for example, because he is sleeping (see, *e.g., H.M. Advocate* v. *Logan, post,* ch. 16). (Scots law may be contrasted with English law in this respect. Since the English law of assault requires that the victim be put in apprehension of immediate personal violence one cannot assault a sleeping person although any injury inflicted would constitute a battery; see Smith and Hogan, pp. 350 *et seq.)*

2. **Fagan v. Commissioner of Metropolitan Police**
[1968] 3 W.L.R. 1120

The appellant was convicted of assaulting a police officer in the execution of his duty, and appealed by case stated to the Divisional Court. The circumstances of the offence are fully set out in the judgment of James J.

JAMES J. "The appellant, Vincent Martel Fagan, was convicted by the Willesden magistrates of assaulting David Morris, a police constable, in the execution of his duty on August 31, 1967. He appealed to quarter sessions. On October 25, 1967, his appeal was heard by Middlesex quarter sessions and was dismissed. This matter now comes before the court on appeal by way of case stated from that decision of quarter sessions.

The sole question is whether the prosecution proved facts which in law amounted to an assault.

On August 31, 1967, the appellant was reversing a motor car in Fortunegate Road, London, N.W.1, when Police Constable Morris directed him to drive the car forwards to the kerbside and standing in front of the car pointed out a suitable place in which to park. At first the appellant stopped the car too far from the kerb for the officer's liking. Morris asked him to park closer and indicated a

S.C.L.—20

precise spot. The appellant drove forward towards him and stopped it with the offside wheel on Morris's left foot. 'Get off you are on my foot,' said the officer. 'Fuck you, you can wait,' said the appellant. The engine of the car stopped running. Morris repeated several times 'Get off my foot.' The appellant said reluctlantly 'Okay man, okay,' and then slowly turned on the ignition of the vehicle and reversed it off the officer's foot. The appellant had either turned the ignition off to stop the engine or turned it off after the engine had stopped running.

The justices at quarter sessions on those facts were left in doubt as to whether the mounting of the wheel on to the officer's foot was deliberate or accidental. They were satisfied, however, beyond all reasonable doubt that the appellant 'knowingly, provocatively and unnecessarily allowed the wheel to remain on the foot after the officer said "Get off, you are on my foot".' They found that on those facts an assault was proved.

Mr. Abbas for the appellant relied upon the passage in Stone's Justices' Manual (1968), Vol. 1, p. 651, where assault is defined. He contends that on the finding of the justices the initial mounting of the wheel could not be an assault and that the act of the wheel mounting the foot came to an end without there being any mens rea. It is argued that thereafter there was no act on the part of the appellant which could constitute an actus reus but only the omission or failure to remove the wheel as soon as he was asked. That failure, it is said, could not in law be an assault, nor could it in law provide the necessary mens rea to convert the original act of mounting the foot into an assault.

Mr. Rant for the respondent argues that the first mounting of the foot was an actus reus which act continued until the moment of time at which the wheel was removed. During that continuing act, it is said, the appellant formed the necessary intention to constitute the element of mens rea and once that element was added to the continuing act, an assault took place. In the alternative, Mr. Rant argues that there can be situations in which there is a duty to act and that in such situations an omission to act in breach of duty would in law amount to an assault. It is unnecessary to formulate any concluded views on this alternative.

In our judgment the question arising, which has been argued on general principles, falls to be decided on the facts of the particular case. An assault is any act which intentionally—or possibly recklessly—causes another person to apprehend immediate and unlawful personal violence. Although 'assault' is an independent crime and is to be treated as such, for practical purposes today 'assault' is generally synonymous with the term 'battery' and is a term used to mean the actual intended use of unlawful force to another person without his consent. On the facts of the present case the 'assault' alleged involved a 'battery.' Where an assault involves a battery, it matters not, in our judgment, whether the battery is inflicted directly by the body of the offender or through the medium of some weapon or instrument controlled by the action of the offender. An assault may be committed by the laying of a hand upon another, and the action does not cease to be an assault if it is a stick held in the hand and not the hand itself which is laid on the person of the victim. So for our part we see no difference in principle between the action of stepping on to a person's toe and maintaining that position and the action of driving a car on to a person's foot and sitting in the car whilst its position on the foot is maintained.

To constitute the offence of assault some intentional act must have been performed: a mere omission to act cannot amount to an assault. Without going into the question whether words alone can constitute an assault, it is clear that the words spoken by the appellant could not alone amount to an assault: they can only shed a light on the appellant's action. For our part we think the crucial question is whether in this case the act of the appellant can be said to be complete and spent at the moment of time when the car wheel came to rest on the foot or whether his act is to be regarded as a continuing act operating until the wheel was removed. In our judgment a distinction is to be drawn between acts which are complete—though results may continue to flow—and those acts which are continuing. Once the act is complete it cannot thereafter be said to be a threat to inflict unlawful force upon the victim. If the act, as distinct from the results thereof, is a continuing act there is a continuing threat to inflict unlawful force. If the assault involves a battery and that battery continues there is a continuing act of assault.

For an assault to be committed both the elements of actus reus and mens rea must be present at the same time. The 'actus reus' is the action causing the effect on the victim's mind (see the observations of Park B. in *Regina* v. *St. George* (1840) 9 C. & P. 483). The 'mens rea' is the intention to cause that effect. It is not necessary that mens rea should be present at the inception of the actus reus; it can be superimposed upon an existing act. On the other hand the subsequent inception of mens rea cannot convert an act which has been completed without mens rea into an assault.

In our judgment the Willesden magistrates and quarter sessions were right in law. On the facts found the action of the appellant may have been initially unintentional, but the time came when knowing that the wheel was on the officer's foot the appellant (1) remained seated in the car so that his body through the medium of the car was in contact with the officer, (2) switched off the ignition of the car, (3) maintained the wheel of the car on the foot and (4) used words indicating the intention of keeping the wheel in that position. For our part we cannot regard such conduct as mere omission or inactivity.

There was an act constituting a battery which at its inception was not criminal because there was no element of intention but which became criminal from the moment the intention was formed to produce the apprehension which was flowing from the continuing act. The fallacy of the appellant's argument is that it seeks to equate the facts of this case with such a case as where a motorist has accidentaly run over a person and, that action having been completed, fails to assist the victim with the intent that the victim should suffer."

Appeal dismissed.

NOTE

Although the court was able to discern a "continuing act" in the appellant's conduct it remains the case that the assault consisted in a wilful failure to get off the officer's foot, which comes close to assault by omission. This would seem inconsistent with the Scottish approach.

b. *The* mens rea *of assault*

H.M. Advocate v. Phipps
(1905) 4 Adam 616

Two men discharged sporting guns at a group of men they believed to be poaching salmon from their father's fishings. One of the men was hit in the eye and seriously injured. At the time of the shooting the suspected poachers were on the opposite bank of the river from the accused, at a distance of about 40 to 50 yards. The shooting took place at night. The accused were charged with assault, or, alternatively, reckless discharge of firearms to the injury of the person. In charging the jury the presiding judge gave the following directions on assault and reckless discharge of firearms:

LORD ARDWALL: "Three views are presented to you in this case. The first is that this is a case of assault, or a verdict to that effect is asked by the Advocate-Depute on behalf of the Crown. On that I agree with Mr. Shaw, that evil intent is of the essence of the charge. The second possible view is that the accused were guilty of recklessness of a criminal character, and the third is the view presented for your acceptance by the defence, that the facts of the case disclose mere misadventure, for which the accused are not responsible in a criminal sense.

On the first of these views of this case I agree, as I have said, with Mr. Shaw, and the authority quoted by him, that in order to entitle you to affirm a verdict of guilty of the charge of assault you must find evil intent proved. Unless you find it proved as a matter of fact that there was evil intent in the minds of the panels, an intention to do bodily injury to these men, you will not return a verdict of guilty of assault by discharging loaded firearms, which is the first charge in this indictment.

On the other hand I cannot agree with the proposition stated to you by Mr. Shaw, that there can be no crime of reckless discharge of firearms merely because the result was unexpected. On the contrary there have been several cases where a verdict of reckless discharge of firearms was found justified in our law where the result was quite outwith the expectation of the accused. Thus a poacher on a dark night seeing something moving fired at it, thinking it was a hare. It turned out to be a man whom he had thus hit. The poacher was convicted of reckless discharge of firearms. Again, on an occasion when crime was the last thing present in the accused's mind, at a wedding festivity, the accused had fired off a gun loaded blank by the way of a salute, and injured a member of the public passing by, who was struck by the cotton wad. Conviction followed. Another case which comes nearer the kind of facts we are dealing with in this case was this. An Aberdeenshire farmer, being disturbed by the too frequent nocturnal visits of a man to his kitchen premises, attempted to surprise him, and when he took refuge in flight, fired his gun at him without any intention to wound him, and hit him in the legs. The farmer was charged with and convicted of reckless discharge of firearms. That shows the sort of case you have to hold has been made out under the charge of reckless discharge of fire-arms, and that is a possible view which you may quite competently see yourselves bound to take of the facts which have been proved before you.

There is yet another possible view which you may take, and which Mr. Shaw has asked you to take. You may come to the conclusion that there was neither evil intent present nor such an amount of recklessness as would justify a verdict of reckless discharge of firearms, but that the facts amount to mere misadventure or an unfortunate chain of misadventures; the unauthorised presence of these men netting this pool; the unfortunate failure of the men to answer when challenged, and the regrettable mischance by which one of the pellets lodged in the eye of one of the men. Was this a mere chain of accidents which the accused could not foresee, and which they were not bound to foresee?

These, then, are the three views on which it is your duty to make up your minds in returning your verdict in this case, and I shall attempt shortly to go over the facts which have been proved, and indicate, as far as I can, their bearing on these questions.

First, then, with reference to the charge of assault. What evidence have you of evil intent? The attitude of the accused has from the first been quite consistent. They said that night at the Castle, they said to the police, and lastly they said in their declaration before the Sheriff, that they had no intention of injuring any one. Now is there any evidence contrary to that? It is suggested that the distance from which they fired was far too short, and that they should not have fired at all. Now as to that you have the evidence both of the gun-maker and of Lord Lovat, and can judge for yourselves, that in the night-time and in uncertain light, as one sees in duck-shooting in early morning, distances are very deceptive and illusive. Even taking it that the distance was only fifty yards, this was an ordinary sporting-gun, and in ordinary circumstances could do not much more than tickle a man hit at that distance, unless some of the shot lodged in such a delicate organ as the eye. Again it is said that the accused knew this river so well that they should have been able to calculate to a nicety the distance across at this point. On the other hand you have it said that they were agitated by the natural excitement of a possible resistance, and the haste of their approach through the brushwood, as they ran down to scare these persons, whom they took for poachers. Turning again to the state of the light. The night is said to have been dark but clear, and what is more important, on the bank behind the men was a clump of wood standing out against the horizon and therefore dimming the light coming thence and making it impossible to say how far the men might seem to one on the opposite bank. For there is no perspective in darkness. It is for you to say whether you find anything proved either in the distance or in the state of the light, which entitles you to say that these gentlemen knew, or ought to have known, that the persons they saw in the shadow on the opposite bank were within shooting distance, and that they fired intending to injure them. I can only say that such a conclusion does not commend itself to my mind.

That is all that seems necessary to say in regard to the question of assault. You are quite entitled to take into consideration the evidence as to the relations which subsisted between the panels and the men whom they are said to have assaulted—to consider whether these men, and especially the fishing ghillie, John Fraser, Cruives— were not the last persons in the world whom the accused would intentionally seek to injure; and whether it is not a more natural explanation to find, that taking them for poachers, they sought to scare them away by firing off shots, and so do what is always considered of importance in such cases, drive the poachers away and secure their nets or some other tangible evidence of their offence. It is said that for this purpose it was unnecessary to fire off four or more shots, as is evidenced by the three empty cartridges found on the ground. That seems to me just the course two men would follow when they were attempting to scare away a larger number of poachers—fire off as many shots as possible and so make a demonstration of force which might impress the poachers with the idea that they had a larger number than two to deal with. It was the safest thing to do, as it might induce the poachers to believe that they were outnumbered and therefore render resistance less likely. Poachers often carry guns, and therefore the fact that the accused fired off so many cartridges seems to me to strengthen the supposition that they fired to scare and not to injure the men at the boat."

NOTES

The requirement of "evil intent" in assault is further discussed in *Smart* v. *H.M. Advocate*, 1975 S.L.T. 65 (*post*). *Cf.* the English rule that assault may be committed intentionally or recklessly—*Venna* [1976] Q.B. 421—and the comments of Lord Moncreiff in *Keay (ante)*.

c. Aggravated assaults

Assault may be aggravated in a variety of ways, most commonly by the degree of injury inflicted on the victim, by the use of a weapon (especially firearms, knives, and the like), and by the character of the victim—the commonest example of this being assaulting a police officer in the execution of his duty.

(i) Specification of the aggravation

Brown v. Hilson
1924 J.C. 1

The appellant, the headmaster of a village school, was convicted of assaulting one his pupils (a boy aged six years) by striking him on the face, and by beating him on the hands, hips and thighs with a pair of leather tawse. The accused brought a bill of suspension in which he averred, *inter alia*, that the complaint was irrelevant.

LORD JUSTICE-GENERAL (CLYDE): "Everything that could be said for the appellant has been laid before us by Mr MacLean in the very careful address which he has just concluded. The first point he makes is that the complaint was irrelevant. Put short, the complaint is in these terms—that the appellant, described as 'School Teacher, The Schoolhouse, Makerstoun, Roxburghshire' did on a specified date, 'in a classroom within the school at Makerstoun,' assault a certain boy, aged six years, and 'did strike him on the face with your hands, and did beat him with a pair of tawse, and with your hands, on the hips and thighs, whereby he was injured in his person.' The ground upon which the relevancy of the complaint is attacked is that, whereas corporal chastisement is a legitimate incident of the relations between schoolmaster and pupil *(Muckarsie* v. *Dickson,* (1848) 11 D. 4), and does not amount to the crime of assault unless the punishment is excessive (see *Scorgie* v. *Lawrie,* 10 R. 610), the complaint ought to have set forth that the alleged assault was an incident of the administration of discipline in the school with regard to the boy as one of the pupils of the school. The complaint does not state that the boy was a pupil in the school, or that the punishment given him was on account of a school offence. I think that represents the real ground of Mr MacLean's attack, but it is right to add that he also maintained that the physical force used should have been specifically described as being in excess of what disciplinary chastisement required and justified.

Now, in the first place, the complaint charges assault in so many words. In the second place, it clearly states that the alleged assault was committed on a very young boy by blows on the face, hips, and thighs, partly with the hands and partly with an instrument of punishment. In the third place, it states that injury to the boy's person resulted from the blows. These statements seem to me to give ample specification of a charge of assault. No doubt, it must always be established to the satisfaction of the tribunal that the act imputed to the accused was done with criminal intent, or with a disregard of duty which infers criminal responsibility. But if the statement of the *modus* would—on criminal intent or criminal responsibility being established—constitute a crime, it is in my opinion sufficient. Judged by this standard, the complaint seems to be relevant.

Mr MacLean founded on the passage in Hume (vol. ii., p. 197) dealing with cases in which it is necessary to the criminality of the act charged, or to the degree of its heinousness, to specify the quality of the person injured or his relation to the accused. He referred also to Macdonald's Criminal Law (p. 333) where the same topic is considered. Hume gives the instances of hamesucken, parricide, adultery, and beating of parents. In Macdonald, the further instance of assaults on officers of the law is given. There is no doubt that, in such instances as these, if (in the one case) there is to be a prosecution for the crime, or (in the other case) if the prosecutor wishes to establish its aggravated character, there must be specification of the quality of the person hurt or of his relation to the accused. But it is a different thing to say that there must be specification of facts in anticipation of something which may be stated *in defence* arising out of the particular circumstances of the relations of parties or the quality of the person injured. The requirements of relevancy do not go so far as this. The defence remains perfectly open, notwithstanding the form of the charge; and it is not the business of a prosecutor to anticipate it in specifying the *modus* of the offence. There was nothing in the present case to hinder or impede the person accused in defending himself on the ground that the force used on the occasion referred to was no more than what was reasonably necessary in the administration of corporal punishment for the purposes of school discipline. In short, no injustice or prejudice was suffered by him in consequences of the form of the complaint."

The court refused the bill of suspension.

NOTE

 Cf. Gray v. *Hawthorn,* 1961 J.C. 13; 1961 S.L.T. 11 *(post).*

(ii) Aggravation by serious injury

Jane Smith or Thom
(1876) 3 Couper 332

The accused was charged with "wickedly and feloniously throwing a child out of a carriage of a railway train when in motion so as to endanger its life, as also assault to the danger of life." It appeared from the evidence that the child had suffered no injury, and counsel for the accused argued that this negatived the aggravation.

 LORD YOUNG in charging the jury said—That it was sufficient to sustain the aggravation *'to the danger of life'* that the child's life had been put in great peril, as it undoubtedly had been, if it was thrown out of the carriage in the manner libelled; and that there was therefore sufficient proof in the case, if they thought the panel guilty, to entitle them also to find the aggravation proved. He further observed, that the crime would have been quite sufficiently, and perhaps with greater correctness, libelled simply as an assault to the danger of life without charging the innominate offence.

Verdict: Not proven.

(iii) Aggravation by the character of the victim: assaulting and obstructing the police

1. **Monk v. Strathern**
1921 J.C. 4

A police officer, returning to his home from his beat in uniform, met a group of young men standing at a street corner. On passing them he asked, "Are you not away to bed yet boys?" (the time was 11.20 p.m.). As the constable was walking away, one of the youths, the appellant, threw a bottle at him which struck him on the back of the head and seriously injured him. The appellant was convicted of assaulting a police officer in the execution of his duty, contrary to s. 12 of the Prevention of Crimes Act 1871. On appeal by stated case to the High Court:

LORD JUSTICE-CLERK (SCOTT DICKSON): "I think the statement of facts in this case does not disclose grounds sufficient to justify an affirmative answer to the only question which is put to us, viz.: 'Whether on the facts proved it was competent to convict the accused?'

The Sheriff-substitute makes no specific finding that the constable was in the execution of his duty. I do not say it was necessary that he should have done so; but, at any rate, in order to warrant a conviction, he should have found facts proved which were sufficient to show that the constable when assaulted was in the execution of his duty. I find no such findings. On the contrary, I think the findings point to the opposite conclusion and show that his duty had terminated at the time when he was assaulted. It is quite true that circumstances might have occurred which might have compelled him to go back to his duty; but there were no such circumstances in this case. All that happened was that he passed some young men standing at the corner, and asked them if they were not away to bed yet; but what he said was not in the execution of his duty. This complaint was brought under the Prevention of Crimes Act, 1871, and under that statute alone, and there was no alternative complaint laid at common law. Accordingly, so far as the complaint is concerned, I think the conviction was unwarranted on the facts which were found proved. I am of opinion, therefore, that the queston should be answered in the negative."

LORD DUNDAS: "I agree. It is an essential part of the statutory charge that the constable when assaulted shall be in the execution of his duty. Now, it is not proved that this constable was so in fact. Indeed, I think that the facts set forth in the stated case go to prove the contrary. All that is said is that he was proceeding in uniform from his beat to his home. The mere fact that he was in uniform does not seem to me to be sufficient to enable us to hold that he was in the execution of his duty. I, accordingly, have come to the conclusion that we must answer the question in the negative. I confess I have done so with considerable regret, because it is clear that a serious and cowardly assault was committed on this constable."

LORD ORMIDALE: "I concur in thinking that the question must be answered in the negative. It seems to me that the facts stated by the Sheriff-substitute negative the idea that this assault was committed while the policeman was in the execution of his duty. He had left his beat where his duties were to be performed, and I do not think that the mere fact that he was in uniform constitutes a valid reason for holding that he was still on duty."

Appeal allowed: conviction quashed.

NOTE

The modern equivalent of the 1871 Act is s.41 of the Police (Scotland) Act 1967, the relevant provisions of which state: "(1) Any person who (*a*) assaults, resists, obstructs, molests or hinders a constable in the execution of his duty . . . shall be guilty of an offence."

2. Twycross v. Farrell
1973 S.L.T. (Notes) 85

A police constable received a message from the headmaster of a local school that the headmaster had just seen some of his girl pupils being approached in the street by a young man selling a magazine which, from a previous incident in the district, the headmaster considered might be pornographic. The police constable drove to the school and saw the appellant holding a magazine and talking to girls from the school. The constable twice asked the appellant what he was doing and then asked for his name and address. The appellant made no answer to the constable, swore at him and then started to run away. The constable then seized hold of the appellant. The appellant then struggled and shouted and was only with difficulty detained until further police constables arrived. The appellant was convicted of resisting, obstructing, molesting and hindering the constable in the execution of his duty and of attempting to resist arrest. Counsel for the appellant contended that since the constable had no reasonable grounds for believing that the appellant had committed a crime he had no right to seize hold of the appellant and that accordingly by seizing hold of the appellant he was assaulting the appellant, against which assault the appellant was entitled to struggle in self-defence. Counsel referred to *Kenlin* v. *Gardiner* [1967] 2 Q.B. 510 and *Ludlow and Others* v. *Burgess* [1971] Crim. L.R. 238. In allowing the appeal and quashing the conviction the court indicated that since there were no findings in the case to support the existence of a reasonable belief by the constable that the appellant had committed an offence, the constable had no right to attempt to stop the appellant from moving smartly away from the spot and that the appellant having been so stopped was entitled to struggle as he did.

Appeal allowed: conviction quashed.

NOTES

Just when a police constable is acting in the execution of his duty is a matter of considerable complexity. In *Rice* v. *Connolly* [1966] 2 All E.R. 649 Lord Parker C.J. suggested the following general guidelines (at p.651): "it is part of the obligations and duties of a police officer to take all steps which appear to him necessary for keeping the peace, for preventing crime, or for protecting property from criminal injury. There is no exhaustive definition of the powers and obligations of the police, but they are at least those, and they would further include the duty to detect crime and to bring an offender to justice."

Despite the generality of this statement, it seems that the police officer's judgment of what is "necessary" for keeping the peace, etc., is not the only consideration, but rather there is an objective test of whether the police officer was legally entitled (either at common law or by statute) to take the steps in question.

3.   Curlett v. McKechnie
1938 J.C. 176

Subsequent to a road accident involving two lorries, the accused made certain false statements to the police for the purpose of concealing a contravention of the Motor Vehicles (Driving Licences) Regulations 1937, art. 16(3) (*a*), and the Road Traffic Act 1934, s.6. They were subsequently convicted of the offence of wilfully obstructing a constable in the execution of his duty. On appeal by stated case to the High Court:

LORD FLEMING: "This stated case arises out of a road accident which occurred at Saltcoats, Ayrshire, and in which two motor lorries were involved. The appellant James Hull Curlett and his son the appellant Hugh Curlett were on one of the lorries at the time, and they are charged in the complaint, along with the appellant James Curlett, who is also a son of James Hull Curlett, but who was not on the lorry; and the charge against them is that of obstructing a police constable in the execution of his duty. The facts alleged in the complaint are as follows:—The appellant James Hull Curlett was not the holder of a licence, and Hugh Curlett, who was the holder merely of a provisional licence, was driving the lorry. That state of matters constituted a contravention of the Road Traffic Act of 1934, section 6, and of Regulations made thereunder. The three appellants, acting in concert and with intent to conceal this contravention, falsely represented to a police constable, who was investigating the circumstances of the accident, that James Curlett, who was a supervisor qualified in terms of the Regulations, was on the lorry at the time of the accident. These facts are said to constitute a contravention of section 12 of the Prevention of Crimes Act, 1871, as extended by section 2 of the Prevention of Crimes Amendment Act, 1885.

The appellants objected to the relevancy of the complaint in the Sheriff Court. The Sheriff-substitute repelled the objection, and thereafter convicted the appellants. Counsel for the appellants stated that he challenged the conviction on other grounds as well, but we heard the parties upon the question of relevancy only.

In order to decide that question it is necessary to consider the statutory provisions which are said to have been contravened. Section 12 of the Prevention of Crimes Act, 1871, provides that, where any person is convicted of an assault on any police constable when in the execution of his duty, such person shall be guilty of an offence against the Act, and shall in the discretion of the Court be subject to certain penalties. Now, it is to be observed that, at least so far as Scotland is concerned, this section does not create any new offence. It was an offence at common law to assault a police constable, and it was an aggravation of such an assault if it was committed while the constable was in the execution of his duty; and all that this section does is to prescribe certain penalties for the offence. The Act provides that offences against it may be prosecuted before a Court of summary jurisdiction, and so empowers such a Court to impose the penalties mentioned in Section 12. That section was amended by section 2 of the Prevention of Crimes Amendment Act of 1885, which provides that its provisions shall apply to all cases of resisting or wilfully obstructing any constable when in the execution of his duty.

The question arises—What amounts to obstruction of a police officer in the execution of his duty? As regards two of the appellants, at all events, a peculiar situation emerges, if the statements in this complaint are true. They were interviewed by a police constable with regard to the circumstances which ultimately led to a criminal prosecution against them and to their conviction, and it is now alleged that they contravened the statutory provisions by giving false information to the constable. As regards the third appellant, what is charged against him is that he told a falsehood in regard to what took place at the time of the accident by saying that he was then on the lorry. No Scottish decision or authority was cited in support of the view that such statements render the person making them liable to criminal prosecution. As regards the relevancy of this particular complaint, I think, however, that the matter is susceptible of being disposed of without going into many of the questions which were discussed before us. In considering what is meant by the wilful obstruction of a police constable in the execution of his duty within the meaning of the Prevention of Crimes

Acts, it is necessary to bear in mind that the words 'wilfully obstructing' are used in association with the words 'resisting' and 'assault,'
and the reasonable inference is that wilful obstruction must have the
same character as the other matters dealt within the two relevant
sections. In my opinion, to bring a case within these sections it must
be proved that the obstruction had some physical aspect. But in any
view, I think it would be straining the language of the statutory
provisions unduly to hold that it covers the case of suspected
persons or other persons making false statements to the police when
the latter are making investigations with a view to deciding whether
there are grounds for criminal proceedings. I have come accordingly to the conclusion that this complaint does not relevantly aver
any offence under the sections which are libelled. That is sufficient
for the disposal of the appeal, as there is no case against the
appellants except under the statutory provisions.

We were referred to two decisions in England—particularly to
the case of *Betts* v. *Stevens* [1910] 1 K.B. 1, where it was held that the
defendant, who was one of the patrols employed by the Automobile
Association, was guilty of a contravention of section 2 of the Act of
1885 in giving warning of the presence of the police to a driver of a
car which was being driven at an illegal speed. The acts of obstruction there alleged were of a quite different character from those we
have to deal with in the present case, and I therefore find it unnecessary to consider whether I should have taken the same view of the
question as was taken by the Court in that case."

LORD MONCRIEFF: "I am of the same opinion. I do not doubt
that the police may be obstructed in the execution of their duty in
cases in which they are engaged in the detection of crime, and,
indeed, am clear that such duties of detection are no less open to
obstruction than are their duties of preventing crime or apprehending a criminal. Accordingly, if the offence of 'obstructing' the police
had been created by statute without words in context such as should
suggest a limitation of the meaning and application of the principal
word, it would have been necessary to consider whether or not the
making of a false statement to the police by the accused, or the
making of a false statement to the police by a person applied to as a
witness, was, in a proper sense, an 'obstructing' of the police. In
solving that question the case of *Betts* v. *Stevens* would have
required consideration. In the view which I take of this statutory
enactment, however, no such question requires to be solved. The
offence is not created as an offence of 'obstructing' the police
without a controlling context. On the contrary, these words, as used
in this statute, have a context, and the statute itself has moreover an

antecedent history, which together are sufficient, in my view, to show that the word 'obstructing' has a definitely restricted meaning.

The first of these statutory enactments was in 1871, and summary powers were given by the Act of that year in the case of an 'assault' on any constable when in the execution of his duty. It is by way of an amendment of the provisions giving summary rights in the case of such an assault that in the later Act the word 'obstructing' is introduced for the first time. It is introduced along with the word 'resisting' the police, and, when I find the word 'obstructing' in a statute in that context and connexion, I recognise that the word is so used as to associate it with physical interference only, and to contrast it with mere adverse influence or trickery."

Appeal allowed.

NOTES

"Obstructing" in this context has been given a very wide interpretation in English law. In *Hinchcliffe* v. *Sheldon* [1955] 3 All E.R. 406, *e.g.*, Lord Goddard C.J. defined it as "Making it more difficult for the police to carry out their duties." In *Rice* v. *Connolly* [1966] 2 Q.B. 414, however, it was held that refusing to answer a police officer's questions did not amount to obstruction (although such refusal must necessarily make it more difficult for the police to carry out their duties). Recent decisions in Scotland have shown a tendency to "water down" the effect of *Curlett* v. *McKechnie*.

4. **Skeen v. Shaw and Another.**
1979 S.L.T. (Notes) 58

Two accused persons were charged in the district court at Glasgow with a contravention of s. 41 (1) (*a*) of the Police (Scotland) Act 1967 in that they obstructed, molested and hindered two police officers then in the execution of their duty and did stand in front of them and threaten them while they had a prisoner in lawful custody. The evidence at the trial was to the effect that after the prisoner had been arrested, the two accused engaged the police officers in a noisy altercation inquiring where they were taking their prisoner and expressing a view that they would have difficulty in taking him anywhere. In the course of the altercation the officers had difficulty in conducting their prisoner towards a police van because the accused were standing in their way. At no time did the accused come into physical contact with the police, nor did they physically threaten them. The stipendiary magistrate (R. Mitchell) found the charge not proven. The procurator fiscal appealed by stated case and the question for the opinion of the High Court was whether the magistrate was entitled to find the charge not proven. The High Court answered the question in the *negative* and remitted the case to the magistrate with a direction to convict.

OPINION OF THE COURT: "Now in finding the charge not proven the magistrate addressed himself to the case of *Curlett* v. *McKechnie*, 1939 S.L.T. 11, and having done so he derived from that case the proposition that where the word 'obstruction' appears in s. 41 (1) (*a*) there is implicit in that word, having regard to the context in which it appears, a physical element or a physical aspect. As he puts it himself, the magistrate says the words 'resist, hinders are ejusdem generis with assault and require an element of physical obstruction'. Having so directed himself it is surprising that the magistrate found the respondents not guilty. Having taken what he did from the case of *Curlett* he ought to have convicted because in finding 2, in the plainest terms, there is demonstrated an element of physical obstruction which required the conviction of the respondents. It is quite sufficient that when veiled threats were being made to the police the magistrate found that the result of the action of the respondents was to cause difficulty to the police in conducting their prisoner and the reason for that difficulty has to do with the respondents who were standing in his way. Since the case of *Curlett* was decided there has been added to the list of words which was considered in that case in the context of the Prevention of Crimes Act 1871 the word 'hinders'. Now we do not propose to consider, and we do not require to consider, whether the word 'hinders' in the context in which it appears also requires a physical aspect or requires a physical element, but that word, by its very introduction, demonstrates how small a degree any physical element must be in the act of persons who place a difficulty in the way of the police in the execution of a purpose in the course of their duty. That is what the word 'hinders' means and even if the act of hindering must contain a physical element the degree of physical element present in this case required the magistrate to convict. Accordingly what we shall do is to answer the question in the case in the negative and we shall remit to the magistrate with a direction to convict."

Appeal allowed.

NOTE

Compare the court's statement about placing a difficulty in the way of the police with Lord Goddard's statement referred to above.

(iv)   Mens rea in aggravated assault.

It is Gordon's view (para. 29-07) that where the aggravation is one of causing severe injury or endangering life it is not necessary to show that the accused intended any such consequence (see, *e.g.,* *Jane Smith or Thom* (1876) 3 Couper 332, *ante*). Where the aggravation relates to the character of the victim, however, the position is not entirely clear. Some cases suggest that knowledge of the victim's character is required, others suggest a lesser standard.

Alexr. and James Alexander
(1842) 1 Broun 28

The accused were engaged in removing goods illegally from a ship lying in the Firth of Clyde when a revenue officer intervened. They attacked him, and eventually threw him in the river and struck him with an oar. They were charged with assault "especially when committed on an Officer of the Revenue in the execution of his duty." An objection was taken to the relevancy of the charge on the ground that it did not aver that they knew the victim to be an officer of the revenue in the execution of his duty.

LORD MONCREIFF: "I do not think that our decision in this case will settle any general question, although it will serve to regulate the drawing of indictments. I hold the major proposition to be correctly laid. I agree also that it is not necessary to set forth, in so many words, that the pannels knew who the individual assaulted was. There may certainly be equivalents. Scarcely one, however, of the many indictments which have been quoted, does not furnish a clearer inference than the present. All that is stated in this libel may have taken place, and yet the pannels have been ignorant of the main fact charged in the aggravation. It is not set forth that the removal of the casks from the ship was by smuggling. A person might have been stationed on board of the vessel, and have attempted to prevent the removal of casks or bags, although he was not a customhouse officer. It is not charged against the pannels, that they did wilfully obstruct or deforce the said officer in the execution of his duty, but merely, that they wickedly and feloniously attacked and assaulted him. Where, then, is it to be collected from this indictment, that the pannels knew this party, and what he was doing? No such necessary inference follows. It seems to me, that the libel should have contained such averments, as to make it perfectly plain, that the pannels were made aware, at the time, of the situation and character of the person whom they assaulted. I admit the point to be attended with doubt, but, on the grounds already stated, my opinion is, that this particular indictment, so far as the aggravation is concerned, is bad."

THE LORD JUSTICE-GENERAL (BOYLE): "The objection which has been stated, in the criticism upon this indictment, is a most important one. I am satisfied that there have been numerous cases, where the same fundamental deficiency, supposing it to be so, has occurred, but in which the indictments have been sustained, and punishments inflicted. In judging of the relevancy of the present libel, we must read the whole minor. The assertion made by the prosecutor, that the pannels had removed from the ship, which the customhouse officer was appointed to guard, several casks or bags, with the intention of conveying them ashore, coupled with the positive averment, that this was done illegally, just amounts to a charge of smuggling. In these circumstances, I agree with the Solicitor-General, that the *onus* of proof is shifted, and that, instead of the prosecutor being required to prove the knowledge of the pannels, it is for them to establish, that they did *not* know the person, whom they assaulted, to be an officer engaged in protecting her Majesty's revenue. It is absurd to suppose, that this person was to walk up and down the vessel, crying aloud every quarter of an hour that he was a customhouse officer. There is enough set forth to satisfy me, that the pannels must well have known his true character, and the object of his interference with their illegal proceedings. I am therefore of opinion, that the aggravation is relevantly charged."

> The court being equally divided, the presiding judge, as is usual in such circumstances gave no vote, and the objection to the relevancy was therefore sustained.

NOTES

Cf. Helen Yoill and Ors. (1842) 1 Broun 480 where Lord Mackenzie's view was that "the minor proposition of indictments, charging the obstructing or assaulting officers of the law in the execution of their duty, must either contain an express statement that they were known to the pannels as such, or set forth such circumstances as necessarily imply this knowledge." In that case it was held that an averment that the accused assembled "for the purpose of obstructing and assaulting" the officers satisfied this requirement. See also, *George McLellan and Ors.* (1842) 1 Broun 478. In *O'Brien* v. *McPhee* (1880) 4 Couper 375 the view was expressed *(obiter)* that once the Crown had established that the accused had assaulted the constables, and that the latter were acting in the execution of their duty, it was for the accused to show "by positive evidence—or that the probability from the whole facts and circumstances disclosed was—that although the persons to whom they offered and used violence were in truth police constables in the execution of their duty, they had no suspicion of that." It seems, however, that to require such exculpatory proof conflicts with the general principles of onus of proof *(ante*, ch. 1). *Cf.* Gordon, para. 29-21, n.72.

d. Justification
(i) Self-defence

1. Fraser v. Skinner
1975 S.L.T. (Notes) 84

A police officer was charged with assault. He pled not guilty and tabled a plea of self-defence. He was convicted and appealed against conviction.

The evidence established that the incident occurred about 1 a.m. on 22 December 1974. The accused with another police officer was then following a mini-car through the streets of Inverness. They formed the view that the car was travelling at an excessive speed. They followed and stopped it. The complainer emerged and adopted an aggressive and offensive attitude. With regard to the incident the sheriff in his findings-in-fact found:—"Complainer's tirade was halted when appellant struck complainer on the left side of his face slightly below the level of the eye with the palm or heel of his hand, though the blow could not be described as a punch. Appellant referred to it as a punch or slap. The complainer fell to the ground although this may have been due to an element of surprise and his being off balance. The appellant believed mistakenly that a contact on his chest with complainer's arm was an intentional aggressive act by him. This belief may have been coloured by complainer's aggressive tirade. . . . The second blow, both of which were admitted by appellant, was also in the nature of a hand off which in fact also landed near the same spot on appellant's face. The complainer's clothes were subsequently noticed to be wet and muddy in such positions as to be consistent with a fall in the road. Two separate bruises were still very noticeable on complainer's face in the morning of the next day and were spoken to by a doctor and also immediately after the incident by complainer's family."

OPINION OF THE COURT: "In short, the sheriff has held that on two occasions the appellant 'handed off' the complainer in circumstances in which he had a reasonable belief and reasonable grounds for believing that he was being assaulted by the complainer and, indeed, the sheriff has accepted that at one stage there was contact between the complainer's arm and the appellant's chest. It is to be noted further that the complainer himself agreed that some involuntary or unconscious contact of his arm with the appellant's chest could have given the appellant the idea that he was being assaulted.

The sheriff has also added in his note that the force used by these blows described as 'hand offs' was meagre although it has to be observed that there were two separate bruises on the appellant's face after the event.

Given these facts relating to the alleged assault which I have mentioned, it is plain that it was sharply in issue whether the Crown had established the necessary criminal intent in the delivery of the hand offs to justify a finding that these hand offs amounted to the crime of assault and the sheriff was clearly faced with a situation in which what was done by the appellant was plainly done in the belief that he had to protect himself. Given these circumstances and given these facts, the test which the sheriff should have applied to the meagre force which was used was whether, in all the circumstances, that force, meagre though it was, amounted to cruel excess, for it is only cruel excess which will defeat a plea of self-defence which is otherwise founded upon the evidence. What the sheriff did was to weigh the matter in too fine a scale and he considered only whether the force, meagre though it was, was excessive. In that he misdirected himself and had he considered the true question, namely whether the force used amounted to cruel excess in all the circumstances he would have been bound to acquit."

Appeal allowed: conviction quashed.

NOTE

Cf. the discussion of self-defence in homicide *(post,* ch. 11).

2.   **H.M. Advocate v. Carson and Another.**
1964 S.L.T. 21

Carson and another man were charged with assaulting a third person "to his severe injury." The second accused lodged a special defence of self-defence, to the effect that he struck the victim in order to prevent him making a homicidal attack on Carson. In the course of his charge to the jury the presiding judge gave the following directions on self-defence:

LORD WHEATLEY: "Ladies and gentlemen, the main evidence in the case—in fact, the only real evidence in the case—to support the special defence is the evidence of the accused Maybury. There is a special defence in relation to the first charge—that is the attack on Downie—and it is that on the occasion libelled he struck Andrew Downie to stop a homicidal attack with a knife by the said Andrew Downie on his co-accused Carson, and that the measures taken were justified.

We haven't had the benefit of hearing what Carson said about it. You had the denial by both Downie and Muir that there was any such attack on Carson; you had the evidence of Henderson and Howie, and it is for you to decide whether there is any room for holding on that evidence, if you accept it, that there was an attack by Downie on Carson, and that it was an attack with a knife of homicidal nature.

The accused said that there was, and if you believe him that he either (a) actually saw such an attack or (b) had reasonable grounds for believing that such an attack was being made, then according to the law of Scotland he was entitled to interfere and intervene in order to prevent such attack because, he would then be justified in killing in defence of his own life against imminent danger or of the lives of those connected with him. That can be reduced from killing. If a man sees another man being unlawfully attacked he is entitled to try to stop that unlawful attack, and if within reason he uses methods that otherwise would constitute an assault he will be excused because his intention is not to commit a criminal assault on the victim but to prevent the victim from carrying out an assault, an illegitimate assault, on another person.

Therefore, if you accepted the story given by Maybury, and were prepared to sustain it, he would be entitled to an acquittal."

NOTE

Defence of another is not, of course, limited to assault, but would be equally applicable in a case of homicide.

(ii) Lawful chastisement

Gray v. Hawthorn
1964 J.C. 69

The appellant, a headmaster of a school, was charged with assaulting an eleven year old boy, one of the pupils. The circumstances of the assault are fully set out in the opinion of Lord Guthrie.

LORD GUTHRIE: "In this case the appellant, who is the headmaster of Lennoxtown Public School, was charged that, on 26th September 1963, in the school, he assaulted Roland Oehme, aged 11 years, a pupil at the school, and administered to the boy excessive punishment with a leather strap on his hands, namely, nine blows within a period of one hour, to his injury. The Sheriff-substitute found the appellant guilty of that charge as libelled, with this modification that he substituted 'eight blows within a period of two hours' for the statement in the complaint. There was a second charge against the appellant, of assault upon another pupil, but that charge was found not proven and need concern us no further.

The findings in fact of the learned Sheriff-substitute are briefly as follows. The boy, Oehme, was a pupil in class Primary 7, and had given no cause previously for complaint regarding his conduct, although he was a poor scholar at the foot of the class. On 26th September 1963, after a period of hymn-singing, this boy and two others were sent by their teacher to the appellant, the headmaster, because their hands and knees were dirty. He punished them by inflicting one stroke on the hand of each boy with a leather strap. He then sent them to wash and to report to him again. On their return he was dissatisfied with their ablutions, and punished them again by giving them each two strokes with the strap. Then he sent them back to their class. After their return to the class they were given an exercise to write, which consisted of sentences dictated by the teacher. Soon afterwards the appellant entered the classroom, and ordered the boys' school-bags to be inspected. Because Oehme's bag was in an untidy state, containing some torn and crumpled bits of waste paper, the boy was again punished by the appellant with a stroke of the strap on his hand. Immediately afterwards the appellant told the boy to produce his exercise book before the appellant had completed a count-down of five, and, when the boy failed to to do so in time, he was again punished in the same way. The appellant then examined the boy's exercise book. He told the boy that the handwriting was not his best, and therefore gave him another stroke from the strap on his hand. The boy was also told to rewrite the whole exercise during the usual playtime break. He was not told that there had been any spelling mistakes in his exercise, but only that his handwriting had been poor. The boy rewrote the exercise during the interval, and it was submitted after the break to the appellant. It contained a misspelling of the word 'decision' which had previously appeared in the first draft of the exercise. He was again punished by the appellant with a stroke of the strap on his hand, and instructed to rewrite the whole exercise again. He was still not informed about the spelling mistake. By this time his hand was swollen and sore from the strokes he had received, and his handwriting on the third attempt was worse. The error in spelling was repeated. When he produced his third effort, it was condemned by the appellant as unsatisfactory, and the boy was punished once more by a stroke of the strap on one hand. He was again instructed to rewrite the whole exercise. On this occasion the spelling mistake was pointed out to him, and he was told to correct it. When the boy returned home for dinner, it was noticed by his parents that his hands were sore and swollen, and that bruise marks were beginning to appear on his right wrist because of the punishments which he had received. Later, after the dinner-break, the boy's father interviewed the headmaster and received from him an explanation. The parent afterwards heard about the incident which was the subject of the second charge, and was influenced by that matter in deciding to make a report to the police. On the following day the boy was seen at the police station, and the constable in charge found that his hands were swollen and bruised, and that the wrist itself was markedly bruised.

The question put in the case is whether, on these findings in fact, the Sheriff-substitute was entitled to find the appellant guilty of assault. There is no doubt that a school teacher is vested with disciplinary powers to enable him to do his educational work and to maintain proper order in class and in school, and it is therefore largely a matter within his discretion whether, and to what extent, the circumstances call for the exercise of these powers by the infliction of chastisement. In general it is true to say that the court will not review the exercise of these disciplinary powers by a schoolmaster, since it cannot interfere with what falls within the scope of his discretion. If what the schoolmaster has done can truly be regarded as an exercise of his disciplinary powers, although mistaken, he cannot be held to have contravened the criminal law. It is only if there has been an excess of punishment over what could be regarded as an exercise of disciplinary powers that it can be held to be an assault. In other words the question in all such cases is whether there has been dole on the part of the accused, the evil intent which is necessary to constitute a crime by the law of Scotland. The existence of dole in the mind of an accused person must always be a question to be decided in the light of the whole circumstances of the particular case. When a headmaster or a teacher is charged with assault on a pupil, such matters as the nature and violence of the punishment, the repetition or continuity of the punishment, the age, the health and the sex of the child, the blameworthiness and the degree of blameworthiness of the child's conduct, and so on, are all relevant circumstances in considering whether there was or was not that evil intent on the part of the accused at the time of the alleged offence.

In the present case it appears to me that the learned Sheriff-substitute has correctly addressed himself to the matter for his decision. In the reasons for his decision contained in the stated case he states: 'I inferred dole only from the excess of punishment in the circumstances narrated.' Just before that statement he says: 'What I found fault with was the succession of punishments and reasons (or lack of just reasons) therefor, as narrated in my findings. At some stage their repetition amounted to what I can only describe as a degree of unjust persecution.' His decision was, therefore, that the actings of the appellant could not be attributed to the exercise of discipline, but inferred that the child was being persecuted, so that dole was established. Other passages in the reasoning of the learned Sheriff-substitute were criticised by counsel for the appellant. But when I consider what he says as a whole, I am fully satisfied that he has not erred in law, and has applied the proper test to the actings of the appellant."

Appeal refused: conviction upheld.

NOTE

Cf. *Brown* v. *Hilson (ante)*. For a discussion of the disciplinary powers of teachers, and the limits of the criminal law in this respect, see Wallington, "Corporal Punishment in Schools" 1972 J.R. 124.

(iii)   Consent

Smart v. H.M. Advocate
1975 S.L.T. 65

The appellant and another man agreed to have a "square-go", during the course of which the appellant inflicted a number of injuries on the other party. He was charged with assault, and in his defence he claimed (*a*) that since the other party had consented to the fight he could not be convicted of assault, and (*b*) that his actings were in self-defence. The jury were directed that consent could not provide a defence to the charge, and the appellant was convicted. He presented an application for leave to appeal against conviction.

OPINION OF THE COURT: "The applicant was found guilty by a majority verdict of the jury of a charge of assault. The charge libelled was that he assaulted Isaac Wilkie, kicked him on the private parts, punched and kicked him about the head and body, pulled out his hair and bit him on the left arm to his injury.

The argument in support of the application proceeded on the basis that the applicant had invited Wilkie to have a 'square go' and that Wilkie consented to this. There was evidence, said to be disputed by the applicant, that Wilkie had been invited on several occasion to have a 'square go' before he finally consented. It is not necessary, in our view, to have regard to this allegation to determine the issues canvassed before us.

Two lines of defence were submitted at the trial. The first was that since Wilkie had consented to fight with the applicant the latter could not be guilty of assault in respect of his actions in that combat by consent. The second was that since the applicant had tabled a special defence of self-defence, that special defence should have gone to the jury. Normally it could only be determined on the evidence whether such a direction was justified, but as this case was presented it appeared that the self-defence founded on was simply that the applicant was participating in an agreed-upon fight and that anything he did was done either to get the better of his opponent or to defend himself against the attack of his opponent. In the course of his charge to the jury the presiding sheriff refused to give effect to these submissions. These arguments were repeated by counsel for the applicant at the hearing of the application. For support of his first contention, based on the parties' consent to fight, counsel said that there was a complete dearth of authority, and he relied principally on a passage in Gordon's *Criminal Law,* at p. 774, where the learned author says: 'If A and B decide to fight each other they cannot be guilty of assaulting each other, so long as neither exceeds the degree of violence consented to or permitted by law.' The author then goes on to say: 'Where the assault does not involve another crime the position appears to be that consent is a good defence provided that not more than a certain degree of injury is caused (*R.* v. *Donovan* [1934] 2 K.B. 498.) What that degree is is undecided and unknown. Consent is not a defence to the charge of murder (*H.M. Advocate* v. *Rutherford,* 1947 J.C. 1, 1947 S.L.T. 3), and the ratio of *H.M. Advocate* v. *Rutherford,* that the attitude of the victim is irrelevant, was applied in the unreported case of *Ian Gordon Purvis* (1964) to exclude a defence of consent in a charge of an assault with a knife to the danger of the victim's life. But it is submitted that consent is a defence to minor assaults whether inflicted for sexual, sporting or other purposes.' We have quoted these passages at length because they represent in effect the argument presented by the applicant's counsel. Leaving aside the question of what constitutes a minor assault, the apparent contradiction in the two passages quoted, and whether the ejusdem generis rule applies to his illustrations, we are of the opinion that the conclusion which Professor Gordon reaches and the submission which he makes are wrong.

An assault is an attack on the person of another. Evil intention is of the essence of assault—Macdonald's *Criminal Law* (5th edition) p. 115. This was reiterated by Lord Justice-Clerk Cooper (as he then was) in *H.M. Advocate* v. *Rutherford* (supra) at p. 6. That is what the presiding sheriff said in the present case. Lord Cooper said that consent was not a defence in a case of murder or culpable homicide. In this he was following the view of Baron Hume in his treatise on *Crimes,* vol. I, at p. 230. This view was followed in *Purvis* (supra) in regard to an assault with a knife to the danger of life. Is there any justification for applying this line of authority to serious assaults but not to minor assaults? In our opinion there is not. Apart from the obvious difficulty of knowing where to draw the line there is nothing in principle to justify the distinction. If there is an attack on the other person and it is done with evil intent that is, intent to injure and do bodily harm, then, in our view, the fact that the person attacked was willing to undergo the risk of that attack does not prevent it from being the crime of assault. If A touches B in a sexual manner and B consents to him doing so (and there is nothing else involved which would constitute a crime under statute or at common law) there is no assault because there is no evil intention to attack the person of B. So, too, if persons engage in sporting activities governed by rules, then, although some form of violence may be involved within the rules, there is no assault because the intention is to engage in the sporting activity and not evilly to do harm to the opponent. But where the whole purpose of the exercise is to inflict physical damage on the opponent in pursuance of a quarrel, then the evil intent is present, and consent is elided. This view consists with the English view as expressed by Swift, J., in giving the judgment of the court in *R.* v. *Donovan* (supra), at p. 506 et seq. This was recognised in the case of duelling when the intention of the participants was to kill the opponent, and we see no reason why it should be different when the duellists have the evil intent of inflicting physical injury on the opponent.

In the circumstances of this case as explained to us we are of the opinion that the sheriff was fully justified in directing the jury that there was no relevant evidence to support the plea of self-defence. It is, accordingly, unnecessary for us to consider the broader question of whether self-defence could ever be a defence in the case of a combat which started by consent.

The applicant's counsel sought to invoke a further argument from the civil law and submitted that the maxim volenti non fit injuria should apply to a case like this and result in an acquittal. In our view, the reasons for rejecting consent as a defence equally dispose of this submission. It follows that the criticisms of the directions in law given by the presiding sheriff in the circumstances of this case are not well founded and that the application must be refused.

Before parting with the case we wish to make one final observation. It is said that the consent was to have a 'square go'. There is no definition, classical or otherwise, of the phrase, and it seems unlikely that any normal person would consent to a fight which could legitimately involve what is contained in the charge, but for the purposes of the argument we accepted that Wilkie did so. We are only too aware of the prevalence of what is alleged to be a 'square go' in one form or another, often leading to serious results. Accordingly, apart from the private interests involved in this case, it is in the public interest that it should be decided and made known that consent to a 'square go' is not a defence to a charge of assault based on that agreed combat."

Application refused.

NOTES

For a detailed examination of the implications of this decision, see Gordon, "Consent in Assault" (1976) 21 J.L.S. 168. The problems are legion. If, e.g., "evil intent" is constituted by "intent to injure and do bodily harm", can the court's treatment of sporting activities work for boxing, since an intention to injure is (presumably) the essence of such a 'sport'?

e. Provocation in assault

The principles governing provocation in assault are broadly similar to those governing provocation in homicide *(post, ch. 11)*: see *H.M. Advocate* v. *Callander*, 1958 S.L.T. 24 *(post)*. There are, however, some differences. The first is that it is clearly established that verbal insults may constitute provocation in assault, but not, it is generally thought, in homicide (see, however, the case of *Berry* v. *H.M. Advocate (unreported, post, ch. 11)*. The second difference may exist in relation to the effect of a successful plea of provocation—see *Hillan* v. *H.M. Advocate*, 1937 J.C. 53 *(post)*.

1. Hillan v. H.M. Advocate
1937 J.C. 53

The appellant was convicted of assault under provocation and sentenced to one month's imprisonment. He appealed against conviction and sentence.

LORD JUSTICE-CLERK (AITCHISON): "The first ground of appeal is that the verdict was unreasonable and cannot be supported, having regard to the evidence. Upon this I am against the appellant. I think there was sufficient evidence to satisfy a reasonable jury that the violence used by the appellant was not justified by any provocation he received, and was unnecessary for his own defence in repelling the attack to which he was subjected. The provocation referred to in the jury's verdict was that the appellant, having been called over to a cabinet in a public lavatory, where he had been preceded by an elderly man, was there assaulted by the elderly man placing his hands upon his person, and saying: 'What about it?' and persisting in that conduct. The jury must have been satisfied that some such immoral gesture took place, and it must be accepted, as the Solicitor-General conceded, that this is what the jury meant by provocation. But so taking it, there was in my opinion, sufficient evidence of excessive violence to support the verdict.

A more serious difficulty arises upon the direction in law given to the jury, which is the main ground of appeal. The appellant had tabled a special defence in these terms: 'That the assault if committed was so committed under provocation and in self-defence justifiably, and that the complainer is a man of such bad character as to render his testimony incredible.' The imputation of bad character was not supported by any evidence.

Provocation and self defence are familiar pleas in criminal trials, and particularly in charges of assault and homicide. But the pleas are not identical although in many cases they overlap. Provocation is frequently a plea in reduction of the quality of the crime, as where it is sufficient to reduce the crime of murder to culpable homicide. But also in certain cases it may amount to a complete defence to the crime libelled, so that on its being satisfactorily established, the proper verdict is one of acquittal. Again, it may neither reduce the quality of the crime, nor afford a complete defence, but only be effectual to establish mitigating circumstances that go to the sentence to be imposed. This distinction between the plea in justi-fication and the plea in palliation should always be kept in view, especially where the panel is not the original aggressor. There are many cases in which both alternatives should be put to the jury. Where the provocation is of such a kind as to justify the retaliation, the panel is entitled to be acquitted; where it is substantial and yet falls short of justifying the retaliation so as not to amount to a complete defence, the panel is guilty under provocation."

Appeal allowed.

NOTES

The confusion between self-defence and provocation is patent in this decision. The case was subjected to probably fatal criticism in *Crawford* *(post,* ch. 11), and Gordon's view is that *Hillan* would probably not now be followed (para. 29-45), although the judicial practice on this seems to vary (Gordon, *ibid.,* n. 47).

2.   **H.M. Advocate v. Callander**
1958 S.L.T. 24

The accused was charged with assaulting his wife and another woman to their severe injury. Evidence was led to the effect that the assault was committed under provocation when the accused dis-covered his wife and the other woman engaging in lesbian practices. In the course of his charge to the jury, the presiding judge gave the following directions on provocation:

LORD GUTHRIE: [After dealing with other matters] "The next question which we have to consider together is this: Are the circum-stances disclosed in evidence today such as would reasonably entitle you on a certain view of the facts to hold that they amounted to provocation? You heard the story told by the accused of the unhappy circumstances of his married life after 1955, after his wife had formed her association with Mrs O'Neil and had indulged with Mrs O'Neil in those unnatural practices between females to which the name of Lesbiansim has been given. Ladies and gentlemen, if a husband discovers his wife in the act of adultery or if a husband learns of his wife's adultery and immediately or shortly thereafter inflicts blows upon his wife, her conduct would amount to provocation. Lesbianism is not adultery, but I do not think that anyone would hold that it is a less serious infringement of the duty of a wife than adultery is, and consequently, if you are satisfied that the husband's actions were influenced by the discovery of his wife under circumstances which indicated that she was pursuing her course of Lesbianism with Mrs O'Neill, that would entitle you to form the opinion that he assaulted her and Mrs O'Neill under provocation. I want to add to that, however, that the mere fact the Lesbiansim was the unfortunate background to this married life would not of itself amount to provocation, because, if a husband has known of his wife's adultery or of her unnatural conduct and does not act under the immediate impulse of his discovery, then, if he assaults her later that is not an act under provocation, but one of revenge, and if you thought that the accused here was not acting under the influence of the discovery of his wife in a compromising situation with Mrs O'Neill, but was merely acting under the influence of what he had known for a long time, then that would not amount to provocation."

NOTES

Cf. H.M. Advocate v. *Hill*, 1941 J.C. 59 (*post*, ch. 11) and *McDermott* v. *H.M. Advocate*, 1974 S.L.T. 206 (*post*, ch. 11).

Cf. English law which maintains that it is only in murder that provocation may operate to reduce the quality of an offence. Thus it cannot operate to reduce a charge of malicious wounding (*Cunningham* [1959] 1 Q.B. 288) or even attempted murder (*Bruzas* [1972] Crim.L.R. 367). The New Zealand courts have held the doctrine to be applicable to the latter offence: *Smith* [1964] N.Z.L.R. 834.

f. Non-intentional injury

As has been pointed out (*ante*, section *b*), the crime of assault is restricted to intentional injury. Reckless injury, or even the reckless endangering of the safety of others, is not, however, beyond the reach of the criminal law.

1. David Smith and William McNeil
(1842) 1 Broun 240

The accused were charged with wickedly, recklessly and culpably discharging loaded firearms into a house, to the imminent danger of the lives of the persons in the house. An objection was taken to the relevancy of this charge on the grounds, *inter alia,* that the indictment did not aver knowledge of the presence of persons in the house or that any injuries were caused.

THE LORD JUSTICE-CLERK (HOPE): "I am of opinion that the act libelled is a crime, and correctly charged as such. Furious driving upon a public road, even when no passengers are to be seen upon it, is an offence, although it may not be worth while to try the case in the Court of Justiciary, unless some person has been injured. The same remark may be made as to Reckless Steering, which has occasioned a collision between two ships, unattended by injury either to persons or lives. If by the argument which was stated in the case of *Young* (1839) 2 Swin. 380, it is meant that in order to constitute an indictable offence, there must be injury to the person, this is clearly erroneous. But if, on the other hand, the doctrine merely is, that there must be a completed act on the part of the pannel, then, in the present case, a sufficient result has been set forth in the alleged act of *firing into* an inhabited house. The averment that the house, into which the gun was discharged, was *'inhabited,'* is explicit enough, and renders an additional averment, that the pannel knew that persons were in the house at the moment, unnecessary. The prosecutor cannot be expected to prove that, before committing the criminal act, the pannel first rung the bell, and inquired if any one was at home. By firing into an inhabited house, the pannel took his chance of that."

Objection to relevancy repelled.

THE LORD JUSTICE-CLERK, in charging the jury, directed them—That in order to constitute the particular crime charged, it was not necessary to prove against the pannel by separate evidence any intention to injure either persons or propery. The act of discharging loaded firearms into an inhabited house, if proved, was of itself sufficient to infer recklessness. It was unnecessary, also, under the present libel, to prove real danger to individuals within the house. The mere firing of the gun into the house constituted the crime, the pannel having taken his chance of the consequences. It would, therefore, be no defence, that the inmates of the house had accidentally left the room when the shot was fired into it, far less that there happened to be a screen which possibly might shield them from danger. If a person standing upon one side of a wall, and hearing the noise of a crowd collected upon the other, threw over some heavy substance, the act was equally criminal, though the crowd chanced at the moment to have moved back from the wall. In the present case, the act done was one by which lives were endangered, and would in all probability have been lost, had it not been for circumstances which the pannel could not have foreseen.

> Verdict: The jury found the accused
> McNeil guilty.

NOTE

Cf. H.M. Advocate v. *Phipps* (1905) 4 Adam 616, *ante*.

2. Quinn v. Cunningham
1956 J.C. 22

The accused was charged with riding a pedal cycle in a reckless manner causing it to collide with a pedestrian, causing injuries to himself and the pedestrian. An objection was taken to the relevancy of the complaint which was brought at common law. The sheriff repelled the objection and convicted the accused. A case was stated for the opinion of the High Court.

LORD JUSTICE-GENERAL (CLYDE): "This stated case arises out of a complaint in unprecedented terms, charging the appellant that he did ride a pedal cycle in reckless manner and did cause it to collide with and knock down Francis Conway, shipyard worker, Dundee, whereby both sustained slight injuries. The complaint was brought at common law in the Police Court in Blairgowrie. An objection to the relevancy of the complaint was taken at the conclusion of the evidence. The objection, as stated in the case, is to the effect that the cause should properly have been brought under the Road Traffic Acts, or with reference to the Highway Code. Although with some hesitation, I am prepared to treat this objection as meaning that the present complaint was not relevant at common law. The objection was repelled by the magistrate. On the evidence he convicted the appellant. The first question put to us is whether the magistrate was right in repelling the objection to the relevancy of the complaint.

It is quite true that the objection to relevancy was not taken at the proper time, and in the ordinary case this would be a conclusive bar to its subsequent consideration. But this well-recognised rule is subject to the exception that the High Court will consider an objection to the relevancy not taken at the proper time if it appears that the complaint cannot be read so as to libel a crime and is therefore fundamentally null—Trotter on Summary Criminal Jurisdiction, p. 324. It would be contrary to justice if this were not so, for, as Lord Mackenzie said in *O'Malley* v. *Strathern,* 1920 J.C. 74 at p. 81, 'This Court will not allow a conviction to stand for what is no crime under the law of Scotland.' The question of relevancy in the present case raises an issue of fundamental nullity, and must therefore be dealt with by us.

The charge in question is brought in respect of an alleged offence at common law. It consists of two separate parts, firstly riding a pedal cycle in a reckless manner, and secondly causing it to collide with someone whereby slight injuries resulted. As regards the second part of the charge, although it may found a claim for civil damages, it clearly does not constitute a crime. As regards the first part of the charge, mere reckless riding or driving of a vehicle has never been treated in Scotland as a crime at common law.

The reason for this is not far to seek. So far as concerns road accidents in Scotland, it is an essential element in the constitution of a crime at common law that there should be either an intention to commit a wrong or an utter disregard of what the consequences of the act in question may be so far as the public are concerned. Culpable homicide is the typical example of the latter form of crime. The essence of culpable homicide is the degree of *culpa* which has in fact resulted in the death. Mere *culpa* plus a death resulting from it does not constitute culpable homicide. As the Lord Justice-Clerk said in *Paton* v. *H.M. Advocate,* 1936 J.C. 19 at p. 22, 'it is now necessary to show gross, or wicked, or criminal negligence, something amounting, or at any rate analogous, to a criminal indifference to consequences, before a jury can find culpable homicide proved.' This represents the standard of culpability which must be established in such cases in order to constitute a crime at common law, based not upon intent, but upon reckless disregard of consequences. It is highly relevant to the present question, since in the text-books furious driving or riding at common law is treated as a subheading of the crime of culpable homicide—Alison's Criminal Law, vol. i, p. 121; Hume on Crimes, vol. i, p. 192. The standard of culpability must be the same, whether its consequences are death or not.

It was just because of the high degree of culpability required to be averred and proved in such cases before a crime at common law could be established that Parliament intervened to make mere reckless driving of a mechanically propelled vehicle a statutory offence. But this lesser statutory offence has never been made applicable to pedal cyclists. And, in my view, it would not be fair nor in accordance with the Scottish system of giving ample notice to accused persons if a charge of mere reckless riding of a pedal cycle were to be sanctioned at common law. Such a practice would sooner or later result in pedal cyclists being punished for the degree of reckless driving which constitutes an offence under statute on the part of drivers of mechanically propelled vehicles. Such a development is one for which Parliament can provide, but for which the Courts cannot.

As the law stands, therefore, this complaint can only be relevant if it libels that degree of recklessness which constitutes the crime at common law, that is to say, a recklessness so high as to involve an indifference to the consequences for the public generally. As the Lord Justice-General said in *M'Allister* v. *Abercrombie*, 5 Adam 366 at p. 370, 'I cannot find that it is part of the law of Scotland that to drive a vehicle culpably and recklessly is a crime, unless there is danger to the lieges.' Accordingly the words 'to the danger of the lieges' as a specification of the degree of recklessness in driving are to be found in the forms of complaint in the Second Schedule to the Summary Jurisdiction (Scotland) Act, 1954. In my opinion, without libelling that high degree of recklessness the complaint is not relevant, for it merely charges a lower degree of recklessness which is not a crime at common law. This Court has more than once observed the importance of adhering to the statutory form of charges, where they are applicable (see *Coventry* v. *Douglas*, 1944 J.C. 13). As the Lord Justice-General said in that case (at p. 20): 'If there is any doubt that the act set forth in the charge comes within the description of a known crime, then the charge is bad. The question is also one of due notice to the accused, and, unless he is given distinct notice that he is charged with a crime according to our law, the indictment or complaint must fall, whatever be the effect of the proof that follows upon it, and however complete the proof of a crime may be.' Judged by this standard the present complaint fails to satisfy what is required, for the words 'to the danger of the lieges,' as an amplification of the recklessness, are not libelled in this complaint. It charges the appellant therefore with a degree of recklessness which does not constitute a crime.

It was maintained that this deficiency was made good in the present case by the second part of the charge. I cannot accept this contention. Mere recklessness by a pedal cyclist followed by an injury to a foot passenger does not constitute a crime in Scotland, any more than mere recklessness in driving followed by a death would constitute culpable homicide. To constitute a crime in either case the recklessness must be such as to involve a disregard of the safety of the public. There is all the difference in the world between a reckless act which in fact happens to result in injury, and a reckless disregard of the safety of the public which in fact does injure someone. The latter but not the former constitutes a crime at common law. In the present case the injury to the foot passenger is in no way connected up with the recklessness, and is not libelled as an element of that recklessness. To hold this complaint relevant would, in my view, introduce a novel and far reaching extension of our criminal law for which there is no precedent and no warrant in principle. In the circumstances, in my opinion, the first question should be answered in the negative."

Question answered in the negative:
conviction quashed.

NOTE

On the court's power to declare new crimes, see ch. 1, *ante*, and the following case.

3. Skeen v. Malik
Sheriff Court of Glasgow and Strathkelvin, August 1977,
unreported

Malik was charged with selling to various children and young persons between the ages of 12 and 16 years quantities of "Evo-stik" glue "well knowing that they were purchasing said cans and tubes intending to inhale the vapours of said glue to the danger of their health and lives, and this you did wilfully, culpably and reck-' lessly, and they did inhale said vapour to the danger of their health and lives." A plea was taken to the relevancy of the complaint. The objection was upheld, and the sheriff stated a case for the opinion of the High Court.

THE SHERIFF: "The case called before me on a plea to the relevancy taken by the respondent. Mr. Findlay, for the respon-dent, submitted first that the charge disclosed no crime known to the common law of Scotland. The Crown were, he submitted, trying to create a new offence against what they considered a social evil but had failed to say so in clear terms. If this was a new offence it must either be brought within the existing rules of law or it must be defined and prescribed as such by Parliament. Alternatively, if there was a declaratory power still subsisting in the High Court of Justiciary it was for that Court and not for the Sheriff Court to determine the relevancy of this complaint. What was charged was the selling of a specific substance which was not of itself an illegal substance, nor was the sale of it illegal though it lead to unacceptable social uses. It was not, said Mr. Findlay, even a crime to sniff glue, though he conceded that, it having been sniffed, might lead to other offences such as breach of the peace, and it is, of course, libelled here that it endangered the health of the individuals sniffing it. Nor, he submitted, did it assist the Crown to aver that the respondent's actings were done 'wilfully, culpably and recklessly'. If it was legal for the accused to sell an inoffensive substance like glue, it could not become a crime for him to do so because he was alleged to have done it recklessly. The words 'wilfully' and 'culpably' were, he submitted, superfluous. Mr. Findlay then instanced the case of a person selling a rope to a man who said he was going to hang himself and said that, under no circumstances could this sale amount to a crime at common law. This, however, was precisely, he said, the situation which the Crown were libelling against the respondent. It could not, he submitted, be a crime to sell Evo-stik, which is not even libelled as a noxious substance, even if it is known that the individual will use it to cause harm to himself.

For the Crown, Mr. Carmichael rejected the suggestion that the complaint did not describe Evo-stik as noxious and, with this, I agree. He submitted that the complaint was based on first principles. He referred to Alison, *Principles of the Criminal Law,* pp. 628 and 629 and to Hume, *Commentaries,* i, pp. 22-23. The crux of the matter was the allegation, he submitted, that the accused's actings were wilful, culpable and reckless. This case, he submitted, was to be equated with those cited in the institutional writers on the administration of drugs. Moreover, culpable and reckless conduct was criminal and the Crown was seeking to extend that principle to cover this particular set of facts. Reference was also made to Gordon on *Criminal Law* (ist. ed.), p. 737, to the cases of *Jean Crawford,* (1847) Arkley 394, and *Milne and Barrie* (1868) 1 Couper 28.

The Crown proposition here is that it is criminal for a shopkeeper to supply a commercial and otherwise innocent substance to an individual, in the knowledge that the purchaser will use the substance in a way that will endanger his or her health. As I understand the Crown argument, criminality lies not in the supply of the substance but in the knowledge on the part of the seller that at the time of the sale he was aware of the use to which the substance might—and it is difficult to see how it can be put higher than a probability—be put. The supply of the substance in this knowledge is said to be wilful, culpable and reckless.

The passages relied on by the Crown in Alison, pp. 628-629, do not appear to me to assist Mr. Carmichael's argument. Mr. Carmichael relied on the passage at p. 628 that to 'furnish medicines for

the purpose knowing the end to which they were to be applied . . .
would unquestionably render [the supplier] liable as art and part'.
But that passage relates to the supply of drugs for the purpose of
committing the crime of abortion and falls within the principle of
concert. In the present case it is alleged the glue was supplied to
persons who were known to have the intention of inhaling the glue,
but to inhale glue is not *per se* a crime in the present law. At p. 629,
again relied on by Mr. Carmichael, it is stated 'that felonious
administration of laudanum or other narcotic or deleterious drugs
with intent to produce stupefaction whether in malice or to facilitate
the commission of any crime is a relevant point of dittay at common
law', but there, the criminality lies, as I understand it, in the
felonious *administration* of the drug. In the present case there is no
question of the accused having administered the drug feloniously or
otherwise. If harm was done here, it was not done by the respondent, it was brought about by the actings of the purchasers who,
their ages are given, cannot be described as infants or below years of
discretion.

Mr. Carmichael submitted that there was such a thing as culpable
and reckless conduct, and that the Crown here was seeking to
extend the principle of reckless and culpable conduct to this particular set of facts. Here he relied on the charge of Lord Justice-Clerk
Hope in *Paton & McNab* (1845) 2 Broun 525, quoted in Gordon,
Criminal Law (1st ed.), pp. 736-737. The standard set forth there,
however, is the same as the standard of care set in the civil law and
anticipates very closely the famous statement of the law on the
extent of duty by Lord Atkin in *Donoghue* v. *Stevenson,* 1932 S.C.
(H.L.) 31 at p. 44. Carelessness as such, however, does not, as I
read the authorities now, of itself amount to a criminal act. In *H.M.
Advocate* v. *Cranston,* 1931 J.C. 28, Lord Justice-Clerk Alness
stated that: 'At one time in our law it was quite sufficient to establish
a charge of culpable homicide that any fault on the part of the
accused resulting in the death of a fellow human being had been
established. I do not think that is the law today. The carelessness
which the Crown must prove according to our conception of the law
today in a case of this kind must be gross and culpable carelessness.'
And this stand was approved by the Criminal Appeal Court in the
case of *Paton* v. *H.M. Advocate,* 1936 J.C. 19; see also Gordon,
Criminal Law (1st ed.) p. 741. MacDonald, *Criminal Law,* p. 101
desiderates 'gross and wicked recklessness in its performance' *i.e.* of
the carrying out a duty.

This raises a number of questions which I have not found it easy to
answer. First of all I find it difficult to apply the concept of gross and
wicked recklessness to the conduct that is alleged here where the act
itself involved nothing other than selling a commercial substance

and where any resulting harm is not the direct result of the sale but of a later supervening act on the part of the purchaser and/or his or her friends. The cases where gross and wicked recklessness have been sustained are cases where there has been something in the conduct of the accused, as by driving recklessly, or using an engine recklessly, which contributed to the resulting injury or death. Where the harm has been caused, not by the original sale, but by an act on the part of the victim, Sheriff Gordon in his *Criminal Law* (1st ed.) states at p. 113 'In this branch of the problem, more than in any other, the idea of responsibility takes precedence over the concepts of causality. If it appears fair to say that the victim had only himself to blame, his death or other eventual injury will probably not be attributed to the original *assailant*: while if his subsequent acts appear excusable, or excite sympathy, or have been "induced" by the original *injury*, the courts will often exert themselves to avoid treating them as *novi actus*.' In the present case there is no question of the respondent being an assailant or of his sale of the Evo-stik glue *per se* involving an injury. Injury only is said to have arisen when the purchasers used the substance in a way it was not intended to be used. It may be that the principles of existing law here are in point to the situation presently canvassed by the Crown but, if so, it humbly seems to me that the Crown's contention involves an extension of existing principles which would fall, it humbly seems to me, within the declaratory powers of your Lordships' Court and not of the Sheriff Court.

Moreover, my difficulty is aggravated, if the Crown is right, when one attempts to delimit the principle for which the Crown contends.

If the Crown here is right there would be no limit to the situations in which a shopkeeper might find himself subject to a similar criminal charge. My difficulty is not just that Evo-stik may be an noxious substance and is after a certain use dangerous, almost anything can be made to be noxious and potentially dangerous depending on the use to which it is put. Some things are more potentially dangerous than others; a penknife, a sword, a pistol, as against a rope; but every one of them could be put to a lethal or dangerous purpose, and the shopkeeper might well be told at the sale they were to be put to a lethal purpose or might very well have good reasons for thinking that they would be so. I do not think, however, it could be successfully argued that the shopkeeper who sold such items to individuals whom he suspects or knows are likely to use them to do harm to themselves or to others—and, in principle, I can see no distinction here,—can be held to have committed a criminal offence. Hamlet, for instance, recognised that the individual 'himself, might his quietus make with a bare bodkin.' If Hamlet's haberdasher was told by Hamlet how the latter intended to use the bodkin he was purchasing—and it being Hamlet he probably would tell him—then if the Crown were right, the haberdasher would be acting criminally to sell Hamlet the bodkin. A shopkeeper who sold a knife to a youth whom he knew to be the leader of a violent gang might be equally described as acting recklessly or wilfully, as could the present respondent in selling glue. What, moreover, would the position be of a tobacconist who sold cigarettes to a chain-smoker whose appearance and cough suggested a bronchial disease or who was aware on information received, that might not have been disclosed to the purchaser, that the latter was suffering from lung cancer? If the Crown is right, such a tobacconist would be guilty of an offence by selling a substance which he knew would further endanger the health and life of the purchaser. Perhaps even more apposite, what of the publican who sells alcohol to a known alcoholic? This is not a novel situation but apart from any provision under statute, it was not suggested that at common law this would constitute a crime. If one considers, moreover, the position of a drug like cannabis and opium, I am led to believe from cases here that the former can be grown and is grown from budgerigar seed. It is certainly available as are other drugs now statutorily defined as dangerous. No authority was cited to me, however, for the proposition that if these drugs were dangerous the possession or sale of them was unlawful at common law. As I understand the history of this aspect of the law the supply of these drugs only became unlawful after Parliament had so declared them. I can see no distinction between the pre-statute situation governing the supply of such drugs and the present non-statutory situation governing the supply of Evo-stik to any customer.

The distinction is sought to be drawn here by the Crown by libelling that the sales were made wilfully, culpably and recklessly. It does not seem to me however, that the word culpably adds anthing to the charge. What was done wilfully here was *prima facie* the sale. If by wilful, here, however, the Crown means that the respondent supplied the purchasers for glue-sniffing knowing that that is what the glue would be used for, and that that was why he supplied it, that would surely be a stronger case than one in which it is averred he did it recklessly. I am not satisfied, however, that even in a situation where the supply was deliberate that a crime would be made out. In this context, I would refer to the case of *Milne & Barrie* (1868) 1 Coup. 28. There the charge libelled the wickedly and feloniously administering to or causing to be administered to or taken by any of the lieges a noxious substance whereby they were put in danger of their lives or injuriously affected in their health. The charge was held irrelevant. I would refer in particular to the judgment of Lord Cowan at pp. 30-31: 'There are here stated a number of alternatives in describing this crime but to arrive at a just conclusion as to whether or not a crime has been charged we are bound to take the lowest alternative, that is in substance administering a purgative whereby injury is done to health. I am of opinion that these words by themselves do not set forth an indictable crime by the law of Scotland. It is not said that it was administered with criminal intent towards the individual. It is not said that it was administered maliciously. It may have been administered from all we can gather from the indictment to a willing person with his own consent. No doubt the words by which the terms commented on are introduced "wickedly and feloniously administered" do touch the mind of the person alleged to have committed a crime, but the crime itself must be well described and charged in the major to give force and efficacy to these words of style. . . . Had the purgative been charged as having been *wilfully and culpably administered that might have amounted to a criminal charge,* but setting these words aside there does not appear to me to be any proper criminal charge.' It will be observed that his Lordship laid emphasis in the fact that the accused there were not said to have administered the drug, and to have placed emphasis on the fact that it may have been administered to a willing person with his own consent. At p. 32 Lord Ardmillan said 'In the present case we must . . . take the lowest alternative charge, namely administering other purgatives whereby the lieges are injuriously affected in their health. There is no malice alleged here, it is not said to be wilful or malicious. It is not said that the substance was disguised as given in anything to conceal it which is very important. It is not said that it was administered against consent. Nor is it said to have been administered without consent. The minor proposition describes the manner of administration which might have been important in the major. According to the major as it stands it might have been administered by prescription by a medical man or at the request of the person as a medicine quite openly or in some usual and simple vehicle. I agree therefore in thinking that the objection ought to be sustained.' Here again it will be observed that his Lordship founded on the fact that the libel did not allege administration by the supplier against the consent of the consumer. If the Crown were alleging here that the substance was wilfully administered by the respondent as in the nature of an assault, that would be one thing but, while it is not, I think there is a fatal hiatus between the act libelled and criminal responsibility in the present law.

If what is alleged in this indictment is in fact happening it is a very grave matter indeed—what Mr. Carmichael called a grave social evil—and, accepting that, it is a matter on which the law ought to be in a position to intervene. If this court, however, were to intervene and hold this complaint relevant, the question still arises how the principle would be limited in practice. If it cannot be limited, and it is a supply of Evo-stik that is to be proscribed, it humbly seems to me that only Parliament could so proscribe it. If a general principle is to be propounded that the supply of a legal substance which can be used to endanger the buyer's health and is supplied in that knowledge then it seems to me that that is either a new principle of law or calls for an extension of some existing principle for which I think only the declaratory or quasi legislative power of the High Court of Justiciary is appropriate. I would think that if the practice is as the Crown has described it there could be fewer cases more apposite for the invocation of that ancient power. So far as this court was concerned, however, I sustained the plea to the relevancy and dismissed the complaint.

The Question respectfully stated for the Opinion of the Court is:—Was I entitled to sustain the respondent's plea to the relevancy?"

NOTE

The matter remains an open question, since the Crown abandoned its appeal against the sheriff's decision to uphold the plea to the relevancy.

g. *Issuing threats*

Assault is conceived of, primarily, as an offence involving physical violence. Oral or written threats of violence may also be within the reach of the criminal law.

1. **James Miller**
(1862) 4 Irvine 238

The accused was charged on an indictment which libelled the "wickedly and feloniously writing and sending threatening letters." An objection was taken to the relevancy of this charge in respect that it did not set forth any crime known to the law of Scotland.

THE LORD JUSTICE-CLERK (INGLIS): "The Court having formed an opinion in this case, they have requested me to state the grounds of it. The major proposition charges the accused with the 'wickedly and feloniously writing and sending, or causing to be written or sent, to any of the lieges, any threatening letter.' Now it is necessary to consider whether this major proposition, as regards its relevancy, obtains support from the use of the words 'wickedly and feloniously,' and it must be observed that, properly speaking, these words have no place in the major proposition. The proper place for these words in an indictment is in the minor proposition, and when they occur in the minor, they express a quality of the act which is there specifically charged; they express that which is essential to the constitution of the crime—a certain condition of mind on the part of the accused at the time of committing the act libelled. I do not say that it is impossible, that these words should have any force or effect in a major proposition; but whatever force or effect they may have, it cannot alter their settled meaning, which is what I have now endeavoured to explain.

Abstracting these words, the crime charged is, 'writing and sending a threatening letter.' Now, that the use of threats is, in certain well-known cases, a crime in the eye of the law of Scotland, will not admit of dispute. A threat to burn a man's house is undoubtedly criminal, and so is a threat to put him to death, or to do him any grievous bodily harm, or to do any serious injury to his property, his fortune, or his reputation. These are all criminal threats; and any one who uses such threats may be punished for the use of them, although he had no intention of carrying them into effect, and no purpose to serve in using them, except it may be the gratification of his own malice or his own caprice. The very using of the threat is in these cases itself a crime. But then, while there is a certain class of threats that are undoubtedly criminal in the eye of the law, there is another and a much larger class of threats that are not so; and even threats that are immoral and unjust may not be of such a kind as to amount to a crime. It is therefore absolutely indispensable, when the criminal law deals with the use of threats as a ground of punishment, that care should be taken to distinguish between these two classes of threats. It seems to follow from this, as a necessary consequence, that the major proposition of a libel which charged the using and uttering of threats would not be relevant, assuming that that means the using and uttering of threats verbally, because there may be the using and uttering of threats in a great variety of cases which would not amount to a crime; and the major proposition which I have supposed, therefore, would be a bad major proposition. On the other hand, it seems clear enough that the using and uttering of a threat verbally of such a kind as I have already adverted to—a threat to burn a man's house, or to take his life, or to do him some grievous harm—would be a relevant point of dittay, and a major proposition setting forth that would set forth a crime known in the law of Scotland.

But here we have the element of writing, and it is that which gives to this case its peculiar importance. The threats here are contained in letters, and the question comes to be, whether the crime of writing and sending threatening letters, or the writing and sending of a threatening letter, is a relevant statement of a crime in a major proposition. Here, again, it seems abundantly clear, that the writing and sending of a threatening letter, in the popular sense of these words, is not in every case criminal, any more then the use of verbal threats is always criminal. For it is only certain threats that are criminal; and it is only if threats of that kind are conveyed in writing, that such writing becomes criminal. It may be also that the threats so conveyed are used for an unlawful purpose, such as extorting money, and thus they may acquire in another way a criminal character. But if in the natural and popular sense these words, 'writing and sending a threatening letter,' do not in themselves amount to a statement of what is criminal, the only question remaining is, whether writing and sending threatening letters, or rather, properly speaking, the term 'threatening letters,' has a technical and fixed meaning in law, and signifies the writing and sending of letters containing threats of that particular kind of which the use is criminal? Now, we have considered the various authorities and the cases that have been cited to us, and upon the whole we have come to the conclusion that there has been no such fixed understanding or practice as to give any definite technical meaning to the term 'threatening letters,' and, consequently, that the major proposition of this indictment, which we read, for the reasons I have already stated, as simply libelling the writing and sending of a threatening letter, is not a relevant major proposition. The objection to the libel is therefore sustained."

                              Objection to relevancy sustained.

2. Kenny and Anor. v. H.M. Advocate
1951 J.C. 104

The appellants were charged on indictment with, *inter alia*, threatening a man with violence "all with intent to intimidate him and to deter him from giving evidence" against the appellants in a criminal trial. On this charge the jury returned a verdict of guilty of threatening violence, but without the intent libelled. An application for leave to appeal against conviction on the third charge was presented to the High Court.

LORD KEITH: "Various points have been taken by the applicants in this appeal, and I can dispose at once of certain of the objections which do not seem to bulk very largely in the case. The facts are that a fracas took place on a common stair in Glasgow, in which the applicants were involved and in the course of which serious injury by cutting with a sharp instrument, a knife or a razor, was occasioned to one of the witnesses, a man Welsh. Welsh was taken to hospital, and some time after his return from hospital—in fact two and a half months after the incident—the two accused called at his house, looked into the house through the top of a window, made certain remarks to him of a threatening character, came round to the door of the house, which Welsh had by this time closed, and made further remarks to him, including one which was that if Welsh came out the accused would mark his face. The charge that was made against the accused on this latter incident (the third in the indictment) was that 'you did climb on to the window ledge of and peer into said house, did shout, knock at the door and threaten said William Welsh with violence, all with intent to intimidate him and to deter him from giving evidence against you in your trial. . . .'

On a suggestion of the Sheriff who was the presiding Judge at the trial, the jury brought in a verdict from which the latter part of the charge was excised, the verdict being that on charge 3 they found the accused guilty of threatening violence without the intent libelled. Such a verdict is, however, open to serious objection. Had the indictment charged the accused with merely threatening violence, the charge would, I think, have been irrelevant and could not have proceeded to trial. In these circumstances, looking to the verdict that the jury has returned, I think the proper course here would be to find that the verdict did not amount to a verdict of a crime of which the accused can be found guilty. Accordingly, so far as the third charge is concerned, I think the accused are entitled to succeed in their appeal."

LORD RUSSELL: "I am of the same opinion. I desire to add only a few words with regard to the conviction on the third charge. It is not every verbal threat that is a criminal offence. It appears to me that the verbal threat libelled in the third charge of this indictment was clearly serious and criminal by reason of the purpose or intent with which the threat was alleged to have been made, that purpose being to intimidate the victim so as to deter him from giving evidence against the accused in their trial due to take place a few days later. I am satisfied that, as framed, that charge did disclose a relevant criminal charge. If that charge had been established by the evidence, it would have been, as it is, a serious offence. As it happened, however, in the evidence adduced relating to the circumstances in which the verbal threat was made, there was no proof of any reference having been made by the accused to the forthcoming trial or of any language used by way of deterring the recipient of the threats from appearing as a witness at the trial. In that situation, since the jury were of opinion that the intent to intimidate and deter was not proved, the result of their verdict was to convict the accused merely of uttering a verbal threat to do violence, without any further specification relevant to infer grievous bodily harm or sinister intent. The failure of the Crown to prove the substance of the sinister purpose contained in the threat so waters down the charge that I have, with some hesitation, come to the conclusion that what was left of the charge did not, on the evidence by which it was supported, amount to a criminal offence. I therefore agree that the conviction on the third charge should be quashed."

Conviction quashed.

NOTE

The Scottish notion of assault and the offence of uttering threats thwarts the diverting English academic debate on whether or not there can be assault by words alone: see, Williams, "Assault and Words" [1957] Crim. L.R. 219 and Smith and Hogan, pp. 351-352.

CHAPTER 11

HOMICIDE

Homicide is the destructon of a living human being (other than oneself). As such it may be criminal or non-criminal. Criminal homicide is divided into murder—which is killing committed with an intention to kill or "wicked recklessness"—and culpable homicide. The latter crime may be subdivided into voluntary and involuntary culpable homicide. Voluntary culpable homicide is simply murder committed under mitigating circumstances, notably provocation or diminished responsibility. Involuntary culpable homicide is really a residual category, comprising those criminal homicides not included in murder or voluntary culpable homicide. Non-criminal homicide is either justifiable killing—as in cases of self-defence—or "casual," that is to say "by accident or mischance" (see Gordon, para. 23-09).

a. A living human being

The *actus reus* of all forms of homicide is the destruction of a living human being. This gives rise to three questions—(i) at what point does a human being begin to exist for these purposes? (this is essentially the distinction between homicide and abortion); (ii) at what point does a person cease to exist for these purposes? (this is a particularly acute problem in relation to the switching-off of life-support apparatus); (iii) how does the law fix the causal connection between the death and the accused's conduct? The second two issues have already been outlined (*ante*, ch. 3). The following cases deal with the first problem.

1. Jean McCallum
(1858) 3 Irv. 187

The panel was charged with the murder of her newly-born child by strangling it with a piece of tape. The evidence showed that the child had breathed, but was not conclusive on whether it had been fully born alive.

LORD JUSTICE-CLERK (INGLIS): "There is no kind of homicide that can be committed except upon a living human being, and, in order to establish here a charge of murder, which is the highest kind of homicide, you must be satisfied on the question, Whether there was a living child, murdered after its birth.

The indictment sets forth, in logical sequence, the facts that the prosecutor undertakes to prove, and which are indispensable to his case. After stating time and place, it proceeds:—'You, the said Jean McAllum or McCallum, having been delivered of a living female child, did, immediately or soon *after the birth* of said child. . . .'

You see, therefore, that the prosecutor must prove that the prisoner was delivered of a living female child, and that the assault leading to the murder of the child was committed after its birth. . . .

The prosecutor must thus prove, as indispensable to his case, that the subject so attacked—the child round whose neck this ligature was tied—was born a living child.

As to what is a living child, there is no difficulty about the law. A child that is not fully born has no separate existence from the mother, and is not, in the eye of the law, a living human being. It is in a state of transition from a *foetus in utero* to a living human being, and it does not become a living human being until it is fully born and has a separate existence of its own.

You may destroy a *foetus in utero*. It has a principle of vitality. And you may destroy it on the eve of birth; or you may destroy it in the course of being born. And all these are very serious offences, and are punishable by law. But they are not murder. And murder is the only charge in this indictment. Now this is extremely important, because unless you are satisfied that that child was alive after birth—that it was completely born a living child—you cannot find a verdict against the prisoner. . . . Everything depends upon what opinion you have as to whether the child was born alive. The case rests entirely on that."

Verdict: Not proven.

2. H.M. Advocate v. Scott
(1892) 3 White 240

The accused was charged with the culpable homicide of her newly-born child by strangling it immediately after birth, or alternatively by refraining from calling for assistance at the birth. Evidence was led by the Crown to the effect that the child had been born alive, had breathed, and had died as a result of manual strangulation. A medical witness for the defence was of the opinion that the injuries could have been caused by the accused in delivering herself of the child, or alternatively that they might have been inflicted before the child was wholly separated from the person of its mother. Counsel for the accused argued that unless the injuries were proved to have been inflicted after complete delivery, there could be no conviction of culpable homicide. In his charge to the jury, the presiding judge gave the following directions.

LORD YOUNG: "If, then, you think that no blame attaches to the prisoner for the death of her child, you will, as I have said, acquit her. If you think that blame does attach to her, then culpable homicide is the name for that blame, resulting as it did in the death of a child which had both cried and breathed. It does not matter in the least, so far as the criminality of the accused is concerned if the injuries were inflicted when the child was partly in its mother's body, and no suggestion of that kind was made at the time by the girl herself."

Verdict: Not guilty.

NOTES

Gordon's view is that Lord Young's approach is correct (para. 32-02). But what exactly is Lord Young saying? Is he saying that it is homicide to kill a child which is not fully born, or could he be construed as saying that a person who inflicts injuries on a child which is not fully born, which result in its death *after* birth, is guilty of homicide? *Cf.*, on the latter point, the English law as contained in the Infant Life (Preservation) Act 1929.

How should Scots law deal with the following problem? A shot a pregnant woman. The twins she was carrying were delivered by an emergency caesarean section, but died a short time later. A court in New Jersey convicted A of their murder (see the case of Anderson, *The Times*, July 17, 1975).

b.   Murder

As has been pointed out, murder is simply one form of unlawful homicide. It is distinguished from other forms of homicide by the particular forms of *mens rea* required. The following cases discuss this requirement.

1.   Cawthorne v. H.M. Advocate
1968 J.C. 32

The accused was charged with attempting to murder four people by firing shots from a rifle at random into a room in which they had barricaded themselves. His intention was apparently to frighten them, rather than kill any of them. At his trial, the presiding judge gave the following directions on the *mens rea* of murder.

LORD AVONSIDE: "In our law the crime of murder is committed when the person who brings about the death of another acted deliberately with intent to kill, or acted with intent to do bodily harm, or, and this is the third leg, acted with utter and wicked recklessness as to the consequences of his act upon his victim. Intent to kill, intent to do bodily harm, acting with utter and wicked recklessness as to the consequences of his act. In murder the Crown need never establish motive or premeditation or plot. Murder is a question of fact within the law, the occurrence of death within the law. It is impossible, ladies and gentlemen, to look into the mind of a man, and when, therefore, you are seeking to evaluate the effect of the evidence in regard to the nature and purposes of an act, you can only do so by drawing an inference from what that man did in the background of all the facts of the case which you accept as proved. In short, you look at all the proved circumstances and events disclosed by the evidence and draw what inference is disclosed as to the nature of the act. Mr Cowie, as I understand it, suggested that in Scots law the crime of attempt to murder was limited to cases in which the Crown had proved intent to kill. That is the first and most obvious branch of the definition of a murderous act. Again I do not agree, and you will take my direction in this matter. Attempt to murder is a charge brought against a man who is alleged to have made an attack on another or other people in circumstances in which, had his victim or victims died as a result of the attack, his offence would have been murder. Thus in my view, and you must accept my view in this court, the law holds it to be murder if a man dies as a result of another acting with utter and wicked recklessness, and that because the very nature of the attack, the utter and wickedly reckless attack, displays a criminal intention. If such an act does not result in death, none the less the criminal intention has been displayed and is of a quality and nature which results in its properly being described as an attempt to murder. And thus, in this case, if you hold it proved that any of the three possible elements of murder have been established, you are entitled to convict the accused man of attempt to murder one or other, some of those named."

The jury returned a verdict of guilty, and the panel was sentenced to nine years' imprisonment. On appeal against conviction:

LORD JUSTICE-GENERAL (CLYDE): "The ground upon which the present appeal against conviction is taken is that under our law, so it is contended, a jury cannot find the appellant guilty of attempted murder unless they are satisfied beyond reasonable doubt that the appellant discharged the firearm at any of the persons named with the deliberate intention to kill. A direction to this effect was asked from the trial judge, who refused to give it, and the question is whether he was correct in so refusing. In my opinion he was.

The crimes of murder and attempted murder are common law crimes in Scotland and I do not find it helpful to seek to draw analogies from alien systems of law where the rules may for various reasons be different. This issue must be determined by the rules applicable to Scots law. In our law murder is constituted by any wilful act causing the destruction of life. (Macdonald on the Criminal Law of Scotland, (5th ed.) p. 89.) The *mens rea* which is essential to the establishment of such a common law crime may be established by satisfactory evidence of a deliberate intention to kill or by satisfactory evidence of such wicked recklessness as to imply a disposition depraved enough to be regardless of consequences. (See Macdonald in the same passage.) The reason for this alternative being allowed in our law is that in many cases it may not be possible to prove what was in the accused's mind at the time, but the degree of recklessness in his actings, as proved by what he did, may be sufficient to establish proof of the wilful act on his part which caused the loss of life."

LORD GUTHRIE: "The main ground of this application for leave to appeal against conviction is set forth in the first reason. The other reasons which were not abandoned at the hearing were subsidiary, and really dependent on the success of the first.

The first part of the first reason is that the trial judge misdirected the jury in respect that he equiparated the *mens rea* necessary for attempted murder with that necessary for murder. As it is stated, I have difficulty in understanding that submission. *Mens rea,* or dole, in our criminal law is the wicked and felonious intention which impels the criminal to commit a crime. It is a state of mind which results in a criminal act, and I fail to see how there can be a distinction between the wickedness resulting in murder, and the wickedness resulting in an attempt to murder. Hume in his book on Crimes, vol. i, p. 21, describes dole as 'that corrupt and evil intention, which is essential (so the light of nature teaches, and so all authorities have said) to the guilt of any crime.'

During the argument, however, it appeared that the complaint of the applicant was against that part of the charge of the trial judge in which he dealt with the intention which is necessary to constitute an attempt to murder. The trial judge stated that 'in our law the crime of murder is committed when the person who brings about the death of another acted deliberately with intent to kill, or acted with intent to do bodily harm, or, and this is the third leg, acted with utter and wicked recklessness as to the consequences of his act upon his victim.' It was not disputed that this is a correct statement of the law in relation to murder if the word 'grievous' is inserted before 'bodily harm'. But it was submitted for the applicant that in a case of attempted murder a jury is not entitled to infer intent to murder from 'utter and wicked recklessness as to the consequences of his act upon his victim'. Therefore, it was argued, the Crown can only succeed in an indictment of attempted murder if it proves deliberate intent to kill or to inflict grievous bodily harm. This contention is expressed in the second part of the first reason. Counsel for the applicant accordingly maintained that the trial judge erred when he directed the jury in these terms: '. . . the law holds it to be murder if a man dies as a result of another acting with utter and wicked recklessness, and that because the very nature of the attack, the utter and wickedly reckless attack, displays a criminal intention. If such an act does not result in death, none the less the criminal intention has been displayed and is of a quality and nature which results in its properly being described as an attempt to murder.'

In my opinion this direction is soundly based in principle and is supported by authority. An attempt to murder is an occurrence, a fact, which can be proved by any competent evidence sufficient to establish it beyond the reasonable doubt of a jury. The intention involved in the attempt cannot, as the trial judge pointed out, be proved by an examination of the mind of the accused. The existence of the intention is a matter of the inference to be drawn from the accused's words, or acts, or both. The inference is easy when the accused has threatened his victim, or has stated his intention to third parties. Again, even in the absence of such statements, the intention may be deduced from the conduct of the accused. Admittedly this deduction will properly be drawn if he has been seen to aim a deadly blow at his victim. Thus it becomes a matter for the jury to decide whether the actions of the accused satisfy them that he intended to murder the victim. A reckless act may well be such as to lead to that inference. For example, as was suggested by your Lordship in the debate, a jury would be entitled to hold intention to murder proved if a criminal recklessly sprayed a courtroom with machine-gun bullets, even if all their Lordships fortunately escaped injury, and it was not proved that the criminal aimed at any one or more of them. As it is put in Macdonald on Crimes, (5th ed.) p. 108, the act manifests the intention. I refer also to Alison on Criminal Law, vol. i, p. 163, where he said: 'In judging of the intention of an accused who has committed an aggravated assault, the same rules are to be followed as in judging of the intent in actual murder, viz. that a ruthless intent, and an obvious indifference as to the sufferer, whether he live or die, is to be held as equivalent to an actual attempt to inflict death.' I think that that is a correct statement of the law of Scotland, and that it fully supports the charge as given by the trial judge.

The view of the trial judge is, in my opinion, in accordance with the fundamental rule of our criminal law that dole may be presumed from the perpetration of the wicked act. The evaluation of the act and the inference to be drawn from it are essentially matters for the jury. I agree with your Lordship that the applicant's attack on the charge of the trial judge fails, and that the application for leave to appeal against conviction should be refused."

LORD CAMERON: "I agree that this application fails. In my opinion those portions of the presiding judge's charge which were submitted to attack by Mr Cowie correctly stated what our law requires to establish the crime of attempt to murder. There are necessarily three elements in murder as defined in our law, (first) proof of death resulting from certain acts, (second) that these acts should be the wilful acts of the accused, and (third) proof of the necessary criminal intent. This intent can be established in the law of Scotland either by proof of deliberate intention to cause death, or by inference from the nature and quality of the acts themselves, as displaying, in the classic words of Macdonald, 'such wicked recklessness as to imply a disposition depraved enough to be regardless of consequences'. Such reckless conduct, intentionally perpetrated, is in law the equivalent of a deliberate intent to kill and adequate legal proof of the requisite *mens rea* to constitute that form of homicide which is in law murder.

Where death does not follow from such an act, or acts, Mr Cowie conceded that, where a deliberate intention to kill is established, that was enough to constitute the crime of attempt to murder. This would necessarily be so whether injury was sustained by the party against whom the attempt was made or not. It was contended, however, that the mere commission of acts directed towards another or others which did not result in death or injury, but were wilful acts of such reckless character that, if death had resulted, the necessary criminal intent sufficient to constitute the crime of murder would be established, did not fall within the category of criminal conduct defined as attempt to murder. This contention, however, appears to me to seek to base a distinction in quality of the crime committed upon a difference in fact which is fortuitous and, in my opinion, irrelevant. It was not suggested by Mr Cowie that such actings would not constitute a crime, but it was maintained that they would do no more than constitute the crime of assault, possibly to the danger of life. I am not able to accept that contention. It seems to me that on principle the quality of the *mens rea* in a case of attempt to commit the crime of murder is not affected by the consequences of the acts constituting the criminal conduct if the *mens rea* necessary to constitute the completed act can be established either by proof of deliberate intent to kill or by the nature of the acts themselves. It would seem both to be logical and to consist with common sense that if the intent to commit the crime of murder can be established in two ways, both should be equally available in proof of the requisite intent of an attempt to commit that crime. After all, the subsumption of a charge of attempting to commit a crime must be that the criminal acts constituting the crime were perpetrated with the intent to commit the complete crime, an intent which was frustrated by circumstances outside or beyond the perpetrator's deliberate control. Therefore it would seem that the quality of the intent is the same in both cases and consequently in principle the proof of intent in both should be the same. This view of the matter would appear to get support from our most recent text writers of authority. Both in Macdonald, (5th ed.) p. 108, and in Anderson, (2nd ed.) p. 155, it is made plain that the necessary intent can be inferred from the acts of the accused. As Lord Anderson put it in dealing with the crime of attempt to murder, 'the intent to murder is held to be proved when the injury done shows utter recklessness as to the life of the victim . . .' This appears to me necessarily to be so, and to be applicable even where by the accident of events no injury has followed upon the acts, because the quality of the criminal intent remains the same, whatever the consequences. The statements of the law contained in Macdonald and Anderson to which I have referred stand without contradiction or doubt cast upon their accuracy in any decided case, nor is there anything in Hume which is inconsistent with them (see, for example, Hume on Crimes, vol. i, pp. 179, 256) and they are entirely in accord with the passage from Alison which your Lordship in the chair has quoted. I therefore think that this attack on the accuracy of the direction given by the presiding judge fails."

                                    Application for leave to appeal refused.

NOTES

How many forms of *mens rea* for murder does this case recognise? See Gordon, "*Cawthorne* and the Mens Rea of Murder" 1969 S.L.T. (News) 41. *Cf.* the treatment of intention and recklessness in *Brennan* v. *H.M. Advocate*, 1977 S.L.T. 151, *ante*. ch. 8.

2. H.M. Advocate v. Robertson and Donoghue
High Court, August 1945, *unreported*

(For the facts of this case see ante, ch. 3 on Causation.) In charging the jury:

LORD JUSTICE-CLERK (COOPER): "Now, every charge of murder, ladies and gentlemen, impliedly includes the lesser charge of culpable homicide. The choice is generally open to a jury—and in this case it certainly is open to a jury—and the matter to which I am now going to direct your attention is the question of the choice in this case between a verdict of murder and a verdict of culpable homicide. The critical factor in determining whether a given act of homicide is murder or culpable homicide only is the view which you take as to the intent with which the assailant acted. Of course, intent is something in a man's mind and can only be proved by inference from his conduct and from the whole surrounding circumstances of the case as these may be established in evidence, but will you please note very particularly that to justify a verdict of murder in this or any other case it is indispensable that the accused should have acted either with the intent to kill or, what is much more common, with wicked and reckless indifference to the consequences to his victim. May I repeat these words—wicked and reckless indifference to the consequences to his victim—and in judging whether that reckless indifference is present you would take into account the nature of the violence used, the condition of the victim when it was used, and the circumstances under which the assault was committed. I have already referred to the medical report, and it is a material point, of course, upon this issue of murder or culpable homicide that the injuries were slight—undoubtedly very slight. The doctors told us what we could have inferred for ourselves without their aid, that an ordinary adult would never have died as the result of those injuries alone. That fact that small injuries were inflicted is obviously in favour of the view that the recklessness—the wicked recklessness—was not present.

The next thing is—what were the weapons employed? Well, so far as the evidence goes, if you accept it, the weapons employed, apart from Robertson's fists or fingers, were bottles—empty bottles—and that is a factor which you may regard as rather indicative of recklessness, because an empty bottle of the size, weight and type exhibited in court before us during these last two days is not the thing which any responsible person breaks over the head of another human being—or tries to.

There is next the condition of the victim. What I mean is this, ladies and gentlemen, if this fracas had occurred between Robertson and a fit young man like Weatherston, the soldier [a witness for the Crown], for one thing there would have been no fatal consequences, and, even if there had been, it would not have been easy I think—it might not have been easy—for a jury to infer reckless indifference to consequences from the infliction of such injuries on a fit young man. But the point which you will have to consider carefully is this, that much less violence if applied to a feeble, old man, to a person whom the assailant must have known was a feeble, old man—if you think he must have known it—may suffice to justify an inference of wicked indifference to consequences. Much less violence in such a case would suffice than would suffice if the victim was a normal healthy adult . . . and you will, accordingly, have to devote some thought to the question—what inference is to be drawn from the fact that this struggle took place and this violence was used, if it was used . . . against this man of 82 whose photograph you have seen . . . and whose description you have heard from his doctor. . . . On the other hand, it is right to add . . . that Professor Sydney Smith did indicate that for his age he was a very muscular man. At p. 160 he said, 'He had good muscular development for 81 years. He was a fine, strong-looking fellow.' So that has certainly to be taken into account against the view of his family doctor . . . that he was a frail old man."

NOTES

In *H.M. Advocate* v. *McGuinness*, 1937 J.C. 37, M. was charged, along with several others, with the murder of S. A number of weapons were used in an attack upon the victim, including a bottle, a hatchet, and a poker. In charging the jury, the Lord Justice-Clerk (Aitchison) said: "People who use knives and pokers and hatchets against a fellow-citizen are not entitled to say 'we did not mean to kill' if death results. If people resort to the use of deadly weapons of this kind, they are guilty of murder, whether or not they intended to kill."

3.   H.M. Advocate v. Fraser and Rollins
1920 J.C. 60

The accused were charged with the murder of a man they had assaulted and robbed. The injuries inflicted on the victim made it clear that a considerable degree of violence had been used. In his charge to the jury the presiding judge made the following comments on the law of murder:

LORD SANDS: "If a person attempts a crime of serious violence, although his object may not be murder, and if the result of that violence is death, then the jury are bound to convict of murder. A striking illustration of this is the case of criminal abortion. There the man has no intention or desire to injure or kill the woman, it is the last thing he wants to do, but if he uses instruments to bring about a criminal abortion and in result kills the woman, that, by our law, is murder. Or, again, take the crime of rape. A man ravishes a woman but has no desire to kill her, yet, if he uses such violence as causes her death, then that is murder. And so it is with regard to the crime you are here concerned with, robbery, and it would be no answer—it was rather suggested in cross-examination—it would be no answer that the violence was connected with the man's seeking to defend himself. If a man is assaulted with violence and those who are assaulting him seek to rob him, he is entitled to defend himself, and, if they use such violence to overcome his efforts to defend himself that they kill him, then that is murder. That aspect of the matter, however, was not pressed so much by the learned counsel; they rather dwelt upon the question of intention. Did the prisoners intend to kill the man? Now, as I have already told you, under the law of Scotland when you have a violent crime like rape or robbery, then in order to convict of murder it is not necessary to show there was intention to kill. No doubt, intention may be taken into account in certain cases where the violence is very slight and the death is as it were a sort of mischance; then, even although the violence is criminal, if there was no intent to kill it would not be murder. I might take the illustration of a thief who tries to snatch somebody's watch. He tries to pull it away and in doing so upsets the man's balance and the man falls on the kerb and has the misfortune to strike his head against the stone and is killed. That would not be murder because there is a certain mischance in the matter. There is no probability or likelihood that you will kill a man by trying to snatch his watch. Then again, if you take the case of somebody who threw a snowball at a man and as a result the man had a shock and it killed him, again, I say, that is a mischance and not what is contemplated and expected. But if a man uses reckless violence that may cause death, and uses that violence in perpetrating a crime, it is murder. You do not require the deliberate intention to kill, but you must have reckless use of force without any consideration of what the results of that use of force may be. It is in that view that you must regard this matter.

You have heard the evidence in regard to the injuries this man suffered, and you must consider whether there was or there was not such reckless violence as shows that these men were determined to rob this man and did not really care what happened to him. There is one aspect of the case which I am afraid you must take into account. I cannot tell you—I should not be stating the law correctly if I were to tell you—that, if a man attacks another man in a park or in the street, and holds his throat so as to prevent him from calling out, or throws him down or pins him to the ground so as to rob him, and the man through that violence suffers death—I am not able to tell you that that would not be murder. It might, however, be in some cases a question of circumstance if the violence were not very great, but this case is on a more unfavourable footing. It is quite clear that this man was not merely held by the throat, he was not merely held down for the purpose of robbing him, but it is perfectly clear, I think, that the evidence shows that the object of the violence was to stun him at all events, if not to kill him, to render him unconscious, and I think that is borne out by the nature of what was done afterwards—taking away the boots and coat. He was struck in the face and on the head, there can be no doubt with the object either of stunning or paralysing him. It was not the case of a struggle to prevent the man calling out or protecting his own; the intention appears clearly to have been to reduce him to such a state that he was incapable either of calling out or resisting the removal of his clothes or anything else, or pursuing and giving the alarm—to make him, as I say, unconscious; and it is for you to judge whether that violence was or was not of that reckless character, regardless of consequences, which involves the crime of murder."

Verdict: Guilty of murder.

NOTE

Given that wicked recklessness is a sufficient *mens rea* for murder, and given that there was evidence of considerable violence having been used by the accused, was it of any particular relevance to the murder charge that the violence was used in the commission of a robbery?

4.   Miller and Denovan v. H.M. Advocate
High Court, December 1960, *unreported*

LORD JUSTICE-GENERAL (CLYDE): "These are two appeals against the verdict of a jury in the High Court in Glasgow. The jury unanimously found each of the appellants guilty of murder. They were both charged with assaulting John Cremin, striking him on the head with a piece of wood, knocking him down, robbing him of certain articles including a sum of £67 of money and of murdering him.

So far as the first named appellant Miller is concerned, as the jury must have found that he struck the fatal blow the verdict was one of capital murder within the meaning of the Homicide Act 1957, s. 5(1) (*a*)—that is to say a murder done in the course or furtherance of theft.

But in regard to the second appellant Denovan there was no evidence that he struck the actual blow and the jury were therefore directed, and rightly directed, that he could only be guilty of non-capital murder owing to the provisions of s. 5(2) of the Act. The jury found him guilty of non-capital murder.

As the presiding judge said in the course of his charge 'This case arises on a background of vice, depravity and violence,' and to appreciate the grounds of appeal it is necessary briefly to set out the circumstances as disclosed in the evidence.

In the indictment the two accused were charged with a series of assaults and robberies on men whom they accosted late in the evenings in the Recreation Ground where this murder is alleged to have taken place. Before the evidence was all led the two appellants pled guilty to all the charges against them respectively in the indictment with the sole exception of the murder charge relating to Cremin.

On the night of Cremin's murder the two appellants had gone to the Recreation Ground late in the evening with the avowed intention of robbing someone. They waited in the vicinity of the public lavatory, Denovan going in to act as the decoy. Cremin visited the lavatory and as he and Denovan were on their way from it Miller suddenly came up and without any warning is alleged to have hit Cremin on the head with a large block of wood some 3 feet 3 inches long which with one blow knocked Cremin senseless to the ground. The two appellants then proceeded to go through his pockets, taking out anything of value. When they had secured all they could find they ran off and left him dead or dying. His body was found a short time afterwards.

My Lords, this cowardly and utterly unprovoked assault was unexplained and unexplainable except as being 'a deliberate attempt to overcome any risk of resistance by Cremin' and so to enable the two appellants in safety to rob his unconscious body of whatever possessions they could find upon it. There was no suggestion of any quarrel or dispute with Cremin or of any resistance on his part which could justify the attack. He was struck down without warning. Both appellants displayed a callous disregard of whatever injuries they may have done him. They centred their whole attention upon snatching all they could from his pockets, rolling his body over on the grass in order to get easier access to them. Once their purpose was achieved they fled into the night and left him to his fate.

But apart from this aspect of the matter there was medical evidence in the case as well. The medical evidence established that the cause of his death was a single blow on his head which fractured his skull and caused a haemorrhage of or into the brain. The blow, according to the medical evidence, was 'a severe one' and 'a violent one' causing, as one of the doctors said, a large fracture and haemorrhage all over the brain. An attempt was made in cross-examination of this doctor to suggest that the fracture might have been caused by Cremin falling forward, to which the doctor replied 'Unless he is struck by a motor car and precipitated on to the ground you would not produce such an injury as this.'

In these circumstances the presiding judge directed the jury that 'If you come to the conclusion that that blow was delivered as a result of Miller hitting Cremin over the head with this large piece of wood in order to overcome his resistance in order that robbery might take place then I direct you in law that there is no room for culpable homicide in this case. If it was homicide at all, in that situation it was murder.' This direction by the presiding judge is attacked in this appeal upon the ground that the judge should have directed the jury that it was open to them on the evidence to return a verdict of culpable homicide.

In our opinion the presiding judge was amply justified in giving the direction which he did given in this case, and there is no basis on the evidence for a finding of culpable homicide. Murder is constituted by any wilful act causing the destruction of life whether intended to kill or displaying such wicked recklessness as to imply a disposition depraved enough to be regardless of consequences. That definition is a well-known one in Scotland. Obviously, therefore it is not essential for the establishment of murder to prove intent to kill. It may still be murder though that intent be absent. For it can still be murder if the jury are satisfied that there was a wilful act displaying utter recklessness of the consequences of the blow delivered. In the present case in our view there was ample evidence to justify a conclusion of that sort.

But it is argued on behalf of Miller that the presiding judge should have left it to the jury to find on the facts whether or not this crime was something less than murder, namely, culpable homicide. In our opinion the evidence in the present case required the presiding judge to direct them that there was no room for a verdict of culpable homicide. If it was homicide at all it was murder. My Lords, there are cases, of course, where the evidence of the circumstances in which the crime occurred is so conflicting that it would be appropriate to leave such a matter to the jury after the distinction between murder and culpable homicide had been pointed out. If, for instance, the issue between these two possible verdicts depended on the weight to be given to conflicting evidence as to the amount of violence used, or upon a question whether death might have been in that particular case a mischance, there may be room for leaving both murder and culpable homicide to the jury for their decision. But it is no part of the function of a judge at a trial to avoid his responsibility by leaving the issue in all cases to the jury to work out for themselves, and that in effect was the contention put before us on behalf of Miller this morning.

The judge has a duty to consider the evidence and has a duty to make up his mind whether any of it is relevant to infer that culpable homicide has been committed. If he arrives at the conclusion that there is no evidence in the case from which such a verdict could reasonably be reached, it is his plain duty to direct the jury that it is not open to them to consider culpable homicide. On the other hand if he finds that there is evidence which might reasonably entitle the jury to return a verdict of culpable homicide then, subject to suitable directions, it is his duty to leave the issue on the weight to be given to the evidence to the jury. (Compare in this connection the decision of the full bench in *Kennedy* v. *Lord Advocate,* 1944 J.C. 171, *per* Lord Justice-General at p. 177.)

In the present case the judge's direction in regard to culpable homicide is challenged on behalf of Miller in particular upon the ground that the judge did not put to the jury certain theories as to how the injuries leading to Cremin's death might have been caused. These theories had no basis in the evidence but were founded upon assumed states of fact for which there was no proof of any kind by anybody. The directions of a judge in a trial must be related to the circumstances of the case as disclosed in the evidence. In the present case there was no scintilla of evidence in support of any of these theories and the presiding judge in his charge very properly completely ignored them. In the present case accordingly in our view this attack upon the presiding judge in regard to his directions relating to culpable homicide completely fails."

Appeals dismissed.

NOTES

A verdict of culpable homicide seems to have been excluded as a matter of law. But which element in the case leads to this conclusion? Was it the extreme violence used, or the fact that it was used in the perpetration of a robbery?

5. H.M. Advocate v. Rutherford
1947 J.C. 1

The accused was charged with the murder of a young woman by strangling her with his tie. He gave evidence that the young woman had asked him to strangle her to death, and had put the tie round her own neck. He admitted pulling the tie, but alleged that he did so only to humour her or frighten her. He did, however, admit that he must have used considerable force, and also that he was aware of the dangers involved in what he did. In his charge to the jury the presiding judge gave the following directions:

LORD JUSTICE-CLERK (COOPER): "The first thing I would say to you is this—rejecting one of the propositions that Mr Milligan asked me to pronounce—the first direction is this, that, even if you accepted the defence on its face value, there is no material before you in this case which would entitle you to treat the accused as guiltless and to acquit him, and I will tell you why. Mr Milligan said that this is a case to be accounted for as a mere accident, a pure misadventure, what is called in our law casual homicide. Now, casual homicide is a well-recognised category in the criminal law of Scotland, as in other countries; and I am going to read you a short passage from an authoritative work which explains what it is, and when I read it you will see why I decline this direction. The passage is this, 'It is casual homicide where a person kills unintentionally, when lawfully employed, and neither meaning harm to anyone, nor having failed in the due degree of care and circumspection for preventing mischief to his neighbour.' Note well the conditions. The writer proceeds, 'Under this class are comprehended all those cases, unfortunately too numerous, in which death ensues, not from any fault in any quarter, but from some misfortune or accident, and where, consequently, the person who is the innocent cause of another's death is more the subject of pity than punishment.' And then he proceeds to give examples. 'Thus, if a person's gun burst in his hand and kill his neighbour; or if the trigger be caught in going through a hedge, and the contents of the piece lodge in his breast; or a horse run away with its rider, in spite of all his efforts, and, though he had no good reason to have believed he would not manage it, and kill a passenger on the road,' and so on—cases, ladies and gentlemen, of pure misadventure. Now, the responsibility is mine, and if I am wrong I shall be set right elsewhere, but I have to direct you in law that on no view of the evidence in this case would you be entitled to accept Mr Milligan's submission that this is a case of misadventure or pure accident or casual homicide as known to the law, and therefore no question of acquitting the accused altogether on that ground can arise.

So much for that. The next point which I have to direct you upon is this—it is a point the Solicitor-General raised, and the direction he asked was that anyone who wilfully kills another person at the latter's request or command is guilty of murder. That, in my opinion, is sound law, and I do so direct you; but I would rather put it more specifically with reference to this case in this form, that, if life is taken under circumstances which would otherwise infer guilt of murder, the crime does not cease to be murder merely because the victim consented to be murdered, or even urged the assailant to strike the fatal blow. To put the matter in popular terms; if there was nothing in this case except the woman's request, and you held that proved, that would not suffice to take the edge off the guilt which otherwise attaches to the assailant. The attitude of the victim is irrelevant. What matters is the intent of the assailant. I think you will see, ladies and gentlemen, that it must be so. It would be a most perilous doctrine to introduce into the law of Scotland, or of any civilised country, that any person was entitled to kill any other person at that other person's request."

Verdict: Guilty of culpable homicide.

What are the implications of Lord Cooper's directions for such issues as suicide pacts and voluntary euthanasia? Presumably a doctor who complies with a patient's request to terminate his or her life is guilty of murder.

In his evidence to the Royal Commission on Capital Punishment, Lord Cooper stated: "The suicide pact would never be charged as murder in Scotland" (para. 5430). Presumably in such cases the circumstances are not such as would "otherwise infer guilt of murder."

c. Self-defence and provocation

These two pleas are very often found "in tandem," and indeed there exists in many of the cases a confusion between the two pleas which stems at least from the time of Hume. This confusion has probably been resolved by the case of *Crawford* v. *H.M. Advocate*, 1950 J.C. 1 *(post)*, but there are still areas of doubt in relation to such matters as excessive self-defence (see *H.M. Advocate* v. *Byfield and Ors.*, unreported, *post.)*

(i) Self-defence

1. Crawford v. H.M. Advocate
1950 J.C. 67

The appellant was charged with the murder of his father by stabbing him. He tabled a special defence of self-defence, and also led evidence of provocation. The special defence was withdrawn from the jury by the judge, but he left open to them the issue of provocation. The jury returned a verdict of guilty of culpable homicide. On appeal against conviction:

THE LORD JUSTICE-GENERAL (COOPER): "The withdrawal of a special defence is always a strong step, but there are circumstances in which it is the duty of the presiding Judge to take that step. I refer to the Full Bench case of *Kennedy* v. *H.M. Advocate*, 1944 J.C. 171, which was concerned, not with one of the recognised special defences, but with the plea of drunkenness presented for the defence in support of the reduction of murder to culpable homicide. In my view, the pronouncements there made regarding the duty of the presiding Judge are just as applicable to the withdrawal from a jury of a special defence as they are to the withdrawal from a jury of a plea of drunkenness. Adapting these pronouncements to the present case, I am prepared to affirm that it is the duty of the presiding Judge to consider the whole evidence bearing upon self-defence and to make up his own mind whether any of it is relevant to infer self-defence as known to the law of Scotland. If he considers that there is no evidence from which the requisite conclusion could reasonably be drawn, it is the duty of the presiding Judge to direct the jury that it is not open to them to consider the special defence. If, on the other hand, there is some evidence, although it may be slight, or even evidence about which two reasonable views might be held, then he must leave the special defence to the jury subject to such directions as he may think proper.

It is next to be observed that in this case self-defence is pleaded in answer, not to a simple assault, but to an act of homicide, admittedly committed by the appellant, and it is so pleaded with the intent of exculpating the appellant upon the view that in the proved circumstances the homicide was justified. Exculpation is always the sole function of the special defence of self-defence. Provocation and self-defence are often coupled in a special defence, and often I fear confused; but provocation is not a special defence and is always available to an accused person without a special plea. The facts relied upon to support a plea of self-defence usually contain a strong element of provocation, and the lesser plea may succeed where the greater fails; but when in such a case murder is reduced to culpable homicide, or a person accused of assault is found guilty subject to provocation, it is not the special defence of self-defence which is sustained but the plea of provocation. I, of course, respectfully agree with Lord Justice-Clerk Aitchison in *Hillan,* [noted *ante*] that self-defence and provocation 'in many cases overlap,' and with Lord Jamieson in *Kizilev?czius,* [noted *post*], that 'in many respects the considerations which apply to them are the same'; but I desire to emphasise that the pleas are not identical but entirely separate and distinct, and that the special defence of self-defence must either result in complete exculpation or be rejected outright. Indeed, I am bound to say that I have considerable difficulty still in understanding how, in the case of *Hillan,* self-defence came to be regarded as a relevant plea.

Now, in the present case, as I have observed, the verdict has reduced the quality of the appellant's act from murder to culpable homicide on other grounds, and the sole question for our consideration is whether there was any evidence on which a reasonable jury could have held that the appellant was justified in stabbing his father to death, with the result that he ought to be exculpated and freed from all penal consequences.

I take briefly the proved facts at and shortly prior to the fatal assault. At least five deep stab wounds were inflicted on the deceased—three in the chest and two in the back. Two penetrated the heart and one the left lung. Death rapidly ensued. The appellant had encountered his father about 6.30 a.m. at the entrance to the lavatory of the house in which the family lived, and the father, still apparently under the influence of a family quarrel which had occurred the previous night, twice ordered him in strong language and with threatening gesture to go to his room. The appellant returned to his room and his father remained in the lavatory, apparently engaged in washing or shaving or preparing to do these things. The appellant procured in his room the sheath knife with which the assault was committed and then deliberately returned to the lavatory, his object, according to his evidence, being to warn his father that, if he assaulted him, he would use the knife. He found his father looking into the mirror. The father turned round, ordered him to get out, and again turned away; and as he turned away the appellant struck the first blow in the shoulder or back of his victim. His father turned round once again and received the further stabs. The father was wearing a shirt and trousers and had no weapon of any kind. Though addicted to strong language and threatening gestures, the father, according to the appellant's own admission, had only once struck him in his life, the incident referred to being a comparatively trifling one which had occurred several years previously when the appellant was a boy of sixteen.

Now, I need not rehearse the familiar requisites of a plea of self-defence. On the facts briefly summarised I am clearly of opinion that it is impossible on any view of the evidence to find the slightest warrant for inferring that the appellant had any justification that morning for the terrible action which he took in any fear for his own safety, or that he was in danger, or had any grounds for so believing. I assume in the appellant's favour that the culpability of his action fails to be reduced because of his physical and mental state, coupled with the provocation which the jury may have been entitled to infer from his unhappy home life. These elements in my view have received full value in the reduction of the verdict from murder to culpable homicide. I cannot find in the general background, nor in the quarrel of the previous night, nor in anything that happened that morning, any grounds for treating the appellant as having acted in self-defence; and, if I had been in the place of the presiding Judge, I should have acted as he did.

As regards the argument urged upon us that the appellant rightly or wrongly thought that he was in danger of his life and the reliance placed upon the case of *Owens,* 1946 J.C. 119 (noted *post*), I should like to say that, when self-defence is supported by a mistaken belief rested on reasonable grounds, that mistaken belief must have an objective background and must not be purely subjective or of the nature of a hallucination. I am of opinion that the appeal fails; and on the question of sentence I see no reason to disturb the discretion exercised by the presiding Judge."

Appeal dismissed.

NOTE

Crawford provides a clear statement of the distinction between self-defence and provocation. The blurring of this distinction has in the past caused confusion, the lasting effects of which may be found in both branches of the law.

2. **H.M. Advocate v. Kizileviczius**
1938 J.C. 60

The panel was charged with the murder of his father by striking him on the face and head with a flat iron. The panel tabled a special plea that on the occasion in question he was acting in self-defence and under provocation. The fatal blows were struck while the deceased was lying in a corner where he had fallen after being struck by the panel. The deceased had attempted to strike the panel with a poker and the iron, but had been disarmed at the point when the fatal blows were struck. In his charge to the jury the presiding judge made the following remarks:

LORD JAMIESON: "Before I come to deal with the evidence, let me just say a word or two about the law. The accused is charged with murder. In order to constitute the crime of murder there must be either an intention to kill or a wilful act so reckless as to show that the person who committed it was utterly regardless of the consequences of what he was doing. You do not have to consider the first branch in this case. It was admitted by the Advocate-Depute—and quite rightly—that the evidence here did not show any premeditated intention to kill. So it is only the second branch that you need consider. Of course, there is no attempt to deny—it is indeed admitted—that the accused inflicted the fatal injuries, but he says that he was acting justifiably; and the special defence is that he was acting justifiably under provocation and in self-defence. Now, these are really two separate pleas, although in many respects the considerations which apply to them are the same. Let me deal first with the question of self-defence. That is a defence which, according to the view which you may take of the evidence and the extent to which, if any, you think that the defence has been established, may have one of two results; on one view it may result in your coming to a decision, that what the accused did was in the circumstances completely justified, in which case your verdict will be one of acquittal. On another view it may result in your finding that what the accused did was not murder but the lesser crime of culpable homicide. Now, to reach the first result, that is to say the result of complete acquittal, you must be satisfied of two things. The first of these is that the accused was in imminent and immediate danger of his own life; he must have had reasonable grounds for apprehension for his own safety, and his alarm must have been well founded, and there must have been no other means of escaping from the danger to which he was subjected. The second point that you must be satisfied on is that the means which he took to overcome the assaults were necessary—in short, that what he did was necessary to save his own life. You would not be entitled to acquit him if, although he had at one time been in danger, that danger had passed before the fatal blow was given. A very good illustration of that is given by Baron Hume, and you have heard quotations from his work on criminal law being addressed to me. He was dealing with the olden times—the times, as Mr. Watson put it, when people carried lethal weapons—but it illustrates, I think, very appositely the sort of rule that you should apply to this case. He gives the instance of a man attacking another with his sword; the other draws his sword to defend himself, but in the course of the fight the original assailant either breaks his sword or is disarmed. In these circumstances the man who has been attacked is not entitled to run the disarmed man through. [His Lordship examined the evidence and then continued]—As I said to you, you are the masters of the facts, but can you say that, after the deceased had been disarmed of the iron and had staggered into that corner where the fatal blow was evidently administered, the accused was at that time in any danger of his life? Because, unless you can say that at that time he was in danger of his life, then I have to direct you that you would not be entitled to acquit him."

Verdict: Guilty of culpable homicide.

3. Owens v. H.M. Advocate
1946 J.C. 119

Owens was charged with the murder of a man called Falconer by stabbing him. The panel lodged a special defence of self-defence, and gave evidence to the effect that he thought Falconer was attacking him with a knife and stabbed him. The jury found him guilty of murder. On appeal, on the ground, *inter alia,* of misdirection in relation to his mistaken belief about the attack made by the deceased:

LORD JUSTICE-GENERAL (NORMAND): "I will now turn to the passage in the charge where the presiding Judge directs the jury on the essentials of a special defence. The learned Judge said:—'If he was completely wrong in thinking'—that is if the appellant was completely wrong in thinking—'there was an object of a dangerous sort in Falconer's hand when he sprang out of bed and there was no such object, then any attack by Falconer following him into the lobby would not have justified the use of a lethal weapon. As I will tell you in a moment with authority the defence must be against an attack which reasonably is understood to be one likely to cause danger to life before it justifies the use of a lethal weapon.'

The first of these two sentences is, in our opinion, a misdirection on the essential elements of self-defence. In our opinion self-defence is made out when it is established to the satisfaction of the jury that the panel believed that he was in imminent danger and that he held that belief on reasonable grounds. Grounds for such belief may exist though they are founded on a genuine mistake of fact. In the present case, if the jury had come to the conclusion that the appellant genuinely believed that he was gravely threatened by a man armed with a knife but that Falconer actually had no knife in his hand, it would, in our opinion, have been their duty to acquit, and the jury ought to have been so directed. Here in the first of the two sentences they are plainly instructed to the opposite sense, and the effect of that direction is not taken off by the obscure sentence which follows and which holds out the unfulfilled expectation of a more complete treatment of the law on the question in a later passage of the charge. The result is that the jury were misdirected on the essential nature of the defence which they were considering, and if they had been properly directed they might have acquitted the appellant. The verdict therefore cannot stand."

Appeal allowed: conviction quashed.

NOTES

Cf. the remarks of the Lord Justice-General in *Crawford (ante).* *Owens* also discusses the burden of proof in cases where a special defence is raised—a question now authoritatively settled by *Lambie* v. *H.M. Advocate,* 1973 S.L.T. 219 *(ante,* ch. 1). For further discussion of the question of error, see ch. 6, *ante.*

4.   H.M. Advocate v. Doherty
1954 J.C. 1

Doherty was charged with the culpable homicide of a man called
Cairns, by stabbing him in the eye with a bayonet. A special defence
of self-defence was lodged by the panel, to the effect that he killed
Cairns while defending himself from an attack by the latter with a
hammer. In his charge to the jury the presiding judge made the
following comments on the plea of self-defence:

LORD KEITH: "Now we come to the point that has really been put
before you, and that is that Doherty acted in self-defence. Self-
defence has been very fairly and fully put before you both by the
Advocate-depute and by Mr MacDonald for the accused, but it is
my duty to state what the law of the matter is with regard to
self-defence, and, although there may be some repetition in this, it
will, at any rate, refresh your minds, and it is a duty that I cannot
avoid.

If the defence of self-defence is held to be established, that results
in the complete exculpation of the accused, that is to say, the
accused is held to be not guilty of culpable homicide. That is the
result of holding self-defence established, but you have got to
consider very carefully the limits of this doctrine of self-defence. It
is my duty in the first place to consider whether there is evidence at
all on which you might hold that self-defence could be established. I
have had considerable difficulty in this case in deciding whether this
was a matter that I should leave to you, but, in the whole circumstances of the case, I think there is evidence on which you will have
to consider this question of self-defence and to decide whether you
think the defence has been established, subject to such directions as
I am now about to give you upon the law of the matter.

Let me remind you first of all of the limits of self-defence in a case
of this kind. First of all, there must be imminent danger to the life or
limb of the accused, to the person putting forward this defence;
there must be imminent danger to his life and limb; and, secondly,
the retaliation that he uses in the face of this danger must be
necessary for his own safety. Those are two fundamental things you
will keep in mind, that there is imminent danger to life and limb and
that the retaliation used is necessary for the safety of the man
threatened. You do not need an exact proportion of injury and
retaliation; it is not a matter that you weights in too fine scales, as
had been said. Some allowance must be made for the excitement or
the state of fear or the heat of blood at the moment of the man who
is attacked, but there are limits or tests that are perfectly well
recognised and which will help you to understand this doctrine by
way of illustration. For instance, if a man was struck a blow by

another man with the fist, that could not justify retaliation by the use of a knife, because there is no real proportion at all between a blow with a fist and retaliation by a knife, and, therefore, you have got to consider this question of proportion between the attack made and the retaliation offered. Again, if the person assaulted has means of escape or retreat, he is bound to use them. If he has these means, then it is not necessary in self-defence to stand up against the other man and in retaliation use a lethal weapon against him. He could defend himself by escape, which is really just another way of ridding yourself of the danger. He could escape or retreat, and then no necessity arises to retaliate by the use of a lethal weapon or in any other way, and, accordingly, that is another of the things in this case that you have got to consider, and to consider very carefully.

Just let me apply the law, as I have endeavoured to indicate it, to the circumstances of this case. Consider the application of those rules here. First of all, it is undoubtedly favourable to the accused that he was attacked or threatened by a hammer, because I do not think you will have any doubt at all that a hammer was a very dangerous thing to be threatened or attacked with, and, therefore, that is a feature favourable to the accused. If the accused had been cornered and had had a bayonet in his hand, it might well have justified a thrust with the bayonet in his self-protection to defend his own life, or to defend himself from very serious injury from the hammer, that is, if the accused were cornered and there was no other method open to him of saving his life or limb. But in this case the circumstances are not all that favourable. First of all, you know he was handed this bayonet by M'Nulty and told to defend himself, and that suggests something—it is for you to consider, it is not for me, but I am only putting this forward as a matter you have got to keep in view—that it suggests something of the nature of a duel, and that is not permissible; you cannot start up a duel with another man and then say, 'But I killed him or injured him in self-defence.' He had friends round about him whom you may think—and it is for you to consider—whom you may think might have helped him or dissuaded Cairns or disarmed Cairns, and again you may think he had a means of retreat. He had an open door to this stair behind him, the stairs down to the yard, and certainly there does not seem to have been any attempt to make an escape by the door, or to get behind his companions Moffat and McNulty, or anything of that sort. Those are circumstances in this case to which you will have to apply your minds, and you will have to decide whether in the light of all those circumstances this was a proper case of self-defence, in which the accused really had no other alternative in his own safety but to thrust at Cairns with the bayonet in the way which has been spoken to in evidence, if you think it is established in evidence that some such thrust was made. It is quite true that you may think that the accused was not altogether to blame, that he was provoked and that he used this bayonet in the heat of the moment. That is perfectly true, and I recognise that, but it is not provocation that has been put forward here; it is self-defence. Provocation is a very different matter, and it really is the provocation that has made this a case of culpable homicide and not of murder; the provocation in that sense has been taken into account, and, of course, provocation would be taken into account in the matter of sentence if you thought that self-defence did not apply here and that the accused is guilty of culpable homicide. In that case, of course, the whole circumstances in which this assault was made by the accused, in which those injuries were caused, the whole question of provocation, heat of blood, and that sort of thing, are proper matters for others to take into account, but you are not really here to consider the question of whether the accused was provoked. I recognise that it may well be said that he was provoked, but the question is, Do you think that he was acting in self-defence?"

Verdict: Guilty.

NOTES

On the question of taking evasive action or using avenues of escape, compare the Scottish approach as outlined above, with that of the Court of Appeal in England in the case of *McInnes* [1971] 3 All E.R. 186. The appellant stabbed another youth in the course of a fight. At his trial for murder the judge directed the jury *inter alia*, that "to show that homicide arising from a fight was committed in self-defence it must be shown that the party killing had retreated as far as he could, or as far as the fierceness of the assault would permit him." On appeal the Court of Appeal took the view that "the direction was expressed in too inflexible terms and might, in certain circumstances, be regarded as significantly misleading." The court preferred the views of the High Court of Australia in *R.* v. *Howe* (1958) 100 C.L.R. 448, that a failure to retreat is only an element in the considerations on which the reasonableness of an accused's conduct is to be judged, or, as Smith and Hogan put it (*Criminal Law* (2nd ed.), p. 231) "simply a factor to be taken into account in deciding whether it was necessary to use force, and whether the force was reasonable."

5.   **McCluskey v. H.M. Advocate**
1959 J.C. 39

The panel was charged with the murder of a man called Ormiston. He stated a special defence of self-defence to the effect that he killed the deceased while resisting an attempt by the latter to commit sodomy upon him. At the trial, Lord Strachan gave the following directions *inter alia* on the question of self-defence:

"Homicide is justified by self-defence only if the homicidal acts are done to save the man's own life. It does not bring the accused within the plea of self-defence if he kills to avoid some great indignity, some attack upon his virtue, or even some bodily harm."

The jury returned a verdict of guilty of culpable homicide, and the panel appealed on the ground, *inter alia,* of misdirection.

LORD JUSTICE-GENERAL (CLYDE): "The first question for this Court arises in regard to the ambit in the law of Scotland of a plea of self-defence. It is contended for the accused that the learned Judge at the trial misdirected the jury in directing them as a matter of law that homicide in this case could only be justified by self-defence if the homicidal act was done by McCluskey to save his own life.

It is, of course, well settled that while a defence of provocation may reduce the crime of murder to culpable homicide, a plea of self-defence, if made out, is a complete answer to a charge of murder and would lead to a verdict of not guilty. Our law has always held that if there are reasonable grounds for a person apprehending that his life is in danger he is entitled to protect himself, provided that the steps which he takes are not in the circumstances cruelly excessive. In such circumstances he will not be guilty of murder. In the present case it is argued that although McCluskey had no grounds for thinking that his life was in any way in danger, a forcible attempt was made by Ormiston to commit sodomy with him, and this was such as to justify McCluskey in defending himself to the extent of taking Ormiston's life. The basis for this extension of the doctrine of self-defence, is, as I follow it, that an attack on the appellant's virtue is as much a justification for taking another man's life as an attack upon his life would have been. No authority was quoted for this extension of the plea of self-defence and I can see no logical nor indeed any other justification for it. Murder is still one of the most serious crimes in this country, for no man has a right at his own hand deliberately to take the life of another. Indeed it is because of this principle of the sanctity of human life that the plea of self-defence arises. Just because life is so precious to all of us, so our law recognises that an accused man may be found not guilty, even of the serious crime of murder, if his own life has been endangered by an assailant, or if he has reasonable grounds for apprehending such danger, and if the steps which he takes to protect his life are not excessive, although they have led to fatal consequences. But I can see no justification at all for extending this defence to a case where there is no apprehension of danger to the accused's life, and indeed, very little evidence of any real physical injury done to the accused himself, but merely a threat, pushed no doubt quite far, but none the less still only a threat, of an attack on the appellant's virtue. Dishonour, it is suggested, may be worse than death. But there are many ways of avoiding dishonour without having to resort to the taking of a human life, and, so far as I am concerned, I do not see how the taking of a human life can ever be justified by the mere fact that there have been threats of dishonour or indignities or even of some bodily harm, which falls short of creating reasonable apprehension of danger to life. Indeed this seems to be recognised in the authorities quoted to us. In Alison's Criminal Law, vol. i, p. 132, the learned author says:—'A private individual will be justified in killing in defence of his life against imminent danger, of the lives of others connected with him from similar peril, or a woman or her friends in resisting an attempt at rape.' It seems to me impossible to assimilate the present case to a woman threatened with rape. For rape involves complete absence of consent on the part of the woman. This is not the situation in sodomy. Hume on Crime, vol. i, p. 223, says:—'The general notion of homicide in self-defence is, that it is committed from necessity; in the just apprehension, on the part of the manslayer, that he cannot otherwise save his own life, and without alloy of any other excusable motive.' The decisions of the Court do not advance the matter since the point has not really arisen in any of them. The case of *Hillan* v. *H.M. Advocate*, [noted *ante*] is of no assistance on the present issue since the observations in that case relate to provocation and not self-defence. This is made clear in the subsequent case of *Crawford* v. *H.M. Advocate*, [noted *ante*] Lord Keith at p. 71.

In my view, therefore, where an attack by an accused person on another man has taken place and where the object of the attack has been to ward off an assault upon him it is essential that the attack should be made to save the accused's life before the plea of self-defence can succeed. For myself I would be slow indeed to suggest that people in this country are justified in taking human life merely because their honour is assailed by someone else. It would be a retrograde step if we were to widen the scope of self-defence so as to enable an accused person to escape altogether in such circumstances. In my view, therefore, the direction given by the learned Judge to which exception is taken was a sound direction, and this ground of appeal is without substance."

Appeal refused.

NOTES

It is difficult to agree with the Lord Justice-General's distinction between rape and sodomy. The fact that the latter crime may be committed with the consent of both parties, while the former necessarily implies absence of consent on the woman's part is an irrelevant consideration in a case involving forcible sodomy.

6.   **H.M. Advocate v. Byfield and Ors.**
Glasgow High Court, January 1976, *unreported*

(For the facts of this case, see *ante*, ch. 6). In his charge to the jury the presiding judge made the following remarks on the question of excessive self-defence:

LORD THOMSON: "Now the last general matter of law that I have to say something to you about, ladies and gentlemen, deals with this question of culpable homicide. . . . Self-defence in the way I have described it to you, ladies and gentlemen, if you hold it established on the evidence, is a complete answer to the charge of murder but you may take . . . a certain view of the evidence which would result in your not sustaining he has established self-defence but taking the view that the circumstances here were such as to entitle the accused to a verdict of guilty against him on the reduced charge of culpable homicide. Let me explain how this can happen. As I have said to you, to constitute murder you have either got to have intent to kill deliberately or you have got to be satisfied that the accused showed such wicked recklessness, as I put to you, totally regardless of the consequences, whether the victim lived or died. If you get a situation where you think that the Crown has failed to prove . . . such a high degree of wicked recklessness but, nonetheless has established to your satisfaction that the accused acted in an unjustifiable way, that would be enough to reduce the charge from one of murder to one of culpable homicide. Moreover, ladies and gentlemen, and this is perhaps closer to the facts of this case, if you took the view that the defence of self-defence was not established either because, . . . the force used in retaliation was excessive or because although the man was petrified, as he says, nonetheless he really ought to have been able to see there was a way of escape and should have taken it: in both those cases the self-defence would fail but in both those cases it would be open to you to say "Well, he shouldn't have done what he did but it is not murder" and in circumstances of that kind the verdict would be culpable homicide. It is sometimes said that this arises from an application of the principle of provocation and you can apply that to this case too. It comes, in a way, to the same thing. If you take the view, upon the whole evidence, that there was provocation by the man Ewart—provocation in the sense of threat of an immediate attack in the way in which it was done—if you take that view and you take the view that the accused's reaction was not such as to constitute self-defence you could nonetheless take the view that although he shouldn't have retaliated at all so as to exculpate himself, nonetheless he was provoked in such a way as to make it understandable why he did react in the way he did and if he simply used too much force or didn't try to escape when he should have done, or the like, then you could bring in a verdict of culpable homicide."

Guilty of murder.

NOTES

Lord Thomson's directions appear to conflict with what was said by the Lord Justice-General in *Crawford (ante)* concerning the effect of a plea of self-defence. They do, however, accord with the view expressed by the High Court of Australia in *R.* v. *Howe* (1958) 100 C.L.R. 448. In *Palmer* v. *R.* [1971] A.C. 814 the Privy Council were of the opinion that excessive self-defence did not have the effect of reducing murder to manslaughter. Similar views were expressed by the Court of Appeal in *McInnes (ante)*.

(ii) Provocation

1. H.M. Advocate v. Kilzileviczius
1938 J.C. 60

(The facts of this case are outlined above.)

LORD JAMIESON: (His Lordship directed the jury that if they found that the panel had used excessive self-defence they might return a verdict of guilty of culpable homicide (as to which see *Crawford* and *Byfield, ante*) and continued): "Very much the same thing applies to the plea of provocation which has been put forward, but I must direct you that in order to given effect to that plea there must be provocation at the time. It is no provocation in the eyes of the law that the deceased had brutally treated the accused's mother, even earlier in that day if there had been any brutal treatment then; or that at some previous time, years before or even days before, he had ill-treated the accused himself. Nor is it provocation that at the time in question he had called him a bastard or used other opprobrious names. You can find that there was provocation only if you take the view that the accused was in the position of being attacked. I think I can best explain what provocation means by giving you a quotation out of one of our text-books [Macdonald's *Criminal Law* (4th ed.), p. 135]. It says: 'The defence of provocation is of this sort:—"Being agitated and excited, and alarmed by violence, I lost control over myself, and took life, when my presence of mind had left me, and without thought of what I was doing." ' Now, you might take the view that the accused here was agitated and excited, that he was alarmed when he saw his father coming at him again knowing the violent man his father was, that he was acting under an emotional strain knowing all that had gone before, what had happened for years and had happened more or less continuously, and that in these circumstances he had really lost his presence of mind. In that case you would be justified in returning a verdict of culpable homicide. If you take the view that the blows that were rained on the deceased man's head by the accused after his father had already been injured, after the flat iron had been taken from him—if you take the view that these blows were administered with complete callousness and with an utter and reckless disregard of the consequences, and in a spirit of hatred—I say, if you take that view, I should be failing in my duty if I did not direct you that you would be failing in yours if you did not return a verdict of murder. On the other hand, if, viewing the evidence broadly and not weighing it in too fine scales, and making allowance for human nature, you reach the conclusion that the accused acted on the spur and in the heat of the moment—but only if you reach that conclusion—you would be entitled to make your verdict one of culpable homicide."

NOTES

The relationship of provocation to self-defence is very marked in Lord Jamieson's directions, particularly in relation to the exclusion of verbal provocation and the emphasis on violence by the deceased.

2. **Berry v. H.M. Advocate**
High Court, October 1976, unreported

Berry was convicted of the murder of a woman. The panel gave evidence that the deceased had taunted him when he had tried unsuccessfully to have intercourse with her, and that he had retaliated by striking her on the head with a brick. In his charge to the jury the presiding judge gave the following directions on provocation:

LORD KEITH: "Well, Ladies and Gentlemen, you have to consider first of all whether you accept that Mrs. Blyth did use these taunts under these circumstances, and if you accept that, then you have to consider, I think, principally whether that constituted sufficient provocation for what the accused says he did, which was to strike the victim upon the head with a brick to the extent and to the effect that you have heard described in evidence. . . .

Ladies and Gentlemen, were these taunts, assuming you believe they were uttered, in your view, sufficient provocation for what the evidence suggests that the accused did. It is the law, Ladies and Gentlemen, that in any case of provocation sufficient to reduce murder to culpable homicide, there must be some degree . . . of correspondence between the provocation and the reaction or retaliation of the accused. It is the law, Ladies and Gentlemen, that the retaliation must not be grossly excessive. It must be the degree of retaliation which you might expect an ordinary average sort of person, carried away by agitation and excitement, to display in the face of whatever the provocation was. You must be able to find, Ladies and Gentlemen, that the person who is provoked completely lost his head, was carried away by passion, so that he utterly lost all capacity for self-control, and that this resulted from what you regard as sufficient provocation.

So, if you take the view, Ladies and Gentlemen, that an ordinary, average sort of a person, in the face of the taunts that Mrs. Blyth uttered would have reacted as the accused did, then you would come to the conclusion that there was sufficient provocation. But if, on the other hand, you found that the ordinary average sort of person in the face of these taunts would not have reacted in that way, then you would find that there was not sufficient provocation."

The jury returned a verdict of guilty of murder, and the panel presented an application for leave to appeal against conviction. The opinion of the court was delivered by Lord Emslie:

THE COURT: "The application is presented upon the basis that there was a misdirection in the judge's charge to the jury and the misdirection is said to arise in those passages in the charge in which the judge is dealing with the question of provocation. Now, the provocation alleged here was that in course of the sexual encounter the lady taunted the applicant with his inadequate prowess, compared him unfavourably to his uncle in that regard and made some critical observations about whether or not he might be the father of his children. This the judge left to the jury on the basis that the jury would be entitled to decide whether the taunts in all the circumstances could amount to sufficient provocation which in law would justify the jury in reducing the quality of the crime charged from murder to culpable homicide. Whether the judge was right to leave that matter to the jury is a matter on which we entertain grave doubt, but we take the case on the footing on which it was presented to us and in the first instance we examine the criticisms of the charge which left it to the jury to decide whether certain verbal taunts could in law amount to provocation such as would justify reducing the quality of the acts done and their consequences from murder to culpable homicide.

For the applicant Mr. Pollock has drawn our attention to a number of passages in the charge. In the first place it was said that the judge misdirected himself and the jury when he spoke of a correspondence, or of the need for correspondence, between the alleged provocation and the acts done. In the second place it was said that there is something illogical in that passage in the charge where the judge mentions that retaliation must not be grossly excessive and yet in the next breath speaks of the individual allegedly provoked having completely and utterly lost his head and control. Finally, it was suggested that the judge misdirected the jury when he invited them to consider not what the ordinary man might do in the face of such alleged provocation, but what the ordinary man would do.

We have, however, in examining Mr. Pollock's criticisms, to read the charge as a whole, and having read it as a whole, we are left in no doubt that the judge in all these passages, was endeavouring to do no more than to assist the jury to decide the vital question, namely, whether the taunts in the circumstances in which they were uttered could properly be regarded by them as provocation of a kind and degree sufficient to justify them in reducing what otherwise would have been murder to culpable homicide. So understood, the particular passages fall into place, and we have come to be of opinion that the attack upon the charge fails and that the application will have to be refused."

Application refused.

NOTES

Lord Keith's directions to the jury raise two important issues:— (a) whether mere verbal abuse can in law constitute provocation or whether, leaving aside the special case of adultery and confessions of adultery, provocation is limited to violence offered to the accused; and (b) the question whether it is necessary for a successful plea of provocation that not only was the accused provoked, but also that the reasonable man would have reacted as did the accused. Unfortunately, neither of these questions is dealt with adequately by the appeal court.

The latter question has been the subject of differing views in Scotland (see, e.g., the views of Lord Cooper in his evidence to the Royal Commission on Capital Punishment, para. 5366, and those of Gordon, paras. 25-37 et seq.). The reasonable man has caused considerable difficulties in English law (see, e.g., the notorious case of Bedder v. D.P.P. (1954) 38 Cr.App. Rep. 133) although the recent decision of the House of Lords in D.P.P. v. Camplin [1978] 2 All E.R. 168 has gone some way to removing these problems.

3.   **H.M. Advocate v. Hill**
1941 J.C. 59

The panel was charged with the murder of his wife and her lover. He shot them both immediately after they had confessed to him that they had committed adultery. In his charge to the jury the presiding judge gave the following directions on the question of provocation:

LORD PATRICK: "Now, as to the law. It is quite plain that a person who inflicts a deadly wound upon another so that the other dies is in the normal case guilty of murder, and, if there were no other facts than these in this case, your duty would be the plain one of returning a verdict of guilty of murder. But the law admits certain circumstances, if they are proved to the satisfaction of the jury, as habile to reduce the facts of a case from the crime of murder to the still serious, but much less serious, crime of culpable homicide. One of the familiar elements which, if proved, will reduce a crime from that of murder to that of culpable homicide is where a man is struck a violent blow and in the heat of the moment then and there strikes back and the other man dies. That element a jury may consider habile to reduce a crime which would otherwise be murder to that of culpable homicide. Now, the law both in Scotland and in England—though probably you need not concern youselves with the law of England—has for several centuries recognised that, if a man catches his wife and her paramour in the act of adultery and in the heat of passionate indignation then and there kills them, his crime is a very serious one, but it is not murder, it is culpable homicide. The same is the law where the man does not actually catch his wife and the paramour in the act of adultery, but where he discovers that they have committed adultery; the discovery is exactly the same thing as if he caught them in the act. If, then, a wife and her paramour were to confess to the husband—who did not previously know that they had committed adultery—that they had committed adultery, and if he then and there killed them in the heat of passionate indignation, the crime would not be murder, it would be the serious crime of culpable homicide. The exception to that law is this: in the case of a man who is struck a violent blow, he must not wait a while and ponder over it and then go and kill his assailant, or, if he does, he is guilty of murder; similarly a man must not discover that his wife has committed adultery and go away and ponder over the matter, while the heat of his blood cools, and then come back and revenge himself by killing his wife; if he does, that is murder. So the matter for you comes down to small compass, though grave in its consequences. If you were to find upon the facts that the prisoner had long known that his wife and Headland had committed adultery, and that after an interval of reflection he came north to Scotland on the 18th of

January to revenge himself, then it would be your duty to return a verdict of murder: but if your view of the facts should be that he came north on the 18th suspecting, it may be, that there was something wrong, suspecting that his wife perhaps had committed adultery, but not sure, and if you thought that, when he got to Scotland and interviewed the two of them, they then confessed that they had been guilty of adultery so that for the first time he knew it, and if you thought that, when he did make that discovery, he then and there killed them in the heat of sudden and overwhelming indignation, it is open to you to return a verdict of guilty of culpable homicide, not of murder. In making up your minds as to what the facts really mean, observe this, that, if you have any reasonable doubt as to whether the accused killed from revenge or killed from sudden indignation and in the heat of the moment, having newly just discovered that his wife had committed adultery, if you have any reasonable doubt, then the accused is entitled to the benefit of that doubt, and your verdict would properly be one of guilty of culpable homicide. . . . So the question is simply this: Are you satisfied that the prisoner killed those two people not in the heat of the moment but after an interval when his blood had cooled—killed them from motives of revenge? Or are you satisfied that he learned for the first time between 12 and 1 on Saturday that those two had been unfaithful to him and that they were still lying to him about their infidelity, and that he then and there in the heat of the moment shot them and killed them. If you think the latter is the truth of the matter, then it is open to you to return a verdict of culpable homicide; if you have any reasonable doubt about the matter, your verdict should be one of culpable homicide; only if you are satisfied that it has been proved that he deliberately shot these two while he was cool and calm, and shot them from motives of revenge, should you return a verdict of guilty of murder."

Verdict: Guilty of culpable homicide.

NOTES

Cf. the cases of H.M. Advocate v. Callander (ante, ch. 10), McDermott v. H.M. Advocate (post).

4. McDermott v. H.M. Advocate
1974 S.L.T. 206

OPINION OF THE COURT: "In this case the applicant was indicted on two charges (1) that he assaulted Alexander Donachie Munro by kicking, punching and stabbing him, inflicting on him injuries from which he died and thus did murder Munro, and (2) that he assaulted

Catherine Fox Bradley. Upon the second charge the jury returned a verdict of not proven, and upon the first charge, a verdict of guilty of culpable homicide.

So far as the first charge is concerned it was not and is not in dispute that a knife caused the injury from which Munro died, and that the knife wound was inflicted by the applicant in the course of a fight with Munro, who was unarmed. No question of accident or of self-defence was in issue at the trial and the case may be approached as one in which the applicant is proved to have killed Munro in the course of an assault. The defence, however, put the question of provocation sharply in issue and counsel for the applicant moved the trial judge to give two directions to the jury.

The first direction sought was that if the jury were satisfied on the facts and on the evidence that, at the critical time when the assault took place, there was complete loss, even if momentary, of self-control by the applicant due to his discovery of an illicit association between the girl Bradley, who was living with him as his wife, and Munro, and that Munro approached the girl with affectionate gestures, which were reciprocated, at the very moment prior to the assault, these circumstances might entitle the jury to reduce the quality of the crime from murder to culpable homicide. The trial judge gave this direction, no doubt upon the view that the circumstances relied on might be thought to be analogous to those disclosed in cases such as *Gilmour* v. *H.M. Advocate*, 1938 J.C. 1, 1938 S.L.T. 72, where a husband kills in a sudden transport of passion when he discovers his wife in adultery. It was in light of this direction that the verdict of guilty of culpable homicide is to be understood.

The second direction sought, which the trial judge declined to give, was that the very same circumstances, taken along with the other evidence in the case, would entitle the jury to return a verdict of guilty of assault only. The application now before us is for leave to appeal against conviction, and the application rests upon the single proposition that in refusing to give this second direction the trial judge was wrong.

In his excellent speech on behalf of the applicant, counsel relied heavily upon the direction given by Lord Justice-Clerk Aitchison in *Gilmour* (supra), the similar direction given by Lord Strachan in the later case of *McCluskey* v. *H.M. Advocate*, 1959 J.C. 39, 1959 S.L.T. 215, and the provision in s. 20 of the Criminal Procedure (Scotland) Act 1887 to the effect that it shall be competent for a jury to convict of any part of an indictment which by itself constitutes, if the facts are proved, a crime by the law of Scotland. He frankly conceded, however, that the directions given in *Gilmour* and *McCluskey* (supra) had never been considered by the appeal court,

that the direction given in *Gilmour* was strongly criticised by Lord
Moncrieff in *Delaney* v. *H.M. Advocate,* 1945 J.C. 138, 1946 S.L.T.
25, who declined to follow it, was regarded with doubt by Lord
Robertson in *Sheppard* v. *H.M. Advocate,* 1941 J.C. 67, 1941
S.L.T. 404 and finds no place in Lord Patrick's charge to the jury in
the case of *Hill* v. *H.M. Advocate,* 1941 J.C. 59, 1941 S.L.T. 401.

The direction given in *Gilmour* was in these terms: 'Under this
indictment it is open to you to convict the accused of part of the
indictment only. That is a matter which is laid down by statute.
When the Crown charges a person on indictment, the jury are never
bound to find the whole indictment proved. The jury may find, if
they choose, only part of the indictment proved, and it is right that I
should tell you that, under this indictment, it is open to you to find
the accused guilty of assault only under charge two. Now, you may
think a verdict of that kind would be a very illogical verdict; and in
one sense it would be an illogical verdict, because, if the accused
struck the blow and death resulted, then there is no doubt that, on a
strict view of the law, it would be difficult to acquit him of responsibility for the death. But then, as I have already told you, the law is
not altogether blind, and there may be in this case circumstances
sufficient to justify you in saying that the accused was wrong in
taking the law into his own hands, but that, if he acted in the first
transport of his passion without appreciating to the full extent what
he was doing, you are not going to hold him criminally responsible
for the death that occurred. The deadly blow was struck under the
most terrible provocation. The accused may have erred in taking
the law into his own hands, but you may say: 'We feel justified, if we
cannot acquit the accused altogether, in saying he shall be found
guilty as for assault only.' That is to say, he would not be found
guilty of murder, and he would not be guilty of culpable homicide
but you would find him guilty of assault only, and that, I direct you
in law, is a competent verdict on this indictment.'

It is to be noted that so far as the report discloses this direction
was not sought by counsel for the defence in terms, and that no
opportunity was afforded to the advocate-depute to present any
argument against the giving of such a direction.

In *McCluskey* the trial judge was Lord Strachan who had been the
advocate-depute in *Gilmour*. It may be taken, therefore, that,
although the case of *Gilmour* does not appear to have been cited to
him, Lord Strachan's direction was given out of respect for the
course followed by Lord Justice-Clerk Aitchison. It was in these
terms: 'You must also consider another matter; whether in this case
you would find the accused guilty only of assault. That point has
been put to me by Mr Maxwell, and I have to direct you that it would
be competent for you under this indictment, should you think of

going so far, to find the accused guilty only of assault. You see, the charge which I read to you begins with the words that the accused did, on the date and at the place in question, assault Andrew Ormiston, and it would be competent for you, if you saw sufficient grounds for doing so, to find him guilty only of that part of the charge against him. But that, of course, could be done only if you saw adequate reason for disregarding the fact that the accused killed Ormiston, if you are satisfied that the killing is proved against him. I put this matter before you. I merely say that I think you should give very careful consideration to the position before you went so far as that . . . ' (1959 J.C., at p. 40).

It will be observed that in this direction Lord Strachan offered no explanation to the jury of what he meant by saying, 'if you saw sufficient grounds for doing so' and 'if you saw adequate reason for disregarding the fact that the accused killed Ormiston' and in the result, if counsel for the applicant's argument is to succeed, it must rest entirely for its soundness upon the direction in *Gilmour*. To that direction we accordingly now return.

In our opinion the direction given in *Gilmour* cannot be supported either in law or logic. Homicide is the killing of another, and where death is brought about by an unlawful act, including an assault upon the victim, it is always homicide and it is always culpable. This was the approach of the institutional writers and, apart from the direction in *Gilmour* (and because of *Gilmour* in *McCluskey*), has been the approach followed invariably ever since in the law of Scotland. If, as Lord Moncrieff said in *Delaney* (supra), a man takes life in circumstances which infer criminal responsibility it is in all cases for the death that he is responsible. In particular, if anyone in the exercise of a criminal act takes life, although the initial act may only be an act of assault, he is liable, if at all, for the taking of the life by the act of assault, and is thus guilty of murder or of the lesser crime of culpable homicide. So far as the lesser crime is concerned, culpability can, of course, vary widely in degree, and the law, which in the words of Lord Justice-Clerk Aitchison 'is not altogether blind', enables the degree of culpability and all proper compassion in each case to be reflected in sentence. What it does not do is to permit any jury to shut their eyes to the crime itself, and to hold the killer criminally responsible merely for the acts which led to death. It is no doubt the case that murder and culpable homicide are frequently charged upon an indictment introduced by the allegation of assault. It is equally true that a jury is entitled to convict of any part of an indictment which by itself constitutes, if the facts establish it, a crime by the law of Scotland (s. 20 of the Criminal Procedure (Scotland) Act 1887). But this latter provision, while on an indictment for murder or culpable homicide it would undoubtedly permit of a verdict of guilty of assault only when the jury were not satisfied that death had been caused by the assault libelled, cannot be invoked as a licence to convict of assault only where it is not in doubt that a crime of homicide has been committed.

In the result we have no hesitation in holding that the trial judge was perfectly correct in refusing to give the second direction sought by the applicant's counsel. The application is accordingly refused."

Application refused.

NOTES

The court appears to have accepted that this case is analogous to the "adultery" cases, without question. This may be a liberal approach to the plea of provocation, but how far does it go? Suppose X found his fiancée "necking" with another man at a party. Would that be sufficient provocation in law?

The doctrine that any assault which results in death must be at least culpable homicide is open to question, especially when coupled with the doctrine that the accused "takes his victim as he finds him"*(ante,* ch.3). The effect would seem to be that the accused must be convicted of culpable homicide if death results, even from a minor or technical assault, and even if death was a completely unforeseeable result of that assault. This of course goes much further than was necessary for the decision of *McDermott's* appeal.

5. H.M. Advocate v. Greig
High Court, May 1979, *unreported*

The panel was charged with the murder of her husband by stabbing him. The deceased was a heavy drinker, and there was a history of violence against the accused at his hands when he had been drinking. The panel had on occasions left the matrimonial home, and had only returned to the home about a week before the killing. On the evening in question the deceased had been drinking, but he had not offered any violence toward the accused, although he was "nagging" at her, and she gave evidence to the effect that she was afraid that he would become violent. When the fatal blow was struck the deceased was sitting in a chair, probably dozing. A special defence of self-defence was tabled. In his charge to the jury the presiding judge gave the following direction on provocation, having first withdrawn the defence of self-defence from the jury on the ground that there was not sufficient evidence to amount in law to self-defence.

LORD DUNPARK: "So, that brings me to the question of provocation. The effect of provocation, if established in a murder trial, is to reduce the killing from murder to one of culpable homicide and that is, as I already explained, an unlawful killing but without the murderous intent. In other words, provocation does not excuse the killing but it affords a reason for it. Now, in the normal case of murder, provocation only operates when the accused is either attacked or is so alarmed by the violent conduct of the other person as to be reasonably apprehensive of his or her immediate safety— and I emphasise 'immediate.'

In other words provocation only takes effect when the first element of self-defence is satisfied, and that is, the imminent danger of attack but one or other or both of the other two elements are not satisfied. That is to say, if the jury is satisfied that the accused is in imminent danger but could have escaped without killing, but instead, attacked and killed the deceased, then self-defence would not apply. The third element is if it was not necessary in his or her defence for the accused to use either the degree of violence or the dangerous weapon which caused the death, then again, self-defence does not apply. I have explained why it does not apply in this case.

The essence of provocation is that the conduct of the deceased which immediately preceded—and I emphasise 'immediately preceded' the killing was so violent or threatening as to deprive the accused momentarily of his self-control—so that in this case she lashed out without stopping to think what she was doing. If this is what happened, it would be quite wrong to find the accused either intended to kill or was so wickedly—and I emphasise the word 'wickedly'—reckless that she should be found guilty of murder— because provocation, in that sense, provoked the act and deprives it of the element of that murderous intent which is of the essence of murder. . . .

Now, there is evidence before you that the deceased was a drunkard, if you like, not an alcoholic but a drunkard in the general sense, that he was a bully, that he assaulted his wife from time to time and that he made her life a misery. But, hundreds, indeed thousands of wives in this country, unfortunately, suffer this fate. The remedy of divorce or judicial separation or factual separation is available to end this torment. But, if, one day the worm turns, if I may use that phrase, not under the immediate threat of violence but by taking a solemn decision to end her purgatory by killing her husband, and by doing that very thing, is she not to be found guilty of murder?

If you are satisfied beyond reasonable doubt that this is what this woman did then you would find her guilty of murder. If, on the other hand you can find some evidence, which I frankly cannot, that the accused was provoked in the sense in which I have defined it, you could return a verdict of guilty of culpable homicide; but only if you can find evidence which either satisfies you that she was so provoked or leaves you with a reasonable doubt as to whether she was so provoked, because, I repeat what I have said before, that you can only convict of murder if you are satisfied beyond reasonable doubt that the accused killed her husband with that intent which is of the essence of murder.

Now, lastly, Mr. Fraser referred this morning to diminished responsibility and suggested that you could return a verdict of culpable homicide on a finding of diminished responsibility. On this matter, I direct you that there is no evidence which you have heard upon which you could reduce the crime from murder to culpable homicide on diminished responsibility. The only basis upon which you could do that would be if you can find provocation in the sense which I have defined it from the evidence in this case."

Verdict: Guilty of culpable homicide.

NOTES

The accused was sentenced to six years' imprisonment (upheld on appeal: High Court, December 1979). While one may respectfully agree with Lord Dunpark's directions on the law of provocation, the case perhaps highlights the unduly restrictive nature of the law with regard to the question of "cumulative" provocation.

On the question of diminished responsibility, *cf.* the case of *H.M. Advocate* v. *Robert Smith* (1893) 1 Adam 34. The panel was charged with the murder of a man who, along with certain others, had subjected the accused to a course of tormenting, taunting and abuse. Lord McLaren directed the jury (by analogy with the case of *Dingwall* (1867) 5 Irv. 466) that "if it were the law that a state of mental disturbance brought on by a man's own fault, by his own intemperance, going the length of producing a physiological disturbance of the brain, might to that extent excuse him, it seems to me that the same result must follow when the disturbance of the mental equipoise was not due to a man's own fault, but to his being subjected to a system of incessant persecution, " and left it to the jury to decide "whether the man's mind was so disturbed by a long system of persecution, culminating in the events of that morning, that, while he was not insane, you might nevertheless reduce the crime from that of murder to culpable homicide." The jury returned a verdict of guilty of culpable homicide.

d. Involuntary culpable homicide

The law on involuntary culpable homicide is not easy to state with any confidence, largely because, as was pointed out, this category of homicide comprises all forms of unlawful homicide not included in any of the other categories. The standard approach, however, is to divide this category into "lawful act homicide" and "unlawful act homicide."

(i) Lawful act homicide

Paton v. H.M. Advocate
1935 J.C. 19

Paton was charged, *inter alia*, with the culpable homicide of a pedestrian by driving his car in a "reckless and culpable manner" and at an excessive speed, so that he mounted a grass verge, collided with two pedestrians, injuring one and killing the other. The jury found the appellant guilty, and he was sentenced to six months' imprisonment. On appeal:

LORD JUSTICE-CLERK (AITCHISON): "There is evidence in the case that the appellant was driving his car at a fairly high speed, and there is also evidence in the case that there was, perhaps, a want of care. The difficulty that the case presents is whether there was evidence that the appellant was guilty of criminal negligence in the sense in which we use that expression. At one time the rule of law was that any blame was sufficient, where death resulted, to justify a verdict of guilty of culpable homicide. Unfortunately, this law has to some extent been modified by decisions of the Court, and it is now necessary to show gross, or wicked, or criminal negligence, something amounting, or at any rate analogous, to a criminal indifference to consequences, before a jury can find culpable homicide proved. It may be that the law on this matter has got to be reconsidered."

> Appeal allowed: conviction of culpable homicide quashed; conviction of a contravention of s. 11 of the Road Traffic Act 1930 substituted.

NOTES

Cf. Andrews v. *D.P.P.* [1937] A.C. 576 and *Quinn* v. *Cunningham* (*ante*, ch. 10).

The sheriff had directed the jury that they could not bring in a verdict of guilty under s. 11, on the ground that a contravention of the statute was not libelled in the indictment. In substituting the conviction of the statutory offence the court relied on s. 3(2) of the Criminal Appeal (Scotland) Act 1926, and s. 34 of the Road Traffic Act 1930.

Although many of the "lawful act" homicide cases arise from road traffic cases, the doctrine is not confined to such cases, see, *e.g.*, *H.M. Advocate* v. *Sheppard*, 1941 J.C. 67 (*ante*, ch. 9). In practice, cases of the *Paton* type are today usually dealt with under s. 1 of the Road Traffic Act 1972.

(ii)   Unlawful act homicide

1.   Bird v. H.M. Advocate
1952 J.C. 23

The appellant, a petty officer in the navy, who had been drinking, was under the impression that a woman had taken money belonging to him. He pursued her along a road, and caused her such alarm and apprehension that she tried to stop and enter a passing car. He grabbed hold of her to prevent her getting into the car, whereupon she collapsed and died of shock. It appeared that she had a weak heart. In his charge to the jury the presiding judge gave the following directions, which were subsequently upheld on appeal:

LORD JAMIESON: "The crime with which the accused is charged is culpable homicide, and I think I can best help you by saying a word or two as to what that crime means. As its name implies, it is simply bringing about the death of another by a criminal act of *culpa* or fault. It differs from the crime of murder in this, that in murder there must either be an intent to kill or a reckless disregard as to the consequences of one's act. In culpable homicide these factors may be absent. It takes many forms, but you here are only concerned with death resulting from violence or assault, and I shall have to explain to you later what exactly I mean by assault. Violence may take many forms. It may be a savage attack causing physical injury resulting in death or it may be a very slight assault. If, having a grievance against a man, another gives him a push, although a slight push, and that knocks him over and he hits his head against a kerb and dies, it may be culpable homicide, and it is no defence to the charge to say that a serious injury was not intended or that death was not in contemplation, and that in that sense the death was accidental. I am going to read to you what was said by one of our Judges, who was at one time Lord Justice-Clerk, in charging a jury. He said [*H.M. Advocate* v.*Delaney,* 1945 J.C. 138, at p. 139]: 'That being so and life having been taken, it is clear that there must be a conviction, unless you are satisfied on the evidence that the taking of life was merely an innocent accident. It may be that those who offer violence, especially violence which is subject to be followed by death, have not had in view the taking of life. They, however, are not accidental in their use of violence. They are responsible for the violence they use, so far as the violence is concerned; and, if consequences follow which they do not anticipate or apprehend, they are also responsible for these consequences. One cannot say "I chose to exercise violence against a person against whom I thought I had a grievance, and it was merely accidental that a probable consequence of that violence followed." '

Now the degree of violence that has been used, as I have told you, may be very slight, but if there was any violence or if there was any assault and death results from it, directly results from it, then the accused person is guilty of culpable homicide. The question of the degree of violence is not really a question for the jury. It is a question for the Judge, if the accused is found guilty, in considering what punishment is to be meted out. Nor is it any defence that the victim was an old person, an infirm person, or a person that suffered from a bad heart, and that if he had been young and healthy the consequences would not have happened. If a person commits an assault, he must take his victim as he finds him. It is not necessary that the death should result from physical injuries. If the result of the treatment that the deceased person has received has been to cause shock and that person dies of shock, then the crime has been committed. If a person is assaulted, although to a slight degree, but is put in fear of serious bodily injury and dies as a result, then the crime has been committed and the person who has committed the assault is guilty of it.

Now I have been talking about assault. Assault, in law, is in some ways a technical term. One talking in ordinary parlance about an assault is rather inclined to think of some serious violence being used, but that, in law, is not necessary. The learned Advocate-depute referred to a well-known book on Criminal Law [Macdonald, at p. 115], in which it is said that every attack upon the person of another is an assault, whether it injure or not; and then it gives an example, that even spitting upon another is assault. Later on it says, "Gestures threatening violence so great as to put another in bodily fear, whether accompanied by words of menace or not, constitute assault. That threatening language was used may be an element in estimating how far the fear of the person attacked was reasonable; but mere words cannot constitute an assault.' So, when I speak about an assault, do not run away with the idea that it means something of a very violent nature. The same applies when I speak to you about violence. The matter was very well illustrated in a case to which the learned Advocate-depute referred me, where an attempt was made to rob a woman. Some force was used but there was no serious physical injury, but she had a weak heart and she died, I think it was a few days later. She died some time later from shock, and in charging the jury a very eminent Judge said this [H.M. Advocate v. Brown (1879) 4 Coup. 225, at p. 227], 'Anyone attacking a person with a view to robbery, and causing his or her death, was guilty of culpable homicide at the least. It was no defence at all that the victim was suffering from heart disease. Therefore, if they were of opinion that this woman died from the shock occasioned by the prisoner's criminal attempt to rob her, he was guilty, not merely of assault with intent to rob, but of culpable homicide.'

Death, however, must result directly from the assault or from the violence used. It must be a direct result, although there may be factors operating such as a diseased heart, and when I speak of it being direct it need not necessarily be the direct result of physical violence, that is to say, the physical injuries received. If a person has been assaulted and there is violence used or if the victim is put in reasonable fear of his or her safety, reasonable fear of further violence, and is suffering from a bad heart which operates as one cause, and as a result dies from shock or emotional shock, as the doctors call it here, that would be enough. So, when you come to consider the facts, you should, I think, direct your attention to this: Did the accused strike the deceased woman? Do you hold that proved? If you do not hold that she was actually struck, did he molest her? Did he lay hands on her and, by his actings, did he put her in a reasonable dread of being attacked to such an extent as caused her to suffer from shock? And, if you find either of these, the other question you have to direct your attention to is this, Was her death a direct result of that?"

Verdict: Guilty.

NOTES

Cf. the cases of *H.M. Advocate* v. *Robertson and Donoghue* (unreported, *ante* ch. 3) and *McDermott* v. *H.M. Advocate*, 1974 S.L.T. 206 *(ante)*, and comments thereon. In *D.P.P.* v. *Newbury and Jones* [1976] 2 All E.R. 365 the House of Lords held that English law did not require actual foresight of the consequences of the unlawful act in such cases. All that was required was an unlawful and dangerous act, *i.e.*, an act which was likely to endanger another.

2.   H.M. Advocate v. Finlayson
1978 S.L.T. (Notes) 18

David Finlayson was charged on indictment (1) with a contravention of the Misuse of Drugs Act 1971, and (2) that he did on 4 August 1977: "unlawfully insert into the person of David William Wilson . . . a syringe containing noxious substances, namely morphine and diazepam, and recklessly inject into the person of said David William Wilson a mixture of said noxious substances in quantities dangerous to health and to life, and . . . did kill him."

David Finlayson appeared for trial before Lord Grieve in Edinburgh on 21 November 1977 and tendered pleas of not guilty in respect of both charges libelled in the indictment. Before the jury was empanelled, a plea was taken to the relevancy of charge (2).

It was conceded by the advocate-depute that, in considering the question of the relevancy of charge (2), that charge should be examined by itself, without any regard to charge (1); and further-more it was admitted that the indictment left it open to the defence to establish that the deceased Wilson had consented to the insertion of the syringe and the injection of the noxious substances, and that the question of assault did not arise. The advocate-depute argued that culpable homicide could result from a lawful act performed with a degree of negligence amounting to recklessness *(Paton* v. *H.M. Advocate,* 1936 S.L.T. 298; 1936 J.C. 19, and *H.M. Advocate* v. *Thomsett,* 1939, unreported, see Gordon on *Criminal Law,* p. 742). Charge (2) did not disclose an intention on the part of the panel to harm the deceased, but it was not necessary in a charge of culpable homicide to libel such an intention where the act which resulted in death was itself unlawful *(McDermott* v. *H.M. Advo-cate,* 1974 S.L.T. 206; 1973 J.C. 8). The unlawful act complained of ought, however, to be capable of being identified as such from the terms of the indictment, and, in the present case, the mere posses-sion by the panel of morphine (a controlled drug) being unlawful, it followed that any act, such as that libelled in charge (2), involving the possession by the panel of morphine, was tainted with illegality (reference was made to *R.* v. *Cato* [1976] 1 W.L.R. 110).

Counsel for the defence argued that in charge (2) no unlawful act had been libelled, the act of insertion of the syringe and injection of the noxious substances not itself being unlawful.

In sustaining the plea for the defence, Lord Grieve observed that, although there were strong arguments in favour of the view that all uses of morphine by a person such as the panel were unlawful, it was necessary to establish that possession by the panel of the drug was unlawful, and that, accordingly, where unlawful possession was not libelled in a charge, such as charge (2), that charge was irrelevant, and that the question of negligence amounting to recklessness did not, in the circumstances, arise.

Plea to the relevancy sustained.

NOTES

For the final disposal of this case, see above, ch. 3. In view of the decision in *Smart* v. *H.M. Advocate* 1975 S.L.T. 65 *(ante,* ch. 10) it is difficult to see how the court could sustain the plea that there was no unlawful act here, the consent of the victim being irrelevant to the question of whether there was an assault committed.

It is futher submitted that the accused's guilt ought not to hinge on whether or not he was lawfully in possession of the drug prior to injection. After all, it is presumably just as unlawful to assault a man by pointing a licensed gun at his head as an unlicensed one.

CHAPTER 12

THEFT

a. Early development

For Hume, theft was restricted to the "unlawful taking" of the property of another. But the early nineteenth-century case-law indicates that the courts were prepared to convict of theft those who appropriated goods in other ways.

1. **John Smith**
(1838) 2 Swin. 28

The accused was charged with theft of money and articles in that he did "find the said money and other articles, and did then and there, or at some other time and place to the prosecutor unknown, appropriate the same to his own uses and purposes, he well knowing the same to be the property of the said John Buchanan, and did wickedly and feloniously steal and theftuously away take the said articles."

He objected to the relevancy of the indictment.

LORD MEADOWBANK: "The Counsel for the pannel has almost admitted himself out of Court; for he admits, that if the pannel had seen the articles drop from the person of the owner, the immediate appropriation of them would have amounted to the crime charged. Now, just take the point a little farther. Suppose, that on the outside of the pocket book he had seen the name of the owner written in legible characters. It must be held that, after this, to pick it up and appropriate it, would be same thing as to do so after seeing it drop from the owner's person. Now, what is the difference in the circumstance that he goes one step farther? He does not see the name of the owner on the outside, but, having opened the book, he finds it written in the inside; and, having thus taken the only means in his power to discover who the owner is, he immediately forms the intention of appropriating it. Suppose the case of a carrier, one of whose parcels had lost the address,—he opens it in order to discover to whom it belongs, and after having done so, forms the design of appropriating it. Can it be doubted, after the decisions which we have given, that he would be held guilty of theft? The principle on which the cases of horse-stealing, referred to in the Information, have been decided, is not,—as is maintained for the pannel,—that the *malus animus* existed at the time of the hiring. It is of no consequence of what character the original possession of the property is. The moment the intention of appropriating the

372

property of another is formed, then the theft is committed. Such appearing to me to be the principle of our recent decisions, it is a source of satisfaction to find, that, although some very vague notions on the subject have at one time been held by those great men who, in England, have adopted the same views as Baron Hume, the more modern practice in that country is the same as our own."

LORD MONCREIFF: "I apprehend it to be quite clear, that the general principle originally laid down by Baron Hume on this subject has been, I do not say altered, but greatly qualified, by recent decisions. A servant who breaks through a trust and appropriates his master's property has, in innumerable cases, been found guilty of theft. So, also, the case of appropriation by a clerk who has the custody of goods, even with the power to sell them, has been held to be theft. Then the case of a person hiring a horse, and appropriating it to his own use, is one very much in point. It is argued, in the Information for the pannel, that to constitute the crime of theft, the felonious intention must have existed from the beginning. I am not prepared to go that length. I think a person may have hired a horse for an honest purpose, and subsequently resolved to steal him; and I am not prepared to say that that would not be a case of theft, although the taking must be libelled in some different way, that if it had taken place at the period of the first hiring. So, also, in the case of theft by a carrier of goods entrusted to his care, the time and place of the offence is not when and where he received the goods, but when and where he formed the felonious intention of appropriating them. Suppose a flock of sheep are found straying on the public road, with the owner's mark on them, surely we should not hesitate to find, that the appropriation of them by another person was theft. The case of a man seeing a person drop a pocket-book, and picking it up and keeping it, is admitted to be a case of theft. But put another case,—that he does not see it drop, but sees a person resting by the side of the road, and when he comes to the spot finds a pocket-book there; and suppose that he either knows the person by sight, or finds his name written in the book,—can it be doubted that the moment he resolves to appropriate it to himself, that moment he commits theft? It is by accident that he has got possession of the goods of another, but so soon as he discovers who the owner is, it is his duty to restore them. It is a very nice question, whether, if the appropriation did not take place till long after the finding, the case would be the same. Whatever may be my opinion as to the alternative charge, I think the libelling of time and place would not, in that case, be sufficient,—too great a latitude being taken in both respects. But the case before us may be decided on the assumption, that at, or immediately after the period of finding, the knowledge of the owner was acquired, and the design of appropriating formed. In that view, I can have no doubt that the Indictment is relevant."

LORD COCKBURN: "The definition which our law gives of theft, is, that it is *contrectatio fraudulosa rei alienae, lucri faciendi causa*— fraudulent taking of the property of another for the sake of lucre. Now, what is meant by this word *taking*? I know no authority, and no principle, for confining it to the act of first possessing. *Lifting* is not *taking*, at least not necessarily; a person may be the recipient of a commodity involuntarily or unconsciously—as by having it put into his pocket secretly, or delivered to him by mistake. He is the *possessor* after this, but not the *taker*. I don't conceive that there can be any taking, in the sense of this definition, without an intention to take. It means appropriation. Accordingly, there are innumerable cases, such as that of servants stealing things committed to their charge, in which the original possessing was quite innocent, but in which *beyond all doubt,* theft is committed merely by the subsequent application of the property to their own use. There is no bringing these cases within the rule, either in its words or in its meaning, without referring it to the appropriation, *no matter when it may occur,* as to the only act of taking. If this be correct, then the original innocence of possessing an article, is not merely no exclusion of the idea of theft afterwards committed by a new act of criminal application, but it has no tendency to exclude it. The guiltlessness of the first occupancy seems to me to be totally irrelevant in reference to the question of subsequent theft. There are two objections stated to this, as applied to the present case. 1st. That there must be an *animus furandi in the first taking*. I agree to this, provided the word *taking* be left to its correct legal sense, of appropriation. But when extended so as to include the original *reception,* it is *quite certain* that the objection is groundless. For there are various cases of clear, and indisputable theft,—such as that of a carrier abstracting a bale committed to him for conveyance,—where property is held to be stolen, because, though got innocently, it is withdrawn by the receiver from its proper destination, and converted to his own use. If the purity of the first acquisition be a defence against a charge of subsequent theft, it would not be easy to say how many have been illegally convicted of stealing. 2nd. The other objection is, that there can be no theft, where the owner, though he retains the property, happens for a time to have *lost the possession*. It would require very strong and positive authority to support a doctrine so full of danger. The import of this principle is, that *lost property can never be stolen*. And if this be law, then it is not theft to pick up a watch the instant that it is dropped and to run; nor to carry off the goods of a known owner which have been thrown ashore from a wrecked vessel whose whole crew has perished; nor for a police officer sent to discover the stolen goods of a known proprietor, and finding them in custody of the thief, concealing this fact and keeping them to himself. This principle would protect the case, where there was a theftuous intention from the first; for if possession by the owner be necessary, the absence of this element cannot be supplied by the motive of the taker. So, if lost goods were advertised, and a person were to search for them with the view of appropriating, and were to find, and to keep them, even this would not be theft. Nor would it be theft for a person observing a man bathing to sink and be drowned, to run off with his clothes lying on the shore, for the old owner, by death, had lost possession of them. I know no authority for such a principle. Rather than adopt it, the law supposes every man who voluntarily takes, or who even accidentally obtains possession of the property of another, to be a sort of trustee or custodier for him. In the cases of servants, clerks, porters, &c. this principle may be thought not to apply, because these persons obtain possession under a direct employment by the owner. But there are cases where this circumstance does not occur. Take the case of property *never received*. An unknown stranger holds a packet addressed to the real proprietor. He gives it to a porter to be delivered to that person, who does not know of its existence. The porter keeps it. I think that this would be theft; and that it would be well charged as such, if the crime were set forth as committed not against the unknown stranger, but against the real owner; because, though not employed by him, the porter having got the parcel, held it as his custodier. I conceive a trust of an analogous description to be imposed by the law upon everyone who happens to take possession, or to find himself in possession, of the property of another; but especially where this is the result of his own act. It may not be his duty to lift the property of another; or, if he should happen to do so, he may lay it down again; but from the moment that he begins to keep possession, knowing whose it is, he holds it for that person; and hence would be entitled to resist its being taken from him."

Charge of theft held relevant.

NOTES

The significance of the decision in *John Smith* lies in the fact that it paved the way for the *actus reus* of theft to be regarded in terms of appropriation, rather than in terms of "felonious taking." Hume's insistence on this latter aspect is understandable in an age when theft was a capital crime, but it led to many inconsistencies of law and logic; in particular his insistence on differentiating the position of "custodiers" and "possessors" could not survive the common sense practice of charging with theft persons who hired goods *bona fide* and subsequently formed the dishonest intention of appropriating them.

2. George Brown.
(1839) 2 Swin. 394

The accused was charged that, having been employed as a watchmaker, and nine people having delivered to him watches for repair between August and December 1838, he did on 7 January 1839 steal the watches.

He objected to the relevancy of the charge.

LORD JUSTICE-CLERK (BOYLE) (dissenting): "I am, in this case, of the opinion that the proper charge against the pannel would have been one of breach of trust. In all these cases, to which I have referred, in which the charge of theft was found relevant, there was a limited mandate, for a temporary purpose, and for a short time. But when I look to the *species facti* in this Indictment, namely that the watches which the pannel is said to have appropriated, were delivered to him, either to be cleaned or to be repaired, I cannot help supposing that it was in the contemplation of all parties, that the operation would require a lengthened possession."

LORD MACKENZIE: "I think that we have already, in numerous cases, departed from the authority of Mr. Hume in this matter. One of the most remarkable instances of this was the case in which we found that the appropriation, by a pannel, of an article found on the highway, the owner of which is well known to him, is theft. We have also decided that a carrier, who appropriates goods given to him to be conveyed to a certain destination, is guilty of theft. The opinion of Mr. Hume in regard to this offence is, that in the case of a regular carrier, it is not theft. So also in the case of a horse hired without any felonious purpose, and afterwards carried off by the hirer, we have decided that a theft is committed. But that decision is contrary to the opinion of Baron Hume, who makes the distinction between theft and breach of trust depend on the character of the first acquiring. Then looking to the charge contained in the present Indictment, I am not able to think that it is less than theft. I cannot see any difference,—except a difference which adds to the difficulty of the theft,—between the case of a watchmaker and that of a carrier. I presume that if a party gave goods into the charge of a carrier, which, instead of being delivered to another person, were to be delivered to himself, the Court would not hold that this made any difference as to the crime committed by the carrier, supposing that he abstracted them. And why shall we say that delivery of a thing, without transferring either the property or the possession, does not bar theft, when the operation to be performed is removal over a certain space, and that it does bar theft, when the operation is the cleaning or repairing of the article. It may be true that there is no absolute limitation in the time which the operation, in the case before us, might require. But in a case such as that before us, the time is not unlimited. It is known that the operation can be performed within a certain time; and it is in the expectation of that time proving sufficient, that the article is given out of the owner's custody. There is this farther circumstance to be taken into account, that in the case of the carrier, the article remains more under the eye of the owner, than it does in that of the watchmaker. On the whole, I am of opinion that we have gone so far, that it is not possible for us to stop. I think we must hold here, as we have done in those other cases to which I have referred, that there was no such transference of the possession as to make the appropriation a less crime than theft. It may be that in practice we have sustained cases as breach of trust, which might properly have been tried as theft. Now, in regard to the argument thus raised, the only answer that occurs to me, is, that theft and breach of trust have not been considered opposed to one another, and that the Court has held them to be similar crimes, to the extent at least of admitting confession of the one, when the *species facti* libelled might perhaps have amounted, in strictness, to the other. I am the more inclined to think that this may have been the opinion of the Court, because I find an opinion to that effect in my own notes. And I am not yet convinced that the conclusion is illogical, which holds that the same act may sometimes fall under two different kinds of offences. If a butler steal wine from his master's cellar, and an indictment is raised against him, under the *nomen juris* of breach of trust, it cannot surely be held that that is equivalent to a decision that the crime was not theft. I agree with the Lord Justice-Clerk, that we are bound to look at indictments, even although no objection is taken, before pronouncing an interlocutor of relevancy. But it is a different thing to say, that if the Prosecutor is satisfied to try the pannel for the lesser crime, the Court ought to interfere with the objection that the *species facti* might have been tried under a harsher name."

LORD MONCREIFF: "I do not think that, consistently with our late decisions, we can come to any other determination than that this is a case of theft. If the principle were, that this crime could not be committed, when the article came into the power of the pannel with the consent of the owner, that principle would exclude from the category of theft the cases of the carrier, the porter, the hirer of the horse. But I apprehend that the decisions which we have given in these cases, proceeded on the fact, that the owner's consent to the transference of the possession is only a qualified and conditional consent, for a special and particular purpose. In the case before us, the pannel gets the watch solely for the purpose of cleaning or repairing it, with the clear expectation and intention of the owner, that it is to be restored to him so soon as that operation is completed. Now, I do not think we can hold this appropriation of the watch, in these circumstances, to be anything but the crime of theft. Although the article came at first lawfully into his possession, the principle of law is, that the felonious taking is at the moment he forms the resolution of appropriating it to his own use."

Charge of theft held relevant.

NOTES

In spite of this decision however the court subsequently decided in a number of cases that theft still required an unlawful taking of possession: see Gordon, para. 14-06.

b. Theft by finding

1.   **Angus McKinnon**
(1863) 4 Irv. 398

A. was charged with theft, in so far as, having at the time and place libelled found a pocket-book and bank notes that had been stolen from or dropped by B, he had wickedly and feloniously appropriated the same to his own uses, well knowing that the same were the property of B, "or at all events that the same were not the property of you the said" A.

LORD JUSTICE-CLERK (INGLIS): "At one time the law of Scotland held, that the finding and appropriation of moveable property under any circumstances did not constitute theft, but that rule has been modified by the decision of this Court in the cases of *Smith* and *Pye* (1838) 2 Swin. 187 so that, under certain circumstances, the finding and appropriation of moveable property does amount to theft. Further than that the old rule has not been relaxed. I think that in this case we are asked by the prosecutor to apply the principle of the judgments in *Smith* and *Pye* to a totally different case. The case of *Smith* was one of appropriation to the finder's own uses and purposes, he knowing who the owner was and the same in the case of *Pye*. They were both exactly in the same position, and it is not unimportant to observe that in the case of *Smith*, where the relevancy of such a charge was first sustained, and which was the only case in which there was any argument, some of the Judges in the majority of the Court, so express their opinion as to lead to the inference that but for the fact that the owner of the money was known to the pannel, and known to him at the time—or almost at the time—when he first took the property, they would not have held the indictment relevant. Whether or not this was a right modification of our old law I give no opinion at present, but it is clear to me that this is all that we have authority for. . . .

The charge as set forth in this indictment does not seem to me to be borne out by the authority of any previous case, or by any correct or intelligible principle of our criminal law. For example, a person finds a thing which is of no great value, he cannot find the owner, and after a considerable period, and having discharged every obligation incumbent on him he appropriates it—whatever may be said of the transaction in a purely honourable point of view, can it be said that that is theft? In dealing with this class of cases we must be very careful, and so draw the line as clearly to distinguish them, even in a moral point of view, from ordinary cases of theftuous awaytaking.

In this libel let us take one alternative, that this pocket-book having been lost or dropped in the month of October on the street of Fort-William, and having been found by the pannel, he did then and there on or near said street, wickedly appropriate it not knowing whose property it was. I say this is the meaning of the last alternative, not because the words 'at all events' are precisely equivalent to 'not knowing whose property it was'; and though, therefore, had this charge stood alone and not as an alternative, it might have been possible to put another construction on it, yet here the alternative is so framed, that I can give it no other meaning than that McGillivray was the true owner, and if the panel did not know that McGillivray was the owner, then he did not know who the true owner was.

It appears to me that this charge might cover the case of a thing being found on the 18th October, and having remained in his possession innocently for a long time, while enquiry was being made concerning the owner, the accused being all that time quite willing to restore the article, but that some time before May 1863, he at last appropriates it to his own use. This clearly does not come up to the crime of *theft*. It may be very questionable in point of *honour,* but it is not that grievous violation of moral right which is implied in *theft.* Such is the case before us, and I should be sorry to pre-judge any other which may arise under the other circumstances with other more specific words, or greater precision in the libelling of the time between the taking and the appropriation, or as to the time of the guilty knowledge on the part of the panel; but for the present I must take these things exactly as I find them in this indictment, and I am of opinion that this charge is irrelevant."

Charge held irrelevant.

NOTES

McKinnon would not be followed today; it is now well-recognised that theft by finding occurs immediately the finder forms the intention to appropriate, whether or not he knows who the owner is and irrespective of exactly when he forms the dishonest intention. But the next case illustrates the difficulty the nineteenth-century judges found with this concept.

2. Campbell v. MacLennan
(1888) 1 White 604.

The accused was charged that "having on the 14th November 1887, within the Inn at Dunvegan, found in money one pound, you did deny having found the same and did appropriate, and thus steal the same."

LORD MCLAREN: "Now, in my opinion, that is not a relevant charge of theft, because everything set out might be true, and yet the accused might not be guilty of theft. I am not prepared to affirm that the mere finding of a £1 note, coupled with a denial of having found it, is tantamount to felonious appropriation. One would like to know who the owner of the note was, and whether the person to whom the accused is said to have denied having found it, had a right to ask the question. The circumstances set out are only these two: that the accused found a £1 note, and that he denied having found it. Now it may be morally wrong to deny having found a £1 note; on the other hand, such a denial, if addressed to a person who had no business to put the question, does not raise a presumption of theft."

LORD RUTHERFORD CLARK: "I am sorry to be obliged to differ, but I differ entirely. We have here nothing to consider but whether this complaint is or is not relevant. The complaint states merely these two facts—that the accused found a £1 note, and that he appropriated it to his own use. Under the new Act 'appropriate' is to be read as 'feloniously appropriate,' but that is really of no importance, for if a person finds a £1 note and appropriates it to his own use, I think that is plainly theft and nothing else."

LORD YOUNG: "A man may find a £1 note, and finding it, may deny having done so, and may appropriate it, and yet not be a thief. He may be a thief, no doubt, but, on the other hand, he may not—the conclusion of theft is not the necessary inference. There must be circumstances entitling a Jury to attribute to the accused the *animus furandi*. A man of large property may find money in the street, and may give it in the way of alms to the next beggar; that is undoubtedly appropriation. Yet who would call it theft, even if the finder had denied having found it? His denial may be a very important circumstance, and if the whole other circumstances point to the conclusion of theft, then he may be rightly convicted. Another important circumstance is that the finder knew who the true owner was, but in this indictment it is not suggested to whom the £1 note belonged, or even that the prosecutor knew to whom it belonged.

I am not prepared therefore to sustain this indictment, and I am the more disposed to take this strict course—if indeed it be a strict course—because I have grave doubts whether this case should ever have been prosecuted. In one sense all crimes are crimes against the public as well as against the individual injured, but where in a case of this sort the individual injured makes no complaint to the authorities, and the friends of the accused come forward and restore what has been taken, it occurs to me that it is not for the public prosecutor to step in and insist in bringing the matter to the test of a criminal prosecution. I think that in cases of this kind—and I do not of course speak of cases of another and more serious description—the public prosecutor ought to act only on the deliberate complaint of the injured person."

Charge held irrelevant.

NOTES

The "new Act" referred to by Lord Rutherford Clark was the Criminal Procedure (Scotland) Act 1887, s. 8 thereof providing that qualifying words such as "wickedly and feloniously" should be implied in indictments charging acts of commission or omission. This is now consolidated in ss. 48 and 312 (*e*) of the Criminal Procedure (Scotland) Act 1975.

c. What can be stolen

Generally, only corporeal moveables can be stolen, although charges of theft of electricity are common. But difficulties may arise when the article is taken not for its own value, but for the value of information it contains.

H.M. Advocate v. Mackenzies
1913 S.C. (J) 107

(For the facts of the case, see *ante*, ch.5 on Attempt.) On the question whether the indictment disclosed a relevant charge of theft:

LORD JUSTICE-CLERK: "As regards the charge of theft, I cannot see any ground for holding it to be irrelevant. The charge is stealing a book, and that charge the prosecutor will have to prove by sufficient evidence. All defences, such as that there was only a trespass and not a theft, will be open to the accused. The indictment seems to hint at the book having been taken, not to appropriate the actual article itself, but in order to obtain the opportunity of copying part of its contents for an illegitimate purpose. That such a taking, although there is no intention to retain the article, may be theft is I think clear. The article is taken from its owner for the serious purpose of obtaining something of value through the possession of it. And that such an action may be theft is shown by the case of a person who desires to enter premises for a felonious purpose, and takes possession of the key by which the security of the premises is protected. Although he has no desire or intention to appropriate and keep the key, he is held to have stolen the key, he having taken it in order to facilitate the carrying out of his criminal intention. In this case the prosecutor charging the accused with stealing a book described fulfils all the requirements of relevancy, and if he can make out by his evidence that the book was taken, and taken with a nefarious purpose, he may be able to obtain a direction in law from the Judge at the trial that what was done constituted a theft of the book. It is quite evident that a book of no real value in itself may be of great value because of what is written in it. I think, therefore, that the charge of theft against the male prisoner must be held to be relevant."

Charge of the theft held relevant.

NOTES

See also *Dewar* (1777) Burnett, 115; Hume, i. 75. Can that case be distinguished from *Mackenzies*? On the question of whether human remains can be stolen, see Gordon, para. 14-44 and also *Dewar* v. *H.M. Advocate*, 1945 J.C. 5 *ante*, ch. 6).

d. Mens rea *of theft*

This is the intention permanently to deprive the owner of his goods. Particular problems have however arisen in relation to persons who taken away motor vehicles. Should they be charged with theft at common law or with a contravention of the Road Traffic Act 1972, s. 175?

Kivlin v. Milne
1979 S.L.T. (Notes) 2

An accused was charged with theft of a motor car, while acting along with another person. The vehicle was abandoned by the accused in a place where the owner was not liable to discover it. It was submitted to the sheriff that in order to establish the crime of theft it must be shown that there had been an intention to deprive the owner of permanent ownership or that the accused had quite recklessly taken away the property and had put it into such a situation that the owner was effectively prevented from getting it back. On appeal by stated case against conviction, the High Court stated:

OPINION OF THE COURT: "The argument advanced by learned counsel for the appellant was to the effect that the necessary conditions to constitute theft had not been established, in that the facts proved did not establish that there was present in the mind of the appellant, on each of the two occasions libelled, the intention permanently to deprive the owner of the motor car of the possession thereof. In the event counsel conceded that it was a matter of circumstances in each case, and having regard to the findings-in-fact we are of the opinion that the learned sheriff in each of the two charges libelled was entitled to draw the inference that the appellant had the intention permanently to deprive the owner of the motor car of the possession thereof, in that he undoubtedly took possession of it without authority and left the car on each occasion in a place where the owner, by reason of his own investigations, was not liable to discover it. In that situation we are of the opinion that the question of law for the opinion of the court, falls to be answered in the affirmative and the appeal will accordingly be dismissed."

Appeal dismissed.

NOTES

So where the vehicle is recovered in a place where the owner is liable to discover it, presumably the charge should be laid under the statute. But what sort of inquires would it be reasonable for the owner to make? In practice, alternative charges of theft and the statutory contravention are often encountered.

e. Clandestine taking and using

The odd crime recognised in *Strathern* v. *Seaforth*, 1926 J.C. 100 (*ante* ch. 1) has been slow to establish itself in Scots law.

Murray v. Robertson
1927 J.C. 1

LORD JUSTICE-CLERK (ALNESS): "This stated case relates to a complaint made by the respondent against the appellant, in which he is charged with clandestinely taking possession of twenty-four fish boxes, the property of certain people who are named, he well knowing that he had not received permission and would not have received permission from the owners, and with using these boxes by filling them with fish and dispatching them to Glasgow, or, alternatively, with the crime of theft. The Sheriff-substitute convicted the appellant on the first of these alternative charges, and the question which we have to decide is whether he was entitled to do so.

The facts in the case, which leave something to be desired in the matter of clarity, at least show this, that the appellant dispatched the fish in question from Ardrossan to Glasgow in boxes which lay in his yard, and which belonged to the persons whose names are mentioned in the complaint. Dealing with the two branches of the first alternative charge in the complaint, there was charged *(first)* clandestine possession obtained, and *(second)* use made of the boxes so obtained. I regard clandestine possession as an essential element in the charge which was made. If the charge sounds in crime at all, it is because possession was alleged to have been taken clandestinely. Now, there is not a vestige of evidence to the effect that possession in this case was so obtained. It is stated in the eleventh finding that it was not shown how—and the learned Sheriff might have added, or when—the boxes came into the appellant's yard, but that it was shown that they might have been deposited there by, or on behalf of, hawkers or owners of fish restaurants in order to get rid of them, or sent in as returned empties by fish merchants who had bought fish from the appellant in his own boxes. From the eleventh article it plainly appears that the possession obtained by the appellant, for aught that is found in this stated case, may have been, and probably was, entirely innocent and legitimate. That the use of the adverb 'clandestinely' was essential to the relevancy of the complaint I have no doubt at all. If that adverb were absent from the complaint, it would, on the face of it, be irrelevant. Accordingly, the appellant founds his appeal upon the fact that there is no finding which supports the view that the possession obtained by him was clandestinely obtained. With regard to the use to which the boxes were subsequently put, in my view, that use cannot, *per se,* be the foundation of a criminal charge. The facts stated disclose, it may be, a civil dispute, and may afford ground for a civil remedy; but I am quite unable to see that they point to any criminal act on the part of the appellant.

The case of *Strathern* v. *Seaforth*, 1926 J.C. 100, to which we were referred, has no application to the circumstances here. The opinions of the Judges who took part in that decision all sound in the word 'clandestine.' Lord Hunter and Lord Anderson both regarded that as the foundation of the charge. For myself, I used the word 'abstracted,' which I regarded, and still regard, as essential to the relevancy of that charge."

Appeal allowed: conviction quashed.

NOTES

For a discussion of this problem, see Gordon, paras. 15-29 to 15-32.

CHAPTER 13

ROBBERY AND EMBEZZLEMENT

a.   Assault and robbery

Most modern charges of robbery allege that the accused "did assault X . . . and rob him of . . .", which might seem to suggest that there are two crimes libelled. But provided there is violence or intimidation of any degree attached to the theft, then the crime is robbery, irrespective of whether there is evidence to prove the specific assault.

O'Neill v. H.M. Advocate
1934 J.C. 98

LORD JUSTICE-CLERK (AITCHISON): "The appellant was indicted on a charge of assault and robbery, the charge being that he assaulted the woman named in the indictment, 'and did knock her head and face against the wall of said close to the effusion of her blood and did rob her of a handbag' containing money and other articles. The case went to trial before a jury, and the jury found the charge of assault libelled in the indictment not proven, but found the appellant guilty of robbery.

The appellant was sentenced to three years' penal servitude, and he now appeals to this Court against the conviction, and also against the sentence.

As regards the conviction, the ground of appeal stated is that the verdict of guilty of robbery cannot be supported, having regard to the evidence. The case, as presented by Mr. Prain, is that the jury having found assault not proven, the facts in the case, while habile to justify a conviction of theft, are not habile to justify a conviction of robbery.

The answer to the question thus raised depends upon what is the true legal definition of robbery. It is well settled that in robbery there must be violence. On the other hand, it is not necessary to robbery that there should be actual physical assault. It is enough if the degree of force used can reasonably be described as violence. I think the law upon this matter is as laid down by Baron Hume in his work on Crimes in words which have never been disputed. In vol. i. (p. 106, paragraph 5), what Hume says is this: 'It is another and an indispensable circumstance that the thing be taken by violence; for herein lies the distinctive character of the crime. But as to this article a great latitude of construction has been received. There may be a robbery without any wounding or beating of the person (and when such violence is used, it may therefore be libelled as an

386

aggravation, as it was in the case of James Andrew); and without any forcible wresting or tearing of the thing from the person; or even any sort of endeavour on the part of the sufferer to detain it. The law means only to oppose this sort of taking, as against the will of the owner; to that which happens privately, or by surprise, and without any application to his will or his fears; and it is understood therefore to be violence, if the thing is taken by means of such behaviour, as justly alarms for the personal and immediate consequences of resistance or refusal.'

Now, that being the law, the distinction between theft and robbery may be very difficult of exact legal definition, and, in the particular case, it may not be easy to say whether the facts amount to robbery or amount to theft only. The question is really one of degree. But, in the present case, I think that there can be no doubt that this woman sustained an injury to her head and also suffered from concussion. We must, of course, take it that these were not the result of assault, because the jury has found assault not proven; but I think it is very clear upon the evidence that the injury which the woman sustained would not have been caused unless substantial force had been used in snatching her bag. Accordingly, I think it is plain that the injury which she suffered was the direct consequence of the snatching of her bag. That seems to me to indicate a degree of violence that places the crime here in the category rather of robbery than of theft.

The case seems to me to be substantially on all fours with the case of *H.M. Advocate* v. *Fegen*, 2 Swin. 25, to which we were referred. In that case, it appears from the report that the accused had come up to the complainer, seized his watch chain, and pulled his watch out of his pocket. The complainer fell, and then the report bears 'whether accidentally or from being tripped he could not say, but he stated that he would not have fallen if he had not been laid hold of.' The Court unanimously held that the degree of violence proved was sufficient to establish the charge of robbery, of which the jury, under the direction of the Lord Justice-General, had found the panel guilty. I think exactly the same may be said in the present case. I think, therefore that the ground upon which this verdict is challenged fails, and that the verdict must stand in the form in which it was returned.''

Appeal dismissed.

NOTES

For a discussion of the problems raised by this case, see Gordon, paras. 16-10, 16-11.

b. Robbery of a ship: piracy

There is only one case this century in Scotland where this has been charged.

Cameron v. H.M. Advocate
1971 J.C. 50

Members of the crew of a British ship were charged on an indictment which set forth that, when the ship was about three miles off the Aberdeenshire coast, they threatened and robbed the master, put him and other members of the crew ashore and navigated the ship eastwards on to the high seas, and thus took masterful possession of the ship and appropriated it to their own use. The word "piracy" was not mentioned in the indictment. They all objected to the relevancy of the charge.

LORD CAMERON: "Piracy is a crime nowadays of rare occurrence, at least in the Courts of this country, and has over the years acquired certain picturesque and picaresque associations. But the crime itself, stripped of the highly coloured detail with which storybook romance has clothed the concept, is in essentials of sordid and squalid simplicity. Mr Douglas, in his careful address, complained that it was not possible to ascertain from the indictment whether the charge was piracy or theft or mutiny or just simply breach of the peace. If it were intended that it should be a charge of piracy, then the prosecutor should libel it as such. His argument ran that robbery was a necessary ingredient of piracy and that the possession obtained by the accused had to be against the will of the robbed and obtained forcibly and for the profit of the perpetrator. This, he said, was not relevantly averred in charge 1. His secondary contention was that, if the indictment did disclose any offence committed on the high seas, it was outside the jurisdiction of the Scottish Courts. I think that reference to section 686 of the Merchant Shipping Act, 1894, sufficiently answers that point, as it covers any offence committed by persons, British subjects or not, in or on board a British ship on the high seas. In any event, the offence itself, so far as the indictment discloses, at least began within territorial waters as appears from the words 'navigate said trawler on to the high seas.'

In support of his basic argument Mr Douglas cited passages from Hume, vol. i, pp. 480 and 482. He criticised the statement in Macdonald, (5th ed.) p. 43, that 'taking possession of a vessel at sea, whether by those on board, or by others, or feloniously carrying off goods or persons from ships, are acts of piracy' as an inaccurate and incomplete statement of the law and not supported by the passages in Hume on which it is apparently based. What was lacking in this bald statement was any indication that robbery was a necessary ingredient of the crime. I agree with Mr Douglas to this extent, that I think that the statement, if taken by itself, and out of context, is less than accurate. In my opinion the 'taking possession' must itself be causally connected with actual violence employed to enable possession to be taken or with the threat of violence. And that this is so would appear to me to follow from the references to Hume on which the statement professes to be based, because, although the sentence in Macdonald is largely a repetition of language used by Hume on p. 482, yet I think that it is clear enough from what appears in the opening sentence of chapter XXIII on p. 480 that the element of violence and compulsion arising out of violence or the threat of it is of the essence of the crime.

Mr Fairbairn, for the accused Massie (in whose argument Mr Shaffer for Innes concurred), adopted Mr Douglas's arguments, but added a further submission that piracy was no more than robbery at sea of a particular kind, and that consequently there must be displayed an intention permanently to deprive the true owner of his property to the gain or profit of the robber. He cited in support of this contention the most recent authority on the matter, *In re Piracy Jure Gentium,* [1934] A.C. 586. He maintained that the words 'appropriate to your own use' was not a phrase which was appropriate to a case of alleged piracy or robbery, however proper to a charge of embezzlement. The distinction between embezzlement and robbery was that in the latter the intention must be to deprive the true owner permanently of his property, while in the former even replacement of the funds embezzled or a proved intention to replace after use by the criminal was no answer to the charge of embezzlement. No doubt the crime of embezzlement is complete even though the money is subsequently repaid or returned in full, but on the particular point raised by Mr Fairbairn, that an intention to deprive permanently is of the essence of theft and robbery and that a gain to the accused must also arise, I am against his contentions. In the first place, the indictment does no more than allege appropriation to the use of the accused: this, I should think, is on the face of it indicative of an intent to dispossess permanently or at least for such indefinite period as to be of permanent character. But, apart from this, Mr Fairbairn could cite no authority for his proposition, which would seem at least to conflict radically with the considerable authority of Hume. At p. 79 in vol. i Baron Hume wrote: 'When once contracted by a proper taking and carrying away, the guilt cannot afterwards be effaced by any course of conduct, not even by an early and spontaneous restitution of the spoil, and much less by payment of the value, or any other atonement or amends.' Whether the intent be permanent or only temporary appropriation, the clandestine or felonious taking of the article constitutes the crime. On the question of profit Hume had this to say (vol. i. 76): '. . . it is certain, that in the ordinary case the *animus lucri* is to be presumed from the act itself of taking away the thing . . . It is also to be remembered, that if the thing is kept, it signifies not for what purpose . . . Every object is lucre in the estimation of law . . .' Now, of course, in these passages Hume was dealing with theft, but I see no possible ground for holding that different principles apply to robbery, which itself is forcible theft. And here I may pause to refer to a later passage in the same chapter, when Hume points out that the display or use of arms or weapons is not a necessary ingredient of robbery. 'Any reasonable fear of danger, arising from a constructive violence, which is gathered from the mode and circumstances of the demand, being such as are attended with awe and alarm, and may naturally induce a man to surrender his property for the safety of his person, is sufficient to make a taking against the will of the sufferer; which is the essence of a robbery. Thus it is robbery to break into a house, and openly to take away effects in the presence of the owner, who, out of terror, makes no resistance, or perhaps, on demand, himself produces the effects or delivers the keys of his repositories, though situated even in another apartment.' (Hume, vol. i, p. 107.)

The matter is put more briefly in Macdonald, (5th ed.) p. 39: 'Robbery is the felonious taking and appropriation of property in opposition to the will of another under whose personal charge it is; and the force that need be used is a matter of degree.' The force referred to is violence or the threat of violence. It will be noted that nothing is said by Hume or Macdonald about the violence or threat of it being such as would be likely to overcome the will of a reasonable man—a point which Mr Fairbairn endeavoured to make and for which he could find no support in authority or text-writer.

If, then, piracy, as Hume would suggest, includes not only privateering without a commission or letters of marque, but also robbery of a ship or of the effects in it, then it may not be necessary to go further than to consider whether what is set out in charge 1, if proved, would constitute robbery of the trawler *Mary Craig*. The question thus is whether there is anything in recent authority to prohibit that course. In the case of *In re Piracy Jure Gentium*, [1934] A.C. 586, the Privy Council were asked to give an answer to one simple question: 'Whether actual robbery is an essential element of the crime of piracy *jure gentium,* or whether a frustrated attempt to commit a piratical robbery is not equally piracy *jure gentium.*' I pause to note that the question itself somewhat confuses the issue by the use of the words 'piratical robbery.' However this may be, the Judicial Committee of the Privy Council, after a full consideration of the authorities, national and international, including our own Baron Hume, returned this answer: 'Actual robbery is not an essential element in the crime of piracy *jure gentium*. A frustrated attempt to commit a piratical robbery is equally piracy *jure gentium.*' After their very full consideration of the law as developed in the jurisprudence of maritime nations, their Lordships (at p. 600) quoted the language of one of Napoleon's commissioners, who said: 'We have guarded against the dangerous ambition of wishing to regulate and to foresee everything . . . A new question springs up. Then how is it to be decided? To this question it is replied that the office of the law is to fix by enlarged rules the general maxims of right and wrong, to establish firm principles fruitful in consequences, and not to descend to the detail of all the questions which may arise upon each particular topic.' Their Lordships also made this observation: 'A careful examination of the subject shows a gradual widening of the earlier definition of piracy to bring it from time to time more in consonance with situations either not thought of or not in existence when the older jurisconsults were expressing their opinions.' Hall, writing in 1924 (International Law, (8th ed.) p. 314), said: 'The various acts which are recognised or alleged to be piratical may be classed as follows: robbery or attempt at robbery of a vessel, by force or intimidation, either by way of attack from without, or by way of revolt of the crew and conversion of the vessel and cargo to their own use.' While it is true that it is said in *In re Piracy Jure Gentium* that a definition of piracy as sea robbery 'is both too narrow and too wide,' the statement I have cited from Hall was quoted without criticism or disapproval. In the case of *In re Piracy Jure Gentium* the Privy Council in the course of their opinion said this (at p. 600): '. . . their Lordships do not themselves propose to hazard a definition of piracy' an observation which precedes the quotation from M. Portalis, Napoleon's commissioner, which I have just cited. I also would decline to incur the navigational hazard of attempting by definition to mark out a safe course among so many expressions of view and opinion as are collected and set out in the opinion of the Privy Council. It would be both unprofitable, and I think in this case unnecessary, to attempt to do so. There is enough, however, in the authorities to make it possible to say that, when a ship is feloniously taken out of the possession of the owner or those in whose charge the vessel has been placed, against their will and by means of violence or threats of violence and, so taken, thereafter appropriated to the use of those who have done so, the crime so committed is piracy *jure gentium*. The essential elements of this crime are no more and no less than those which are requisite to a relevant charge of robbery where that crime is committed in respect of property on land and within the ordinary jurisdiction of the High

Court. I therefore conclude that, where the facts set out in an indictment relevantly allege robbery of a ship by members of her crew, that will constitute a relevant charge of piracy, whatever may be the future ambit of the crime of piracy *jure gentium.*"

Objection to relevancy repelled.

NOTES

All the accused in this case were convicted of piracy. Their appeals against conviction were all dismissed; the High Court on appeal approved of Lord Cameron's decision on what constituted piracy in Scots law.

c.   Embezzlement: what is it?

Many attempts have been made to define this crime, mostly with no success. Various suggested definitions are catalogued by Gordon, paras. 17-01 to 17-04. None are particularly satisfactory, but the essence of the crime appears to be in the failure to account for goods or funds entrusted to the accused.

Edgar v. Mackay
1926 J.C. 94

A solicitor received instructions from clients to recover payment of a sum of money. Although the instructions had been given in August 1924, by November of that year nothing appeared to have been done and the clients cancelled the solicitor's mandate. In fact the solicitor had collected various sums of money but had not told the clients this. Meantime another solicitor was instructed who discovered what had happened. In November 1924 the clients wrote to the original solicitor saying that if they did not receive some sort of accounting from him, they would refer the matter to the authorities. Subsequently repeated applications failed to produce any satisfaction and in September the following year the agent was arrested by the police. On the day of his arrest he finally accounted to his clients for the sums collected. He was convicted of embezzlement. On appeal against conviction:

LORD JUSTICE-CLERK (ALNESS): "The considerations which lead me to the conclusion that the inference of dishonesty should receive effect are these. In the first place, there is the length of time which elapsed between the cancellation of the appellant's instructions and the demand for the money which he had collected, on the one hand, and, on the other, the date of his arrest in September of the following year when he sent the money. Many months had elapsed, and nothing was done by the appellant. In point of fact, to use a colloquial expression, he received a very large amount of rope before the drastic step of arrest was taken. Apart from the length of time, there is also what I regard as a crucial fact, to which I have already incidentally adverted, that no explanation consistent with honesty was at any time, so far as I know, tabled by the appellant to those who corresponded with him or who interviewed him. There is no suggestion in the letters which he wrote, no trace in the interviews which his brother solicitor had with him in Dumfries, of any reason assigned by him, consistent with honesty, why he delayed to forward the money which belonged to Campbell & Son and which, I take it, was then in his pocket. There had been a threat by them, as I read the correspondence, of civil and criminal proceedings, and yet no explanation was offered. A further consideration which weighs with me is that no payment was made by the appellant until after his arrest. To these facts I would add that the discovery that he had collected the money at all was made, not in consequence of anything which he communicated to Campbell & Son, but from the investigations of others. I confess that, for myself, I should like to have known what the appellant said in the witness-box. The case discloses that he was examined. I presume that he offered some explanation of his conduct. I think I am bound to assume, from the conclusion which the learned Sheriff reached, that he rejected any explanation which may have been given. If he had accepted it, it is inconceivable that the learned Sheriff could have reached the conclusion which he did. Therefore, I treat the case as if it contained the statement that any explanation, assuming it to have been given, was not accepted by the judge.

In these circumstances it appears to me that there is no competing theory in this case, as it comes before us, to displace what I regard as the inevitable conclusion from the facts found by the Sheriff that the money in question was fraudulently appropriated by the appellant. It may be impossible to state—indeed, it is generally impossible to state in such cases—the precise date at which that misappropriation took place. Nor is it necessary. It would be unfortunate in the interests of justice if the law were otherwise. Therefore, deciding the case, as we must do, on the facts before us, it appears to me that the only reasonable conclusion from these facts is that the appellant was guilty of the offence with which he was charged. In these circumstances, I am of opinion that the question of law stated by the learned Sheriff should be answered in the affirmative."

Appeal dismissed.

d.   Distinguishing theft from embezzlement

This has never been an easy task for the Scots courts and still gives rise to problems today. Gordon at paras. 17-05 to 17-23 discusses the various criteria which have been used to distinguish the two crimes, some of which arise more as a matter of sociological "labelling" rather than as a matter of law. The subject is also made more difficult by the fact that Hume's ideas concerning custodiers and possessors persisted well into the 19th century.

1.   **Cathrine Crossgrove or Bradley**
(1850) J. Shaw 301

The accused was a pawnbroker charged with theft of articles pledged with her.

LORD MONCREIFF: "There is no doubt that this case must turn on somewhat nice distinctions; and the cases which have been already decided, as to whether any particular *species facti* amount to embezzlement or theft, are sufficiently puzzling; but it appears to me that this case differs from that of the watchmaker, which has been cited in argument, and the analogous one of money being entrusted to a messenger, to be carried to the bank, and appropriated by the party on his way. In the present case, the party who pledged the property, by that act not merely gave a right of possession, but a title to the goods themselves, which, by lapse of time, became absolute, and enabled the party to sell, and give a valid right to all the world."

LORD IVORY: "There is a great distinction between a lawful possession *de facto*, and a legal possession *proprio jure*. Here the latter was the right which the prisoner is alleged to have had, and it seems to me impossible to draw any distinction between the appropriation of the goods pledged, before the period when the sale might lawfully take place, or the proper title of the pawnbroker, and his unlawful retention of any surplus pence which might be realised thereby, over and above the amount advanced, together with interest thereon, at proper rates; yet no one would undertake to say that the latter case would be one of theft."

LORD JUSTICE-CLERK (HOPE): "Looking to the legal import of the indictment, and the nature of the contract of pledge, I think embezzlement or breach of trust is the appropriate *nomen juris* in the circumstances. It is quite different from those former cases, where only a limited and temporary custody, unaccompanied with any title of property in the things themselves, had been given, for the purpose of having something done by the party who committed the offence. In this case a contract is set forth. It is for breach of that contract that the prisoner is charged; and I am of opinion that the criminal violation of a contract of trust constitutes the offence known by us as breach of trust or embezzlement, and not that of theft."

Charge held irrelevant.

NOTES

Despite these remarks by the judges, the charge of theft was almost certainly correct. For a critique of the decision, see Gordon, para. 17-08.

Where someone has custody of an object for a limited time and purpose only there may be a choice of charges: but appropriation which has taken place after the accused has obtained the object for a short time or limited purpose may be theft, at least if this is libelled in the charge.

2. William Taylor Keith
(1875) 3 Couper 125

The accused was an auctioneer who was instructed to sell a piano at a private house. If this was unsuccessful, he was entrusted with it to sell it at a public roup. He was charged that having failed to sell it at the house he took it to an auction room and "thus having obtained the temporary custody of it, he pawned it, appropriated the money thus realised and stole it."

LORD ARDMILLAN: "In order relevantly to have charged theft of the piano, the indictment would require to have set forth that the custody given was for some specific purpose, and for a short time. It is not sufficient to be able to gather that it was so, or may have been so, by implication from the terms of the charge. Where the custody is not for a short time and not for a specified purpose, and the article is appropriated, a sort of trust is constituted, and the crime is breach of trust. But where the custody is for a short period and for a specified purpose, as, for example, to take a box to a railway station, the crime is theft: and so also where the purpose of the custody is such as to exclude all separate possession, such as a butler in charge of wine, or a shepherd of sheep, the appropriation is clearly theft. But in order to libel either crime relevantly, the prosecutor must set forth specifically the elements which go to constitute and to distinguish the crime. As these are not here stated, I think the objection to this charge of theft, as distinguished from the alternative charge of breach of trust, must be sustained."

Charge held irrelevant.

NOTES

This is a rather unsatisfactory case, especially since it is easy to argue that albeit the piano was "entrusted" to the accused, this *was* for the limited purpose of sale.

In any event, the whole aura surrounding the distinction between the two crimes is pervaded by the consideration that one should not convict persons in responsible positions with the lowly crime of theft.

3. H.M. Advocate v. Laing
(1891) 2 White 572

The accused was a solicitor who received sums from a client for the purpose of discharging a heritable security. He failed to carry out his instructions and paid some of the money into his own bank account. He was charged with theft.

LORD KINCAIRNEY (in charging the jury): "It was contended that an agent could not be said to steal or embezzle his client's money if he employed it in carrying on his business, as, for example, in making a payment to or on behalf of another client. I do not assent to that argument. There seems no doubt that if an agent receives money on behalf of a client, and uses it for his own purposes, he is guilty of theft or of embezzlement, whether he lodges it in his bank account, or employs it in his business, or pays it on account of other clients. But in any case there must be proof of his dishonest and felonious intention. . . .

If one receives money merely to pass it on to another, his crime, if he feloniously appropriates the money, would be theft. If he gets it under an obligation to account for the like amount, the felonious appropriation would be embezzlement. The distinction nowadays is rather technical than substantial."

Accused convicted of embezzlement.

NOTES

But Laing did not even begin to carry out his instructions. Should not he have been convicted of theft as libelled?

If someone is given a power of administration over a fund or goods entrusted to him, then a misappropriation concomitant with the accused exceeding his mandate appears to be theft and not embezzlement.

4. Kent v. H.M. Advocate
1950 J.C. 38

LORD JUSTICE-GENERAL (COOPER): "The first charge related to a transaction (or series of transactions) too complicated for brief summary. It is sufficient to say that it was concerned with the disposal of a consignment of apple puree, valued at over £500, consigned to the Danish Bacon Company in Edinburgh by a firm in Northern Ireland and eventually sold by the appellant to a third party. The charge was brought when it later transpired that the price had neither been paid nor accounted for by the appellant. . . .

I pass on to the point which was the subject of keen argument, and it has occasioned me much perplexity. In drafting the indictment the Procurator-fiscal, whose difficulties in disentangling an obscure series of business deals must have been grave, provided as a narrative to charge one a statement to the effect that the appellant had been authorised by the Danish Bacon Company and by the Northern Ireland firm to dispose of the consignment in question; and it was on the footing that he had been so authorised that the charge of embezzlement of the proceeds was then built up. It now appears—I shall not say by express concession from the Crown, but rather from an examination of the evidence—that no support, or no sufficient support, can be found for any inference that the appellant was ever authorised either by the one company or by the other or by anyone else to dispose of the consignment. Accordingly, since the indictment went to the jury in the form indicated, and as their attention was pointedly directed to this very matter in the course of the Sheriff-substitute's charge, the verdict as returned is not supported by the evidence.

But that is not necessarily the end of the matter in view of the duty laid upon us by section 3 (2) of the Criminal Appeal (Scotland) Act, [1926,] and our over-riding obligation not to sustain appeals unless we are satisfied that there has been a substantial miscarriage of justice. It is at that stage of the matter that my difficulties have chiefly arisen. I am bound to say that from my reading of the evidence the impression conveyed is that the appellant is in a dilemma in this respect, that the facts proved mean either that he stole the consignment or that he embezzled its proceeds. But he was never charged with stealing the consignment. The Solicitor-General maintained with force that from the verdict which they returned the jury must have been satisfied on four points—(first) that the consignment never at any time belonged to the appellant; (second) that he disposed of it; (third) that he was authorised to dispose of it; and (fourth) that he failed to account for the price; and he maintained that, even on the assumption (which I have indicated is my own view) that the third of the propositions was not justified by the evidence, nevertheless, the remaining three propositions sufficed to satisfy the requirements of section 3 (2) that the jury must have been satisfied of facts which led to the conclusion that the appellant was guilty of another offence, to wit, theft. He asked us therefore to substitute for the conviction of embezzlement of the proceeds a conviction of theft of the consignment."

> Conviction for embezzlement quashed: motion to substitute verdict of guilty of theft refused, 'as unwarranted in the circumstances.'

NOTES

So embezzlement seems to be restricted to cases where the goods or money appropriated are in the accused's possession lawfully, where he has started upon a course of dealing with them and where he has carried out some unauthorised action with the goods or money; provided also there is some dishonest intention to appropriate.

e. Mens rea of embezzlement

This is generally thought of as being the intention to appropriate money or goods due to another without his consent. The absence of proof of this will provide a defence.

Allenby v. H.M. Advocate
1938 J.C. 55

LORD JUSTICE-CLERK (AITCHISON): "The appellant was tried and convicted in the Sheriff Court at Aberdeen on a charge of embezzlement. He was managing director of a company called Benjamin Allenby, Limited, and as such he acted as fish salesman for a number of trawl owners. It is common ground that he failed to account to four of these trawl owners in respect of sums amounting in all to upwards of £900. The practice of the appellant was to pay all the moneys he received from purchasers of fish into a common fund. I do not think that there was anything wrong in that, because, as was explained to us by Mr. Burnet, a purchaser might on the same morning buy from half a dozen trawl owners, and make out one cheque to the appellant as fish salesman, and, therefore, the keeping of a common fund in the first instance was perfectly right and proper. The method of the appellant was then to pay out by means of his own cheques on the common fund to the different owners the sums due to them from time to time. It is in evidence that the books of the appellant were kept with scrupulous accuracy. Nothing was concealed. Not a single penny went into appellant's own pocket, except in the sense that he utilised the common fund for the purpose of making disbursements on behalf of all the trawl owners. It was part of his own business to make such disbursements. What happened was this—there is really no dispute about the facts—that he used some of the moneys that belonged to the four trawl owners in question to make advances to other trawl owners, whose moneys he applied when necessary in the same way. Now, there is little doubt that strictly speaking that was an irregular thing to do. It would have been better for the appellant to have kept separate accounts, and, although the moneys went into a common fund in the first instance, to have apportioned it and paid it over with the least possible delay, charging disbursements, when made, each against its own proper account. But while this would have been strictly the proper course to follow, I cannot find in what the appellant did any evidence of embezzlement; but, as we have not gone fully into the facts and as there is a clear ground of judgment in the terms of the charge, I say no more about that.

When the learned Sheriff came to charge the jury he said this (I read one passage only): 'If Mr Allenby did choose to act as fish salesman for those other ships, and if he did utilise moneys belonging to the four ships mentioned in the indictment for the purpose of meeting liabilities of those other ships, I must direct you that that in law amounts to embezzlement.' In my judgment, that was a misdirection. The passage I have read was calculated to convey to the minds of the jury that it was enough that the moneys had been used in the way they were by the appellant. I respectfully think that was a misdirection. Without laying down that a dishonest intention may not be inferred from an immixing of moneys, I think that this case was so exceptional that the jury should have been told explicitly that, unless they were satisfied that the appellant had acted dishonestly, they were bound in law to acquit him of the charge. No such direction was given. I think it was vitally important that it should have been given, having regard to two facts in the case—(1) that there appears to have been some kind of practice prevailing in the fish business in Aberdeen not dissimilar to the practice followed by the appellant; and (2) because the only accountant called in the case who had investigated the appellant's books said, not merely that they were kept with scrupulous accuracy and that nothing was concealed, but also that he could find no evidence of dishonest intention at all, and he had expressed that view to the proper authorities. When the leading witness for the Crown gives evidence of that kind one would require very clear and strong evidence before the Court would be justified in disregarding it; but, as I have already said the whole evidence is not before us, and it is enough for the disposal of this case that the direction given by the learned Sheriff was inadequate. On that ground I move your Lordships that the appeal be allowed, and the conviction and sentence set aside."

LORD WARK: "Speaking for myself, I do not think that there ever can be a conviction of embezzlement unless the jury find evidence of dishonest intention, although evidence of dishonest intention may be afforded either by acts which are deliberate or by acts which are reckless. . . .

I do not think it is necessary to make any reference to the authorities which were quoted to us except to say that the present case is one in which it was, in my opinion, much more necessary to direct the jury's attention to the question of honesty or dishonesty than either in the case of *Duncan* J. Shaw 270, or in the case of *Lee* 12 R.(J.) 2, 5 Coup. 492. In the case of *Lee* there was an admission that the accused had immixed funds of his client with his own and that he had used them for his own purposes, and in the case of *Duncan* there was a clear admission that the accused had used money with which he was entrusted for the purpose of paying his own private debts. And yet in both these cases it was thought necessary by the learned judge who presided at the trial to point out that it was a matter for the jury to consider whether the accused acted honestly or dishonestly. In this case I have no doubt, as I have said before, that that question should have been put. Towards the end of his charge the Sheriff came very near to putting it, because he said to the jury, 'You will consider whether or not the man did what he did, believing he was entitled to do it.' But then, that part of the charge is just as defective as the other to which your Lordship has referred, because the Sheriff did not go on to direct the jury, as he ought to have done, as to what the consequence would be of taking one view or the other of what the accused believed."

Conviction quashed.

NOTES

But was Allenby's defence a simple denial of dishonesty, or a specific claim that he was entitled to act as he did? Perhaps both.

CHAPTER 14

FRAUD

In each case of common law fraud the Crown must prove that the accused achieved some definite practical result as a result of a false pretence. Fraud is distinguished from the separate crime of uttering by the fact that in the latter, all that is required is that some article, in practice usually a document, is passed off as genuine towards the prejudice of another person, whether or not actual prejudice is suffered.

a. The false pretence

1. **Tapsell v. Prentice**
(1910) 6 Adam 354

A hawker was convicted on a complaint which set forth that "within the shop at . . . occupied by J. McB., you did assume the name of Mrs. G. and did pretend that you were manageress of a company of travelling gipsies who were about to encamp in the neighbourhood for several weeks, and that you intended to purchase provisions for said gipsies from the said J. McB. to the value of £30 sterling or thereby, and relying solely on the truth of said representation did thus induce him to purchase from you a rug in excess of its proper value, and you did thus defraud the said J. McB." She appealed to the High Court by bill of suspension.

LORD JUSTICE-CLERK (MACDONALD): "I am quite clear that the bill of suspension must be sustained without making any comment on, or proposing to detract from the authority of, any case that has been quoted to us. I do not think these cases have any bearing upon the present case. The act that is charged here is selling a rug in excess of its value, which is a thing that is done any day, and is not a criminal offence. Then it is a curious form of charge to say 'in excess of its value,' when we are not told what the prosecutor thought was the true value of the rug, nor what was the price paid. I think the charge is hopelessly irrelevant, and that is really sufficient to dispose of the case.

But further, it is said that this person is a fraudulent person and assumed a false name and represented that she was manageress of a company of travelling gipsies who were about to encamp in the neighbourhood, and that she intended to purchase provisions from the complainer, and did thus induce him to purchase the rug. Now, the person who bought the rug is presumably as capable of estimat-

401

ing its value as anyone else, and though, no doubt, the suggestion is that the object of his purchasing it was to keep the gipsies, as it were, thirled to his shop, yet misstatements of that kind do not amount to falsehood, fraud, and wilful imposition in the criminal sense. The cases cited to us were all cases of misrepresentation about the article sold. In the horse case, *Turnbull* v. *Stuart,* 25 R. (J.) 78, the purpose was to get a better price for the horse by representing that it had been hunted by Mr and Mrs Younger, well-known people. There is nothing said here to suggest that this woman made any misrepresentations about the rug or its value. I therefore think that on this ground also the conviction must be quashed."

LORD ARDWALL: "Two obvious criticisms can be made on this complaint. In the first place, there is no statement that any money passed, and so far as the complaint goes the rug said to have been sold may never have been paid for to this day. Secondly, we are not told what the proper value of the rug was, nor how much in excess of that was the price agreed upon. That, again, seems to me to be a defect in this complaint, apart from other things. But the most serious defect is the want of any statement that there was any fraudulent misrepresentation regarding the article sold. It is said that the accused made certain representations about herself and a gang of gipsies which she was taking about the country. These are just the ordinary lies which people tell when they want to induce credulous members of the public to purchase goods, or to do something for them. But these representations are not directly connected with the rug, which may have been a perfectly good one. Now, there can be no crime in such a sale as is here alleged unless the fraudulent misrepresentations relate directly to the articles to be sold. I am therefore of opinion that all the allegations of misrepresentation made in this complaint are irrelevant, and that the conviction must be set aside."

LORD SALVESEN: "I am very far from commending the conduct of this accused, but I agree that there is no relevant charge. The complaint should at least have contained a statement that the complainer not merely purchased the rug but paid the accused for it. If there was only a purchase without payment, it could never be said that this accused got any advantage, or that the purchaser suffered any injury by her false pretences."

Conviction quashed.

NOTES

This case illustrates the difficulties facing the common law in relation to business dealings, where the spectre of criminality is hard to find. With regard to advertisements in the normal course of business, dealers are far more likely to fall foul of the Trade Descriptions Acts than the common law of fraud, unless there is some clear element of dishonesty.

2. Strathern v. Fogal
1922 J.C. 73

A father and his sons were charged with (1) having entered into a fraudulent scheme for obtaining from the tenants of shops owned by the father payments for a continuation of their tenancy, by falsely representing that the shops had been let to the sons, and that, unless the payments were made, the tenants would be ejected; and (2) having made returns to the City Assessor which did not include grassums received from the tenants of the shops, intending that the figures thus returned should enter the valuation roll, as they did; and with thus having defrauded the rating authorities of the rates and taxes assessable in respect of the grassums. The sheriff-substitute dismissed the complaint as irrelevant. On appeal by the procurator-fiscal:

LORD HUNTER: "I have formed a clear opinion, agreeing in this with the Sheriff-substitute, that the complaint sets forth no specific and relevant averments of criminal fraud committed against the tenants of the accused Myer Fogal. According to the complaint, the accused and three of his sons, two of whom are also charged with the offence, 'having entered into a scheme to fraudulently obtain from the tenants of said shops payments of money in respect of said tenants being permitted to continue in the tenancy of the shops already occupied by them, or to obtain a grant of new lets of such shops, by pretending to them that a *bona fide* let of said respective shops had been entered into between you Myer Fogal, as proprietor, and you Harris Fogal, Lion Fogal, presently of Bleicherweg, Zurich, Switzerland, and you Joseph Fogal, as tenants, and that unless said payments were made said tenants would be ejected,. . . did . . . fraudulently obtain from the respective tenants specified in the second column, in respect of the lets of the shops specified in the third column, the amounts respectively specified in the fourth column, all of the first schedule hereto annexed, which sums you forthwith appropriated to your own uses.' As I read the complaint at first, I thought the suggestion was that the accused Myer Fogal was not entitled to exact any premium for the renewal of the leases or the grant of new leases. Some, if not all, of the members of the jury might think that was a natural meaning to attach to the words. But it was admitted that the accused Myer Fogal was quite entitled to bargain with his tenants for the payment of a sum of money as a condition of their being allowed to remain in occupation, or to get from new tenants a higher rent than he had obtained from old tenants, and to obtain that increase by receiving payment of a grassum. Nor do I see that it would have been any crime on the part of Myer Fogal and his sons to arrange that the sons should be put in possession, if the tenants refused to agree to the landlord's terms. Apart from any specific arrangement, what crime would have been committed by threat to dispossess? It was contended that the crime was committed by pretending that a *bona fide* let of the shops had been entered into between the parties. There is no specification of the language employed to create a belief in the minds of the intending tenants of the existence of, or terms of, the lease. I do not, however, think that a false statement by the parties accused upon this matter renders them liable to be prosecuted for the crime of defrauding the tenants, whatever civil rights might thereby be conferred upon the latter for reduction of the leases or damages. The misrepresentation, if made, did not in any real sense affect the subject of the bargain, but was essentially collateral, though it might be material and induce the contract.

The appellant relied upon the authority of *Hood* v. *Young,* 1 Irv. 236, and *Turnbull* v. *Stuart,* 25 R. (J.) 78, 2 Adam 536. In the former of these cases Hood and another were charged with fraud 'in so far as they fraudulently and feloniously formed the design to expose two unsound horses or mares belonging to them, or one or other of them, to public sale, and, with a view to obtain higher prices for them, fraudulently to represent that they were the property of a farmer, who had worked them for a year bygone or thereby, and that they were sound and good workers, and only parted with because the owner was about to emigrate.' These statements were repeated by the auctioneer to intending purchasers who attended the sale. The accused was convicted and a note of suspension refused. This case was followed in the later case of *Turnbull,* where a false and fraudulent description of horses had been made to an auctioneer which was inserted in the sale catalogue. Both these cases were before the Court in *Tapsell* v. *Prentice,* 1911 S.C. (J.) 67, 6 Adam 354 [noted *ante*]. . . . That case appears to me to be authority for our holding that the complaint, so far as it charges the accused with defrauding the tenants, is irrelevant.

As regards the alternative charge, I am unable to agree with the Sheriff-substitute. The alleged offence is that the accused defrauded the rating authorities of a large sum of money by supplying false information to the Assessor as to the return from the property. It is also said that the false information was supplied with the intention that it should be inserted in the Valuation-roll; and that it was so inserted, with the result that the accused escaped payment of rates for which they were, or at all events the accused Myer Fogal was, liable. I am of opinion that the facts averred in the complaint, if proved, establish a common law offence."

First charge held irrelevant;
Second charge relevant.

NOTES

So the first charge in *Strathern* v. *Fogal* really concerned an objectionable but non-criminal course of action, while the second charge was clearly fraud. But the finding of Lord Hunter that the statements made by the accused in the first charge were merely collateral has been criticised: see Gordon, para. 18-28. There was still a pretence which was false; and it still had a practical result. On the question of collateral statements, see also *Richards* v. *H.M. Advocate, post.*

3. Richards v. H.M. Advocate
1971 J.C. 29; 1971 S.L.T. 115

The accused was convicted of fraud on an indictment which charged: ". . . that having formed a fraudulent scheme to induce the Corporation of the City of Edinburgh to dispone in feu the property known as Hillwood House and policies in Corstorphine, Edinburgh, by means of false pretences as to the party desirous of obtaining such feu and the purposes for which it was desired you did in pursuance of said scheme (1) between 1st February 1968 and 1st February 1969, both dates inclusive, in Edinburgh, cause Walter Erfyl Burns, [and others] to pretend to the said Corporation in verbal and written communications that said Walter Erfyl Burns desired to purchase for the private residential use of himself and his family the foresaid property . . . and did thereby induce the said Corporation on 8th January 1969 to make an offer to feu the said subjects to the said Walter Erfyl Burns for a price of £4,000 which offer was accepted on behalf of the said Walter Erfyl Burns on 21st January 1969, the truth being that the said Walter Erfyl Burns had no intention that the said subjects should be used for the private residence of himself and his family and that you intended to acquire the said subjects for your own purposes and you did fraudulently induce the said Corporation to do an act which they would not otherwise have done, namely to accept the said Walter Erfyl Burns as the genuine offerer to purchase in feu said subjects for the private residential use of himself and his family and to enter into missives with him thereanent."

The accused sought leave to appeal against his conviction on the ground, *inter alia*, that the indictment was irrelevant in that: (i) the facts set forth in support of the first charge did not constitute a crime known to the law; (ii) the said misrepresentation did not relate to a past or present fact but to future intention; (iii) the alleged misrepresentation set forth in the first charge related to a matter collateral to the contract alleged to have been induced.

LORD JUSTICE-CLERK (GRANT): "The substance of [the first] two reasons is that, as the misrepresentation libelled relates not to a past or present fact but to a future intention, the charge discloses no crime known to the law of Scotland. It seems to me that 'future intention' is an elliptical and somewhat ambiguous phrase. Assuming, for the moment, that the misrepresentation libelled is of intention only (and the Crown do not concede this), it is one of *present* intention as to future conduct. This, I think, was how [counsel for the appellant] treated the matter and I shall do likewise. I shall also proceed meantime on the basis (which again is disputed by the Crown) that there is no difference in principle between a misrepresentation by A of his own intention and the causing by A of a misrepresentation to be made as to the intention of a third party.

So far as I can trace, the appellant's argument on this branch of the case derives no support from Hume or Alison, neither of whom appears to draw a distinction between misrepresentation of a 'fact' and misrepresentation of 'intention.' It is a distinction, however, which was made in *Hall* (1881) 4 Couper 438, where Lord Young held an indictment libelling fraud irrelevant because the misrepresentations averred related not to past or present facts but to intention as to future conduct. A new indictment, framed to meet this objection, later came before the High Court on a different point, but at that stage no comment was made on Lord Young's ruling on the earlier indictment. [See *Hall* at p. 500.] Then we come to an *obiter dictum* of Lord Ashmore in *Strathern* v. *Fogal,* 1922 J.C. 73, at p. 82, to the effect that the complaint (which had been held to be irrelevant for another reason) was also irrelevant because the false pretences alleged related to future conduct. Finally, the appellant relied strongly on the case of *Regina* v. *Dent* [1955] 2 Q.B. 590, which, if it represents the law of Scotland, is directly in point here.

In my opinion, however, it does not and, despite the reasoning of Devlin, J. (as he then was), I can see no reason in principle why it should: for it seems to me that a man's present intention is just as much a fact as his name or his occupation or the size of his bank balance. Quite apart from general principle, however, we find as far back as 1849 the case of *Chisholm,* J. Shaw 241, in which Lord Justice-Clerk Hope sat with Lords Wood and Ivory. The main question in that case related to the relevancy of a cumulative charge of fraud and theft on the same *species facti*. There was a further question, however, as to the relevancy of the fraud charge *per se*. The misrepresentation libelled was that the accused had promised to pay the price of certain goods at specified places at a future time. On the amendment of the libel (at the suggestion of the Court) by the insertion of a statement that the accused had entered upon the transactions with the intention of not paying for the goods, the libel was held relevant. This decision seems to me to be directly in point here as does that in the later case of *Macleod* v. *Mactavish* (1897) 2 Adam 354, (1897) 5 S.L.T. 150. There the sole misrepresentation was that the accused intended to remain in his employer's service for another half year. On a bill of suspension being taken the complaint was held to be relevant and the conviction upheld. One may also take into account the 'board and lodging' cases (*cf.* Macdonald, at p. 56) and the specimen form of complaint set out in the Summary Jurisdiction (Scotland) Act, 1908, and repeated with one small amendment in the Second Schedule to the consolidating Act of 1954 thus: 'You did obtain from C.D. board and lodgings to the value of 12s. without paying and intending not to pay therefor.' (The phrase 'and intending not' was originally 'or intending.') If the appellant is right, it is difficult to see how such a complaint could be relevant. We were also referred to Gordon on Criminal Law (1st ed.), in which the authorities are reviewed at pp. 546 to 548. His conclusion that 'a statement of present intention as to future conduct can ground a charge of fraud' is, in my opinion, fully justified by authority.

For these reasons I am of opinion that subheads (i) and (ii) of the first ground of appeal must fail.

In his argument on subhead (iii) [counsel for the appellant] relied mainly on the cases of *Tapsell* v. *Prentice*, (1911) 6 Adam 354 and *Strathern* v. *Fogal*. On their facts, however, these cases are clearly distinguishable from the present. No doubt there are many cases where the future use of heritable subjects is of no moment to the seller and may be a matter extraneous to the actual contract for the sale of those subjects. Here, however, on the face of the indictment (and I am not, of course, concerned at this stage with what may or may not have been established in evidence) the future use of the subjects was of crucial importance and was an essential governing factor in the completion of the contract for the sale of those same subjects. It cannot, in my opinion, be treated merely as a matter collateral to the contract."

> The indictment was held relevant and grounds of appeal (i)—(iii) were rejected, but conviction quashed on other grounds.

Richards illustrates just how wide the Scots law of fraud has become and how it compares to the convoluted statutory provisions contained in the Theft Acts of 1968 and 1978 in England. The common law in Scotland is certainly flexible enough to deal with situations such as "cheque-card frauds" which have perplexed courts elsewhere. Two such cases have recently been examined in England: in *R.* v. *Kovacs* [1974] 1 W.L.R. 370, an accused had presented to various suppliers her cheque card along with cheques which she knew would not be honoured. She was convicted under the then existing s. 16 (1) of the Theft Act 1968 of obtaining a pecuniary advantage by deception. It was argued that she had deceived not the bank, but the person to whom she had presented the cheques. However, the Court of Appeal held that she had obtained the pecuniary advantage for herself from the bank in increasing her overdraft by inducing the suppliers to believe she was entitled to use the cheque card when she was not. In *R.* v. *Charles* [1977] A.C. 177 the House of Lords held that when the drawer of a cheque accepted in exchange for goods, services or cash used a cheque card, he made to the payee a representation that he had the actual authority of the bank to enter on its behalf into the contract expressed on the card that it would honour the cheque on presentment for payment.

4. D.P.P. v. Ray
[1974] A.C. 370

An accused person and four friends went to a Chinese restaurant intending to have a meal there and pay for it. After eating the main course they decided not to pay for it but remained until the waiter went out of the room. They then ran from the room. They were convicted of obtaining a pecuniary advantage by deception contrary to s. 16 (1) of the Theft Act 1968. By s. 15 (4) of that Act "deception" is defined as "any deception . . . by words or conduct . . . including a deception as to the present intentions of the person using the deception." The Divisional Court quashed the conviction and the D.P.P. appealed to the House of Lords.

LORD MACDERMOTT: "My Lords, the respondent with four other young men entered a restaurant on the evening of September 30, 1971, and he and three of his companions then ordered a meal. When this order was given the respondent intended to pay for his meal. The meal was duly served and there were no complaints. But after the respondent and the others had eaten it they had a discussion and decided to run out of the restaurant without paying. Some 10 minutes later they did so while the waiter was absent in the kitchen. By then they had been almost an hour in the restaurant and, until they ran out, had maintained the demeanour of ordinary customers. . . .

The magistrates' court found that the respondent had practised a deception, and that, having made himself liable for a debt in respect of a meal, had by his deception dishonestly evaded payment. The court accordingly found the case proved, convicted the respondent and fined him £1. It subsequently stated a case for the High Court which set out the facts and findings I have mentioned and asked whether, upon a true construction of section 16 of the Theft Act 1968, the respondent was rightly convicted. . . .

To prove the charge against the respondent the prosecution had to show that he (i) by a deception (ii) had dishonestly (iii) obtained for himself (iv) a pecuniary advantage. . . .

No issue therefore arises on the ingredients I have numbered (iii) and (iv). Nor is there any controversy about ingredient (ii). If the respondent obtained a pecuniary advantage as described he undoubtedly did so dishonestly. The case is thus narrowed to ingredient (i) and that leaves two questions for consideration. First, do the facts justify a finding that the respondent practised a deception? And secondly, if he did, was his evasion of the debt obtained by that deception?

The first of these questions involves nothing in the way of words spoken or written. If there was deception on the part of the respondent it was by his conduct in the course of an extremely common form of transaction which, because of its nature, leaves much to be implied from conduct. Another circumstance affecting the ambit of this question lies in the fact that, looking only to the period after the meal had been eaten and the respondent and his companions had decided to evade payment, there is nothing that I can find in the discernible conduct of the respondent which would suffice in itself to show that he was then practising a deception. No doubt he and the others stayed in their seats until the waiter went into the kitchen and while doing so gave all the appearance of ordinary customers. But, in my opinion, nothing in this or in anything else which occurred *after* the change of intention went far enough to afford proof of deception. The picture, as I see it, presented by this last stage of the entire transaction, is simply that of a group which had decided to evade payment and were awaiting the opportunity to do so.

There is, however, no sound reason that I can see for restricting the inquiry to this final phase. One cannot, so to speak, draw a line through the transaction at the point where the intention changed and search for evidence of deception only in what happened before that or only in what happened after that. In my opinion the transaction must for this purpose be regarded in its entirety, beginning with the respondent entering the restaurant and ordering his meal and ending with his running out without paying. The different stages of the transaction are all linked and it would be quite unrealistic to treat them in isolation.

Starting, then, at the beginning one finds in the conduct of the respondent in entering and ordering his meal evidence that he impliedly represented that he had the means and the intention of paying for it before he left. That the respondent did make such a representation was not in dispute and in the absence of evidence to the contrary it would be difficult to reach a different conclusion. If this representation had then been false and matters had proceeded thereafter as they did (but without any change of intention) a conviction for the offence charged would, in my view, have had ample material to support it. But as the representation when originally made in this case was not false there was therefore no deception at that point. Then the meal is served and eaten and the intention to evade the debt replaces the intention to pay. Did this change of mind produce a deception?

My Lords, in my opinion it did. I do not base this conclusion merely on the change of mind that had occurred, for that in itself was not manifest at the time and did not amount to 'conduct' on the part of the respondent. But it did falsify the representation which had already been made because that initial representation must, in my view, be regarded not as something then spent and past but as a continuing representation which remained alive and operative and had already resulted in the respondent and his defaulting companions being taken on trust and treated as ordinary, honest customers. It covered the whole transaction up to and including payment and must therefore, in my opinion, be considered as continuing and still active at the time of the change of mind. When that happened, with the respondent taking (as might be expected) no step to bring the change to notice, he practised, to my way of thinking, a deception just as real and just as dishonest as would have been the case if his intention all along had been to go without paying."

LORD MORRIS OF BORTH-Y-GEST: "It is clear that the respondent went into the restaurant in the capacity of an ordinary customer. Such a person by his conduct in ordering food impliedly says: 'If you will properly provide me with that which I order, I will pay you the amount for which I will become liable.' In some restaurants a customer might have a special arrangement as to payment. A customer might on occasion make a special arrangement. Had there been any basis for suggesting that the respondent was not under obligation to discharge his debt before he left the restaurant that would have been recorded in the case stated. All the facts as found make it unlikely that it would have been possible even to contend that in this case the debt incurred was other than one which was to be discharged by a cash payment made before leaving.

If someone goes to a restaurant and, having no means whatsover to pay and no credit arrangement, obtains a meal for which he knows he cannot pay and for which he has no intentions of paying he will be guilty of an offence under section 15 of the Theft Act. Such a person would obtain the meal by deception. By his conduct in ordering the meal he would be representing to the restaurant that he had the intention of paying whereas he would not have had any such intention. In the present case when the respondent ordered his meal he impliedly made to the waiter the ordinary representation of the ordinary customer that it was his intention to pay. He induced the waiter to believe that that was his intention. Furthermore, on the facts as found it is clear that all concerned (the waiter, the respondent and his companions) proceeded on the basis that an ordinary customer would pay his bill before leaving. The waiter would not have accepted the order or served the meal had there not been the implied representation.

The situation may perhaps be unusual where a customer honestly orders a meal and therefore indicates his honest intention to pay but thereafter forms a dishonest intention of running away without paying if he can. Inherent in an original honest representation of an intention to pay there must surely be a representation that such intention will continue. . . .

It was said in the Divisional Court that a deception under section 16 should not be found unless an accused has actively made a representation by words or conduct which representation is found to be false. But if there was an original representation (as, in my view, there was when the meal was ordered) it was a representation that was intended to be and was a continuing representation. It continued to operate on the mind of the waiter. It became false and it became a deliberate deception. The prosecution do not say that the deception consisted in not informing the waiter of the change of mind; they say that the deception consisted in continuing to represent to the waiter that there was an intention to pay before leaving.

On behalf of the respondent it was contended that no deception had been practised. It was accepted that when the meal was ordered there was a representation by the respondent that he would pay but it was contended that once the meal was served there was no longer any representation but that there was merely an obligation to pay a debt: it was further argued that thereafter there was no deception because there was no obligation in the debtor to inform his creditor that payment was not to be made. I cannot accept these contentions. They ignore the circumstances that the representation that was made was a continuing one: its essence was that an intention to pay would continue until payment was made: by its very nature it could not cease to operate as a representation unless some new arrangement was made."

LORD REID (dissenting): "If a person induces a supplier to accept an order for goods or services by a representation of fact, that representation must be held to be a continuing representation lasting until the goods or services are supplied. Normally it would not last any longer. A restaurant supplies both goods and services: it supplies food and drink and the facilities for consuming them. Customers normally remain for a short time after consuming their meal, and I think that it can properly be held that any representation express or implied made with a view of obtaining a meal lasts until the departure of the customers in the normal course.

In my view, where a new customer orders a meal in a restaurant, he must be held to make an implied representation that he can and will pay for it before he leaves. In the present case the accused must be held to have made such a representation. But when he made it it was not dishonest: he thought he would be able to borrow money from one of his companions.

After the meal had been consumed the accused changed his mind. He decided to evade payment. So he and his companions remained seated where they were for a short time until the waiter left the room and then ran out of the restaurant.

Did he thereby commit an offence against section 16 of the Theft Act 1968? It is admitted, and rightly admitted, that if the waiter had not been in the room when he changed his mind and he had immediately run out he would not have committed an offence. Why does his sitting still for a short time in the presence of the waiter make all the difference?

The section requires evasion of his obligation to pay. That is clearly established by his running out without paying. Secondly, it requires dishonesty: that is admitted. There would have been both evasion and dishonesty if he had changed his mind and run out while the waiter was absent.

The crucial question in this case is whether there was evasion 'by any deception.' Clearly there could be no deception until the accused changed his mind. I agree with the following quotation from the judgment of Buckley J. in *In re London and Globe Finance Corporation Ltd.* [1903] 1 Ch. 728, 732: 'To deceive is, I apprehend, to induce a man to believe that a thing is true which is false, and which the person practising the deceit knows or believes to be false.'

So the accused, after he changed his mind, must have done something intended to induce the waiter to believe that he still intended to pay before he left. Deception, to my mind, implies something positive. It is quite true that a man intending to deceive can build up a situation in which his silence is as eloquent as an express statement. But what did the accused do here to create such a situation? He merely sat still.

It is, I think apparent from the case stated that the magistrates accepted the prosecution contention that '. . . as soon as the intent to evade payment was formed and the appellant still posed as an ordinary customer the deception had been made.' The magistrates stated that they were of opinion that '. . . having changed his mind as regards payment, by remaining in the restaurant for a further 10 minutes as an ordinary customer who was likely to order a sweet or coffee, the appellant practised a deception.'

I cannot read that as a finding that after he changed his mind he intended to deceive the waiter into believing that he still intended to pay. And there is no finding that the waiter was in fact induced to believe that by anything the accused did after he changed his mind. I would infer from the case that all that he intended to do was to take advantage of the first opportunity to escape and evade his obligation to pay.

Deception is an essential ingredient of the offence. Dishonest evasion of an obligation to pay is not enough. I cannot see that there was, in fact, any more than that in this case.

I agree with the Divisional Court [1973] 1 W.L.R. 317, 323: 'His plan was totally lacking in the subtlety of deception and to argue that his remaining in the room until the coast was clear amounted to a representation to the waiter is to introduce an artificiality which should have no place in the Act.'

I would therefore dismiss this appeal."

Appeal (by a majority) allowed:
conviction confirmed.

NOTES

This English case is included here merely as an illustration of the difficulties inherent in trying to legislate on the meaning of "deception." In England, s. 16 of the Theft Act 1968 has been radically altered by the Theft Act 1978; the particular circumstances encountered in *D.P.P.* v. *Ray* would now be covered by s. 3 of the 1978 Act which creates a new offence called "making off without payment." This offence does not require proof of deception, and dishonesty need not be present at the outset of the transaction but only when the accused makes off without having paid the bill.

Ironically, this is the situation which is envisaged by the common law of Scotland, where charges alleging that the accused obtained goods or services "without paying or intending to pay" are undoubtedly relevant and frequently encountered in practice. In Scotland the argument so extensively canvassed in *Ray* as to whether it was possible to "split up the transaction" would in practice be of no validity, emphasis being focused on the end result.

b.   The practical result

Adcock v. Archibald

1925 J.C. 58

A coal miner was convicted of fraud in that he induced his employers to do something they would otherwise not have done, namely, crediting him with a bonus payment to which he was not entitled. Adcock had tampered with the "pin" on a fellow miner's hutch of coal so as fraudulently to represent that he was responsible for mining that particular coal. He appealed by bill of suspension on the broad ground that his pretence had not actually caused any loss to his employers.

LORD JUSTICE-GENERAL (CLYDE): "The grounds of suspension are to be found in the circumstance that, while in this as in other pits the miners are paid on the amount of the coal gotten by them, there is in force a minimum rate of wage per shift; and, if the wage of any particular miner, earned on the coal gotten by him, falls short of the minimum shift-wage, he receives a 'make-up' representing the difference. The suspender's point is that the increase in the amount of wage (calculated on the coal gotten by him)—which was paid to him in consequence of his having tampered with the pins—did not equal, still less exceed, the difference between the wage to which he was entitled in respect of the coal gotten and the minimum shift-wage. He did not, in short, actually succeed in getting anything more out of his employers than the minimum shift-wage, to which he was in any case entitled. On this he argues that, at most, he was guilty of no more than attempted fraud.

It is, however, a mistake to suppose that to the commission of a fraud it is necessary to prove an actual gain by the accused, or an actual loss on the part of the person alleged to be defrauded. Any definite practical result achieved by fraud is enough. In the present case, the employers were undoubtedly induced, by the fraudulent tampering with the pins, to credit the accused with wages, for coal gotten by him, to an extent to which they would not otherwise have done so. They were also induced to credit his fellow-miner with wages for coal gotten by him to a less extent than they would otherwise have done. This was the definite practical result of the accused's fraud. It is not, in my opinion, any answer to say that such result did not involve the employers in paying more than the minimum shift-wage.

I think, accordingly, that the bill of suspension should be refused."

LORD HUNTER: "I agree. A fraud may be committed, although in the result the person defrauded may not have suffered any pecuniary loss. The essence of the offence consists in inducing the person who is defrauded either to take some article he would not otherwise have taken, or to do some act he would not otherwise have done, or to become the medium of some unlawful act. In the present case I think it was relevant to aver that a wrongful act had been done by the accused, with the result that the company were induced to do something they would not otherwise have done. That being so, it is of no account to consider whether in the result the colliery company have not in fact been out of pocket."

Appeal dismissed.

NOTES

For a trenchant critique of the decision in *Adcock*, see Gordon, para. 18-16, n. The only "practical" result was the making of the entry in the books, the triviality of which is in stark contrast to the practical results commonly encountered as giving rise to charges of fraud, such as obtaining property by deception. See also *Wm. Fraser* (1847) Ark. 280 *(post)* where Lord Cockburn at p. 312 remarked that any deceit that injures and violates the rights of another is punishable.

c.   *The causal connection*

Mather v. H.M. Advocate
(1914) 7 Adam 525

The accused was charged that ". . . on 7th June 1913, having purchased and obtained delivery of nine cattle through the Farmers' Mart Limited, Brechin, within their premises at Park Road, Brechin aforesaid, you did on said date and within said premises fraudulently tender to John William Henderson, Cashier of the said Farmers' Mart Limited, a cheque for £189. 2s. 6d., in payment of the price of said cattle, which amounted to £183. 12s. 6d., and of a balance of £5. 10s., due by you on a former transaction, the said cheque being drawn by you on the West End Perth Branch of the British Linen Bank, you having no funds in said Bank to meet said cheque and well knowing that said cheque would not be honoured, and you did thus defraud the said Farmers' Mart Limited, of the sum of £183. 12s. 6d." An objection to the relevancy of the charge was repelled and the accused was convicted after trial. On appeal to the High Court:

LORD JUSTICE-GENERAL (STRATHCLYDE): "I think this indictment relevantly charged the accused with telling a falsehood, but telling a falsehood *simpliciter* is not a crime by the law of Scotland. I think it is equally clear that it does not charge the complainer with fraud according to the law of Scotland; because it appears that he actually had purchased and obtained delivery of the nine cattle, and had obtained credit for the former debt of £5. 10s., before granting the cheque in question in this case. It is not a relevant statement of a crime to say, as the indictment does, that when the accused granted the cheque he knew that he had no funds at the bank to meet the cheque. Is it then relevant to infer fraud to add that he well knew that the cheque would not be honoured? I think not.

In plain language what he did was this. Having obtained delivery of the cattle—I know not how long before the cheque was granted—he said to the seller of the cattle: 'Here is a written order upon A.B., who will pay you the money,' well knowing that A.B. would not pay the money. That was a falsehood, but it was not the means by which he either secured delivery of these cattle or obtained credit for £5. 10s. I do not for a moment doubt that the law is as stated in the cases to which we were referred, viz., that if a person obtains goods or money by issuing a cheque he having no funds in bank and knowing the cheque will not be honoured, he commits a fraud. The essence of that statement lies in the little preposition 'by,' which is lacking in this indictment. That, I think, is a fatal flaw.

Therefore I am of opinion that the conviction ought to be suspended and liberation granted."

Appeal allowed.

NOTE

So *Mather* seems to be authority for the proposition that a successful defence to fraud may be run if the pretence was not the cause of the actings of the dupe.

d. Uttering as genuine

Passing off an article (usually a document) as genuine will normally found a charge of uttering, provided it is towards the prejudice of another. But what about "false documents"?

Simon Fraser
(1859) 3 Irv. 467

LORD INGLIS: "The second charge of this indictment is in a different position; it is libelled in the major proposition as forgery, and the uttering, *as genuine,* of a forged execution. The *species facti* libelled in the minor, to support this charge, is, that the panel, being a sheriff-officer, procured one John Forrest, to *subscribe* his own name on a blank piece of paper, adding thereto the word 'witness,' that he then wrote or procured to be written, above the said subscription, an execution of citation, and then subscribed the writing with his own name, as the officer making the service, 'you the said Simon Fraser intending said execution of citation to pass for, and be received as, a genuine execution of the service of the said criminal libel, certifying that a copy thereof had been delivered by you to the said John Cunningham personally.' And further, it is libelled, that the panel 'did use and utter, *as genuine,*' this forged execution of citation, knowing the same to be forged, by delivering the same, '*as genuine,* to the said Donald Macbean,' &c.

There is here, unquestionably a charge of falsehood; and the falsehood consists in knowingly making and uttering a formal writing containing a false statement. It is stated that John Forrest *subscribed* the paper, adding the word witness to his name; and it is obvious, therefore, on the face of the indictment, that John Forrest wrote his name there, intending that it should be used as a *subscription* to some writing to be afterwards written above it. It is not alleged or suggested that John Forrest intended his subscription to be used for any other purpose than that to which it was applied by the panel, or that the panel, having obtained this subscription for one purpose, used it for another and unauthorised purpose. The fair construction of the libel therefore is, that John Forrest put his subscription on the blank sheet of paper, for the purpose of its being used as that of witness to the execution. The case, therefore, is the same in effect as if John Forrest had subscribed after the execution was written out. And the charge thus resolves into an allegation, that the panel and Forrest wrote and subscribed a document, which falsely stated that they, as officer and witness respectively, had made a service which never was made, and uttered that document as a true execution.

This statement constitutes a serious charge of falsehood against both the panel and Forrest, and such a charge is, beyond doubt, a relevant point of dittay. But, in my opinion, it is not a relevant charge of forgery.

Forgery, at least as it is understood in modern times, consists in making and uttering a writing, falsely intended to represent and pass for the genuine writing of another person. And, accordingly, the charge of uttering, which is generally the most important part of the indictment for forgery, is invariably libelled as 'the using and uttering, *as genuine,*' that which is not genuine, but forged. The ordinary style of our indictments thus shows, that *forged* and *genuine* are precisely opposite and contradictory terms; and, consequently, that which is forged cannot be genuine, and that which is genuine cannot be forged.

But, if the panel and John Forrest were to be be tried for writing and subscribing a writing, containing a false statement, that they made a service which they never made, the first fact to be proved by the prosecutor would be, that the writing was made and subscribed by them, or, in other words, that it is their *genuine writ.* In a merely colloquial sense, the term 'genuine' is sometimes loosely enough employed, but when applied to a writing, its only proper sense is, that the writing is the act or deed of the person whose act or deed it professes to be. In the scientific study of the evidences of Christianity, one becomes familiar with the distinction between the genuineness and the authenticity of the books of the New Testament,—the term 'genuineness,' as applied to them, expressing merely the fact that they were written by the persons whose names they bear, apart altogether from any question as to the truth or credibility of their contents. For a writing, though genuine, may contain nothing but falsehoods. A genuine letter, containing a false and scandalous libel, is a good ground for prosecuting the writer for libel, because it is his genuine production, and the first step towards making him answerable for writing it, is to prove that it is genuine. And so here, supposing the panel and Forrest were both charged in terms of the minor proposition of this indictment, they must be proved to be the authors of the false execution, before they could be made responsible for it; or, in other words, it would be indispensable as the foundation of the charge against them, as laid, that the execution should be proved to be their genuine production. The offence, therefore, which they have committed, is not the using and uttering as genuine that which is not genuine; and yet that is the charge in the major proposition of this indictment.

I am quite aware that, in our earlier practice, the distinction between forgery, properly so called, and other species of the *crimen falsi*, was not much observed or acted on, the more ordinary classification, as given by Sir G. Mackenzie, being falsehood committed by *means of writing*, falsehood by witness, falsification of the coin of the realm, and the using of false weights and measures. But it is quite impossible to read that learned author's enumeration of the various kinds of falsehood, committed by means of writing, without being satisfied that falsehood by means of writing, and forgery, can never be convertible or commensurate terms. Indeed, it is historically true, as stated by the counsel for the panel, that forgery is not a *nomen juris* in our older law; nor is it until modern times, that the name has been distinctively applied to one particular kind of the falsehoods committed by means of writing. But that it is now used only in this definite and restricted meaning, I hold to be proved by the invariable style of our indictments, and by the fact that the Crown counsel, with all their sources of information, have not been able to produce to us a single example of an indictment for forgery, which, in its minor proposition, libelled anything short of the making and uttering, by the accused, of a writing falsely intended to represent and pass for the genuine writing of another person.

I am therefore of opinion, that the second charge of forgery and uttering is irrelevant."

LORD NEAVES: "The forgery of a writing may be committed in two ways; either by the person signing the name of some one else to a writ, or by bringing a false writ to a true signature. As there were two ways in which Mahomet and the mountain might be brought together, so there are two ways in which a forged bond may be made, either by signing a false name below the bond, or by writing the bond above the genuine signature without permission, and in that way fabricating the thing as a whole, it not being the genuine instrument of the party. But the falsehood must be in the external execution of the writing, and not in the signification or narrative of the deed. A man who signs his own writing, and tells a lie in it, is not guilty of forgery. There is a plain distinction between the fabrication of the *corpus* of the writing, and the falsehood of the allegations contained in it."

Charge of uttering held irrelevant.

NOTES

On this case, see Gordon, paras. 18-45 to 18-48. On the question of whether articles other than documents can be uttered, see *Bannatyne* (1847) Ark. 361.

CHAPTER 15

RESET

The crime of reset, originally limited to reset of theft, has been extended to include the retention of goods obtained also by robbery, fraud or embezzlement. The *mens rea* is "guilty knowledge" and an intention to detain the goods from the owner, although *Latta* v. *Herron* (1968) 32 J.C.L. 51 *(ante)* suggests that "wilful blindness" may be sufficient. The *actus reus* of this crime does not normally give much difficulty, except in those situations where the doctrine of "being privy to the retention" of the goods applies. It is worth noting that this concept is almost entirely the work of Macdonald, whose views have subsequently been approved by the High Court. The following cases are all concerned with this aspect of the law.

1. H.M. Advocate v. Browne
(1903) 6 F. (J.) 24

The accused was charged along with others with stealing a sum of money in banknotes, some for large amounts. The evidence showed that on the day of their arrest and for some days previously, the accused had been in possession of similar notes. The numbers of the stolen notes were not proved. In the course of charging the jury:

LORD JUSTICE-CLERK (MACDONALD): "Now, gentlemen, supposing you feel yourselves not able to come to the conclusion that the prisoners at the bar were the thieves—that is to say, were privy to the theft at the time it took place, you then need to consider the further question, whether or not they, being in possession of money that you are satisfied was stolen money, were guiltily in possession of that stolen money—in other words, whether they can be found guilty of receiving stolen property knowing it to be stolen. Now, as regards that, I must tell you that it is not necessary according to law that the actual property which is said to have been received guiltily has ever passed into the personal possession of the receiver at all. If a man steals a bundle of notes out of a man's pocket, and after that informs another man that he has got these notes, that he has stolen them, or if the other man saw him stealing them and knew that they were stolen, then if the other man connived at it remaining in the possession of the thief or being put in any place for safe custody, such as hiding it in a cupboard, he is guilty of receiving feloniously even although he never puts his fingers on the notes at all. Reset consists of being privy to the retaining of property that has been dishonestly come by.

Now, assuming that you do not think that the theft is made out, the question comes to be whether you are not satisfied that all these three men knew that this large amount of property which was between them was stolen property, and were doing their best to dispose of it by arrangements which were made in opening accounts with banks, and so on, and whether, whichever of them had the money in his possession at the time they were apprehended, they were all privy to that money dishonestly come by being in the possession of the individual who happened to have it in his pocket or bag—if you are satisfied of these facts you would be quite entitled to find that they were all guilty of reset.''

The accused was convicted of reset.

NOTES

On this point see also *Gilbert McCawley,* High Court, July 1959, unreported, discussed in Wallace, "Reset without Possession (1960) 5 J.L.S. 55. The case concerned a passenger in a stolen car who was convicted of reset at common law. Such persons are of course often tried under s. 175 (1) (*b*) of the Road Traffic Act 1972.

2. Clark v. H.M. Advocate
1965 S.L.T. 250

An accused was charged along with a man Mackenzie with theft of 38,800 cigarettes, 1½ lbs. of tobacco and a sum of money. He was convicted of reset of 13,000 cigarettes. He appealed against conviction on grounds of insufficiency of evidence and on alleged misdirection by the sheriff on the material elements necessary to constitute the crime of reset.

LORD JUSTICE-CLERK (GRANT): "The main evidence against the appellant was as follows. His fingerprints were found on a package of 100 of the stolen cigarettes. He had seen these and the other stolen cigarettes in Mackenzie's house shortly after the housebreaking, he had handled some of them and it is a fair inference from the evidence that he knew they were stolen. He then accompanied Mackenzie to a bus depot where they both sat down at a table in the canteen with the witness Walkinshaw. Mackenzie handed over a parcel containing 1,000 cigarettes to Walkinshaw who agreed to try to sell the cigarettes on Mackenzie's behalf at 30s. per 200 package to his fellow employees. No payment was then made but it was arranged that Walkinshaw should meet Mackenzie in the Kenmore public house that evening and hand over the proceeds. All this happened in the presence and hearing of the appellant though there is no evidence that he took part in the conversation. The appellant was again with Mackenzie in the Kenmore that evening, but was not present in the lavatory when payment was made there by Walkinshaw to Mackenzie.

In these rather unusual circumstances the learned sheriff charged the jury to the effect that reset 'consists in knowingly receiving articles taken by theft, robbery, embezzlement or fraud and feloniously retaining them, or being privy to the retaining of property that has been dishonestly come by. It is reset for a person to connive at a third party possessing or retaining the stolen goods, even if the person charged never laid a finger on the stolen property.' This passage comes from Macdonald on *Criminal Law*, 5th edition, page 67 and goes back to at least the second edition of that work published in 1877. The learned sheriff then quoted to the jury a passage from Lord Justice-Clerk Macdonald's charge in *H.M. Advocate* v. *Browne* (1903) 6 F. (J.) 24, at page 26 (11 S.L.T. 353) to the following effect:—'I must tell you that it is not necessary according to law that the actual property which is said to have been received guiltily has ever passed into the personal possession of the receiver at all. If a man steals a bundle of notes out of a man's pocket, and after that informs another man that he has got these notes, that he has stolen them, or if the other man saw him stealing them and knew that they were stolen, then if the other man connived at it remaining in the possession of the thief or being put in any place for safe custody, such as hiding it in a cupboard, he is guilty of receiving feloniously even although he never puts his fingers on the notes at all. Reset consists of being privy to the retaining of property that has been dishonestly come by.' The learned sheriff then went on to warn the jury that merely knowing that the thief has stolen property is not enough—there must be connivance. He then reviewed the evidence and left it to the jury to decide whether, on that evidence, connivance had been established.

Some time after retiring, the jury returned for further directions as to what was meant by connivance. In the course of his further direction the learned sheriff stated, *inter alia:* 'I think that you would be entitled to draw an inference from the fact that he did nothing whatever to inform the police or anyone of that sort that stolen property was being disposed of, and that might raise an inference of connivance, but you have got to find this thing called connivance or whatever it is first of all, the mere fact that the accused was in company with the thief is not by itself sufficient.'

It was on this direction by the learned sheriff that counsel for the appellant launched his main attack. He did not attack the passages from Macdonald, *Criminal Law*, 5th edition, page 67 and from the charge in *H.M. Advocate* v. *Browne (supra)* to which I have referred as being unsound in law, but said that they must be read on the basis that connivance involved some overt act, something on the accused's part of an active character. With this the learned Solicitor-General appeared to agree and such an interpretation would be in line with that placed on connivance in the consistorial sphere. (Cf. *Thomson* v. *Thomson*, 1908 S.C. 179, per Lord President Dunedin, at page 185).

On that basis, the passage which I have just quoted from the learned sheriff's charge was, in my opinion, a misdirection in law. It was a direction that connivance could be inferred from mere inactivity and I do not think, nor did the Crown argue, that in a case such as this, it properly can. The Crown argument appeared to be that the charge, read as a whole, was adequate and sound in law. This direction, however, was given at a time when the jury were clearly puzzled as to what connivance involved and it was the last direction they received on that matter before finally retiring to consider their verdict. In those circumstances it is impossible to say, in a narrow case such as this, that the jury, if properly directed would still have convicted the appellant. I would, accordingly, allow the appeal and quash the conviction.

I may say that I have considerable sympathy with the learned sheriff in the difficult task which he had in charging the jury in this case. He had to rely on *dicta* in Macdonald and in *Browne* which, I confess, I do not fully understand and which I have some difficulty in reconciling with the principle laid down both in Hume on *Crimes* (volume I, page 113) and Alison on *Criminal Law* (volume I, page 328) to the effect that it is fundamental to the crime of reset that the stolen goods be received into the accused's possession. It may be noted that when Hume ((*supra*), page 114) refers to 'privity and connivance' in a case of reset, he is dealing (as appears from the example which he cites in the passage immediately following) with the type of case where the stolen goods are found in the accused's premises. That is a very different type of case from the present and I would think that, in the type of case with which Hume was dealing, 'privity and connivance' are relevant, not so much to the question of possession, as to the question of intention to retain the goods as against the true owner. (I am not, of course, concerned here with the case where an accused, though not in actual possession, may be found guilty art and part. That was not an issue in the present case.) Furthermore, the facts in the present case appear to be far removed from those in *Browne*. These, however, are issues which go much wider than those argued in the present case and I express no concluded opinion upon them."

LORD STRACHAN: "I confess that I have some difficulty in reconciling the directions of the Lord Justice-Clerk in *Browne* with the statement in Hume on *Crimes* (volume I, page 113) that: 'It is the fundamental circumstance in the description of this crime that the stolen goods are received into the offender's possession' and the similar statement in Alison on *Criminal Law* (volume I, page 328) that: 'It is indispensable to this crime that the goods are received into the prisoner's keeping'. In the present appeal, however, counsel for the appellant did not maintain that the directions in *Browne* were wrong, and the Solicitor-General seemed to concede that when Lord Justice-Clerk Macdonald spoke of the 'other man' conniving at the stolen goods remaining in the possession of the thief, he meant connivance which involved some positive act. In these circumstances this is not an appropriate case in which to question the soundness of the directions in *Browne*. Those directions and the corresponding statements in Macdonald on *Criminal Law*, appear to have remained unquestioned for more than sixty years and they could not be overruled without hearing adequate argument on both sides. I content myself therefore with the observation that in an appropriate case they may have to be reconsidered.

The directions in *Browne*, however, came to be of vital importance in the present case, and it was by no means easy to apply them to the facts, because of the difficulty in being certain as to what Lord Justice-Clerk Macdonald meant when he used the word 'connived'. The sheriff was obviously puzzled by that word, and so were the jury for they returned to Court and asked for further guidance. I have considerable sympathy with the sheriff's difficulties, but in response to the jury's inquiry and in explanation of the word connivance, he directed them as follows:—'I think that you would be entitled to draw an inference from the fact that he [i.e. the appellant] did nothing whatever to inform the police or anyone of that sort that stolen property was being disposed of, and that might raise an inference of connivance'. In my opinion that was a misdirection for I cannot hold that the crime of reset is committed by merely refraining from reporting to the police that stolen property is being disposed of. I am further of opinion that having regard to the circumstances in which that misdirection was given the conviction cannot stand, because I think it probable that the jury would have acquitted the appellant had that misdirection not been given."

Conviction quashed.

NOTES
For a comment on the decision in *Clark*, see Gordon, para. 20-18.

3. McNeil v. H.M. Advocate
1968 J.C. 29

A person was convicted of reset after being found in a car carrying stolen goods. The accused had introduced the thief of the articles to another person who was to reset them. He appealed against conviction on the grounds of alleged misdirection by the sheriff.

LORD JUSTICE-GENERAL (CLYDE): "As regards the first ground of appeal the Sheriff-substitute in the course of his charge to the jury defined reset as including, *inter alia,* a situation where the accused, although not in actual possession of stolen property, was privy to its retention from the owner. This direction was challenged as unsound.

It is, however, in conformity with the direction to the jury given by the presiding judge in the case of *H.M. Advocate* v. *Browne,* 6 F. (J.) 24, at p. 26. (Compare Macdonald on Criminal Law, (5th ed.) p. 67.) The argument for the applicant was that the soundness of this direction had been doubted in the case of *Clark* v. *H.M. Advocate,* 1965 S.L.T. 250. But in the first place the observations as to the soundness of the direction made by the Lord Justice-Clerk and Lord Strachan in the latter case were *obiter* in that case. In the second place the Court in *Clark's* case was not referred to the unreported decision in 1959 by the High Court in *H.M. Advocate* v. *McCawley,* 23 July 1959. In *McCawley's* case objection was taken to a direction that the crime of reset consists in knowingly receiving articles taken by theft or being privy to the retaining of property which had been dishonestly come by. . . . The Court held that this direction was sound in law and affirmed the correctness of the direction in *Browne's* case. (Compare Hume on Crimes, vol. i, p. 114.)

In my opinion, therefore, the direction of the Sheriff-substitute in the present case was correct, and if an accused is privy to the retention of property dishonestly come by, he may be guilty of reset, although he is not in actual possession of the goods."

Appeal dismissed.

NOTES

So Macdonald's view in *Browne* is apparently still the law. But what is connivance? In *Clark* all that really happened was that the High Court held that the sheriff's definition was wrong; nowhere does the court say what 'connivance' really means.

CHAPTER 16

SEXUAL OFFENCES

a. Rape

1. **William Fraser**
(1847) Ark. 280

A man was charged with raping a woman by having intercourse with her while inducing her to believe he was her husband, and alternatively with "fraudulently and deceitfully obtaining access to and having carnal knowledge of a married woman" by pretending to be her husband, or otherwise conducting himself, and behaving towards her so as to deceive her into the belief that he was her husband. The accused objected to the relevancy of the indictment.

LORD COCKBURN: "Now, I can gather nothing from our books, except that the crime of rape consists in having intercourse *without the woman's consent.* It is sometimes said that it must not only be without her consent, but *forcibly.* But this is plainly said loosely; merely because where consent is withheld, force is generally resorted to. It is not meant that there must be positive physical force, as a substantive element; but only that constructive force which is implied in the absence of consent. It is in the absence of consent that the essence of the crime consists. Force is only the *evidence,* and the *consequence,* of the want of consent, but is not necessary for the constitution of the crime. Hence, the crime is unquestionably committed wherever consent is *impossible, though there may be no force;* as in the cases of intercourse with children, or lunatics or with women in intoxication, or in faints, though these may not have been produced by the ravisher. An insane woman, instead of requiring force, may actively concur; but because she cannot consent, the connexion is rape.

In applying this principle to the case before us, there is a statement in the indictment which, in one view, settles, or at least supersedes, the question at issue. It is averred, and of course offered to be proved, that the intercourse was '*against, or without her will.*' If this is to be assumed, no question of relevancy is raised. But this interpretation of the libel would not decide, but might only postpone, the decision of the point. If the prosecutor was to maintain that the constructive want of consent implied in the fraud was sufficient, or if the Jury were to ask instructions on this matter, the question would arise on the trial. Moreover, I presume that the prosecutor does not mean to say that there was any *positive* dissent, or any *positive* absence of consent, but only intends to set forth that want of consent which is implied in the alleged deception practised on the woman. If this be the proper view of the libel, then the question may be held to be regularly raised now.

And my opinion upon it is, that obtaining access to the person of a female by this deception, does not amount to the crime of rape. I reach this result solely because the want of the woman's consent is not implied, either legally or practically, in the circumstance of her yielding from misrepresentation.

There is nothing better known to the law, or more familiar to its practice, than the difference between consent *withheld,* and consent given, but *given through fraud.* It would be idle to state examples of a distinction so certain and so common.

Now, the prosecutor's argument proceeds entirely on confounding these two things. Its substance is, that there was no consent, and indeed that the prisoner's fraud reduced his victim to a state of non-free agency, exactly as if he had taken advantage of her having been in childhood, or in lunacy, or as if he had drugged her himself. The plain fallacy of this, however, is, that it assumes consent given under misapprehension, to be not given; an assumption not warranted by legal principle, and repugnant to the actual truth.

There is certainly nothing impossible or absurd in the idea of a person being induced to consent by a trick. And this very indictment states a fact which necessarily implies that this was the case here. It sets forth, that 'you (the prisoner) *did deceive her into the belief that you were her husband.'* If this was her belief, it includes her consent. No doubt it was a consent procured by deceit: but still it was procured. The victim was not in the condition of a female intoxicated, deranged, or under age, where there is no consent *de facto.* It is said that there was no consent to intercourse *with the prisoner.* But there was; only the consent was given on the erroneous conviction that he was her husband. She was misled as to his name and identity; but her consent to intercourse *with the very individual beside her,* is involved in the fact of her believing that she was his wife."

> Charge of rape held irrelevant,
> but alternative charge relevant.

NOTES

The particular crime charged in *Fraser* is now a statutory offence: s. 2 (2) of the Sexual Offences (Scotland) Act 1976, formerly s. 4 of the Criminal Law Amendment Act 1885. See also *H.M. Advocate* v. *Montgomery*, 1926 J.C. 2 *(post).*

2. Charles Sweenie
(1858) 3 Irv. 109

An accused person was charged with raping a sleeping woman and
also with "wickedly and feloniously having carnal knowledge" of a
sleeping woman. He objected to the relevancy of the indictment.

LORD DEAS: "I have no doubt at all that the act charged in this
indictment, is a crime cognizable by this Court. To suppose the
contrary, would be to suppose that any female,—it may be a virgin,
pure in thought and in act,—may, while asleep, without her knowledge or consent, be deprived of her virtue, rather than have yielded
which, she would have yielded her life, and may even, by being
made a mother, be brought to open shame, and yet that the perpetrator of this grievous wrong shall be liable to no punishment. This is
a proposition too repugnant, not only to our moral nature, but to
the plainest principles of our criminal jurisprudence, to be for a
moment entertained. Let it be,—as was held by the only Judge who
dissented from the judgment in the gambling case of Greenhuff and
others (2 Swin. 236), and who was so scrupulously jealous of what
has been called the native vigour of our criminal law,—that we are
not to introduce new crimes,—that an offence, to be indictable,
must either come within the range of some known term, or fall
within the spirit of some previous decision, or within some established general principle; still, I can see no difficulty in holding, that
the wickedly and feloniously invading, by stealth (as is said in this
indictment), the bed of a woman while asleep, and having carnal
knowledge of her person without her consciousness or consent, is an
offence of an aggravated kind, which might easily enough be
brought (if that were necessary), within the range of more than one
known term, and which certainly falls as well within the spirit of
previous decisions, as within the established general principle, that
every one who inflicts upon another, without that other's consent, a
grievous and irreparable personal injury, must be answerable for
having done so at the bar of criminal justice.

The more difficult question, however, remains, whether the
offence be the crime of rape?

The prosecutor defines rape to be carnal knowledge of a woman
without her consent. This, he says, is all that it is necessary to libel as
a general rule, and that the cases where anything more has been
stated, or requires to be stated, are exceptional. It is obvious, if this
be so, that nearly all the cases that have occurred have been exceptional, and that we have scarcely had an example of the general rule.
Accordingly, it is said, that all the cases of adults who have a will,
are exceptional, and that it is because such cases are exceptional,

that force has been and must be libelled as having been used to overcome the person, or the will. I cannot concur in this view. It appears to me that, according to all practice and authority, the libelling of force or concussion, applied either to the person or the will, is necessary, as a general rule, to the relevancy of the charge of rape; and that the cases where this is dispensed with, are exceptional. The prosecutor holds the case of infants to be rather an instance of the general rule than an exception. But, on his own shewing, it would not be a good instance, for it goes beyond his definition of the crime,—the libel, in such cases, never bearing, 'without her consent,' but being, in modern practice at least, altogether silent on the subject of consent, of which an infant is presumed to be incapable. Of the alleged general rule, as applied to the case of an adult, (I mean the mere libelling that carnal knowledge was had of the woman without her consent), we have really no instance; not even in the case mentioned by Hume, of the bedfast cripple of sixteen, whose alleged inability to make resistance, can only have been inability to make *successful* resistance, for what was charged against the panel was, 'the shameful deflowering, *forcing*, and abusing' of the girl.

I do not say that force must, in every instance, be libelled. The case of girls of tender years is an instance to the contrary; resting, however, not so much on the fact, that they have neither appetite nor will in the matter, (for in some cases, and to some extent, they may have both), as on a presumption of law, introduced and established to prevent the evils to society and the demoralization which might otherwise follow, and which presumption, accordingly, is not allowed to be redargued. It may be that idiots fall within the same principle. (I say nothing of insane persons who are not idiots, whose cases may depend on their own circumstances and on degree). But I regard instances of children and of idiots as exceptional; and it does not follow, that, because an exception is made of cases in which by law, or both by law and nature, the parties are totally disqualified from consenting, an exception shall equally be made of the case of a woman who might have consented if awake, although she neither did nor could consent, being asleep.

Beyond the case of parties whom the law holds incapable of consent, we have no recorded instance of the element of force being altogether omitted in the libel. I mean force different from that which is necessarily implied in the act of sexual intercourse,—for there is a plain fallacy in confounding what is essential to the act, even when consented to, with the force necessary to obtain opportunity to perform the act."

Charge of rape held irrelevant, but nonetheless held to disclose a relevant crime.

On the question of what force (if any) is required for rape, Lord Ardmillan in *Sweenie* at p. 137 said "any mode of overpowering the will, without actual personal violence, such as the use of threats, or drugs, is force in the estimation of the law—and . . . any degree of force is sufficient in law to constitute the crime of rape, if it is sufficient in fact to overcome the opposing will of the woman."

3. H.M. Advocate v. Logan
1935 J.C. 100

A man was charged with raping a woman "while she was in a state of insensibility from the effects of intoxicating liquor supplied to her by you for the purpose of rendering her incapable of resistance." In the course of charging the jury:

LORD JUSTICE-CLERK (AITCHISON): "The Crown case is that the woman was doped with drink. If you thought that the Crown had proved that the woman was plied with drink, and drink of a deadly kind, the nature of which was concealed from her, in order to overcome her resistance, you could find a verdict of guilty of rape; but if the position was that the woman was not given the drink for the purpose of overcoming her or making her incapable of resistance, but had taken it of her own free will, and it had not been given to her for a criminal purpose, and she became insensible, and advantage was then taken of her in her insensible condition, then, in the eye of the law, the crime would not be rape but indecent assault only. Now, you may think that a very odd distinction, but it is there on the authorities. A similar question arose many years ago, as far back as 1858, in what is known as the case of *Sweenie*, (1858) 3 Irv. 109. That was a case where a man took advantage of a woman while she was asleep. There was no drugging of her to put her to sleep, and the Court held that it was a crime by the law of Scotland. The crime, so far as it is possible to define it, comes within the category of indecent assault. There may have been a reason for the decision in *Sweenie's* case, because in 1858 rape was one of the pleas of the Crown (as it still is), but also it was a capital offence, and the judges were very unwilling to extend the definition of rape so as to bring any new class of crime within the category of a capital offence. That may explain the decision, and, in any event, it is binding on me; and, applying it here in this case, it comes to this, that if you are satisfied on the evidence that Logan was a party to doping this woman for the purpose of overcoming her resistance, so that advantage might be taken of her, and advantage was taken of her, then he would be guilty of rape and there would be no answer to it. On the other hand, if the woman through indulgence—even if she was being invited or coaxed to drink—voluntarily took drink and just got insensible through it, and it was not doped or given her for the purpose of making her insensible, and advantage was taken of her in her insensible condition, then the crime is not rape, but indecent assault."

> The accused was convicted of
> indecent assault.

NOTES

The reference to "pleas of the Crown" is of no significance today, except as a reminder that rape is in the exclusive jurisdiction of the High Court. *Logan* is also clear authority for defining rape in terms of "overcoming the will of the victim" rather than in terms of force as implied by the institutional writers: see Hume, i. 302 and Alison, i. 209.

4. H.M. Advocate v. Montgomery
1926 J.C. 2

A man was charged with raping a woman. She was at the time married to her second husband. The accused pretended to be her first husband, who was dead. The charge was brought under s. 4 of the Criminal Law Amendment Act 1885. In charging the jury:

LORD HUNTER: "The charge is that the accused had intercourse with a Mrs Baxter by representing to her that he was James Anderson to whom she had been previously married. The charge therefore is that the accused personated James Anderson, and by personating James Anderson induced Mrs Baxter to have intercourse with him. The Act of 1885 provides by section 4 that 'whereas doubts have been entertained whether a man who induces a married woman to permit him to have connexion with her by personating her husband is or is not guilty of rape, it is hereby enacted and declared that every such offender shall be deemed to be guilty of rape.' With a provision couched in these terms before me, I do not feel I should be justified in throwing out this charge as irrelevant, although I entirely appreciate the point that proof of the crime in this case will be an exceedingly difficult thing for the Crown. The woman here, in the belief, and on quite good information, that her first husband was dead, has married again; but, of course, if her first husband was not dead the second marriage is of no consequence. I therefore do not think that the circumstance of a second marriage can be taken into account in considering the relevancy or irrelevancy of this charge. Supposing the question had been this—and I am of opinion this is the way the Act of 1885 is to be tested—supposing James Anderson had disappeared and had been reported to be dead, and the accused had come and had induced the woman to believe that he was in point of fact James Anderson while he was not, and had thereby persuaded her to let him have intercourse with her, I cannot doubt that the words of the Act of 1885 are apt to cover the case. If that be so, I cannot see that any difference is introduced by the circumstance that the woman has meantime gone through a ceremony of marriage with another man. If she was satisfied that James Anderson was before her in the flesh, the second ceremony of marriage was invalid—it did not constitute marriage between her and the person now living with her as her husband; and therefore the means by which she was induced to have connexion was by the accused personating her husband. That being so, I am prepared to repel the objection taken to the relevancy of this indictment and to allow the case to proceed, although I think the Crown will have great difficulty in establishing the charge."

> The objection to relevancy was repelled and the case produced to trial. The accused was found not guilty.

NOTES

Section 4 of the Criminal Law Amendment Act 1885 is now s. 2 (2) of the Sexual Offences (Scotland) Act 1976.

5.   H.M. Advocate v. Grainger and Rae
1932 J.C. 40

Two men were charged on indictment with assaulting a woman, having carnal knowledge of her person while she was in a state of insensibility or unconsciousness from the effects of intoxicating liquor, and ravishing her. They objected to the relevancy of the indictment on the ground that these averments were not relevant to infer the crime of rape.

LORD ANDERSON: "Rape (save in the exceptional cases of pupils and idiots) is the carnal knowledge of a woman forcibly and against her will—Macdonald's Criminal Law, (4th ed.) p. 175; Hume on Crimes, vol. i., pp. 301-302; Alison's Criminal Law, vol. i., p. 209. Accordingly, it was urged by the accused, the crime cannot be committed unless a woman is in a condition, physically and mentally, to exercise her will power and offer resistance. In the present case the libel sets forth that the woman was in a condition when she was incapacitated, by reason of intoxication, from offering any resistance to her assailants or from exercising her will power in the way of giving or refusing consent. The offence charged, accordingly, it was said, does not amount to rape. This contention seems to me to be well founded. It is not alleged that the accused supplied the woman with the liquor with which she became intoxicated. Had this allegation been made, the charge of rape might have been sustained, as it has been decided that it is rape to have connexion with a woman whose resistance has been overcome by drugging her—Macdonald's Criminal Law, (4th ed.) p. 176; Hume on Crimes, vol. i., p. 303; Alison's Criminal Law, vol. i., p. 212; *Fraser* (1847) Ark. 280; *Sweenie* (1858) 3 Irv. 109. It might be suggested that the present case falls to be assimilated to that of an idiot female; but this does not seem to me to be a true analogy. The idiot has, in law and in fact, no will; in the present case the woman assaulted had a will, the activity of which was but temporarily suspended by her intoxication. The true analogy seems to me to be the case of the woman who is taken advantage of while asleep. Such an offence is not rape—Macdonald's Criminal Law, p. 175; *Sweenie.* Just as a sleeping woman is temporarily in a state of unconsciousness wherein she is incapable of exercising her will power, so here it seems to me that the woman was in the same temporary condition of unconsciousness by reason of intoxication. The objection to relevancy must therefore be sustained.

As I have indicated, what is said to have been done by the accused, although not rape, is a criminal offence—the crime of inflicting clandestine injury on a woman—Macdonald's Criminal Law, (4th ed.) p. 178. But the crime must be indicted as such, and not as rape."

Objection to relevancy sustained.

NOTES

This case is considered authority for charging the innominate offence of "clandestine injury to women" and is a good reminder of the flexibility in charging enjoyed by the Crown, free from the necessity of selecting a *nomen juris* for each crime: see Criminal Procedure (Scotland) Act 1975, s. 44.

b. Incest

1. **H.M. Advocate v. R.M.**
1969 J.C. 52

A man was charged with incest, contrary to the Incest Act 1567. At the material time the girl in question was both the illegitimate daughter of his wife and also his own adopted daughter. He challenged the relevancy of the indictment on the ground that in neither case did the relationship between himself and the girl bring them within the prohibited degrees for the purposes of the Act.

LORD JUSTICE-CLERK (GRANT): "Whatever may have been the situation before 1567, the argument before us proceeded on the basis that since that date incest in Scotland has been a statutory crime depending upon whether the parties concerned come within the prohibited degrees as laid down by the Act of 1567 and certain verses of the 18th chapter of Leviticus which are incorporated thereby as part of the law of Scotland. The Crown further contended that, in a case of adoption, these prohibited degrees had been extended by the Adoption Acts. I note in passing that, in construing those verses of the 18th chapter of Leviticus which form part of the law of Scotland, the text to be looked at is that of the Geneva Bible of 1562, which was the current text when the 1567 Act was passed—*Solicitor-General* v. *AB*, 7 Adam 306, 1914 S.C. (J.) 38. We have been provided with copies of this text, taken from the original Bible in the National Library—an advantage which might not be shared by all persons who were in doubt as to whether they were within the prohibited degrees or not.

The first question, accordingly, is whether a man and his wife's illegitimate daughter are within the prohibited degrees laid down in the verses of Leviticus, chapter 18, which are made part of our law by the Act of 1567. In the absence of any subsequent statutory provision which affected, directly or indirectly, by inclusion in or exclusion from the prohibited degrees in the 1567 Act, the 'relationship' just mentioned, we must decide the question posed in the light of the situation as it was when the 1567 Act became law. It is, I think, common ground that, if the 'relationship' founded upon by the Crown on this branch of the case did not fall within the prohibited degrees 400 years ago, it falls not within those degrees today.

It is not in dispute that the relevant verses of Leviticus, chapter 18, are verses 6 to 17 inclusive, verse 18 having received its death-blow in *Solicitor-General* v. *AB*. It is also well settled that verse 6 is a general prohibition, of which verses 7 to 17 are examples only—*i.e.* they are not an exhaustive catalogue. The argument for the Crown is, as I understand it, this: that the girl here is, in the words of verse 6, 'the kindred of his [*i.e.* the accused's] flesh' and, in particular, that the present case falls in terms within the opening words of verse 17, namely, 'Thou shalt not discover the shame of the wife and of her daughter . . . .' This, it is said, includes both lawful daughter and illegitimate daughter and is accordingly directly in point here. Support for this latter proposition is sought in the (translators'?)

side-note to verse 9 in regard to 'thy sister.' The side-note expounds this as 'Either by father or mother, borne in marriage or otherwise.' I have three comments on this side-note: (*a*) I am extremely doubtful as to whether it has any interpretative value; (*b*) if it has, it relates to verse 9 only and not to verse 17; and (*c*) in the context it seems to me to deal not with legitimacy and illegitimacy but with legitimate relationships of the half-blood. Much has been done by legislation in recent years to ameliorate the lot of the bastard. It was not suggested, however, that anything in that legislation affected his position, so far as concerns relationship by blood or affinity, as it has existed over the centuries. The operation of the 1567 Act depends (verse 6 of Leviticus, chapter 18) on there being 'kindred of his flesh' involved: and although the necessary 'kinship' may be by consanguinity or affinity, it can only be by one or the other. Whether or not there can be any blood relationship in the legal sense (and for the purposes of the law of incest) between a bastard son and his mother (*cf*. Hume on Crimes, vol. i, p. 452) or a bastard daughter and her father, it has been clear over the centuries that there is no blood relationship recognised by our law between the illegitimate child on the one hand and the blood relations of his or her natural parent on the other. In this respect the unfortunate child is, and has been treated as, *filius (or filia) nullius*. The illegitimate nature of the link between bastard and natural mother is such that the chain of relationship between the child and his or her mother's blood relations is broken *ab initio*. Yet it is this same so-called link that is relied upon by the Crown as founding the alleged relationship by affinity between the accused and his wife's illegitimate daughter.

In principle I can see no reason why that link should be stronger in supporting affinity than it is in supporting consanguinity. Indeed the reverse might be the case. The question in issue is one on which there is no direct authority and the text-book writers exercise some caution, although, so far as they go, they seem to me to be generally against the Crown. Hume *(loc.cit.)* stresses the denial by the law to the bastard child of 'any privileges or advantages of blood,' to which denial I have already referred. And he appears to doubt whether, even in a case of intercourse between a bastard and his mother, there is incest in the statutory sense. If that be so, *a fortiori* there would be no incest in the circumstances now being discussed. Alison (Criminal Law, vol. i, p. 565) is more categorical: 'Incest is not committed by bastard relations, how near soever.' That would seem to me to cover, not merely cases depending on alleged consanguinity, but also cases, such as the present, where the alleged affinity is based fundamentally on a bastard link which (to mix the metaphors) will not hold blood. I should add that I agree with the views which Alison expresses on the case of *Johnston* (1705). The interlocutor and verdict in that case puzzled Hume *(loc.cit.)*, but they seem to me to support, so far as they go, the argument for the accused here. Macdonald (5th ed., p. 148) is fairly categorical, and I preface the relevant passage by saying that, apart from certain factors which have no relevance to the issues which we have to decide here, if A commits incest with B, B equally commits incest with A. The passage reads thus: 'Bastards cannot commit incest, unless it be where the mother of a male bastard have intercourse with him, she being the only person whose relationship is recognised in law, but even this has never been decided.' Erskine (Inst., IV, iv, 57) appears to take a view more favourable to the argument advanced for the Crown, but it is right to note that in Nicolson's edition of 1871 the editor has a warning foot-note referring to the passages above referred to in Hume and Alison and to the original relevant passage in the first edition of Macdonald, published in 1866.

So far as decided cases are concerned, there is no authority directly in point. The facts in *H.M. Advocate* v. *Black*, 1 Adam 312, were (for the purpose of this branch of the argument) indistinguishable from those in this case. The accused there was charged with incest with his step-daughter and pleaded guilty. It was not until after that plea had been tendered that the accused's advisers and the Crown ascertained that the 'step-daughter' was in fact his wife's *illegitimate* daughter. That having been ascertained, the Crown withdrew the libel. The only other case to which I would refer is *Philp's Trustees* v. *Beaton*, 1938 S.C. 733. I do so because the learned Solicitor-General sought some support from certain *dicta* in the opinion of Lord President Normand in that case. The facts there were somewhat complicated and it is right to point out that it was a case dealing not with the criminal law of incest but with the civil law of marriage. It is not, and was not suggested to be, a case that is directly in point here. It is a case, however, the decision and *dicta* in which tend to confirm my view, already expressed, as to the weakness of an 'illegitimate' link in tracing an alleged relationship between A and B.

The practice of the Crown as exemplified in *Black* and as operated, we were informed, at the present day has, of course, no direct relevance to this first question which we have to answer. On the other hand there appears to be no record of any successful prosecution since 1567 in any case where a man has had intercourse with his wife's illegitimate daughter. Such intercourse is no doubt utterly reprehensible. The question, however, is whether it is the crime of incest under an Act which for over 300 years until 1887 carried the penalty of death (unless the pains were restricted) and even now can carry the not entirely modest sentence of imprisonment for life.

Having regard to what I have already said, I should be slow to hold that the facts libelled in the first branch of the first alternative charge are relevant to infer incest unless there were clear statutory provisions upon which I could properly so hold. I can find none, and, for the reasons I have given, I am satisfied that on the first branch of their objections the defence must succeed.

I turn accordingly from illegitimacy to adoption, out of which the second branch of the objections to relevancy arises. This raises a much shorter and much narrower point than the argument with which I have just dealt. It is not suggested that, as enacted, the provisions of the Act of 1567 struck in any way at intercourse between persons whose only tie is that of adoption. Indeed, it was not till 1930 that adoption achieved legal status in Scotland and, not surprisingly, there is nothing in the 18th chapter of Leviticus or the 1567 Act to hint in even the vaguest terms that adopter and adopted might come within the prohibited degrees therein laid down. On this matter, and on the question of marriage between adopter and adopted, the Adoption of Children (Scotland) Act, 1930, was silent. In 1949, however, certain provisions were enacted which now appear in section 12 (3) of the consolidating Adoption Act of 1958. They are to the effect that 'for the purpose of the law relating to marriage, an adopter and the person whom he has been authorised to adopt under an adoption order shall be deemed to be within the prohibited degrees of consanguinity. . . .' These provisions, it is said, not merely prohibit marriage between the parties concerned, but also bring them within the penal ambit and prohibited degrees of the Act of 1567. Had that been the intention of Parliament, it would have been a simple matter, when the provisions were first enacted, to insert, after the word 'marriage,' some such phrase as 'and of the law of incest' or even 'and of the criminal law.' Marriage is basically a civil matter and incest is a criminal matter. The argument for the Crown, however, is that, so far as prohibited degrees are concerned, the law of marriage and the law of incest have been in Scotland, since 1567, two sides of the same coin. Having regard to the difference (which in some cases may be of substantial importance) between 'heads' and 'tails,' I am not sure that the learned Solicitor-General's metaphor was an entirely happy choice. His point, however, was clear. It was to the effect that the Incest Act of 1567 and the immediately succeeding Act (1567, cap. 16) 'anent lauchfull marriage' etc. set out the law respecting prohibited degrees (a) in regard to incest on the one hand and (b) in regard to marriage on the other in such terms as were identical in effect, and that this identity had continued in essence till the present day. There may be some historical foundation for, at any rate, part of this view, although it is necessary to stress that the two Acts, although related in substance and objects, were separate Acts, one criminal, the other civil, and that their phraseology even in regard to what might be called common ground differed to a marked degree. Nor am I satisfied that the two branches of the law have kept consistently in step throughout the centuries. I am by no means clear, for example, as to how one equates the decision in *Solicitor-General* v. *A.B.* a criminal case, with the prohibition (civil) in the concluding words of chapter XXIV, para. 4, of the Act 1690, cap. 7. Whatever the statutory effect of these words may be, they appear to indicate a view of the civil law different from that taken of the criminal law, not merely as it was at the time, but as it had been since 1567, in *Solicitor-General* v. *A.B.*

Apart from that, however, there seems to me to be a much more cogent objection to the argument for the Crown. I would accept that, if it is enacted that persons within certain degrees may marry, then any provision making it a criminal offence for such persons to have sexual intercourse is impliedly repealed: for legislation legalising a marriage must inevitably imply that the parties thereto and indeed parties eligible to contract such a marriage) do not, by having sexual intercourse, commit a criminal offence. It does not follow, however, that the converse holds good. Clear language is required for the creation of a criminal offence, particularly when it can carry a sentence of life imprisonment. The provision founded upon by the Crown debars marriage, but I am unable to see how it creates a criminal offence by bringing adopter and adopted within the ambit of the law of incest. Had the legislature intended so to do, it could (and, I think, would) have done so by the addition of a few simple words. Should it wish to do so now, the remedy is equally simple. On this second branch of their argument the defence, for the reasons I have given, are also entitled, in my opinion, to succeed."

Objection to relevancy upheld.

2. Vaughan v. H.M. Advocate
1979 S.L.T. 49

An accused person was charged that, acting along with the mother of a small boy, he forced the boy's penis into the mother's vagina and did cause him to have incestuous intercourse, contrary to the Incest Act 1567. The accused was not related to the mother or the son. The trial judge repelled a defence objection to the relevancy of the indictment which was to the effect that since the accused was not within the forbidden degrees, he could not be guilty as actor, but only as art and part; since the 1567 Act applied only to the former, the indictment was irrelevant. The accused was convicted after trial. On appeal,

LORD JUSTICE-CLERK (WHEATLEY), (with whom Lords Kissen and Thomson concurred): "At the trial diet the applicant, who had pled not guilty at the pleading diet, withdrew his plea of not guilty and challenged the relevancy of the incest charge. This challenge was repelled by the trial judge and the case proceeded to trial on a not guilty plea. Learned counsel for the applicant, repeating the submission which he advanced to the trial judge, argued before us as follows. The applicant could not commit incest with this boy as actor. They were not within the forbidden degrees referred to in the Incest Act of 1567. In the circumstances he could only be said to be guilty art and part.

This, however, was a charge based on a statute which related to a restricted class of persons, and there was no provision in the statute other than in respect of a person who has had sexual intercourse with another person within the prohibited degrees. The group of persons covered by the Act was a narrow one, namely those persons contained in the 18th chapter of Leviticus. The Act of 1567 has accordingly to be read in a restricted sense and cannot be extended beyond a literal and narrow translation: *Solicitor-General* v. *A.B.*, 1913 2 S.L.T. per Lord Justice-General Strathclyde at pp. 397-398 and Lord Salvesen at p. 402, and *H.M. Advocate* v. *McKenzie* per Lord Justice-Clerk Grant at pp. 82 et seq. Where an Act sets out in terms the persons struck at by the Act, a person who does not fall within the stated category or categories cannot be convicted on the ground that he assisted in the commission of an offence under the Act: Lord Justice-General Inglis in *Robertsons* v. *Caird* (1885) 5 Couper at p. 668. Hume on *Crimes,* vol. i, at p. 447, deals with the restricted classes of persons covered by the Act of 1567, but makes no mention of guilt by accession in incest. This is in significant contrast to his reference of guilt art and part in the crime of rape— vol. i, p. 305. Counsel conceded that a person could be convicted of incest art and part if that person fell within the forbidden degrees, but argued that this extension did not go beyond that to a person who did not fall within the forbidden degrees.

Counsel then proceeded to deal with the argument which he anticipated (correctly) would be advanced by the Crown, namely the argument presented to the trial judge. Section 46 of the Criminal Procedure (Scotland) Act 1975 enacts that: 'It shall not be necessary to state in any indictment that a person accused is "guilty, actor or art and part,'' but such charge shall be implied in all indictments'. Section 216 of that Act provides that: 'A person may be convicted of, and punished for, a contravention of any statute or order, notwithstanding that he was guilty of such contravention as art and part only'. He submitted that s. 46 was purely procedural, that s. 216, in relating its provisions to any statute, constituted a generality, and that on a general rule of construction such a generality should not derogate from statutes which are restrictive: Maxwell on *The Interpretation of Statutes* (12th ed.), p. 196. Accordingly the generality of s. 216 is not sufficient to extend the limited class of persons named in the Act of 1567 to a person not within that specific class as actor or art and part.

The learned advocate-depute, before dealing with the argument under s. 216 aforesaid, submitted that there had been for some time the view that a person could be guilty art and part of a statutory crime. Hume on *Crimes*, vol. ii, at p. 239, says: 'The charge of art and part is suitable alike to accusations of every sort; to an indictment on a British statute, which creates some new offence, as to one laid at common law, or on any of our old Scottish acts'. The advocate-depute conceded that a statute might be so framed that only a person in a special capacity could be charged, as in *Robertsons* v. *Caird* which turned on the exact provisions of the Debtors (Scotland) Act 1880, s. 13, but maintained that one does not start with any particular presumption that art and part is excluded in any particular statute. The Act of 1567 related to those people who can be actors in the crime of incest, but does not exclude its applicability to persons who are art and part in the commission of the offence. The cases cited on this point relate only to the position of the actor. In the case of rape a female can be guilty art and part. There is accordingly no reason why in incest a male should not be convicted art and part in circumstances such as were here present. In any event, if he was wrong in this, s. 216 aforesaid was sufficient in itself to make the conviction a valid one.

In our opinion, the issue here can be determined simply by reference to s. 216, whatever the position may have been prior to the passing of s. 31 of the Criminal Justice (Scotland) Act 1949, which was its predecessor. It is not without interest to note that s. 31 of the 1949 Act is prefaced by the words, 'For the removal of doubts', words which have been excluded from s. 216 in the consolidation statute of 1975. It is quite clear that the restrictive principle relied upon by counsel for the applicant must be applied to the case of the actors in the crime of incest. It is accordingly logical to look primo loco at the persons who are said to be the actors in the offence, to see whether they fall within the forbidden degrees. If they do not, then that is the end of the case. But if they do, is there any reason in principle why, if the act and the actors fall within the provisions of the Act, a person who is art and part in the commission of the offence should not be equally guilty? Counsel for the applicant conceded that a person could be guilty art and part provided that person fell within the forbidden degrees. Having regard to the roles which they play, it is difficult to see why there should be a distinction between such a person and one who does not fall within the forbidden degrees. The gravamen of the offence is the act of sexual intercourse between persons within the forbidden degrees. The abettor who is art and part is linked by reason of his accession to the crime. In our opinion, the argument that the generality of the provisions of s. 216 do not derogate from the restrictive provisions of the Act of 1567 proceeds on a misconception and is ill-founded. The act and the classes of actors remain the same and are in no way extended. All that s. 216 does is to make a person who has abetted in the commission of the act between the actors a person who has also to accept responsibility for the offence, in accordance with the general principle of our law. On that ground alone we are satisfied that the argument advanced by counsel for the applicant must fail. We accordingly do not require to consider the application for leave to appeal against sentence, and both applications will be refused."

Appeal dismissed.

NOTES

Gordon's view (2nd ed. para. 5-10) is thus confirmed, although the court in *Vaughan* did not find it necessary to overrule *Robertsons* v. *Caird:* statutory offences are subject in general to the same rules of art and part as those charged at common law. On the whole question of reform of the law of incest in Scotland, see the proposals of the Scottish Law Commission in its Memorandum No. 44 'The Law of Incest in Scotland (1980).

c. *Shamelessly indecent conduct*

1. **McLaughlan v. Boyd**
    1934 J.C. 19

A publican was charged in the police court, *inter alia*, with using lewd, indecent and libidinous practices towards a number of persons who came to his bar in the course of their work. In each case the evidence was that he had seized the other person's hand and placed it on his own private parts. There was no evidence of the age of these persons. He was convicted by the magistrate. On appeal by stated case, the charges were challenged on the ground that the words "lewd, indecent and libidinous practices" could not be used to describe an assault on a person of the age of puberty.

LORD JUSTICE-GENERAL (CLYDE): "To deal only with the charges in the indictment on which conviction followed, it appears that the accused over a considerable period of time has given himself up to conduct with other men of a grossly and shamelessly indecent kind. The incidents were repeated and followed each other at short intervals. Some of the charges on which conviction was pronounced were libelled as assaults by the appellant placing his hand upon the private parts of certain persons named; in other cases the charge was libelled as the use of lewd, indecent, and libidinous practices by the accused 'seizing ↓the hand of his victim ↓and placing it on ↓the appellant's own ↓private parts.'

The main question which has been debated is as to whether there is in Scotland, at common law, any such offence as indecency or lewdness when committed upon a person who is not proved to be below the age of puberty. In support of the argument that indecent or lewd conduct in such circumstances is not a crime by the common law of Scotland, reference was made to the statutory provision introduced by section 11 of the Criminal Law Amendment Act of 1885, which affirms that gross indecency between two male adults, or indecency committed by one male adult on another male adult, is a crime. But it is, in my opinion, impossible to maintain on the authorities that, by the common law of Scotland, indecent conduct committed by one person upon another only constitutes a crime when the victim of that conduct is below puberty. Whether the victim is male or female, it has, no doubt, always been a serious aggravation that the victim was near the age of puberty or below it. There are obvious reasons for this; but the cases quoted to us negative the idea that indecency or lewdness ceases to be a crime as soon as the victim is proved to be above the age of puberty. If a hard-and-fast line at that age is not warranted by the authorities, it is impossible in principle to fix any standard of age; although (according to circumstances) the age of the victim may be an important consideration.

It would be a mistake to imagine that the criminal common law of Scotland countenances any precise and exact categorisation of the forms of conduct which amount to crime. It has been pointed out many times in this Court that such is not the nature or quality of the criminal law of Scotland. I need only refer to the well-known passage in the opening of Baron Hume's institutional work (Hume on Crimes (3rd ed.) ch. i), in which the broad definition of crime—a doleful or wilful offence against society in the matter of 'violence, dishonesty, falsehood, indecency, irreligion' is laid down. In my opinion, the statement in Macdonald's Criminal Law (4th ed., p. 221), that 'all shamelessly indecent conduct is criminal,' is sound, and correctly expresses the law of Scotland. No doubt there may be in particular cases circumstances of aggravation, but I am not prepared to rule out of the category of crime any shamelessly indecent conduct, and I am not prepared to infer, from the circumstances that section 11 of the Act of 1885 affirmed the proposition that shamelessly indecent conduct by one male adult in relation to another was criminal, that such conduct was not, or could not have been, the competent subject of prosecution in Scotland before.

That being so, the only question that remains in this stated case is whether the magistrate, by convicting of assault in the *modus* libelled in some of the charges, and of lewd practices in the *modus* libelled in the others, has gone wrong. I do not think so. It is not material that the charges are stated as charges of assault attended with indecency, or as charges of lewd practices. It is, in short, plain to my mind that it is impossible to attribute to the conviction as it stands any injustice to the accused at all.

Lastly, complaint was made that the magistrate, in narrating the facts proved under the various charges, has not stated in so many words that the indecent assaults or lewd practices were committed against the consent and without the will of the victims. But it is impossible to read the findings in fact in relation to the charges made as consistent with the notion that there was any consent on the part of the persons who were abused in this way. I suggest that both the first and second questions ought to be answered in the affirmative."

Appeal dismissed.

2. Watt v. Annan
1978 S.L.T. 198

An accused was charged on summary complaint with shamelessly indecent conduct in that he showed an obscene film to a number of persons in a hotel. The complaint also narrated that the film: "was liable to create depraved, inordinate and lustful desires in those watching said film and to corrupt the morals of the lieges". An objection to the relevancy of the complaint on the grounds that it did not disclose a crime at Scots law was repelled and the accused went to trial. The evidence disclosed that the film had been shown to members of a private club and that the showing had taken place in private in the lounge bar of the hotel, the door of which had been locked by the accused to keep out the public and non-subscribing members of the club. The accused was convicted and appealed by stated case.

LORD CAMERON: "The statement that 'all shamelessly indecent conduct is criminal' makes its first appearance in the first edition of Macdonald's *Criminal Law* and is repeated in all subsequent editions without comment or criticism in any decided case. It was approved by Lord Clyde in *McLaughlan* v. *Boyd,* 1933 S.L.T. at p. 631 when he declared it to be sound and correctly expressing the law of Scotland. It is true that this observation was obiter but it was concurred in by the other members of the court and has not been since subjected to criticism or doubt. It is clear however that, as the Crown maintained, it is not the indecency of the conduct itself which makes it criminal but it is the quality of 'shamelessness', and the question is what is the content of this qualification? It was accepted, and rightly so, in the submission for the Crown that the conduct to be criminal, in such circumstances as the facts in the present case disclose, must be directed towards some person or persons with an intention or knowledge that it should corrupt or be calculated or liable to corrupt or deprave those towards whom the indecent or obscene conduct was directed. Whether or not conduct which is admittedly indecent or obscene is to be held criminal will depend on proof of the necessary mens rea and upon the facts and circumstances of the particular case. It would be impracticable as well as undesirable to attempt to define precisely the limits and ambit of this particular offence, far less to decide that the nature of the premises or place in which the conduct charged has occurred should alone be decisive in transforming conduct which would otherwise be proper subject of prosecution into conduct which may do no more than offend the canons of personal propriety or standards of contemporary morals. If it were considered desirable or necessary that this was a chapter of the criminal law in which precise boundaries or limits were to be set then it might be thought that the task is one which is more appropriate for the hand of the legislator.

In the present case there is no dispute that the film displayed amply deserved the description of indecent or obscene or that its display was calculated or liable to corrupt or deprave the morals of those who viewed it, whether they were consenters or otherwise. The question is then narrowed to this, whether the circumstances of the display as found by the sheriff in this case were such as to render the conduct of the appellant shamelessly indecent. It was strongly urged for the appellant that the circumstances here lack that necessary element of publicity or affront to public morals which is essential to commission of the offence. The argument derived its force from the citation of opinions in the context of obscene publication cases ranging from *Robinson* (1843) 1 Broun 590 to the more recent decisions already cited in *McGowan* v. *Langmuir* 1931 J.C. 10 and *Galletly* v. *Laird.* 1953 J.C. 16. These decisions however and the judgments pronounced in them must be considered in light of their own facts. In particular, they arose out of admitted publication in respect that the books or prints were offered for sale to members of the public and were on public display. Nothing which is said in them therefore casts directly or by implication any doubt on the soundness of that broad general statement of the law founded upon by the Crown which has stood unchallenged for over a century. Neither the publicity nor the privacy of the locus of the conduct charged necessarily affects far less determines the criminal quality of indecent conduct libelled as shameless. That this is so can be readily inferred from the context in which this statement of the law appears, particularly in Macdonald's first edition and in those subsequent editions which were revised by the Lord Justice-Clerk himself. In my opinion therefore it is not essential to relevancy of a charge of shamelessly indecent conduct that it must be libelled that the conduct in question occurred in a public place or was a matter of public exhibition. The case of *Mackenzie* v. *Whyte* ((1864) 4 Irv. 570) makes it clear that the offence of indecent exposure, an offence against public morals, 'consists of a person exposing himself in a state of nudity in a public place or where he can be seen by a multitude of persons' (see per Lord Justice-Clerk at p. 577). It is therefore no more essential that an offence of shamelessly indecent conduct, within which category indecent exposure falls, should be libelled as having been committed in a public place than it is in a charge of lewd and libidinous practices, which is an offence whether committed in domestic privacy and secrecy or in a place of public resort (see *McLaughlan* v. *Boyd*).

The criminal character of the act of indecency must therefore depend on proof of the necessary criminal intent as well as proof of the nature of the conduct itself and of the circumstances in which it takes place. Conduct that may be legitimate and innocent in the laboratory of the anthropologist may well be shamelessly indecent if carried on or exhibited in other places or circumstances, and whether these can be characterised as private or public may be no matter. In any event, it may well be asked what should be the criterion of 'publicity' as opposed to 'privacy' which is to determine the critical issue of deciding that conduct which might otherwise be regarded only as in conflict with accepted morals becomes in breach of the criminal law. To this question the submissions for the appellant provide no answer and the obscene publication cases are no guide. In these circumstances and for these reasons I am of opinion that the appellant's attack on the relevancy of this complaint fails and the first question should be answered in the affirmative. The answer to the second question posed in the case is to be found in the facts found by the sheriff. Prior notice of the display of this film had been given not only by members of the club but by others, presumably not members of the club. Membership of the club was based upon no special qualification nor subject to a period of application or probation. Membership was enjoyed on a weekly basis and on payment of a modest weekly subscription. Prima facie any person could apply for and, so far as the rules disclose, in fact receive the privilege of membership on tendering to an appropriate official at any time or place the modest sum of 10p for which he could enjoy the privileges of the club for a period of three weeks without further payment. It is significant that while the club has a treasurer it has, again so far as the rules disclose, neither secretary nor time or place of meeting, nor any regular mechanism for intimation of meetings. Further, as appears from finding (22), the door of the room in which the club meeting was held was only locked by the chairman after the display of the film of the club outing and before the showing of the film in question. It is found by the sheriff that the locking of the door was to keep out the public during the showing of the film libelled and also to keep 'non-subscribing members' out; that is, those in arrears with their subscriptions. There is nothing therefore in this finding to negative the idea that any person could be enrolled there and then as a subscribing member of the club on payment of 10p and thus enjoy the benefit of viewing this admittedly obscene film.

In light of these undisputed facts it appears to me idle to maintain that this was a performance in circumstances which were inconsistent with affront to public decency or morals. Even if it were to be argued that a mere domestic and gratuitous entertainment of family and friends by a display of such a film would not attract penal consequences the facts found in the present case bear no resemblance to any such situation. So far as the findings-in-fact disclose there was little, if any, control over indiscriminate access in premises to which the public had a right of entry to an exhibition, the character of which it is not in dispute, was accurately described in the complaint and in the sheriff's finding-in-fact. The appellant's conduct was intentionally directed towards whoever could avail himself of the opportunity to be present and it was conduct which the sheriff, in my opinion, was entitled to find was calculated or liable to deprave or to corrupt in light of the admitted nature of the film. Having regard to these findings, to the whole circumstances in which this film came to be exhibited, the audience to which it was displayed and the admitted purpose for which the audience had been gathered together, I am of opinion that the sheriff was entitled to reach the conclusion at which he arrived and that the second question should also be answered in the affirmative."

Appeal dismissed.

NOTES

The success for the Crown in *Watt* v. *Annan* is having the effect that prosecutions for "obscenity," which in England have been bedevilled by the difficulties inherent in the Obscene Publications Acts, are proceeding in Scotland at common law; see *Robertson* v. *Smith*, 1979 S.L.T. (Notes) 51. For a critique of *Watt* v. *Annan* and the whole concept of "shameless indecent conduct," see Maher, "The Enforcement of Morals Continued" 1978 S.L.T. (News) 281; Gordon, "Shameless Indecency and Obscenity", (1980) 25 J.L.S. 262.

d.   Living on immoral earnings
Soni v. H.M. Advocate
1970 S.L.T. 275

A landlord owned or controlled about 22 furnished houses in Glasgow of which he let eight to women whom he knew to be prostitutes. He was charged with and convicted of knowingly living in part on the earnings of prostitution, contrary to s. 1 (1) (*a*) of the Immoral Traffic (Scotland) Act 1902. He appealed to the High Court on three grounds: (1) that the sheriff misdirected the jury in that he directed them that they would be entitled to convict if the evidence showed that the accused was participating and assisting in the activities of the prostitutes notwithstanding that the charges made for the houses were reasonable and normal and not exorbitant; and (2) in any event there was no evidence upon which the jury could have found that he was participating and assisting in the activities of the prostitutes and (3) that there was no evidence of exorbitant charges.

LORD JUSTICE-CLERK (GRANT): "The applicant was charged on indictment and convicted of a contravention of s. 1 (1) (*a*) of the Immoral Traffic (Scotland) Act 1902 as amended by the Criminal Law Amendment Act 1912, s. 7. The conviction, in terms of the jury's verdict, was that during the period libelled he had knowingly lived in part on the earnings of prostitution. He was sentenced to nine months' imprisonment. Against both conviction and sentence he now seeks to appeal. . . . The first ground of appeal is in the following terms: 'The presiding judge misdirected the jury in that, having correctly directed them on s. 1 (3) of the Immoral Traffic (Scotland) Act 1902, that there was no sufficient evidence that the applicant had been proved inter alia "to have exercised control direction or influence over the movements of a prostitute in such a manner as to show that he was aiding and abetting or compelling her prostitution with any other person or generally" he then directed them in law that the applicant would be guilty of the offence libelled if the evidence showed that he was participating and assisting in the activities of the prostitutes notwithstanding that the charges made for the houses were reasonable and normal and not exorbitant.' It is right to say here that what the sheriff-substitute did in fact say was not that 'the applicant would be guilty' but that the jury 'would be entitled to convict.'

Before turning to examine and determine the arguments submitted on this ground of appeal it is desirable to give a digest of the facts. The applicant owned or controlled about 22 furnished houses in Glasgow. Eight of these he rented to women whom he knew to be prostitutes. At the trial the Crown maintained that the rents charged for these latter houses were exorbitant or 'prostitute rents' and that in the circumstances the applicant by receiving the rents was living at least in part on the immoral earnings of the prostitutes who rented the houses.

Counsel for the applicant argued strongly that where a house was rented for occupation to a prostitute, and was not provided solely and specifically by the landlord to enable the prostitute to carry on her trade, then the only way by which the landlord could be convicted of a contravention of s. 1 (1) (a) (supra) was to establish that the rent charged was exorbitant, or what has been described in other cases as a 'prostitute rent'. In support of this submission he founded on a passage from the speech of Viscount Simonds in *Shaw* v. *Director of Public Prosecutions*, [1962] A.C. 220 at p. 266; (1961) 45 Cr. App. R. 113 at p. 146. If this were well founded, then the learned sheriff-substitute had obviously misdirected the jury in law when he told them the applicant could be guilty of the offence libelled even if the evidence showed that the charges made for the houses were reasonable and normal and were not exorbitant.

In our view the limitation which counsel for the applicant sought to place on the conditions under which a conviction can be obtained in circumstances such as prevailed here is too restrictive. Each case must be considered on its own facts. The authorities indicate that where a landlord lets a room specifically and exclusively for the purpose of enabling a prostitute to carry on her trade an offence under the section may be held to be committed: see *R.* v. *Thomas* [1957] 1 W.L.R. 747, (1957) 41 Cr. App. R. 117 and the observations thereon by Viscount Simonds in *Shaw* (supra). The same situation arises where knowing that the woman is a prostitute and likely to carry on her trade in the premises, the landlord charges a rent in excess of normal, extorting it from the prostitute upon no other ground than that she is a prostitute—Lord Reid in *Shaw*, at p. 271. And, of course, a person may be convicted if he is brought within the provisions of s. 1 (3) of the Act as amended. These, however, are not the exclusive ways in which the section may be attracted. Circumstances may vary infinitely and in any given case the question is whether in the words of the subsection it is proved that the person accused has been living in whole or in part on the earnings of prostitution.

We were informed that this is the first case of its kind which has come before the courts in Scotland for an authoritative determination. There have, however been a number of cases in England under kindred statutes, and, in consequence of these, and in particular of the case of *Shaw,* it was accepted (and properly so) by both sides of the Bar that there could not be a contravention of the subsection simply if the premises were let for occupation, even if the landlord knew that the tenant was a prostitute and must be assumed to have known that she would ply her trade there. Something more than that is required. Counsel for the applicant maintained that the only thing that could be 'something more' was exorbitant rent. Why should there be such a limitation? There seems to be no reason in principle. The passage from Viscount Simonds in *Shaw,* at p. 226, on which the whole argument was hinged, must be read in its context. His Lordship was there dealing with a case such as that of *R. v. Silver* [1956] 1 W.L.R. 281, 40 Cr. App. R. 32, where the facts were that in the various charges libelled the landlord had let a flat at a high rate to a prostitute, knowing that she was a prostitute and that she intended to use the flat for the purposes of prostitution. Viscount Simonds, who found *Silver* (supra) a difficult case and expressed no final opinion on it, said that it was a tenable view that in such a case the landlord could be convicted of an offence upon the ground that the rent is exorbitant. He did not say that in another set of circumstances no other determining factor could apply. Elsewhere in his speech the noble Lord, after pointing out that a prostitute is entitled to be provided with goods and services in the same way as other people, without an offence being committed, goes on to make a distinction. He says at p. 263: 'I would say, however, that, though a person who is paid for goods or services out of the earnings of prostitution does not necessarily commit an offence under the Act, yet a person does not necessarily escape from its provisions by receiving payment for the goods or services that he supplies to a prostitute. The argument that such a person lives on his own earnings, not hers, is inconclusive. To give effect to it would be to exclude from the operation of the Act the very persons, the tout, the bully or protector, whom it was designed to catch.' The latter category is not confined to those who might be caught by virtue of s. 1(3). At p. 264 he adopts with approval terms used in previous cases such as 'coadjutor' (i.e. an assistant) and 'trading in prostitution'. All this points to a wider range of possibilities than counsel for the applicant asserted. When the case of *Shaw* was in the Court of Criminal Appeal, Ashworth, J., who read the judgment of the court stated (at p. 229): 'It was further submitted that there was no evidence that the appellants charged inflated prices for the prostitute's advertisements, and that therefore *Thomas's* (supra) case was distinguishable. This submission is not well founded, and involves a misunderstanding of the relevance of the inflated rent in that case. The purpose of tendering evidence as to the rent was to show that the room was not let for normal accommodation, but for the prostitute's professional purposes, and although, in the absence of such evidence or other evidence implicating the accused, it might be difficult to prove the charge in the case of a room being let to a prostitute, such evidence was not, in our view, an essential element in the prosecution's case.'

In the House of Lords, Lord Reid said at p. 271: 'But I am far from saying that a landlord can never be guilty of living on the immoral earnings of his tenant. To my mind, the most obvious case is where he takes advantage of her difficulty in getting accommodation to extract from her in the guise of rent sums beyond any normal commercial rent. In reality he is not then merely acting as a landlord; he is making her engage in a joint adventure with him which will bring to him a part of her immoral earnings over and above rent. And there may well be other ways in which he can make himself a participator in her earnings and not merely a recipient of rent. The line may be a difficult one to draw, but juries often have to decide broad questions of that kind.'

While proof of payment of an exorbitant rent may be a factor, and possibly a telling factor, in the issue, it is not an essential one. In its absence, proof that the accused was living on the immoral earnings of prostitution might be difficult, but that is not to say it is impossible. We therefore reject this argument by counsel for the applicant. . . .

So far as the second ground of appeal is concerned, it was agreed that there was ample evidence to support the point that the applicant knew that the women concerned were prostitutes. Counsel for the applicant submitted, however, that there was not sufficient evidence to warrant a reasonable jury finding that the applicant was participating and assisting in the activities of the prostitutes in such a manner as would bring him within the terms of s. 1 (1) (*a*) of the statute. It is not necessary to go into all the evidence in detail. There is, however, ample evidence that the sole reason why some of the prostitutes came to Glasgow was to carry on their trade there, that the applicant was aware of this and that he gave them priority as tenants. There is also clear evidence that the dominant purpose of the lets was not to provide a place to live in but to provide a place where the prostitutes could carry on their trade. At least two of them speak to obtaining a change of house, not because their accommodation was unsuitable for living in, but because the new accommodation was more suitable for prostitution. The prostitutes had no means of support other than prostitution and it was, to say the least of it, in the applicant's interest that their earnings should cover their rent as well as their other outgoings—and that their earning power should be reasonably substantial and should be affected, on a conviction for soliciting, by a fine and not by imprisonment. . . .

In our opinion the evidence that he was participating and assisting in such ways as we have just described and that, for example, he was giving them premises more suited for their activities, discussing the installation of a telephone to facilitate bookings and counselling them against conduct which might get them involved with the police and a possible cutting off of their income, can properly be regarded as showing a personal involvement with their immoral activities designed to secure and advance his own financial interests. This is a view which the jury were entitled to take. The matters which we have mentioned clearly distinguish the position of the applicant from the ordinary case of a person providing services at a normal rate in the normal way. We are accordingly of opinion that the second ground of appeal also fails.

In support of the third ground of appeal counsel for the applicant argued that it was impossible for the jury to come to any decision that the rents were exorbitant in the admitted absence of any evidence of comparative rents for comparative properties. He made a similar submission at the trial, and the presiding judge left it to the jury to decide whether they should accept that, but indicated that there was other evidence, albeit not very much, which would entitle them to find the point proved in the absence of such comparative evidence.

We are of the opinion that while comparative evidence might have been the best way of establishing that the rents were exorbitant, it is not necessarily the only way. We are also of the opinion that although the evidence on the point is not strong there was sufficient to entitle the jury to hold that the exorbitancy had been established. The evidence about the applicant's proposal to 'cook' the returns to the Inland Revenue, wherein the rents would be shown as being about only half of the rents actually being charged could be regarded as a legitimate touchstone of what normal rents ought to have been. . . .

In the whole circumstances therefore we are of the opinion that the application for leave to appeal against conviction should be refused and that the conviction should stand."

Appeal refused.

NOTES

Section 1 (1) (*a*) of the Immoral Traffic (Scotland) Act 1902 is now s. 12 (1) (*a*) of the Sexual Offences (Scotland) Act 1976.

CHAPTER 17

OFFENCES AGAINST PUBLIC ORDER

a. Mobbing

Although this is still thought of in conjunction with the old crime of rioting, the *nomen juris* "mobbing and rioting" is inapplicable today since the abolition of the Riot Act 1714. Modern indictments for the crime still however refer commonly to the accused "forming part of a riotous mob."

Sloan v. Macmillan
1922 J.C. 1

Three coal miners, who were on strike from their colliery, were convicted of forming part of a riotous mob, which, acting of a common purpose with a view to unlawfully compelling a number of persons who were then working at the colliery to abstain from working, and, in breach of the public peace and to the alarm of the lieges, invading the colliery at 2.30 a.m., demanding that the said workmen abstain from work, threatening them with violence if they did not so abstain, unlawfully compelling them to abstain from working and stopping the carrying on of work at said colliery. They appealed to the High Court.

LORD JUSTICE-CLERK (SCOTT DICKSON): "What they did was to set out from a place some distance from this pit for the purpose of stopping the voluntary workers, who were at the pit to preserve the works so that, when the strike was over, the miners might at once get access to the workings and carry on their employment. It is found as a fact that seventeen people went to this pit for the purpose of ordering the fires to be drawn so that the workings should be drowned out, and of enforcing their orders. That was obviously an illegal purpose, and the suggestion, which is made in article 16 of the stated case, that Alexander Sloan and his associates did no more than use peaceful persuasion to the voluntary workers, is simply nonsense. Sloan went there with several of his associates and, for the purpose of intimidating the workers there, persistently lied—as he now represents in the argument to us—to the police and to some of the voluntary workers by stating that he was backed up by hundreds of desperate men. In point of fact he did intimidate the workers there, and the fear which Sloan and his associates engendered was a perfectly justifiable fear that, if the voluntary workers did not do what they were asked to do, grievous bodily harm would happen to them. By what is now said on his behalf to be his lying representations Sloan succeeded in getting the men in the pithead to cease stoking the fires and to raise the men in the pit up to the pithead. I think it is impossible to hold that there was anything of the nature of peaceful picketing on this occasion, and, if it is the belief that this was peaceful picketing the sooner that belief is dispelled the better. It was not peaceful picketing; it was riotous conduct which is liable to punishment. The result was that five men, three of whom are the appellants, and twelve or thirteen others who were personally present at the pithead, succeeded by threats of what would happen to the voluntary workers, if not by actual violence, in carrying out the illegal purpose which they had set out to achieve; and so terrified the voluntary workers—who are quite entitled to work at this pithead if they pleased—that they gave up their work so that the workings were liable to be destroyed. . . .

The charge is that the appellants formed part of a riotous mob which, acting of common purpose with a view unlawfully to compel certain people who were then working at the colliery to abstain from doing what they were quite entitled to do, carried out their purpose. There is no rule of law apart from the Riot Act and the decision to which Mr Sandeman referred, *Gollan* (1883) 5 Couper 317, which says anything about the number of persons required to constitute a mob. But I think the law is that the number of people required to constitute a mob depends on what these people do, the violence they show, the threats they use. In this case the three appellants through their spokesman, Sloan, lied persistently to the police and to the workmen in order to produce terror on the part of the workmen, and did produce terror by saying that there were hundreds of desperate men outside. That seems to me to be enough to make the appellants constitute part of a riotous mob, when one considers the threats, their character, the time when they were uttered, and the result they produced, for they succeeded, by these illegal threats, in frightening the men who were working to do what the mob desired. That to my mind was quite sufficient to justify the Sheriff in coming to the conclusion in fact that there was here a riotous mob assembled for the illegal purpose of compelling the voluntary workers to abstain from doing the work they were doing."

LORD SALVESEN: "It is not necessary that any actual violence shall be used in order that a mob may be deemed riotous; it is sufficient if the mob assembles for the purpose of intimidating people in the lawful performance of their duties. If no resistance is made to the intimidation, perhaps violence will never be used. But the very object of intimidation, if it is to be effective, is to induce the belief in the minds of those intimidated that, unless they submit, worse things will happen and the thing will be done forcibly.

Accordingly I see no ground in law—and our province is limited to reviewing the Sheriff upon points of law—for holding that this conviction was otherwise than perfectly justified by the facts which the Sheriff has found proved.

I express no opinion as to whether a riotous mob may not consist of no more than five persons."

Appeal dismissed.

NOTES

Lord Salvesen's doubt as to how many persons constitute a "mob" has never been resolved. On the rule that mere presence in a mob will make a person responsible for everything done by it, see Gordon, paras. 40-13 *et seq.*

b.   *Breach of the peace*

1.   **Raffaelli v. Heatly**
1949 J.C. 101

An accused person was convicted on a charge that he conducted himself in a disorderly manner, peered in at a lighted window of a dwelling-house in a street about 11.50 p.m., put residents in the street in a state of fear and alarm and committed a breach of the peace. He appealed to the High Court.

LORD JUSTICE-CLERK (THOMSON): "Mr. Thomson [counsel for the appellant] has argued to us with his usual persuasiveness that there were no sufficient facts found to justify the conclusion reached. Mr Thomson says that the facts as found are no more than that the accused walked down the street and stopped on a public pavement and stared through a chink of some curtains into the room of a dwelling-house in which there was a light and that he did so on two occasions. Mr Thomson says that there was no evidence that anybody was alarmed or disturbed. None of the three women who gave evidence said that they were upset. There was no evidence as to what was going on in the house into which the appellant looked, and Mr Thomson says that was really no evidence at all that there was anybody alarmed or that anything took place that might be reasonably expected to alarm anybody.

It is usual to charge this offence as a breach of the peace, because it is a species of disorderly conduct; where something is done in breach of public order or decorum which might reasonably be expected to lead to the lieges being alarmed or upset or tempted to make reprisals at their own hand, the circumstances are such as to amount to breach of the peace.

It seems to me in the present case there are sufficient facts to entitle a judge to draw the inference of disorderly conduct in that sense. It was argued that the earlier findings related to an earlier date, but the fact remains that on the very night when the offence took place this Mrs Price was keeping watch and she had been so upset about the matter that she informed the police, but she was afraid to inform her own husband as to the situation in case he would through distaste be tempted into a breach of the peace. All that, taken in conjunction with other facts found, in particular with the fact that the accused returned to this particular window and again looked into this window, seems to me thoroughly to warrant the conclusion which was reached."

Appeal dismissed.

2.   **Young v. Heatly**
1959 J.C. 66

A schoolmaster was convicted of breach of the peace. He appealed by stated case.

LORD JUSTICE-GENERAL (CLYDE): "This is a stated case from the Burgh Court of Edinburgh, arising out of a complaint in which a depute headmaster at a technical school in Edinburgh was charged with four breaches of the peace, or alternatively with four contraventions of a subsection of the Edinburgh Corporation Order, 1933. The charges arose out of four separate interviews which the depute headmaster had in his room at the school, at each of which he and a pupil alone were present, and at each of which he was alleged to have made grossly improper remarks and suggestions to a pupil aged sixteen or seventeen. After hearing the evidence, the police judge found the appellant guilty of each of the four charges subject to certain very minor modifications, and he sentenced him to sixty days' imprisonment. . . .

It is said that to establish breach of the peace the acts in question must take place in public and produce alarm in the minds of the lieges and offence to public decorum. Here it is said that the incidents referred to in the complaint each took place in the master's private room at the school, and on each occasion only the appellant and one youth were present. There is no finding of alarm being created to spectators or the public, none of whom either saw or heard what took place, nor is there any finding of alarm to the boys themselves. In these circumstances it is said that the facts do not establish a breach of the peace.

Breach of the peace, however is an offence the limits of which have never been sharply defined. It is so largely in each case a question of circumstances and of degree. It is well settled that it can take place in a private house—*Matthews & Rodden* v. *Linton*, 3 Irv. 570. Moreover, although normally evidence of alarm on the part of third persons is produced in cases of this sort, such evidence is not essential. As Lord M'Laren said in the case of *Ferguson* v. *Carnochan*, 2 White 278 (at p. 282): 'It is enough if the conduct of those who are found brawling and using the offensive language is such as to excite reasonable apprehension that mischief may ensue to the persons who are misconducting themselves, or to others.' In the later case of *Raffaelli* v. *Heatly,* 1949 J.C. 101, there 'was really no evidence at all that there was anybody alarmed or that anything took place that might be reasonably expected to alarm anybody'— see Lord Justice-Clerk at p. 104. Yet the conviction was sustained. As the Lord Justice-Clerk said, 'It is usual to charge this offence as a breach of the peace, because it is a species of disorderly conduct; where something is done in breach of public order or decorum which might reasonably be expected to lead to the lieges being alarmed or upset or tempted to make reprisals at their own hand, the circumstances are such as to amount to breach of the peace.' Lord Mackay (at p. 105) referred to the argument that it was essential that the witnesses should say that they personally were alarmed or that they were annoyed, and he then observed: 'I do not think the definition allows that. If acts are repeated and are calculated to cause alarm and annoyance and are indecorous, I think that is enough.' It follows therefore that it is not essential for the constitution of this crime that witnesses should be produced who speak to being alarmed or annoyed. At the same time, however, I consider that a very special case requires to be made out by the prosecution if a conviction for breach of the peace is to follow in the absence of such evidence of alarm or annoyance. For then the nature of the conduct giving rise to the offence must be so flagrant as to entitle the Court to draw the necessary inference from the conduct itself.

The present case, in my opinion, does fall within this special category. The disgusting nature of the suggestions made, the fact that they took place within a matter of hours with a series of adolescent boys, and the fact that they were made to pupils by a depute headmaster to whom they would normally have looked for help and guidance—all these facts would in the special circumstances of this case justify the inference which the judge clearly drew, and would entitle him to hold a breach of the peace proved. But such a result could not have followed apart from these special circumstances. In my opinion, therefore, the first question and the second question should be answered in the affirmative. So far as the third question is concerned (namely; Was the sentence harsh and oppressive?) the revolting conduct established in this case appears to me amply to warrant the sentence which the Court thought fit to impose."

Appeal dismissed.

NOTES

Raffaelli v. *Heatly* and *Young* v. *Heatly* again confirm that proof of actual alarm or annoyance is unnecessary to support a charge of breach of the peace, although Lord Clyde obviously regarded the situation in *Young* as somewhat of a special case. That case is also considered another authority for the proposition that breach of the peace can be committed in private, if the conduct is (objectively) calculated to result in public annoyance. The subjective intention of the accused (if any) appears to be ignored. See also *Turner* v. *Kennedy* (1972) 36 J.C.L. 249, referred to in Gordon para. 41-10, n. 29. In *Montgomery* v. *McLeod,* 1977 S.L.T. (Notes) 77, where the accused was convicted of breach of the peace after refusing to "move on" when requested to do so by the police, Lord Justice-General Emslie commented: "There is no limit to the kind of conduct which may give rise to a charge of breach of the peace. All that is required is that there must be some conduct as to excite the reasonable apprehension [that mischief may ensue] or such as to create disturbance and alarm to the lieges in fact." See also *Palazzo* v. *Copeland,* 1976 J.C. 52 (*ante,* Ch. 6) where it was held that it was no defence to a charge of breach of the peace that the accused acted in order to stop a breach of the peace.

CHAPTER 18

OFFENCES AGAINST THE COURSE OF JUSTICE

a. Perjury

Before a false statement on oath or affirmation can constitute perjury the statement must have some materiality, as well as being relevant and competent evidence.

1. **Hall v. H.M. Advocate**
1968 S.L.T. 275

The accused was convicted of perjury in that at the trial of William Stark and others (see *H.M. Advocate* v. *Stark and Ors.,* 1968 S.L.T. (Notes) 10) he "did depone that he did not . . . make to [a] detective sergeant [certain statements] and, in particular, that . . . he gave a knife to J.S. and that he saw J.S. stick the knife into a boy's back, the truth as he knew being that he did make said statements . . ."

LORD JUSTICE-CLERK (GRANT): "Counsel, in his argument for the applicant, has raised here a point of considerable interest. His client was convicted of perjury in the Court below. The perjury alleged was the giving of false evidence, at an earlier trial at which he was a witness, to the effect that he had not made a particular specified statement to the police. At the earlier trial, the Crown sought to lead evidence of the making of that statement to the police, presumably in order to discredit the applicant who had denied in the box that he had made it. Objection was then taken by the defence, and the presiding judge, after hearing evidence of the circumstances in which the statement had been made, allowed evidence of it to be received. He rejected the defence submission that the statement was inadmissible by reason of its being in the nature of a precognition.

At the trial of the accused a somewhat analogous situation arose. The Crown, having based their case on the alleged falsity of the applicant's denial on oath that he had made the statement to the police, could not, of course, establish their case without leading evidence that the statement had in fact been made. When they sought to do so, the defence objected to the admissibility of that evidence on, basically, the same grounds as had been argued in the earlier trial. The presiding judge in this case adopted the same course as Lord Avonside had done previously. He heard evidence of the circumstances in which the statement was made. He agreed with the conclusion which Lord Avonside had previously reached and held that the statement had not been a precognition or a statement in the nature of a precognition, and evidence as to the statement was admitted. That evidence is, of course, crucial to the conviction of the accused. In these circumstances, today, for the third time, the admissibility of evidence of the making of that statement has been challenged.

Counsel for the applicant founded strongly on the case of *Kerr* v. *H.M. Advocate,* 1958 J.C. 14, 1959 S.L.T. 82, and, in particular, on certain dicta by Lord Justice-Clerk Thomson, at pp. 19 and 20. The case of *Kerr* (supra) is, however, to my mind, a very different one from the present. The Court in *Kerr* were not dealing, as we are here, with the admissibility of evidence given at a trial in which the applicant was a witness only and not an accused and which took place before the trial at which the applicant was convicted. To my mind the crux of the matter here is whether Lord Avonside was right in admitting the evidence in question at the earlier trial to which the applicant was not a party. I must say that I would need strong reasons for interfering in a case like this with the decision made, on a question of competency of evidence, by a judge in a trial on an indictment which is not before us in the present case. It is unnecessary to decide, in this case, whether or not Lord Morison's statement of the law, in regard to such a case as the present, in *Angus* v. *H.M. Advocate,* 1935 J.C. 1, in the last paragraph of his opinion at p. 6, does or does not go too far. He begins that paragraph by saying: 'The judge at the trial, subject to any statutory appeal which there may be, is the final judge of the admission or rejection of evidence at a trial. It is quite impossible for one judge at a trial for perjury to review the decision of another judge on the admissibility of evidence which he has allowed in a trial before him.' (1934 S.L.T. 501.) I should perhaps add, for the sake of clarity, that the phrase 'judge at the trial' at the beginning of that quotation referred, of course, to the judge who presided at the trial at which perjury is alleged to have taken place. Nevertheless, whether Lord Morison's statement of the law goes too far or not (and I express no opinion on this) I am satisfied that it is only for the most exceptional reasons that the presiding judge at the perjury trial (and indeed this Court in an appeal in which that presiding judge's decision on admissibility is attacked) should review the decision of the judge at the trial at which the perjury is alleged to have taken place, on the question of the admissibility at that earlier trial of evidence which is part of the subject matter of the charge of perjury.

In the present case, so far from thinking that Lord Avonside went wrong, I think that, on the facts as disclosed to us, his decision was right.

I should add, secondly, in regard to the case of *Kerr,* that certain circumstances there were extremely special. They are narrated in the opinion of Lord Justice-Clerk Thomson, towards the foot of p. 18 of the report. I think it was probably because of these special circumstances that he appears to have taken the view on the facts of that case, that there was some onus on the Crown to establish the admissibility of the evidence which had been admitted by the presiding sheriff was hearsay evidence admitted in the Court below. Briefly, the situation in *Kerr* was that the evidence designed for no other purpose than to discredit a defence witness in advance and that the circumstances in which the alleged statement was made to the police had not been elucidated in evidence. Here we are in a very different situation. No question arose of discrediting the present applicant *in advance* at the earlier trial at which he gave evidence as a witness. Furthermore, the circumstances in which the statement was made by the applicant to the police have been elucidated in evidence, as I have indicated, both before the presiding judge at the earlier trial and before the presiding judge at the trial of the applicant. They both reached the same decision and, in my opinion, they reached the proper decision.

In my opinion, one should, in general, be very slow to confer on statements made to the police by potential witnesses the confidential status which attaches to precognitions in the proper sense of that word. There is an obvious and basic difference between the two, although the former may in certain circumstances merge into the latter as, for example, in *McNeilie* v. *H.M. Advocate,* 1929 J.C. 50, 1929 S.L.T. 145. There the police officer, who obtained a statement from a defence witness the day before the trial, appears to have been doing so, not as a preliminary to a precognition which was to be taken by the procurator-fiscal but, as still happens because of the brief period between the lodging of the defence list of witnesses and the trial, as something which was to serve the purpose of the precognition which would otherwise have been taken by the procurator-fiscal. We have a very different situation here.

I would accordingly refuse the application."

LORD WALKER: "I agree that the application should be refused. Counsel for the applicant's argument raised the delicate question as to the distinction between a statement made on a previous occasion which may properly be the subject matter of evidence under the authority of s. 3 of the Evidence Act 1852 and one which has the character of precognition and so may not.

Broadly speaking, I think that there is an important distinction between statements made to the police in the course of their investigations before apprehension and statements taken after apprehension on the authority of the procurator-fiscal for the purposes of a trial. The latter are prima facie of the nature of precognitions, but that does not mean that the former may not also be precognitions. Whether they are or not seems to me to depend very much on the circumstances and on the nature of the particular statement. If I may borrow, with respect, the phraseology of Lord Justice-Clerk Thomson in *Kerr* v. *H.M. Advocate,* 1958 J.C. 14, 1958 S.L.T. 82, a statement which appears to have 'filtered through the mind of another person' might probably be regarded as precognition, and one which appears to be 'pure and undefiled' might not.

In the present case the police in the course of investigating a case of stabbing, and before reporting the result of their investigation to the procurator-fiscal, took a statement from a potential witness, the present applicant. The statement was detailed and lengthy and was taken down in writing. I do not see anything in the circumstances or in the tenor of the statement to suggest that its contents may have filtered through the minds of the police. At the subsequent trial for stabbing the applicant was adduced as a witness for the Crown. The advocate-depute desired to examine him on whether he had made the statement to the police which ex hypothesi was different from the evidence being given by him. That was a course rendered competent by s. 3 of the Evidence (Scotland) Act 1852, but it was objected to on the ground that the statement to the police was a precognition. After hearing evidence and argument the trial judge repelled the objection. I think that on this issue the onus was on the objector to satisfy the judge that the statement was truly a precognition and I am not satisfied that in rejecting this objection the trial judge erred. The evidence of the applicant denying that he made the statement to the police was, in my opinion, a valid basis for the charge of perjury. And in the trial for perjury objection was again taken to the Crown using the statement to the police as evidence that the applicant's denials in the first trial were perjured. Again there was evidence and argument but the trial judge repelled the objection, and I cannot say he erred in doing so."

NOTES   Appeal dismissed.

The case of *Hall* is of course concerned mainly with the admissibility of evidence of the statement to the police, and whether it was in the nature of a precognition. But the denial by the witness that he had made the statement and evidence that he *had* made the statement both required to be rehearsed in the witness's trial for perjury, and there seems little doubt that the issue of materiality and relevance was satisfied. But what would have happened if evidence of the original statement had been held inadmissible? Presumably no proceedings for perjury would have followed. Section 3 of the Evidence (Scotland) Act 1852 is now consolidated for the purposes of criminal cases in ss. 147 and 349 of the Criminal Procedure (Scotland) Act 1975.

2. **H.M. Advocate v. Cairns**
1967 J.C. 37

The accused was charged with perjury in that when giving evidence at his trial for the murder in Barlinnie Prison of a man Malcolmson of which he was acquitted he gave evidence that he did not assault and stab Malcolmson, the truth being as he well knew that he did assault and stab him.

He pled to the relevancy of the indictment on the grounds that it was incompetent, irrelevant and contrary to natural justice and criminal practice in Scotland. His arguments were heard by a bench of three judges in the High Court.

LORD JUSTICE-CLERK (GRANT): "The plea in bar of trial and the objections to competency and relevancy are three different facets of what is basically the same point. The question raised in each case is whether, if an accused person is acquitted at his trial, having given evidence on oath denying the crime charged, the Crown is entitled thereafter to charge him with perjury in respect of that evidence. In seeking to persuade us to answer that question in the negative Mr Bennett based his argument on the maxim that no man can be made to thole an assize twice for the same matter (Hume, vol. ii, pp. 465-467) and on considerations of practice and natural justice.

As Hume points out (at p. 466), the prosecutor cannot evade the maxim by altering the shape of the former charge and laying the second libel 'for the same facts, under a new denomination of the crime,' *e.g.* by charging fraud instead of forgery. On the other hand, for the maxim to apply, the previous trial 'must have been for the same crime, depending upon the same evidence, and not for what is truly another crime.' [Macdonald on the Criminal Law of Scotland, (5th ed.) p. 272]. Thus it is well settled that a person who has been tried and acquitted, or tried and convicted, on a charge of assault may subsequently be tried on a charge of murder if, after the first trial, the victim dies *(Cobb or Fairweather,* 1 Swin. 354; *Stewart,* 5 Irv. 310). That is so notwithstanding the fact that the Crown will seek to establish at the second trial the assault which was the sole *de quo* at the first. The supervening event changes the character of the offence and the second charge is one which could not possibly have been made at the earlier trial.

In the present case the Crown are, in my opinion, in an even stronger position than in the cases to which I have just referred. The perjury charged in the present indictment is alleged to have occurred in the course of the earlier trial. Not only could it not have been the subject of a charge at that trial, but it is a crime wholly different and it is libelled as having taken place at a different place and on a different date. In *Fraser*, 1 Irv. 66, Lord Justice-General McNeill points out (at p. 73) that a person may be tried if he has never been in jeopardy *for the offence with which he is charged;* and in *Dorward* v. *Mackay*, 1 Coup. 392, Lord Neaves refers (at p. 397) to the 'plain identity' of charges which is needed if the maxim is to apply. The panel here has never been in jeopardy for any offence libelled as having been committed in the High Court at Glasgow on 1st March 1966 and I can find no identity between the present charge and the charge of murder of which he was acquitted. Evidence will no doubt be led tending to show that, as is set out in the indictment, he did in fact assault and stab Malcolmson, but that seems to me to be of no more avail to the panel than it was in *Cobb or Fairweather* and *Stewart*. It is identity of the charges and not of the evidence that is the crucial factor. In my opinion, the plea that the panel has tholed his assize clearly fails."

LORD WHEATLEY: "I now turn to examine Mr Bennett's argument that what the Crown proposed to do in this case, namely lead evidence of the assault on Malcolmson by the panel, was contrary to equity, natural justice and criminal practice in Scotland.

In the first place he argued that humane considerations should preclude the panel from being exposed to the *de facto* ordeal of having to undergo what was tantamount to a second trial of having assaulted and stabbed Malcolmson. A corollary of this was that if he was convicted of the present charge, he would suffer the *de facto* guilt of the original charge of which he had already been acquitted. Yet the second trial, which brought about this unfortunate result, would take place at a later date, when the dice might be more heavily loaded against the panel. The original jury would have had the advantage of evidence which was fresher in the minds of witnesses; evidence vital for the defence might not be available at the second trial; real evidence might be lost or destroyed; the Crown might have obtained further evidence in the interval which strengthened the Crown case; and the second jury might have read the previous case in the press, to the detriment of the panel.

Once again Mr Bennett's argument proceeds on a misconception. The points which he made might have had validity if what was being considered was whether the panel should be charged again with the crime of assaulting and stabbing Malcolmson. What in fact will be investigated at the trial on the present indictment is whether the panel committed perjury at his original trial. If in the establishment of an essential part of that charge the Crown are in a better position—or a worse position—than in a previous trial when an entirely different charge was being investigated, that seems to me to be a matter of no relevance so far as the competency of the second charge is concerned, or of the evidence adduced in support of it. The issue in the present case is the truth or otherwise of the allegation that the panel committed perjury on the occasion libelled, and I do not see why the evidence on that issue should be circumscribed because some of the facts relevant to the charge were the subject matter of a jury's verdict on a previous occasion in relation to an entirely different charge.

So far as criminal practice in Scotland is concerned, this can only date back in this context to 1898, when the Criminal Evidence Act of that year came into operation. As far as I know, Mr Bennett was correct in saying that this was the first time within that period that an accused person has been charged with perjury in relation to his denial on oath in the witness box that he had committed the offence with which he was charged. If it has been a practice in the past not to charge an accused with perjury in such circumstances, this is not a practice which has been hallowed by our criminal courts. The Lord Advocate is master of the instance in criminal proceedings and if such a practice has existed, it is a practice of Lord Advocates and not of the Court. With the discretion which is vested in him in these matters, there is no reason why a Lord Advocate should not decide in a particular case to depart from a practice which his predecessors have observed, and indeed circumstances may arise when he may feel that in the public interest it is his duty to do so. The Court cannot interfere with that discretion—it can only hold that a particular charge libelled is incompetent or irrelevant on some legal ground. If the charge is competent and relevant, as I consider the present one to be, it is not in my opinion open to the Court to refuse to entertain it because the Lord Advocate has in his discretion departed from the practice of his predecessors. I accordingly do not consider that this point has any substance.

Mr Bennett in his final submission seemed to accept that his argument on practice had little validity and switched his argument from practice to equity. If the Crown were right, he argued, then every accused person who gave evidence to the effect that he did not commit the offence libelled against him was liable to be charged with perjury at the discretion of the Lord Advocate, irrespective of whether he was convicted or acquitted of the original offence. One result of this would be that every innocent accused would have to decide whether he dared go into the witness-box to deny the offence with which he was charged, because, if the prosecution witnesses were believed, he was liable to find himself charged with perjury. This seemed to me to be an unrealistic plea to extremities, and to ignore the whole basis of our system of public prosecution in Scotland, which has its ultimate foundation in the person, in the impartiality and in the discretion of the Lord Advocate. This system has stood the test of time and, while it remains, there is no reason to suppose that the standards of fairness, impartiality and equity will be relaxed. Extreme cases may be conjured up, but the proper exercise of his discretion by Her Majesty's Advocate in Scotland is the guarantee against excesses and abuses or unfairness, injustice or inequity in bringing prosecutions. I do not consider that the fears expressed by Mr Bennett have any foundation in the normal case. On the other hand, if his argument is sound to the extent that no such prosecution could be taken for perjury irrespective of the circumstances, however blatant they may be, then the administration of justice could easily fall into disrepute. Considerations of equity operate in different ways, and while our Courts have always been jealous to protect the legitimate rights of individuals and to see that the individual is not exposed to injustices, they have a duty towards the general public and the maintenance of a proper standard of justice. To give a general immunity to accused persons to commit perjury, however blatant, and perhaps even publicly boast of its success, would only bring the law into disrepute. To fetter the Lord Advocate in his right to prosecute for perjury in what he conceives to be appropriate circumstances would in my view be doing something contrary to the public interest. If it were otherwise, and Mr Bennett's submission was well-founded, there would be a bonus for successful perjury or subornation of perjury, and the administration of justice might be openly flouted without redress. I do not consider that the decision which I have reached or my reasons therefor will lead to the wholesale prosecutions for perjury which Mr Bennett envisaged, or place an accused person in the normal case in the dilemma which he postulated. In my opinion the discretion of the Lord Advocate will confine such charges to those cases where the public interest seems to require that a prosecution should proceed.

In the whole circumstances, therefore, I would repel the objections tabled on behalf of the panel and pass the indictment for trial."

Objections to competency and relevancy repelled.

NOTES

Individuals such as Cairns are rarely prosecuted for perjury, but in this case there would have been good evidence that the denial of murder was false, had the perjury trial proceeded. In fact the accused died before the trial diet. For a case on subornation of perjury, see *Wilson, Latta and Rooney*, February 1968, unreported, *ante*. ch. 5.

b. Misleading the police

Kerr v. Hill
1936 J.C. 71

LORD JUSTICE-GENERAL (NORMAND): "In this case the appellant appeals against conviction and against sentence. He was charged in the Sheriff Court at Paisley with falsely representing to the police that he had seen a pedal cyclist struck by a motor omnibus belonging to Young's Bus Services, as a result of which the pedal cyclist was thrown onto the pavement. The results of this representation to the police are set forth in the charge. It is said that he caused the officers of the Renfrewshire Constabulary, maintained at the public expense for the public benefit, to devote their time and service to the investigation of the false story told by him, and did temporarily deprive the lieges of the services of the officers, and rendered the lieges, and particularly drivers of motor omnibuses belonging to Young's Bus Services, liable to suspicion and accusations of driving recklessly.

The appeal is by way of a bill of suspension and liberation, and the ground of the appeal against conviction is that the charge is *funditus* null, because it discloses nothing that is a crime according to the law of Scotland. It was admitted, and rightly admitted, by counsel that it is a crime to give information falsely of a crime against a named individual; but it was contended that, unless some individual is named, no crime is committed. It was further maintained that, unless information given to the police was not merely, as in this case, that somebody was knocked over by a motor omnibus, but also that the motor omnibus driver was guilty of criminal negligence or the like in driving the omnibus at the time, the giving of that information, although it was false, was not criminal.

I do not agree with the contentions put forward on behalf of the appellant. The story which the appellant told to the police was an invented story; it was told to the police with the intention that they should commence criminal investigations, and it had in fact that result. In my opinion, the giving to the police of information known to be false, for the purpose of causing them to institute an investigation with a view to criminal proceedings, is in itself a crime.

Great injury and damage may be caused to the public interest, which is mainly to be regarded, by a false accusation, although no individual is named or pointed at by the informer. A charge which is perfectly general, and leaves the public at large open to suspicion, does nevertheless constitute a crime if it is falsely made. That the appellant when he gave the information to the police did not actually charge a particular crime, but left open the possibility that the knocking over of the pedal cyclist might have been the result of an innocent accident, is also, in my opinion, immaterial. The point is that the criminal authorities were deliberately set in motion by a malicious person by means of an invented story. That is the essence of the crime, and, when these essentials are present, I think that a crime is committed. Accordingly, I am of the opinion that the appeal against conviction fails."

Appeal dismissed.

NOTES

    Kerr v. *Hill* was the first case of its type and is now used as the standard authority for this type of charge. It is one of the few twentieth-century examples of the courts creating a new crime, which should be more properly be the task of the legislature. On the declaratory power generally, see Ch. 1, *ante.*

c.　Failure to attend as a witness

1.　**H.M. Advocate v. Mannion**
1961 J.C. 79

Hugh Kelly Mannion and Frances Egan or Mannion were charged on the following indictment:—"That between 17th August and 7th September 1960, both dates inclusive, in the house occupied by you at 22/7 Muirhouse Medway, Edinburgh, or elsewhere in Scotland to the Prosecutor unknown, you did form a criminal purpose to hinder and frustrate the course of justice, in pursuance of which you, knowing that you were required to give evidence for the prosecution in the trial of Samuel McKay, now a prisoner in the Prison of Aberdeen, at a sitting of the High Court of Justiciary, Glasgow, commencing on 13th September 1960, on charges of attempting to open a lockfast place and theft by opening a lockfast place, did leave your said house and go into hiding somewhere to the Prosecutor unknown for the purpose of avoiding giving evidence as aforesaid, and the diet of said trial having been deserted *pro loco et tempore,* and a new diet appointed for trial in said High Court on 7th November 1960, you, again knowing that you were required to give evidence as aforesaid, continued to hide for the purpose aforesaid until said Samuel McKay had been tried in said High Court, all with intent that your evidence would not be available to the prosecution and with intent to hinder and frustrate the course of justice, and you remained in hiding until 6th December 1960, when you were apprehended by officers of police, and you did attempt to defeat the ends of justice." The accused pled to the relevancy of the indictment.

LORD JUSTICE-CLERK (THOMSON): "I have listened very carefully to the ingenious argument which Mr Stewart has presented in support of this motion. Mr Stewart's argument really comes to this, in the end of the day:—That until a man has actually received a citation to come to a criminal court, it is open to him to take any steps he likes to remove himself from the possibility of being called upon to give evidence, and that, while this may be socially reprehensible, it is not criminal. I find myself unable to agree with this proposition, and I do not think that I am doing anything revolutionary in failing to agree with it. It seems to me to be clear that if a man, with the evil intention of defeating the ends of justice, takes steps to prevent evidence being available, that is a crime by the law of Scotland. Evil intention, of course, is of the essence of the matter and must be established. This indictment clearly narrates the evil intention of the accused to avoid being called upon to give evidence, and that is sufficient to make the indictment relevant. Accordingly I refuse the motion."

Objection to relevancy repelled.

NOTES

For a comment on the case of *Mannion*, see Gordon, para 48-41.

d. Escaping from lawful custody

Quite apart from the crime of prison breaking, there are situations where escaping from custody will itself be criminal.

H.M. Advocate v. Martin and Others
1956 J.C. 1

A prisoner escaped from a working party outside the prison. He and two others who assisted him were charged with attempts to defeat the ends of justice. All three objected to the relevancy of the indictment.

LORD CAMERON: "It was admitted by Mr Elliott that a criminal libel, to be relevant, does not require to name a specific crime or be stamped with any particular *nomen juris*. Nevertheless he maintained that the facts set out must be such that, if proved, they would infer the commission of what is already recognised as a crime by the law of Scotland. Much of Mr Elliott's very careful argument was devoted to demonstrating what he maintained to be the limits of the well-recognised offence of prison-breaking, but the accused in this indictment are not charged with prison-breaking, nor are they charged with assisting or being art and part in the crime of prison-breaking. I was referred to the closing passages in Baron Hume's work on Crimes and Alison's Principles and Practice of the Criminal Law, dealing with the offence of prison-breaking. It is significant that both those writers were writing at a time when modern ideas of places of confinement for persons under sentence had not been developed and when prisons, in the words of Alison, were in the main 'gloomy abodes.' Further, it must be borne in mind that the chapter in Hume (vol. i, p. 401) which deals with breaking prison comes in that section of his work which relates to the category or the genus of offences against the course of justice of which the offence of prison-breaking is itself a species or illustration, and the chapter in Alison's Principles (vol. i, p. 555) which deals with the same matter begins with the significant opening paragraph which I quote: 'The act of prison-breaking, however natural to the inmates of those gloomy abodes, cannot be overlooked by the law, as being a violation of the order and course of justice, and a direct infringement of regulations essential to the peace and well-being of society.' So it is quite plain that the writer of those words regarded the act of breaking the type of prison in use when he wrote as being an act in violation of the order and course of justice, and an act in direct infringement of regulations essential to the peace and well-being of society. In an authority which is familiar, to which Mr Elliott drew attention, the case of *Bernard Greenhuff* in 1838, 2 Swin. 236, Lord Cockburn in his dissenting judgment, upon which Mr Elliott laid much reliance, said this (at p. 274): 'I may only say at present, that I am far from holding that the Court can never deal with any thing as a crime, unless there be a fixed *nomen juris* for the specific act, or unless there be a *direct precedent.* An old crime may certainly be committed in a new way; and a case, though never occurring before in its facts, may fall within the *spirit* of a previous decision, or within an established *general principle.* And such is the comprehensiveness of our common law, that it is no easy matter for any newly invented guilt to escape it.'

In my opinion, the offence of escaping from lawful custody, as lawful custody is nowadays defined in section 12 of the Prisons (Scotland) Act of 1952, is an offence which falls within an established general principle, even although there might not be a precise precedent directly in point. However that may be, I do find that in the recent case of *Turnbull*, 1953 J.C. 59, an indictment libelled that an accused person formed a criminal purpose to hinder the course of justice by effecting the escape from lawful custody of Hugh Kelly Mannion, then a prisoner in the prison of Edinburgh, by fraud and the uttering of forged documents. The relevancy of that indictment was challenged, and was sustained by the Lord Justice-Clerk, and therefore it seems to me that, even if a precise precedent were required for the form of indictment which appears in this case, the case of *Turnbull* does provide such a precedent. But, in my opinion, there can be no doubt that to form a criminal purpose to hinder the course of justice by effecting escape of a prisoner from lawful custody, or by taking other steps to frustrate the ends of criminal justice, is and always has been a crime by the common law of Scotland, and that those who aid the escape are equally guilty with the prisoner who by their aid escapes from lawful custody. What is libelled in this indictment is very plainly an attempt to hinder the course of justice and frustrate its ends by seeking to assist a sentenced criminal to escape or evade the penalty of his crime. That is an offence against public order and against the course of justice. If I am correct in that view—and if I am wrong, I can be corrected—then that is the end of the matter, because what is libelled here is but one species of a well-recognised and undoubted genus of crime.

Mr Elliott, however, argued strongly tht to hold the facts in this libel relevant would be to designate a new crime in the law of Scotland and that, because nowadays the High Court has no power to declare new crimes, his plea to the relevancy must be sustained. I express no view upon the very careful and interesting argument which Mr Elliott submitted on the extent to which the power to declare new crimes still remains with the Courts to-day, or, if it does, in what circumstances it could or should be exercised, because I do not find it necessary to invoke that power in determining the relevancy of this indictment."

Objections to relevancy repelled.

e. Contempt of court

Gordon (at para. 51-01) is certainly correct in saying that contempt of court is in many ways a crime *sui generis*. The cases considered here concern contempt by a witness, the media and a solicitor.

1. H.M. Advocate v. Airs
1975 S.L.T. 177

LORD JUSTICE-GENERAL (EMSLIE): "This is a petition and complaint addressed to the High Court of Justiciary by Her Majesty's Advocate, relating to the conduct of the respondent, Gordon Airs, when adduced as a Crown witness on oath at the trial of certain persons, including William Gibson Anderson, upon an indictment charging them with conspiracy and other crimes. The trial began in the High Court at Glasgow on 28 April, 1975. The petition narrates refusal by the respondent to answer certain questions which the trial judge had directed him to answer, and stat. IX of the petition is in the following terms—'That the refusal to answer said questions was a gross contempt and high offence offered to the Supreme Criminal Court of Scotland, to which your petitioner deems it his duty to call the attention of the court.' The respondent has lodged answers to the petition and at the hearing before us has, by his counsel, insisted in his second and third pleas-in-law which are respectively a plea to the competency of the petition and a plea to the relevancy of the averments therein. He did not seek to present argument in support of his first plea-in-law which rested upon the proposition that the petition was premature and it was accepted that if his second and third pleas fell to be repelled plea 4 must be repelled of consent. Plea 4 it should be mentioned rests upon the proposition that the respondent was not in contempt of court.

Before turning to the submissions made in support of the challenge to competency and relevancy it is desirable to set out briefly the facts which, happily, are not in dispute. In particular, the terms of the indictment are agreed to be those in the copies before us and the transcript of evidence produced and referred to in the petition is accepted as a true and accurate record of the whole of the evidence of the respondent at the trial.

So far as the indictment is concerned the charge libelled against Anderson and his co-accused was one of conspiracy, by various specified criminal means, to further the purpose of an association of persons known as the Scottish Army of the Provisional Government. . . . It was in course of the Crown case in proof of that charge that the respondent was adduced as a witness.

From the transcript it appears that the respondent is chief reporter of the *Daily Record* newspaper. He took the oath when called to testify and explained that in August 1974 he was, in the course of his calling as a journalist, interested in making contact with extremist nationalist organisations in Scotland and that he took steps to do so. In the result he made contact with Murray, one of the men on trial, and through him a meeting was arranged which eventually took place in September, initially at Bannockburn. The respondent was accompanied by a photographer and from Bannockburn they were taken in a van to a ruined castle which we were informed was later proved to have been Plean Castle. The respondent there had a conversation with one of his fellow passengers in the van at a point some distance away from the others. At this point in his evidence-in-chief the respondent was asked if he saw the person with whom he had this conversation in court. His answer was: 'The trouble is before I got to the meeting I had to give an undertaking that on no account at any time would I reveal who was at the meeting.' The advocate-depute then invited the trial judge to direct the witness to answer. The trial judge did so and when the question was repeated the respondent said: 'I feel this is in conflict with the undertaking I gave in that the National Union of Journalists have a code of professional conduct in that you shouldn't divulge a source of information.' He was again reminded by the trial judge that he could claim no privilege to refuse to answer but in spite of this he repeatedly refused to answer the question as to the identity of the person with whom he had had the conversation at Plean Castle. The advocate-depute then elicited from the respondent what had passed at the meeting with the man he refused to identify. It was in these terms—'he wouldn't say his name. He said he was a member of the military council . . . of the A.P.G.' and it is not disputed that A.P.G. meant Army of the Provisional Government. The man also added that 'they knew that the editor was English and that he had better leave the country, or something'. All that remains to be said of the respondent's evidence-in-chief is that he was again invited to identify the man who claimed to be a member of the military council and that he again refused to do so in spite of a warning that refusal might be contempt of court, and in spite of a further direction from the trial judge in these terms—'Well, Mr Airs, I am afraid I must direct you that this is a question which you must answer under sanction that if you do not answer it, if you disobey my direction, you will be in contempt of court.' The trial judge thereupon declared as follows—'Well, this matter will have to be dealt with as contempt of court. Steps must be taken Mr Advocate-Depute but it is better than it should be dealt with by another judge than myself.' This declaration led to the entry in the minute of proceedings in these terms: 'The court directed that the matter of contempt of court should be dealt with by another judge.'

To complete the necessary background of fact for the purposes of disposal of the petition we have little to add. Firstly, as appears from the examination-in-chief of the respondent two witnesses had previously identified the man who met and conversed with the respondent at Plean Castle as the accused Anderson. These witnesses were not cross-examined on this point but it has to be said that they were associated with Murray in accompanying the respondent to the meeting. Secondly, certain other witnesses for the Crown called later in the trial also identified the man in question as Anderson. Finally, before counsel for Anderson began his cross-examination of the respondent he announced that Anderson did not dispute that he was the man with whom the respondent had the conversation at Plean Castle and had no objection to being identified by the respondent. The respondent thereafter identified Anderson.

One further preliminary matter falls to be mentioned. Counsel for the respondent informed us that he did not intend to argue that a journalist enjoys any privilege, on grounds of confidentiality or otherwise, which entitles him to refuse to answer any proper questions adduced as witness before the court. On the authority of the cases of *Attorney-General* v. *Clough* [1963] 1 Q.B. 773 and of *Attorney-General* v. *Mulholland* and *Foster* [1963] 2 Q.B. 477 the law of England denies the existence of any such privilege in journalists and it could not be suggested that in the law of Scotland a different rule would apply. In our opinion, counsel was well founded in so saying and lest there be any doubt upon the question we declare without hesitation that the law of Scotland differs not at all from the law of England upon the position of the journalist as a witness.

In support of the plea to the competency counsel's argument for the respondent can be shortly stated. Contempt of court of the kind alleged in this petition is a crime. Anomalously, it may be dealt with by the court before which it occurs but where the inherent power of that court to punish contempt is not exercised, the only competent way of proceeding against the alleged offender is by indictment or summary complaint. This submission was made under reference to ss. 1 and 2 of the Criminal Procedure (Scotland) Act 1887 and it was pointed out that by s. 74 of that Act all statutes, laws, regulations and usages inconsistent or at variance with the provisions of the Act are repealed. The terms of the petition and complaint itself, said counsel, disclose that the respondent is now being charged with a crime for the respondent's refusal to answer when directed to do so by the trial judge is therein described as a 'gross contempt and high offence', and since in substance this is an attempted prosecution of the respondent by an incompetent means the petition should be dismissed. In making this submission, counsel pointed out that all those prosecuted for crime are entitled to all the protection afforded to an accused by our criminal law and procedure and that to allow this petition to proceed would be unjust since it would deny the respondent that protection.

In our opinion this argument fails because it rests upon false premises. It is not in doubt that where commission of a crime is alleged, the only competent forms of prosecution are prosecutions upon indictment or by summary complaint. Subject only to the single qualification we mention later contempt of court is, however, not a crime within the meaning of our criminal law. It is the name given to conduct which challenges or affronts the authority of the court or the supremacy of the law itself, whether it takes place in or in connection with civil or criminal proceedings. The offence of contempt of court is an offence sui generis and, where it occurs, it is peculiarly within the province of the court itself, civil or criminal as the case may be, to punish it under its power which arises from the inherent and necessary jurisdiction to take effective action to vindicate its authority and preserve the due and impartial administration of justice (see *H.M. Advocate* v. *Cordiner*, 1973 S.L.T. 125, at p. 126). In some, but in no means all, cases the facts which constitute or may constitute contempt of court may also constitute a criminal offence and render the offender liable to prosecution, but, save as expressly authorised by s. 33 (3) of the Summary Jurisdiction (Scotland) Act 1954, which permits a prosecutor in the sheriff court to proceed by 'formal complaint' against a witness for certain defined acts which are deemed to be contempts, the charge will not be of contempt of court but will be of the commission of a crime known to the law of Scotland under its appropriate nomen juris, for example, perversion of the course of justice, assault, breach of the peace and the like. Where upon a given set of facts which would constitute contempt of court as well as a crime the Lord Advocate initiates a criminal prosecution the court will very properly not exercise its power to deal with the matter as contempt. Where, however, the Lord Advocate in appropriate cases does not choose to prosecute the court may deal with the matter as a contempt at its own hand or may do so if the matter is brought to its notice by the well established and competent process of petition and complaint, which may be at the instance of the Lord Advocate or any other interested party. In this case it is nothing to the point that the respondent was brought before the sheriff on petition shortly after his evidence had been given for this is a purely preliminary procedure which may or may not lead to prosecution. The Lord Advocate has, we are informed, decided not to initiate criminal proceedings against the respondent and has, instead, presented to this court this petition and complaint. By this petition the Lord Advocate does no more than to allege the commission of an offence against the court itself and in performance of his duty and no doubt mindful of the direction of the trial judge, calls the attention of the court thereto. The petition so states and notwithstanding the use of expressions such as 'gross' contempt and 'high offence offered to the Supreme Criminal Court of Scotland' the petition is, in no sense, an attempted prosecution upon a criminal charge for it neither bears to be nor is it concerned with the matter of complaint as the subject of criminal prosecution. In short, the argument for the respondent, well presented though it was, fails fundamentally because contempt of court as such is not a crime within the meaning of our criminal law, including the statutes governing its procedure, and because the petition, which does no more than to call attention to a contempt of this court, in no sense purports to initiate any prosecution.

In support of the plea to relevancy counsel for the respondent argued that before a witness who could claim no privilege would be legally required to answer a question, the question had to be not only competent and relevant but also 'necessary' or 'useful', and since there is nothing in the petition or in the transcript to show that the question put to the respondent was either 'necessary' or 'useful', there are no relevant averments of failure in a legal duty to answer, and accordingly no relevant averments of contempt. This argument was founded upon certain observations of Lord Denning, M.R., and Donovan, L.J., in the cases of *Mulholland* and *Foster* (supra). It will be recalled that these cases arose out of proceedings before a tribunal of inquiry to which the Tribunals of Inquiry (Evidence) Act 1921 applied. The tribunal was investigating security matters connected with spying offences and the issue before the Court of Appeal was whether journalists who had refused to disclose their sources of certain information enjoyed a privilege based upon confidentiality. The observations of their Lordships, accordingly, must be understood within the context of a consideration of the remit of the tribunal, but with all respect to their Lordships, if they intended to say that the 'necessity' or 'usefulness' of a competent and relevant question must be demonstrated in all proceedings before the courts before a legal duty to answer it can arise we cannot agree that this represents the law of Scotland. In our opinion there is a legal duty to answer any question which is both competent and relevant. A relevant question is one the answer to which a judge or jury is entitled to hear in reaching the decision upon the facts, although the precise weight and bearing which ought to be attached to the answer can never be determined until all the evidence has been led. Indeed it is hard to figure any circumstances in which a relevant question could, in course of a trial or proof, be judged unnecessary or not useful but, if such circumstances were ever to arise, and they could only be quite exceptional circumstances, there remains a residual discretion in the court to excuse a witness, who seeks to be excused upon a ground of conscience, from answering a relevant question in accordance with his legal duty. In so saying we are content to observe that the test of the existence of the legal duty in accordance with the law of Scotland is the one expressed by Parker, C.J., in the case of *Clough* (supra) in which judgment was given before that of the Court of Appeal in *Mulholland* and *Foster*. Further, we do not consider that, properly understood, the opinions delivered in the cases of *Mulholland* and *Foster* are, to a material extent, in conflict with the views we have just expressed.

The 'necessity' contemplated by Lord Denning is, it will be observed, 'necessity' in the sense only that the question was one 'that ought to be answered to enable proper investigation to be made'. A competent and relevant question in proceedings before the court is prima facie necessary in the comparable sense in that it seeks an answer habile to assist the court in question in resolving the issue of fact committed to its determination. The observations of Donovan, L.J., in which he substituted the word 'useful' for 'necessary' were, it is clear, made with reference only to the residual discretion which any court must retain and which we have held to reside in the courts of Scotland.

What we have said so far is sufficient for disposal of the plea to relevancy which, like the plea to competency, falls to be repelled. We must, however, add that if the test of 'necessity' or 'usefulness' had fallen to be applied to the questions which the respondent declined to answer, that test would have been satisfied with ease. Indeed it is not difficult to conclude that the answer sought was of the highest materiality. The respondent deponed that he had been escorted to a secret rendezvous by one of the accused—Murray— and that his informant had specifically stated that he was a member of the military council of the Army of the Provisional Government. The indictment specifically libelled that the conspiracy charged was to further, by criminal means, the purposes of this very organisation. In these circumstances it would be difficult to envisage a more material and important question than the one which sought from a witness of obvious credit the identity of the associate of Murray and the maker of a statement of so potentially incriminating a character. Indeed, prima facie, the most reliable evidence of identification of the accused concerned was most likely to come from the respondent and might have been of critical importance had the jury formed doubts as to the credibility and reliability of those other witnesses who, before and after the evidence of the respondent was given, identified Anderson as the man who met the respondent at Plean Castle.

In the whole matter, having repelled pleas 1, 2 and 3 for the respondent, we also repel plea 4 for it cannot now be disputed that the respondent's refusal to identify his informant, in the circumstances disclosed in the transcript, was a contempt of the High Court of Justiciary. . . . To refuse to answer a competent and relevant question in the High Court and, indeed, in any court of law for whatever motive, is a challenge to the rule of law which can only be regarded as serious contempt meriting in ordinary circumstances severe penalty.

In this case, however, we accept that Mr Airs acted from what he conceived to be honourable professional motives, and did all in his power in advance of the trial to be released from the undertaking which he had given. Further, it was represented to us, and it may well be the fact, that Mr Airs may have been under the the misapprehension that the questions had to be shown to be necessary or useful before he could be required to answer them. Finally, we have to bear in mind that the vital identification was in the end made after the intervention of Anderson's counsel.

In these special circumstances, although Mr Airs should have recognised that the trial judge was the sole arbiter of the necessity of an answer being given to the questions, and although the undertaking by Mr Airs was given primarily in the commercial interests of his newspaper, we propose to deal with Mr Airs with special leniency and to restrict the penalty to one of a fine of £500.

Let us, however, sound a note of clear warning. Now that all possible causes of misapprehension have been dispelled, any witness, including any journalist witness, who declines to answer a competent and relevant question in court must realise that he will be in contempt and be liable to incur severe punishment."

Accused convicted.

2.   Hall v. Associated Newspapers Ltd. and Others
1978 S.L.T. 241

A person was detained by the police in connection with a murder inquiry. While he was in police custody an article was published in the *Daily Mail* newspaper describing the inquiry and revealing considerable personal details regarding the person in custody. That person was subsequently charged by the police and appeared on petition at Haddington sheriff court several days later charged with murder. He presented a petition to the High Court alleging that the publication of the article constituted a gross interference with the course of justice. He further craved the court to consider whether the article amounted to contempt of court and to prohibit the newspaper proprietors from publishing any further articles of a similar prejudical character until the conclusion of his trial. At the initial hearing of the petition it was argued by the respondents that there was no contempt, in that publiction of the article had occurred at a time before the court's jurisdiction to deal with prejudicial matter had arisen. In view of the difficulty surrounding this point, the case was remitted to a Bench of Five Judges.

OPINION OF THE COURT: "The law of contempt of court covers many diverse forms of conduct one of which is conduct that is liable to prejudice the administration of justice generally, or in relation to the case of a particular individual. Its source is to be found in the indispensable power which is inherent in every court to do whatever is necessary to discharge the whole of its responsibilities. As

Erskine says in the *Institute*, I.2.8: 'every power is understood to be conferred without which the jurisdiction cannot be explicated'. One particular aspect of this power is the power to punish summarily conduct which impedes the court in the exercise of its functions and this represents an exception to the rule that those accused of offences shall be tried with the benefit of all the procedures which are provided for their protection by the criminal law. Hume on *Crimes* (3rd ed.), ii, pp. 138 et seq., treats of this exception thus: 'In that view, every Judge, of whatsoever degree, has power to punish summarily, and of his own motion, all such disorders or misdemean-ours, committed in Court during the progress of a trial, as are a disturbance of the Judge in the exercise of his functions. . . . It is equally indispensable, to repress, in the like speedy and effectual manner, all attempts which may be made with relation to any trial depending at the time, or which has recently been so, to slander the proceedings of the Court, or depreciate the character, or sully the honour, of the Judges; or to impose on their wisdom, and pollute the channels of justice, to the prejudice of a fair and an impartial trial.' Thereafter, having given examples of instances of contempt, including examples of publication of prejudicial matter, Hume goes on to say (ii, 143): 'These are instances of wrong or misdemeanour, for which the offender may be tried and convicted, without calling an assize, at any period of the proceedings.' From what we have said so far two conclusions may be drawn. In the first place it is of vital importance that the court should guard jealously, in the interests of justice, its inherent jurisdiction to vindicate the fair and impartial administration of justice and, as a corollary, to protect persons charged with crime and liable to be tried for such crime or other as may be libelled against them, from actions on the part of others which may prejudice their prospects of fair and impartial trial. In the second place it is just as important that this indispensable and special jurisdiction which exposes offenders to summary punish-ment should be confined within proper and necessary limits.

What are these proper and necessary limits? The language of the institutional writers is not sufficiently precise to identify with accuracy the point of time from which the court's jurisdiction in contempt by publication of prejudicial material can be exercised. All that can be deduced from their various works is that the court's twofold jurisdiction to prohibit the publication of prejudicial material, and to punish the publishers of such material, appears to require that there are before the court at the time of publication proceedings which are pending, that is to say, proceedings which can properly be said to have commenced. In the case of the civil courts there is no difficulty in defining the time at which proceedings can be said to commence, and that time is the time of service of the summons or petition or, in the sheriff court, the service of the initial writ. At that time the court becomes responsible for the fair and impartial administration of justice in the proceedings, and the litigant becomes entitled to the court's protection against action by others which is likely to prejudice the fair and impartial resolution of the issues in these proceedings. When, however, can it be said for the purpose of defining the starting point from which the contempt jurisdiction of the criminal courts begins to run, that there are proceedings which have commenced which have brought the case of an individual within the court's protection?

The respondents' answer to that question is that the relevant time, in cases which are governed by solemn procedure, is the time of full committal or at least not earlier than the time of committal for further examination. In examining that attractively simple answer we recognise that with the exception of the case of *Stirling*, 1960 J.C. 5, there is no reported case in which the High Court exercised a jurisdiction to prohibit the publication of prejudicial material, or to penalise such a publication as contempt, save in circumstances in which a prohibitory order was sought, or in which the publication complained of occurred, after there had been a full committal of an accused person for trial. That there is such a jurisdiction after that stage has been reached admits of no doubt but in none of the cases was the court called upon to decide whether the jurisdiction might lie at any stage earlier than that of full committal.

As we have seen Hume makes it clear that the jurisdiction to punish summarily for contempt, including the kind of conduct which is complained of in this petition, exists 'at any period of the proceedings'. Further it may be deduced from the authorities that there will exist 'proceedings' for the purpose of this special jurisdiction when it can be affirmed that the court has become seised of a duty of care towards individuals who have been brought into a relationship with the court. Lord Trayner in *Smith* (1892) 3 White 408, for example, at p. 413 put the matter thus: 'The High Court of Justiciary is a supreme Court, vested with all the powers necessary for the protection of itself and its proceedings, and of those under its care. The prisoner Smith [who, incidentally had not yet been brought before the High Court and who had not been indicted] is in the latter category'. In principle, accordingly, the starting point of the contempt jurisdiction in the administration of criminal justice will be the moment when it can be said that proceedings have commenced so as to bring about a relationship between the court and a person charged with crime, who may ultimately stand trial, in which the person concerned has come under the care of the court and within its protection. In the field of the civil law, proceedings have an identifiable common starting point and are continuous thereafter. This is not so in the administration of criminal justice for, as the decided cases show, proceedings relevant to the emergence of the jurisdiction in contempt may begin at different points of time. It is well settled, for example, that it is not necessary that the service of an indictment should be preceded by procedure on petition or committal until liberation in due course of law or even by arrest (cf. *McVey* v. *H.M. Advocate* (1911) 6 Adam 503). In one sense, accordingly, the commencement of proceedings may be the date of service of an indictment. Proceedings on petition are no more than one of the normal and separate stages in the process of apprehending, charging, and bringing an accused person to trial. Yet it is undoubted, having regard to the principle which is derived from the authorities, that proceedings for the purpose of the contempt jurisdiction of this court and of its jurisdiction to make prohibitory orders have commenced at least from the stage of committal for trial. At that stage the person accused is just as much entitled to the protection of the court as the person who has been indicted and it is as an accused person that he enjoys that protection even although for various reasons he may never be indicted and may never proceed to the stage of trial. That protection, be it noted, is afforded not only in the interests of the person accused but in the wider interest of the fair and impartial administration of justice. Let us now consider what may be regarded as the step which in most cases will immediately precede full committal on petition, namely, committal by the court, in the person of the sheriff, upon petition, for further examination. At this stage the person so committed is a person accused who may, if all the succeeding steps in the process of the administration of criminal justice are taken, ultimately require to stand trial.

Can it be said that proceedings have not begun by the stage of committal for further examination and that no proceedings commence until the court commits the same accused person, who has already been deprived of his liberty by order of the court, until liberated in due course of law? There can be no reason whatever in principle for answering that question in the affirmative. Any distinction between committal for further examination and full committal on the same petition would be quite arbitrary and indefensible. Lord Fleming, in *Stark* v. *H.M. Advocate*, 1938 S.L.T. at p. 518 said: 'I have always understood that an accused person in that position' (i.e. a person who has been committed for further examination) 'was under the protection of the Court'. In this observation Lord Fleming correctly stated the law and the corollary of that is that the right of an accused person to claim protection, and to be protected, against prejudicial publications has emerged at least at the stage of committal for further examination, by which stage at least it is clear that relevant proceedings have begun.

The process of apprehending, charging, and bringing a person to trial does not, however, begin only where an accused is brought before the court on petition. It will normally begin—and this is what happened in the case of the petitioner—by the arrest of the accused by the police upon a specific charge followed by the grant of warrant by the court to bring him before the court with a view to his possible committal for further examination or until liberated in due course of law. At the stage of arrest there is, just as at the stage of committal for further examination, a person accused of crime who, if the subsequent steps in the process are taken, may ultimately stand trial on the charge on which he has been arrested or other charges. In order to discover whether it would be legitimate to say that proceedings which bring into existence a relationship between the court and a person charged with crime have commenced at the moment of his arrest the question which must be answered is whether a person arrested is within the protection of the court. At that stage the person concerned is vested with rights which he can invoke and which the court is under a duty to enforce. He must be informed of the charge on which the arrest has been made and must be brought before the court (a magistrate) not later than in course of the first lawful day after he has been arrested (s. 321 (3) of the Criminal Procedure (Scotland) Act 1975). This is the modern definition of the common law right of an arrested person to be carried 'with all convenient speed before a magistrate . . . to be dealt with according to law' (Hume, vol. ii, 80). Further a person arrested on any criminal charge becomes immediately entitled to have intimation sent to a solicitor that his assistance is required and informing him of the place to which such person is to be taken for examination. This is provided by s. 19 (1) of the Criminal Procedure (Scotland) Act 1975 and s. 19 (2) and (3) not only provide further rights in that regard but empower the sheriff or justice to delay examination on declaration for a defined period to allow time for the attendance of the solicitor. Apart from these statutory rights a person arrested may not lawfully be interrogated lest he may incriminate himself and it would be strange indeed if an arrested person should be guarded by the court against interrogation which, if permitted, could elicit prejudicial if not incriminating evidence, but were not to enjoy any protection at the hand of the court itself against conduct on the part of others likely to prejudice the fairness and impartiality of any trial he may be called upon to stand. We have no doubt that it can be said that from the moment of arrest the person arrested is in a very real sense under the care and protection of the court and we are quite unable to see any relevant or material distinction between the situation vis-à-vis an accused person created by arrest and that which clearly exists at the time when an accused person is committed on petition for further examination. From the moment of arrest the process of apprehending, charging and bringing a person to trial has begun and the beginning of that process is one of two points of time at which relevant proceedings have commenced so as to bring into play the contempt jurisdiction of the court where prejudicial publication is concerned. Although for the purposes of our decision upon the point taken in this petition it is, strictly speaking, unnecessary to do so, we think it proper to say that the second of these points of time will be where a petition is presented to the court for warrant to arrest a named person and the warrant is granted. At that time the court, in the person of the sheriff, is informed of the identity of the person accused on prima facie information and grants its authority for his apprehension for the purpose of being formally charged and thereafter, it may be, of his committal for further examination or until liberation in due course of law with a view to possible trial on indictment. At this point of time it cannot be disputed that the court has become seised of proceedings against an individual which, if they move through all subsequent stages of the process, will end in trial. The machinery of the administration of criminal justice has in these circumstances been set in motion by the court itself and there is no more ground in logic or expediency, and certainly none in authority, for denying to such an accused person, any more than to a person who has been arrested, the full measure of protection against the injury which he may sustain by the publication of material prejudicial to a fair and impartial trial.

We are content to know that the results of our examination of the limits of the jurisdiction of the court in Scotland for the purposes of the law of contempt by publication have led us to a conclusion as to the starting point of this jurisdiction which is identical to that adopted by the High Court of Australia, and which is not very different from the starting point recognised by the law of England (vide *James and Others* v. *Robinson* (1963) 109 C.L.R. 593 and *Att.-Gen.* v. *Times Newspapers Ltd.* [1974] A.C. 273, the speech of Lord Diplock at p. 308). In light of these results it follows that although the reasons on which the court proceeded or appeared to proceed in *Stirling* are not sound, the decision at which the court arrived was correct and represents accurately the law of Scotland. In so saying, however, we add, without hesitation, that we disapprove of the dicta in the judgment of the court in that case tending to suggest that the court's jurisdiction in the matter of contempt by prejudicial publication or by other conduct may run from the time at which a crime is suspected and investigation by the criminal authorities has begun. It is, of course, perfectly obvious, as has been pointed out repeatedly in earlier cases and, indeed, in other jurisdictions that the administration of justice may suffer just as much injury as the result of publication or other conduct by the Press or by any other person or agency before the court's jurisdiction in contempt can be invoked , as it may suffer by publication or other conduct thereafter. The avoidance of such injury prejudicial to the course and interests of justice before the court's special jurisdiction arises is, however, left to the control of the general criminal law and if there is any reason to believe that the power of our criminal law as it is may not, in practice, be a wholly effective mechanism for that purpose then it is for consideration whether it should not be strengthened by legislation.

Before parting with the petition at this stage we wish to say for the sake of completeness that, by parity of reasoning, when a person is involved in our summary procedure the jurisdiction of the court to treat prejudicial publication as contempt will arise at the time of arrest or of service of the complaint, whichever is the earlier.

Finally, we wish it to be understood also that we recognise that prejudicial publication may take place when the publishers, whoever they may be, are unaware that the person who is the subject of the publication in connection with a particular crime has been arrested or that a petition warrant for his arrest has been granted by the court. Excusable ignorance of these facts will of course always be a factor of importance if and when the question of penalty comes to be considered. Since, however, the risk of prejudicial publication which may fall to be treated as contempt is normally likely to arise only in relation to notorious crimes attracting wide public interest, it is not unreasonable that those who have it in mind to publish material which may be prejudicial to the administration of justice, in relation to a particular crime or crimes, should be put upon their inquiry."

Publication held to be
contemptuous.

NOTES

As will be apparent, prior to the decision in *Hall* the question of exactly when the court's jurisdiction to deal with contempt arose was governed by the rather unsatisfactory case of *Stirling*. The passage in the latter case which caused the difficulty is to be found in Lord Clyde's judgment in 1960 J.C. 5 at p. 11: "Any independent interviewing of possible witnesses by representatives of the Press, while the investigations by the Crown authorities are in progress, constitutes interference with the authorities' public duty, and, usually, will impede their investigations, as the Lord Advocate has pointed out. If the result of these interviews is published in the Press before the trial is over, this may well constitute contempt of Court."

These *dicta* were specifically disapproved in *Hall*, and the question of contempt will not now arise unless a specified individual can be said to be under the protection of the court. But it is interesting to note that the control of other potentially prejudicial conduct is left to the general criminal law, presumably by invoking the charge of attempting to pervert the course of justice. In *Skeen* v. *Farmer*, Glasgow Sheriff Court, September 1979 unreported, a journalist was charged on summary complaint with this crime, but the charge as laid was held to be irrelevant. A subsequent Crown appeal against the decision was abandoned. For a discussion of *Hall* and other issues see *McLean*, "Contempt in Criminal Process" 1978 S.L.T. (News) 257. See also generally, the Phillimore report on Contempt of Court (Cmnd. 5794 (1974)).

3.   Muirhead v. Douglas
1979 S.L.T. (Notes) 17

A solicitor was convicted of contempt of court. He appealed by bill of suspension.

LORD CAMERON: "The matter arose out of a summary criminal proceeding in which the complainer had been instructed on behalf of one accused of a contravention of s. 3 of the Road Traffic Act 1972. A plea of not guilty had been tendered on the client's behalf and trial fixed for 7 September 1978 on which date the complainer attended and, on his client's behalf, adhered to the plea of not guilty. The trial was one of three listed for that day's sitting of the court and was second on the list. The time the plea was tendered was approximately 11.15. Thereafter the complainer left the court and proceeded to his office, which is said to be only 100 yards or thereby from the court buildings. According to the complainer's own statement in the bill he asked the agent instructed in the first trial for its likely duration, and was given an estimate of two hours. In point of fact the trial came to a premature conclusion by the tender of a plea of guilty after the evidence of only two of the Crown witnesses. The complainer alleges that he left 'instructions' that he was to be 'contacted on the conclusion of the first trial'. It appeared that the 'instructions' related to a private arrangement with the court officer. It was said in the bill, but not admitted by the respondent, that this is in accordance with 'normal procedure at Dunfermline Sheriff Court'—though nothing is said as to the proximity of other solicitors' offices to the court buildings.

Shortly after his return to his office the complainer narrates that, as he was going on holiday the next day, he would take the opportunity of conducting some other outstanding professional business. This was the making of an adoption report to the court in his capacity as curator ad litem. To do this he required to visit the proposed adopters who (it is said) 'lived close to his office' and obtain the information he required for his report. The complainer does not say for what length of time he expected to be absent on this inquiry, but does state he informed his receptionist he was leaving the office. He does not however state that he informed her where he was going, how long he would be absent, or what to do if a message came from the sheriff court intimating that the first trial was concluded. The complainer goes on to aver that he returned shortly after noon but 'due to an oversight' did not inform his receptionist of the fact. Having dictated his report the complainer avers that he returned to court at about 12.25 and then learned that the first trial had come to a premature conclusion at about 12.05. During the complainer's absence a message was received by the receptionist, who merely noted that the complainer was to 'contact the Respondent's office on his return'. She did nothing more as, according to the complainer, she had not been informed that there was any urgency in the matter.

The complainer avers that when he appeared before the sheriff at approximately 12.30 he informed him of what had occurred and made full apology. After hearing explanation and apology the sheriff found that the complainer's absence was 'in itself contempt of court' and convicted him of that offence and imposed a fine of £25. According to the complainer's statement in the bill: 'the sheriff indicated that in his opinion the Complainer should not have absented himself from his office while there was a possibility that he might be recalled to court'. The complainer's version of the events of that morning so far as his own actions are concerned is not admitted by the Crown, but its general accuracy was not challenged.

On that assumption of fact the complainer pleads that his actings did not amount in law to a contempt of court and that in any event the sentence was harsh and oppressive.

In moving that the bill be passed and the conviction quashed, counsel for the complainer submitted that, while his conduct might call for a measure of censure, it did not fall within the category of contempt of court. For conduct to be held as contempt it was necessary that there should be an element of deliberation, of wilful disobedience of an order of court or non-compliance with its requirements or a deliberate intention to interfere with or obstruct the course of justice. In the circumstances disclosed in the bill and not challenged or contradicted by the Crown, this was no more than a case of carelessness and a series of unfortunate mistakes in which the element of intent or wilful disregard of the interests of the court was absent. Such a failure as was here disclosed could therefore not be characterised as 'contempt of court'. Carelessness as disclosed here, while deserving of censure, was not contempt in the absence of any fact indicative of an intention to ignore or flout an order of court or hinder the due administration of justice. In support of this wide proposition, counsel relied on the case of *Pirie v. Hawthorn*, 1962 S.L.T. 291; 1962 J.C. 69 and the judgment of Lord Clyde. That was a case in which a youth of 17 was charged on summary complaint. He failed to appear at the trial diet when his case was called, and in respect of that failure was held as in contempt in spite of the explanation tendered for his initial failure. This was to the effect that the complaint had been handed over to the accused's father, who forgot to inform the accused of his obligation to appear on the date and at the time stated in the complaint. The reason for the omission was said to be pressure of urgent farming duties. The Lord Justice-General said (1962 S.L.T. at p. 293): 'There was no wilful defiance of the Court at any stage and no wilful failure to appear at the proper time or to explain why appearance was not made in the morning. The essential element in contempt of court is thus absent'. On this statement two comments may be made. First, the sole allegation against the complainer was of wilful disobedience to the order of the court. When this was shown to be erroneous there was no alternative allegation against him of carelessness or reckless disregard of the citation, and it was in these particular circumstances that Lord Clyde made these observations. In the second place, as Lord Clyde had only recently given judgment in the case of *Stirling v. Associated Newspapers Ltd.*, 1960 S.L.T. 5; 1960 J.C. 5, in which no issue of wilful or deliberate attempt to interfere with or pervert the course of justice was raised, it is clear that in the case of *Pirie* the court was not limiting and was not intending to limit the boundaries of contempt in the way for which counsel contended. Further, recent decisions such as that in *Hall v. Associated Newspapers Ltd. and Others*, 1978 S.L.T. 241, make it abundantly clear that the element of deliberate intent to cause prejudice to the administration of justice is not an essential element in contempt. Indeed, counsel was constrained to concede that there could be such a degree of carelessness or disregard of obligation leading to interference with or material disruption in the course of the administration of justice as to be equiparated with wilful or deliberate disobedience or interference. I therefore think that the complainer's argument so far as based on the judgment in the particular circumstances of *Pirie v. Hawthorn* is unsound.

It would be undesirable in this case to endeavour to define the limits of conduct which may be held to constitute contempt of court. The variety and quality of the acts or omissions which in particular cases may fall within that description are not capable of precise delimitation or formulation. On the other hand it may be said that where there has been in fact a failure to obey or obtemper an order or requirement of a court such a failure demands satisfactory explanation and excuse, and in the absence of such may be held to constitute a contempt of court of varying degree of gravity. I can see no reason in principle and there is certainly none in authority, for an assertion that failure due to carelessness alone may in no circumstances constitute contempt of court. The question in my opinion is essentially one of fact and circumstances, in which the position and duties of the party alleged to be in contempt are necessarily material considerations.

Being of this opinion I turn now to the facts which are stated by the complainer in his bill.

In considering these it must be kept in view that the complainer is experienced in court practice. He must therefore be held to be well aware that the prediction of the duration of summary criminal proceedings is a hazardous matter. For a variety of reasons cases may break down, collapse or be protracted and such events are not to be forecasted with any degree of assurance, far less certainty. The first trial before the sheriff came to premature conclusion on a plea of guilty tendered during the presentation of the prosecution case and when the complainer's case called neither he nor his client were present, and the complainer could not be found although a call was made to his office. This caused a delay and interference with the work of the court and a hindrance in the administration of justice for which at the time there was neither explanation nor excuse. Prima facie there was therefore a plain and serious dereliction of duty on the part of a practitioner directly causative of an interference with the administration of justice in that court. Such a dereliction, in the absence of satisfactory and sufficient explanation could in my opinion be properly held to be a contempt of court. The explanations offered by the complainer are set out in the bill and have already been narrated; not all of the statements made by him are accepted as accurate or admitted by the Crown, but let it be assumed they are correct so far as they go. To what do they amount? They disclose a series of errors and mistakes operating with cumulative effect for which the complainer was solely and directly responsible. Instead of remaining within the precincts of the court the complainer not only returned to his own office without making adequate arrangements to ensure that he was immediately informed of the end of the first of the listed cases and without any firm assurance of its probable duration, but did not inform his own receptionist of at least the possibility of an urgent telephone call from the court nor give her instructions how to deal with it. Next, he leaves his office to conduct other professional business than that for which his services in court had been retained. He does not inform his receptionist or any of his staff of his whereabouts or of the

probable duration of his absence. Then, his other business completed, he returns to his office without informing his staff of his return
or even inquiring if any message had been received from the court.
It is only after finishing a report in some adoption proceedings in
which he was curator ad litem that the complainer returned to the
court. As he was going on holiday the following day it is plain that
the complainer seized on a chance, as he thought, of completing his
report in the adoption proceedings in the expected or at least
hoped-for interval between tendering his 'not guilty' plea and the
calling of the diet of trial. In face of all this I think it is plain enough
that the complainer deliberately chose to take a risk that he might
for his own personal professional benefit bring about (as in fact he
did) an avoidable and quite possibly serious delay in the due dispatch of the court's criminal business. In light of this and of the
wholly inadequate measures taken by the complainer, I think that
the sheriff was entitled to hold that the complainer's conduct
amounted to a contempt of court.

For that contempt the complainer rendered himself liable to a
penalty; he says it is 'harsh and oppressive'. The sum involved is
itself of little moment. The complainer's conduct displayed a levity
of regard for his professional duty both to his client and to the court,
and I am far from thinking that in the admitted circumstances the
penalty imposed was harsh and oppressive.

In my opinion the bill should be refused."

NOTES

Since *Muirhead*, there has been at least one other instance in Scotland
where a solicitor was made the subject of contempt proceedings: *Macara* v.
Macfarlane, 1980 S.L.T. (Notes) 26, but in that case the solicitor successfully appealed by bill of suspension against his conviction.

INDEX